VISIONS OF LUSCOMBE
The Early Years

by
James B. Zazas

VISIONS OF LUSCOMBE
The Early Years

by
James B. Zazas
Published as part of the
"Aviation Heritage Library Series"
by

SunShine House, Inc.
P.O. Box 2065
Terre Haute, IN 47802
© Copyright 1993 James B. Zazas
All Rights Reserved

(812) 232-3076

Publishers: Alan Abel, Drina Welch Abel
Editorial Assistants: Colleen Brannon, Mitzi Nichols, Donna Hardesty
Layout/Design: Karen Horn
Cover Design: Fred Jungclaus
Color Separations: Ropkey Graphics, Inc., Indianapolis, IN

First Edition, First Printing
Printed in the United States of America
ISBN 0-943691-09-5

The Aviation Heritage Library Series is published to preserve the history of the men and women, and of their airplanes, during the era of the Golden Years of Aviation. The books in the series include:

The Welch Airplane Story by Drina Welch Abel
It's a Funk! by G. Dale Beach
The Luscombe Story by John C. Swick
The Earhart Disappearance - The British Connection by James A. Donahue
Ryan Sport Trainer by Dorr Carpenter
Aeronca — Best of Paul Matt
Ryan Broughams and Their Builders by William Wagner
The Corsair and other— Aeroplanes Vought by Gerald P. Moran
Peanut Power by Bill Hannan
Paul Matt Scale Airplane Drawings, Vol. 1
Paul Matt Scale Airplane Drawings, Vol. 2
Roosevelt Field — World's Premier Airport by Joshua Stoff & William Camp
WACO — Symbol of Courage & Excellence by Fred O. Kobernuss
The Taylorcraft Story by Chet Peek
Visions of Luscombe, The Early Years by James B. Zazas

Dedication

To Dad —
Who made it all possible.

George J. Zazas
(1926 - 1990)

*Jim Zazas with his
father, George Zazas.*

Preface

Several years ago a friend of mine, James B. Zazas, a DePauw University graduate, while still serving a hitch with the military flying C-130s from Pope Air Force Base, North Carolina, noticed an ad on the post bulletin board. It announced one of the pilots on the Base was looking for a partner to buy a one-half interest in his Luscombe 8A. Jim succumbed and was soon "tooling around" in this lively performer, using it, in part, to "court" the future Mrs. Zazas.

Some months later, his owner-partner was getting married and wanted "out" of the partisan arrangement. Jim obliged and thus possessed 100 percent of this "rag-wing" beauty! As of the date of this writing he still does and has flown it extensively including a coast-to-coast trip from Kitty Hawk to San Francisco and return.

Between June 1982 and March 1984, Jim gave his Luscombe a complete overhaul featuring a gleaming yellow paint job trimmed with glossy black. He flies the "Canary" (as it is dubbed) to participate in the various sport aviation activities of the Southeast.

Jim, a talented writer for numerous military and civilian aviation publications, became so captivated with this popular "tail-dragger" he decided to research and write about its manufacturer's heritage, the Luscombe Airplane Corporation. His was an in-depth challenge to trace its development from dreams to reality.

The dreamer was Donald A. Luscombe, a great man who left his mark within the aircraft industry for the superb design, manufacturing processes and quality performance of all-metal light aircraft. This corporate biography will give the reader an insight into the man and the people who surrounded him assisting in the pursuit of his inceptive ideas through final fruition. And so was born what will be a two volume story of Don Luscombe and his Visions!

Following separation from active duty in the Air Force in 1984, Zazas joined Piedmont Airlines (now USAir) as a Flight Officer flying 727, 757 and 767 jets domestically and transoceanic. During his "off duty" hours he proceeded with his writing. Research on Jim's book has consumed a time span of some eight years! He has toured this country widely in pursuit of factual data and personal interviews with those who knew and worked with Don Luscombe during his many years in the aircraft industry. Governmental historical records and archives have been scrutinized as well in search of "the story." Although Don was primarily a promoter and seller of ideas, his consuming interest, following flights in France during World War I, centered on the means to manufacture airplanes.

This book relates how Don's interest in flying and aviation grew. His first acquisition was an OX-5 powered JN4 "Jenny" biplane in which he learned to fly. A Laird Swallow followed — and then his first venture into airplane manufacturing, the formation of Central States Aero Company in the Davenport, Iowa, area. Here, in late March 1927, the first "Monocoupe" was born. The "Monocoach" followed as did the "Monoprep" and "Monosport." It was a never-ending task for Don to raise funds to proceed with his corporate goals of airplane design and production and, from time to time, reorganization was necessary. Formation of the Monocoupe Corporation followed and, eventually, the Luscombe Airplane

Company situated in the Kansas City area.

Advances were made in the design and manufacturing techniques along the way utilizing sheet aluminum, extruded aluminum spars and formed ribs. In early 1934, the famed "Phantom" appeared preceding a company move to West Trenton, New Jersey, which was completed in early 1935. Shortly following this move and to attract greater operating capital, Luscombe Airplane Development Corporation was chartered under the laws of that state. From here emerged the "Luscombe 90" prior to formation of yet another change to Luscombe Airplane Corporation two years later in April of 1937 as "development" work had been completed.

Don and his small group then concentrated on designing and producing an all-metal light airplane, the "Luscombe 50," from whence came the famous advertising slogan "No Wood — No Nails — No Glue"! The line of increased power Continental engine Model 8s followed.

Reaction to this latest design, coupled with the fine flying performance of these new aircraft, was stimulating, catching the interest of not only the flying fraternity but would-be pilots as well. The Warner Brothers Studio, reacting to public acclaim, arranged to do a short film clip featuring this unique construction technique — and so it was completed at the Luscombe plant for showing country-wide!

It was during his never ending quest for operating capital that Don met Leopold H.P. Klotz who poured much needed funds into the organization, acquiring controlling stock issues along the way. In April of 1939, due to conflicting views within management, Don stepped aside, leaving control of the business in the hands of Mr. Klotz. And so it was that Don, his wife, and several associates loyal to Don left West Trenton taking up residence in the same general area in nearby Pennsylvania.

Always a dreamer and entrepreneur, Don asked his friend and former Chief Engineer, Frederick J. Knack, to design a new experimental all-metal four-place high-wing airplane. Hence, in August 1939, an attractive monoplane featuring a gull-wing was developed at Fred's house in Willow Grove, Pennsylvania while actual construction of the prototype took shape nearby at Don's estate in Gwynedd Valley. During this time period various other enterprises were set in motion. Don organized yet another of his companies in early 1942, the Luscombe Engineering Company, Inc., whose output was quite diversified.

Jim's unique style for combining the stringent lines of company detail with human interest anecdotes of the true-life players make this story most readable.

To lovers of flying, of aviation, of enterprise and adventure and MONO-COUPES and LUSCOMBES — "take off"!

A. Edgar Mitchell
Luscombe Alumnus
Hatboro, Pennsylvania
January 1992

Acknowledgments

Writing a book is a team effort. Without the help and encouragement of many different individuals and organizations, this book would not have been possible. I am indebted to the following individuals for their total support in this project:

Alan Abel, Drina Welch Abel, Jerry and Delores Adkison, Bruce Akers, Jon Aldrich, Andy Austin, Brian Baker, Dorothy Driggs Baker, Melvin Barron, John and Alice Bergeson, T.R. Boyd, Bob and Carol Brown, Tom and Margaret Bruce, Lee and Geraldine Brutus, Ken Bryant, Loren and Adele Bump, Charles E. Burgess (dec.), Mrs. Winona Burgess, John Butler (NARA), Dick Cavin, Kenneth E. Cericola, Kathy Coghill, Jerry and Lucy Coigny, Joe and Ellen Cole, Mike Collins, Doug and Laurie Combs, Bob Coolbaugh, Jack and Golda Cox (EAA), Edgar S. Davis, Jules de Crescenzo (dec.), Steve Davis, Cathy Dick, Rick Duckworth, Capt. Carlos Dufriche, Kent Dragnett (dec.), Mrs. Connie Dragnett, Eric and Annie Edelson, J. Elliot Eggleston, Marty and Bee Eisenmann, Wayne Evans, Susan Ewing (NASM), Lyle L. Farver (dec.), Mrs. Carol Farver, Stephen D. Feldman, Alex and Evangeline Filis, Mrs. Fran Fitzwilliam, Lee Flick, Calvin Folkerts, Dale Folkerts, William E. Force (dec.), Mrs. Dottie Force, Chuck Forrester, Keith Funk, Robert Funk, Ross Funk (dec.), Mrs. Naomi Funk, William Grady, Dwayne Green, Howard P. Greene, Rolfe Gregory, Carl Gunther, Dan Hagedorn (NASM), Jim Harvey, R.S. Hirsch, Otto Hoernig, David Hutchison, Todd Huvard, Frank Johnson (dec.), Mrs. Leah Johnson, Joe Johnson, Howard and Ella Jong, Butch Joyce, Fred and Martha Jungclaus, Lucille Luscombe Kapitan, Glenn and Pauline Kauffman, John C. Kelly, Alfred "Fritz" and Marion King, Leopold H.P. Klotz, Leo J. Kohn, Jean Kornblut, Jo Kotula, James M. Kovakas, A.R. Krieger, William T. Larkins, Moody Larsen, Linwood and Emilee Lawrence, Jerome "Jerry" Lederer, John Lengenfelder, Lane Leonard, Red Lerille, Wayne Livengood, Andrew Love, James H. Luscombe, James T. Luscombe (dec.), Ora May "Brownee" Luscombe, Murry Main, G. Paul McCormick, John McCulloch, Owen McGrath, Ben Melcher, Mike Melfa, Mark Meyer, A. Edgar and Lorry Mitchell, Merle and Wanda Mueller, Tom and Evelyn Murphy, Eugene and Jan Norris, Betty Luscombe Numerof, Dennis Parks (EAA), Austin Perdue (dec.), Robert J. Pickett (dec.), Stephen Pitcairn, John Polhemus, Eric and Debbie Preston, Ron and Donna Price, Marta Purvis, Carol Rex, Henrietta Roberts, Ken Roberts, Bill and Ginny Robinson, Frederick "Rick" Ropkey, Bert Rowe, Eugene and Bonnie Ruder, Ignatius and Sissie Sargent, Ed Saurenman, Mike Schenk, LaDean Seago, Bill and Jane Shepard, Eleanore Luscombe Shurtz (dec.), Paul Silberman (NASM), Graham M. Simons, Chris Stuhldreher, Norman Summey, Quinton Sweeney, John Swick, Brent Taylor, Cecil Taylor, Robert Taylor, Stan Thomas, Della Tinsley, Chizuko Ueno, John Underwood, Nora Walkup (FAA), Truman "Pappy" Weaver, Gar Williams, Walter Winazak, Tom Woodburn, Bill Wright, Margie Wright, Mrs. Barbara Zazas, George J. Zazas (dec.), Karen Q. Zazas, Robert C. Zazas, Sylvia Zazas (dec.) and Wanda Zuege.

In particular, I would like to thank the Monocoupe and Luscombe factory alumni and family members who opened their hearts, memories and homes to this wandering researcher/author. Without their candid input, this project would have never been possible.

Special recognition must be given to Dorothy Driggs Baker, Chuck and Winona Burgess, Jerry and Lucy Coigny, Marty and Bee Eisenmann, Mrs. Fran Fitzwilliam, Keith Funk, Rolfe Gregory, Howard Greene, Frank and Leah Johnson, Howard and Ella Jong,

Al and Marion King, Jerry Lederer, Mrs. Ora May "Brownee" Luscombe, Ben Melcher and Tom Murphy. These gracious factory alumni and family members, as well as others I may have forgotten to include, spent considerable time proof-reading various sections of my manuscript, each adding or correcting passages as necessary.

To this end, a distinctive and most heartfelt appreciation must be given also to Ed and Lorry Mitchell. When my first calls for information went forth, both were there and most willing to offer whatever they could. These two wonderful folks spent innumerable hours proof-reading my many manuscript copies from the first chapters to the completed work. Ed and Lorry, you have given more than you will ever realize.

The Monocoupe chapters would not have been possible without the support of Red Lerille and, in particular, John Underwood. John graciously allowed me unrestricted use of the copious notes, letters, documents and correspondence he collected preparing his excellent work, Of Monocoupes and Men.

Furthermore, a great deal of Monocoupe history and related information was provided by Jim Harvey, a most knowledgeable Monocoupe historian, one-time editor of the Monocoupe Flyer and the proud owner of a Monocoupe 90A.

Similarly, I owe a great debt of gratitude to Mike Schenk, Velie historian and Monocoupe enthusiast. He opened his many files and served as tour guide during my visit to the Quad Cities.

The "Golden Age of Air Racing" details were edited by air racing historian Major Truman C. "Pappy" Weaver (Ret.). His notes and comments, supplementing those of Jim Harvey, added much to the overall accuracy of this book.

This book involved many fine folks at many museums and archives. To this end, I would like to offer a special thank you to the fine folks at the Air Force Museum, Experimental Aircraft Association Museum/Archives, the National Air and Space Museum, the National Archives, the Library of Congress and the Aviation Heritage Library. Each showed me the "proper" way to find the answers I sought.

Similarly, I would like to thank James M. Kovakas and Jean Kornblut of the U.S. Department of Justice, Freedom of Information/Public Affairs Office, for their help and patience during my many visits to review wartime Vested Claims Committee documents.

I would be remiss if I forgot to mention the many Monocoupe enthusiasts and "Luscombe Lovers" worldwide who offered encouragement. To this end, recognition must be given to John and Alice Bergeson of the Luscombe Association; Loren and Adele Bump of the Continental Luscombe Association; and Bob Coolbaugh, Jim Harvey, and Bud and Connie Dake of the Monocoupe Club. These untiring individuals, and all who have helped them through the years, have kept the "spirit" of the Monocoupe and Luscombe airplanes alive and well. Thank you all for your support and patience.

Similarly, two great organizations, the Experimental Aircraft Association and the Antique Airplane Association, have kept the antique/classic movement growing and prosperous worldwide. Their many-fold activities and dedication to aviation will keep the Visions of Luscombe flying for years to come.

A special note of thanks goes to La Dean Seago and Margie Wright, my courageous interview tape transcribers. Each patiently endured the horrors of putting on paper my often "chatty" conversations with Luscombe alumni.

Likewise, another very special thank you is extended to Fred Jungclaus, my meticulous artist who made the fine STANAVO Luscombe Phantom rendering and Phantom profiles. Ours is a unique relationship as I grew-up in Indianapolis, Indiana, with his parents only a few houses in one direction and his nephew a few houses in the other direction. Little did I know then Fred and I would share a two common denominators — this book and flying. Each have proved immensely rewarding.

The excellent Monocoupe drawings are the handiwork of R.S. Hirsch. He has captured the Monocoupe's classy style and "sexy" grace in his fine drawings. His work is often found in the <u>American Aviation Historical Society Journal</u>.

Many of the photographs depicted in this book were obtained from a variety of sources, including Monocoupe and Luscombe factory alumni, private collections, libraries and contemporary publications. Dorothy Driggs Baker, Chuck and Winona Burgess, Lyle and Carol Farver, Jim Harvey, Frank and Leah Johnson, Howard and Ella Jong, Leo J. Kohn, A.R. Krieger, William T. Larkins, John Lengenfelder, Ed and Lorry Mitchell, Ron Price, Ignatius and Sissie Sargent, Mike Schenk, John Underwood and others graciously loaned photographs from their unique collections.

The color photographs were obtained from original, 16mm "home movie" film shot by Ignatius and Sissie Sargent. In turn, 4x5 color transparencies were made from individual frames under the discerning eye of Norman Summey and his assistant, Diane Fitzpatrick. Their special talents added "life" to this project.

Preparing a book often requires the use of many unique facilities. I would like to thank Todd Huvard, Mike Collins, Carol Comer, Dave Mallette, Fonda Hughes and rest of the fine staff at <u>The Southern Aviator</u> for the use of their Macintosh computers and darkroom.

A special thank you is extended to Mike Collins, the magazine's untiring editor. He took time from his busy schedule to make sure all my "t's" were crossed and all my "i's" were dotted when he wasn't scrutinizing my copious use of developer and photographic paper.

I would like to extend my most sincere appreciation and thanks to the fine folks at Aviation Heritage/SunShine House. In particular, I would like to thank Drina Welch Abel, a most gracious and sincere lady who first proposed she publish my work. Likewise, my most heartfelt thanks goes to her two sons, Alan and Greg, both of whom offered much encouragement and support at all stages of this project. In addition, special recognition must be given to Karen Horn, Colleen Brannon and Mitzi Nichols. These most helpful ladies had their patience tried on many occasions while I barraged them with my constant revisions.

Likewise, I had encouragement from family, including Barbara Zazas, Eric Edelson, Bob Zazas, Joe and Ellen Cole, Alex and Evangeline Filis, and Della Tinsley.

A simple "I want a copy of your book!" from friends including John Kelly, Chris Stuhldreher, Cathy Dick, Chris Percey, Terri Loncar, Wanda Zuege, Jeff and Thorny Little and many others kept me moving forward.

To this end, I would like to thank Chizuko Ueno for reasons only I can appreciate.

Anybody who has ever written a book learns very quickly such an endeavor becomes a soul-searching and consuming labor of love, an almost demanding mistress. Fortunately, I had a "real" woman at my side who appreciated the wily ways of this project. I would like to thank my wife, Karen, for her untiring, if not hand-wringing patience and understanding during the lengthy course of this project. Though stuffed file boxes, countless letters, faded photographs, scattered cassette tapes and assorted research paraphernalia littered the home, she allowed me a freedom to pursue this project few women on this earth would tolerate. Thank you, Karen, and good luck in all your future endeavors.

Finally, words cannot express the many contributions my late father, George J. Zazas (1926 - 1990), made to this project. He allowed me a virtually unrestricted freedom to pursue my many endeavors in life, always offering encouragement tempered with the love and concern of a parent. This first few chapters of this book were written during his heroic battle with cancer. The balance was written after his death. I regret he never saw the completed product, but I know he would have been proud.

About the Author

Jim Zazas was born in Tampa, Florida, in 1955, yet grew up in aviation-rich Indianapolis, Indiana. The model airplanes of his youth quickly gave way to flying real Cessnas, Pipers and Stearmans, including four years at DePauw University, Greencastle, Indiana, where he graduated in 1977 with a B.A. degree in Political Science. Concurrently, Jim was commissioned through the AFROTC program at Indiana University and started Undergraduate Pilot Training at Columbus Air Force Base, Mississippi, in February 1978.

Twin-engine Cessna T-37B and Northrop T-38A jet trainers soon lead to four-engine airplanes, most notably Lockheed C-130E/H transports. A five-year tour followed at Pope Air Force Base, North Carolina, where he flew Lockheed's rugged and reliable "Herky Bird." Though exciting, including four deployments to Europe and as an Aircraft Commander in Operation Urgent Fury (the Grenada Invasion), Jim separated from the U.S. Air Force and joined Piedmont Airlines as a pilot in early 1984.

Today, Jim flies the Boeing 757 and Boeing 767ER for USAir. Though flying "warbirds," restoring antique airplanes, wilderness canoeing and writing for several flying safety, military aviation and sport aviation publications are included in his many hobbies, Jim enjoys flying his 1946, rag-wing Luscombe 8A most of all. In May 1986, Jim undertook a fifteen-day, coast-to-coast, no-radio adventure in his Luscombe from Kitty Hawk, North Carolina, to San Francisco, California, and return.

Currently, Jim is restoring a recent acquisition, the one-off Luscombe "Gull-Wing" or, as it is better known, the Weatherly-Campbell "Colt."

Introduction

Writing a book is an experience bar none. The mind, body and very soul of a writer meld to create the work. In essence, this work becomes a disembodied extension of the author's persona. Much like an artist who splashes life's color across a tapestry, the writer puts life to paper. In the end, the final product in the hands of the reader makes this experience all worthwhile.

Undertaking such an endeavor requires a measured degree of extreme patience and luck. The spectrum of rewards for such perseverance range from positive accolades to depressing frustrations.

Visions of Luscombe required input and contributions on many levels. On numerous occasions, contributors had to draw upon memories of events that took place fifty or more years ago. Some of these recollections were joyous, others were embarrassing and a few, no doubt, were painful. Without this devoted input, this book would not have been possible.

The idea for Visions of Luscombe was conceived on a balmy, North Carolina evening in early August 1983. At the time, my hail-damaged 1946 Luscombe 8A was undergoing an extensive restoration. To ensure accuracy in this project, I sought information relating to the correct paint schemes of the period, proper instrument placement, upholstery and so forth.

Using available publications, most notably John Underwood's excellent work, Of Monocoupes and Men, and Joseph Juptner's factual, U.S. Civil Aircraft series, I set upon my task. However, much to my dismay, I soon discovered a tremendous lack of concise, alternative information. Furthermore, simple investigations revealed this information often conflicted with other published information, most notably magazine articles, then readily available.

Why did these differences exist? I found myself constantly asking, "What is the 'real story'?"

My interest piqued, I called John Bergeson, Luscombe Association Chairman, and Loren Bump, Continental Luscombe Association President for help. Each suggested I contact the few Luscombe alumni and family members they had on their membership rosters for the information I sought. Likewise, I made several telephone calls to Robert Taylor, Antique Airplane Association President, and netted similar results.

It took only a few letters and telephone calls to these factory alumni to realize my humble search had lead me to a dynamic branch of American aviation history rarely told. More was involved than a simple biography of Don Luscombe or rehashed descriptions of the airplanes that bear his name. A genuine need existed to accurately detail the goals and visions of Don Luscombe from his earliest aviation endeavors in the mid-1920s to the loss of his company shortly before the outbreak of hostilities culminating in World War II.

This period in United States and world history was fraught with many challenges and misery. A beleaguered world was recovering from one major world war and was about to enter another. The economy of the greatest economic power on Earth at the time was in shambles. Indeed, times were tough!

Yet, Don Luscombe and a handful of other clairvoyant individuals were able to produce and sell airplanes for the private owner against almost overwhelming odds. These individuals raised money any way they could and built these airplanes without government assistance! Little did they realize the significant contributions they were making to aviation history.

I decided to write a book about Donald A. Luscombe, his visions, his airplanes and the men who shared these ambitions. To this end, I decided to concentrate my efforts in this volume to Don's early years, the period encompassing Don's childhood to mid-1939.

I endeavored to tell this story, seeking the bulk of the information I needed from the living Luscombe family and factory alumni and, in turn, share it with fellow Monocoupe enthusiasts and "Luscombe Lovers." At first, my simple goal was to explain this history in a one hundred page book, complete with photographs and drawings. Very quickly, I realized this attempt was impossible; too much needed to be told in so few pages.

In the end, I settled for a volume that would faithfully present the clairvoyant insights of Don Luscombe, the promoter. Likewise, I aimed to share his many successes and heartaches, including the important contributions of the dedicated men — and women — that rallied around Don. At the same time, I felt obligated to offer descriptions relative to the corporate and financial background necessary for Don to achieve these objectives.

I didn't know it at the time, but much of the information I uncovered often contradicted with many popular Monocoupe/Luscombe airplane and design stories handed down through the years. Much of this lore and legend has been accepted as "fact" by many Monocoupe and Luscombe enthusiasts.

To find the "truth," I decided factory alumni, family members, corporate records, court documents and archival material would constitute the basis for accuracy in my book. I soon found myself becoming a detective as I uncovered these recollections and records buried by time. Quite often and much to my dismay, I found many worthy records irretrievably lost to natural calamity, ignorance or general lack of interest.

My quest for accurate information took me well beyond the few Luscombe family and Monocoupe/Luscombe factory alumni members provided initially. In time, this list expanded to almost two hundred names and other sources of information. Weekend hobbies and weekday free time were often sacrificed in countless libraries, archives, private homes and offices. I was allowed to tape, copy and photograph whatever was needed.

Though my research widened and my correspondence files bulged, it was the Monocoupe and Luscombe factory alumni — the men who designed the airplanes, bucked the rivets or made the decisions to keep the company a going concern — who remained my best source of accurate information. In many cases, the wives of these admirable gentlemen offered equally important insights and information through personal interviews. As a direct result, a great many close and lasting friendships evolved from this project.

These interviews proved indispensable. Perishable memories were recorded and preserved. In many instances, these interviews offered details that escaped my note-taking and correspondence. I found these tapes invaluable when writing a particular section, especially if the interviewee had died since the time of the interview.

I made every attempt to have another source, a confirmation, before ink went to paper. Written sources such as corporate and government documents, legal filings, company Board of Directors' minutes and personal correspondence proved invaluable. Many are quoted to give the reader a greater insight and meaning into certain complex events.

Specific dates were determined from variety of sources, but the most important proved to be the pilot logbooks of Don Luscombe, Ig Sargent, Eddie Davis, Al "Fritz" King, Bill Shepard and Aline Brooks. Each revealed an accurate time-line of airplane test flights, modifications and, surprisingly, noteworthy corporate events.

Accuracy was my foremost goal. Yet, despite my best efforts or due to the information I had in hand at the time of this writing, I am sure inaccuracies and omissions will come to light; this fact cannot be discounted.

I actually look forward to learning more about this fascinating era of American aviation history from others whom might be able to offer a broader, more "accurate" insight. History needs to be shared and appreciated.

Any mistakes made in this work are mine alone. I endeavored to separate the "chaff from the wheat" and capture the "real story" before I was ready to publish this book.

I hope I have succeeded.

Donald A. Luscombe
(1895 - 1965)

ELEANORE LUSCOMBE SHURTZ COLLECTION

Promoter,

Entrepreneur,

Visionary

ELEANORE LUSCOMBE SHURTZ COLLECTION

Contents

Dedication

Preface

Acknowledgments

About the Author

Introduction

Chapter 1	Every Story Has Its Beginning	*1*
Chapter 2	One Has to Learn How to Walk, Before He Can Run	*9*
Chapter 3	Perfecting the Breed	*21*
Chapter 4	A Time for Change, A Chance for Survival	*31*
Chapter 5	A Time for Determined Action	*59*
Chapter 6	Tinker, Tailor, Engineer, Genius, and Romance	*75*
Chapter 7	Metal, Mass Production and Kansas City	*87*
Chapter 8	New Places, Smiling Faces	*107*
Chapter 9	Looking Up, Getting Better	*127*
Chapter 10	"Well... We Tried Everything Else"	*145*
Chapter 11	Making the Grade — The Quest for an All-Metal Airplane	*161*
Chapter 12	Prelude to Success	*179*
Chapter 13	No Wood! No Nails! No Glue!	*195*
Chapter 14	Rainbow's End	*209*
Chapter 15	Forces Greater Than He	*225*
Chapter 16	Post Luscombe, Luscombe	*237*
Footnotes		*253*
Appendix A	Monocoupe Brochure Reprints	*263*
Appendix B	Monocoupe Specifications	*269*
Appendix C	Individual Luscombe Phantom Model 1 Histories	*277*
Appendix D	Individual Luscombe "90" Histories	*293*
Appendix E	Luscombe Airplane Development Corporation Distributorships for 1937	*297*
Appendix F	Luscombe Phantom, Luscombe "90," Luscombe "50" and Luscombe "65" Specifications	*299*
Appendix G	Luscombe Phantom, Luscombe "90," Luscombe "50" and Luscombe "65" First Flight Analysis	*301*
Bibliography		*305*
Addendum		*309*
Index		*315*

*"Was it a vision, or a waking dream?
Fled is that music: Do I wake or sleep?"*
John Keats (1795 - 1821)

Chapter One

Every Story Has Its Beginning

Visions. They are perceptions, an often intensely personal illumination or intelligent foresight focused within the mind and spirit. They may be brief, like a wisp of smoke in a gentle wind, or they may be intense, powerful enough to shake the body and soul to its very core of existence. They may be clairvoyant, portending events to be, or they may be a summation of experiences, a simple answer to end a difficult day's work.

Donald A. Luscombe had his vision — build, market, sell, advertise, *PROMOTE* an affordable, responsive, sturdy, personally owned, mass produced airplane. The "all-metal" portion of this perception was still many years distant. Luscombe took time and tremendous personal effort to develop and mature this vision into reality. He nursed this vision, he cradled it, loved it and often cursed it. Regardless of obstacles, Don persevered, prevailed and followed his vision until it was ripped from him by forces more powerful than he.

Don Luscombe was often torn between two objectives. One half of his complex personality desired the promoting or selling of his ideas. The other half wrestled with the means to manufacture or produce these ideas. In the final analysis, he settled for both. Don was neither a designer nor an engineer. He possessed neither the necessary engineering skills nor the mechanical ability to undertake such endeavors. But what he lacked, he compensated by surrounding himself with friends, acquaintances and employees who possessed these learned and "natural" abilities.

Luscombe was fortunate, however. He had the drive, the desire and the ability to follow his visions. He did not know what drove him, but he knew what he wanted. And being so driven, he usually achieved and received credit for the visions he promoted.

Donald A. Luscombe was born in Iowa City, Iowa, on May 25, 1895.[1] He was the second son of James Liddle Luscombe and Minnie Ellen Hartle Luscombe. An older brother, James Torring Luscombe, was born February 10, 1894. A younger brother, Robert Hartle Luscombe, was born August 7, 1900.

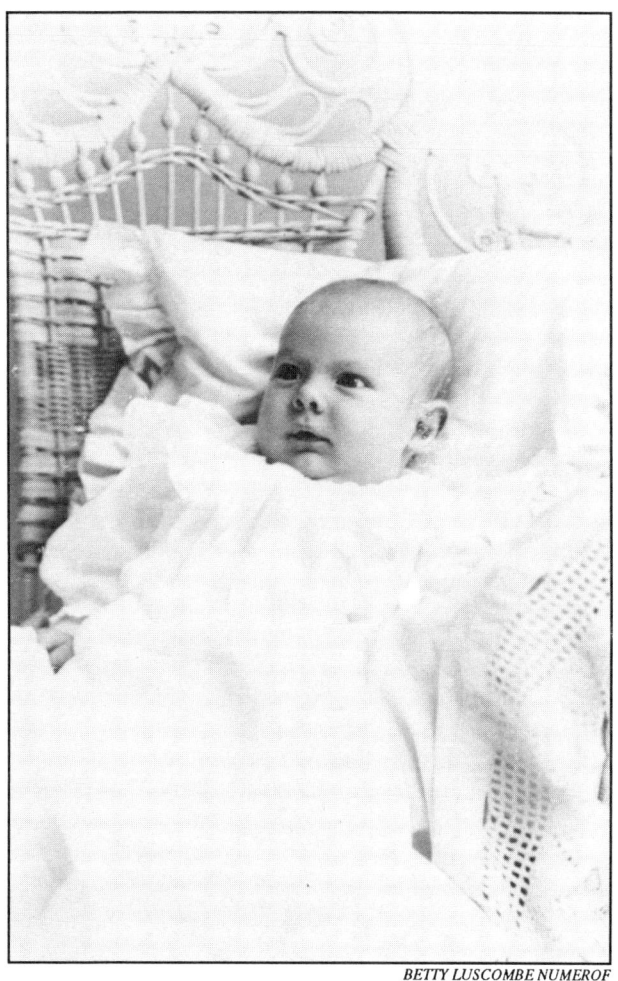

Five months old, Don Luscombe captured the hearts of his parents, James and Minnie Ellen.

The family was neither wealthy, nor was it poor. A modest home provided shelter and warmth for the Luscombes from the Midwest's fickle weather that ranged from hot, humid summers to the bone chilling winters.

Though the Luscombe name traces its origin to French-Norman ancestry, the family background is solidly English.[2]

Don's father was a tall, somewhat thin man. The first born of three children and the eldest son of a yeoman farmer, James Liddle Luscombe was heir

James Liddle Luscombe

Minnie Ellen Hartle Luscombe

Cabinet photograph mark used by James Liddle Luscombe. Circa 1890-1900.

apparent to a small farm called Leigh in the parish of Aveton-Grifford, Kingsbridge, Devon, England. Born at Albert Road, Finchley, London, England, he came to the United States in May of 1871 when his parents emigrated. Family records suggest Don's paternal grandfather, James Torring Luscombe (December 6, 1838 - January 12, 1873), was a member of the Queen's guard. Don's paternal grandmother, Mary Liddle Luscombe (March 25, 1838 - May 14, 1916), was a dressmaker.[3]

Upon arriving in the United States and full of hopes for a better life, the family took a train to the end of the line, in this case Iowa. They settled in Iowa City where Don's grandfather earned a respectable reputation as an artisan carpenter.

James Liddle Luscombe (July 25, 1868 - November 4, 1928) met his future wife, Minnie Ellen Hartle, in Iowa City. Minnie Ellen (December 24, 1874 - March 11, 1959) was the youngest of ten children born to her parents, George Hartle and Sarah Dansdill Hartle. James and Minnie were married in the Christian Church, Iowa City, Iowa, on January 1, 1893.

When his sons were born, James was a commercial photographer for the nearby University of Iowa and owned the Luscombe Studio on Dubuque Street in Iowa City. He was an accomplished artist, also.

Minnie was a good housewife and caring mother. She tended always to the needs of her growing children, James (called Torring by the family), Don and Bob. Sadly, tragedy struck the Luscombe family when Don was barely fifteen months or so old. Brother Torring died from diphtheria and was buried in the family plot in Iowa City.

Growing up, Don shared many of his father's avid hunting and fishing interests. Hunting dogs, mostly beagles, were kept in outdoor pens near the family home. But it was his father's photography work that often captured the greater part of Don's attention. He spent many hours tinkering with his father's cameras and darkroom equipment. As such, photography developed into one of Don's favorite hobbies, a keen interest that stayed with him through the balance of his life. Bob, on the other hand, was keen with numbers. He enjoyed mathematics and preferred a more analytical approach to his hobbies. He loved to tinker with things mechanical. Iowa City, a closeknit community located some thirty miles south of Cedar Rapids and sixty or so miles west of Davenport, was nestled on the banks of the meandering Iowa River that flowed gently through the heart of the Hawkeye State's breadbasket. Farming was the lifeblood of the community. Though Don worked in the fields occasionally to earn extra income, farming was not his forte.

Growing up, he believed better opportunities existed. Marketing or better yet — promotional advertising — offered the challenge, fulfillment and personal recognition he sought. Don soon proved adept at promoting, and to a very small measure, writing. He could be most persuasive when he needed or wanted to be. Coupled, these skills served Luscombe well throughout his life. Quite often, these same abilities "shielded" him from difficult family and business problems, whereas at other times, these same attributes got him into trouble with family, associates and creditors.

Before he was fifteen, Don earned money deliv-

Chapter One: Every Story Has Its Beginning 3

ering newspapers. Additionally, he ran a small printing press at home, financed by borrowed money from family, friends and neighbors. In turn, he would print and promote almost anything that crossed his machine's palate. To further enhance his income, Luscombe solicited and wrote advertising for the local newspapers.

Other early promotional advertising jobs involved early dirt track auto-racing. He wrote the programs, printed them and distributed same throughout the local area. Don Luscombe was recognized as a promoter. He was good at his craft, a "natural" in his field. His promoting skills were praised as often as they were cursed. Yet, regardless of his promotional ability, Luscombe often had difficulties managing his financial resources. These problems were demonstrated at an early age. Years later, when previous lenders asked Luscombe for reimbursement, they learned a small part of his personality; he would borrow money, but all too often, he would not (or could not) repay it. This detractive tendency plagued Don Luscombe the rest of his life.

Don was an adventurous youngster. However, his unbounded enthusiasm and zest for life got him into trouble on occasion. Once, while still in his teenage years, Don promoted a large dirt track race which offered generous cash prizes. Local merchants were asked to ante-up money to cover the race's expenses and promotion in return for some pre-race and race-day publicity. The race was run, but the prize money till came up short. Reportedly, Don had used some of the funds for his own benefit. He could have been severely reprimanded, even thrown in jail then and there, but the merchants thought better. Any lawyer fees and associated court costs would total more than any monies that could be returned. Don got off with no more than a stern lecture from his father and a modest loss of respect from area merchants.

BETTY LUSCOMBE NUMEROF

During these dirt track racing days, Don had little more than a cursory interest in the cars. He was intrigued, however, by the mechanical modifications these cars

(Top center) Don Luscombe as a four-year-old.
(Bottom left) Seven years old and not camera shy, Don Luscombe poses for his father's lenses.
(Bottom right) Don always had a soft spot in his heart for animals, dogs more than any. A fourteen-year-old, Don (right) poses with his brother, Robert, and his father, James L., at the family home.

ELEANORE LUSCOMBE SHURTZ COLLECTION

BETTY LUSCOMBE NUMEROF

(Left) Sitting on the porch at the Marcy Street family home, Bob Luscombe (left) and Don Luscombe (right, center) pose with their mother, Minnie Ellen (center) and two aunts.

(Below) Magical, almost mystical eyes, Don's good looks broke many young ladies' hearts at college.

BETTY LUSCOMBE NUMEROF

ELEANORE LUSCOMBE SHURTZ COLLECTION

Though farming was not Don's forte, he did help in the fields on occasion to earn extra money.

ELEANORE LUSCOMBE SHURTZ COLLECTION

possessed to increase their performance. No doubt, Don was more interested in these enhancements as being a means to better his promotional pitch and advertising base than he was in the purely mechanical design and construction improvements.

Don loved the challenge of promoting and relished the opportunity to publicize a product. Once done, however, he would often sit back and let somebody else "carry the ball" after he had "built it up." As such, Don became the consummate promoter who enjoyed *promoting* a product to success, but cared very little for *managing* a product to success.

Another interesting aspect of Luscombe's personality was his controlled anger. It was cool, calculated and most effective. Though he could be verbally harsh at times, he was never physically abusive towards anyone nor threatened them. On the flip side of the coin, Don could be very gregarious. He could display great warmth and care towards others during very difficult times. These positive qualities and his natural charisma endeared other individuals to follow Don in pursuit of his quests, regardless of the difficulties presented, simply because they *believed in him.* But the major soft spot in Don's heart was his unyielding love and admiration for animals. He never displayed any anger towards any animal. And of all creatures on the earth, he loved dogs more than any other. Growing up, as in later years, Don always had a pet dog nearby.

As college days approached, Don turned his sights to the nearby University of Iowa. He enrolled in the school's Liberal Arts College in September 1914, and took courses in English, public relations and advertising. He shied from the math and science

(Right) Don A. Luscombe strikes a rigid pose before his World War I ambulance.

(Below) The horrors of World War I France surrounded Don Luscombe during his tour of duty.

ELEANORE LUSCOMBE SHURTZ COLLECTION

ELEANORE LUSCOMBE SHURTZ COLLECTION

courses.

While attending the university, Don was very involved in retail advertising and promotion on many levels. He held several local and national accounts, including one from a respected coast-to-coast men's clothing chain. Additionally, Don became a member of the Phi Kappa Psi fraternity and was initiated into this fraternal organization on October 12, 1915. Though educated at a well-known and respected school, Don later wrote, *"Most of my education came from making money so I could attend school."* No doubt he was referring to his teenager "print shop" days and his college advertising experiences.

The future was bright for Don and his college friends and fraternity brothers, yet war clouds billowed on a distant European horizon and offered chilling implications their future might involve combat. Though President Woodrow Wilson adopted a policy of neutrality and promised our "boys" would not fight on foreign soil, American loyalty to France and a developing anger towards the Germans regarding their invasion of neutral Belgium slanted public opinion towards the Allied nations plight. Many Americans thought United States participation was imminent.

On April 2, 1917, President Woodrow Wilson called a special session of the U.S. Congress. He asked for a "declaration of war" against Germany. In his stirring speech, Wilson said, *"The world must be made safe for democracy."* A strong sense of patriotism gripped America and many "boys" and men volunteered to help the British and French forces. Don was restless and volunteered to go overseas. Barely two-and-a-half years into his college work (he finished his winter term in March 1917), Luscombe joined six other Iowa volunteers in offering their services to Uncle Sam as members of the Ambulance Corps.

A local Iowa City newspaper printed the exciting news. Under the banner "Six More to Serve Country, Another Patriotic Quintet of Iowa Boys to Aid Government Ambulance Corps," Don Luscombe was mentioned as one of six going to Allentown, Pennsylvania, in May or early June (1917) for training before being ordered to France. The article continued by quoting the Army Medical Corps officer who inspected the men as saying, *"This is a fine group of young men, much better than the average, as to physical attributes and mental and moral caliber."*

Don's ambulance unit, an "American Sanitary Section," was assigned to French forces, but was soon transferred to elements of the American Expeditionary Forces. His rank was Private First Class. Don had barely arrived in the Paris sector when the horrors of war were thrust upon him. Broken buildings, torn bodies and shattered lives offered grim and constant reminders of man's inhumanity towards his fellow man.

Don Luscombe's first airplane flight was in a 1916 French Voisin pusher biplane similar to this aircraft. AVIATION HERITAGE LIBRARY

He often looked to the skies for relief from the human misery around him and watched in awe as the tiny airplanes swooped, soared and chased in combat. His desire to fly intensified as stirring stories of aerial heroism found their way to his ambulance unit. Eager to experience firsthand the fascination of flight, Don bartered his way into the cockpit. Offering a pack of cigarettes or a friendly handshake, Don eventually convinced the French pilots at a nearby Paris-sector based Escadrille to take him aloft occasionally while airplanes and crew were ferried from one location to another.

Don Luscombe wanted to fly and now he was. Circling the Abbey de Chartres in World War I France, in a French Voisin pusher biplane, Don was elated. The experience was wonderful; it was his first airplane flight!

Donald A. Luscombe — a son of an Iowa City, Iowa, photographer, a former University of Iowa student and now an ambulance driver in World War I France — could only look from his lofty vantage point, marvel at the red-roofed monastery and many sights below him, and dream of the future. France, in all its pastoral and tranquil beauty, was embraced in an ugly war. But it was the flying that offered this lad of twenty-one an escape from the grim horrors that surrounded him. Don may have sensed he wanted to be a substantial part of this new endeavor man called "flying." Though he didn't realize it then, history would prove later he would be a convincing leader in the new arena called "aviation."

Don Luscombe's memorable experience over the Abbey that day placed a formulative vision within him — the adventure he experienced should and would be shared by others. In time, he would learn he could be "paid" for promoting and providing the means of this new, if not intensely personal, adventure by those who could afford to do so. Years later, when Don was pursuing

ELEANORE LUSCOMBE SHURTZ COLLECTION

A photograph of the oil painting Don purchased of the Abbey de Chartres. This photograph was taken by Don Luscombe, and is one of many photographs taken by Don which are included in this book.

other endeavors, an oil painting of the Abbey was exhibited at a New York City gallery on 57th Street. It caught his eye and his heart. He had to have the painting there and then, at all costs — so intense was his desire, so strong were the memories of better, more rewarding times. With his wife's urging, Don bought the painting for $300. Quite possibly through these World War I flights and, in particular, the flight over Abbey de Chartres, Don realized his future would involve aviation in one manner or another.

Sitting on the front porch of the Luscombe family home on Marcy Street in Iowa City, Robert and Don Luscombe pose with Clara Hadley (Bob's fiance) and Eleanore True Luscombe, Don's wife. BETTY LUSCOMBE NUMEROF

At last, the Great War ended in Europe. The Armistice was signed on November 11, 1918. The Americans "over there" were coming home. Don was anxious to return home and start his own advertising business. Don's exemplary efforts with the French forces did not go unnoticed; he was recognized for heroism in a belated citation from 42nd Division French General Commandant de Baresout. Dated 12 January 1919, the citation order stated:

"A very brave and devoted driver. Without regard for bullets and shells has time and time again gone up to the most advanced postes (sic) to bring back wounded. Distinguished himself particularly before the Canal du Nord and on the Aisne during attacks of August and September."[4]

Returning to Iowa City, Don was reunited with many home-town friends and associates. Together, they talked of future goals and dreams. Eventually, Don returned to school during July 1919, and stayed there until February 1920, the end of the academic year. Don Luscombe never completed the requirements for his degree. Instead, he elected to forego any further college and decided to pursue advertising full-time where he maintained active accounts.

Shortly after his return from Europe, fate intervened and played a grand hand; Don met his future wife, Eleanore True. Four years his junior, a public relations major at the university and a member of Gamma Phi sorority, she was introduced to Luscombe by his cousin, who just happened to be a sorority sister of Miss True. Eleanore True was swept off her feet. Don Luscombe was known as a "lady killer" in those days. His slim build, overall good looks, dark hair and expressive grey eyes made many female hearts skip a beat or two.

Obviously, Don saw something special in Miss True. Barely two weeks after their first date, he proposed marriage. However, Miss True came from a strict family. She was very worried how the family would react to the news, especially since she had ended a recent engagement to another fine lad a couple weeks earlier. When Don suggested, *"Let's keep it a secret,"* needless-to-say, Eleanore True was utterly flabbergasted by the proposal, yet she accepted.[5]

The happy couple went to Tipton, Iowa, and were married on December 12, 1919. However, they kept the news of their marriage secret until the following Valentine's Day. To further conceal their marriage, the newlyweds dated other friends over the holiday period. Upon learning of her daughter's marriage, Eleanore's mother went into a rage. She wrote to Dean Auner of the University of Iowa to find out more about Don Luscombe. Her beloved daughter's new husband had broken virtually all the rules for social protocol. How dare he marry her only daughter without "asking for her hand!" And, she wondered, *"Who is this Don Luscombe?"* The Dean replied, answering the questions regarding Luscombe's character. He added Don was an *"O.K. sort of fellow, but not too industrious in school."*

In September 1920, several months after the couple revealed they were, in fact, married, they moved to nearby Davenport, Iowa, to start their lives together. Don became the advertising manager for Dave Newsted, proprietor of a small men's clothing store chain in Iowa and neighboring Illinois. Additionally, the new couple bought a lovely frame home where their home life became very pleasant.

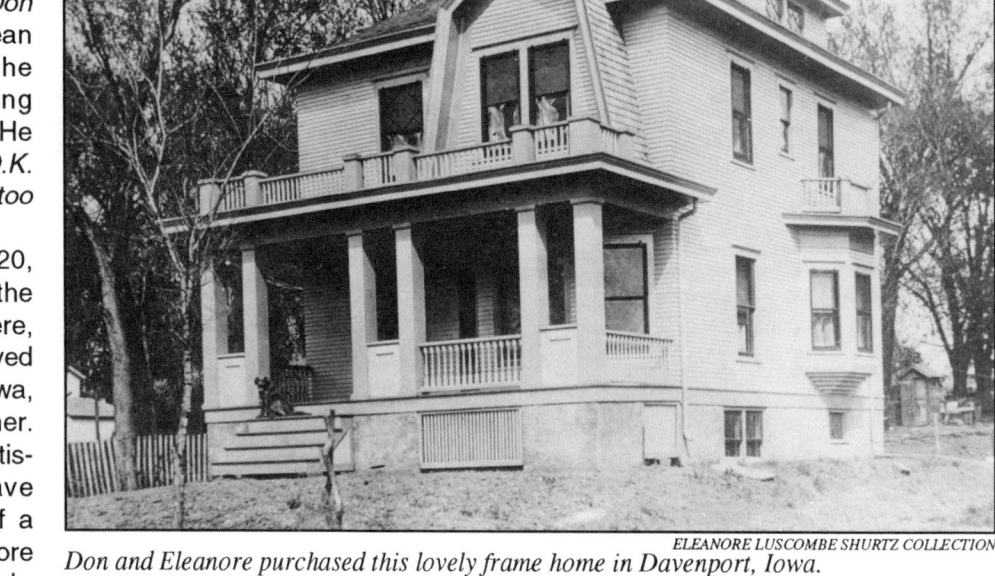

Don and Eleanore purchased this lovely frame home in Davenport, Iowa. — ELEANORE LUSCOMBE SHURTZ COLLECTION

On February 9, 1922, the Luscombes had their first child, a lovely daughter they named Patricia Irene Luscombe. Their happiness was short lived, however. The baby had a severe respiratory condition which could not be treated. Sadly, the child died less than three weeks later.

Although Don and Eleanore were heartbroken, they buried their grief in their work and activities in and around the house. Within a couple years later, Mr. Newsted sold his store in Iowa, thus, leaving Don to seek employment elsewhere. In turn, he started his own small business and called it the Luscombe Advertising Agency, locating his office in Davenport's prestigious Whitaker Block business district.

One of Don's first promotional ventures was convincing store owners to purchase advertising in specially printed copies of Charles Dickens' classic novel, *A Christmas Carol*. To sway business owner opinion, Don prepared a small, pocket-sized brochure detailing the advantages of such advertising. This pamphlet related the huge market potential of Christmas and "the millions of dollars invested each year in developing the idea that human kindness proves profitable during Christmas as it does no other time."

Merchants by the dozen were convinced. For a ten-cents-per-copy investment, a merchant could hand out free copies of a classic novel and carry their store's Christmas advertising message on the inside and back covers. Additionally, Luscombe convinced these store owners and managers that such an enterprise *"will gain a recognition not to be found in the customary channels of developing 'The Christmas Spirit.'"* The mold was set. Don Luscombe believed he could promote anything, including "Christmas Spirit," and often make a handsome profit for himself.

Don traveled quite often to further his many ideas. During one eleven to twelve week stint during the summer of 1925, Eleanore Luscombe returned to Iowa City to stay with Don's folks while he traveled throughout the eastern United States. On her behalf, Eleanore put the time to good use; she returned to school, though she never completed the requirements for her degree.

While Don's advertising ventures proved successful, his aviation interests remained strong. A small airfield near Davenport garnered his increasing attention. The ambitious activity at this small airfield rekindled his desire to fly.

He soon became a regular visitor.

"He whose honor depends on the opinion of the mob must day by day strive with the greatest anxiety, act and scheme in order to retain his reputation. For the mob is varied and inconsistent, and therefore, if a reputation is not carefully preserved it dies quickly."
Benedict [Baruch] Spinoza (1632 - 1677)

Chapter Two

One Has To Learn How To Walk, Before He Can Run

Clayton Folkerts' first airplane was an open air contraption that never flew.

The Bettendorf Airfield where Don Luscombe learned to fly, according to a Davenport-area newspaper, was "located between the Milwaukee tracks and the Mississippi River and Duck Creek and the old Zimmerman Foundry." Owned and operated by Frank C. Wallace, a former race car driver, a "retired" barnstormer and then general manager of the nearby Bettendorf Railroad Car Company, this 117 acre expanse offered few physical obstructions for any flying student or visiting pilot. Three or four small hangars were located on the field. Though most of the based airplanes were Standards, several JN-4 "Jenny" airplanes, a "Tommy" Morse, and a Laird-Swallow were frequent visitors. Weekends were always busy.

Adjacent to this field, Frank Wallace had a cozy summer cottage on the muddy banks of the Mississippi River. His place was a popular watering hole for the local area flying crowd wishing to visit and swap stories about auto racing and airplanes. Don was a frequent visitor at the Wallace Field and enjoyed hobknobbing with the local pilots and politicians.

Frank Wallace was born in 1889 in Davenport. Interested in aviation at an early age, he and his younger brother, Frederick, formed the Wallace Brothers Aero Company in 1919 and established Wallace Field. His flying school taught more than 70 students to fly. Brokering Curtiss OX-5 engines for several years, Wallace decided to limit his activities to private flying in early 1925.

During one of his many visits, Don learned Wallace had a crated OX-5 Curtiss JN-4 "Jenny" in storage. Fondly remembering his flying adventures in France, Don decided to buy the JN-4. With partner and close friend Ray Shriker, he purchased the Curtiss Jenny for $825.[6] Don wasted no time learning how to fly the Jenny. He was a quick learner. Reportedly,

Don's first airplane was a Curtiss JN-4 "Jenny" similar to the one shown here. Though Don enjoyed flying the "Jenny," it was heavy, cumbersome and drafty. Don soon formulated his many observations into a design that would be lighter, stronger and offer its occupants good protection from the elements.

Don Luscombe, dressed in the uncomfortable flying clothing of the day, peers from the cockpit of his Curtiss JN-4.

he soloed after four hours of dual instruction. His flying education consisted of whatever he could read on flying, coupled with Frank Wallace's personal tutoring.

While steamboat and river barge crews eked a difficult living on the mile wide Mississippi River, Don logged many pleasurable hours flying his Jenny above them. His varnished wood and doped fabric covered airplane became a familiar sight over Bettendorf and downtown Davenport on the Iowa side of this commanding river and Rock Island and Moline on the Illinois side. These four cities, including East Moline, encompass an area often referred to as "The Quad-Cities."

Don quickly observed the Jenny had many qualities left to be desired for someone who enjoyed the "finer" things in life, such as nice clothes and a warm house. The Jenny proved to be heavy, cumbersome and drafty. Yet, despite any of its perceived shortcomings, Don fell in love with this somewhat sluggish aircraft and enjoyed flying the Jenny whenever he could. The Jenny's flying days were short-lived as Don's partner nosed the airplane into the Mississippi River while attempting a takeoff. The airplane was towed from the river and the damage was assessed. Within days, Don traded the Jenny for an OX-5 Laird Swallow. However, Ray Shriker chose not to join Don in this new venture.

Often, while flying the Jenny and later, the Laird Swallow, Don made mental notes regarding these airplanes' good and bad qualities. Few positive attributes tallied in his mind. Although he enjoyed flying both aircraft, particularly the Jenny, Don was annoyed by the Jenny's overall size and weight. It was cumbersome on the ground and required at least two people to move it. Once in the air, the aircraft was slow to respond to a pilot's input. In each case, the Jenny's and the Laird Swallow's heavy, 90 hp Curtiss OX-5 engine did little to improve the overall performance potential.

After Don's partner nosed the Curtiss JN-4 "Jenny" into the Mississippi River, Don's second airplane was an OX-5 powered Laird Swallow.

As the last straw, the fact that both airplanes were "open cockpit" made Don's mental tally all the more upsetting. This uncomfortable characteristic was reinforced by memories of his earlier flights with the French pilots in the exposed front seat of a French Voisin. Always a dapper dresser, Don cared little for the traditional flying clothing of the period, e.g. leather helmets, tight fitting goggles, bloused pants and often ill-fitting, blister-producing boots.

Not all of Don's observations were negative. Some perceptions were surprisingly revealing and positive. Wallace Field was a favorite rest and relaxation spot for many Midwestern barnstormers. Frank Wallace would let these pilots use his hangar to repair a broken airplane. Don, in turn, observed several barnstormers with cracked-up ships repair a broken wood fuselage with longerons made of welded steel tubing. From these observations, Don later remarked, *"This was one of the enterprises where the repair business began an infant manufacturing company."*

Don Luscombe's unsettled mind churned these observations into something tangible. He decided to build an airplane one couldn't buy on the current market. Don soon formulated the positive attributes he would prefer in an airplane. He pictured a graceful design, one that was lighter, stronger, more responsive and offered its occupants good protection from the elements. It would have neither a radiator nor a lot of wood struts and flying wires. A high-wing design was a must to improve overall visibility. Remembering the modified dirt track racers of earlier days, Luscombe realized "his" aircraft would need a lightweight, yet powerful engine. No suitable, American-made power plant was available, so Don purchased a 55 hp French "Anzani." Did Don Luscombe envision an aerial "sports car?"

While Don formulated his idea, he came across a cartoon depicting the Belgian-designed Demonty-Poncelet. This most unusual, if not ponderous looking, side-by-side seating monoplane offered some intriguing possibilities. The comic strips of the day often anticipated future inventions and changes. Don pondered the alluring nature of the side-by-side design for a moment and asked himself, *"Why not?"* Weight and drag would be pared considerably by such a design. Similarly, complicated fuel and payload problems would be solved easily by keeping all close to the airplane's center-of-gravity. He sent a letter requesting further information on this design from its builders. Though other enclosed cabin designs existed, primarily larger biplane projects, it was this cartoon that set Don on his path towards a side-by-side configuration.

While he toyed with his airplane design ideas, Luscombe realized these requirements, if built into a tandem seating aircraft, would not offer any significant weight, performance and creature comfort improvements. However, a side-by-side design with a completely enclosed cabin area would offer easy access, no wind problems, less noise and more comfort, all while wearing normal or non-flight clothing.

During the summer and early fall of 1926, Don pursued his enclosed cabin airplane ideas relentlessly and soon put them into a mock-up form. When he wasn't working at his advertising business in Davenport, Don was at Frank Wallace's dirt floor hangar in nearby Bettendorf, much to the quiet discomfort of Don's wife, Eleanore.

Don used wood lath and cardboard to make a rough cabin frame. Other readily available construction items, such as oil cans, were used for seats. Using only homemade sketches, he built the cabin based upon an average sized human body, namely, himself. At times, Don confided with friends, he was at a loss as to what direction he should take with some aspect of the overall mock-up. Aeronautical engineering was a very imprecise science then, at least according to Don's beliefs. Often, when a part was needed, he would go to a nearby department store with his younger brother, Bob, and select what was needed. They would look at a certain piece, such as steel tubing, then discard it only to select a slightly

BETTY LUSCOMBE NUMEROF
Robert H. Luscombe, Don's mechanically minded younger brother, was good with numbers and helped Don and Clayton Folkerts design the first Monocoupe. Circa 1928.

larger (they thought stronger) piece. While Don labored on his project, many of his friends considered him *"as an overgrown kid playing with mud pies."*

In a candid letter to aviation historian John Underwood, Don reflected the idea of an enclosed cabin *"prompted some harsh remarks from the helmet and goggle boys that one could not fly properly without feeling wind on the face."* Obviously, very few people took Don's airplane ideas seriously.

Originally, Don never intended to build airplanes as a business. Instead, he longed for an airplane that would permit him to fly for pleasure. But as the mock-up took shape, Don realized there existed a tremendous production potential and profit in his airplane ideas. Furthermore, he recognized he needed financial support if his conceptions were to evolve beyond any flimsy wood and cardboard homebuilt mock-up. Don presented his resourceful ideas to about a dozen of his friends and local businessmen at Wallace's Airfield. He described how aviation was evolving rapidly to be more than just military and public conveyance endeavors. Furthermore, he explained in great detail the current and future need for a two-place, side-by-side, enclosed cabin airplane. Airplanes, much like automobiles, needed to be designed and produced for the common man — the private owner.

Luscombe continued. Airplanes available to the private owner were, in most cases, war surplus or modified military types, predominantly open-cockpit airplanes. He explained the future trend would be towards airplanes possessing an enclosed cabin thus, eliminating many of the hazards, degraded comfort and marginal performance these ex-military ships offered. Value, performance and reliability were terms Don used to describe what a future customer would want in any aircraft purchase. In conclusion, Don quipped, *"You don't want to take your girl flying and have her sit behind you?"*

Many of those individuals present agreed with Don's surprisingly clairvoyant outlook and lent their financial support. A new corporation was created to turn Luscombe's positive ideas into production reality. Thus, on October 12, 1926, the Central States Aero Company, Inc., was formed.

The capital stock of this new endeavor was set at $10,000 and was divided into two hundred shares of par value of $50 each. One hundred shares of par value stock aggregating $5000 was to be subscribed and paid for before the corporation commenced business. Anxious to start this new business, the businessmen involved in this creative venture wasted no time collecting the needed funds.

As listed in the State of Iowa Incorporation Records, the new company was officered by Frederic E. Zeuch, president; Tom J. Korn, vice-president; Robert L. Block, secretary and Rudy A. Moritz, treasurer. The directors were listed as Frederic E. Zeuch, Tom J. Korn, Donald A. Luscombe, Rudy A. Moritz, Warren T. Zeuch, Burton E. Forster, Frank C. Wallace, Ferdinand C. Korn, Robert Luscombe[7] and Robert L. Block. Most of the individuals named in this charter were prominent Bettendorf and Davenport businessmen. Several held positions in the nearby Bettendorf Railroad Car Company, and within Deere & Company and the Velie Motors Corporation, the latter two companies being well respected firms in nearby Moline, Illinois. All participants were interested in establishing and developing commercial aviation in Davenport.

Little did those gentlemen realize the impact of their actions. They had just given added impetus to a developing and soon-to-be immensely popular standard by which most side-by-side seating, enclosed cabin, high-wing light airplanes were to be built. Likewise, it is doubtful they realized the mass production methods that would be developed and employed to build these airplanes. Soon, the Wallace Field was leased to operate and test their airplanes. Though a club house, fuel facilities and a repair shop were located on the field, there were no plans to operate a commercial field.

Don Luscombe had his vision. He developed it, he promoted it, and those who listened, bought it. Luscombe's vision evolved, slowly at first, into a credible reality. Not being an aeronautical engineer, Luscombe could not design the airplane he sought. However, he could appreciate the difficulties involved in such an endeavor. Don had a lot of volunteer help, but often complained he had no one sufficiently knowledgeable or dependable to design and build the proposed Central States Aero Company (CSA) airplane. Don needed expertise, but who would be willing to undertake such a venture? Don's questions were soon answered.

Milton Miller, a novelties salesman from nearby Dubuque, Iowa, frequently visited Wallace's airport as an outlet for his ambition to fly. He always made it a point to visit Don and see the progress of the airplane mock-up. During one of their conversations, Miller told Don of a young, handyman farmer he encountered in northern Iowa who had built his own single-seater airplane and had self-instructed to learn how to fly it. More importantly, Don learned this young farmer's desire to build airplanes and be paid for it was stronger than his desire to farm. This adventurous aviator's name was Clayton Folkerts.

Don immediately informed his investors of this young lad. In October 1926, three Central States Aero Company executives, including Don Luscombe, interviewed Folkerts at Miller's Miller-Palmer Company in Dubuque. When Don and the other executives met Clayton Folkerts for the first time, they were impressed immediately with this self taught, natural-born "aeronautical engineer" and the many ideas he proposed. They gave Folkerts a free hand as to the

Chapter Two: One Has To Learn How To Walk, Before He Can Run

ideas, design and building of the CSA's new airplane.

Folkerts, on his behalf, was inspired by the bright horizons the Central States executives painted. If all that was said was true, the future looked very positive indeed. They asked him to come to Bettendorf to build their first airplane, a two-place, side-by-side design with a preference towards a steel-tube fuselage. Clayton Folkerts agreed immediately. He signed a one year contract with CSA, valid from October 18, 1926, to October 15, 1927, to:
1. Design, manufacture, study and experiment with aeroplanes in accordance with the plans of the Central States Aero Company;
2. Devote his full time to work and give his best efforts to it, and;
3. Cooperate with Central States Aero Company to the best of his ability.

Clayton was made a superintendent and started work at CSA at a rate of $35 per week for a one year period. After spending a few days setting-up shop in Wallace's hangar, Clayton set forth to build a prototype airplane. It quickly became apparent to all present at Wallace Field that Clayton Folkerts was much more than a handyman farmer who loved to tinker with engines, machines and things aeronautical. Like other eager and young farmers turned aviation pioneers — Clyde Cessna, for example — Clayton Folkerts was almost obsessed with the desire to build, and fly, a successful airplane design of his own making.

By way of background, Clayton Folkerts was born on November 9, 1897, near Wellsburg, Iowa. He was the seventh born of a family that consisted of seven boys and three girls. His German immigrant parents, Atho and Johanna Voss Folkerts, moved the family to a farm two miles east of Bristow, Iowa, in 1901. Always an easy going individual with an innate instinct for creativity and mechanical design, Clayton shared this attribute with his brothers and father. Mathematics was another study Clayton loved. Incidentally, Clayton's father came from Germany to escape military service. Mechanically inclined, he built a well-equipped shop. Atho didn't restrict any of his boys' outside interests as long as the farm chores were completed. School was hard for Clayton because of his German family background, anti-World War I sentiment and his lack of interest. He dropped out of school in the tenth grade and stayed home to help on the farm and tinker.

Clayton's interest in aviation developed when his father returned from a state fair in 1914 and told his boys about the flying machine he saw. He was enthralled by the lively stories his father told. Within weeks, the impressionable sixteen-year-old visited a county fair in nearby Oelwein, Iowa, and saw his first airplane. Clayton Folkerts' interest was piqued. He sought books on aviation, but desired magazines for recent information. Once, while on a trip to Chicago carrying a load of hogs or cattle to market, he made it a point to visit a magazine stall that sold airplane periodicals. It was there he discovered the Heath Aeroplane and Supply Company. A mesmerized Clayton spent the balance of the day browsing through Ed Heath's cornucopia of aeronautical hardware. Clayton studied any available theory. His expanding knowledge was supplemented by Heath Company books, magazine articles and other data he collected.

Using ideas from magazines, such as *Popular Mechanics* and the popular biweekly *Aviation*, Folkerts built his first airplane during the winter of 1916-17. It was powered by an seven horsepower Indian motorcycle engine he purchased from a neighbor, Harm Frey, for three dollars. Frey disposed of the engine

Clayton and Harold Folkerts pose before the Folkerts #2.   HAROLD FOLKERTS

because he believed the crankshaft and main bearings were worn-out and put everything in a dishpan. Clayton and a brother, Edward, soon discovered they could purchase replacement parts for the engine in nearby Waverly, Iowa, which was about twenty-five miles east of the family farm. Soon, the engine was running in first-class condition. The family's farmhouse basement became his workshop.

Clayton whittled his own propellers and determined his own wing curves. The six foot diameter propeller was driven by a motorcycle roller chain with a 4 to 1 reduction. The fuselage was made of four bamboo poles, which served as the longerons. The wingspan was sixteen feet with a four foot chord. Clayton employed "eyeball engineering" to determine the strength of the parts he used. He rarely missed his calculations!

His first taxi test ended in near disaster as the structure broke in half when one of the monoplane's two, 20 inch diameter bicycle wheels hit a ditch. Both longerons to the tail broke, letting the forward section nose over, breaking the propeller. Undaunted, Clayton picked up the pieces and returned to the shop. Never once swearing nor cursing, he set forth to rebuild and improve his design.

This later version featured several innovations. A set of ailerons, eight inches wide and five feet long, were added to the wing's trailing edge. Additionally, a new, four foot propeller was bolted directly to the crankshaft with four carriage bolts. Clayton made many runs across the field testing his improved design. When there was a little snow on the ground, he was able to check his track to see where he became airborne. His early designs were made mostly from scrap lumber, baling wire, junked iron, tin, discarded bicycle parts, braided clothesline and other items found around the farm. At best, these early "aeroplanes" could only "hedge hop."

Built mostly of bamboo and baling wire, the Folkerts # 3 sported a converted Model T Ford 20 hp motor for power. HAROLD FOLKERTS

Money was tight for Clayton's endeavors. Fortunately, the family was most understanding and willing to see him succeed in his aviation adventures. One brother, Edward, was a teacher at a nearby school and financed many of Clayton's early aeronautical projects. Another brother, Henry, was a high school student and contributed money to his brother's enterprising endeavors, as well. The fact Clayton Folkerts designed and built his own airplanes is remarkable in itself. More remarkable is the fact he never had any formal flight instruction, yet he taught himself the early basics of how to fly with crossed rudder pedal wires!

Clayton's next design, the "Folkerts #2" as it was called, was built during the winter of 1918-1919. It was a beautiful, almost dainty biplane that featured a wing curve patterned after a factory rib he had mail-ordered. This airplane had a wingspan of 21 feet, six inches, was 16 feet long and weighed about 275 pounds. Powered by a 2-cylinder, 13 hp air-cooled Spacke Cycle Car engine removed from a motorboat, Clayton gained a lot of local attention with this design. Occasionally, he featured this airplane at the local county fairs as a part of an airplane/automobile ride attraction to raise funds for their projects. Bannered under an oilcloth sign, HOME-MADE SINGLE PASSEN-

HAROLD FOLKERTS
The Folkerts #3. Clayton Folkerts taught himself how to fly in this craft.

Chapter Two: One Has To Learn How To Walk, Before He Can Run

GER AEROPLANE, brother Minno sold 20 cent admission tickets to see the airplane. In conjunction with this promotion, brother Ed ran a homemade pusher car, or "wind buggy," which featured a rear-mounted propeller, on the fairground's race track for 25 cents a ride.

When Clayton wasn't demonstrating his airplane, he was practicing takeoffs and landings. As with the "Folkerts #1," he was able to hop his biplane design only a few feet off the ground and only for very short distances. The "Folkerts #2" had the unnerving tendency to noseover which always broke the propeller. Sadly, this design met its demise when a storm lodged it squarely in the crotch of a large tree near the family homestead. Years later, Clayton recounted this design could have flown *if* the wing's angle of incidence had been less. His third design, the "Folkerts #3," was built between 1921 and 1923, and was his first design to actually achieve any appreciable sustained flight. The "Folkerts #3" featured low pressure tires made from cut down truck tires. These tires were intended to absorb landing loads. The fuselage longerons, wing ribs and wing spars were made from bamboo fishing poles purchased at a local hardware store. Bicycle spokes were used for bracing wires, with many of the turnbuckles coming from these spokes. The fuselage, wings, and tail were covered with doped cloth.

The most remarkable aspect of this design was its power plant — a highly modified Model T Ford engine which, at best, delivered 25 horsepower. Clayton cut off the water jacket and mounted the engine inverted. The crankcase was cut such that only three main bearings remained. Hard oil cups were screwed to each connecting rod and main bearing. A drip oiler from an old Overland automobile was used to supply oil to each cylinder. A six-and-a-half foot wood propeller was attached directly to the flywheel flange.

To test this engine, a test stand was made around a ten inch fence post that was used to secure the family's cow yard fence. Brother Ed would swing the propeller to crank the engine while Clayton manipulated the throttle. Their few tests proved successful.

Content that all was in order, the modified Ford engine was removed from the test stand and bolted to the airplane. Clayton leaped into his machine while Edward waited patiently nearby to swing the propeller. When Ed swung the prop for the first time, it broke at the hub flange and fell to the ground. Afraid the prop could have hit him if the engine had fired, Ed politely told Clayton, *"I've had all of this aeroplane business I want!"* and decided to quit. Undaunted, Clayton installed another crankshaft and had the motor running smoothly. Soon, Clayton was hopping fences while he flew from field to field.

However, another pesky problem quickly developed; the Model T engine was prone to severe overheating. As such, Clayton's hedge-hopping was limited to flights generally less than a minute. Though he kept working on a solution, even attempting flights when the outside temperature was twenty degrees below zero, Clayton was never able to solve this problem.

Somehow, Clayton discovered he could purchase a World War I surplus, 2-cylinder, 28 hp Lawrance aircraft motor for about $75. He ordered one and quickly installed it upon arrival. The vibrations it created when it ran were horrendous and tended to pull the bracing wires loose. Clayton solved this problem by adding more braces and employing a little more rebuilding, but the vibrations were still troublesome. By now, Clayton was making run after run practicing takeoffs and landings. Eventually, he made a moderately successful flight but, once more, he "flew" only a few feet off the ground.

Taking off from a hay field during one flight of

Clayton Folkerts and his Folkerts #4 in Dubuque, Iowa, circa 1926.

HAROLD FOLKERTS

almost a mile in length, Clayton failed to clear some telephone wires at the end of another field and landed in a neighbor's cornfield. The resulting nose-over damaged the airplane, but not extensively. The "Folkerts #3" was dismantled and no further flights were made.

Folkerts' fourth design was constructed in late 1923 or early 1924. By this time, Clayton was twenty-six years old and had spent better than seven years building and trying to fly airplanes. Never discouraged, he was determined more than ever to make a design he could truly fly. The "Folkerts #4" used the same Lawrance engine from the number three airplane. It was reliable, light and proven. This new airplane design was built to be unaffected by vibration. This monoplane featured a geodetic wood construction, was twelve feet long and had a twenty-six foot wingspan with a four foot chord. Two ash wood struts, one for each wheel, were used for the landing gear. The airplane was estimated to have weighed about 350 pounds.

Clayton's first flight in the "Folkerts #4" occurred in September 1924, and was undertaken with some initial secrecy. Before this momentous flight, however, he confided in his younger brother, Harold, about the upcoming test hop. Together, they made preparations, which included making a trip into town to buy some "high test" fuel. Clayton believed the best time for any test flight was at daybreak, so he and Harold tiptoed quietly from the house early one morning, taking care not to wake any of the family. The parents knew Clayton's first test flight was near, but never gave the idea much thought as they had heard the boys talk about it quite often.

The airplane was parked near a grove of maple trees on the east side of the family's barn. Clayton positioned fourteen-year-old Harold alongside the fuselage to handle the ignition switches while he turned the propeller to draw fuel. Then Clayton called for *"Contact!"* and Harold threw the switches. The motor started immediately. Clayton let it idle to warm the aluminum cylinders. Then, after a thorough warming, he shut down the engine to adjust the rocker arm clearances, now out of tolerance due to internal expansion. All valves were adjusted to Clayton's discerning satisfaction.

Once more, Harold manned the switches while Clayton swung the prop. Once more, the Lawrance caught the first time and ran smoother and faster than before. In the meantime, poor Harold was holding on to the airplane for dear life to keep it from moving. Clayton ran back around and hopped into the cockpit, ready for takeoff. Confident all was in order, Clayton opened the throttle. After a short, rough ride over a stubble oats field, Clayton was airborne and was soon flying about thirty feet off the ground. He held the stick forward to allow the airplane to gain speed which might be necessary to clear some fences ahead of him. Very shortly, Clayton eased the responsive "Folkerts #4" to an altitude of a hundred feet or more. The airplane's noise awakened the family to the startling fact their aeronautically-minded son was actually in the air making his first true solo flight.

Soon, after making a wide and gentle left-hand turn, the stubble field reappeared before Clayton. He gently retarded the throttle and glided to a perfect landing. His momentous flight covered several miles of gently sloping Iowa farmland. A breathless and excited Harold ran over to his older brother and exclaimed, *"Gee, that was great flying and not even a bounce in the landing!"* Clayton had hoped a second flight later in the day would relieve him from his farm chores, but this was not to be the case. The family had several cows that needed to be milked. Later, following a second flight, Clayton believed himself to be a full-fledged pilot.

Diverging from the vibration-prone, 2-cylinder Lawrance engine, Clayton turned his thoughts towards a more suitable four cylinder engine. Thus, he and his father, Atho, went to Waterloo, Iowa, and found a motorcycle shop selling four cylinder Henderson engines. A complete motor, less flywheel, could be purchased for $210. They promptly placed an order for one. While he waited for the new engine to arrive, Clayton turned out a stub shaft on a lathe to mount the propeller. In turn, he whittled a four foot propeller. When the engine arrived, Clayton mounted his propeller to the engine and started it. The combination ran as smooth as a Singer sewing machine.

Clayton then turned his attention towards building a new airplane to accommodate the new engine. He called this new design the "Folkerts #5." Once more, he used a wood latchwork design. The wingspan was twenty feet with a four foot chord. He used the same wing curve as used on the Lawrance-powered airplane. Clayton had high hopes for this design, but its flying success could be summed-up in three words — *"It wouldn't fly!"*

By now, however, Clayton had captured the interest of Milton Miller who asked him to bring his airplanes to Dubuque, particularly the last two designs, and put them on display. Clayton agreed. Clayton flew his "Folkerts #4" on many occasions, but decided to leave the "Folkerts #5" alone. He hoped to expand his own airplane endeavors into a commercial venture with Miller's backing. Initially, Clayton's plans were to develop the "Folkerts #4" into a two-seater airplane. Miller — himself an OX-5 Jenny pilot — was trying to convince the Dubuque city commissioners to build an airport to stimulate commerce. Miller had a small factory in the city that built small gliders out of balsa wood for storekeepers to give away as novelties.

Milton Miller was well aware aviation interest

was keen in the Midwest. He placed an article in the local paper describing Clayton and his airplanes as an attempt to woo public support for his airport ideas. Sadly, very little if anything positive resulted from this public relations effort. However, Miller was successful in introducing Folkerts to Don Luscombe. Suddenly, here were two men seeking the same goal—build a lightweight personal airplane for commercial production. Folkerts had the technical aptitude; Luscombe possessed the promotional genius. Their meeting wasn't exactly a marriage "made in Heaven," but the potential for both to succeed in their common goal *was* there.

Prototype Monocoupe under construction. Note the Folkerts designed one-piece wing. JIM HARVEY

Their first joint purchase was a tablet of graph paper and some wing curve pamphlets from the Bureau of Standards in Washington, D.C. Soon, Don and Clayton began their first rough sketches. Fortunately, their were no government regulations in existence then to influence their calculations or design outlook. Initially, Luscombe and Folkerts were besieged with advice on how best to build the new airplane or what materials to use. Don insisted on a welded steel tube fuselage, others offered wood and fabric ideas.

At one point, a tolerant and understanding Frank Wallace confided with Folkerts. *"Clayton, be patient and listen to all the suggestions of how to build the airplane and then go ahead and build it as you think best, because I have faith in your ability."* In the end, Clayton's common sense and uncanny intuition prevailed. He didn't like cables and pulleys and avoided them wherever possible. Instead, he opted for the more reliable and positive operation of bell-cranks and push-pull tubes. Folkerts' wooden wing structure endured as did Luscombe's steel tube fuselage requirement. The fact Folkerts worked from instinct and used no blueprints or drawings made his efforts all the more remarkable. Only the unlighted, white-washed walls of Frank Wallace's hangar shop were used to make the various sketches and drawings for the design.[8]

Ironically, for all the intuitive genius Folkerts possessed, he lacked a basic airframe building skill—welding. Wasting no time, he learned this industrial art to help him and Luscombe turn their new project into reality.

Briefly joining Folkerts in this new aviation endeavor was Don Luscombe's younger brother, Robert. He held an engineering degree and was good with complex mathematical computations and formulas. Bob Luscombe was asked to find a suitable airfoil for the new design. The final result, after a relatively short four to five month team effort, was a dainty, high wing strut-braced, side-by-side seating, apple green painted monoplane featuring a Clark-Y airfoil. The landing gear utilized discarded Curtiss Jenny wheels and tires.

The semi-cantilever wings were made of one section with a span of thirty feet and a five foot chord. The spars were constructed of selected airplane spruce while the ribs were made with basswood webs and spruce capstrips. One-sixteenth inch piano wire was used to shape the trailing edge. The wingtips were squared, whereas later wing designs incorporated an elliptical shape. Two, ten gallon fuel tanks were mounted in the wing, one on each side of the fuselage. The wings were covered with Flightex Grade A fabric. Finally, the wings were supported by struts made of tubular chrome molybdenum steel.

The fuselage pinched towards the rear, a feature that contributed to the new airplane's streamline appearance and reduced cross-sectional area. The internal fuselage structure was of a welded Warren truss construction. All chromemoly tubing was 20 gauge (.035), except for an 18 gauge (.049) member used to take the loads from the wing struts. Once more, Flightex Grade A fabric was used to cover the fuselage. Only one cabin door was provided, with this being on the right side.

According to later company advertising, this new airplane's stout construction ensured the weakest member of the fuselage was 13% stronger than design load factors required. Uniquely, this new and

18   Visions of Luscombe: The Early Years

The prototype Monocoupe makes its debut at Wallace Field.   ELEANORE LUSCOMBE SHURTZ COLLECTION

Another view of the prototype Monocoupe. This airplane featured an all moving fin, but later models had more conventional fin and rudder.   ELEANORE LUSCOMBE SHURTZ COLLECTION

A proud Clayton Folkerts stands beside the prototype Monocoupe. Circa April 1927.   AVIATION HERITAGE LIBRARY

exciting airplane had an all moving tail. Other features included a slightly staggered side-by-side seating arrangement in a completely enclosed cabin with dual controls. This seating arrangement allowed good shoulder room and reduced the cross-sectional area of the fuselage which Folkerts and Luscombe believed would improve overall performance.

Powered by a 60 hp, five-cylinder Detroit Aircraft Engine Corporation "Air-Cat" radial engine turning a Hartzell wood propeller,

Chapter Two: One Has To Learn How To Walk, Before He Can Run 19

Aerial view of the Moline Airport grounds in 1926.

MOLINE AIRPORT BROCHURE, CIRCA 1926.

this new airplane was boasted to have a 100 mph maximum speed, an 85 mph cruise speed and a very docile 37 mph landing speed.[9] The configuration provided everything Luscombe desired in an airplane. Gone was the need for the leather or cloth helmets and goggles. Gone were clumsy climbs over the top of the fuselage to enter the cockpit. Now, a pilot and passenger could open a door like an automobile, step inside and ride in an enclosed compartment. And, perhaps just as important, the owner could taxi to the hangar and push it in unassisted.

In late March 1927, the prototype airplane was ready for its first flight. At the risk of alienating his host, Frank Wallace, Don Luscombe asked Earl K. "Rusty" Campbell, then the general manager of the nearby Moline Airport, to make the first flight. Campbell had come to Moline some time earlier, made the right connections and garnered local public and financial support for his aeronautical endeavors. He was respected by the press and politicians for his word on aeronautical matters. Additionally, he was a general partner in the Campbell-De Schepper Airplane Company, an early fixed-base operation located on Franing Field and Weaver Farm, a leased 1,600 feet by 2,700 feet natural sod pasture which made-up the Moline Airport. As an enticement, Don hinted he had future plans for Moline's industrial center. Considering all factors, Campbell was pleased

E.K. "Rusty" Campbell

MOLINE AIRPORT BROCHURE, JAMES B. ZAZAS COLLECTION

and told Don he would fly the airplane whenever it was ready.

Interestingly, Don's request may have been a veiled attempt to keep a tepid political battle between two aviation factions in the Davenport area from exploding into a nasty war-of-words. Hard feelings existed between a Mr. Ralph Cram, editor of the *Davenport Democrat* newspaper and proponent of the Davenport Aero Club, and Frank Wallace. Cram was promoting a future airport for the city that could handle the Airmail's Liberty engine powered airplanes. His group believed their interests were threatened in some way by, and therefore opposed to, those of Frank Wallace's barnstorming breed who operated from the Bettendorf Railroad Car plant property. Committed to neither side, Don sought to tread the middle line and maintain some peace.

The first flight of the new monoplane occurred on Wednesday, April 6, 1927, at the Moline, Illinois, airport. Wallace Field in Bettendorf was too wet from an earlier heavy rain, so the plane was trucked to Moline where Campbell could make the initial flight. The dainty monoplane weighed in at slightly more than seven hundred pounds and hinted some startling performance. A quick swing of the propeller and Campbell was soon on his way.

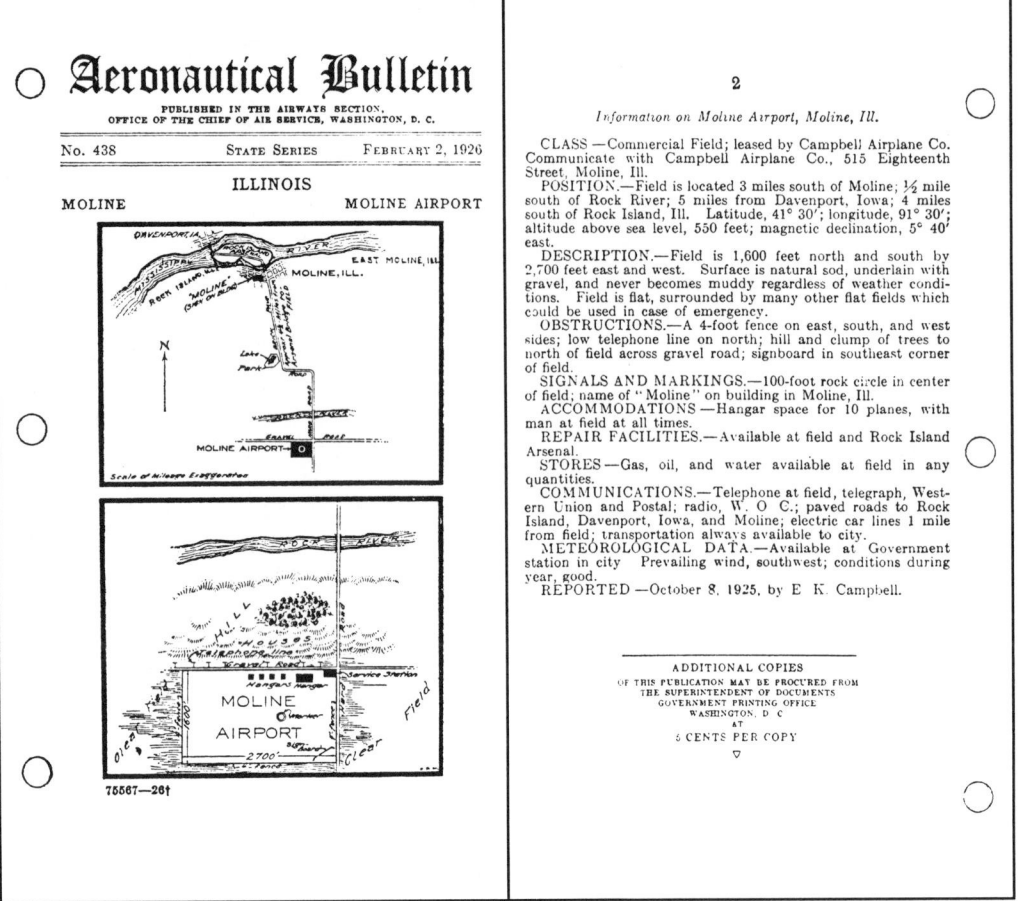

Moline Airport Brochure/Airport Grounds Diagrams. JAMES B. ZAZAS COLLECTION

The day was clear quite breezy as Campbell taxied to his takeoff point. Then, surprisingly, Campbell and the new prototype were airborne following a takeoff roll of barely more than a hundred feet. The Detroit "Air-Cat" purred approvingly while Campbell made a few, cautious trips around the grass airfield. Upon landing, Campbell was most enthusiastic about the new airplane's sprightly performance, revealing responsive and light control forces. *"The plane is certainly O.K.,"* he told a local newspaper reporter. In his brief test report, he later reported, *"Great future — but you don't fly this thing, you only wish it!"*

However, other pilots who had the early opportunity to fly the new design complained about the aircraft's "chancy" stall characteristics. Since there were no adjustable fittings installed on the wing struts for rigging, it was necessary to send one or more struts back to the weld-shop for shortening of the wing fittings. Don Luscombe later recounted this fact in a letter to *Of Monocoupes and Men* author, John Underwood, and added the airplane wing had a tendency to fly left wing low. Furthermore, in this same letter, Don mentioned: *"It was also apparent that merely staggering the passenger's seat to provide the pilot elbow room was inadequate and that the inside cabin dimension must be extended on subsequent models."*

Anxious to demonstrate their new airplane, Central States Aero Company personnel invited the general public to witness a test flight scheduled only days after the airplane's initial flight. Stories were carried in the local newspapers heralding this event. Several hundred people converged on the Moline Airport to see the airplane put through its paces. Amidst a developing interest, Don realized he needed a catchy name for the new design. His attention was drawn to a toy model airplane his friend, Milton Miller, was developing called the "Mono-Kite." Knowing that two passenger, enclosed automobiles were called coupes and the fact his new airplane was a monoplane, Luscombe called his new airplane the "Monocoupe." Incidentally, this idea became the trade name for the design. Three Teal ducks, arranged in a stylized echelon formation, became the company's trademark. Reportedly, Don took this idea from Miller's "Mono-Kite" box design.

When asked what contributed to the airplane's swift nature, Don supposedly answered the fuselage's pinched shape gave a "push from behind" and, therefore, enhanced the airplane's speed. Don often related he chose the Teal, the fastest of the duck family, to represent his fledgling company's proud accomplishment.

Central States Aero Company's new airplane soon proved immensely popular with all who had the privilege and honor to fly it. All were impressed by the aircraft's high performance while using relatively little horsepower. In time, these positive attributes became synonymous with the name Monocoupe. Soon, many of Don's friends clamored to have a Monocoupe built for them.

"It is quality rather than quantity that matters."
Lucius Annaeus Seneca (circa 4 B.C. - A.D. 65)

Chapter Three

Perfecting the Breed

Lineup of three early Monocoupes at Wallace Field, Bettendorf, Iowa. JIM HARVEY

Don Luscombe and Clayton Folkerts realized Frank Wallace's wood frame hangar was too small to meet any anticipated demand. New facilities needed to be found fast. As luck (or Divine Providence?) would have it, the Tabernacle Building in nearby Bettendorf became available. Seven years earlier, traveling evangelist Billy Sunday had this small tabernacle erected on a corner lot a few hundred yards north of the Bettendorf Railroad Car plant. Now, Sunday was gone and the empty clapboard building was available.

A quick survey of the facilities revealed it was suitable for the Central States Aero Company's growing airplane business, even though completed airplanes would have to be towed or dismantled and trucked to Wallace Field (barely a mile east of the tabernacle) and reassembled. CSA leased this former church building for $45 a month. The company elected to maintain the corporate offices at Don's old advertising offices, 318-319 Whitaker Building in Davenport, while the field and factory were set-up in Bettendorf.

Additional help was hired to meet the growing demand for the new Monocoupe. One of the first employees hired was Chester Loose of Davenport, Iowa. He was an excellent mechanic and had an uncanny knowledge of airplane construction and repair, yet it was his welding ability that set him head and shoulders above his peers. He was made foreman of the fuselage, tail plane and metal work departments. Other employees were added to the employee rosters. These individuals included Beverly "Bud" Washburn and Ernest Hagenmueller. Respectively, they were made foreman of the wood working and wing department and foreman of the fairing and fuselage installation department. By late spring 1927, Central States Aero Company had seven or eight full-time employees on its roster. Don's position was listed as the corporation's general manager.

Don lost one valuable employee during this teething period, his younger brother, Robert. He told Don he had a family to raise and intimated Don's aviation endeavors would not pay the bills. Robert soon entered a non-aviation related profession, yet maintained an active interest in his older brother's entrepreneurial endeavors, if nothing more than owning a few shares of stock in the company.

Orders for the new Monocoupe began to arrive daily. But just when Don Luscombe thought things couldn't be better for his airplane manufacturing enterprise, he was faced with a very difficult dilemma. The new Air Commerce Act of 1926 nearly grounded his new airplane before it ever went into production and presented a serious challenge to Luscombe's aviation promotion and management endeavors. During the fall and early winter months of 1926, rumors had been circulating for some time the Government would soon regulate all interstate commercial and civil aviation activities, including the manufacture and licensing of airplanes and engines. Airmen pilot licensing was said to be included. All too soon, these rumors proved true.

To manage the sudden proliferation of new airplanes and power plants, new government regulations went into effect which required government approval of all designs manufactured following 1927. The Approved Type Certificate program and its resulting numbering system was created. Similarly, this act required all airmen and aircraft mechanics be qualified and properly certificated. As a consequence of this new regulation, Don Luscombe himself was required by law to be "certificated." On August 9, 1927, Luscombe was issued Commercial Pilot certificate number 94 by the aeronautical branch of the Department of Commerce. Don Luscombe's application was included in a select group of more than 330 pilots who were licensed that day.

At the time, no written or flight tests were required. Any pilot who was flying commercially was given a commercial license. Folklore relates many pilots of that era were quite "independent" characters and the inspectors had to use a lot of salesmanship (buy drinks, etc.) to convince them to fill out their applications. The Aeronautics Branch of the U.S. Department of Commerce was charged to supervise and enforce the new regulations.

Central States Aero Company morale slumped. Despite Clayton Folkerts' remarkable intuitive genius, the company had neither the in-house expertise nor the finances on hand to interpret and implement these regulations. Don did not care what obstacles stood in his path; these problems would be solved. To fulfill these stiff requirements, the Central States Aero Company had to present various drawings, stress analysis studies and production blueprints to the government to support their designs. The Department of Commerce, Bureau of Air Commerce, wanted cold, hard facts on paper before certificating an airplane — not intuitive or TLAR (That Look's About Right) engineering.

Don solved his Monocoupe certification woes by contracting for the services of Jerome F. "Jerry" Lederer, an adept aeronautical engineer employed at the time with the U.S. Mail Service in Maywood, Illinois. Don flew to Maywood with E.K. Campbell to interview Lederer and offer him the job. Returning home, Don knew he made the right choice. Concurrently, Lederer was president of Aerotech, Inc., an airplane and airport design company based in Streator, Illinois. When Lederer assumed his new role at Central States Aero, it became his responsibility to do the necessary structural analysis and drawings to get the new Monocoupe certificated.

Lederer's educational background included a Bachelor of Science degree with a B.S.C. mechanical engineering/aeronautical option from New York University (1924). After graduation, he remained at N.Y.U. as an assistant instructor and worked for Dr. Alexander Klemin, the school's director of the Guggenheim Fund for the promotion of aeronautics. During that period, Lederer installed, calibrated and operated the school's wind tunnel, eventually acquiring a Mechanical Engineering degree. Lederer left N.Y.U. in 1926 and accepted a position with the U.S. Air Mail Service. Thus, he became the mail service's first and only aeronautical engineer.

To assist him at Central States Aero, Lederer brought with him Frederick J. Knack, a young, bright and talented engineer and an Aerotech, Inc. employee. Like Lederer, Knack was a New York University graduate (1926) and earned an aeronautical engineering degree from New York University's Guggenhiem School of Aeronautics (1928). Knack would gain greater recognition while under Luscombe's employ a decade later. Lederer hired Bud Whelan, also. He was an Iowa native and a University of Iowa engineering graduate. Clifford T. Smith, a draftsman, was hired at the same time. Lederer and his small staff spent many long hours at their drafting boards to resolve the government certification requirements. Six months later, their laborious efforts were successful.

At the same time, the Detroit "Air-Cat," the engine of choice for the new Monocoupe, was meeting its certification requirements. Central States Aero Company morale rebounded with the prospect of an Approved Type Certificate for the Monocoupe, powered by an "approved" engine. While the CSA engineers toiled to gain the necessary and eventual approval, word of the Monocoupe's startling performance and exquisite handling characteristics spread rapidly, including inquiries from as far as Australia. Visitors around the country began to appear before the company's doors. Quite often, their first question was, *"What must I do to get one?"* Don and his fledgling staff could only answer, *"Pay in money as we need it. If you want to come in and help build it, there will be no extra charge."* Many accepted this invitation, often bringing their own engine to hasten delivery.

Jerome F. "Jerry" Lederer JEROME LEDERER

This move on Don's behalf proved to be a masterful stroke of public relations goodwill. Ruffled feathers were eased while valuable labor was delegated to work on other orders. Luscombe would use this same technique in later years to soothe tempers and gain additional time, labor and, if necessary, money to complete the work at hand.

The first production Monocoupe (s/n 1, registration 1025) was made ready for its first test flight in July 1927. A local pilot, Douglas Harris, undertook the initial test flight. Harris remained to make other early production Monocoupe test flights and, in turn, became the CSA's first chief test pilot. This particular Monocoupe was registered with the Bureau of Air Commerce as "experimental" at the request of the factory. The airplane maintained a brisk flying schedule and was used to demonstrate the Monocoupe's performance as well as to season "Air Cat" motors prior to installation on production Monocoupes.[10]

Monocoupe 1025, s/n 1, with Detroit "Air-Cat" engine. JIM HARVEY

As more orders were booked, visitors of another kind beckoned to the company — salesmen. Engine, paint and aviation parts representatives visited the company with increasing frequency. One of the first to solicit CSA's account was dope and paint expert Tom Colby, the Aviation Manager of Berry Brothers Paints, Inc., of Detroit, Michigan. His company was well known for the "Berryloid" line of high quality aircraft finishes.

Don gave Colby the CSA dope and paint account. In turn, Colby stayed to personally paint and handfinish an early production Monocoupe (1026, s/n 4 or 5). This particular airplane was painted an overall maroon with a brilliant gold trim and was completed in late July 1927 and sold for $2285. Colby and Berry Brothers retained the Monocoupe paint account until Monocoupe production ceased more than a decade later. Tom Colby remained one of Don Luscombe's most ardent supporters.

Monocoupe 1026 was delivered to George A. Weis, a Stearman and Stinson distributor from Mineola, Long Island, New York. Not long afterwards, Weis became Central States Aero Company's first Monocoupe distributor. Prior to its delivery, Weis' Monocoupe was displayed in the front window of the People's Light Company office in Davenport. Many of Davenport's residents took advantage of this early August 1927, promotional display to see CSA's handiwork.

Incidentally, while Weis was enroute to his Roosevelt Field, Long Island, New York base, a call was received from the Ford Motor Company in Detroit, Michigan, inviting him to demonstrate his sprightly monoplane. Weis consented and deviated his flight plan to Detroit. His Monocoupe was soon the subject of a close examination by a small army of Ford Motor Company engineers. Afterwards, Weis continued towards his New York home, a journey that proved more adventurous than he bargained. Along the way, he experienced at least seven engine failures. Central States Aero Company exchanged the engine at no charge.

By August, at least two other Monocoupes were produced and delivered. One went to Sebring, Florida (possibly 1027, s/n 6), and the other to a happy buyer in Lincoln, Nebraska.

Very shortly after Central States Aero Company started Monocoupe production, an event of tremen-

An early production Monocoupe strikes an appealing pose. This airplane was painted by Tom Colby and delivered to New York airplane dealer George Weis. JIM HARVEY

Eleanore Luscombe and her only son, James True Luscombe. Circa 1928.

dous international significance occurred that had a profound influence on the company's future—Charles Lindbergh's solo Trans-Atlantic flight. Though the private aviation sector was developing, this one flight created a substantial demand for a "Flivver" or sport-type airplane.[11] Subsequent appeal for an affordable, responsive, reliable, privately owned light airplane literally "took off." In turn, a lot of people and companies began making airplanes. By some accounts, this number swelled eventually to an incredible three hundred separate concerns made or anticipating making airplanes.

Don Luscombe and Central States Aero Company were ready to offer a good product but, unfortunately, faltered meeting the demand. The Monocoupe quickly became a very popular aircraft, but the Detroit Aircraft Engine Corporation's "Air-Cat" power plant proved to be a major thorn in any production or promotion effort. Either deliveries of the engines fell behind schedule or worse, the engine simply fell apart in flight. If this 5-cylinder radial engine didn't throw push-rods, it consumed spark plugs at a prodigious rate. These very serious shortcomings bottlenecked Monocoupe production and created delivery problems for the fledgling company. Obviously, Luscombe and Central States Aero Company had to resolve these problems if their popular aircraft was to survive.

As a temporary solution to these engine woes, Don purchased several foreign-manufactured power plants, including the five cylinder, 60/80 hp, German designed and built Siemens-Halske engines from T. Claude Ryan. Slightly larger and heavier than the Detroit "Air-Cat," Don later recounted, *"We splurged and bought five of them."*[12] Other foreign-designed and built engines were considered, also. In most cases, however, these engines were used only once with the customer furnishing the power plant. Examples included the British "Cirrus," the British "Genet" and the French "Anzani."

Interestingly, the "Anzani" was never rejected as a regular Monocoupe engine. Commitments for the "Anzani" were made about the same time as the "Air-Cat." Perhaps the decision to use the "Air-Cat" was made because, as Don later wrote, "it arrived first." Overall, very few "Anzani" engines were used because, being foreign-built, they were expensive and hard to obtain. The British designed, 4-cylinder in-line, "Cirrus" engine was quite heavy in actual Monocoupe use and presented its owners some delicate weight and balance problems. Reportedly, test pilot Doug Harris had to use an appreciable amount of power on landing to maintain elevator control.[13] The 5-cylinder, 88 hp English Armstrong-Siddeley "Genet" was used a couple times, also. The latter were supplied by a pair of Canadian customers. In each case where a foreign engine was employed, the Central States Aero Company staff had to manufacture a variety of motor-mounts necessary to accommodate changes in weight and balance. As a result, engine cowls were custom tailored and odd-shaped oil tanks became the norm. Seldom did any two ships look alike.

Extremely nose heavy, this Monocoupe used a Cirrus engine.

The summer months were a busy time for Central States Aero Company and Don Luscombe, now the company's vice-president and general manager. Not only were the first three production Monocoupes completed, but Don became a proud father. Don's first and only son, James True Luscombe, was born on August 4, 1927. Though never a doting father, Don Luscombe made attempts to spend some time with his only son. Often, this time was at the airport taking little Jimmy for airplane rides or just taxiing around the field. Eleanore Luscombe, on her behalf, was a very caring and loving mother, but not to the point of being "overly protective." Interestingly, she never flew with Don during this period. It was not she was afraid of his abilities as a pilot. Quite the contrary — Eleanore Luscombe was amazed by her husband's piloting skills. She was concerned for her only son and did not want to see him orphaned as a result of a flying accident.

Interestingly, both the Air Commerce Act of 1926 (by its very nature requiring airplane manufacturers employ qualified, often well paid aeronautical engineers) and James Luscombe's birth shaped and further molded Don Luscombe's complex personality. Sadly, both events, as they respectively matured and developed, offered occasional cause for resentment and jealousy for a fiercely competitive Don Luscombe in his later life.

In late July or early August 1927, the Fargo Aeronautics Club, Inc., bought an early production Monocoupe (1427, s/n 7) and sponsored their pilot, Vernon L. Roberts, to race it in the Class A race of the 1927 National Air Races' "New York - Spokane Air Derby." First and second place prize money totaled $15,000. Roberts' sponsors bought the airplane to participate in this September 24th and 25th race and to promote aviation in the Fargo area. Roberts, a barnstormer from Fargo, North Dakota, went to Bettendorf to help build his Monocoupe racer. He called his craft "Miss Fargo" to honor his sponsors and hometown. In the late August, Roberts test flew his new airplane for the first time. Barely a week later, he headed towards New York to race it.

The actual race proved more exciting than he had bargained. Between New York and Fargo, Roberts experienced twenty-one forced landings caused by burned spark plugs and thrown push rods. But the worst was yet to come in North Dakota. While the local press and politicians waited for their hometown hero to land, Roberts' "Miss Fargo" lost its propeller while crossing the threshold. An unfazed Roberts coasted his propeller-less Monocoupe up to an astonished crowd, the "Air-Cat" still turning. An awestruck bystander gasped, *"Fly without a propeller!"*

Despite these problems, Vern Roberts was impressed with the Monocoupe. The airplane was an enlightening change from the uncomfortable and somewhat sluggish open cockpit biplanes he flew while barnstorming. Don Luscombe's promises of a comfortable, sporty and fast enclosed cabin airplane were true. For services rendered, the Fargo Aeronautics Club literally gave this Monocoupe to Vern Roberts. During the balance of the fall months, Roberts flew his Monocoupe to promote aviation and the Monocoupe. Roberts enjoyed his airplane tremendously and often sang its praises to an admiring crowd.

Test pilot Vern Roberts and Don Luscombe. AVIATION HERITAGE LIBRARY

Winter's icy breath signaled an end to Roberts' aerial sojourns and he returned to Bettendorf in his Monocoupe whereupon he disassembled it for winter storage at the factory. Shortly thereafter, the airplane was dismantled to salvage its fittings and wing. Several improvements had been made to the Monocoupe design since this particular Monocoupe first graced the skies; thus, the Central States Aero Company considered Roberts' Monocoupe to be an "experimental plane." Roberts made a bold decision. He uprooted his family in early 1928 and moved to Moline to help Don Luscombe attain his airplane goals. For his efforts, Roberts was rewarded a factory manager position. Upon Doug Harris' departure in early 1928, Roberts became the company's chief test pilot. Then and later, Vern Roberts' many contributions added much to Monocoupe lore. His "need for speed" never diminished and, as such, he offered Don Luscombe's fledgling airplane a unique blend of engineering and air racing expertise. Similarly, Roberts proved to be a very capable and respected salesman. All factors contributed to the rapidly growing popularity of the Monocoupe.

Behind these gratifying scenes, Clayton Folkerts used whatever "free time" he had to good advantage. For Folkerts, it was not enough for him to design

Powered by a 28 hp Henderson motorcycle engine, Clayton Folkerts used this geodetic parasol to commute between Moline and the family farm. HAROLD FOLKERTS

and improve the Monocoupe, often he needed to *build* his ideas. Thus, a new personal design (not associated with the company) took shape at Wallace Field. Folkerts' endeavor was a small, single-place geodetic construction monoplane he later called and registered with the Department of Commerce as the "Folkerts Parasol." Powered by a 28 hp Henderson engine, Folkerts built the airplane in six months. When it flew, Folkerts reported a 70 miles per hour top speed and a 35 miles per hour takeoff speed. Folkerts used his airplane on occasion to commute from Davenport and Moline to the family farm in Barstow.

The "Air-Cat" engine situation continued to plague Central States Aero management and annoy Luscombe's Monocoupe promotional efforts. Though considered by many to be "a step in the right direction," the "Air-Cat" was vexed by a host of corporate problems in addition to its reliability problems, most of which were now corrected. The lack of money was perhaps the biggest dilemma faced by the Detroit Aircraft Engine Corporation to keep this 5-cylinder power plant in production. In an attempt to improve the "Air-Cat's" image, uplift the Detroit Aircraft Engine Corporation's image and sell more engines, Capt. Eddie Rickenbacker, the power plant's sponsor, carried an advertisement in an industry trade publication detailing the positive side of the "Air-Cat" and Monocoupe combination. The ad drew several hundred responses.

Despite this noble attempt, Rickenbacker's engine enterprise was soon bankrupt, leaving Don Luscombe in a quandary. Of the thirteen "Air-Cat" engines produced, Don had acquired nine, at least one snatched from an engine test stand only hours before a sheriff was to confiscate it. Don and CSA needed a reliable power plant if their airplane manufacturing endeavors were to continue. At year's end, Central States Aero Company had produced twenty-two Monocoupes. Twenty-five employees were listed on this growing company's employee roster.

The Monocoupe's popularity incurred the wrath of other airplane manufacturers. Don Luscombe later reflected upon this phase in Monocoupe history and recounted this experience in a letter to John Underwood: *"The biplane manufacturers didn't exactly like the threat of something new and encountered a 'stop Monocoupe' movement which embraced many libelers' accusations. In fact, on one occasion we were ruled out of the State of Connecticut."* Don put these problems aside and directed his actions towards the factory's deteriorating engine supply problem. By late December 1927, or early January 1928, this situation became acute. Operating with the full support of the other CSA executives, Don turned to Willard L. Velie, Jr., the aviation-minded son of well known and respected carriage and automobile maker Willard L. Velie, Sr., a powerful force in Midwestern business. The Velies had money and the technical experience to help Central States Aero Company.

An artist's rendition of the expansive Velie plants in 1928. JAMES B. ZAZAS COLLECTION

Velie, Sr., owned and operated an expansive auto plant, the Velie Motors Corporation, located just across the Mississippi River in nearby Moline, Illinois.

Chapter Three: Perfecting the Breed 27

A Velie automobile strikes a classy pose in front of the Velie mansion. JAMES B. ZAZAS COLLECTION

This prosperous manufacturer had a sales agents network that stretched around the globe. Besides making automobiles, the Velie Motors Corporation was experienced in designing and manufacturing their own engines. In 1919, the company designed and built the first six-cylinder valve-in-head motor. Velie motors were noted for their endurance, quietness and long life.[14]

The younger Velie, himself quite interested in aviation, listened intently while Don promoted the positive attributes of his new company and the bright outlook for his airplanes. Don stressed the importance of a reliable power plant to keep his airplanes flying, and added the questionable performance of the "Air-Cat" engine was the cause of many of his sales and delivery problems. In conclusion, Don proposed Velie Motors Corporation build a suitable, more reliable engine. An impressed Willard, Jr., presented Don's convincing pleas to his father, a grandson of farm equipment maker John Deere. Reiterating many of Luscombe's convincing arguments at the family's Mediterranean style marble, stone and brick mansion — the "Velie Villa" — the younger Velie stated emphatically and enthusiastically the future of the family business should involve aviation.

Willard Velie, Jr., wanted to make his own mark in business and, as such, he set his goals toward aviation. However, he lacked the necessary funds, factory space and employees to undertake such a difficult and potentially risky venture. A meeting was set during the first week of January 1928, for Don to present his ideas firsthand to the senior Velie. Once more, Don was most pervasive in his presentation. Spreading out a briefcase full of inquiries and a picture of his Monocoupe before an astonished Willard Velie, Sr., Don Luscombe began the most important sales pitch of his life.

"Mr. Velie, the whole world recognized the famous Velie wrought-iron buggy, and everyone is familiar with your pioneering of a better automobile. Now there is a new form of transportation for the private owner in the foreseeable future, and I think I have hit upon an acceptable design that will lend itself to production methods despite the fact that my own resources will not permit the attempt. You have a wonderful engine plant and a more dependable, small aircraft is badly needed. Here is a picture of the vehicle and here are 400 inquiries from a small adver-

The "Velie Villa" was made of stone, brick and imported marble. This renovated building serves as a popular Moline restaurant today. FRAN FITZWILLIAM

tisement in a magazine of limited circulation. We need engines — a Velie engine! Your local aviation expert, Mr. Rusty Campbell, has tested this job and I believe will be willing to give you an unbiased report on its potentialities."

After carefully weighing the facts, the older Velie agreed to study Don's request further. At first, the elder Velie was not particularly interested in pursuing an airplane engine manufacturing role, but Velie and his automobile company had their backs against the wall. Other reputable automobile manufacturers, e.g. Ford, had made deep inroads into Velie's automobile market share. Velie needed something to keep his company a going and profitable enterprise.

By way of background, Willard Lamb Velie, Sr., was a prominent figure in many diversified endeavors besides manufacturing and finance. "Will" Velie — as many folks called this well-liked gentleman — was an avid outdoor enthusiast and loved fishing and hunting. Additionally, Velie was an ardent golfer. Willard Velie, Sr., was born on May 10, 1856, the son of S.H. Velie and Emma Deere Velie. His mother was the daughter of John Deere, the famous farm implement manufacturer. Velie's association with Deere & Co. began in 1889 as a clerk. Later, he was promoted to various positions, including sales manager. In 1895, Velie was elected the director and secretary of the company.

In 1900, Velie resigned his position at Deere & Co., but remained in an advisory role, and founded Velie Carriage Company. In 1908, Velie started the Velie Motor Vehicle Company, later changed to the Velie Motors Corporation. In 1911, the Velie Engineering Company was organized to manufacture trucks. Many thousands of these trucks were used in World War I to transport men and material. According to some accounts, Velie Motors Corporation produced some 250,000 to 300,000 vehicles during the twenty years the factory was in business. Between 1908 and 1918, Willard Velie, Sr., was chief of the Executive Committee of Deere & Co. and was second-in-command under President Ben Butterworth.

Mr. Velie married Anne Floweree of Helena, Montana, on May 21, 1890. They had two children, Willard, Jr., and Marjorie. Willard L. Velie, Jr., was born in the family's home in Moline, Illinois on July 2, 1896. He attended the Moline schools and entered Yale University for college. However, these studies were interrupted by World War I. Velie, Jr., enlisted and served several months in France as an officer. After the war, the younger Velie started working in his father's shop. Over the next decade, Willard Velie, Jr., held various sales positions, later being appointed to serve as the Velie Motors Corporation vice president in 1927.

While "Will" Velie, Sr., pondered his decision to help Central States Aero Company, the Bureau of Air Commerce notified CSA executives an Approved Type Certificate would be forthcoming. In January 1928, the Monocoupe was awarded Approved Type Certificate (ATC) number 22. This model was called the Monocoupe Model 22. Thus, the Monocoupe Model 22 became the first light, cabin monoplane to be approved and certificated for production in the United States under the new regulations.

The Velies took careful notice of this event. The Monocoupe was now a "government approved" airplane. This approval solidified their decision to act. They began to quietly purchase CSA stock and soon had a controlling interest. Throughout late January and early February 1928, rumors abounded that Velie's expansive enterprises would absorb the smaller Central States Aero Company. The younger Velie tried to quash these rumors by telling local reporters, *"We are not interested in the (Central States Aero) enterprise other than that we will probably build motors for planes."*

However, this situation changed very quickly. On February 24, 1928, Mono-Aircraft, Inc., of Moline, Illinois, was capitalized for $150,000 to manufacture and distribute airplanes. The Velies had decided to enter full-scale airplane production. In early March, the Central States Aero Company directors agreed unanimously to sell their Iowa-chartered corporation to the Illinois-chartered corporation. Willard L. Velie, Jr., was named president and Don Luscombe was retained as a vice-president and sales manager. George A. Stange was appointed secretary and treasurer. The senior Velie was named a director and Chairman of the Board.

In March 1928, the Central States Aero Company ceased to exist as a separate entity and, in turn, became Mono-Aircraft, Inc., a subsidiary of the Velie Motors Corporation. All existing Monocoupe tooling, dies and paperwork were moved from Bettendorf to the Velie factory, thus providing almost three hundred thousand square feet of floor space and all facilities and machinery consistent with a large automobile production plant. Brochures were prepared that touted the plant could produce one Monocoupe per day or upwards of fifty per week, if needed.

The Monocoupe
Registered Trade Mark

Manufactured by
Mono Aircraft, Inc.
Moline, Illinois

Chapter Three: Perfecting the Breed 29

MOLINE—THE QUAD CITY AIRPORT

Irresistible to Sportsmen

AT LAST, a modern plane for the private owner! Smart in line and appointment. Offering the last word in performance, economy of operation, strength and reasonable first cost.

You and your passenger sitting side by side on velour upholstered seats and in velour-lined cabin, find it possible to converse with motor at full throttle. Wear a straw hat and smoke if you wish.

Figure twenty-five miles to the gallon and hop off for five hundred miles without fatigue. Unstick in a hundred feet, cruise at eighty-five and land at less than thirty, enjoying visibility you never thought possible.

Tubing construction, high safety factor throughout, Detroit Aircraft Engine Corporation 60-70 air-cooled motor. Weight, empty, 600 lbs; span, 30 ft.; length, 20 ft. Early deliveries at Davenport, Iowa, or Moline, Ill., at $2285.

Distributors interested in complete details may address inquiries to

The Central States Aero Co.
Davenport, Iowa

BE MODERN — USE THE AIR MAIL

MOLINE—THE QUAD CITY AIRPORT

A Velie-Built Automobile
WITH A VELIE-BUILT
Airplane-Type Motor

VELIE cars are Velie-built in their entirety in the Moline plant, including motors, bodies, front and rear axles, fenders, sheet-metal parts, upholstery and paint.

Velie builds two lines of automobiles—Model 60, 118-inch wheel base, and Model 50, 112-inch wheel base. Both are powered by the famous Velie-built, airplane-type motor, with full forced-feed lubrication to all moving parts—a motor noted for its stamina, long life and remarkable quietness.

In the Velie cars is incorporated all that exceptional manufacturing facilities and experience of a quarter of a century of quality-building can give, plus the care and attention to detail permitted by a production policy which has always placed quality ahead of quantity.

Every attribute that a fine car should possess is found in Velie. Beauty of line and finish, sterling performance with dependability, backed by a reputation for remarkably long-life Velie cars, offer even more—distinctive design.

The Velie Model 50 Standard Six is built for those who desire durability and low automobile transportation costs, as well as comfort, convenience and pride of ownership that heretofore only higher-priced cars have afforded. It possesses features not found in any other American Standard 56-inch tread, six-cylinder, four-door sedan in its price class.

Prices $1165 to $1635 F. O. B. Moline—War Tax Extra

VELIE MOTORS CORPORATION, Moline, Ill.

VELIE
AMERICA'S LONG LIFE CAR

"BEAT 'EM TO IT" — USE THE AIR MAIL

"For I dipped into the future, as far as the eye could see;
Saw the vision of the world, and all the wonder that would be:
Saw the heavens fill with commerce, argosies of magic sails,
Pilots of the purple twilight, dropping down with costly bales."
Alfred, Lord Tennyson (1809 - 1865)

Chapter Four

A Time For Change —
A Chance For Survival

The history of Velie Motors Corporation's contribution to transportation is reflected in this photo. Left to right, Velie-built carriage, Velie-built automobile, Velie-built Monocoupe airplane. The building in the background is the just completed Monocoupe assembly hangar. MIKE SCHENK

Both Willard Velie, Sr., and Willard Velie, Jr., had high hopes for their latest enterprise, Mono-Aircraft, Inc. Each wanted their airplane manufacturing company to succeed, prosper and dominate the private airplane market. With their hearts set on quality, the Velies wanted to "make only the best."

The Monocoupe was proving itself to be an excellent and very popular design and a successful production run was anticipated. The former Central States Aero Company jigs, tools and dies had been moved to the former carriage factory and the first Velie built Monocoupe was expected to rollout in mid to late March 1928.

Monocoupe airplanes were still being sold with a variety of engines and prices. Standard equipped, 60 hp "Anzani"-powered Monocoupes sold for $2750 and 80 hp "Anzani"-powered Monocoupes sold for $3000. If the customer desired, a Ryan "Siemans," 70 hp engine, could be installed. This version listed for $3750. Willard Velie, Sr., decided it was time to design, build and mate a more reliable engine to this exciting airplane. Velie, Sr., requested Don Luscombe obtain an "Air-Cat" engine for further study. Don hedged as he had just sold the last "Air-Cat" to John Livingston, then an airport operator in Monmouth, Illinois. Velie did not care for excuses. *"Get me an engine!"* he thundered.

Don acted swiftly. A sixty mile drive with Frank

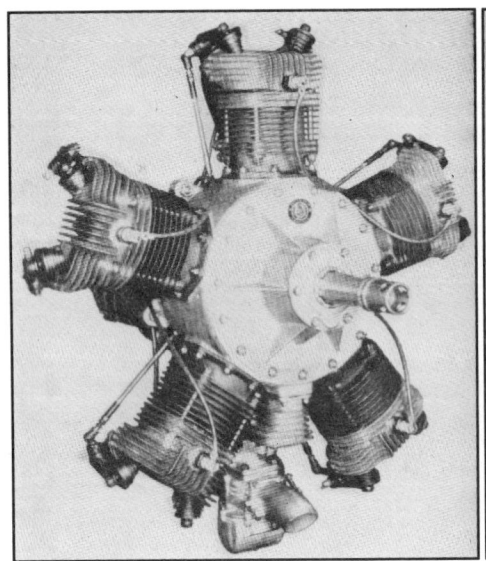

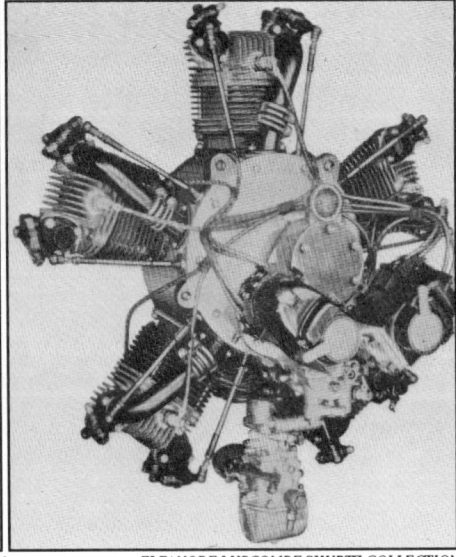

Front view of a Velie M-5 engine. This engine developed 55-62 horsepower.

A rear view of the Velie M-5.

Wallace and a bottle or two of Wallace's finest Scotch whiskey later (despite Prohibition times), Don was able to coax the engine from Livingston. Don had the "Air-Cat" in the Velie plant within hours after his "purchase," whereupon it was quickly disassembled by Velie's inquisitive engineers.

Within six weeks, the Velie Motors Corporation was making an air-cooled aircraft engine of its own design called the Velie Model M-5. This five cylinder engine developed 55 hp at 1815 rpm and developed a maximum of 62 hp at 2000 rpm at sea level.

Before the M-5 was flight-tested, this engine was run for fifteen hours on a test block within the factory, then it was installed on a Monocoupe. With Vern Roberts at the controls, the first flight of this new engine occurred on March 21, 1928 at the Moline Airport. A large crowd of Velie and Mono-Aircraft employees were on hand to watch these first tests. No major discrepancies were noted during this successful flight.

Further experimental work was needed before the M-5 engine was ready for production, including a required series of fifty hour Department of Commerce tests. But, within days of the test flight, a very satisfied Velie, Jr., announced the Velie Motors Corporation would enter into full scale airplane engine production. Thus, at the time, Mono-Aircraft, Inc. became the only company in the United States to manufacture its own airplanes and the engines to power them.

Upon closer examination, the Velie M-5 was virtually a carbon-copy of the Detroit "Air-Cat." Few changes were made and, as such, copied many of the "Air-Cat's" shortcomings, including severe overheating. Complicating the situation, E.K. Campbell complained of broken tractor and lawn mower blades — the new Velie engine was dropping an inordinate amount of cast iron on the Moline airport grounds.

Aware his reputation was at stake, Willard Velie, Sr., directed his engineers to find a solution. He made it clear cost was not a consideration. An improved M-5 engine was developed quickly. The actual changes were few, but they proved most effective. The most notable alteration involved throwing aside the "Air-Cat's" original iron heads and utilizing aluminum heads. Sodium valves were incorporated, also.

Despite these changes, however, the new Velie M-5 design remained so close to the "Air-Cat" that Velie Motors Corporation was charged in a subsequent patent suit fourteen months later (June 1929) and had to pay damages to the LeBlond Aircraft Engines Corporation of Cincinnati, Ohio, the holders of the "Air-Cat" patents acquired from the Detroit Aircraft Engine Corporation's receivers.

An early Velie Monocoupe sits before the National Air Transport hangar at the Moline Airport.

Monocoupe fuselage frame of steel tubing was formed with precision and welded into one unit. MIKE SCHENK

The senior Velie cast aside any initial skepticism and went to great lengths to insure the success of his new aviation venture. Once, when float arms bending in the Zenith carburetors used in the M-5 engine were causing a rash of forced landings, Velie appealed directly to the top management of Stromberg Carburetors for a solution. Stromberg wasn't particularly interested in Velie's plight, especially when they considered Velie's airplane operation as creating only a limited carburetor demand without any appreciable production potential. But, Velie was undaunted.

In a dramatic gesture, the elder Velie opened his shirt, revealing his chest. *"Gentlemen,"* he said addressing the startled executives, *"civilian aviation will be set back ten years unless we can get a carburetor that will function. Here is my bare chest."* Velie got what he wanted. And Velie M-5 reliability improved dramatically. In the process, Cornelius Barnett "Scotty" Burmood, a Moline-area pilot, mechanic and previously a Stromberg carburetor technical representative, joined the Mono-Aircraft payroll.

Burmood related his feelings about the new carburetor to several Mono Aircraft employees in the following poem:

Here's to the Monocoupe,
That wonderful bird of flight.
It flies from pasture to pasture,
And back in a pasture it lights.
And every time it flies, it poops.
And everytime it poops, it lights.
Whether it flies or whether it lights,
It all depends on the new carburetor.
And that's the way it was.

On March 30, 1928, a photograph depicting the first Mono-Aircraft, Inc. produced Monocoupe (4138, s/n 14) sporting a Siemens SH-10 engine appeared in the *Moline Daily Dispatch*, a local newspaper. An enthusiastic Don Luscombe told the *Dispatch* this new Monocoupe would sell for approximately $2500.

Concurrently, Mono-Aircraft officials announced

34 Visions of Luscombe: The Early Years

Monocoupe wing construction at the Velie factory.
Here, the robust wing framework, buildup from routed spruce spar I-beams and basswood ribs with spruce cap-strips, are ready for covering.
FRAN FITZWILLIAM

they were considering erecting a $5000 assembly hangar at the Moline Airport. This building would give the company a field close enough to the factory where completed airplanes could be trailered, reassembled and test flown. With new equipment being installed daily, these officials hinted upwards of fifty airplanes a day were to be produced!

Several days later, Jerry Lederer notified the Moline Chamber of Commerce he would move his concern, Aerotech, Inc., into new offices in the Velie Motors Corporation. Besides its work on the Monocoupe, Lederer told the Chamber that Aerotech, Inc. had considerable airplane and airport design experience for such clients as the Texas Aircraft Corporation, the Monarch Airplane Company and the Gillis Construction Company. Lederer and his handful of Aerotech employees went to work immediately to gain government approval of the Velie-powered Monocoupe.

Behind these public announcements, there was a flurry of activity at the Velie factory. Velie and Luscombe were anxious to display the Monocoupe at the Detroit Board of Commerce sponsored All-American Aircraft Show in Detroit, Michigan. Nearly forty manufacturers were scheduled to display their products at this aviation pageant. Three Monocoupes sporting different power plants were flown to Detroit and displayed in the Detroit Convention Hall at this April 14 through April 21 event and included an "Anzani," a "Cirrus" and a "Velie."

Making his first airplane flight ever, Mr. Willard L. Velie, Sr., flew to the show in a Fairchild with E.K. "Rusty" Campbell as pilot. Velie's son joined his father on this flight, also. A six-place Travel Air, flown by Campbell's assistant, Roy T. "Stub" Quinby, carried other Moline officials invited by Velie to attend.

JAMES B. ZAZAS COLLECTION
Wing rib sandbagging tests. One rib is supporting all the sandbags shown, 500 lbs. total.

JAMES B. ZAZAS COLLECTION
The strain of this test was four times greater than the landing gear would be subjected to under the most severe conditions.

JAMES B. ZAZAS COLLECTION
Sandbagging the tail assembly. This test was also four times what was to be expected under the most strenuous maneuvers.

Chapter Four: A Time For Change — A Chance For Survival   35

Moving production line of Velie M-5 engines. Each man had a specific task to perform. Engine was complete and ready for testing at the end of line.   JAMES B. ZAZAS COLLECTION

During the show, Ford "Trimotor" designer Bill Stout and Ford Corporation President Henry Ford were most interested in possible production of the sprightly Monocoupe. Reportedly, the pair approached Willard Velie, Sr., to sell. Scotty Burmood later recounted Velie was not about to "pry loose from it."

By the end of April 1928, Don Luscombe could count almost fifty new Monocoupes had been built in the Velie factory. More could have been constructed, but the M-5 engines could not be manufactured fast enough to keep pace with airplane production. Velie solved this bottleneck and ordered an increase in motor production.

On May 3, 1928, Mono-Aircraft proudly announced total orders for the Monocoupe exceeded a half-million dollars. A mid-spring sales surge, no doubt the result of the favorable showing and press coverage the Monocoupe received in Detroit, required the company to increase production to one hundred ships a month. To handle this increased production schedule, ground was broken for a new, 60 x 106 feet, concrete block and concrete floor hangar at the Moline Airport. Intended to be used to assemble Monocoupe airplanes, this structure was built for the Campbell-DeSchepper Airplane Company at a cost of $7500 and was situated immediately west of the National Air Transport (NAT) hangar on the field.

Prior to this decision, a portion of the NAT facility was leased by Mono-Aircraft to assemble new Monocoupes. But unlike the NAT facility, this new hangar would neither be heated nor would have extra rooms for offices and storage. In winter, the heated NAT hangar would be used to assemble airplanes and the new hangar would be used for storage of parts and completed airplanes.

June 1928, proved to be a newsworthy month for Mono-Aircraft. Twenty-five year old Mrs. Phoebe Omlie of Memphis, Tennessee, a well-known and respected aviatrix, arrived at the company and announced she would race a Velie-powered Mono-

Mounting engine and installing controls on Velie Monocoupes. The plane was then carefully inspected throughout, after which the wing was firmly attached. MIKE SCHENK

Charles A. Lindbergh poses before an early Monocoupe. ELEANORE LUSCOMBE SHURTZ COLLECTION

coupe in the 1928, 6300 mile National Air Tour, competing for the Edsel Ford Trophy and a $12,000 first place prize. She was to be the only woman to enter this race and she was to fly it solo! Omlie's appearance and comments netted several new Monocoupe orders.[15] Initially, her entry was the only "flivver" plane originally scheduled to fly this arduous trek, but another Monocoupe was later entered.

American humorist, Will Rogers, made a brief stop at the Moline Airport during June. Spotting a Velie Monocoupe, Rogers told everybody present he liked the airplane. The press published his comments. . . and a few more Monocoupe orders followed.

On June 22, Velie Motors received word the government approved their engine and received the Department of Commerce's "Highest Rating." The Velie M-5 was issued engine ATC number 4.[16]

Joining this exciting news was word Charles A. Lindbergh had visited a Madison, Wisconsin, airport a week earlier, noticed a Monocoupe on the field and remarked it looked like a fine ship. He asked the owner for the opportunity to fly it. He returned from his flight with much enthusiasm and high praise for the Mono-Aircraft product. His comments were carried by an aviation-hungry media and more Monocoupe orders arrived at the company shortly thereafter. Quite possibly, the aircraft Lindbergh flew may have belonged to then Governor Fred Zimmermann of Wisconsin, a licensed pilot.

Factory fresh Monocoupe airplanes were trucked to the Moline Airport, assembled and then test flown. Circa Summer 1928. SIMPLIFIED FLYING, JAMES B. ZAZAS COLLECTION

On July 14, Mono-Aircraft officials announced yet another concrete floor hangar would be built to handle Monocoupe storage and assembly. These officials stated this new 60 x 100 feet hangar, set to be built on the northwest corner of the airport, was needed because the company had outgrown its other hangar(s). Monocoupe production was said to be four-and-a-half airplanes a day.

In August 1928, the Velie M-5 powered Monocoupe was awarded Approved Type Certificate number 70 and was called the Monocoupe 70. Besides the engine on the nose, this Velie-powered Monocoupe used the same airframe as its "Air-Cat"/"Siemans" powered cousin, the Model 22. Priced originally at $2500 Flyaway Moline, this sporty airplane was repriced to sell for $2675 Flyaway Moline.

A quarter page advertisement in the *Moline Daily Dispatch* stated "Buy it and Fly it for $2775. Complete instructions are included under the competent direction of E.K. (Rusty) Campbell." Velie Mono Sales, the local Monocoupe dealership, paid for this ad.

In retrospect, the Monocoupe 22 and Monocoupe 70 airplanes sported at least three different tail configurations. Besides the better known classic style, there was a somewhat triangular shaped fin with a squared oval combination as well as a more rounded, half circle shaped rudder that used a similar rakish fin.

Another unusual Monocoupe feature was the placement of the design's only door, usually on the right side. However, the customer had the option of ordering a Monocoupe with the door on the left side. This arrangement allowed the pilot his choice of having the throttle in his left or right hand. These Monocoupes became known as "left-hand" and "right-hand" Monocoupes.

Don Luscombe, now generally content with the Velie M-5's reliability, was most anxious to promote the company's airplanes and boost sales. Orders were being received on a regular basis. Luscombe wasted no time taking advantage of the Monocoupes' increasing popularity and quickly developed a sizable Monocoupe dealer program and marketing network. Private airplane owners, Monocoupe enthusiasts and airport owners/operators served as a broad extension to Luscombe's plans by marketing and selling Mono-Aircraft airplanes.

Don's endeavors reaped substantial rewards, particularly in the Western and Southern United States. A new dealership, the Monoplane Aircraft Company, based in Los Angeles, California, became the Monocoupe distributor for California, New Mexico, Arizona, Nevada and Utah. James B. Carpenter headed the dealership while the dapper-dressed John B. Hinchey became sales manager.

Before the year was out, Don had established Monocoupe dealers and distributors throughout the country, including John G. "Tex" Rankin, who became the Monocoupe distributor for Oregon and Washington, and John Livingston of Aurora, Illinois, whose territory included northern Illinois and Iowa. Phoebe Omlie held the Southern states as her territory. A Mr. C.W. Shaw, co-owner of Travel Air Ways of Dallas, Texas, completed arrangements to become the Monocoupe distributor in Texas.

While developing this network, Don withdrew from most day-to-day contact with his Mono-Aircraft employees. Instead, he put his promotion skills to work where they worked best, in the company of the rich and affluent of aviation's elite. Up and coming air race pilots of the day, even "The Lone Eagle," Charles A. Lindbergh, were counted among his many friends.

Though other airplane manufacturers developed similar distributor programs, none did so with the fervor demonstrated by Don Luscombe. He was intent the Monocoupe would capture the lion's share of the market for privately-owned airplanes. He was not to be disappointed. Then, Don did something characteristically "Luscombe." He decided to take an intuitive and innovative marketing approach to promote his airplanes — magazine advertising. The result exceeded his wildest imagination!

Luscombe had been working on a small booklet for some time. Titled *Simplified Flying,* this fifty-four page production described the basics of flying, from simple aeronautical theory through advanced flight training. As written in this booklet, *"the purpose of this book is to set forth certain fundamentals of flying for one taking up aviation for pleasure and personal transportation."* Ample descriptions of the Monocoupe, vivid photographs depicting its sturdy construction and Velie air-cooled engine, and informative specifications of each were included. The book concluded with a fifteen page section listing the common aeronautical terms and their definitions.

Don presented his booklet in mid-July as part of a two page color ad in *Liberty,* then a popular bi-weekly magazine. The booklet was offered at ten cents per copy and drew almost 19,000 responses. Mono-Aircraft and the local post office had to hire extra help to handle the sheer volume of inquiries.

His novel promotion idea worked! And the name Monocoupe became recognized far and wide. A point of interest, this ad was the first time an airplane had been advertised in a major national magazine.

Vern Roberts assisted Don in his Monocoupe promotion endeavors. At first, Roberts was sent to "familiar territory" — North Dakota, South Dakota, Minnesota, etc., — to sell Monocoupes. But, unlike Don's penchant to hob-knob with the well-to-do and participate in the country club style of living they enjoyed, Roberts was more frugal in his initial salesman approaches with prospective clients.

The following yarn demonstrates Vern Roberts' more humble approach to his clients. Shortly after he had joined the Mono-Aircraft organization, Roberts learned the value of a company-paid expense account from none other than Willard L. Velie, Sr. Returning to Moline from his first trip somewhat late on a Friday night, Roberts handed his expenses to Velie's secretary as Mr. Velie had already gone home. Roberts was quite concerned the expenses he incurred during his sales trip might upset his employer. The following Monday, Roberts was summoned to Mr. Velie's office, *"Now!"*

"Mr. Roberts, is this your expense account?" the senior Velie inquired holding a small stack of papers in his hand.

"Yes, sir. I tried to keep expenses down by staying with friends and with them, everything the most economical."

Velie leaned forward, his eyebrows furrowed, *"Listen, I don't want any cheap-skates working for me. After this, you stay at the best hotels, take your friends out to eat. . ."*

Vern Roberts was relieved — he was so sure he was going to get chewed-out for his "extravagant" expenses. Roberts realized he would be able to continue his sales work — and air racing — in style. Unlike Don Luscombe, however, Vern Roberts remained "close to the troops" and earned the unwavering respect of his fellow employees.

Don was held in awe by many of the Mono-Aircraft employees. Many were swayed by his charismatic manner and ability to remain positive despite such difficult times. Where many employees were friendly with Roberts, others elected to stay with Don Luscombe because they "believed in him."

Willard Velie, Sr., had good reason to be "loose" with his money. Before 1928 drew to a close, the Velies, Don Luscombe, Vern Roberts and Mono-Aircraft advertising could (and would!) boast ninety percent of all *light-planes* owned in the United States were Monocoupes. By the same token, each could exult almost ten percent of all licensed *airplanes* in the United States were Monocoupes.

Don was exuberant! He could vaunt the aircraft as setting *"a new standard of uniformity and interchangeability of parts."* The Monocoupe was still the lowest priced government-approved airplane at the time.

The Monocoupe's appeal and performance contributed to successes in other fields of aerial advertising and promotion, most notably for air races and air derbies. Vern Roberts became a perennial air race winner and placed very well in several events at the 1928 National Air Races at Mines Fields, Los Angeles, California, held later in the year. He took a stock Monocoupe 70, called "Little Sweetheart" (NR-7323, s/n 199), to these races and finished "in-the-money." He placed fourth in the 510 cubic inch Civilian Free-for-All race at 101.37 mph winning $200 and fourth in the San Francisco to Los Angeles

Phoebe Omlie and her Monocoupe 70, "Chiggers." This photo was signed by Omlie to Frances Fitzwilliam, then secretary to the company's treasurer, George Stange. FRAN FITZWILLIAM

California Class A race earning $150.

In the Light Plane Speed and Efficiency Races, Roberts placed 2nd in both races flying his Monocoupe 70. A Charles LaJotte placed 3rd in the Speed Race and 5th place finish in the Efficiency Race, flying a stock, Velie powered Monocoupe 70.

Likewise, two Monocoupe 70 airplanes were flown in the 1928 National Air Tour by Jack Atkinson and Phoebe Omlie, the first woman to pilot an airplane in this event. Both aviators embarked on the Ford Reliability Tour, a grueling 6300 mile odyssey often flown over rough terrain and included stops in thirty-two cities! Omlie, who later called herself "assistant to president of Mono-Aircraft" in a *Who's Who in Aviation* biography, became the first woman to fly alone across the great American desert. Omlie's adventure and her progress made front page newspaper stories. Yet, this news was often bittersweet.

Near Marfia, Texas, Omlie tipped her Monocoupe, named "Chiggers" (NC-5878, s/n 58), while landing. In a display of superior sportsmanship, Atkinson gave Omlie his ship (NC-5877, s/n 57) and stayed behind to effect repairs to Omlie's Monocoupe. Atkinson finished 19th and Omlie finished 24th in this torturing air derby.

Shortly after the race, Omlie stated many of the participating pilots had signed a petition to the Detroit Board of Commerce airing several grievances, including poor hotel accommodations and that the formula used for rating the airplanes was not just. In addition, she charged the race officials had refused an accounting of the prize money awards. In a letter written to her mother, Omlie wrote, *"The signers had taken up the matter merely to prevent the recurrence of such things in future tours. We realize air tours are a new thing and perfect management can be achieved only through some failures."*

These races afforded an airplane manufacturer tremendous promotion and publicity value. Furthermore, these races were used as a testing ground for new designs and ideas. The lessons learned from these races were often carried to the factory. Quite often, the favorable results gained from racing an airplane were incorporated into improved airplane designs. The Monocoupe was no exception.

Beyond the air racing scene, a Monocoupe was modified with a pair of Edo Aircraft Corporation floats. Crocker Snow and Theodore Kenyon of Skyways, Inc., a Boston Airport Fixed Base Operation, undertook this modification making subsequent flight tests in late August and early September. At one point, their olive green and cream Monocoupe was flown with three occupants crammed in the cockpit. The event received considerable attention with the local media.

These wins and showings, coupled with Don Luscombe's intuitive and impressive marketing schemes, virtually made the name Monocoupe a

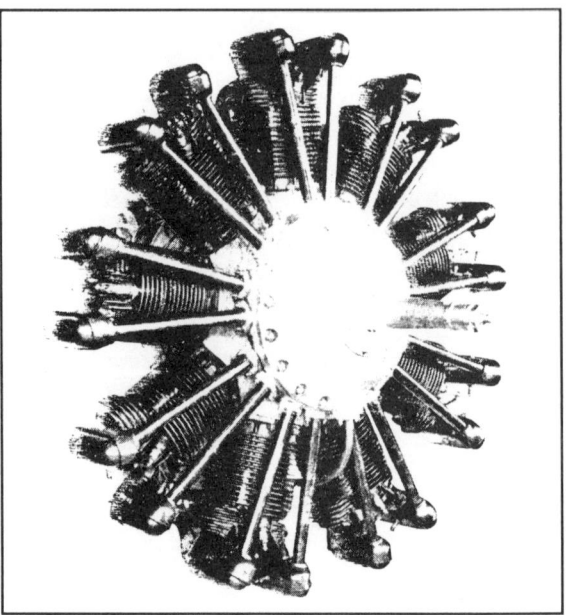

The Velie ML-9, designed to be used in to the Monocoach, was rated at 170/180 hp. JAMES B. ZAZAS COLLECTION

MONO-AIRCRAFT BROCHURE

household word in the aviation fraternity at the close of 1928. Similarly, the favorable design innovations attained from the air racing Monocoupes were incorporated into the production airplanes which helped make the Monocoupe the "high performance" airplane it was touted to be.

By year's end, some 278 Monocoupes had rolled through the Mono-Aircraft doors, despite that production had slowed to three airplanes per week. During the waning months of 1928, a new Mono-Aircraft design and a new Velie power plant made their debut. The new airplane was called the "Monocoach," a four-place airplane. The new power plant was the Velie M-9, an air-cooled, nine-cylinder 180 hp engine.

The Monocoach, a high-wing monoplane, was developed during the fall of 1928 to satisfy customer requests for a four place cabin monoplane. It was first flown on October 24, 1928, with company test pilot Vern Roberts at the controls. Flight testing was projected to continue well into the spring of 1929 before any government approval was anticipated. The Monocoach's project engineer was none other than Clayton Folkerts.

Unlike its more gracefully styled brethren from which it evolved, the first Monocoach was a rather boxy looking airplane with a wide, split-axle type landing gear. This stout gear greatly reduced the chance of damage due to landing on rough ground. Company engineers, however, were dissatisfied with this design and endeavored to improve its aesthetic qualities.

The Monocoach's overall length was 26' 8", the height was 8' 7" and the wingspan was an even 39 feet with a 75 inch wing chord. Gross weight was 3092 lbs, empty weight was 1919 lbs and useful load was listed as 1173 lbs.

The Monocoach possessed a robust structure. The fuselage was built-up from welded 1025 and

4130 chromemoly tubing formed into a rigid, truss form. Wood formers, all covered in fabric, gave the fuselage its tapering shape. The steel tubing, fabric covered fin and rudder were manually adjustable on the ground whereas the horizontal stabilizer could be adjusted in flight.

Bucket-type, folding-back seats were included for front seat occupants while a bench-type seat was provided for the rear seat passengers. A step was provided on each side of the cabin for easy entry. Dual controls, a skylight in the cabin roof and large, side windows that slid up and down were standard. The cabin walls were soundproofed and the interior was upholstered in mohair. The Monocoach possessed a striking "Berryloid" finish. Painted an overall gloss black, the airplane was tastefully trimmed in a bright orange-yellow. Of course, the customer had the choice of other colors and schemes.

JIM HARVEY

(Above) Monocoupe 113 — "Powered by Velie."

(Right) Chic Florence Klingensmith takes delivery of her Monocoupe 113.

Concurrently, a new engine was designed and built to be used primarily on the Monocoach. Called the Velie ML-9, this 9-cylinder, 180 hp engine was engineered mostly through the efforts of A.R. Weigel. The ML-9 was similar in appearance to the Wright J-5 "Whirlwind," but was smaller and had the magnetos placed on the accessory section instead of the nose. To undertake needed testing, a Travel Air 4000 biplane was borrowed and the ML-9 was mounted to it. This combination flew for at least 100 hours.

When the first Monocoach was built, an ML-9 was removed from the Travel Air and fitted to this prototype Monocoach (X-8900, s/n 5000). Though it proved quite reliable, some problems were encountered and further work on the ML-9 was soon abandoned as being too costly and time consuming. The Wright J-5 "Whirlwind" was selected to power the Monocoach.

But 1928 was not to end without its share of tragedy. Willard L. Velie, Sr., died suddenly in his home on October 24, 1928. Ill for only 24 hours, the pioneer auto maker, financier, outdoorsman and aviation entrepreneur died from a heart attack aggravated by an embolism in his right leg. To honor this gregarious industrialist, the Velie plants were closed the following day. Similarly, a flight of five Monocoupe airplanes flew a classic "V" formation above the funeral procession at Moline's Riverside Cemetery.

The death of Willard Velie, Sr., cast a tremendous burden of responsibility on the younger Velie's shoulders. Willard Velie, Jr., tried to calm his workers' fears they would soon be unemployed by telling them he planned to increase automobile production. But, as events unfolded, this was not to be the case.

JOHN UNDERWOOD

Velie Motors Corporation announced on November 27, 1928, it would discontinue permanently the manufacturing of automobiles. Furthermore, a work-weary Willard Velie, Jr., announced negotiations were in progress to sell the Velie plants except for the parts engaged in airplane manufacturing. To this end, Monocoupe airplane and Velie engine production would be increased.

At Mono-Aircraft, 1929 promised to be a very busy and rewarding year. Rumors abounded, new ideas and new airplane designs were to be intro-

Spartan, but functional, Monocoupe 113 cockpit. JIM HARVEY

Phoebe Omlie boards her Monocoupe 113 Special as part of a publicity stunt meant to gain Moline resident support for a new tax levy. Omlie flew this Monocoupe to more than 23,000 feet and set a woman's altitude record, but was later denied after certifying officials questioned the accuracy of the barograph recording. FRAN FITZWILLIAM

duced. The engineering department hummed with activity developing these innovations to keep pace with a rapidly unfolding market and an increasingly fickle aviation public. More and more pilots shied from the slow, lumbering biplanes of the period and opted for something faster, something sexier, something with a single wing. Many of these pilots looked towards the Monocoupe.

Folkerts, Lederer, Knack, Whelan and Smith were quite busy fulfilling the demands thrust upon them. And Luscombe found himself increasingly on-the-road promoting his company's airplanes.

One of the first of new aircraft to be offered for 1929 was the Monocoupe Model 113 (ATC #113). This new airplane, basically an improved derivative of the Velie-Monocoupe, featured a longer wing, a split-axle landing gear with oil-draulic struts and an uprated, 65 hp Velie M-5 power plant. Two heavy-duty wing struts were on each side of the cabin, giving the Monocoupe 113 a large safety factor. The Approved Type Certificate was issued during February 1929.

The Monocoupe 113 was 19' 9" long and 6' 3" high. Its forgiving "Clark Y" airfoil wing had a span of 32' with a 60" chord. Top speed was an impressive 98 mph, cruising speed was 85 mph and landing speed was a very docile 37 mph. Other figures included a 1350 lbs gross weight, an 848 lbs empty weight and a 502 lbs useful load.

A few Monocoupe 113 airplanes were modified with a Warner 110 hp "Scarab" engine and were groomed primarily for racing events. This model became the Monocoupe 113 Special and was approved originally for production under Group 2 Approval #2-120.

As was inherent in all Mono-Aircraft airplanes, performance, ruggedness and maneuverability were the Monocoupe 113's trademark. The Flyaway Moline price was $2675 initially, but was later increased to $2835 by late August 1929.

Heads turned in late January when an attractive blond haired, female pilot arrived from Fargo, North Dakota, and announced her intention to purchase a spanking new Monocoupe 113. Florence Klingensmith desired to be a barnstormer and talked several businessmen in her Fargo, North Dakota, hometown into backing her. After a check-out flight with Scotty Burmood, Klingensmith was on her way home in her prize Monocoupe 113 (7838, s/n 277). Soon, this chic lady would return to *race* Monocoupes!

The Monocoupe 113 quickly became the darling of Phoebe Omlie. On May 30, 1929, Omlie announced to an excited press she would try for a new altitude record in a Monocoupe 113 "Special." Two weeks later, she would try for the record at Moline or near her home in Memphis, Tennessee. Omlie's record attempt was a part of a campaign to gain public approval of a proposed municipal tax levy to purchase the Weaver Farm and Franing Field property that constituted the Moline airport.

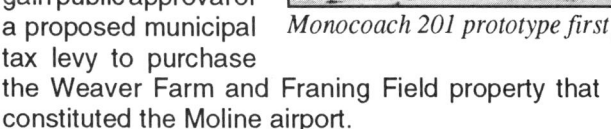

On June 29, 1929, about four o'clock in the afternoon, Omlie donned her winter flying clothing, climbed into her Warner 110 horsepowered Monocoupe and started her attempt for the record. Slightly more than two hours later, she returned to a cheering crowd. The papers bannered the news, "NEW ALTITUDE MARK IS SET BY WOMAN FLYER." Omlie had climbed to 24,500 feet.

Phoebe Omlie basked in the glow of the publicity, until reports filtered from Washington, D.C., that questioned the accuracy of the barograph recording. Though the figures varied (17,467 feet established the record and 23,996 feet was the maximum recorded), certifying officials were anxious for another check. Without hesitation, Omlie told a questioning public she would make another attempt on the record. By now, however, her racing schedule began to fill rapidly and she was unable to make another attempt on the woman's altitude record.

Concurrently, Don Luscombe was anxious to meet a developing demand for the Monocoach, using the more reliable Wright J-5 "Whirlwind" radial engine. The result was a very capable airplane that cruised at 110 mph, with a top speed of 128 mph while maintaining a docile 50 mph landing speed and a range of 550 miles. The Monocoach was awarded

Monocoach 201 prototype first flew on October 24, 1928.   FRAN FITZWILLIAM

JIM HARVEY

Monocoach 201 flown by Don Luscombe and others during a national, coast-to-coast tour sponsored by the Elks Club.

The Monocoach 275 cabin was roomy and comfortable. FRAN FITZWILLIAM

ATC number 201 on August 16, 1929. Keeping with company policy then in effect, this four-place airplane adopted the ATC number in its name and became known as the Monocoach Model 201. At least twelve Monocoach 201 airplanes were constructed and delivered to satisfied customers. The Bureau of Air Commerce bought at least two, also.

Regardless of these impressive figures, individuals involved with its design and manufacture were inclined to extract even more from the airplane's overall appearance and performance. Their efforts created an improved version called the Monocoach Model 275 which made its first flight March 29, 1929. The Approved Type Certificate (ATC #275) was issued November 13, 1929.

Priced at $8250 Flyaway Moline, this model became available in mid-November 1929, equipped with a 7-cylinder, 225 hp Wright J-6 (R-760) engine. Outside of increases in useful load and takeoff performance, overall performance improved marginally. At least seven Monocoach Model 275s were produced.

Overall, the Monocoach series proved to be a popular and rugged performer. Don Luscombe flew a Monocoach Model 201 (NC-8969, s/n 5004) on a national promotional tour, sponsored in part by the Elks Club. Everywhere he stopped, Don touted the aircraft's inherent ruggedness, spirited performance, impressive load carrying capability and tremendous overall utility. Other pilots involved in this tour included Lieutenant Edgar Schmind, a Mono-Aircraft representative, and company secretary George Stange.

Incidentally, the latter two gentlemen flew a Monocoach to get a glimpse of the airship *Graf Zeppilin* in late August 1929, while the giant, German airship was touring the United States. Intercepting the Zep some 120 miles southwest of Moline, their airplane was one of several Monocoupes in the air used to escort the blunt-nosed airship on its slow approach to The Quad-Cities.

The Monocoach netted favorable publicity in other well-reported, aerial activities. Race pilot Ike Stuart flew a Monocoach in the "Philadelphia to Cleveland" Air Derby and placed a very respectable second place behind a slightly faster Alexander Aircraft Co. "Bullet." Moreover, Don entered a Monocoach Model 201 in the 1929 National Air Races at Cleveland as a promotional gesture. This impressive showing as well as various promotional flights made during the air race week resulted in a wave of interest in this airplane.

But the Model 201's $7950 price tag kept many prospective buyers from purchasing the Monocoach despite the fact it was the cheapest four-place cabin airplane flying. Potential sales were further depressed when the more expensive Model 275 was introduced with its $8250 Flyaway Moline price tag. Regardless, at least three Monocoach 275 airplanes were purchased by the Department of Commerce.

Years later, Don Luscombe mused the Monocoach *"was a good airplane, but Stinson made it tough for us."* No doubt Luscombe inferred the Stinson SM8A was a deserving airplane, though less expensive to buy than the Monocoach.

Another "new" Mono-Aircraft, Inc. design to be government certificated in 1929 was the Monoprep Model 218 (ATC #218), basically an open cockpit trainer version of the immensely popular Monocoupe Model 113. The origin of this side-by-side seating design began as a requirement for a helmet and goggles type trainer from West Coast dealer Jack Frye. John Hinchey, now the West Coast Monocoupe distributor through his company, Mono-Aircraft Sales and Service, took Frye's requirements to the factory in October after the 1928 National Air Races. Within a week, the first pre-production Monoprep (s/n 6000) was built sporting a Goettingen airfoil, a wide-track oil-draulic landing gear and a Velie M-5 engine.

This airfoil performed quite well in the cool, autumn weather around Moline, but proved totally inadequate in the warmer California skies. After a high-spirited pilot bent the wing struts in a roll, company officials agreed a total redesign was in

Chapter Four: A Time For Change — A Chance For Survival   45

Chummy comfort was needed to stay warm in the open cockpit Monoprep. JAMES B. ZAZAS COLLECTION

order. A vastly improved airplane, featuring an new airfoil, landing gear changes and some general streamlining, appeared during the early spring months of 1929, yet the ATC was not issued until August 30, 1929.

Powered by a Velie M-5 engine, the production Monoprep was 21' 0" long, 6' 3" high with a wingspan of 32' using a "Clark Y" airfoil section with a 60" chord. Gross weight was 1288 lbs, empty weight was 783 lbs and useful load was 505 lbs. Maximum speed was listed as 92 mph, cruising speed was 80 mph with a slow landing speed of 37 mph. Cruising range was 290 miles consuming 4 gallons of fuel per hour. Standard features included oil-draulic landing gear struts and two doors.

Almost overnight, the redesigned Monoprep became an excellent and very popular trainer. Advertising of the day touted schools could *"cut instruction prices... yet double-up on profits!"* Almost sixty units were made which were large numbers, at least according to Mono-Aircraft standards. Buyers included Embry-Riddle Company of Cincinnati, Ohio, Philadelphia Air Transport of Norristown, Pennsylvania, and Hinchey's Mono-Aircraft Sales and Service of Los Angeles, California. At least a dozen Monopreps were bought by Mono-Aircraft dealers and retained as demonstrators.

Not all Mono-Aircraft airplanes were Velie or Wright powered. In an effort to address the needs of the sportsman pilot on a tight budget, Mono-Aircraft developed the Monosport Model 1 (ATC #249) dur-

Monosport Model 2 with 100 hp Kinner K-5 engine. JOHN UNDERWOOD

Summer 1929, a Monosport Model 2, equipped with a pair of Edo floats, undergoes a series of tests on the Rock River. FRAN FITZWILLIAM

ing early to mid-1929. Powered by a reliable 7-cylinder, 110 hp Warner "Scarab" radial engine, the Monosport Model 1 was based on the popular Monocoupe 113 design and was influenced by Vern Roberts' highly modified Monocoupe 70 "Little Sweetheart." The Monosport Model 1 Approved Type Certificate (ATC #249) was issued on October 4, 1929.

Perhaps the biggest difference between the Monosport and the Monocoupe 113 was the wing design — the Monosport had elliptical wings. Additionally, the Monosport had an oleo landing gear. Both features became standard equipment on later Mono-Aircraft designs. The Monosport Model 2 (ATC #250) was identical to its Warner-powered cousin, but this model had a 100 hp Kinner Airplane Motor Corporation K5 mounted on the nose.

With respect to performance and specifications, the Monosport Models 1 and 2 had a maximum speed of 129 mph, a cruising speed of 110 mph and a range around 530 miles. Yet, their prices at the factory differed appreciatively. The Monosport Model 1 was offered initially at $6350 Flyaway Moline (later reduced to $4500) whereas the Monosport Model 2 was offered at $5750 Flyaway Moline (later reduced to $4250 in May 1930). Both Monosport models proved ideal for aerobatics and racing. Though the actual numbers vary slightly according to sources, at least nine, possibly eleven, Monosport Model 1 and seven Model 2 airplanes were produced.

Interestingly, Monosport Model 1, serial numbers 2000-2002 and 2005, were originally awarded Group 2 Approval #2-134 at 1,650 lbs. gross weight. Likewise, Monosport Model 2, serial numbers 2003 and 2004 were originally awarded Group 2 Approval #2-135 at 1,650 lbs. gross weight.

Enthralled with the Monocoupes' reputation for performance, Smith Reynolds, scion to the R.J. Reynolds Tobacco Company of Winston-Salem, North Carolina, bought a Monosport Model 1 (NC105K, s/n 2005).

Don Luscombe, an ardent air race and air derby fan, vigorously promoted the new Monosports. His marketing efforts were enhanced by the racing pilots' skills as each met with success. Both airplane designs placed very well in various contests entered during the year.

Don Luscombe had a lot of help with his Monocoupe air racing/air derby promotions and marketing efforts. Several pilots, including Phoebe Fairgrave Omlie, Mono-Aircraft assistant test pilot C.B. "Scotty" Burmood, company employee R.T "Stub" Quinby

Clockwise: Monosport Model 1 and cockpit as shown in 1929 factory brochure.

JAMES B. ZAZAS COLLECTION

and lovely Florence Klingensmith preferred to race Monocoupe aircraft, often placing first or placing "in-the-money" in their various classes or events. They served an important role in that every win or show resulted in more orders for Mono-Aircraft airplanes.

This quartet of enthusiastic air racing pilots called themselves the "Monocoupe Rockets" and often represented Mono-Aircraft's racing endeavors. They combined their innate flying skills and superb showmanship to create a virtually unbeatable air racing team, all backed by a most enthusiastic Don Luscombe and Mono-Aircraft Corporation. In time, other pilots sponsored by the company were included in this elite group.

The 1929 National Air Races at Cleveland and other races/derbies held during the year yielded impressive results using Mono-Aircraft, Inc. airplanes and pilots. The first women's National Air Derby was

Chapter Four: A Time For Change — A Chance For Survival 47

(Above) The "Monocoupe Rockets" racing and display team. Left to right are C.B. "Scotty" Burmood, Florence Klingensmith, Phoebe Omlie and R.C. "Stub" Quinby.

JOHN UNDERWOOD

(Above) John Hinchey christens Phoebe Omlie's Monocoupe 113 Special "Miss Moline."

(Right) Phoebe Omlie poses before her Monocoupe 113 Special, "Miss Moline."

JAMES B. ZAZAS COLLECTION

Vern Roberts and his Monocoupe 70 "Little Sweetheart." JOHN UNDERWOOD

won by Phoebe Omlie flying a Warner "Scarab" powered Monocoupe 113 Special called "Miss Moline" (NR-8917, s/n 297). She was awarded two trophies for this win — the "Standard Steel" trophy for her first place finish in the light plane division and the "Aerol" trophy for the most efficient performance of all planes in flight.

The Air Derby's circuitous course stretched from Santa Monica, California, to Cleveland, Ohio, and covered a distance of 2753 miles. Miss Omlie covered this vast distance in an elapsed time of 25 hours, 10 minutes and 36.5 seconds. Besides winning this Air Derby race, Miss Omlie won the Women's 50 mile race, also. In the All Ohio Derby, Vern Roberts placed third flying his Velie-powered Monocoupe 70, "Little Sweetheart."

But it was the pylon races where Vern Roberts piloting ability glowed bright. Flying a Monocoupe Model 113, Roberts won the 10 lap, five mile closed course event for motors of 510 cubic inches displacement with an average speed of 129.18 mph earning $500. Quinby placed second flying his Warner-powered Monocoupe with a 128.09 mph average speed, winning $400.

In closed course races for motors of larger displacement (720 cubic inches), Vern Roberts flew his "Little Sweetheart", now sporting a Warner 110, to a second place finish with an average speed of 128.84 mph, while "Stub" Quinby stayed close behind for a third place finish with an average speed of 128.15 mph. Roberts and Quinby earned $375 and $187, respectively, in this race.

As if these results were not impressive enough, Kinner Motors chief test pilot Leslie Bowman took a second place finish flying a Kinner K5-powered Monosport 2 (NC-113K, s/n 2006) in the Miami Beach to Cleveland Air Derby. He pocketed $750 for his efforts. Perhaps the secret to Roberts' participation in several events almost simultaneously (and, possibly, those of other Monocoupe pilots) throughout the year was the uncanny ability of his racing team being able to change only the engine and fairings on the same airplane!

In a letter to John Underwood, Scotty Burmood reflected: *"We had the engine installations, fairings, etc., down pat so well that we could race it in the 60 hp Class events, then, one hour later race it in 110 hp Class with a Warner using the same airplane. We could change these engines just like changing a tire on an automobile."*

Vern's active racing schedule required he hand over his factory test pilot duties to Byron Hatch, a Mono-Aircraft employee with considerable flying experience. Other pilots employed as test pilots included Basil and Joe Russell from Portland, Oregon. Both had established flight schools in Portland, Oregon and Vancouver, Washington. Sadly, the latter was killed in an airliner accident near San Clemente, California, in 1930.

The Russell Brothers, Joe and Basil. Both brothers were Monocoupe test pilots. JAMES B. ZAZAS COLLECTION

Mono-Aircraft's many triumphs during 1929 were mixed with change and tragedy. Weary of trying to manage the vast Velie enterprises after his father's untimely death, Willard Velie, Jr., started to divest himself of much of the company's concerns, including Mono-Aircraft, Inc. On March 11, 1929, it was announced Mono-Aircraft, Inc. would become a part of Allied Aviation Industries, Inc., a St. Louis based holding company, via a cash and stock-swap deal. The parent company, Augustine & Co., was controlled by Floyd Augustine and several prominent St. Louis bankers and brokers.

Allied's officers included W.C. Fergeson as head of the Executive Committee and John A. Love, president of Love, Bryan & Company and a director of Fokker and Universal Aviation, as Chairman of the Board. Don A. Luscombe was chosen to be the vice-president. These company officials told the local press they had purchased a controlling interest in

Mono-Aircraft from W.L. Velie, Jr., and that the new corporation owned the patent rights to the Velie engine, but the transactions did not include any part of the Velie factory.

Furthermore, these officials said their company owned all the capital stock of three other aviation concerns — the Lambert Aircraft Engine Corporation, the Aviation Accessories Corporation and the Hurricane Aircraft Engine Company. The assets of the Mono-Aircraft were taken over by the Lambert Aircraft Engine Corporation. The Hurricane Aircraft Engine Co. took over the assets of the Velie Motors Corporation insofar as they pertained to the manufacture of aircraft engines.

In a statement to the press, the new company announced, *"These two companies will continue operations for the present in Moline, but it is contemplated that they will eventually be moved to St. Louis."*

A Mono-Aircraft Board of Directors meeting was scheduled for March 18, 1929, to discuss the sale and dissolution of Mono-Aircraft, Inc. A special meeting of the Mono-Aircraft stockholders was held April 22 to officially finalize the sale. On May 14, a Certificate of Dissolution of "Mono-Air-craft, Inc." [sic] was filed in the Illinois Office of the Secretary of State.

Velie engine production continued under the direction of Samual B. Lambert, at one time the president of the Lambert-Graves Auto Agency of St. Louis. Sam was joined in this new venture by his cousins, Maj. Albert B. and J.D. Wooster Lambert. The Lamberts had been Lindbergh backers.

Eventually two engine models were produced, 55/60 hp and 85/90 hp, the latter called the Lambert R-266 and was produced by the Lambert Aircraft Engine Corporation, the successor to the engine division of Velie Motors Corp. The R-266 was announced formally on December 11, 1929.

Work had been in progress for more than a year to design and build this new power plant. The new engine weighed 180 lbs whereas the Velie engine was a slightly heavier 210 lbs. As of mid-December 1929, government approval had been granted to start production, but the official ATC certificate had yet to be issued. Furthermore, Sam Lambert stated to an excited press that 25 experimental motors were in production and he expected the new engine would be in full production by early spring 1930. Ironically, only Mono-Aircraft, Inc. (and its successors) would use Lambert engines in any appreciable quantity. When the Monocoupe production ended more than a decade later, Lambert engine production ended as well.

Amidst this flurry of corporate activity came word Willard L. Velie, Jr., had died suddenly on March 20, 1929, in the home of a Mono-Aircraft employee. Reportedly, Velie was returning home from a meeting with his attorneys finalizing some details regarding the sale of Mono-Aircraft, Inc. to Allied Aviation Industries. He intended to stop at the residence to discuss some business related matters. Velie was still alive when company employee Scotty Burmood arrived to render assistance, but died before medical help could arrive. The official cause of death for the 33-year-old Velie was stated to be a heart attack.

Once more, company employees were dumbstruck by the news, especially that Velie, Jr.'s, death occurred so soon after that of his well-liked father. Don Luscombe tried to quell employee and potential buyer fears regarding Monocoupe production status by stating the Mono-Aircraft purchasers planned to continue airplane production in Moline indefinitely and these plans would not be affected by Mr. Velie's death. Don Luscombe, then thirty-four

A sight to behold! Three Monosport Model 1 and Model 2 airplanes grace the Moline Airport. Les Bowman's Kinner-powered Monosport Model 2 sits in the middle. Circa August 1929. JAMES B. ZAZAS COLLECTION

years old, was retained by the holding company and became Mono-Aircraft, Inc.'s president and general manager.

Despite the best sales and promotion efforts of Don Luscombe and his aggressive sales force, the introduction of several new models and the impressive air race/derby wins, Mono-Aircraft's productive design and sales frenzy soon came to a sudden slowdown. The bottom fell out of the American stock market in October 1929. In the first month of this market "crash," almost 1300 banks closed. Stockholders agonized with a paper loss of almost 15 billion dollars.

Sales wavered while bankers, businessmen and pilots attempted to sort-out how the "crash" would affect them. Many adopted a "wait-and-see" attitude. In the end, airplane orders slowed dramatically, then plunged precipitously. Gone were the gala, almost heady, free-wheeling activities common only a few months, even years before. Money and jobs suddenly became extremely tight and scarce. The nation was gripped in a Great Depression that would last almost a decade.

Mono-Aircraft, Inc., like many of its contemporaries, was ill-prepared to weather this financial storm. However, through perseverance, innovation, tenacity, good luck and plain old hard work, Don Luscombe and Mono-Aircraft proved their mettle as survivors.

Though lean years were forecast, many manufacturers, including Mono-Aircraft, brought forth some of their best and more enduring designs during this most difficult period. Dreamers and schemers were forced to be innovative to stay in business and remain "competitive."

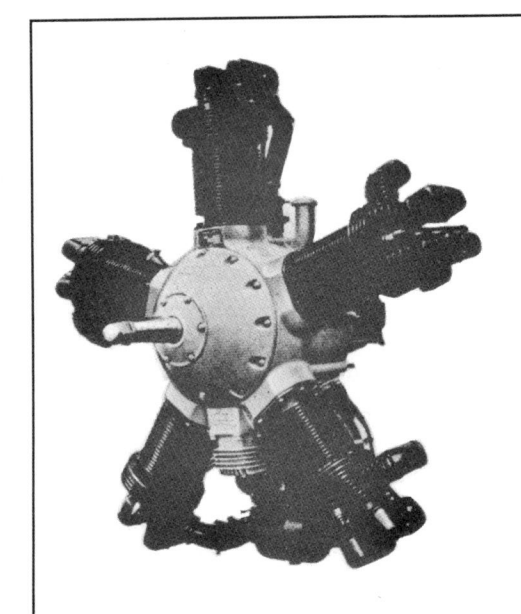

Name of Engine:	KINNER K-5.
Manufactured by:	Kinner Airplane & Motor Corporation, 635 West Colorado Boulevard, Glendale California.
Type:	5 cylinder, radial, air cooled, 4 cycle. (Approved Type Certificate No. 3.)
Department of Commerce Rating:	90 H.P. at 1810 R.P.M.
Displacement:	372 cu. in.
Compression Ratio:	5.0 to 1.
Dimensions:	Length, overall .... 32 1/4"
	Diameter, overall .... 43"
	Bore .... 4 1/4"
	Stroke .... 5 1/4"
Weight:	278 lbs. (without starter or hub).
Fuel Consumption at Rated H.P.	Not more than .60 lbs. per H.P. hr.
Oil Consumption:	Not more than .025 lbs. per H.P. hr.
Lubrication:	Circulating oil system, pressure feed to front and rear main bearings and to link pins which are all of the plain type, through grooved master rod bearing.
Ignition:	Dual Scintilla.
Carburetion:	1 Stromberg NAR-5-A or Holley.
Spark Plugs:	2 per cyl. B. G. No. 4 Hornet.
Price:	$1,800 f.o.b. Glendale.

GUIDE TO PRE-1930 AIRCRAFT ENGINES

Name of Engine:	THE LAMBERT R-266.
Manufactured by:	Lambert Aircraft Engine Corp., Moline, Ill.
Type:	5 cylinder, fixed radial, air cooled.
Department of Commerce Rating:	90 H.P. at 2375 R.P.M.
Displacement:	266 cu. in.
Compression Ratio:	5.55 to 1.
Dimensions:	Length, overall .... 30 3/8"
	Diameter, overall .... 33"
	Bore .... 4 1/4"
	Stroke .... 3 3/4"
Weight:	(Minus equipment) 214 lbs.
Fuel Consumption at Rated H.P.	Not more than .55 lbs. per H.P. hr.
Oil Consumption:	Not more than .025 lbs. per H.P. hr.
Lubrication:	Pressure and Dry Sump.
Ignition:	Scintilla Dual.
Carburetion:	Stromberg NAR-3.
Spark Plugs:	2 per cyl. (Champion).
Price:	On application.

GUIDE TO PRE-1930 AIRCRAFT ENGINES

A Vital Message to SCHOOLS

Cut Instruction Prices... *yet* Double-up on Profits!

You Can Do It With *The Monoprep*

Especially Designed for Economical Training

MAINTENANCE and operating costs of the MONOPREP are but a mere fraction of the expense attached to the average training plane.

That's why schools with Monopreps on the line can offer student training for less money and still enjoy larger profits than their competitors.

Often the same purchase money puts two *Monopreps* instead of a more expensive plane into service, which means two students in the air during the same hour. The side by side training permits the instructor to cover each lesson thoroughly *while the student is in the air*. This feature alone saves hours of time.

The MONOPREP embodies every qualification desired in a training plane.

Inquiries are invited for distributor and dealer franchise contracts. Write or wire today for full information.

MONO-AIRCRAFT, Inc.
Builders of the Monocoupe, Monocoach and Monoprep
Moline, Illinois, U. S. A.

Note these Monoprep Features—

Perfect vision all directions.
Oildraulic landing gear struts.
Two doors.
Friese type ailerons.
High lift wing.
Slow landing speed.
Gas consumption 4 gals. per hr.
Five hours fuel.
Flyaway price $2675.

Increased Enrollment Accrues to the School with the MONOPREP

Know these *Monocoupe* Facts

Ninety Percent of American light planes in 1928 were—
Monocoupes

More Monocoupes sold during first year of production than any other commercial plane in history of the industry. Service Stations in over a hundred airports.

Out of the large number of Monocoupes in service in 1928, the majority in hands of amateurs, there were fewer fatal accidents than sustained by the few well known multi-motored planes in service which were piloted by men of long experience.

Monocoupes have never failed to win prize money in any race meet although they were always matched against motors of approximately twice the horsepower or more.

No commercial airplane is subjected to the vigorous stunting given the Monocoupe. There has never been a structural failure.

It is not only approved by the Department of Commerce but all materials and workmanship viewed by a government inspector on duty at all times.

Instruction time before solo has proven materially less.

A new standard of uniformity and interchangeability of parts. The Monocoupe is one of the very few planes sold with a guarantee that includes the plane and motor as a single unit.

MONO-AIRCRAFT CORPORATION
A Subsidiary of
Allied Aviation Industries
MOLINE, ILLINOIS

The Monocoupe is still the lowest priced approved plane in the world and will continue to give the greatest value for every dollar.

$2675
Flyaway at Moline, Illinois

A Deluxe Edition of Pursuit Performance

▲

Custom Built for

$6350

Flyaway at Moline, Illinois

▼

FOR the sportsman pilot seeking high speed, maneuverability, built-in strength to withstand the rigors of any stunt maneuvers, coupled with all year 'round comfort and distinctive luxury, the new Monosport captures the fancy of every pilot able to qualify for its ownership.

Since its first introduction it has beaten in speed everything powered with the same engine. It takes every acrobatic maneuver known to the book with remarkable ease.

There are over 800 r. p. m. in reserve with full load. Despite its helicopter characteristics nothing is slighted —navigation lights, the panel is filled with the best instruments, seats are wide and roomy, large luggage compartment, upholstered in genuine leather, Bendix brakes, Oildraulic shock struts, steel propeller, five hours in gasoline. Colors are optional.

Smart in appearance, comfortable, strong, maneuverable, fast—$5750 with Kinner engine—$6350 with Warner engine—deliveries fifteen days after acceptance of order.

Additional information on request.

MONO AIRCRAFT CORPORATION
Division of Allied Aviation Industries, Inc.
MOLINE, ILLINOIS - U. S. A.

Photo by Holmberg Air Mapping Co.

The *Monocoach*

WELCOMES COMPARISON

In performance—comfort—dependability—luxury and *VALUE*, the new Monocoach welcomes comparison with all other quality production aircraft. Nothing else will prove so conclusively—so decisively—the supremacy of this four passenger cabin plane.

Altho designed and engineered especially to meet the growing demand of the private flyer for a family and guest plane, the Monocoach has proven itself invaluable for business and passenger service. Powered by the Wright W.W. J-6, it has an excess of reserve power and a speed of 133 miles per hour.

Is offered at about two-thirds the cost of the slightly larger cabin planes and approximately the same price as the conventional open three place biplanes, equipped with engines of less horsepower.

Price: $8,250 flyaway Moline, Ill.

Specifications and Performance Data

High wing monoplane
4 place enclosed cabin
Color.............optional
Upholstery.........mohair
Span............... 39 feet
Length............. 26 feet, 8 in.
Height............. 7 feet, 8 in.
Wing Area......... 222 sq. ft.
Weight—Empty ....1919 pounds
Weight—Full Load .3092 pounds
Fuel Capacity....... 63 gallons
Engine...........Wright W.W.J-6
Horsepower .... 225 h.p.
Landing Speed...... 48 M.P.H.
High Speed......... 132 M.P.H.
Cruising Speed..... 117 M.P.H.
Cruising Range..... 650 Miles
Ceiling ....22,000 feet
Climb, per minute... 1,200 feet

Dual Control; Hamilton or Standard Steel Propeller; Eclipse Starter; Bendix wheels and brakes; Split type landing gear; Oildraulic shock struts; Navigation lights; Pioneer Compass and Air Speed Indicator; Thermo-Pete oil pre-heater; Consolidated Instrument Board.

*Department of Commerce Certificate of Approval
Number 201*

MONO AIRCRAFT CORP. MOLINE ILLINOIS

Builders of the *Monocoupe, Monosport, Monoprep, and Monocoach*

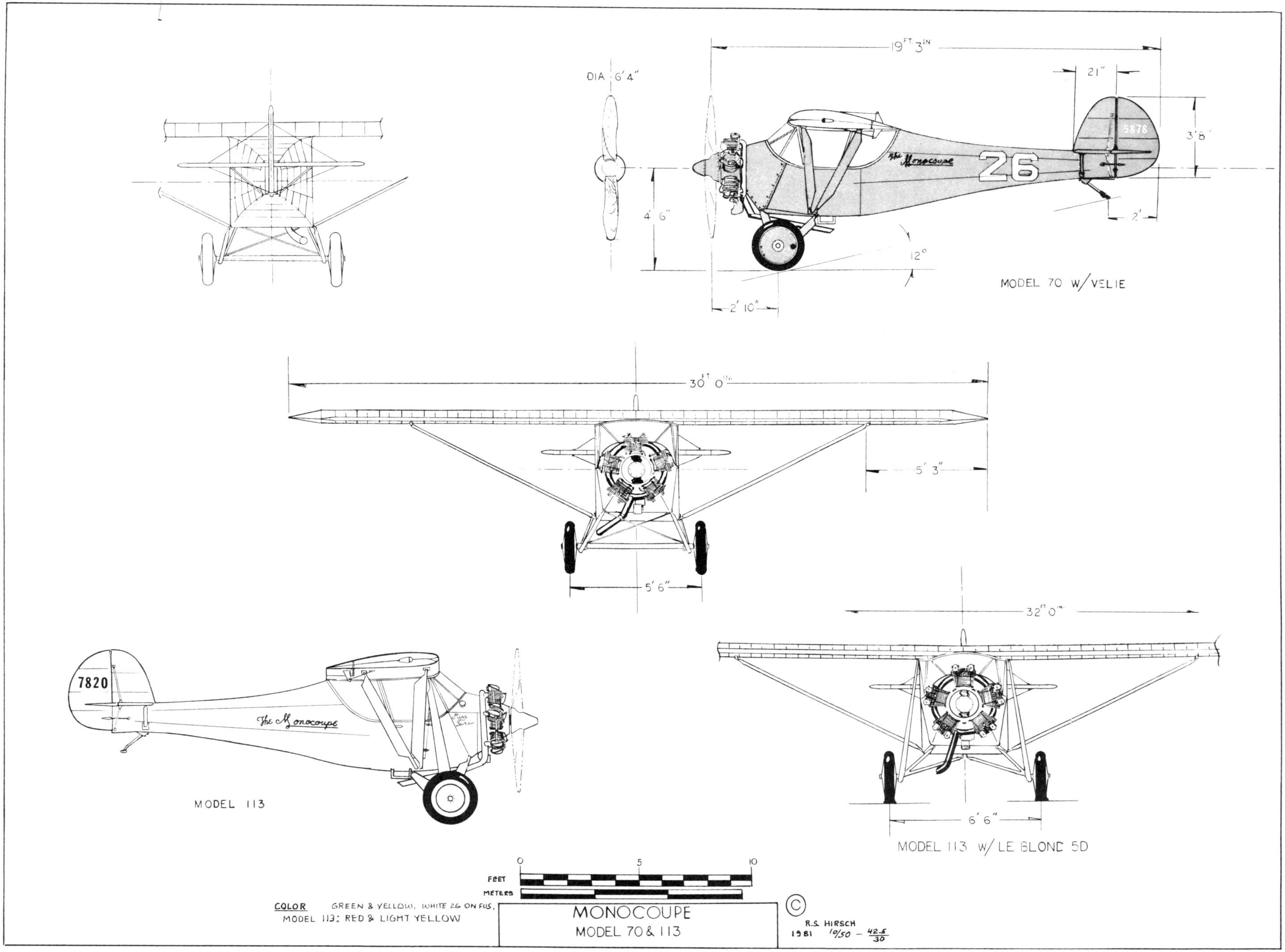
DIA 6'4"
19 FT 3 IN
21"
3'8"
2'
4'6"
12°
2'10"
26
5878
The Monocoupe
MODEL 70 W/VELIE
30 FT 0 IN
5'3"
5'6"
32 FT 0 IN
6'6"
7820
The Monocoupe
MODEL 113
MODEL 113 W/ LE BLONC 5D
0
5
10
FEET
METERS
COLOR GREEN & YELLOW, WHITE 26 ON FUS.
MODEL 113: RED & LIGHT YELLOW
MONOCOUPE
MODEL 70 & 113
©
R.S. HIRSCH
1981 10/50 - 42.5/30

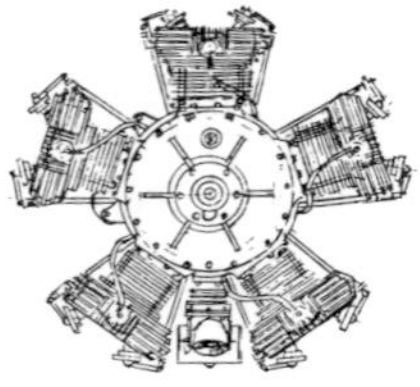

VELIE 5

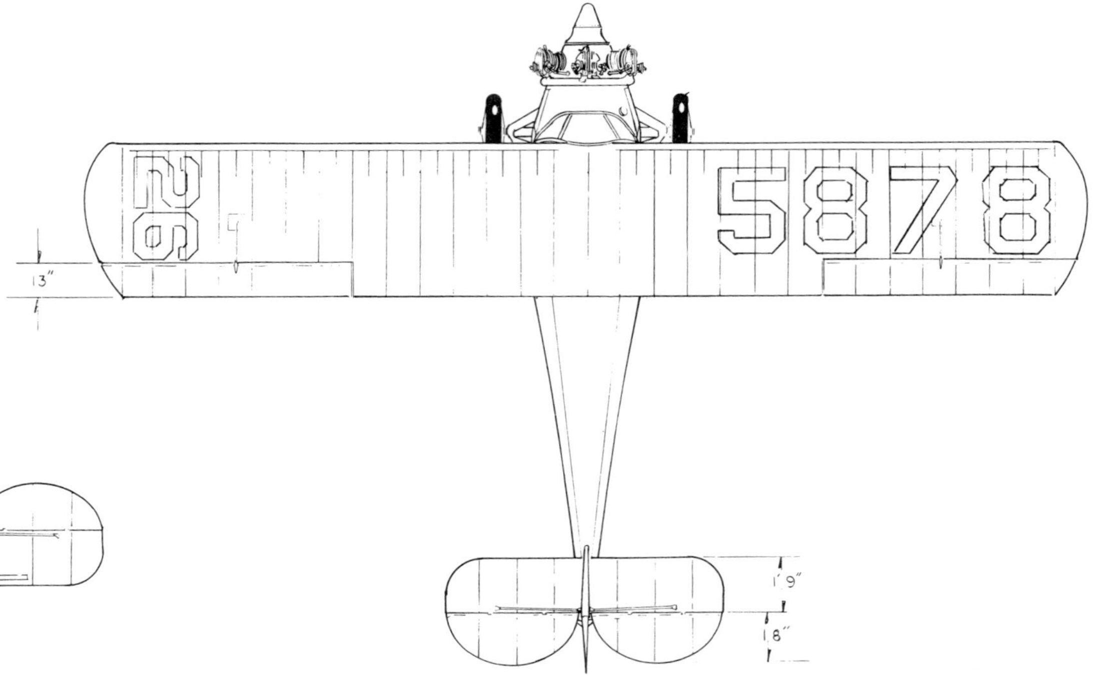

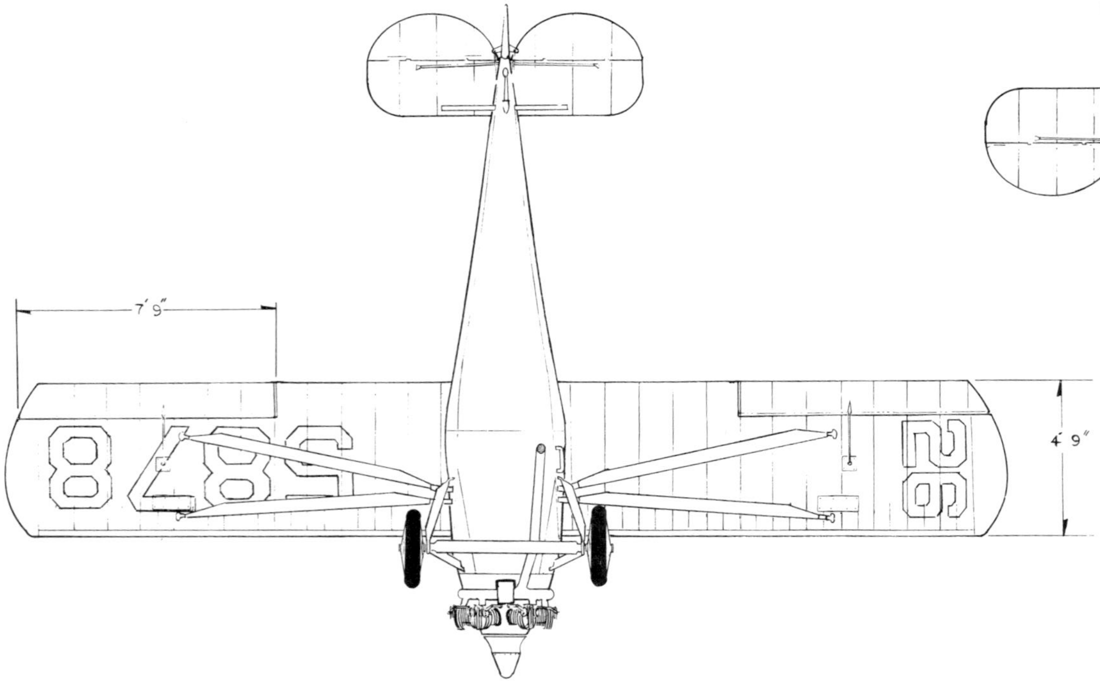

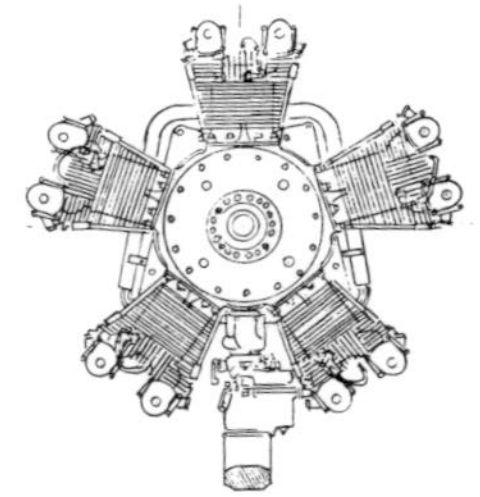

LE BLOND 5D

MONOCOUPE MODEL 70 & 113

SHEET 2

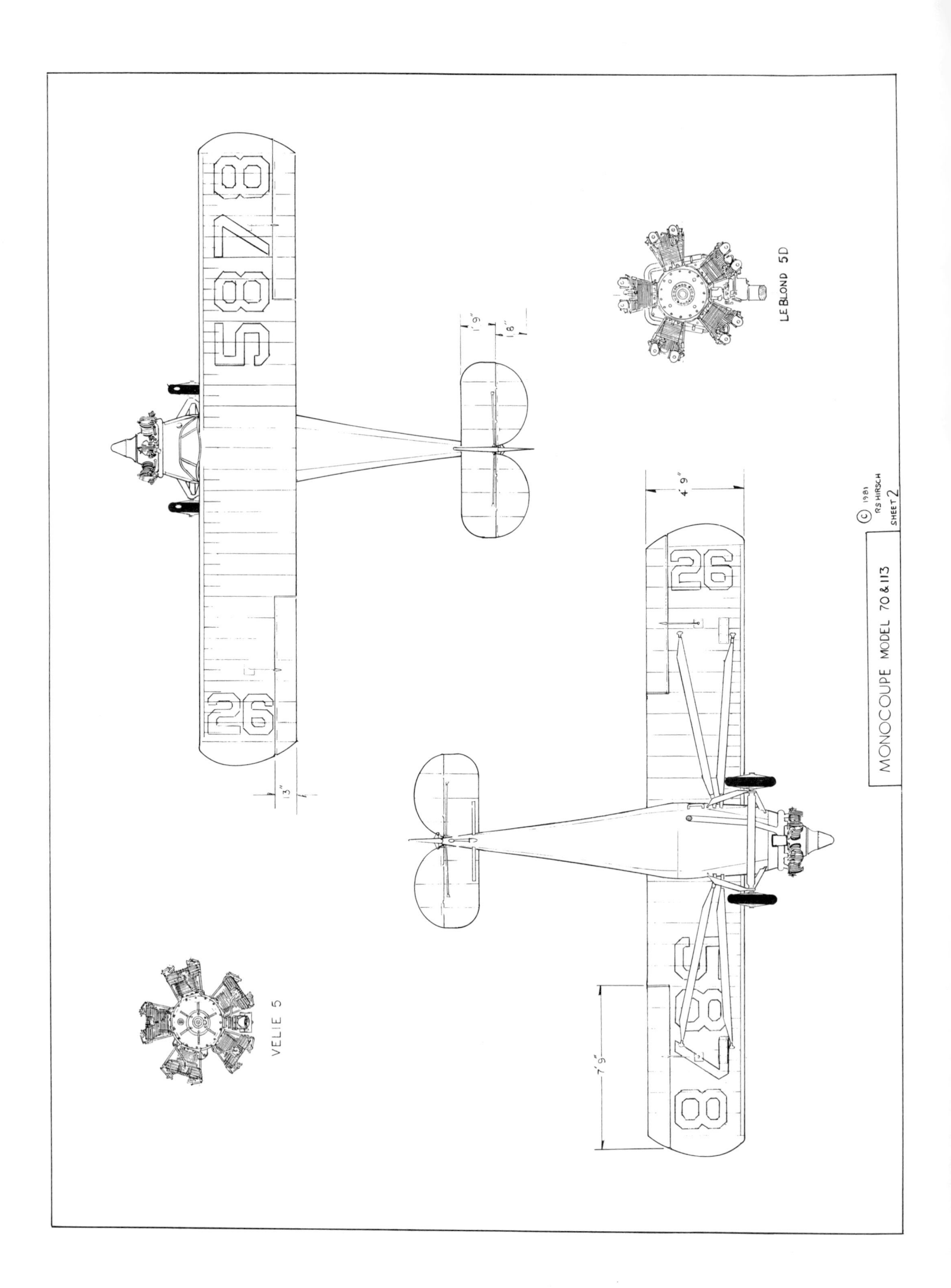

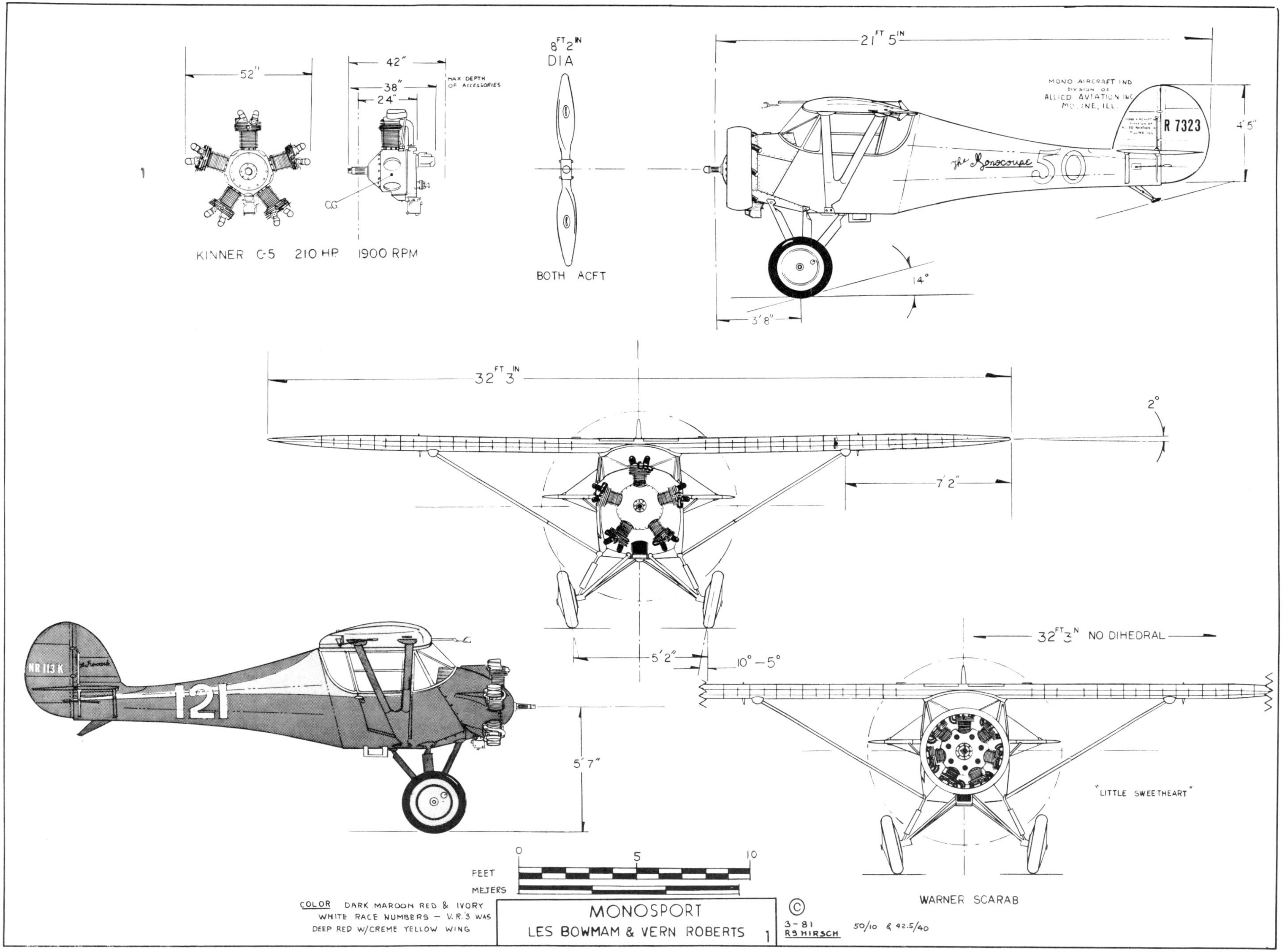

52"
42"
38"
24"
MAX DEPTH OF ACCESSORIES
C.G.
KINNER C-5 210 HP 1900 RPM
8 FT 2 IN DIA
BOTH ACFT
21 FT 5 IN
MONO AIRCRAFT IND
DIVISION OF
ALLIED AVIATION INC
MOLINE, ILL.
R 7323
4'5"
the Monocoupe 50
14°
3'8"
32 FT 3 IN
2°
7'2"
5'2"
10° — 5°
32 FT 3 IN NO DIHEDRAL
NR 113 K
121
5'7"
"LITTLE SWEETHEART"
WARNER SCARAB
0
5
10
FEET
METERS
COLOR DARK MAROON RED & IVORY
WHITE RACE NUMBERS — V.R.'S WAS
DEEP RED W/CREME YELLOW WING
MONOSPORT
LES BOWMAM & VERN ROBERTS
1
©
3-81
RS HIRSCH
50/10 & 42.5/40

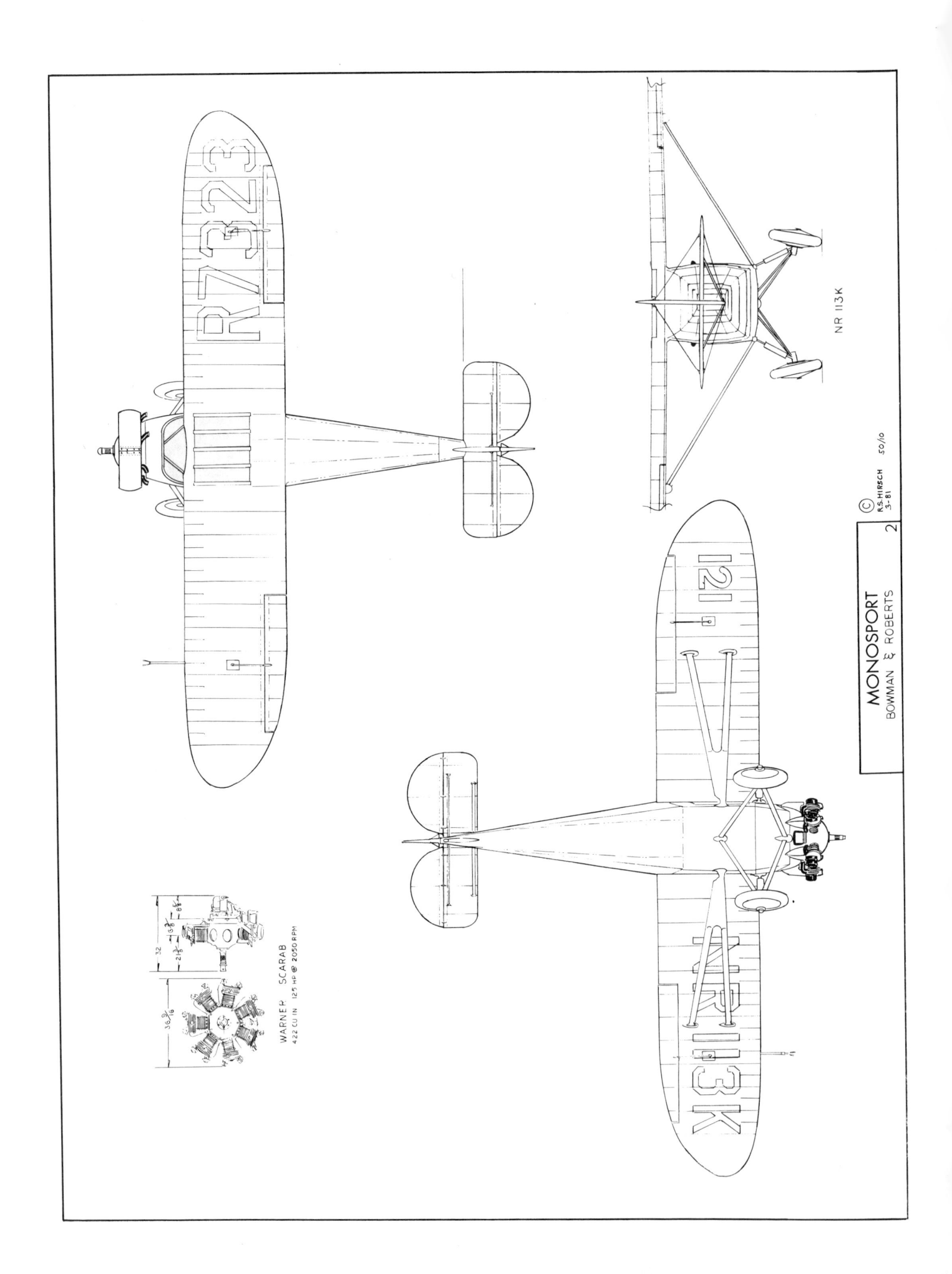

MONOSPORT
BOWMAN & ROBERTS

WARNER SCARAB
422 CU IN 125 HP @ 2050 RPM

NR 113K

© R.S.HIRSCH 3-81 50/10

*"What through strength fails? Boldness is certain to win praise.
In mighty enterprises, it is enough to have had the determination."*
Sextus Propertius (54 B.C. - A.D. 2)
Elegies, I, X, 5

Chapter Five

A Time For Determined Action

Owning an airplane in the late 1920s and through the 1930s was an expensive proposition, even for the well-heeled in society. Vern Roberts once summed the general mood of the period by commenting, *"Even if we gave them away, few could afford the upkeep."* Money, being tight, had to be stretched to cover a multitude of costs such as labor, overhead and supplies. Often, labor was the first expense to suffer and filling the manpower gap required less "labor-intensive" designs without a decrease in quality, performance or value. A new design had to stand on its own reputation if it and its parent corporation were to survive.

With few new models and engineering challenges offered for the immediate future, Jerry Lederer left Aerotech, Inc./Mono-Aircraft, Inc. in early 1930 to work for the Studebaker Corporation in South Bend, Indiana, which was developing a transport airplane designed by engineers at Wright Field, Ohio.[17] In turn, Frederick J. Knack assumed the chief engineer position at Mono-Aircraft.

Clayton Folkerts stands beside the prototype Monocoupe 90, one of several airplanes he helped design. JIM HARVEY

Additionally, Luscombe's carefully developed Monocoupe dealer network was besieged by the Curtiss-Wright Aircraft Company. Its Flying Service division was aggressively developing its own sales and service program. Most Monocoupe dealers capitulated to Curtiss-Wright Flying Service's better offers for sales. Some dealers were simply "bought-out" by the competition. E.K. "Rusty" Campbell became a Curtiss-Wright distributor in Mono-Aircraft's backyard, the Moline Airport. Though he sold an occasional Monocoupe, he did not carry a Monocoupe distributorship.

Don Luscombe turned to his remaining dealers, distributors and, quite often, associates and friends to sell Mono-Aircraft's airplanes. His tenacity in the face of difficulty prevailed once again and, in time, he was able to rebuild his company's dealer network.

Don wrote and printed a series of small, twelve page pamphlets proclaiming "1930 Will Be a Monocoupe Year." These pamphlets were given to distributors and anybody who requested Monocoupe airplane information. (A couple examples, "Setting Tongues A-Wagging" and "You Certainly Look Funny in That Outfit" are reprinted in Appendix A).

To further stimulate sales and maintain a positive cash flow, Don decided to market and sell airplanes to those individuals who could afford to buy his product. The "sportsman pilot" — the pilot who enjoyed flying for fun or weekend recreation — was high on his list. So, too, were the well-known racing pilots of the day.

In a concerted effort to capture and keep these fliers' interest in the company's airplanes, Mono-Aircraft introduced at least three new airplanes during 1930 — the Monocoupe 90, the Monocoupe 110 and the Monocoupe 125. Each design offered the buyer value, utility and performance for his hard-earned money.

The Monocoupe 90 made its debut in mid-January 1930, and was presented to an excited public a month later at the International Aircraft Show in St. Louis. The government gave its seal of approval to the design and awarded the Monocoupe 90 Approved Type Certificate number 306 on April 2, 1930. Though similar in appearance to earlier Monocoupe airplanes, this Clayton Folkerts designed streamlined monoplane was developed from Vern Roberts' racing experience. The Monocoupe 90 used the same ply covered leading edge and stiff trailing edge wing as the Monocoupe 113, yet the airframe was fifteen inches longer and four inches wider. An economical, 90-hp Lambert R-266 radial engine provided the power.

The prototype Monocoupe 90 in January 1930. Vern Roberts' racing experience provided the basis for this design. JIM HARVEY

Consequently, this new design boasted some very respectable figures — 120 mph top speed, 105 mph cruising speed, a 37 mph landing speed and a 525 statute mile cruising range. An enthusiastic Don Luscombe exclaimed the new ship could be operated at 1 1/2 cents per mile.

The instrument panel was well arranged and equipped with Navy specification instruments. Standard equipment included an air speed indicator, altimeter, tachometer, oil temperature gauge, oil pressure gauge, clock, ignition switch, throttle, mixture controls and navigation lights. All was surrounded by a neatly trimmed interior that offered six inches more leg room. Dual controls were standard. Wheel brakes were provided on the left side only.

The landing gear was a split type with oildraulic shock struts. These struts were fastened to the lower longerons instead of the upper ones as used earlier.

Much thought and care went into the Monocoupe 90's streamlining. All tie rod terminals were located within the structure and, consequently, offered no drag. The stabilizer was adjusted by a novel arrangement of two springs, each variable to tension by a control under the pilot's seat. One spring pulled back on the elevator control, the other pulled forward.

Rudder and ailerons were operated by standard steel cables, the elevator by steel tubing. Two welded aluminum fifteen gallon fuel tanks, each with direct reading gauges, were built into the wing on each side of the fuselage. The entire fuselage was made of steel construction covered with fabric. The wing was made of spruce spars and ribs covered with fabric.

Ten color combinations of five colors were available. A Hamilton-Standard steel propeller was standard equipment. Priced at $3375 Flyaway Moline, the company proved it could produce an economical airplane that was comfortable and easy to fly.

If the prospective buyer so desired, enough parts to complete an overhaul of a Lambert R-266 could be bought for an extra $75. Items included five cylinder barrels, five pistons with rings, ten valve guides, ten rocker arm bushings, ten spark plugs and a complete set of gaskets. No doubt this sales effort was a disguised marketing ploy by the company to rid itself of surplus Lambert engine parts and stock.

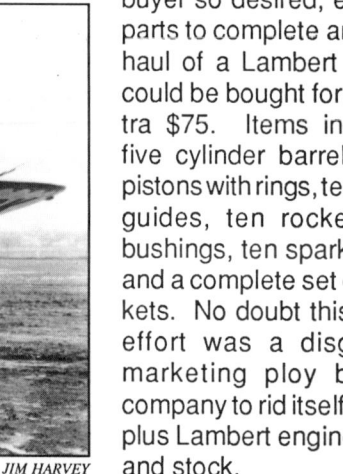

Recognizing the new Monocoupe 90's sales potential, Mono-Aircraft officials acknowledged that production of other less efficient designs might be terminated. Shortly after the Monocoupe 90 received its ATC, Don Luscombe hinted:

"... production of the (Mono)sport would probably be abandoned, due to the fact that the new Monocoupe embodies all the features that made the sport so popular at a lower price."

Monocoupe 90 production was to start at a rate of two airplanes daily by the middle of April. Interestingly, the Monocoupe 90 design remained in production for almost twenty years! This longevity speaks

Chapter Five: A Time For Determined Action   61

well for the overall appeal and utility of the design.

Meanwhile, a most unusual Monocoupe project took shape within the bustling factory walls. Coined the Monocoupe 501, this chubby-looking airplane was designed by Fred Knack and was intended to be the Monocoupe 113's replacement. The project was abandoned when the Monocoupe 90 proved to be superior in every respect of valve and performance.

Concurrently, the company unveiled a new, two-cylinder, 40 hp engine designed for use in motor gliders. Sam Lambert introduced this new engine, called the Lambert H-106, to an enthusiastic press on March 31, 1930, and said it would enter full production within a month. The diminutive H-106 engine used Lambert R-266 cylinders, pistons and as many R-266 parts and assemblies as possible. This engine was block tested and perfected at the former Velie factory between the winter of 1929 and the spring of 1930.

Intended to replace the Monocoupe 113, this Monocoupe 501 airplane, designed by Fred Knack, lost on all counts to the superior Monocoupe 90.

JIM HARVEY

Sam Lambert and Scotty Burmood successfully tested this engine on a Monoprep on a balmy, early April, Sunday afternoon. Both returned from their

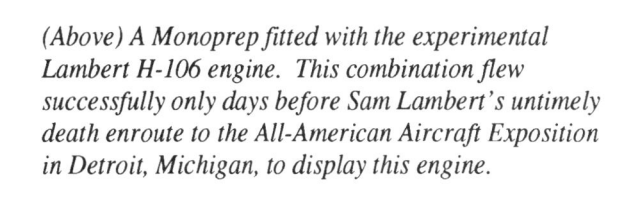

JIM HARVEY

(Above) A Monoprep fitted with the experimental Lambert H-106 engine. This combination flew successfully only days before Sam Lambert's untimely death enroute to the All-American Aircraft Exposition in Detroit, Michigan, to display this engine.

(Left) The diminutive, 35 hp Lambert H-106 engine. Weighing only 102 pounds, this engine was test flown successfully in early April 1930.

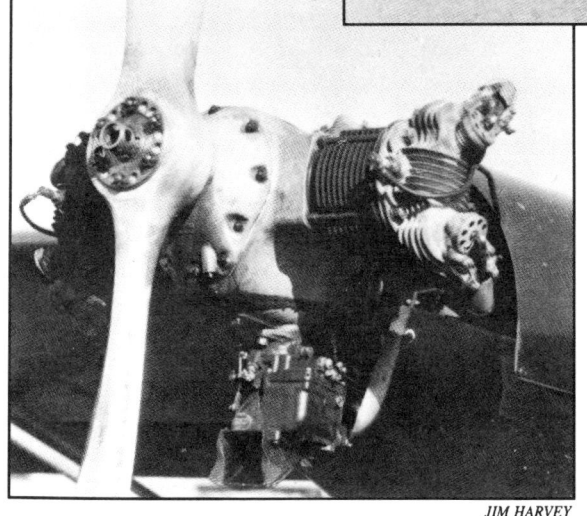

JIM HARVEY

flights enthusiastic about the engine's future. Lambert expected to find a favorable market for the H-106. Anxious to promote this engine, he made plans to attend the All-American Aircraft Exposition to be held in Detroit, Michigan, the following weekend. This excitement was to be short lived, however.

Just as a small avalanche of orders for the new Monocoupe 90 began to arrive, Lambert Aircraft Engine Corporation was dealt a stunning blow. Sam Lambert, 36, was killed in a Monocoupe accident near South Bend, Indiana, on April 7, 1930, while enroute to the Detroit show. The reported cause of this accident ranged from a broken propeller as a consequence of a high-speed dive to speculation that an experimental Lambert H-106 engine carried in the cockpit broke loose and jammed the controls.

According to witnesses at Shockley Field, north of South Bend, Lambert's ship suddenly nosed-down, followed by a spin an instant later and the right wing appeared to collapse. One thousand feet above the earth, a propeller blade departed the aircraft and was followed almost immediately by the Lambert R-266 engine torn from its mounts. The engineless Monocoupe made one complete loop and crashed on the backside of a second loop.

Company employees were dumbstruck when news of Sam Lambert's death reached Moline. Scotty Burmood, Mono-Aircraft chief mechanic, and Pacific Coast Sales Manager John Hinchey flew to South Bend to examine the wreckage. Both declared Lambert's metal propeller, bent and straightened from previous mishaps, had failed and was responsible for this calamity. Except for a few H-106 engine parts, very little remained worthy of salvaging.[18]

Don Luscombe was saddened by the loss of his good friend and fellow pilot. This tragedy aside, Don now had to run an airplane company *and* an aircraft engine company. Don made a careful review of the Lambert Aircraft Engine Corporation. He realized the present company was saddled with a tremendous inventory of obsolete material. There was little need for Velie engines or parts. In time, Don would use his creative marketing and promoting abilities to lessen this burden.

At the same time, Don began to question the input of his company's previous owners. He believed many Velie employees had contributed little to the overall success of the company when it was under Velie's control and, as such, felt Mono-Aircraft had become *"an old soldiers home,"* a place where the older workers and retiring Velie auto workers could work at a slower pace.

Don was frustrated, no doubt, by the many fickle market forces that tried to besiege him. But now, the company was no longer under Velie control and no longer had Velie money to keep it afloat. Don had to keep his company solvent any way he could. Creativity, perseverance and gut determination would see him through the difficult times.

Perhaps as an effort to maintain a positive cash flow, Don and other factory officials surveyed the former Velie mansion with plans to turn it into a flight school and dormitory for prospective Monocoupe buyers. Though actual flight training would take place at the Moline Airport, these future Monocoupe owners would have a comfortable place to rest while learning how to fly. All plans were dropped when it was determined the renovation of the now dilapidated "Velie Villa" would be prohibitively expensive.

At least three other Monocoupe designs made

West Coast dealer John Hinchey strikes a confident pose shortly after taking delivery of his Monocoupe 110.   JIM HARVEY

their debut during the spring and summer months. The first was the Monocoupe 110, another high wing, side-by-side seating Mono-Aircraft design tailored to appeal to the sportsman pilot and, very quickly, the racing pilot. The Monocoupe 110 was basically a Monocoupe 90 adapted for a 110 hp Warner "Scarab" engine. The Monocoupe 110 received its Approved Type Certificate (ATC #327) on June 16, 1930.

The performance improvements were startling! This 1611 lbs gross weight monoplane boasted a 133 mph top speed, a 112 mph cruise speed and an impressive 480 statute mile cruising range — all for $4500 Flyaway Moline. Very quickly, this sprightly airplane became the darling of the light airplane racing community.

The airframe was identical to the Model 90 with few exceptions. A metal propeller and 6:50 x 10 wheels were standard equipment. Optional equipment included wheel pants, a Heywood engine starter, a battery, navigations lights, a tail-wheel and a norrow-chord, "Townend" ring cowl.

Dean of American Air racing, Johnny Livingston poses confidently before his new, stock Monocoupe 110.   JIM HARVEY

Early versions of the 110 had an oleo gear arrangement not unlike that found on the popular Monocoupe 90. Later versions featured the better known — and faster — faired Vee and streamlined wire-braced arrangement, mostly racing gear. Several Monocoupe 110 airplanes were modified and groomed for air racing uses. Thus, the Monocoupe continued in the ranks of the racing circuit. A few were altered with a deep chord "Townend" speed-cowl ring to further boost speed. Eventually, at least fifty Monocoupe 110 airplanes were built, including seven "Clipwing," Warner 145/185 powered "Specials."

At least one Monocoupe 110 earned a respectable notch in air racing history. Built at the Moline factory in the early part of 1930 and delivered as a stock airplane (less wheel pants and "Townend" ring), this soon-to-be-famous Monocoupe 110 (NC501W, s/n 533) was bought by crack aerobatic and racing pilot, Johnny Livingston. Over the next few years, Livingston's impressive racing accomplishments would earn him the title "Dean of American Air Racing." In many races, Livingston's Monocoupe 110 outperformed airplanes with twice, sometimes three times

John Livingston's Monocoupe 110 as it appeared before modifications made this airplane an almost "unbeatable" competitor.   JIM HARVEY

the available horsepower.

The Monocoupe 90-J was another new design introduced during the balmy, 1930 summer months. Virtually identical to the popular Monocoupe 90, the 90-J sported a 90 hp Warner "Scarab Junior" with a "Townend" speed-ring cowl. Priced $3950 Flyaway Moline, this design was awarded ATC #355 on August 20, 1930. At least two Monocoupe 90-J examples are known to have been built, both in 1931, yet future company advertising continued to show this particular airplane available for at least one year afterwards.

A third design introduced during mid-1930 was the Monocoupe 125 and was awarded Approved Type Certificate number 359 on August 23, 1930. This airplane was a 125 hp Kinner B-5 powered version of the sprightly Monocoupe 110. The 125 was offered as an option for those buyers who preferred a Kinner power plant versus a Warner power plant. Monocoupe 125 production was extremely limited. Only four examples of this airplane were built, with two going to the Aeronautics Branch of the Department of

Commerce. The Monocoupe 125's selling price in mid-1930 was $4500 Flyaway Moline, but later was raised to $4750.

Vern Roberts wasted no time taking advantage of the performance gains embodied in the new Monocoupes and, soon, used these advances for racing. Much like Johnny Livingston's Model 110, another stock Monocoupe 110 was prepared to be flown by Roberts. Concurrently, a Monocoupe 125 was groomed for racing. It took little time before the rumor mill was abuzz which airplane was faster. The stage was set for some exciting racing between Roberts and Livingston.

Meanwhile, a local political problem completely beyond Don Luscombe's control came into play; the lease on the Moline Airport property was to expire on November 7, 1930. A local referendum had been voted upon in late 1929 to raise the necessary money to buy the Franing Field and Weaver Farm property and passed. But a mistake had been made in the tax levy computations and the election was later declared invalid. Another referendum was held in early May 1930, but lost.

For the want of one decimal place, Rock Island County lost its chance to own the Moline Airport property. Instead of collecting $50,000 in new revenue, the city and county stood to collect only $5,000. The job and payroll costs of this mistake were to prove much greater than anybody expected, including the distinct possibility a major airplane/engine manufacturing concern would not become firmly rooted on the airport grounds.

Don announced to a stunned local public the loss of this election would force Mono-Aircraft, Inc. and Lambert Aircraft Engine Corporation to move from Moline, quite possibly as soon as early fall.

Similarly, Curtiss-Wright Flying Service announced they were abandoning plans to erect a $125,000 hangar and office building on the field. Indeed, National Air Transport reconsidered their future maintenance base construction plans, also. These discouraging announcements made the local population realize the importance of their airport.

As the local politicians and the Moline Association of Commerce sought a way to extend the lease or buy the property outright, Mono-Aircraft and Lambert engine production continued on a regular basis. No formal plans were entertained to interrupt this production, at least for the near future.

Shortly after Mono-Aircraft announced their

An OX-5 Command-Aire Model C3C flies overhead the Moline Airport. The Mono-Aircraft assembly/storage hangar is on the left, the National Air Transport hangar is center and the Campbell-de Schepper Airplane Company hangar is on the right. Circa 1931.

JAMES B. ZAZAS COLLECTION

Monocoupe super salesman Bart Stevenson and a Monocoupe 110

Roy T. "Stub" Quinby poses before a Monocoach at the 1929 National Air Races.

Vern Roberts stands ready to meet the competition.

possible move, company officials were deluged with mail and telephone calls from almost fifty communities asking that the company consider locating their business in their respective cities. Many communities offered generous financial incentives and virtually all the cities offered the use of their airports and facilities at no charge. Don Luscombe thanked these communities for their interest. He told the local media the company would not move unless forced to do so.

Perhaps the only favorable news offered the beleaguered Mono-Aircraft employees during 1930, was the Monocoupe's impressive domination of the racing scene. These wins held the Monocoupe name before the public eye and kept a few orders flowing into the company.

The Monocoupe racing legacy received a positive, international boost when Lord John E. Carberry, a former World War I Flight Lieutenant in the British Naval Air Corps and a former member of British peerage, paid a cordial business visit to Mono-Aircraft, Inc. on June 4. He was in town to take delivery of the prototype Monocoupe 110 (NC503W, later G-ABAR, s/n 5W40) to Europe to compete in the "Challenge de Tourisme International." Incidentally, this Monocoupe was to be the only American-made airplane in the race. Lord Carberry and his mechanic placed sixth in this difficult race. No doubt they would have placed better, even won, if they had succeeded in the required roadability test. The Monosport's one-piece wing proved to be the racers' downfall — their competitors had folding wings.

Phoebe Omlie returned to Mono-Aircraft in early June, whereupon she announced her plans to race a Monocoupe in the upcoming Iowa State Air Tour. "Stub" Quinby was listed to participate in this local race, also. Before undertaking this race, however, Quinby raced a Monocoupe in a June 1930, Rockford Air Meet, a two-day event held west of Chicago, Illinois. He placed first in the stunting contest and second in a free-for-all race. He was beaten by Charles "Speed" Holman who raced a

66   *Visions of Luscombe: The Early Years*

300 hp Laird.

As the summer progressed, Monocoupes placed well in other local air tours. Phoebe Omlie raced her ship in the Indiana State Air Tour. Barton Stevenson, a Mono-Aircraft salesman-pilot, flew a Monocoupe in the Nebraska State Air Tour.

On July 13, speed kings Vern Roberts and "Stub" Quinby swept a series of air races held during the dedication of the Monticello, Iowa, airport. Roberts flew his "Little Sweetheart" to a first place finish in a free-for-all race and earned a first place finish in a race for small airplanes. Quinby, flying a stock Monocoupe, placed second in two races and third in another race. Roberts, Quinby and Stevenson — billed as the "Three Rockets" — thrilled the crowd of 4,000 people with a dazzling display of formation aerobatics in their Monocoupes. Quinby kept the pace lively with a series of spectacular solo acts. Johnny Livingston and his brother, "Bite," took first and second place finishes respectively in the dead-stick landing contest.

Perhaps the most unusual race design to grace the Moline Airport ramp during the summer months was a small, 90 hp "Cirrus" powered racer. Called the "Mono-Special" by factory workers, this diminutive racer was identified as the Mono-Aircraft, Inc. "mystery ship" by the Moline and Davenport press. Developed initially as a joint venture between Clayton Folkerts and Vern Roberts on their free time, with accomplished welder Chet Loose adding his expertise, Mono-Aircraft, Inc. soon became involved and provided a shop and materials in return for any publicity benefits. Clayton Folkerts designed the craft; Vern Roberts was to be the pilot.

A grueling 5,500 mile race, sponsored by the American Cirrus Company, was the motivation to build this racer. More than $36,000 was posted as prize money with $15,000 going to the first place winner. A free, 90 hp "Cirrus" engine was provided to every bonafide entrant.

Johnny Livingston and Vern Roberts made the preliminary test flights in the polished bright red, mid-wing racer. Roberts, now suffering from occasional bouts of severe dizziness (perhaps Meniers Disease), was forced to relinquish his Mono-Special piloting duties to "Stub" Quinby. Johnny Livingston was scheduled to fly the ship in the race, but he became ill also, and was unable to race.

Quinby and the little racer did very well in the early part of this race, often averaging 192 mph. Sadly, the sleek racer was damaged in a takeoff accident near Douglas, Arizona, pinning a slightly injured Quinby beneath the wreckage. The Mono-Aircraft "mystery ship" had to be withdrawn from the race after completing 2885 miles, much to the disappointment of the local press and race fans who followed the daily progress.

Soon repaired, the Mono-Special was flown briefly at the 1930 National Air Races, but it drew hardly any notice. Quinby placed well in other, lesser known local races during the balance of the year, often finishing first or second. An improved Mono-Special appeared during the summer of 1933 and was called the "Folkerts Special." Later still, this airplane became known as the Folkerts SK-1 (SpeedKing 1) and was flown by veteran race pilot Harold Newmann.

Phoebe Omlie returned to the factory in late July to oversee construction of her new Monocoupe

JOHN UNDERWOOD

(Above) Clayton Folkerts and the Mono-Special. This 90 hp, Cirrus powered, aircraft was entered in a 5,500 mile race sponsored by the American Cirrus Company.

(Right) A good side view of the Mono-Special shortly after its debut in July 1930.

JOHN UNDERWOOD

racer. Employees hoped for a repeat of her winning performance of a year earlier. In early August, Omlie was invited to the White House to visit President and Mrs. Herbert Hoover. Behind these festive scenes, the calamitous effects of the Depression were taking hold. Sales fell sharply. Soon, the Mono-Aircraft, Inc. and the Lambert Aircraft Engine Corporation were in grievous financial trouble.

Allied Aviation Industries officials undertook negotiations with several concerns to sell their Mono-Aircraft and Lambert Aircraft Engine Corporation subsidiaries. Fokker Aircraft, at the time a subsidiary of General Motors, offered a stock exchange plan as the means to gain control.

During the course of these delicate negotiations, Floyd Augustine, head of the Allied Aviation Industries, denied rumors that General Motors had purchased Allied Aviation for $2,000,000. Furthermore, he admonished the local press that publicity could scuttle the deal. In the end, the deal did collapse leaving the St. Louis-based brokers scrambling to find a buyer elsewhere. These negotiations brought forth a flood of rumors. One unfounded rumor said the Curtiss-Wright Aircraft Company would take over. The rumors served no advantageous purpose and only caused the employees to fret about their future.

Despite the mixed bag of air race victories and corporate setbacks, Luscombe persevered to improve sales. His mind was always active, always thinking of ways to achieve that end. Don was confident and determined he and his company would weather the nation's financial storm swirling about them.

On August 9, a sudden, natural storm struck the Moline Airport with 55 mph winds. The huge doors of the Curtiss-Wright hangar were ripped from their hinges, then laid on the ground so gently that no glass was broken.

Next door, Mono-Aircraft employees did what they could to protect several, specially prepared Monocoupe 110s being made ready for the National Air Races. The storm soon ended and, much to their relief, not a plane had been damaged.

Five days after this storm, veteran race pilot Johnny Livingston arrived to take delivery of his new overall yellow and red trimmed Monocoupe 110. Livingston had only ten days to get his airplane ready for the 1930 National Air Races at Chicago. Wasting no time, he hurried to his Aurora, Illinois, home to prepare.

Livingston would race this airplane stock in the 1930 NAR. He would not undertake until after the races the many, careful modifications that would endear this particular Monocoupe in the hearts of air racing enthusiasts.

The 1930 National Air Races at Chicago held great promise for Mono-Aircraft, Inc. and its airplanes. Don Luscombe and many air racing enthusiasts were not disappointed. Vern Roberts, "Stub" Quinby and Phoebe Omlie were scheduled to race the factory's specially prepared Monocoupes. Of course, John Livingston was there with his glistening airplane.

Monocoupes virtually swept away the competition. They garnered first place finishes in eleven of fifteen races entered during the August 23 to September 1 spectacle. Additionally, Monocoupes placed second in ten of these events as well as third in nine events entered. Moreover, the swift Monocoupes placed first in each of the three Air Derby races in which they were entered. Finally, of the fifteen events entered by Monocoupes, five of them were for airplanes of greater horsepower.

Vern Roberts won most events handily. But a hard-charging Livingston gave Roberts a good race in a couple of races by trailing behind only by tenths of a second! For example, in the Civilian's Closed Course Race of 800 cubic inches displacement, Roberts placed first with an average speed of 145.58 mph. Livingston and Quinby followed in second and third places with speeds of 145.40 and 140.01, respectively.

Employing an often used race tactic, Roberts rose his airplane on the last pylon of the last lap, then dove towards the finish line. The crowd thundered with excitement!

But Livingston wasn't Roberts only close competition. During one 25 mile pylon race, Les Bowman stayed on Roberts' tail, flying a speed-ring cowl modified Monosport 2. Likewise, Bart Stevenson, flying a Lambert-powered Monocoupe, garnered at least one first, and two second, and three third place finishes.

In the Woman's Closed Course Race of 800 cubic inches displacement, Phoebe Omlie took first place flying a Monocoupe 113 Special with a 139.97 mph average speed. Gladys O'Donnell placed second with a close 139.84 mph average speed flying a Warner-powered Monocoupe.

Much as they had done a year earlier, Vern Roberts, "Stub" Quinby and Phoebe Omlie collected huge cash prizes at the 1930 NAR. Often, these winnings exceeded $2,500, quite a handsome prize when one considers the average weekly wage in 1930 was barely $35. Other Monocoupe pilots and cash winners included Wesley Smith, Bart Stevenson, Scotty Burmood, Marti Bowman and, of course, Johnny Livingston. Many of these names would be immortalized in air racing's "Golden Age."

In light of the Monocoupes' domination of these races, well-known air race commentator, Cy Caldwell, commented the races should have been called the "Monocoupe National Races" instead of the National Air Races. Don Luscombe used these remarks in future Monocoupe advertising and sale brochures.

Though he did well in these races, Johnny Livingston was not happy with his many second place finishes. Livingston wanted dearly to win these races. Addressing this goal, he began to modify and streamline his "Coupe." His goal was to have the fastest Monocoupe. His approach was methodical and he kept an accurate record of changes, noting changes and performance gains. Livingston would spend many hours modifying his Monocoupe. By the end of 1930, his changes included the addition of wheel pants and discarding the collector ring and the long, trailing exhaust stack.

By the year's end, Don Luscombe was ecstatic! He could boast, and rightfully so, Monocoupe airplanes had won 63 percent of the total prize money offered for the events in which they were entered during 1930.

In spite of the new and innovative designs introduced and the brief sales flurry they generated, the financial situation worsened within the company. In an effort to maintain a positive cash flow, Mono-Aircraft slashed prices commencing in August 1930, to move stock on hand. For example, the popular Monocoupe 113, offered originally at $2835, was marked-down to $1895.

At the time, Mono-Aircraft officials stated they had about twenty-five Monocoupe 113 airplanes available to be sold at this low price, the only model affected by the price decrease. Very few other models were left in stock as they were being sold almost as fast as they were being built.

Mono-Aircraft and its employees were hamstrung by the Depression. Don tried to allay fears the factory was in dire financial shape and promoted vigorously the positive attributes of the Monocoupe. However, further attempts to sell the Monocoupe beyond the sportsman or racing pilot clientele proved all but fruitless.

Likewise, most employee attempts to pool their creative energies to offer the public a better product were thwarted. They had to "make do" with what they had on one hand and improve the same on the other. There simply wasn't enough money available at the time to pursue all new airplane ideas and offer any significant new designs.

Airplane manufacturers learned quickly their creative energies had to be channelled productively while management redirected its marketing efforts. Those companies which took careful stock of their predicament and elected to pursue more realistic marketing plans survived. Those that didn't soon fell victims of the Depression. By year's end, some 110 "aircraft companies" could count themselves as survivors from the almost 215 that had been doing business at the start of the year.

For many casualties of the Depression, simple hope was replaced by the simple, yet fundamental, need of just staying alive. Being able to stay open meant more to many airplane company executives and workers than being able to turn a profit. By this time, total income in the country had fallen almost in half from its 1929 level. Since the stock market crash of 1929, almost 85,000 businesses failed. Except for a very few more fortunate individuals, the Depression squashed any hope of better times in the minds of many.

Sadly, despite Don Luscombe's and his employees' determined efforts, Mono-Aircraft, Inc. was forced to slow production, eventually ceasing most operations during the late fall and well into the winter months of 1930 and 1931. The company was within a hairline of becoming a "victim" of the Depression.

On December 30, 1930, both Mono-Aircraft, Inc. and Lambert Aircraft Engine Corporation were placed into receivership. Robert A. Cole, Mono-Aircraft's director of advertising, was appointed receiver by Peoria, Illinois, Federal District Court Judge Louis FitzHenry. Cole was considered an investor "friendly" with the companies' and the creditors' goals. Moline's Association of Commerce assisted the companies in developing a reorganization plan. But other creditors were not happy. Pioneer Instrument Company and other concerns initiated legal proceedings against Mono-Aircraft and Lambert Aircraft Engine Corporation for collection of debts in Federal Court in Peoria, Illinois.

On January 7, 1931, Judge Louis FitzHenry ruled in favor of the companies and issued an injunction to stop the creditors' actions while the companies reorganized. Furthermore, the Judge ordered airplane manufacturing operations to continue. Cole was instructed to operate the companies as a "going concern." During this period and as an attempt to regain control of the companies, Luscombe raised nearly $50,000 and petitioned the court requesting that both corporations be allowed to sell their assets to the newly formed Luscombe Company of St. Louis.

In this petition, Luscombe stated one of the main causes of the Mono-Aircraft's current woes was related to overproduction in 1929, which required sweeping price reductions in 1930 to sell airplanes to remain competitive. He stated further the 1931 outlook was encouraging as a per unit profit potential existed. Moreover, Luscombe stated he believed he would be able *"to secure a major portion of the machine work for the Warner aircraft engine this coming season which will reduce overhead ratios for our own engine."*

In his proposal letter, Luscombe laid blame for many of the Mono-Aircraft's immediate problems on the investment brokers, *"who were concerned with* the making of immediate profits from the flotation of stock and far overestimating the market, declining to consider the time element for development."

Luscombe continued, "The immediate distress of this broker group puts the companies in a precarious position, but at the same time creates the rare opportunity for the creators of the Monocoupe idea to gain control of the companies and to preserve an industry of great promise to Moline."

In his reorganization plan, Luscombe proposed: "... To ruthlessly shrink present figures of value used in the capital structure of Mono-Aircraft, Inc. and Lambert Aircraft Engine Corporation, set up a new company, ignoring intangible values, basing all figures on the basis of immediate liquidation, then offering to share the opportunity with Moline citizens.

"After securing permanent and fixed assets with a first mortgage, offer convertible 6 percent bonds with warrants for additional common stock to be exercised if the affairs of the company progress with the rapidity with which it seems destined."

Luscombe's offers were rebuffed as the creditors demanded more money. They wanted the full $78,000 purchase price.

On January 10, 1931, Robert Cole announced the Mono-Aircraft reorganization plan would include moving to an airport that would allow locating the plant on the field. Such a move would save $20,000 in heat and transportation. Cole stated such a move would separate Mono-Aircraft from Allied Aviation Industries.

Negotiations were started on many levels to find a suitable investor willing to purchase the floundering Mono-Aircraft.

Scarab

Name of Engine:	WARNER SCARAB.
Manufactured by:	Warner Aircraft Corp., 20263 Hoover Ave., Detroit, Michigan.
Type:	7 cylinder, fixed radial, air cooled, 4 cycle. (Approved Type Certificate No. 2.)
Department of Commerce Rating:	110 H.P. at 1850 R.P.M.
Displacement:	422 cu. in.
Compression Ratio:	5.2 to 1.
Dimensions:	Length, overall .... 29"
	Diameter, overall ...... 35 1/2"
	Bore .... 4 1/4"
	Stroke .... 4 1/4"
Weight:	270 lbs. (without starter or hub).
Fuel Consumption at Rated H.P.	.55 lbs. per H.P. hr.
Oil Consumption:	.025 lbs. per H.P. hr.
Lubrication:	Force feed.
Ignition:	Dual Scintilla Magnetos.
Carburetion:	1 Stromberg.
Spark Plugs:	2 per cyl. A.C.
Price:	$2,700.

GUIDE TO PRE-1930 AIRCRAFT ENGINES

Scarab-Junior

Name of Engine:	WARNER SCARAB-JUNIOR.
Manufactured by:	Warner Aircraft Corp., 20263 Hoover Ave., Detroit, Michigan.
Type:	5 cylinder, fixed radial, air cooled, 4 cycle.
Department of Commerce Rating:	90 H.P. at 2025 R.P.M.
Displacement:	301 cu. in.
Compression Ratio:	5.2 to 1.
Dimensions:	Length, overall .... 28 1/2"
	Diameter, overall ...... 36 1/4"
	Bore .... 4 1/4"
	Stroke .... 4 1/4"
Weight:	230 lbs. (without starter or hub).
Fuel Consumption at Rated H.P.	.55 lbs. per H.P. hr.
Oil Consumption:	.025 lbs. per H.P. hr.
Lubrication:	Force feed.
Ignition:	Dual Scintilla Magnetos.
Carburetion:	1 Stromberg.
Spark Plugs:	2 per cyl. A.C.
Price:	$1,900.

New Super-Performance

Under All Conditions for
The Monocoupe "90"
at $3375.00

TAKE it point for point—a plane that is comfortable in all weather without getting dressed up to look funny. It's companionable—you can smoke and talk, no weather too rough, one man moves it in and out the hangar, a power plant that requires less concern over motor service and maintenance than one gives his automobile, one that you can rebuild after the second year for $75.00—with a landing speed of less than 37 miles an hour—guaranteed top speed of 120 miles an hour and a fuel cost of less than 1½ cents a mile—an initial cost far below anything on the market, and regardless of some of the queerest yarns, some of the Jenny experts who have never flown such an airplane tell, it is so easy to fly that it's almost a shame to take money for showing a prospect how to operate it.

The unprecedented popularity of the new design necessitates your order being placed at least three weeks in advance.

Monocoupe "90" Performance
High speed . . . . . . 120 M.P.H.
Landing speed . . . . . 37 M.P.H.
Cruising speed . . . . 105 M.P.H.
Climb . . . 1100 ft. per min.
Horse power . . 90
Length overall . . . 20 ft. 5 in.
Span . . 32 ft. 0 in.
Cruising range . . . . 525 miles

$75.00 Buys
Parts for complete overhaul of Lambert R-266 Engine
5 Cylinder barrels
5 Pistons with rings fitted
10 Valve guides
10 Rocker arm bushings
10 Spark plugs
Complete set of gaskets

MONO AIRCRAFT CORPORATION
MOLINE, ILLINOIS

A CLEARANCE SALE OF 25 BRAND NEW AIRPLANES AT UNPRECEDENTED VALUES

The Monocoupe 60

Price $2835—Now Priced at $1895

¶ A surplus of service parts prompts the immediate clearance of "built up" and "in process" materials of this popular airplane to make factory room for other models. ¶ These airplanes are standard, new and guaranteed in every respect, in fact they are yet to be assembled. (Approved Type Certificate No. 113)

MONOCOUPE 60

Specifications and Performance

Two passenger
Useful load .... 522 lbs.
Span .... 32 ft.
Length .... 19 ft. 9 in.
Height .... 6 ft. 3 in.
Fuel Capacity .... 25 gals.
Engine .... Velie M5 60 h.p.
High Speed .... 98 M.P.H.
Cruising Speed ...... 85 M.P.H.
Cruising Range ...... 550 miles
Landing Speed .... 37 M.P.H.
Weight (Full Load) ... 1350 lbs.

INASMUCH as we must carry service parts at all times, only twenty-five planes of this type will be assembled at this price from service stocks. Never has such value been offered the flying public. Therefore, it behooves interested parties to make commitments without delay. ¶ Orders will be accepted in turn without favor. A deposit of $500 must accompany orders. ¶ In the sale are several factory reconditioned planes of this type which have been accepted in trade and which are offered at prices ranging from one thousand dollars to fifteen hundred dollars.

Remember, this offer is for immediate acceptance only and it may be years before such an opportunity can be duplicated.

Bargains in Used Planes With Factory Guarantee

Kinner Monosport
Less than 10 hrs. $2950

J5 Monocoach
Special upholstering
50 hrs. $4250

J6 Monocoach
Less than 40 hrs. $5500

Monocoupe 90
Demonstrator, 50 hrs. .. $2500

MONO AIRCRAFT CORPORATION

MOLINE, ILLINOIS

"A SWEEPING VICTORY for *Monocoupe*"

Summary of Events—*National Air Races*

Chicago, August 23 to September 1

MONOCOUPES placed first in 11 of the 15 events in which they they were entered, including both open and closed type planes and were in a power class of from 275 to 800 cu. in. engine displacement.

MONOCOUPES placed second in ten of these events.

MONOCOUPES placed third in nine of these events.

MONOCOUPES placed first in each of the three Air Derbies in which they were entered.

MONOCOUPES won 63% of the total prize money offered for the events in which they were entered.

Of the 15 events entered by MONOCOUPES one-third of them were for planes of greater horse power.

THE AIR RACES held at Chicago this year have been responsible for a sizable increase to the already large MONOCOUPE following. Many of the oldtimers have been converted and realize that for real speed and efficiency the MONOCOUPE with its cabin comfort and general high performance qualities represents the last word in airplane design.

There must be a reason! Performance such as shown by MONOCOUPES during the 1930 National Air Races is not obtained by mere coincidence. The speed and efficiency shown by these sturdy little planes are the result of years of manufacturing experience and experimental work and engineering skill devoted exclusively to the production of a light plane giving a maximum of performance with a minimum of power.

All of the MONOCOUPES entered in the various events of speed and efficiency were strictly stock models with the same trim lines and embodying the same comfort as found in all our planes. If you have not flown the new MONOCOUPE arrange for a demonstration today and experience the thrill of super performance and the comforts of flying that only can be found in a cabin plane.

Department of Commerce Approved Type Certificates have been granted to MONOCOUPES powered with Lambert R 266, Warner Jr., Warner 110, and Kinner B5 engines. Top speeds of the MONOCOUPES vary from 120 m.p.h. to 148 m.p.h., depending upon the power plant used.

Prices from $3375.00 to $4500.00 fly away Moline

MONO AIRCRAFT CORPORATION
MOLINE, ILLINOIS, U.S.A.

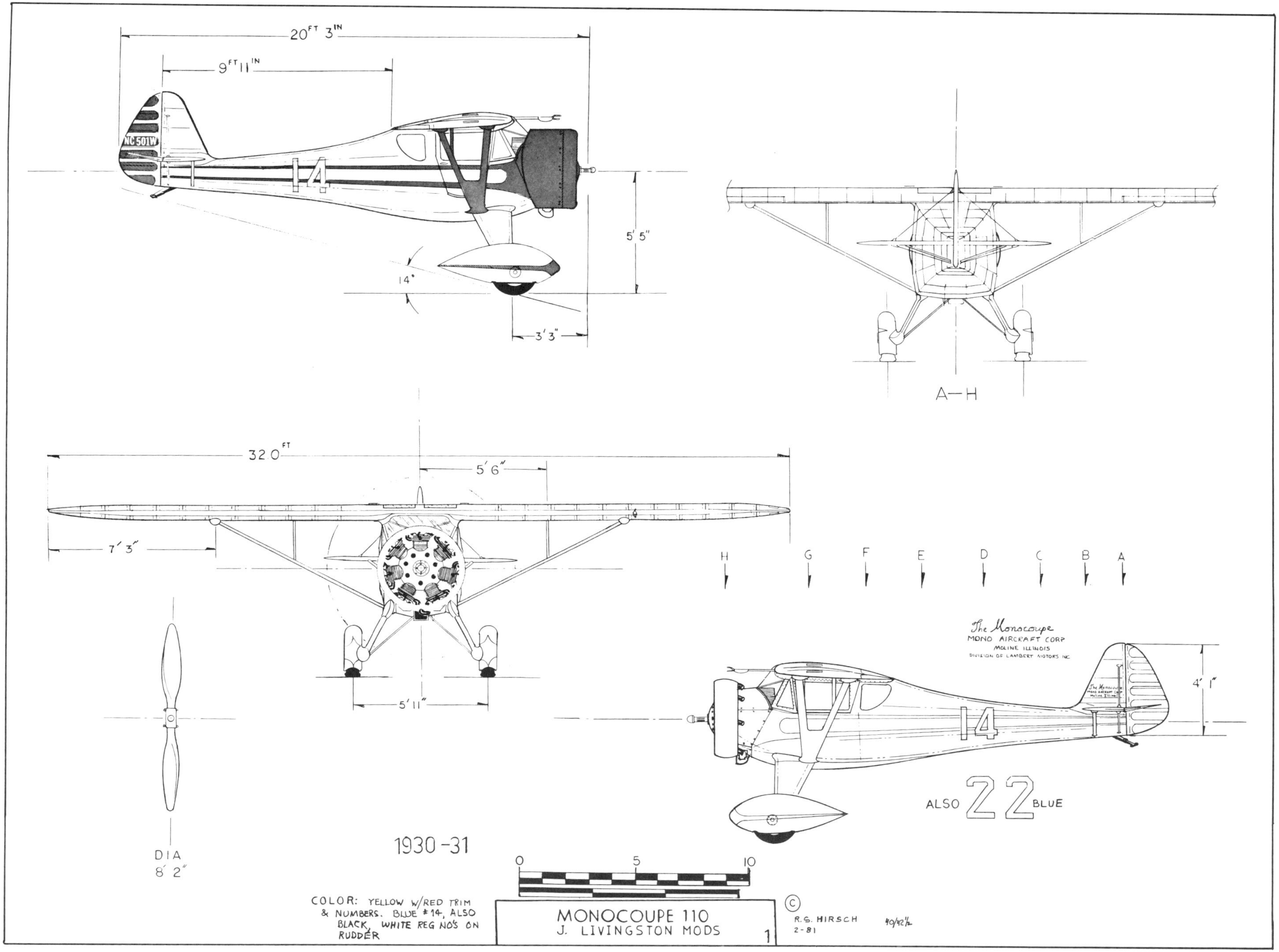

20FT 3IN
9FT 11IN
NC 501W
14
5' 5"
14°
3' 3"
A—H
32.0FT
5' 6"
7' 3"
5' 11"
H G F E D C B A
The Monocoupe
MONO AIRCRAFT CORP
MOLINE ILLINOIS
DIVISION OF LAMBERT MOTORS INC
4' 1"
ALSO 22 BLUE
DIA
8' 2"
1930-31
0 5 10
COLOR: YELLOW W/RED TRIM & NUMBERS. BLUE #14, ALSO BLACK, WHITE REG NO'S ON RUDDER
MONOCOUPE 110
J. LIVINGSTON MODS
1
© R.G. HIRSCH 2-81
40/42½

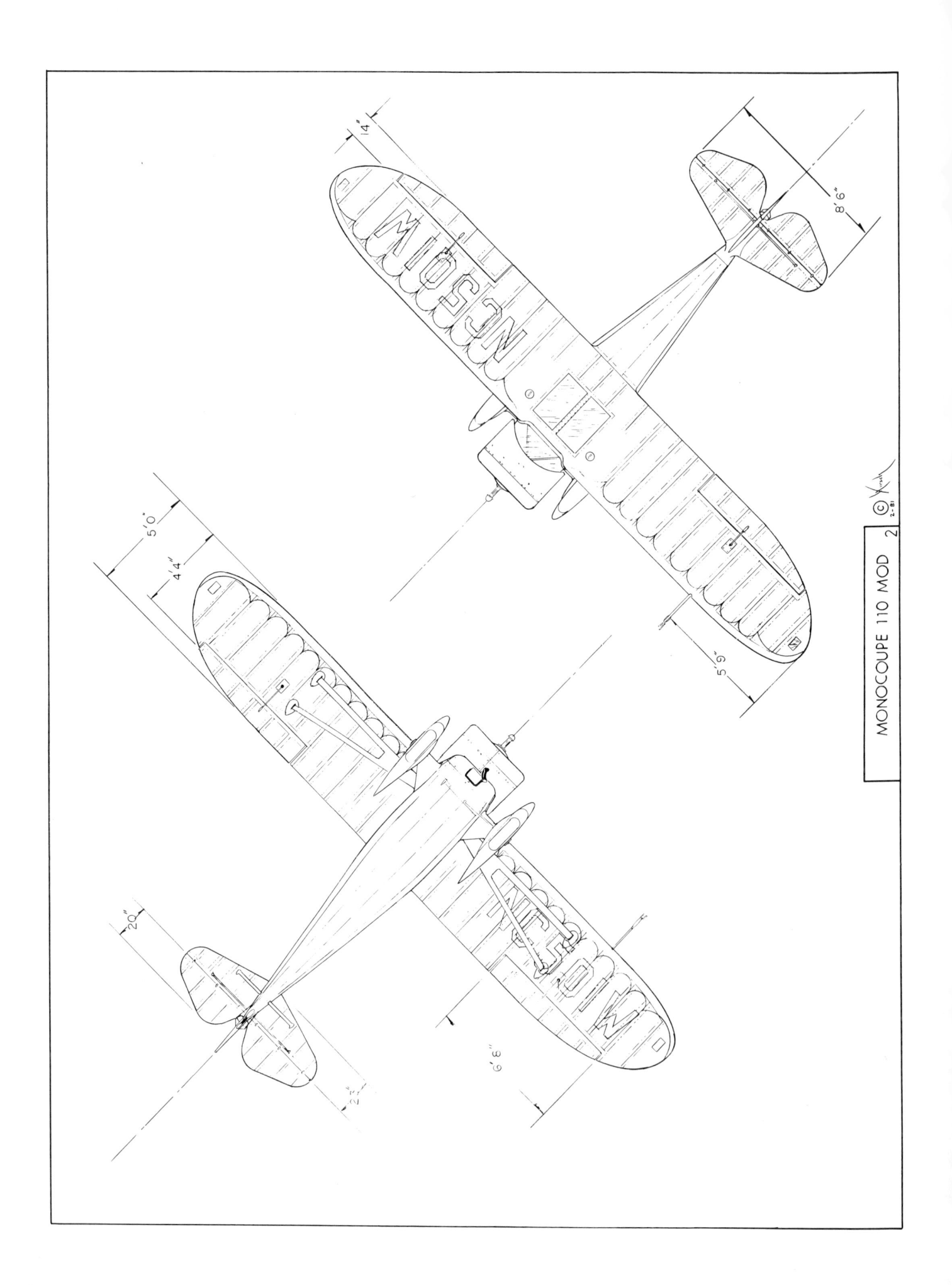

MONOCOUPE 110 MOD

*"Genius... is the capacity to see ten things where the ordinary man sees one,
and where men of talent sees two or three,
plus the ability to register that multiple perception in the material of his art."*
Ezra Pound (1885 - 1972)

Chapter Six

Tinker, Tailor, Engineer, Genius and Romance

The Monocoupe Model "D" with a revised tail. This tail design was carried over from Ivan Driggs' earlier airplane designs.

ELEANORE LUSCOMBE SHURTZ COLLECTION

Receiver Robert Cole's announcement the factory may move played little on the racing enthusiasm demonstrated by the Mono-Aircraft pilots and fans. Monocoupes continued their domination of various air races and derby events.

Moline-made ships came home with a bunch of trophies from the Miami Air Meet held in early January 1931. Quinby, Roberts, Livingston, Omlie, Bowman and others beat the competition handily, including more powerful U.S. Army airplanes that were entered. Johnny Livingston hit an astounding 146.14 mph in his Monocoupe 110 and took the honor as having the highest average speed of the meet.

Behind these festive scenes, tense negotiations continued to sell the company. Fortunately for Don Luscombe and Mono-Aircraft, Phil De Cameron Ball soon entered the picture as a major player. Ball, a major Mono-Aircraft stockholder, was a colorful individual and was well-known in the St. Louis area for his many successful business ventures, including the Ball Ice Machine and various cold storage plants. An avid sportsman, Ball owned the St. Louis Browns, a major league baseball team in addition to Sportsman Park in St. Louis.

On June 8, 1931, Ball announced his plans to purchase both Mono-Aircraft and the Lambert Aircraft Engine Corporation from Allied Aviation Industries. This deal was subject to approval from Federal District Judge Louis FitzHenry. Furthermore, he announced his intentions to move the aircraft manufacturing operations into the old Ryan Aircraft factory at Lambert Field near St. Louis where the new concern would be more efficient an operation. Ball asked Don Luscombe and Vern Roberts to join the new company he planned to call Monocoupe Corporation (Incidentally, as of this writing, this building is a part of the massive McDonnell-Douglas Aircraft Company complex in St. Louis.) The judge gave his approval to the plan in mid-July 1931, despite some last minute charges by creditors of wrongdoing in the deal. Thus, with the stroke of a pen, Ball became Don Luscombe's new "guardian angel."

Commencing the early summer 1931 months, Mono-Aircraft men and equipment moved from Moline, Illinois, into the former Ryan Aircraft Company plant in Robertson, Missouri, a suburb of St. Louis. On August 1, the now renamed Monocoupe Corporation started business.

Don Luscombe was retained as president and general manager. Additionally, Don became the president of the new Lambert Engine and Machine Corporation with its offices and production facilities remaining in Moline, Illinois.

Despite Phil De Cameron Ball's generous infusions of capital, the years 1931, 1932 and 1933 were to be slow for Mono-Aircraft, Inc. and, later, the Monocoupe Corporation, its engineers and employees. The slump in orders affected everyone from design and engineering to sales and production. The combined talents of these men were all but wasted by the crippling Depression that gripped the nation.

Auspiciously, Mono-Aircraft (later, the Monocoupe Corporation) was able to build and sell airplanes during this very difficult period. Regardless of the despair of the time, airplanes were still being designed, built and sold. A very small segment of society still had the funds available to partake in such an extravagant hobby. Likewise, Ball made sure money was available when needed to cover day-to-day expenses and payroll.

The tiny Mono Midget was powered by the Lambert H-106 engine and could outfly anything in its class

Shortly before Monocoupe operations moved to Robertson, a sleek little racer bearing the Mono-Aircraft name made its debut. This airplane was called the "Mono Midget."

Designed and built by fuselage department foreman Chester Loose, with Clayton Folkerts assisting, Mono-Aircraft employees donated their free time to build this racer. Reclaimed scrap and other materials gathered around the factory were used to build this airplane.

The Mono Midget weighed-in just under 700 pounds, including pilot and a full tank of gas. Mono-Aircraft management donated a 40 hp, H-106 engine, one of two built by the company. Though one of two of these little engines had been tested on a Monoprep, management decided not to begin production of the little two cylinder engine after Sam Lambert's tragic death. In turn, they gave the Mono Midget group the remaining parts of the experimental engines built.

The Mono Midget cockpit was quite cramped, but five-foot, nine inch Scotty Burmood wriggled into the cockpit to undertake the first test flight on May 10, 1931. Reportedly, his knees were almost tucked up to his chin.[19]

The airplane's flight characteristics proved satisfactory, but the performance was startling! Loose and Folkerts wasted no time entering their Mono Midget in races around the Midwestern United States. Their diminutive airplane outflew everything in its class.

Over time, the Mono Midget underwent some

streamlining and name changes. At the 1932 National Air Races at Cleveland, for example, a much-improved version appeared as the "Loose Special." Harold Neumann had the honors of flying this craft.

Sadly, this racer met its demise at the Moline Airport when a hapless pilot spun it into the ground from 700 feet.

For those individuals who could not afford an airplane, many took great interest in the varied and exciting activities of those who could. They read the newspaper stories and listened to the radio for information. Air races, derbies and air shows offered many less fortunate a chance to forget their woes and share in the excitement of the day. A glowing ray of hope developed from this interest that private aviation would not only survive, but flourish.

Enhancing Monocoupe Corporation airplanes' appeal were the many victories these swift designs tallied in several prestigious races. Overall, 1931 proved an astounding year as Monocoupe racers won more than 50 percent of all available prize money.

Johnny Livingston was ready for the 1931 air racing season. Sporting a much-modified racer, he flew his long-wing Monocoupe 110 to victory after victory. At the Miami Air Races held in January, Livingston garnered two first place finishes and a second. Five months later at the Omaha Races, Livingston and the Coupe captured seven firsts, one second and one third.

Shortly before entering in the 1931 National Air Races at Cleveland, Livingston began to modify the cowl on his Monocoupe. He developed a longer cowl that consisted of two flat pieces wrapped around and connected to the speed ring. To determine the effects of these and other modifications, Livingston would whitewash his airplane and fly it through a rain cloud. After landing, he would carefully note the airflow disturbances from the resulting streaking. In turn, he would make the appropriate corrections.

On August 25, shortly before the start of the 1931 National Air Races at Cleveland, a confident Livingston took his Monocoupe to the Warner Aircraft factory in Detroit, Michigan, for an overhaul and a horsepower boost to 125 hp.

At these races, John Livingston and his yellow and red trimmed Monocoupe, race number 14 emblazoned on it side, visited the winner's circle on numerous occasions. He racked an impressive seven victories and two second place finishes of twelve events entered. His race earnings amassed to an incredible $6,180. When one considers two bits and a dime could buy a good dinner for two, these earnings were a lot of money.

Livingston would thrill the crowd with hairpin turns at the pylons. His vertical banks only a scant twenty feet or so above the ground added much to his

Race number 14 emblazoned on its tail and still sporting stock "long" wings, Johnny Livingston poses with his much modified Monocoupe 110 shortly before the start of the 1931 National Air Races. JIM HARVEY

Vern Roberts' stock Monocoupe 110 at the 1931 National Air Races at Cleveland. This swift racer gave a slightly faster Johnny Livingston a run for his money. JIM HARVEY

developing legend. He would finish his display of superb airmanship by doing a series of victory rolls at the conclusion of each race.

Before the 1931 air racing season was out, Johnny Livingston and his much-modified Coupe took home forty-one first place finishes, nineteen seconds, four thirds and one forth — all from sixty-five starts! Not to be outdone, Vern Roberts, Bart Stevenson and Florence Klingensmith took a sizable share of first, second and third place finishes.

Once again, as she had done in 1929 and 1930, Phoebe Omlie won the 1931 Women's Transcontinental Handicap Air Derby. She flew a Monocoupe 113 Special in this Santa Monica, California, to Cleveland, Ohio, handicapped race and collected $3,000 in prize money. Aviatrix Mary "Mae" Haizlip of St. Louis flew a Lambert-powered Monocoupe to a second place finish in the same race and collected $1,800.

At some point during the waning days of 1931, Vern Roberts left Monocoupe. Contrary to popular belief, there was no "falling out" between Roberts and Don Luscombe. Instead, Roberts' bouts of severe dizziness grew worse and he felt he could no longer fulfill his job satisfactorily.[20]

Engineering work during this period was slow and consisted mostly of airframe or power plant modifications to improve performance. To this end, Frederick J. Knack, as chief engineer, addressed his efforts. Knack was a thorough engineer. There was no "second best" or "it'll do" in his vocabulary. However, Knack had a temper which would rise now and then. According to a former engineering associate and close friend of Knack, this temper would be present *"only if the end result of any design problem was not intuitively discernible by his associates."* On many occasions, Knack would listen patiently and consider carefully the advice of his associates. Then, he would make his decision and move onward.

Knack enjoyed a good engineering challenge. However, if he finished a project at one firm and there was no further engineering problems to be resolved, he would move on to another firm that offered a current design opportunity. Such was Knack's character. Fortunately, Don Luscombe and the Monocoupe Corporation had such an engineering challenge to keep Knack in the company. Reports were filtering from the field the Monocoupe was "too small" for pilots of wider and taller stature. In turn, management instructed the engineering staff to find a plausible, cost-effective design resolution to this problem.

Knack relished in the challenge to design this somewhat larger, two place aircraft. His diligent efforts, commencing during the winter of 1931, resulted in a sprightly new design that became known as the Monocoupe "Model D."

Designed by Fred Knack, the prototype Monocoupe Model D was powered by a Warner "Scarab," 125 hp engine. Circa December 1931. ELEANORE LUSCOMBE SHURTZ COLLECTION

Basically, the Model D evolved from the Monocoupe 110 airframe. The beneficial modifications gleaned from air racing Monocoupes were evaluated and incorporated. To accommodate larger and taller pilots, the cockpit was widened six inches and the wing was constructed in two panels to allow extra headroom.

Work on the Model D progressed slowly from blueprints to prototype. Eventually, the test aircraft was made ready by late 1931 or early 1932 powered by a Warner 125 hp engine. But the airplane design still eluded the qualities Luscombe desired. Furthermore, progress towards Department of Commerce certification and approval was moving at a snail's pace.

As the corporation entered into 1932, Don Luscombe continued to seek new and innovative means to sell his airplanes. One particular successful idea was the Monocoupe Corporation's Deferred Payment Plan. According to a company brochure, the corporation had *"previously declined all forms of time payment plans due to the sincere conviction that they were excessive in cost for the customer."* No doubt economic reality set in and forced a rethinking of corporate strategy.

According to the plan, a prospective Monocoupe buyer had to be a person of reasonable responsibility and acceptable to the Bureau of Air Commerce. Furthermore, the buyer had to make a fifty percent down payment on the Monocoupe of his choice and the balance paid off in twelve equal monthly payments. Very simply, this plan simplified Monocoupe ownership for some and enabled purchase for others who could not afford to do so previously.

Don was keen to the many hardships presented by the Depression, but he was keen to the many opportunities for "survival" presented by the current economic times, also. Luscombe sought ways to keep the public's interest in their airplanes. Proclaiming the Monocoupe to be "America's Most Representative Small Airplane" for 1932, Don returned to the flashy sales brochure as a means to tout the company's few available models then in production and get potential buyers to part with their hard-earned money.

These models included the Velie M-5 powered Monocoupe 70-V, the Lambert R-266 powered Monocoupe 90, the Warner "Scarab" powered Monocoupe 110 and the Kinner B-5 powered Monocoupe 125. In April 1932, these four airplanes sold respectively for $2395, $3375, $4485 and $4350. All prices were Flyaway Robertson.

According to advertising of the day, a 100 hp Kinner K5 could be substituted on the Monocoupe 125. Thus, the airplane became a Monocoupe 100. Price was listed as $3475 Flyaway Robertson.

To lend a degree of credibility, Don had several of his well-known friends lend their names in Monocoupe advertising. Peter Brooks contribution was one notable example.

Reginald Langhorne Brooks, better known by the nickname "Pete" his mother had given to him, was an avid sportsman pilot, an accomplished stunt pilot, a collector of aerobatic trophies, president of the exclusive Aviation Country Club in Hicksville, Long Island, New York, and a nephew of Lady Astor. In

The Monocoupe
Program for 1932

WE BELIEVE THE PRIMARY purpose of an airplane is to render fast, economical transportation with the utmost comfort. We will adhere to designs which discriminate between merely airport use and highly efficient cross-country utility.

PRICES:
$2395 to $8500.

TOP SPEEDS:
115 miles per hour up to—well, maybe 200 miles per hour.

ENGINES:
Velie M5; Lambert 90 h. p.; Warner 110 h.p.; Kinner 100 h.p.; 125 h. p.; 150 h. p.; and Wright Whirlwind J6-5 225 h. p.

TIME PAYMENTS:
We hope to offer a conservative and sensible plan for deferred payments eliminating the excessive carrying charges.

AGENCIES:
The present Monocoupe dealer and service stations are now augmented by Curtiss-Wright Flying Service.

MONOCOUPE CORPORATION
Lambert, Field
ROBERTSON, MO.

AERO DIGEST, APRIL 1932

Peter Brooks — ELEANORE LUSCOMBE SHURTZ COLLECTION

addition, he was a Monocoupe owner. Somewhat eccentric and always a practical joker, Brooks was one of Don's closest friends and keenest financial backers.

Brooks was regarded as "nuts" or "crazy" by friends and associates, but in a friendly way. Brooks was involved in a serious airplane accident and suffered a fractured skull as a result of hitting a telephone pole while rolling upright from an inverted approach to a landing. A steel plate was inserted in his head. As a result of this unfortunate accident, Brooks' personality changed slightly, but he kept his keen sense of humor for a good practical joke.

Brooks had purchased a Monocoupe 110 from Don earlier and "sang the praises" regarding this aircraft's exemplary and sprightly flying characteristics. Incidentally, Brooks flew a thrilling acrobatic demonstration in his Monocoupe 110 (NC12345) at the 1931 National Air Races at Cleveland and won the acclaim of attending pilots and spectators.

Peter Brooks' Monocoupe 110. Brooks flew a thrilling aerobatic demonstration at the 1931 NAR in this airplane. — ELEANORE LUSCOMBE SHURTZ COLLECTION

In the letter Don used in his advertising, Brooks wrote: *"I have never in five years of flying enjoyed a ship which has so perfectly convinced me that flying from a private ownership point of view is thoroughly practical, highly original and economical to a point where owners of higher priced automobiles can buy a Ford and own a Monocoupe and enjoy the privileges of flying without giving up their homes, divorcing their wives and drowning their children to afford the cost."*

Yet, for all the positive acclaim and advertising, Don Luscombe and Monocoupe Corporation did stumble, although very rarely. The Monocoupe 70-V, awarded ATC #492 on September 1, 1932, stood-out as an oddball in the almost legendary lineup of Monocoupe airplanes and the traditional performance, maneuverability and value they conveyed. Sporting the Velie M-5 power plant and identical in structure to the Monocoupe 90, the Monocoupe 70-V was presented as an alternative to those buyers seeking a low-priced airplane.

Though economically priced, the Monocoupe 70 was recognized for what it was — a corporate ploy to rid itself of surplus Velie M-5 engines rather than an honest effort to offer the flying public something new. As best can be determined, only one Monocoupe 70-V was ever built and delivered.

Without a doubt, the company went "backwards" with this particular design as performance and value were traded for basic economy. Yet, disregarding any underlying corporate strategy or cash infusions, the company was still in dire financial straights and any potential sale was better than no sale at all.

While Don Luscombe and the Monocoupe Corporation struggled to sell their products, Curtiss-Wright Flying Service had aggressively developed its distributorship program to the point it could announce proudly it was the "national distributor for the Monocoupe." A full page ad carried in the February 1932 issue of *Aero Digest* proclaimed this development. According to this ad, almost thirty fixed base operators throughout the United States held Curtiss-Wright Flying Service dealerships. Similarly, Curtiss-Wright Flying Service held the exclusive distributorships for Travel Air, Cessna, Curtiss-Robertson, the deHavilland Moth and other Curtiss-Wright products.

Despite this intense if not intrusive competition, a perennial ray of hope continued to shine upon Don Luscombe and the Monocoupe Corporation. The 1932 racing season proved equally if not more impressive than the previous year. Once more, Johnny Livingston's Monocoupe took center stage in many races during 1932. Though he placed second, behind Steve Whitman, in the Miami Races' 500 cu. in. race, Livingston was keen to win more races and made plans to further modify his gaily painted Coupe.

In May 1932, Livingston took his Coupe to Lambert Field, St. Louis, to effect several key modifi-

The Monocoupe 70-V, of which only one was built, traded performance for economy. JAMES B. ZAZAS COLLECTION

cations. These modifications eventually resulted in his Monocoupe, originally certified under ATC # 327, being recertified in the Group 2 Approval category as #2-452. To many, his ship became known as the "Livingston Special."[21]

When Livingston arrived at the mid-May 1932 Omaha Races, his Monocoupe featured a "clipped-wing" design of his own. Though Livingston designed these wings, the Monocoupe factory built them new and did not use old wings simply "clipped." Livingston referred to his creation as a "Short-wing Monocoupe."

Livingston's first true test his new wing occurred at these races. He was not disappointed! Livingston and the Coupe took six first place finishes, two thirds and one fourth. But, Livingston was still not satisfied.

In early August 1932, Livingston returned to Detroit to install a 145 hp, Warner 145 "Super Scarab" engine. Concurrently, he formed and fitted a new, bumped cowl that reduced the frontal area and faired further rearward than the original cowl. Johnny Livingston believed he and his Coupe, complete with midget wheels, pants, special fairings and other key airframe modifications, were now ready for the Cleveland National Air Races.

The 1932 National Air Races at Cleveland saw more Monocoupes entered than in any National Air Races previously. Some twenty-seven Monocoupe pilots registered and, in turn, won twenty-eight places in the money! Spunky Florence Klingensmith won the most money with Johnny Livingston second and Art Carnahan third on the list.

Johnny Livingston entered several of the faster races and, in turn, had to face faster competition. He won the Cincinnati Trophy race, finished third in two events and garnered a respectable fourth place in the competitive pylon events.

Although Livingston's Coupe could easily surpass 200 mph, often trading wins with other fiercely competitive pilots, a somewhat somber Livingston and Don Luscombe realized the racing days of the Monocoupe were numbered. The Monocoupe's winning streak had reached its pinnacle. The competition was getting faster.

Livingston enjoyed several more victories during the balance of 1932 and early 1933 before he sold his "Livingston Special" to Jack Wright of Utica, New York, less than a year later. In turn, Wright enjoyed several air race victories in this highly-modified "Coupe."

The Monocoupe wins and Luscombe's marketing strategies continued to net sales. Orders for new airplanes trickled into the company which kept the Monocoupe employees employed, though actual production averaged less than three airplanes per month. Less than thirty-five Monocoupe airplanes were delivered in 1932.

As the corporation entered 1933, only three basic Monocoupe models were offered — the Monocoupe 90, the Monocoupe 110 and the Monocoupe 125. Prices, Flyaway Robertson, were $3375, $4750 and $4500 respectively. Optional equipment and prices on all models included wheel pants ($150), Townend Ring ($45), Goodyear "Airwheel" tires ($25), chrome plated controls and collector ring ($30), left hand throttle in addition to center ($20) and tail skid wheel ($15). In addition, Lambert R-266 engine repair kits were offered for $100. Don could reflect Monocoupe airplanes had been sold to happy customers throughout the United States, Europe, South America, Africa and Australia. He hoped such interest would continue.

Meanwhile, Fred Knack had become disgruntled

by the Model D's slow development pace and soon left the corporation in early 1933 for a position at the General Aviation Corporation in Dundalk, Maryland. However, Fred Knack's and Don Luscombe's paths would continue to cross as each required the other to solve a respective engineering problem or design endeavor.[22]

Filling Knack's position was Ivan H. Driggs, an aeronautical engineer of impeccable, if not enviable, engineering experience and background. Due to his many and dedicated engineering efforts in light aircraft aviation, Driggs has been called by many the "Father of the Lightplane."

Driggs was born on April 8, 1894, and grew-up in Lansing, Michigan, where he attended various schools. He entered Michigan State College in 1912, but left in March 1914, during his sophomore year, for the opportunity to join the Burgess-Dunne Company in Marblehead, Massachusetts, where he worked as a draftsman on the U.S. Navy's Burgess-Dunne seaplane. (Incidentally, this airplane was awarded the Collier Trophy in 1915.)

He returned to his Lansing, Michigan, home where he prepared designs and layouts for the Motor Wheel Corporation for the next three years. At the same time, he continued his aeronautical engineering education with correspondence courses through the University of Chicago. On January 1, 1916, Driggs married his high school sweetheart, the former Eva Wright.

About this time, Driggs, who was twenty-two years old, built his first airplane in a barn and test flew it from a grassy meadow behind their home in Lansing. This airplane soon disappeared and later, reportedly, became a part of Pancho Villa's rag-tag air force.

Yearning to get back into aviation at the beginning of the World War I, Driggs wrote a letter to Orville Wright expressing his desires. In turn, Wright telegraphed, *"Come on!"* Driggs accepted a position at Dayton-Wright in Dayton, Ohio, which was building the first American-made deHavilland-4. His new job required him to practically make over the many drawings of the original British ship. Later war work found Driggs assigned to McCook Field, Dayton, Ohio, where he assisted Lincoln Nelson on the development of the Nelson Machine Gun Synchronizer.

After the war, Driggs worked on an enclosed cockpit monoplane for the 1920 Gordon-Bennett Races in France. Orville Wright was the Consulting Engineer and Driggs ran the numerous wind tunnel tests in collaboration with Mr. Wright. Thereafter, Driggs worked with Wright on the development of the Cabin Cruiser and the OW-1 (OW Aerial Coupe). The latter was a four passenger, enclosed cabin design and was the last plane designed by Orville Wright. Additionally, Driggs was an accomplished private pilot. Together, Driggs' engineering and flying abilities gave him an unparalleled insight in light aircraft design and development.

In 1924, financed by the Johnson Airplane and Supply Company, Driggs designed and built the DJ-1, a cabin monoplane powered by a stock Henderson motorcycle engine. This unique design, nicknamed the "Bumblebee," won all races in which it was entered and gar-

In 1933, Johnny Livingston sold his shortwing Monocoupe 110 to race pilot, Jack Wright, who, in turn, enjoyed several victories in this airplane. Shown here, NC501W was returned to the factory for further modifications. JIM HARVEY

nered the interest of many prominent aviation officials at the 1924 Dayton Air Races.

In 1925, using his own financing, Driggs started the Driggs Aircraft in Dayton, Ohio. His first effort involved modifying the DJ-1 design into the Driggs "Dart" Model 1 for the United States Army Air Corps. This small monoplane was powered by a 30 hp, 2 cylinder Wright-Morehouse engine. The Driggs Dart Model 2 followed in 1926. A very light, open cockpit two place biplane, the Dart 2 was powered a 3 cylinder, 30 hp "Anzani" engine.

Driggs next design was the Driggs "Coupe." Built in 1926, at the request of Captain Eddie Rickenbacker, this enclosed cabin airplane possessed a chummy, side-by-side seating arrangement, brakes, steerable tailwheel, folding wings and trailing edge flaps. The Coupe's power plant was a 60 hp, 5 cylinder "Air-Cat" power plant. Incidentally, the Driggs Coupe became one of the first designs to use this engine.

Capt. Eddie Rickenbacker, former McCook Field chief engineer and engine designer Glenn D. Angle and airplane designer Ivan Driggs stand before a Driggs "Coupe" powered by an early "Air-Cat" power plant. The Coupe and "Air-Cat" combination was used to showcase Rickenbacker's new engine.

DOROTHY DRIGGS BAKER

Driggs held several patents and wrote a series of early technical memorandums in 1925 and 1926. Titled "The Light Airplane," these noteworthy abstracts, published in National Advisory Committee for Aeronautics (N.A.C.A.) journals, influenced the rational design of airplanes.[23]

In the Citation nominating Driggs for the prestigious Spirit of St. Louis Medal, these papers were recognized as: *"providing the designer with the necessary tools to cover the influence of various variables on aircraft performance quickly and sufficiently accurate for immediate use on practical problems."*

In September 1927, Driggs moved his fledgling company to Lansing, Michigan, and sought outside financing. Incorporation papers were filed and the Driggs Aircraft Corporation was formed. A Board of Directors was selected, with Driggs elected as the company's vice president, chief engineer and general manager. A $100,000 stock issue was authorized.[24]

During its brief existence, the company built light biplanes primarily for the commercial and pilot training market. Emphasis was placed on safety to ensure the would-be pilot would not kill himself learning how to fly. Examples of Driggs Aircraft Corporation airplanes included the respected Driggs Dart Model 2, the Driggs Coupe and the advanced Driggs Skylark.[25]

In summary, Driggs provided the Monocoupe Corporation an engineering talent virtually unmatched by other competitive, light airplane companies. Sadly, for all the genius Driggs possessed, it was squandered on completing the Monocoupe Model D design. Regardless, Driggs persevered and endured any hardships the job presented. Life was hard and disappointing during the Depression, harder still for those poor individuals who had no jobs.

The conditions and circumstances that surrounded Driggs were heartbreaking. To escape, Driggs would immerse himself in his work, absorbed in the design challenges. When he wasn't working, he would often tinker with a radio receiver.

Ivan Driggs was a kind and considerate man, always willing to take the time to explain a design detail to others. One who listened intently to Driggs' explanations was a young and eager draftsman named Ben Melcher. By way of background, Ben Melcher was born in Mount Vernon, Missouri, on December 26, 1909, and was raised in the "Show Me State." The son of a school teacher, Melcher and his family moved many times, including a two year stint in Colorado. Eventually, the family returned to Missouri and settled in Websters Grove, a small town not far from St. Louis, where Melcher completed high school.

He continued his education at Park College in Parkville, Missouri (north of Kansas City), where he studied to be a chemical engineer. However, his plans changed somewhat suddenly and unexpectedly. While in his junior year, Melcher attended an air show in Kansas City. He was impressed by the many airplanes he saw and the creative "freedom" they

Distinguished inventor, designer and businessman Bill Lear boards his Robertson-built Monocoupe 110.

ELEANORE LUSCOMBE SHURTZ COLLECTION

offered. He decided then and there he wanted to be an aeronautical engineer. Furthermore, he decided he wanted to learn how to fly. Melcher convinced his parents to let him quit school and learn how to fly, which he did.

Shortly after he completed his flight training, Melcher got a job working for the Curtiss-Wright Aircraft Company in St. Louis as a draftsman. During this time, he attended night school at Washington University where he took several aeronautical engineering courses, but never completed the requirements for his degree.

The Curtiss-Wright job consisted of doing layouts on the "Kingbird," a new twin-engine transport being designed and built for either American or Eastern Air Lines. However, Melcher was laid off eventually requiring him to seek another job.

Melcher enjoyed engineering and drafting, but these jobs were quite scarce. Fortunately, Driggs needed a qualified draftsman and prevailed upon Luscombe to find one. Melcher met with Driggs and Luscombe, and was soon hired.

Melcher's first day on the job revealed much about Don Luscombe's generally easy-going personality and management style. A brief meeting between the two gentlemen set the stage for a professional, if not personal, relationship that would last the balance of their lives.

The engineering department at the St. Louis factory was on an upper floor, a short flight of stairs from Don's ground floor office. Driggs was away on a trip during Melcher's first day at work and was unavailable to answer Melcher's questions about company policy. So, Melcher decided to ask the boss instead.

About noon time, Melcher went downstairs, noticed the door was open to Luscombe's office, stuck his head in and asked, *"How long a lunch hour do we have?"*

Luscombe gazed towards Melcher and responded in a authoritative tone of voice, *"Come in here for a minute."* He looked the new engineer squarely in the eyes and asked, *"Do you know what your job is around here?"*

Melcher replied, *"Yes, I think so."*

Luscombe continued, *"Well, I don't care if you take half an hour or an hour-and-a-half for lunch, or you can take the afternoon off and play golf if you want to. Just as long as you get your work done!"* Melcher realized then his new boss was firm, yet fair. And, he recognized Luscombe's desire to "get the job done," regardless of the obstacles. He went to lunch with a new found admiration for Don Luscombe.

Under Driggs' leadership and Melcher's careful drafting, a second Model D prototype evolved and was completed during the summer of 1933. This airplane was powered by a Warner 145 hp "Super Scarab" radial engine and featured a revised vertical tail. By September, the tail group was revised once again, its graceful design suggestive of Driggs' earlier work. Certification problems kept the company from realizing any near-term production goals beyond the flying prototypes.

Don flew this prototype throughout the Eastern United States to solicit orders. Yet customers would have to wait almost a year before delivery. In early October 1933, Phil De Cameron Ball died from a heart attack leaving the Model D certification program, if not the entire Monocoupe Corporation's future, in serious jeopardy.[26]

Don and his employees were stunned by Ball's passing. Once more, Don tried to calm his employees' fears about the corporation's future. But a usually sanguine Don began to harbor his own fears about future employment.

Moreover, Don's fervor promoting Monocoupe

Corporation airplanes and his constant traveling had extracted another, more personal toll. Differences with his wife, Eleanore, regarding household income versus buying-on-credit and issues concerning little Jimmy's care served only to exacerbate their differences. During the spring of 1933, Don and Eleanore Luscombe separated and eventually divorced. However, they maintained close contact throughout the ensuing years.

Don was not an uncaring father. During the summer of 1933, little Jimmy stayed with Don's parents in Iowa City. Don, anxious to spend the Fourth of July holiday with his only son, flew to Iowa City in a Monocoupe. Don announced his arrival with a low pass over the family home.

Upon landing, Don told his eight-year-old son this Fourth of July would be special. Thereupon, Don proceeded to purchase every firecracker and firework he could find in Iowa City. That night, little Jimmy Luscombe and his five-year-old cousin, Betty, were treated to the most incredible fireworks display ever seen around Iowa City.

Over a period of time, Don Luscombe had met a new lady, Ora May "Brownee" Wellington. Petite in figure, her dark brown eyes burned with a desire to learn how to fly and explore the world. The nickname, Brownee, was given to her by her mother when she was a youngster.

Don and Brownee met, originally, on a train to Kansas City in late 1928. Barely twenty-two years old at the time, Brownee was traveling from her San Diego, California, home to stay with her aunt and uncle in Kansas City, Missouri. She was extremely interested in aviation and, ironically, her parents were sending her there to *"get away from airplanes."* As Brownee boarded the train with her banjo-ukulele, she was given a stern warning from her father to guard her pocketbook and *not* to talk to strangers.[27]

Enroute, the train stopped in Olathe, Kansas. Brownee disembarked and promptly proceeded to get into a foot race with several other teenagers who were on the same train. Running alongside the train, she ran headlong into a dark-haired stranger with the most magical grey eyes. Both Brownee and the stranger tumbled to the ground.

The stranger picked Brownee up and asked if she was all right. Very embarrassed, she hopped quickly back on the train. However, she was smitten by the overall good looks of the stranger. She hoped he would be on the train to Kansas City.

ELEANORE LUSCOMBE SHURTZ COLLECTION

The second prototype Monocoupe Model "D" with revised tail and sporting a Warner 145 engine. The "D" model Monocoupe had a cockpit six inches wider than the the Monocoupe 90/110 from which it was derived.

As luck would have it, he was. He came to the observation car where Brownee was sitting with her train friends. In this case, there were about twenty military academy cadets headed home for the holidays. Being close to Christmas, everybody was singing Christmas carols with Brownee strumming out the chords on her small banjo uke. The more Brownee played, the more the stranger became interested in her banjo and the India ink drawing of an airplane upon it. The drawing depicted a Velie Monocoupe.

The stranger asked Brownee why she had an airplane drawn on the banjo. Brownee replied she had flown an airplane like it in San Diego. Then, without pausing, she proceeded to tell the stranger how to fly. She had read a small booklet recently that described in great detail how to fly and she recited in great detail the book's contents. Brownee had all but memorized the booklet. The stranger displayed great interest in what Brownee had to say. Brownee sensed this interest and continued with more excitement about flying and how to fly.

As the train approached the Kansas City terminal, the stranger introduced himself as Don Luscombe. He stated he had been forced to land near Olathe, Kansas, due to weather. Furthermore, he revealed he had written the book, *Simplified Flying,* to which Brownee was referring. Extremely embarrassed, Brownee became quite angry at the gentleman for not revealing his true identity earlier. Though Luscombe continued to St. Louis, he called Brownee on several occasions when he was in Kansas City. A quiet courtship soon developed.

ONLY THE TEST OF TIME BRINGS OUT THESE FACTS

"90"
Lambert R-266 Engine
Fly-away Field, Moline
$3,375.00

"110"
Warner 7-cyl. Engine
Fly-away Field, Moline
$4,750.00

"125"
Kinner B-5 Engine
Fly-away Field, Moline
$4,750.00

•

See it at
THE DETROIT SHOW

MONOCOUPE for 1931 Is the Year's Outstanding Development

More pilots have won prize money for speed and efficiency with MONOCOUPES than any other airplane.

More MONOCOUPES are flown by strictly private owners and amateur pilots than any other two place plane.

MONOCOUPES offer more features of comfort, high performance combined with economical maintenance than are found in any other airplane at any price.

Although MONOCOUPE imitators have failed to equal MONOCOUPE performance the important trend in modern design is indicated by this imitation.

More MONOCOUPES have been sold in 1931 to date than in the same period of any other previous year. The financial backing of the MONOCOUPE has never been greater at any time nor its dealer organization stronger.

The Monocoupe
Registered Trade Mark

MONO AIRCRAFT CORPORATION
MOLINE, ILLINOIS, U.S.A.

*"Therefore doth heaven divide
The state of man in diverse functions,
Setting endeavor in continual motion;
To which is fixed, as an aim or butt,
Obedience: for so work the honeybees,
Creatures that by a rule in nature teach
The act of order to a peopled kingdom."*
William Shakespeare (1564 - 1616)
Henry the Fifth [1598 - 1600],
Act I, Scene ii, Line 183

Chapter Seven

Metal, Mass Production and Kansas City

Luscombe Phantom 272Y.   ELEANORE LUSCOMBE SHURTZ COLLECTION

The waning months of 1933 signaled an end to a bleak year for Luscombe and the chance for a new beginning. The Monocoupe Corporation was being devastated by the Depression and was beset with corporate problems. Sales were poor and Phillip De Cameron Ball's death left employees bewildered and wondering about their future livelihood. Similarly, Don Luscombe perceived any future with the Monocoupe organization would not be promising. Phil De Cameron Ball's assets were to be liquidated upon his passing. Plans were entertained to sell the tooling and dies individually, but in the end, Ball's airplane concerns were to be sold intact.

Don was especially upset by Ball's passing. Ball was Don's closest mentor, a guardian angel for many of Luscombe's endeavors. According to former associates, Don often spoke of Ball in an almost reverent tone of voice. Now, as Ball's holdings faced liquidation, Don wanted to leave. He needed to get out. If he was to make his *own* mark in aviation, his move had to be now or never.

Don Luscombe took a long, hard look at the market and the needs of the private owner and reasoned the days were numbered for personal airplanes made by a wood, nails and glue process. Being basically a handmade product, the Monocoupe was labor intensive and was not well adapted to the use of production machinery. Therefore, it did not lend itself to mass production. By their very nature, wood/ tubing/fabric aircraft were specialized products and required qualified craftsmen to produce them.

A better idea had to be found to build a durable, sturdy, reasonably priced airplane without incurring major increases in production and labor costs. Additionally, this new airplane had to offer the customer value and utility without being costly to operate.

Once more, Luscombe's uncanny marketing instincts guided him to build an airplane of an all-metal, monocoque construction. He believed this construction method would lend itself to be mass produced, utilizing die cut and stamped parts that were interchangeable. Thus, mechanics with minimal experience could assemble the aircraft in minimum time.

Don realized the initial costs for purchasing and installing the necessary machinery would be high and, in turn, would create a somewhat expensive product initially. However, the per unit costs would decrease as more units were produced. Whether Don Luscombe's all-metal aircraft notions evolved solely from a personal inspiration, a culmination of observations from various sources or as a promotional "gimmick" to increase personal airplane sales cannot be said for certain. What can be said for certain is Don was intrigued by some metal airplane work by A.K. Longren taking place at Kansas City's Municipal Airport and, in particular, in the old Butler Blackhawk airplane plant.

Mr. Longren, an aeronautical genius who was well known in aviation circles for his many innovative airplane design endeavors, particularly in the Kansas City area, was experimenting with a metal monocoque construction method which involved a "stretch-press" process.

The Longren stretch-press process was a simple, yet ingenious manufacturing operation. Metal parts were made by "stretching" metal sheets over maple wood forms, molds that often weighed in the excess of two hundred pounds. The metal was held in place by clamps or "holding jaws." A hydraulic press would "push" these wood forms upwards into the metal. The major shortcoming of this endeavor was more metal sheets were lost in this process than were formed successfully.

Ultimately, Longren ran out of money trying to perfect and advance this technique, but not before producing an all-metal biplane that featured a full monocoque fuselage with compound curves and minimal internal structure.[28] Despite any shortcomings, Don believed Longren's stretch-press was a possible solution to his all-metal airplane production vision. He leased the equipment and, shortly thereafter, leased one of the two buildings that comprised the Butler Blackhawk Airplane facilities and soon moved into the space vacated by Longren. The Butler Blackhawk facilities were leased for $75.00 per month. Luscombe's initial capitalization for the entire endeavor was $100,000.

The Butler Blackhawk Plant at Kansas City, circa 1933. This equipped aircraft factory on the Kansas City Airport was rented for $75.00 per month. ELEANORE LUSCOMBE SHURTZ COLLECTION

Thus, during October 1933, a new airplane company joined the scene, the D.A. Luscombe Airplane Company, Manufacturer of Airplanes. However, the name was changed later to the Luscombe Airplane Company, a proprietorship.[29]

The facilities themselves were not impressive, but they were very functional. The plant faced east and consisted of two main buildings, each about forty feet wide and one hundred fifty feet long. The building Don leased had the engineering department near the front, adjacent to the administrative offices, while the punch presses, band saw and heavy machinery were located farther back. Outside, a dirt road passed these buildings. A railroad track adjacent to the airport offered the possibility to have parts and equipment shipped by rail, if necessary. Interestingly, the building Don leased did *not* contain the Longren presses.

Behind these buildings were two large hangars, about fifty feet to a side. Both were open in front. Luscombe intended to use one of these hangars to assemble his new airplane. The other hangar was occupied by a previous tenant.

Initially, Don took a suite of rooms on the second floor of the President Hotel in Kansas City which became, more or less, his office. A great deal of his early work to raise money and promote his fledgling company was done by Don from these quarters.

To save expensive labor and overhead costs, Don restricted his new company's activities to the assembling of airplane parts manufactured by companies that specialized in their manufacture. In turn, these parts would be shipped to Don's company to be heat-treated, finished and installed.

Starting a company is one major headache, but staffing a new company is quite another. For his vision to develop and mature, Don needed bright, intuitive and qualified people to design and build his airplanes. Furthermore, Don needed money to fulfill his latest vision. His task was made more difficult by the ravages of the Depression and the money scarcity it created. Fortunately, he had a lot of friends, associates and contacts in "well-heeled" circles willing to support his aviation endeavors. These relationships had developed during Don's Monocoupe airplane days.

One of the first individuals hired was Ivan Driggs. In fact, Driggs joined Luscombe in his departure from Monocoupe Corporation in October, 1933. Almost immediately Don instructed Driggs to design an all-metal, two place monoplane. Following Driggs to Kansas City was Ben Melcher. He had worked extensively with Driggs for almost a year at Monocoupe on the D-145 design and certification. [30]

Lyle L. Farver joined this embryonic team on November 1, 1933. Farver was a close friend and engineering associate of Driggs. Their professional and social relationship dated from mid-1928 when the two worked together at the Driggs Aircraft Corporation in Lansing, Michigan.

Lyle Farver was born in Columbia Corners, Michigan, on May 8, 1905. He attended school there until eighth grade, then attended Unionville High School nearby. His class consisted of fourteen students. After graduating from high school, Farver enrolled in Michigan Agriculture College in Lansing, Michigan. However, before he enrolled, he got a job working as a sub-station operator at the Municipal Power Plant. The work was grueling for Farver — his eight hour shifts were staggered throughout the week and made it hard for him to attend class and study. Farver did not complete school and got a job at the Reo Motor Car Company in the Apprentice Department to pay his bills and learn more about engineering.

Farver met Driggs during his freshman year in college. He had an idea for a 4-cylinder cam engine and needed a qualified engineer to evaluate his idea. Driggs Aircraft Corporation was nearby. Thus, Farver sought Ivan Driggs for his expertise and advice.

From the meetings that followed, Farver was offered the opportunity to do stress analysis for Driggs. On July 20, 1928, this opportunity became a full-time job. Thus, a close, professional relationship started and flourished.[31]

At least four other individuals joined the new organization — "Pops" Stroeble, Edward Nemechek, Anthony Bevelo and Ross Funk. Stroeble, a capable mechanic, was hired as a machinist and the plant caretaker. Uniquely, he was the plant caretaker when A.K. Longren occupied the facilities. Prior to his employment with Longren, Stroeble worked for the Cessna Aircraft Company in Wichita, Kansas.

Additionally, Stroeble understood the Longren process and how to work metal over maple wood end forms. He had been involved in building the dies used in creating Longren's airplane. As Don Luscombe's new two-place airplane developed, Stroeble was placed in charge of all jigs, dies and fixtures.

Stroeble slept at night in the portion of the plant that housed the Longren presses. He awoke often to check all was well. He and his wife had a small room to themselves near the administrative offices. With affordable housing scarce (by Depression standards), this on-site watchman arrangement worked well for both Stroeble and Luscombe.

Edward Nemechek, on the other hand, was hired to be the shop foreman in charge of production. A somewhat slender individual, he was a very capable and qualified machinist. Anthony Bevelo was very good with dope and fabric and was hired to do the majority of the wing work. Italian by birth and some-

CHARLES E. BURGESS

"Pops" Stroeble peers from door at the Butler Blackhawk Plant. Besides being an accomplished mechanic, Stroeble understood how to work and form metal using the Longren press.

what heavy in stature, Bevelo was very friendly to all who worked with him.

Rounding out the basic staff was Ross Funk. Funk came to work for Luscombe as an accomplished mechanic with considerable experience with LeBlond Aircraft Engine Corporation radial engines.

By way of background, Funk's aviation interest began after reading an article about the Heath Parasol in *Popular Mechanics*. He bought a set of plans and began building a Heath. Soon, Ross found himself working for R.K. LeBlond in Cincinnati, Ohio. In his free time, he studied aeronautical engineering at the nearby University of Cincinnati. He took flying lessons at Lunken Airport in an OX-5 International biplane.

When the stock market went belly-up in 1929, Funk returned to the family farm near Kansas City. A few years later, Ross and his new bride, Naomi, lived with Stroeble briefly in the Butler plant. Funk was introduced to Longren and his stretch-press process, eventually working with Stroeble and Longren until hired by Don Luscombe.

utilize his scant financial resources in the most prudent manner. Building a new design required tremendous financial backing from many sources.

Peter and Aline Brooks were a couple of individuals Don sought initially for help. Pete offered money where he could, but his wife, Aline, probably invested the most funds. Aline Brooks was accomplished in her own right. She was the first woman to fly from New York to Mexico City and return in a stock Monocoupe 90. When she and Pete married on May 25, 1933, they flew separate Monocoupes on their 17,500 mile honeymoon adventure.

Aline was very wealthy, also. Her father owned the Bamberger Department Stores of Newark, New Jersey. Aline invested heavily in Don Luscombe's airplane endeavors. Reportedly, she was a "silent partner" in his Kansas City operation. Unlike her playful husband, Aline Brooks was a serious lady and an accomplished artist. Her handiwork can be seen today in New York's La Guardia Airport Marine/Air Terminal.

Other individuals who listened to Luscombe's convincing pleas and conveyed their financial support included: banker Charles "Bunnie" Hinsch of Cincinnati, Ohio; Colonel Clarence Young, formerly Assistant Secretary of Commerce for Air Commerce, residing in New York City; Roger Wolf Kahn, a well-known orchestra leader from New York City; Donald D. Cooke of New York City; George Wales Hard of New York City, heir to the Singer Sewing Machine empire; George A. Thorne of New York City; Malcolm McAlpin of Morristown, New Jersey; William Barclay Harding of Red Bank, New Jersey; Tom Colby, Aviation Division Manager of the prosperous Berry Brothers Paint Company; and Carl B. Haun of Blackwell, Oklahoma, an oil man. A host of other established financial supporters and backers could be tallied on Luscombe's side. Most of these individuals owned or had owned a Monocoupe.

Brownee Wellington fulfilled the necessary initial secretarial duties for Don's growing Kansas City operation. LYLE FARVER

Joining Don in the main offices was none other than "Brownee" Wellington. Brownee fulfilled the necessary secretarial duties. From this basic staff, Don Luscombe set out to build his new airplane. Others would be hired in due course, but Don had to

Don could embrace many other aviation notables, as well. Included were Jimmy Doolittle, Eddie Rickenbacker, Clare Bunch, Ben O. Howard, Harold Neumann, Earl Ortman, Steve Wittman and Roscoe Turner to name but a few.

Sadly, as a reflection of his "promote-it-to-the-hilt" personality, Don often embraced these friendships, not for friendships in true spirit of "friendship," but for the marketing, financial and promotional value they held. All too often, as Don alienated one set of friends, he cultivated another set.

Regardless of the financial backing available, or what appeared on the surface to be available, life was very difficult for the Luscombe Airplane Company staff. The engineers were paid $25 to $35 dollars a week and the balance of the staff took home barely two-thirds that amount.

On rare occasions, they were not paid at all and, instead, were handed I.O.U.s. These I.O.U.s were paid in full as soon as Luscombe was able to do so. (It was not until *after* his move to West Trenton, New Jersey, that Luscombe was unable to meet payroll on a regular basis.)

The housing situation was a concern for many. Several employees, such as Brownee Wellington, were fortunate to have parents or relatives who lived in the area where they could stay. Other more fortunate individuals had their own homes. However, some employees had to sleep in the plant or make alternative arrangements. Times were tough and jobs were scarce, but the employees had a roof over their heads.

Development of Don's new airplane started almost as soon as Driggs, Melcher and Farver had a table on which to work. Fresh from his work on the D-145 project, Driggs envisioned an aircraft with similar lines. However, this new airplane was not to be a redesigned or "metalized" version of the D-145 Monocoupe.

Melcher assisted with the many drawings while Farver undertook the very important stress analyses. The landing gear stress analysis was done by a local engineer with considerable experience. Driggs selected a NACA 2412 airfoil for the wing. Quick to stall at low speeds, ideal for landing, the NACA 2412 exhibited low drag characteristics at higher speeds, thus, optimizing the design's overall performance range.

By the end of 1933, Driggs and his small staff had completed a preliminary set of drawings. From

Ivan Driggs at Kansas City, circa August 1934. DOROTHY DRIGGS BAKER

these drawings, Nemechek and Stroeble built the wood forms and jigs necessary to start construction of the new airplane.

Though the Longren equipment was available, it was never used to make any parts. True, Don had leased this process with the intention of using it to make parts for his airplanes, but Driggs, Farver, Melcher, Nemechek and Stroeble decided against using it. The equipment could not make the various skins to the correct tolerances needed. They generally agreed, however, if several airplanes were to be built, the Longren process had merit for producing less critical or precise pieces.

Furthermore, Don could not afford to absorb any associated material loss costs incurred during production, e.g. misshaped or deformed parts, torn skins, etc. Hence, he decided to forgo any further effort towards using the Longren press.

JAMES B. ZAZAS COLLECTION
Ben Melcher

92 Visions of Luscombe: The Early Years

ELEANORE LUSCOMBE SHURTZ COLLECTION

ELEANORE LUSCOMBE SHURTZ COLLECTION

(Above) No wood was used in the wing-ribs. All ribs were stamped from duraluminum giving increased strength and longer life with a cost saving in manufacture.

(Upper Left) The prototype's rudder petals were also stampings. A provision was made for operating brakes without taking feet off the rudder petals or to lose the advantage of the extra leverage the heel affords as compared to that of the toe.

(Left) Rear bulkhead was also made from a duraluminum stamping and could be fabricated in less than five minutes. Such stampings assured absolute uniformity in the fuselage shape, thereby contributing to the correct fit of the other parts.

ELEANORE LUSCOMBE SHURTZ COLLECTION

(Left) The prototype Phantom fuselage was assembled in a rotating, wood jig. Notice the fuselage form in the background used to assure proper fit before assembly.

ELEANORE LUSCOMBE SHURTZ COLLECTION

(Right) The prototype Phantom's fuselage takes shape. Each section was slightly crowned to give rigidity and stiffness.

ELEANORE LUSCOMBE SHURTZ COLLECTION

Chapter Seven: Metal, Mass Production and Kansas City 93

Work continues on the Phantom fuselage. The tail fin section is being attached in this photograph.

Luscombe Phantom 272Y (s/n 1) rests in its wooden jig. Note the rivet detail around the door frame.

Interior shot of Luscombe Phantom 272Y (s/n 1) under construction. Note the contour of the metal seats. Circa February 1934.

(Left) The prototype Luscombe Phantom (s/n 1) rests on its landing gear. Note that this airplane did not possess side straps and wires to brace the gear.

ELEANORE LUSCOMBE SHURTZ COLLECTION

(Right) A top view of the robust Luscombe Phantom wing.

CHARLES E. BURGESS

Obviously, it was disappointing to all — especially Luscombe — the new airplane would have to be built by hand, a labor intensive, costly and time-consuming process. Don acknowledged his "mass production" ideas would have to wait a while longer until the proper equipment and talent could be found.

Step-by-step, piece-by-piece, the new airplane came together. Building the wing structure was a relatively straightforward process, but constructing the fuselage proved to be a very tedious, time-consuming endeavor.

To form the fuselage skins, a wood mock-up (complete with bulkheads and stringers) was made and served only as a guide as to the correct shape and contour. As the various skins were hammered out, they were laid upon this mock-up to ensure correct conformity prior to any riveting.

To facilitate the actual construction, the new airplane's fuselage was made of top and bottom skins joined along the sides of the fuselage by a one inch duraluminum splice strip. Hardwood jigs were made to build this fuselage, but they proved difficult in actual use for several reasons.

First, this jig was designed to hold the bulkheads at their proper station while the contoured skins were laid upon the assembly, trimmed and filed to size, and the rivet holes drilled. Then, the skins were lifted from the jig to remove the burrs and metal chips caused by the drilling before returning the skins to their proper position on the jig. Parker-Kalon sheet metal screws, frequently called "P-Ks," were then used to secure the skins ("Clecos" did not exist then) to the bulkheads and to each other while they were riveted.

Second, a central rod or axle ran the length of the fuselage jig that allowed the entire fuselage to be rotated to make the bottom accessible for riveting. Because of this axle's position, little room was afforded the individual given the task to crawling inside the fuselage to buck the rivets.

Finally, as the .065 inch dural sheet skins were riveted, various pieces of the jig had to be disassembled and removed by hand through the forward portion of the fuselage. This procedure added another time-consuming step.

Before driving, these rivets had to be heat-treated. When the fuselage sections were ready to be riveted, Stroeble would heat the rivets to 950 degrees Fahrenheit and quench them in cold water. Then, the rivets had to be driven within the first half hour after heating, or they would become too hard and brittle to drive. (A year or so later, a new rivet material was developed by the Aluminum Company of America [ALCOA] so rivets could be driven "as purchased" and became stronger as they were worked).

The Aluminum Company of America of Pittsburgh, Pennsylvania, was contracted to fabricate the airplane wing's front and rear spar I-beam extrusions. On paper, these extrusions appeared simple to make, but proved difficult to meet the required tolerances and strength in actual construction.

These fabrication problems were soon surmounted and the first airplane took shape during February and March of 1934. Don was encouraged by the progress and applied to the Department of Commerce, Aeronautics Branch, for an identification mark assignment. As the fuselage and wing sections were completed, they were moved into one of the two hangars adjacent to the plant.

All control surfaces were made of tubular steel and were fabric covered. Noteworthy, the horizontal stabilizer was made from tubular steel, also, but was covered in sheet duraluminum.

During March, April and May, other employees were added to the Luscombe Aircraft Company employee roster. Keith Funk, Ross Funk's younger brother, was hired. He was followed soon afterwards by Alfred "Fritz" King.

King, who had met Luscombe during earlier Monocoupe days, was hired as a mechanic. Additionally, he kept his airplane — an American Eagle — at the Kansas City Municipal Airport in the hangar adjacent to Don's leased hangar. Prior to his employment, King had many opportunities to witness the work taking place a few hundred feet away from his hangar and thought about looking for a job.

Sometimes, getting hired with Don Luscombe was being present with a needed skill at the right time. When King actually asked for a job, Don inquired, *"Do you know how to splice cable?"* King replied he did.

"You're hired!" Luscombe responded enthusiastically.

Keith Funk, on the other hand, had little aviation experience, but was keenly interested in airplanes. Finance and accounting were his strengths. Don put Keith in charge of the company's stockroom and tool crib.

Perhaps the most prominent individual to join the employee roster during this time was Nick Nordyke. Dutch by birth and a metalsmith by trade, Nordyke was working in Kansas City as a welder and metalsmith at the Libby Welding Company when Don asked him to join his airplane company.

Additionally, Nordyke had done work for many of the local area automobile repair shops. Respected and well-known for his metal repair work, it was his power-hammer work that set Nordyke head-and-shoulders above his peers. Nordyke could take a sheet of steel or aluminum and create on a power-hammer whatever shape was needed.

Luscombe soon learned of Nordyke's incomparable ability, sought him out and offered him a job. He accepted. In the final analysis, it was Nordyke's exper-

>Have you written for the advance dope on the new Luscombe metal plane which will change all standards for airplane comparisons?
>
>**LUSCOMBE AIRCRAFT CO.**
>**KANSAS CITY, MO.**

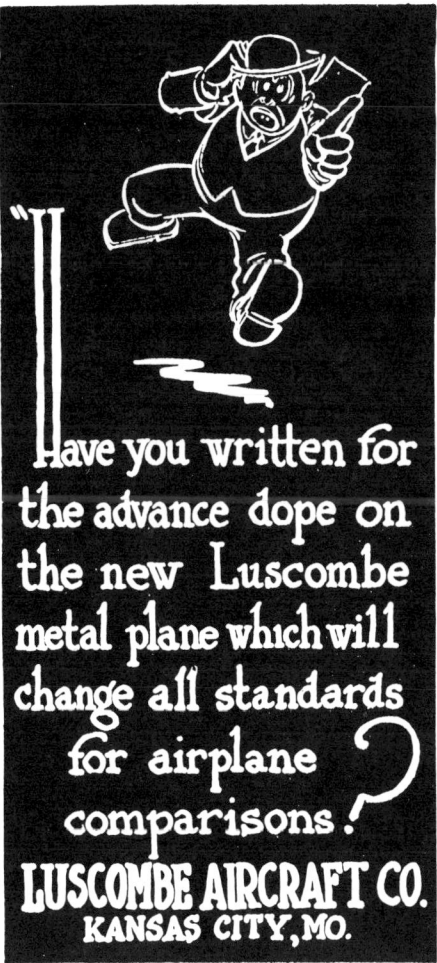

AERO DIGEST, MARCH 1934

The prototype is rolled out.   JOHN UNDERWOOD

96 Visions of Luscombe: The Early Years

Anxious to get some publicity photographs, Don Luscombe has the prototype Phantom moved to a grassy area and its tail supported to represent a flying attitude. The bumped cowling, unique to this one variant, is shown to a good advantage. Don often used picture postcards, such as this one, to describe his company's work. Here, Don tells his former wife, Eleanore, of work yet to be accomplished.

ELEANORE LUSCOMBE SHURTZ COLLECTION

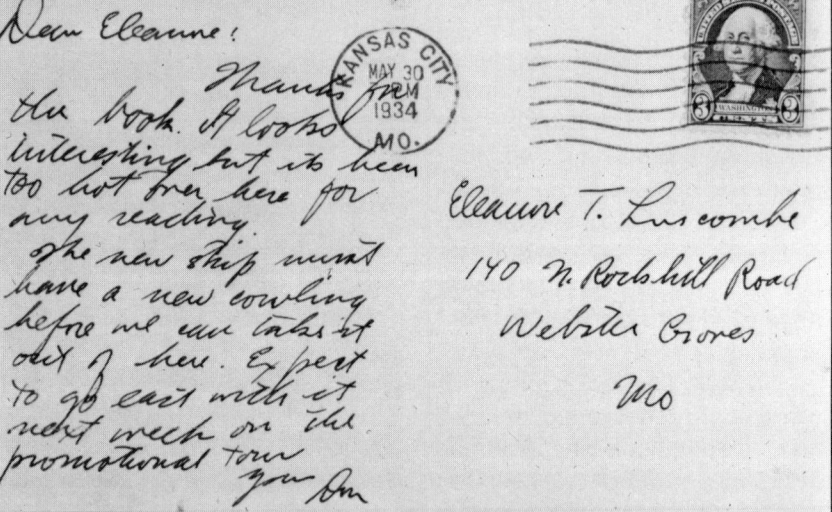

ELEANORE LUSCOMBE SHURTZ COLLECTION

tise that brought Don Luscombe's metal airplane visions to life and production feasibility.

A local area draftsman, Vernon Outman, was hired to assist the small but growing engineering department.

By late April or early May 1934, the first airplane was assembled, not for flight, but for photographs. And, it was at this time Don Luscombe came very close to losing his dream to the wind. With great expectation and little fanfare, the new airplane was rolled-out.

Don was eager to tell the world of his new airplane. He had been heralding his new design in the popular aviation periodical, *Aero Digest*, for several months, but now he needed some dramatic photographs. Taking advantage of a mild spring morning, the staff assembled the new metallic gray/green painted airplane on a grassy area not far from the hangars. Small, temporary sheet metal screws held most components together, not the required rivets, bolts and nuts.

The new airplane was placed in a tail-high, takeoff flying position, its tail supported by a flimsy tripod. Don snapped his pictures hurriedly as a breeze started to develop. Those workers who assisted Luscombe barely got the airplane disassembled and returned to the hangar before a vicious thunderstorm moved through

The Phantom fuselage was designed to withstand tremendous loads. Here, almost 19,000 lbs. of sand bags are loaded on the robust fuselage during a required Department of Commerce test. The fuselage passed without so much as a wrinkle!

ELEANORE LUSCOMBE SHURTZ COLLECTION

the area.

This new airplane was a sight to behold and represented an engineering marvel, if not a revolutionary design for a cabin monoplane. The aesthetic, streamlined fuselage was made of duraluminum monocoque construction supported by 17ST duraluminum bulkheads. This design allowed all loads to be carried through the skin and did not require any internal stringers between the frames. Furthermore, any structural repair could be completed without complete dismantling.

Don was particularly interested in having his new aircraft be sturdy, almost at the expense of practicality. Built like a heavily riveted tank of World War One, the new airplane's riveted fuselage was incredibly strong and rigid. This point was aptly demonstrated during a required Department of Commerce stress test. Almost nine *tons* of sandbags and lead shot bags were loaded on the fuselage without so much as a wrinkle!

The empennage consisted of sheet duraluminum with the moveable control surfaces made of welded steel tubing covered with doped airplane fabric. The elevator and rudder were statically balanced. Additionally, the horizontal stabilizer leading edge angle of attack could be adjusted in flight by an ingenious jackscrew trim operation.

The wings featured extruded duraluminum metal I-beam spars and die-cut, stamped dural metal ribs. The leading edge was covered in dural sheet. The entire wing framework was covered in Grade-A fabric. Narrow chord ailerons spanned more than half of each wing. Both wings were supported by a pair of streamlined vee-struts.

Electrically-driven, shot-welded, narrow chord stainless steel flaps, located about a foot inboard of the wing's trailing edge and spanning half the wing, allowed the operator to move the flaps to any desired position at virtually any speed. If electrical power was not available or if the pilot desired to avoid discharging the battery while the engine was not running, the flaps could be cranked down by hand, also. (Later Department of Commerce certification, however, restricted the use of flaps above 149 mph.) Likewise, two 16.5 gallon gravity-feed fuel tanks were installed, one in each wing.

In sum, the fuselage, tail and wing components offered a greater uniformity and strength than could be found in wood parts. Any need for wood, nails and glue was practically eliminated. Production costs were kept to a minimum since many parts were already blanked or formed by dies, then assembled at the plant.

Interestingly, the only wood incorporated into the new design was located along the center of the fuselage fairing just aft of the cockpit and inside the leading edge of the vertical fin and the horizontal stabilizer. The wood in the fairing dampened or eliminated any drumming noise that could be created by airloads or engine/airframe vibrations.

The cabin was moderately roomy, with skylights in the top and rear. Windows included on the airplane's two large, unobstructed doors added to the tremendous visibility in all side directions. Adequate ventilation was provided while keeping the occupants safe from hazardous engine fumes.

Don's newest airplane was the first light airplane to use "Plexiglas." The windshield, the small fairings adjacent the windshield and the overhead and rear windows were Plexiglas. The side windows were actual glass. [32]

The instrument panel was large and high (restricting over-the-nose visibility somewhat) and offered sufficient room to add radios or optional equipment. All flight and engine instruments were held by rubber mounts to dampen any vibrations. Dual control sticks were furnished. Finally, the seats featured coil-spring cushions and were removable to allow use of seat-type parachutes.

The semi-cantilever landing gear, perhaps the aircraft's greatest weakness, was very clean aerodynamically and had oil-draulic struts with a five-and-a-half to six inch deflection. Hayes Autofan wheels and brakes were used and featured 6:50 x 10 low pressure, twenty-one inch General "Streamline" tires.

JAMES B. ZAZAS COLLECTION
Instrument panel of the prototype Luscombe Phantom

The tail wheel assembly was an ingenious design that used both a leaf spring, attached to a yoke supporting a small hard rubber tire and, for additional shock absorption, a stack of vertically mounted rubber disks carried inside the fuselage. This design was light, offered low drag and was very cost effective.

Finally, a Warner "Super Scarab" radial engine powered the airplane. Rated at 145 hp at 2050 rpm, this seven-cylinder power plant was enclosed in a bumped cowl design that provided cooling of all cylinders and enhanced the airplane's overall streamline appearance.

Ben Melcher gives test pilot Don Joseph some last minute advice. Joseph made the initial Phantom test flight and other early flights in the airplane before relinquishing his duties to local pilot Bart Stevenson.

ELEANORE LUSCOMBE SHURTZ COLLECTION

Standard equipment included an adjustable Hamilton-Standard metal propeller, a battery, a generator, an electric engine starter, fire extinguisher, wheel brakes, dual controls and navigation lights. Options included a radio, landing lights, parachute flares and ignition shielding.

Don planned to offer his new creation at the bargain price of $6,000. However, when he considered the prevailing low wages of the time and the amount of "handmade" work involved in building this new monoplane, he soon realized only the "well-to-do" could afford this airplane. The average sportsman pilot had little chance to afford one. When one considers a Ford V-8 Sedan cost between $700 and $800 at that time while an Oldsmobile or Buick cost some $300 more, it was obvious only a very few could afford Luscombe's new airplane.

As such, Don soon tailored his marketing plans to *"those privileged to enjoy fast flying and who continually seek finer contentment in the more permanent type of material possession."*

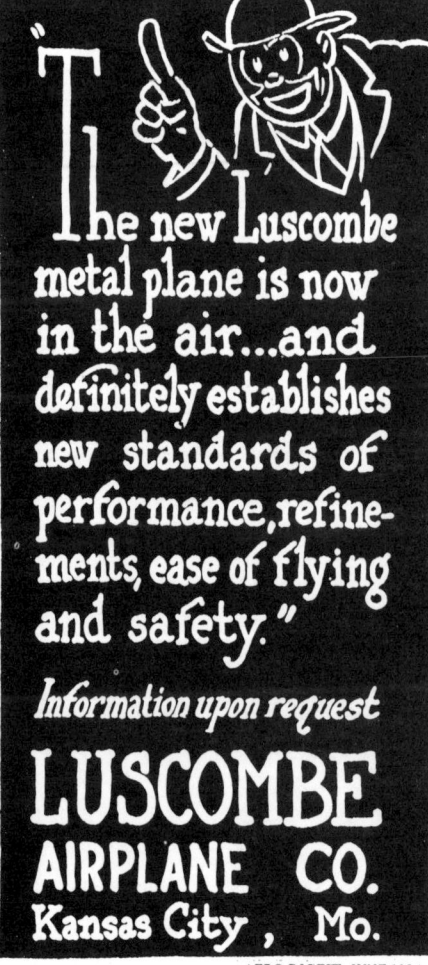

"The new Luscombe metal plane is now in the air...and definitely establishes new standards of performance, refinements, ease of flying and safety."

Information upon request

LUSCOMBE AIRPLANE CO.
Kansas City, Mo.

AERO DIGEST, JUNE 1934

The prototype was reassembled using the necessary rivets, bolts and nuts for the first flight scheduled in early May 1934. To undertake this prototype's first flight, Don Luscombe sought the help of a friend and test pilot from his Monocoupe Corporation days in St. Louis.

Don Joseph was called. Joseph owned and operated a flying service in St. Louis, occasionally loaning Luscombe an airplane when needed for business. Joseph did some barnstorming on the side, occasionally hopping passengers to help make ends meet.

Taking off from the airport's cinder-covered runways (the runways were not concreted until 1937), Joseph cautiously put the new airplane through its paces during this first flight. Luscombe, Farver, Driggs, Melcher and others watched their collective creation circle the field. As Joseph returned to land, somebody made the wisecrack, *"Well, it looks like he's gonna try and land it now,"* an almost derogatory remark implying he couldn't land the airplane. Don Luscombe shot back, *"What do you mean, 'gonna try and land'?"* Everybody present had a good laugh and the tension of the moment was relieved.

Over the next two weeks, Joseph undertook other test flights in the new airplane. He recognized quickly it had tremendous performance and potential, i.e. "potential for sales" and a "potential for groundloops."[33]

Don's new airplane exceeded all predictions and performance goals. The airplane had a top speed of 168 mph, a 140 mph cruise speed, a 45 mph landing speed and stalled at 40 mph. Cruising range was 560 statute miles. As a bonus, the airplane was aerobatic. Other specifications included a 1,950 lb gross weight, a 1,300 lb empty weight and a 650 lb useful load.

The landing gear was ac-

Chapter Seven: Metal, Mass Production and Kansas City 99

Another publicity postcard, Phantom 272Y displays the "Watters" cowl designed to improved engine cylinder cooling. Note the mention of "other models" available.

WARNER SUPER SCARAB
145 H. P. Span 31 feet; length 20 feet 10¼ inches. Useful load 650 pounds. Cruising range 560 miles. Completely equipped, $6,000. Other models with Warner Junior or Warner Scarab from $3,500 up.

ELEANORE LUSCOMBE SHURTZ COLLECTION

knowledged as the aircraft's weakest point. Though incredibly strong, the compression of one strut — with no compensation on the other strut — served only to aggravate the tendency to swerve, thus, setting into motion the potential for a nasty groundloop or noseover.

Don Luscombe later related his feelings about this aspect of his new airplane's personality when he said, *"You could master the violin easier than the fancy footwook needed to avoid grouncllooping."*

Upon completing the initial test flights, Joseph relinquished further duties to Barton Stevenson. Stevenson, a former Monocoupe company pilot and dealer, ran the Stevenson-Weeks Air Service located about a quarter mile from the Butler Blackhawk facilities. Stevenson's partner in this endeavor was Henry Weeks of Kansas City, Missouri.

While flight testing continued, Luscombe applied to the Department of Commerce, Aeronautics Branch, on June 11, 1934, for a

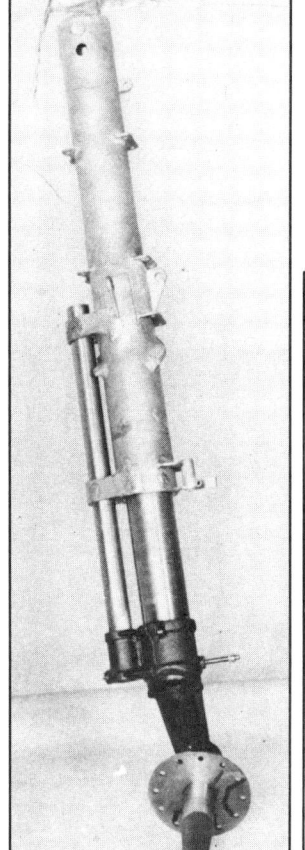

The New Luscombe "Phantom"
Check these advantages and refinements for comparison:
1. Metal monocoque fuselage.
2. Fuselage sectional repair.
3. Fireproof.
4. Full oildraulic landing gear.
5. Two unobstructed weather-proof doors.
6. Metal spars and ribs.
7. Ball-bearing controls throughout.
8. Electrically operated flaps.
9. Complete electrification, completely fused.
10. Motor driven generator.
11. Electric starter.
12. Built-in radio.
13. Landing lights.
14. Rubber suspended, flush mounted instruments.
15. Streamlined wheels and tires.
16. Adjustable rudder pedals with heel brakes attached.
17. Eight cubic feet luggage space.
18. Rear cabin window.
19. Removable coil spring seats.
20. Wheels adjustable against ground looping.
21. Dust free carburetor intake.
22. Battery protection against motor heat.
23. All wires in aluminum conduits.
24. Shimmy-proof and puncture-proof tail wheel.
25. Dural control sticks.
26. No wood, nails, or glue.
27. Forty-five miles landing speed.
28. One hundred sixty-eight mile top.

Luscombe Airplane Company
834 Richards Road   Kansas City, Mo.

(Right) Even the landing gear strut itself was refined to improve the Luscombe Phantom's landing characteristics.
(Far right) Much time and effort were directed towards improving the Phantom's wily landing characteristics. One solution involved adding flying wires to add rigidity to the gear.

HOWARD JONG   CHARLES E. BURGESS

permanent identification mark assignment. The number "272Y" had been applied previously as a temporary identification mark. On June 22, Luscombe received his reply — 272Y became the unlicensed aircraft identification mark assignment for the Luscombe 1. Being a "test" aircraft, an "NC" could not be applied to this particular airplane initially, but was used when the design was granted an Approved Type Certificate.

Originally, Don called his new airplane the "Luscombe Model One." Later, in the application for the Approved Type Certificate (dated July 3, 1934), the airplane was referred as the "Luscombe Coupe." But this name was crossed out and the name "PHANTOM," in Don Luscombe's handwriting, was inserted. Likewise, when Don made the application for the Commercial License, the "Model One" was crossed out and the name "Luscombe Phantom Model One" was inserted. However, to the aviation world, the new aircraft became known simply as the "Luscombe Phantom."

Interestingly, the origin of the name may have developed some time earlier during a conversation between Don Luscombe, Ivan Driggs and Lyle Farver. Don was at a loss for a name when Driggs referred jokingly to the new airplane as the "Phantom." An incredulous Don Luscombe retorted, *"How would you like to own some stock in the Phantom Airplane Company?"* No doubt each gentlemen had a good chuckle. Regardless, the name stuck.

Phantom flight testing continued through the hot, summer months. Few major problems were uncovered except a recurring engine overheating problem. Further tests revealed the "bumped" cowling failed to provide adequate cooling.

A new tunnel-type cowling was developed — the "Watters" cowl — and soon replaced the original installation. This new cowl provided forced and cockpit-controllable cooling of the cylinders. Likewise, this cowling provided easy access to the engine and accessories for inspection, repair or valve adjustment.

Further testing revealed the flaps tended to seriously degrade the performance of the ailerons at low speeds with the flaps extended. Thus, future Phantom production saw almost two feet removed from the flap assembly's outboard section.

The landing gear continued to be the new airplane's major stumbling block. The early gear tended to wobble at times, setting into motion a chain of events (differential braking, etc.) leading to a nasty groundloop. Don once commented, *"Anything that can be done to the landing gear of the Phantom is an improvement."*

Efforts were made to stabilize the gear. One idea involved adding stainless steel streamline wires to the structure. These wires extended from the gear struts mid-section to the side of the fuselage at its widest point. This improvement was not utilized in 272Y, but was applied to most, if not all, later-built Phantom airplanes.

Now that he had a flying airplane, Don set his sights towards the 1934 National Air Races in Cleveland, Ohio, in September to demonstrate his new airplane to a most curious aviation public. But first, he needed to get the government's approval for his airplane before he could proceed with production.

With this goal in hand, Driggs, Melcher and Farver completed the necessary engineering paperwork. In early July, Luscombe applied for an Approved Type Certificate (ATC) to permit manufacturing. On July 28, 1934, Department of Commerce, Aeronautics Branch Inspector George Gay inspected the new Phantom and prepared his Operations Inspection Report. He recommended the Luscombe Phantom Model 1 be approved for an Approved Type Certificate.

On August 18, 1934, the United States government awarded the Luscombe Airplane Company ATC number 552 for the Luscombe Phantom Model 1. Luscombe was free to start production.

Early published stories and advertising detailing the Luscombe Phantom related the aircraft could be powered by either a Warner 90 hp "Scarab Junior" or a Warner 125 hp "Scarab" engine. The Warner 90 version was priced to sell at $3500. However, any production of these lower horsepower versions were abandoned as Don Luscombe realized the discriminating pilot wanted performance in a "high-performance" airplane, often caring little for "economy."

The ink was barely dry on the ATC when Don instructed his three-man engineering department to design a four-place airplane. Lyle Farver, as directed by Ivan Driggs, undertook these initial layouts. Though some thought and, possibly, some effort had been expended previously on a four-place idea, Luscombe believed the time was ideal now to design, build and introduce a companion aircraft to complement his just-certificated two-place Phantom.

The four-place design, as it evolved, was a scaled-up version of the Phantom. Little was changed from the basic Phantom design except for an increase in wingspan, a revised tail group and the installation of a more powerful engine. Almost 60 percent of this new design had parts in common with the Luscombe Phantom Model 1.

Work started almost immediately to produce new Phantom airplanes. Don had to hire more help to meet the increased workload. One of the newly hired was Charles E. "Chuck" Burgess. An accomplished mechanic, a former Ford V-8 automobile engine expert and a former steel mill worker, Burgess was working at a nearby Ford Motor Company dealership when his friend, Nick Nordyke, told him of the new positions available at the Luscombe Airplane Company. Burgess told Nordyke he was very interested for he had planned to leave the Ford dealership shortly and would be looking for a job.

Nordyke, in turn, asked Luscombe if his friend could join the company. Don agreed and Burgess was accepted immediately. Soon, he was working as a sheet metal mechanic in the fuselage department. Chuck Burgess would wear many hats during his employment with Don Luscombe and the corporation. His many, insightful contributions would add much to the overall future success of Luscombe's airplane endeavors.

By way of background, Burgess was born in Pueblo, Colorado, on February 27, 1905, and moved to Kansas City when he was five. Burgess' father was a steel worker. From an early age, Burgess was intrigued by airplanes. He desired always to get into aviation, but his father wanted him to work in the steel mills in the Kansas City area. After grade school, Burgess labored alongside his father in a rolling mill cutting and shaping railroad rails. A promised job within the factory never materialized. Thus, a dismayed Burgess left his position.

While in the sixth grade, he enrolled in a course at the Sweeny Automobile School in Kansas City and soon demonstrated a very strong mechanical aptitude. Burgess enjoyed this training immensely and decided to become a mechanic. Initially, Burgess worked on engines, mostly in motor boats and automobiles. Then he met Hugh Libby, owner of the Libby Welding Company, and was hired to maintain Libby's racing boat engines. Much to his delight, Burgess did some experimental airplane work for Libby, as well.

After this stint, Burgess returned to school and took a course in engineering. In late 1931 or early 1932, Burgess' good grades, drafting expertise and mechanical ability landed him a position with Ford Motor Company in Kansas City as their V-8 engine repairman. He was responsible for repairing the "bad order" engines, those engines in which problems materialized in tests as they came off the assembly line. The harsh economic conditions of the time caught-up with Burgess and he was laid-off. Fortunately, a local Ford dealership recognized Burgess' talents and quickly hired him. During his employ with Libby and Ford, Chuck Burgess had become good friends with Nick Nordyke.

C.E. "Chuck" Burgess peers from inside the cockpit of a later-built production Phantom. Note the intricate work required to form the four-piece windshield assembly. LYLE FARVER

The rush to build new airplanes was often hindered by the lack of money. Don cajoled and convinced his many financial backers and friends to ante-up more dollars. Quite often, Pete and Aline Brooks were Luscombe's only source of much-needed money.

Moreover, this rush created some tremendous production problems. One of the biggest headaches still rested with the wood jigs needed to make the fuselage. Another headache was making the circular fuselage bulkheads. Made from 1x1x1/8 inch aluminum alloy angle, they had to be hammered around a big circular wooden block. In both cases, the process was tedious and very time-consuming.

102   Visions of Luscombe: The Early Years

The balmy Kansas City summer days soon gave way to more pleasant autumn weather. To Luscombe Airplane Company workers, the shorter days brought relief to the sweltering summertime heat often found inside the factory. To Don Luscombe, these shorter days signaled the fast approaching National Air Races at Cleveland.

With one Phantom flying and at least four more in various stages of construction, Don made preparations to attend the annual National Air Races. Though the aviation world buzzed with printed and spoken word of his new airplane, Don—being one to seek the flair and flash of publicity—wanted this event to be the formal debut of his revolutionary all-metal airplane.

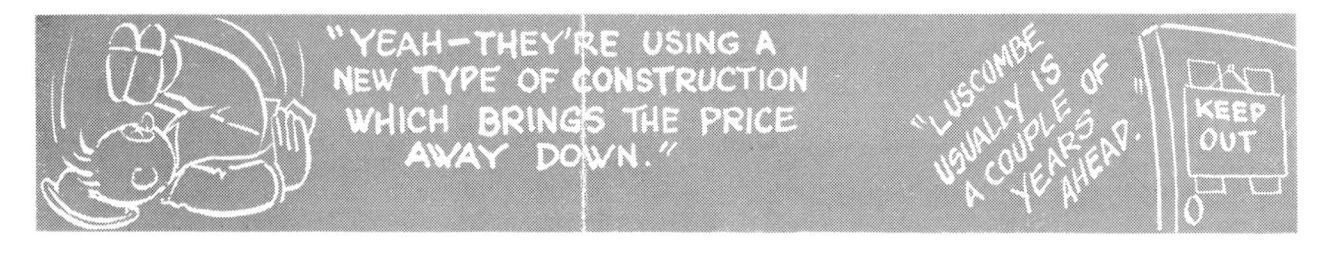

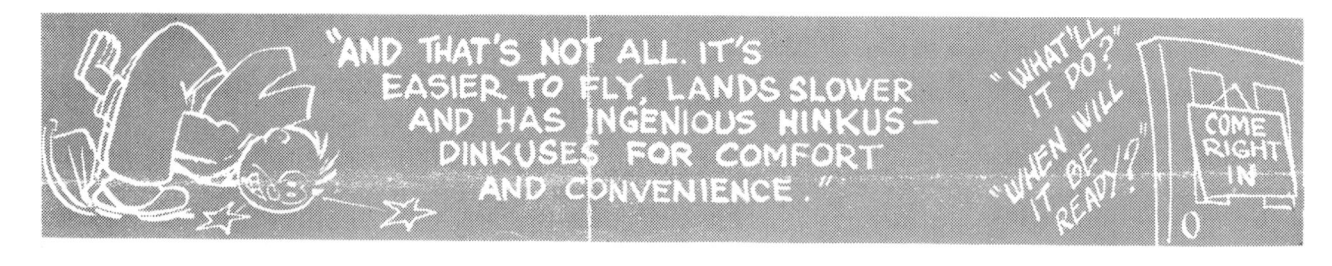

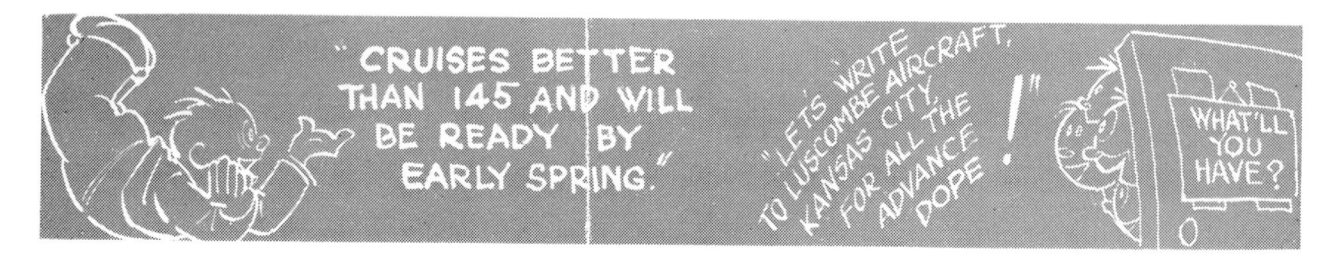

Already, Don had generated considerable interest in his Phantom through a series of advertisements that appeared in *Aero Digest* (shown below) during the summer months. Similarly, Don wrote a detailed story about his company's new airplane and the advantages of all-metal construction which appeared in the September 1934, issue of *Aero Digest*. By plan or coincidence, this particular issue was billed as the National Air Races edition and was found in quantity at these prestigious races. Nevertheless, many of Luscombe's financial backers were anxious to see how "their" project would be received. In the end, they were not disappointed.

Shortly before the start of the 1934 National Air Races, Don Luscombe headed east towards New York City in NC272Y. He flew into the city's North Beach Airport (La Guardia Airport today) and joined Pete and Aline Brooks who planned to fly their Monocoupe to the popular and "trendy" air races. Together, the trio headed west for Cleveland. Everywhere they stopped enroute, people were awed by the Phantom.[34]

The Luscombe Phantom was a star among the non-racing aviation community at this September 1934 event. Don flew his airplane daily before an enthralled crowd, most notably in the well-publicized "Progress Parades." Likewise, all who got a chance to fly with Don in NC272Y came away shaking their heads in disbelief. The airplane was everything Luscombe said it was. . . and more!

Many accolades were given Don and his Phantom during and after the races. Perhaps the best compliments paid to Luscombe, and private aviation in general, appeared a month later in the popular publication, *Aero Digest* (October 1934). Writing in an almost editorial tone, Dr. Alexander Klemin, Dean of New York University's Daniel Guggenheim School of Aeronautics, stated in his opening paragraph:

"This year's National Air races at Cleveland left the impression that the racing constructors were lagging behind the less romantic designers of transport and private planes. The explanation is not hard to seek. It takes a good deal of money to develop and build an entirely new racing airplane, it is cheaper simply to install a more powerful engine, and backers are scarce. Otherwise, the races were highly successful, with the paid-in attendance reaching a maximum of possibly 90,000 on Labor Day, indicating an immense public interest. After meeting visitors who casually came in their own planes, learning that there were forty-five privately-owned Monocoupes and as many Fairchilds and Wacos on the field, and after seeing Don Luscombe's new cabin job (described last month in AERO DIGEST), one was convinced that private aviation was forging ahead."

The writer continued to describe that contestants relied more on "suped-up" engines than design ingenuity to improve performance. He suggested:

"... the cantilever landing gear on Luscombe's new cabin job is a better undercarriage for a racing craft than most racing chassis seen at the field."

Regardless of the sincerity behind the many compliments received, the Phantom's $6000 dollar price tag discouraged many potential buyers. Furthermore, behind-the-scenes debate regarding the aircraft's tricky landing characteristics did little to encourage other possible sales.

Luscombe knew he had to sell his airplanes if he was to survive. It was simple, economic sense. But no one was buying. Don decided to return to the East Coast (New York City, Boston, etc.) and demonstrate the Phantom to those people who could afford to buy his new airplane. Additionally, many of Don's keenest financial backers lived on or near the East Coast and had yet to see something more substantial for their efforts than a small black and white postcard-sized photograph, a balance sheet or a letter or cable from Luscombe seeking more money.

He planned to head towards Boston initially, then fly southward, stopping at various airports along the way. Don's promotional tour came to a quick, sudden and embarrassing halt on September 17, 1934, when he nosed over while landing the Phantom at the Boston Airport. Though shaken by the experience, Don emerged unhurt.

Fortunately, the damage was relatively minor and consisted of a few dents to the bottom of the fuselage, replacement of sheared rivets, straightening the top of the rudder and fin, in addition to repairing a few cuts on the top of the wing. Within a week, Don Luscombe and the Phantom were in the air.[35]

At some point during his tour, or shortly thereafter, Don was confronted with the proverbial pot of gold at the end of the rainbow. Various backers told him his future was dim in Kansas City, a point Luscombe acknowledged readily. They suggested he move East.

Don had always known the "real" money was in the East. By moving his aircraft company east, he would be closer to the source of those who could afford to buy his product, i.e., the young and affluent pilots of the East Coast "Country Club" set.

Don weighed other categorical aspects for the move. He would be closer to the raw materials needed to produce his airplanes thereby reducing material shipping costs. Likewise, he would be close to good engineering firms who could offer needed advice and help. Additionally, he would be closer to export facilities. Don could develop and reap a worldwide market for his airplanes. Finally, he would be near Washington, D.C., and the Department of Commerce offices that certified his airplanes.

Yes, the East Coast held many positive solutions to his current corporate production and sales woes.

But the real incentive came when Wall Street money men hinted they would offer Don and his company whatever money was needed, only if he would move his operations closer to New York. Luscombe was dazed by their most generous offer.

Before he got any real money, however, he had to make the actual move east. [36]

Almost immediately, Don began planning for the move. But first, he had some pending family matters to handle. He and Brownee were married on October 13, 1934.

Don continued to advertise his airplanes in widely-read publications. *Aero Digest* continued to be one of his favorites.

A Summer 1934 view of the Mercer County Airport, West Trenton, New Jersey. This quaint location would be the future home of Luscombe's fledgling airplane company.

ELEANORE LUSCOMBE SHURTZ COLLECTION

By late October or early November, a fifth fuselage was readied for the jigs. Nick Nordyke's skill on the power hammer was a source of inspiration to all around him. But Don had little time to congratulate him or his fellow workers for their exemplary construction efforts. He had a new factory site selected and immediately had to make the necessary preparations for the move east. Don did have time, however, to formally announce the planned move to the workers of the company's new location — the Mercer County Airport in West Trenton, New Jersey!

The selection of the Mercer County Airport site is attributable to Jerry Lederer. Though several civic groups and various Chamber of Commerce officials wooed Don Luscombe to West Trenton, including Jack Gillis (an avid aviation enthusiast who kept his airplane based at Mercer County for several years), it was Lederer who convinced Don this site was the best to relocate his company.

Lederer, then working for the Department of Commerce, Civil Aeronautics Branch, knew of Don's intentions for a move eastward. After consulting with Don as to what he needed in a new plant site, Lederer set out to find a suitable location, if such an East Coast site near New York City was available.

As luck would have it, Mercer County Airport's previous tenant, the Thropp Flying Service, had run out of money and its lease was due to end January 1, 1935. Lederer became aware of this situation and quickly informed Don the premises would be vacated shortly. Negotiations were started through Walter O. Lochner, Mercer County's secretary of the Chamber of Commerce. County solicitor Phillip S. Vine prepared the lease in its final form.

The West Trenton site was perfect! Located in a very pastoral and picturesque part of central New Jersey, the airport was close to New York City (barely an hour's travel by train), Philadelphia and Washington, D.C., and had much to offer. Besides a trio of 2400 to 2700 foot grass runways, there was an 80 foot x 100 foot brick hangar available with a 15 foot office extension along one side. Furthermore, the Department of Commerce maintained a 24 hour weather observation and teletype service on the field. This function provided the equivalent of an around-the-clock, on-site watchman service.

The deal included a frame building and garage known as the Caretaker's House. Located at the edge of the field and approximately 1700 feet northwest of the main hangar, this building would become the future Luscombe residence.

Specifically, the airport (in 1934) was located one mile northwest of Trenton Junction and 5.5 miles northwest of Trenton, New Jersey. The airport's elevation was 225 ft. and it rested on a rectangular plot 2700 ft. by 2370 ft. Three sod runways were on the field; 2700 ft. NW/SE, 2400 ft. E/W and 2340 ft. NE/SW. The name MERCER, made of crushed stone, was embedded on the field some 900 feet north to northeast of the main hangar.

This main hangar was located along the Trenton Junction-Harbourton Road, approximately 800 feet northwest of Ridge Road. The Caretaker's House, formally the Airport Inn, fronted the Trenton Junction-Harbourton Road and was approximately 2500 ft. northwest of Ridge Road. The name Trenton Junction-Harbourton Road was later changed to Bear Tavern Road during the middle to late 1930s.

On October 17, 1934, Don signed a three year lease effective January 1, 1935. The yearly rent was set at $500 and was to be paid quarterly. Besides use of all the aforementioned buildings, the lease gave the

The West Trenton, New Jersey, site was perfect for Don's airplane company. This aerial photograph, taken from an early 1930s pilot publication, shows the facilities to a good advantage.

JAMES B. ZAZAS COLLECTION

Luscombe Airplane Company the right to manufacture airplanes on the premises and unrestricted use of the runways as necessary for any test or conduct of business. Use of all utilities, storage facilities and fuel tanks was included.

According to a Trenton newspaper of the era, Luscombe sighted the many advantages of moving to West Trenton and added: *"... since our dealer organization is made up of people who fly airplanes in the various States of our country, we believe that you will be pleased to find Mercer Airport the destination for a great many flying visitors as guests."*

While many Kansas City workers pondered their future with the Luscombe Airplane Company, Don Luscombe netted a Phantom sale from one of his backers. Carl B. Haun of Blackwell, Oklahoma, told Luscombe in late November he wanted a Phantom airplane. He confirmed this order in early December.

On December 17, 1934, Bart Stevenson undertook a brief test flight of the second Luscombe Phantom built, NC275Y (s/n 101). On December 19, 1934, Mr. Haun became the proud owner of this first production built Luscombe Phantom Model 1. [37]

This first production Phantom exhibited several improvements over the prototype model. Notable changes included a slight decrease in flap size (to prevent a "blanking" effect on the ailerons), internal improvements in the vertical fin's construction and a slight lengthening of the fuselage turtleback fairing. Most changes enhanced production capability and eased associated labor costs.

Haun's enthusiasm for the aircraft faded quickly as he found the new airplane's tricky and unforgiving landing characteristics not to his liking. He requested the company repurchase his airplane. Barely five days later, the Luscombe Airplane Company bought back the aircraft from Haun. Fortunately, Don held a Phantom deposit in hand from Reginald and Aline Brooks and, thus, was able to repurchase the aircraft.

The excitement of this first sale and subsequent resale January 12, 1935, as well as the sale of at least two more Phantoms, was lost in the rush to close business in Kansas City. Any manufacturing was terminated one week before Christmas. New opportunities and new adventures were waiting for Luscombe and his employees in West Trenton, New Jersey. Some would follow, others would stay.

There was much work that needed to be done — all in the midst of a cold, almost cheerless winter.

106   *Visions of Luscombe: The Early Years*

December 1934 roll-out of NC275Y, the first production Luscombe Phantom.   ELEANORE LUSCOMBE SHURTZ COLLECTION

(Right) Aline Rhonie Brooks, a very accomplished pilot, sits in the cockpit of Luscombe Phantom, NC275Y.

AVIATION HERITAGE LIBRARY

(Left) Peter and Aline Brooks pose beside their Luscombe Phantom (s/n 101) on a cold, windswept Kansas City ramp.

JOHN UNDERWOOD

*"To persevere
In obstinate condolement is a course
Of impious stubbornness; 'tis unmanly grief:
It shows a will most incorrect to heaven,
A heart unfortified, a mind impatient."*
William Shakespeare (1564 - 1616)
Hamlet [1600-1601], Act I, Scene ii, Line 92

Chapter Eight

New Places, Smiling Faces

The main hangar at Mercer County Airport as seen from the Trenton Juncton-Harbourton Road (later called Bear Tavern Road). All corporate and engineering offices were located on this side of the hangar until other arrangements were made. Circa 1934. — ELEANORE LUSCOMBE SHURTZ COLLECTION

The slowdown and eventual shutdown of Kansas City operations and the subsequent start-up of West Trenton production was smooth and orderly. Commencing from late October 1934, and extending through early March 1935, men, equipment and material were moved overland to Mercer County Airport. What couldn't be carried in or towed behind an automobile was loaded on trucks.

The first Phantom, NC272Y, was disassembled and loaded aboard a truck. As the prototype of the series, the airplane had served its days admirably as the rugged test bed for a new design, while heralding the construction advantages and inherent value of an all-metal light plane to a skeptical "general aviation" world. At the time, no one knew what strange and unusual uses awaited this airplane in West Trenton, but history would later point to several.

Money was extremely tight for the move. Don

Looking southeast towards the main hangar from a grassy area adjacent to one of the runways. ELEANORE LUSCOMBE SHURTZ COLLECTION

Luscombe prevailed upon his backers to offer whatever they could to cover the costs. In turn, he informed those employees making the move east they were basically on their own, with respect to on-the-road meals and lodging, but gave them fifty dollars apiece to defray any fuel and auto maintenance costs.

Don and Brownee Luscombe were among the first to head east. Leaving shortly after January 1st, they carried what few possessions they owned in a new 1935 Pontiac. The family dog rode comfortably in the back seat.

Upon arriving at West Trenton, Brownee was aghast at the dreary weather, but she forged ahead. She set-up housekeeping in the nearby Hotel Stacy-Trent in Trenton as the Caretaker's House was not in any condition for immediate occupancy. In the meantime, Don tended to his new office at Mercer County Airport.

However, business matters in Kansas City required him to return on several occasions. The Phantom sale to Carl Haun, its subsequent repurchase and resale to Pete and Aline Brooks in early January required his presence.

Don consummated the sale of at least two other Phantom airplanes in Kansas City. The first was to Bryan Sheedy of New York, who bought Phantom NC276Y (s/n 102) on January 5, 1935. Another Phantom was sold to Donald D. Cooke of Tenafly, New Jersey, on January 22, 1935. This airplane was assigned Department of Commerce license number NC277Y and possessed serial number 103.

Soon, other employees packed their meager belongings and motored towards West Trenton. Fortunately for some, surface transportation was no major problem. For example, Ivan Driggs had two cars that needed to go east, a Hudson and a Model A Ford. He opted for the Hudson and asked Fritz King to drive the other.

Driggs left Kansas City in late January 1935.

The clean graceful lines of the second production Luscombe Phantom, NC276Y (s/n 102), ELEANORE LUSCOMBE SHURTZ COLLECTION
are highlighted in this photograph. This airplane was sold to Bryan Sheedy of New York City, New York. Note the tailwheel arrangement employed in these early production Phantoms.

Chapter Eight: New Places, Smiling Faces   109

With the Hudson chugging, he and his family pulled their little mobile trailer behind them. However, severe winter weather forced them to leave it in Washington, Pennsylvania, as a raging blizzard made driving extremely hazardous through the Appalachian Mountains. Driggs became increasingly worried for his family's safety as the trailer slipped and slid behind them. Placed in storage, they would retrieve this trailer the following spring.

Upon arriving in Trenton, Driggs checked into the Hotel Stacy-Trent. As luck would have it, the hotel manager was a friend of Driggs from their Michigan State University days. Driggs played on his sympathy a bit and, in turn, was told he and his family could reside in the hotel.

Lyle Farver, with his wife, Carol, soon followed. Sadly, their few personal belongings were stolen from their car shortly after they arrived in West Trenton. Driggs and family offered to clothe and shelter them. Chuck Burgess and Nick Nordyke rode together. They were joined by Nick's wife, Bertha. Fritz King and Charlie Peacock, another Kansas City employee, followed driving Driggs second car with a tow of personal items.

King owned the remains of a Fleet Model 2 which he bought to rebuild after it had been almost completely destroyed in a hangar fire. He loaded the parts on a trailer, including an experimental power boat belonging to Chuck Burgess. Ross Funk, wife, Naomi, and brother, Keith, joined the makeshift convoy.

NC276Y and NC275Y shown together on the Mercer County Airport ramp.   HOWARD JONG

(Right) As seen from the Trenton Junction-Harbourton Road, the former caretaker house on the Mercer County Airport property was Don Luscombe's residence. Today, this stately building is the Mountain View Country Club restaurant and clubhouse.

ELEANORE LUSCOMBE SHURTZ COLLECTION

(Left) In late 1934 and early 1935, Don Luscombe sent several "handmade" prospectuses to potential investors. Quite often, Don's keen sense of humor would compliment this sales effort. Here, Don described this photograph as "An income producing adjunct for sales dept."

ELEANORE LUSCOMBE SHURTZ COLLECTION

110   Visions of Luscombe: The Early Years

DOROTHY DRIGGS BAKER

(Left and Below) Bryan Sheedy pays a visit to the Luscombe Airplane Company in his Luscombe Phantom, NC276Y. Note the sign on the hangar has not yet been repainted.

ELEANORE LUSCOMBE SHURTZ COLLECTION

On March 1st, this group said good-bye to family and friends in Kansas City and started east. In addition to the Fleet biplane and the boat, each carried a large number of Fleet wing ribs.

The reason why King had these ribs relates to a previous effort by King to earn extra money to afford rebuilding his Fleet. Recognizing a need for replacement Fleet ribs across the country, he traded an old motorcycle for a set of maple wood forms and hammered out Fleet wing ribs in his spare time. At $6 a rib, few people could afford this price, so King traded ribs for parts to rebuild his Fleet. The quality was impeccable and soon his replacement ribs were in demand. The move to Trenton, however, required he forfeit this lucrative endeavor. He gave the maple wood dies to "Pops" Stroeble who planned to stay behind.

Closing out the Kansas City operation were Ben Melcher, "Pops" Stroeble, Ed Nemechek and Vernon Outman. One could say they literally "turned off the lights" at Luscombe's former airplane plant. Melcher made sure all bills were paid and ensured all equipment owned by the Butler Blackhawk Airplane Company was reinstalled in their original locations. These duties complete, Melcher and Outman drove east while Stroeble and Nemechek later elected to remain in Kansas City.

As employees arrived in New Jersey, they contacted Don Luscombe to let him know they had arrived. In turn, he gave them their new assignments while jigs, dies, tools and other equipment were installed. For example, Ben Melcher was asked to ensure all equipment was installed in such a way as to improve production efficiency. Through this assignment, Melcher became the Plant Manager, a position he held for the next four years. Likewise, Chuck Burgess became fuselage assembly foreman, Nick Nordyke became the sheet metal department foreman, Fritz King became the wing department and final assembly foreman while Keith Funk was placed in charge of the stock-room and tool crib.

Working closely with his dedicated team, Don's factory was able to begin Phantom production by early April 1935. Confident and optimistic, he issued shop orders to build twenty-five Phantoms. Sub-contracts were let to other nearby companies to fabricate parts, dies, jigs, extrusions and tools.

To ease his start-up costs, Don restricted his company's activities to the assembling of parts manufactured by firms that specialized in the manufacture of these parts. Minor heat-treating and finishing work was to be accomplished at the factory.

Teicher Manufacturing of Brooklyn, New York, for example, was sub-contracted to drop-hammer various metal pieces including the landing gear fairing parts. Yet, it was Nick Nordyke's genius with the power-hammer that prevailed when any fuselage panels needed to be formed.

Concurrent with these activities, the engineering department undertook extensive time versus cost and man-hours required versus units produced studies to determine the best means to achieve Luscombe's Phantom production goal. Lyle Farver, in a personal interview with this author, explained this process was more "calculated guesswork" than analytical fact finding.

In the meantime, Luscombe sought capital. He worked closely with his many financial backers, always seeking ways to enhance the financial viability of his company.

During this time, several Wall Street bankers offered him, once again, all the money he could want or need, but now made clear they would do so only if they gained 51 percent control of the company. Don declined. It was HIS company and HIS dream; no one was going to take it away from him, at least, not now. Don Luscombe was a proud man. He believed steadfastly he could drum up support for his company the old-fashioned way — he would ask for it.

Don Luscombe was a suspicious man, also. He was leery of bankers and the banking industry in general. He did not trust their smiling lures of money and generous repayment plans. He was afraid once he accepted their offers, he would lose control of his company or its future course.

To further his money raising endeavors, Don would stay up late into the night, with Brownee assisting, writing letters to anyone whom he thought would lend a friendly ear for his vision. Often, he would randomly pick names and addresses from various aviation publications.

Don was "driven" in this endeavor. Even in sleep, it controlled his personality. On occasion, he would awake from a deep sleep and yell *"I've got it!"* He would then proceed to spend the balance of the night writing a letter seeking money in an innovative way from an incredulous, yet potential backer.

In the final analysis, Don Luscombe was fortunate. Even though times were tough financially and the Depression still maintained a tight grip on the nation, many well-heeled individuals and corporations gave Luscombe a positive nod.

Don knew in his heart his fledgling company and all-metal aircraft designs held great promise for the future. Given the proper financial boost, it could forever change the general aviation aircraft industry. He needed to set forth his goals on a national and global level.

Currently engaged in the research and development of metal airplanes, Don's company could offer the potential investor and airplane purchaser more

The first West Trenton-built Luscombe Phantom (NC278Y) under construction.   ELEANORE LUSCOMBE SHURTZ COLLECTION

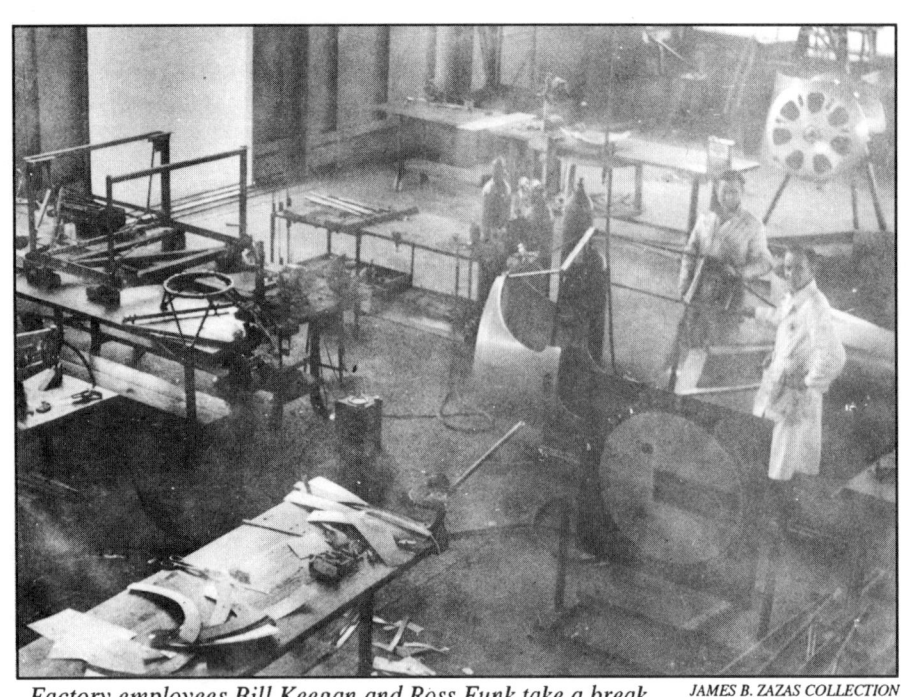

Factory employees Bill Keegan and Ross Funk take a break from work. During this period, the shop had few tools.

JAMES B. ZAZAS COLLECTION

than simple fabrication of metal airplanes — it would offer the innovative ideas, engineering talent and mechanical skills necessary to build these airplanes. Ever the consummate promoter, Don was cognizant his new corporation had to have an appropriate corporate name, a deserving identity to tout before the public's eye.

On April 17, 1935, the Luscombe Airplane Development Corporation was chartered under the laws of the State of New Jersey. The Board of Directors consisted of Ivan Driggs, Lyle Farver, Ora May (Brownee) Luscombe and Don Luscombe. At their first meeting, Don Luscombe was elected president of this new corporation. Thirty thousand common shares, no par, and fifteen hundred preferred shares at $50 were authorized.

In a typical, "Luscombe-esque" worded statement sent to potential investors, Don said, *"Shares are offered primarily to those in aviation whose activities and opinions are valuable to the growth and development of aviation in America and who are in position to benefit the company with sales accruing from their endorsement of its products."*

Don's airplane visions remained intact and in his control, at least for now. But he had to keep interest in his company if he was to maintain and gain financial support.

Don prepared and had printed a small, twenty page pamphlet describing the company's extensive experience building all-metal airplanes and its overall production potential. The text discussed the merit of having various designs of different configurations, cabin sizes and power plants to cater to any public or military need. Furthermore, all designs would be made from similar tools and dies to keep tooling costs low.

Several drawings were included in this pamphlet to visually tout the aforementioned corporate goals and engineering efforts. Included were: the "Ghost," essentially a luxury, four-place Phantom powered by a 420 hp Pratt and Whitney radial and priced at $12,000; the "Spectre," a five place, twin-engine, high-wing executive design priced in the $12,000 range; the "Small Transport," an executive and feeder transport aircraft envisioned to sell for an incredible $30,000; the "Sprite," a tricycle gear, two place, Ford V-8 powered aircraft aimed at the amateur pilot market; and, finally, the "Harpie," a 420 hp radial engine powered pursuit aircraft.

Though the designs described never saw production, they served Luscombe well promoting the engineering, production and marketing potential of the Luscombe Airplane Development Corporation.

Even as this pamphlet was printed and distributed, several financial backers expressed interest in owning a Phantom. For Don Luscombe, a sale equated to "more money in the bank." Don was all too happy to receive these airplane orders. He could beg for money only so long. He needed to sell airplanes if he was to stay in business.

George A. Thorne, Jr., a Luscombe backer, placed and later confirmed a Phantom order in late March 1935. His aircraft, NC278Y (s/n 104), became the first Phantom assembled in West Trenton. Though the fuselage had been built in Kansas City, the balance of the aircraft was jigged and constructed at the Mercer County Airport. Within hours after it was inspected by Department of Commerce Inspector George Gay on July 8, 1935, Thorne picked-up his gleaming Luscombe Phantom aircraft. [38]

This sale gave Don little financial breathing room. He had a multitude of bills to pay and still had to meet payroll. Though several workers stayed with Luscombe through this very lean period, others pressed for their paychecks, they were tired of any further I.O.U.s or Don's repeated offers of stock in the company.

Ivan Driggs was one such individual who was

discontented with Don's financial promises. He had a family to support and his pleas to Luscombe to be paid cold, hard cash often went unheeded. In frustration and anger, Ivan Driggs resigned his chief engineer position. He left the company in late April 1935, and accepted a chief engineer position at Fairchild Aviation Corporation in nearby Hagerstown, Maryland.[39]

Lyle Farver replaced Driggs as the Luscombe Airplane Development Corporation's chief engineer. He was saddened to see his good friend and mentor leave upset, but he understood the reasons why. Farver soon put these concerns aside and concentrated on his work. Most energies now were directed towards a four-place aircraft and a lower horsepower version of the Phantom.

Soon, other employees elected to leave as well. Ed Nemechek left for a position at Glenn L. Martin in nearby Baltimore, Maryland, while a couple of employees departed and signed-on with Sikorsky Aircraft in Stratford, Connecticut, or Chance Vought in East Hartford, Connecticut. Only Farver, Melcher, Burgess, King, Nordyke, the Funk brothers and a scant few others elected to stay with Luscombe.

Regardless of these financial and employee problems, Don persevered. Furthermore, he was still able to sell another Phantom airplane. In late spring, he received an order from his first foreign customer, Dr. A.K. Tschudi of Bergamo, Italy.

Actually, the good doctor's wife, Mrs. A.K. Tschudi, placed the order. Obligingly, Don took his special customer on a demonstration ride. This excursion turned "exciting" upon landing when Luscombe applied the brakes a little too hard and rolled the Phantom gently on its back. Both occupants emerged unscathed. Don was embarrassed, but Mrs. Tschudi was

Don Luscombe stands under the wing of Pete Brooks' repainted Phantom. LYLE FARVER

(Above) Dr. K. Tschudi and Phantom HB-EXE (s/n 105), near his Bergamo, Italy, home.

(Right) Somewhere in Africa, a camel and rider saunter nonchalantly past Phantom HB-EXE. Sadly, this airplane was lost in an accident on April 8, 1937.

Photographed in Ithaca, New York, Phantom NC277Y is shown to a good advantage. Note the tailwheel position.

AVIATION HERITAGE LIBRARY

impressed by the airplane's overall strength and crashworthiness! She gave Luscombe a deposit for the next Phantom airplane to be built.

With money in hand for this aircraft, Luscombe ordered the instruments, engine and propeller. Interestingly, this Phantom possessed the last Kansas City-built fuselage. Future Phantom fuselages would be fabricated totally in West Trenton. [40]

By early July 1935, the Tschudi airplane was completed and was assembled to check rigging, test flown (most likely by Don), then quickly disassembled for shipment to Europe. Painted an overall white with a distinctive black trim and lettering, the airplane (s/n 105) carried the Swiss registration, HB-EXE, on the fuselage and on the wings.

Dr. Tschudi and his wife later flew their Phantom extensively throughout Africa. Sadly, the aircraft was lost in a crash on the continent on April 8, 1937. No further information is known as to the exact location of this unfortunate accident nor is any information known as to the injuries, if any, sustained by the occupants.

During this period, Don and his wife, Brownee, wanted to have a child of their own. Though little Jimmy Luscombe often visited, Don and Brownee decided to adopt a child. They sought help from Dr. Whiteis, the family doctor in Iowa. He was unable to help the couple, so Don and Brownee turned to Quaker Society of Philadelphia. Sadly, these plans went awry and Don and Brownee's dreams of being parents went unfulfilled.

The long summer months allowed Don little rest, but he and his employees were entertained by an air show held at Mercer County Airport. Pete Brooks entertained the crowds with an enthralling aerobatic routine in his Warner-powered Monocoupe 110.

Concurrently, Ben Melcher was treated to a little corporate humor. One of Melcher's duties required he maintain a sufficient supply of materials in inventory necessary for production. One day, Ben realized the supply of chile saltpeter, a material used to heat treat small metal parts and rivets, was low. So, he dutifully placed an order for a generous supply with a local chemical warehouse. When he told the girl who answered his call that he wanted 50 pounds and if they could send it out to the factory, the sweet voice on the other end inquired, *"How many men do you have out there?"*

All fun times aside, the economic realities of manufacturing and supporting a new airplane design were soon forced upon Luscombe. He had to face the unsettling prospect of brokering and absorbing repair costs for some previous Phantom airplanes sold.

In early August, Thorne told Don he wanted to get rid of his ship, as did Pete Brooks. Sheedy had nosed his Phantom over and was awaiting repairs. In the meantime, Cooke had sold his airplane to sugar fortune heir Frank Spreckles on the West Coast who, in turn, informed Don he was experiencing serious engine overheating problems. [41]

Additionally, reports from the field suggested the Phantom's tricky landing characteristics were depressing further potential sales. Don was furious at these reports and directed the engineering department to resolve the landing gear problems and the overheating problems. Despite these many woes, Luscombe pressed onward and continued to pursue different avenues to raise capital for his company. Eventually, his many efforts bore fruit in two areas.

The first idea involved creating a small refueling and maintenance operation not unlike a fixed base operation. The relatively close proximity of the Mercer County Airport to Newark Terminal, then the world's busiest airport, and its location along the airways between Washington, D.C., Philadelphia and New York City made it a logical place to stop, relax and refuel. Furthermore, the on-site maintenance facilities and low rent made the airport attractive for any individual seeking a place to base his aircraft.

Don recognized this need, but it was Fritz King who developed the gas concession and, to a small degree, the maintenance repair operation at Mercer County Airport. Luscombe, in turn, received money from King via rent payments and a small percentage of any fuel sales.

King, on his behalf, used his rebuilt Fleet biplane for flight instruction to earn extra money. Brownee

Luscombe was one of his first students. Similarly, Don Luscombe, Chuck Burgess and many others flew the airplane regularly to maintain required proficiency.

Luscombe's second idea involved the creation of an "apprentice program," a school-like environment to teach unskilled individuals the basics of metalworking, mechanics and aeronautics. He recognized there was a current need and ever increasing demand for people qualified with metal working experience. Larger military and civil aircraft plants were accepting applicants as soon as they completed training. The fact he lost a few of his key employees to larger, more established aircraft companies hardened his decision to act.

But it took two enthusiastic individuals to convince Luscombe how best to proceed with his apprentice school idea. On September 23, 1935, Don had a most welcome visitor. Ignatius "Ig" Sargent of Boston, Massachusetts, flew to West Trenton in his Monocoupe 110 to visit Don and to discuss the possible purchase of a new Luscombe Phantom airplane.

Sargent had never seen a Phantom before except in magazine advertisements. In fact, during his honeymoon a few months earlier, Sargent told his new bride, Frances, he was going to buy one of these new all-metal airplanes. He was so impressed by the airplane that he wrote to Luscombe requesting more information. Don's reply was a slick, postcard-sized picture of Phantom 272Y on the front and a detailed description of the airplane on the back.

Briefly joining the Sargents during their honeymoon was their close friend and Ig's former college roommate, Edgar Steuart Davis. Like Sargent, Davis shared an infectious enthusiasm for the Phantom. Each expressed a strong desire to ultimately own one of Don Luscombe's "all-metal" airplanes.

Sargent met Luscombe for the first time at the Detroit Air Show at the Detroit City Airport during mid-August 1935. Though this show was more "static" in nature and involved no aerial activities, Sargent had the opportunity to talk to Don Luscombe at length about the Phantom. At the end of their conversation, Luscombe offered an invitation for Sargent to visit the plant, which was gladly accepted.

So it was barely a month later that Sargent, who had recently completed his sophomore year at Harvard University, was treated like royalty during his visit to the factory. Even though the hangar was virtually empty and only a few parts lay scattered here and there, Luscombe rolled out the proverbial red carpet for his guest and did his best to promote his fledgling company.

Don Luscombe showed Sargent every phase of Phantom construction while describing the very bright future for privately owned, all-metal airplanes. Sargent, on his behalf, was impressed by what he saw and heard.

However, he had yet to fly a Phantom. The company's demonstrator, NC272Y, was undergoing repairs from an earlier mishap. A red-faced Luscombe explained to Sargent he had nosed-over the company's only demonstrator airplane a few months earlier while giving the wife of a prospective customer a demonstration flight.[42]

Alfred "Fritz" King built this Fleet Model 2 from a burned-out wreck and, later, used it for flight instruction and proficiency. CHARLES E. BURGESS

Regardless, Sargent placed an order for a Phantom airplane and gave Luscombe a $2000 deposit. Luscombe was astonished and grateful. Sargent and Davis, who also ordered a Phantom about the same time, had both recently moved to New York City and planned to enroll in the Casey Jones School of Aeronautics during the fall of 1935. But these plans changed quickly. Within days of placing their Phantom orders, Sargent received a call from Luscombe. *"We're working on your wings now. Why don't you come down here and help us build the damn airplane?"*

Sargent and Davis were all too excited about the prospect of owning a new Phantom NOT to accept the offer. When Sargent made a quick trip to check on the progress of his airplane, he discovered the only work accomplished was a pair of wing spars resting on a pair of saw horses awaiting ribs. Somewhat dismayed but anxious to get his Phantom built, Sargent elected to work for Luscombe. Ig Sargent and Eddie Davis started work at the Luscombe Airplane Development

Corporation on September 30, 1935.

During the next nine months, Ig Sargent and Eddie Davis made the almost daily, 45 minute aerial commute from New York City's North Beach Airport (La Guardia Airport, today) to Mercer County Airport in Sargent's Monocoupe 110 or by train when the weather negated *any* possibility of flying. Occasionally, Sargent would use a friend's 240 hp Stinson Detroiter or Eddie Davis would fly his Davis D-1-W monoplane.

Eddie Davis and Chuck Burgess pose in front of a Stinson. CHARLES E. BURGESS

Once at the factory, each joined the shop crew then in place and worked together on their respective Phantom airplanes. Sargent and Davis were each paid $18 per week as mechanics, even though each had invested a couple thousand dollars in the Luscombe Airplane Development Corporation.

During the course of their employment with Luscombe, Sargent and Davis were given a considerable amount of stock in the LADC. In late 1935, this over-the-counter stock was priced at $.50 a share. Three years later, the stock sold for $2.00 to $2.50 a share.

Ig Sargent's and Eddie Davis' presence and their desire to build their own airplanes bolstered Don's "apprentice program" concept. Soon, he hoped, there would be more people producing his airplanes, perhaps at no direct cost to him. The idea was intriguing and promising.

The mere thought of having this kind of enthusiastic help on the floor lifted Luscombe's morale. Before him were two, affluent individuals who enjoyed working on their airplanes. Don sensed others would follow. However, if this idea was to move forward, the proper instructors had to be located and hired, a course of instruction developed and prospective students interviewed and accepted.

Luscombe decided to "test the waters" regarding this scheme. He broached the idea for this apprentice program in a letter to Ivan Driggs dated September 26, 1935. (Don was still attempting to woo Driggs back to the company). In it he said: *"There should be a way to stay in business without having to depend on profit from airplane sales. . . . We are now tooled to the point where we can use certain inexperienced labor. The country is filled with boys with money who are 'problems' in college. They are interested in mechanics and aeronautics.*

A six months semester at $1200. They work in the shop during the day and classes three nights per week. They earn $15 per week and pay us only $10 for their dormitory. They get actual and live problems in building an airplane which they can sell to advantage because of their knowledge when they are through. Twenty-five students twice a year pay the entire direct labor, salary and burden. We stay in business if we sell only six airplanes."

Ivan Driggs did not respond to this plea. But Don, the sort of individual who could embellish an idea at the expense of sound accounting principles, liked what he had written. He carried his abstracts a step further.

During late September and early October, Luscombe approached Dr. Alexander Klemin, Dean of New York University's Daniel Guggenheim School of Aeronautics. He told him in a letter: *"We can absorb fifteen or twenty young fellows with the proper background for six month periods, work them in the shop during the day and tutor them in the evenings. We certainly do not want to be known as a school but by being exposed to actual shop problems, not old crackups, but to live examples of procedures the workman does become a better student."*

Dr. Klemin was most interested in what Luscombe had to say. He replied the plan might be too late for the current summer term students, but suggested Luscombe come to the University during the spring term and outline his plan to the sophomores and juniors. Thus, several could fit it in their plans for the summer of 1936.

Additionally, Dr. Klemin wrote several of his university students and stated, *"I believe this would be an opportunity for gaining shop experience while paying your way and securing a mechanics license which might be very helpful later on. Shop experience is also a great help as preparation for drafting or engineering work. May I suggest that you look into this matter."*

Don was encouraged. His "apprentice program" idea was taking hold. More importantly, the idea held great promise as a legitimate means to raise much needed working capital. No doubt Don Luscombe had a good chuckle. Imagine, students paying for the privilege of attending this school and, in turn, being paid a salary to do it.

Simple arithmetic showed why Don was keen to this idea. He reasoned if 100 men paid $575 for six months tuition, the company would receive $57,500. From this amount, if the students were paid back $390 in salaries, totalling $39,000, the company would have $18,500 to cover general expenses *and* the benefit of their labor.

Don wrestled with this idea through the early autumn months, eventually putting forth his ideas to the stockholders. It was a "last-gasp" effort to remain solvent. Meanwhile, Don approached other schools for technical know-how and academic assistance. Though Dr. Klemin showed interest in Luscombe's "apprentice program" idea initially, it was two Cornell University professors in upstate New York who answered Luscombe's requests positively, professors K.D. Wood and C.W. Terry.

Keith Funk. Circa 1936. KENNETH E. CERICOLA

Professor K.D. Wood agreed to direct the courses of study while C.W. Terry, formerly of the Department of Machine Design at Cornell, would take a semester's leave of absence to directly supervise and teach the actual shop practice. However, Wood was schooled as a stress analysis engineer and an aerodynamicist and soon deferred all responsibilities to Terry who held, also, both a pilot's and mechanic's license; K.D. Wood held neither. As such, he thought Cy Terry could do a more creditable job of organizing and instructing the classes.

Additionally, the foremen would teach the students assigned to their respective departments how to do the work performed in those departments which entailed actual production work. The foremen were responsible for the quality of the parts made and these parts were checked by a member of the inspection department.

Occasionally, one or two of the foremen were asked to teach a classroom period or two and describe his department's work to the whole class. This benefited the entire class as it expanded the students' knowledge of work done in all departments, even though they worked in one or two departments during their student training.

For example, Ross Funk was asked to teach detail parts fabrication while Chuck Burgess, the fuselage assembly foreman, and Nick Nordyke, the sheet metal foreman, would teach sheet metal techniques. Later, Keith Funk was asked to teach basic accounting and stock control principles.

Don envisioned most teaching would involve actual, on-the-job training. After completing the six month course, the students would become full-time, paid employees. For the first time in many months, Don Luscombe could breath a sigh of relief. He felt his all-metal airplane venture might succeed after all.

Perhaps another bright horizon for Don was a deal hammered-out with Fleetwings Aircraft of nearby Bristol, Pennsylvania. During September 1935, Fleetwings offered to produce parts, most notably Phantom landing gear fillets, on their new drop hammer. Additionally, the company proposed to make the landing gears. The most intriguing aspect of the Fleetwings' proposal was to make the Phantom's number two bulkhead from stainless steel and shot-weld same. Luscombe's engineers studied the proposal, but nixed the last idea.

As 1935 drew to a close, Don prepared initially a two page document, then a finely printed four page document, detailing the new, six month "apprentice program." He placed a small advertisement in a local newspaper, also. The response was surprising — almost a hundred men responded to Luscombe's call.

Concurrently, Don approached his company's stockholders with his school ideas in a letter. He needed their continued support if the "apprentice program," as well as his company, were to succeed and survive. In this letter, he stated the following:

"During the past three weeks I have interviewed not less than a hundred young men with college training of technical nature, among them many graduates of aeronautical colleges and have received as many as a hundred letters daily from a small advertisement.

Over thirty of these men have indicated their willingness to supply own salaries for six months in return for the experience and tutoring we are in a position to give.

I am satisfied we can receive not less than ten thousand applicants by using classified advertising. We can take one hundred men.

The arithmetic for six months is then as follows:

100 men at $575 for tuition	$57,500
We pay them back in salaries	39,000
To cover all of our general expenses	$18,500

This means that if we have $2751.49 for a bill of materials we could sell at that figure and still stay in business on a no profit basis.

Since our nearest competitor (Fairchild) sells at $5300 and put out over a hundred ships last year, and since we cruise twenty miles an hour faster than their top speed and have the advantage of metal construction and all it entails, we are confident that we could equal such an out-put, sell for $1,000 less and still net $1,000 per sale, on the basis (sic) of making an education as a by-product supply all direct and indirect labor and general expense.

On the other hand if we can sell readily at the Fairchild figure of $5300, allow 20 percent sales discount and receive $4240 for the ship at wholesale, we would pay $472 for assembly labor and $472 for burden, and thereby make our cost with overhead $3695, with a net profit which we dare estimate at $80,000 annually.

Before accepting the checks for tuition which are already coming to us, we must begin to fill orders and not only save all of our invested money, but show definite and assured returns.

Otherwise we will be forced to give away our very fine development and accept a loss to all of us as investors."

Don concluded his letter with a sobering prophecy: *"... There is no time for delay as we must give an immediate answer to the men who are ready to come. Those who have invested money must <u>concern</u> themselves. It will be recalled that our idea was predicated upon the belief that each person taking part would concern himself in our cooperative effort to get this business under way. It is difficult to over emphasize the heart breaking efforts that have been made by the immediate organization here at Trenton to preserve the equity of the investing group in the face of so little supporting helpfulness on the part of those who pledged their interest at the onset.*

We have evolved a plan that is ready for execution and which can be made to net handsome returns.

Please permit me your immediate response, declaring what responsibility or interest you will assume in the matter. Shall we give it away or save our investment?"

Though many investors bristled at having to spend more money to keep Luscombe afloat, the stockholders pledged their support for the "apprentice program." Plans were made to start the first class in mid-January 1936.

Meanwhile, Thanksgiving arrived and presented the factory workers a truly thankful holiday. Don and Brownee Luscombe hosted a small, Thanksgiving dinner for the few employees residing in the West Trenton area. The dinner was not bountiful, but the men were grateful. A sort of "family" atmosphere grew and prospered during those early West Trenton days.

This relationship played an important role in the company's overall survival. On several occasions, Don was unable to meet payroll. Though many employees grumbled, many persevered and remained loyal to Don despite the many hardships.

In mid-December 1935, William B. Shepard paid Luscombe a visit. Shepard, a 1933 Cornell electrical engineering graduate, was intrigued by the new "Apprentice Program" scheduled to start soon. Tired of working for an inventor near Hartford, Connecticut, and wanting to get a job in aviation, Shepard learned of Luscombe's new program through his former college professor, K.D. Wood.

Bill Shepard was a rated pilot, also. He started his flight training in July 1930, flying a Fleet biplane and received his private license in late August. Shepard was keen to aviation more so than electricity. He worked at an FBO in upstate New York as a mechanic's helper, line boy and occasionally hopped rides for passengers. By then, he held a limited commercial license.

When he left this FBO, Shepard went to work for an inventor who was developing various applications for photo-electric cells. However, this work lasted until December 1935, when he heard Luscombe was looking for young engineers to work in West Trenton.

When Shepard arrived, Luscombe painted a rosy picture of his company's production capability. Sitting behind his desk, Luscombe highlighted this point by picking up a stack of papers and told Shepard, *"Here are the orders for twenty-five Phantoms."* Shepard was impressed. Obviously, *this* new aircraft company was going to thrive and survive if it had already netted twenty-five Phantom airplane orders.

Chapter Eight: *New Places, Smiling Faces* 119

With little hesitation, Shepard enrolled in what was to become the program's first class. At least twelve other equally enthusiastic young men joined him.

Only later did Shepard learn a sobering truth. The twenty-five orders Luscombe picked-up from his desk were not bonafide or confirmed airplane sales, but were, instead, "shop" orders issued eight months earlier to build twenty-five airplanes. Once more, Don Luscombe demonstrated his inane ability to promote a product, this time his company's sales prospects, even though the truth was "bent" slightly.

During their same conversation, Don boasted, *"Bill, we'll have one hundred boys out there in the shop."* Within two years, this prophecy was fulfilled, with several students to spare.

Don's rosy outlook served its purpose — it lured prospective students. Students enrolled in the new program and Don Luscombe, in turn, was rewarded with working capital to keep his company afloat.

The Luscombe Airplane Development Corporation would survive.

Super-Scarab

Name of Engine:	WARNER SUPER-SCARAB.
Manufactured by:	Warner Aircraft Corp., 20263 Hoover Ave., Detroit, Michigan.
Type:	7 cylinder, fixed radial, air cooled, 4 cycle.
Department of Commerce Rating:	145 H.P. at 2050 R.P.M.
Displacement:	499 cu. in.
Compression Ratio:	5.3 to 1.
Dimensions:	Length, overall .... 28 $\frac{1}{2}$"
	Diameter, overall .... 36 $\frac{1}{4}$"
	Bore .... 4 $\frac{5}{8}$"
	Stroke .... 4 $\frac{1}{4}$"
Weight:	305 lbs. (without starter or hub).
Fuel Consumption at Rated H.P.:	.55 lbs. per H.P. hr.
Oil Consumption:	.025 lbs. per H.P. hr.
Lubrication:	Force feed.
Ignition:	Dual Scintilla Magnetos.
Carburetion:	1 Stromberg.
Spark Plugs:	2 per cyl. A.C.
Price:	On application.

Phantom

LUSCOMBE AIRPLANE DEVELOPMENT CO.
TRENTON, N.J.

120 *Visions of Luscombe: The Early Years*

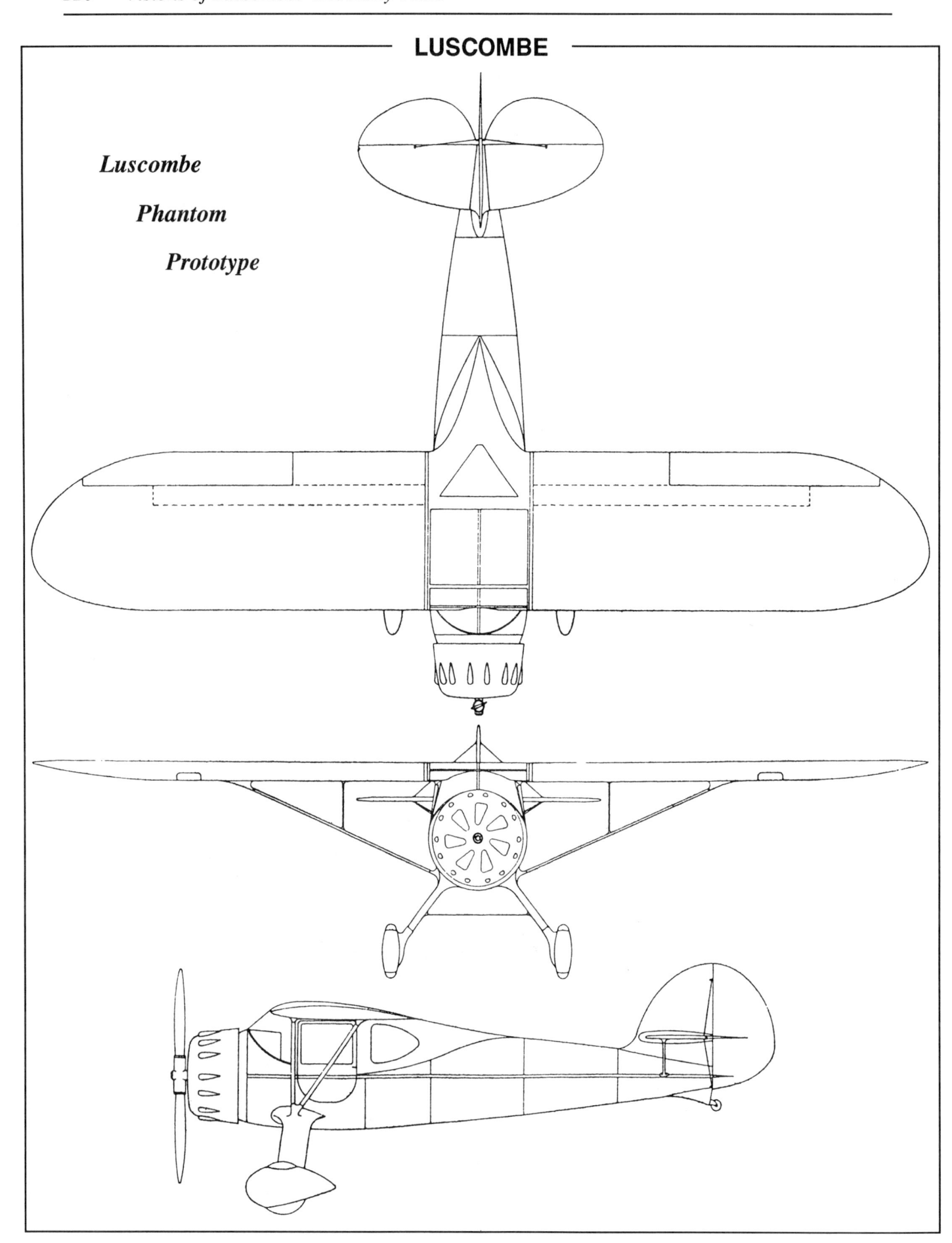

LUSCOMBE

Luscombe Phantom Prototype

Chapter Eight: New Places, Smiling Faces 121

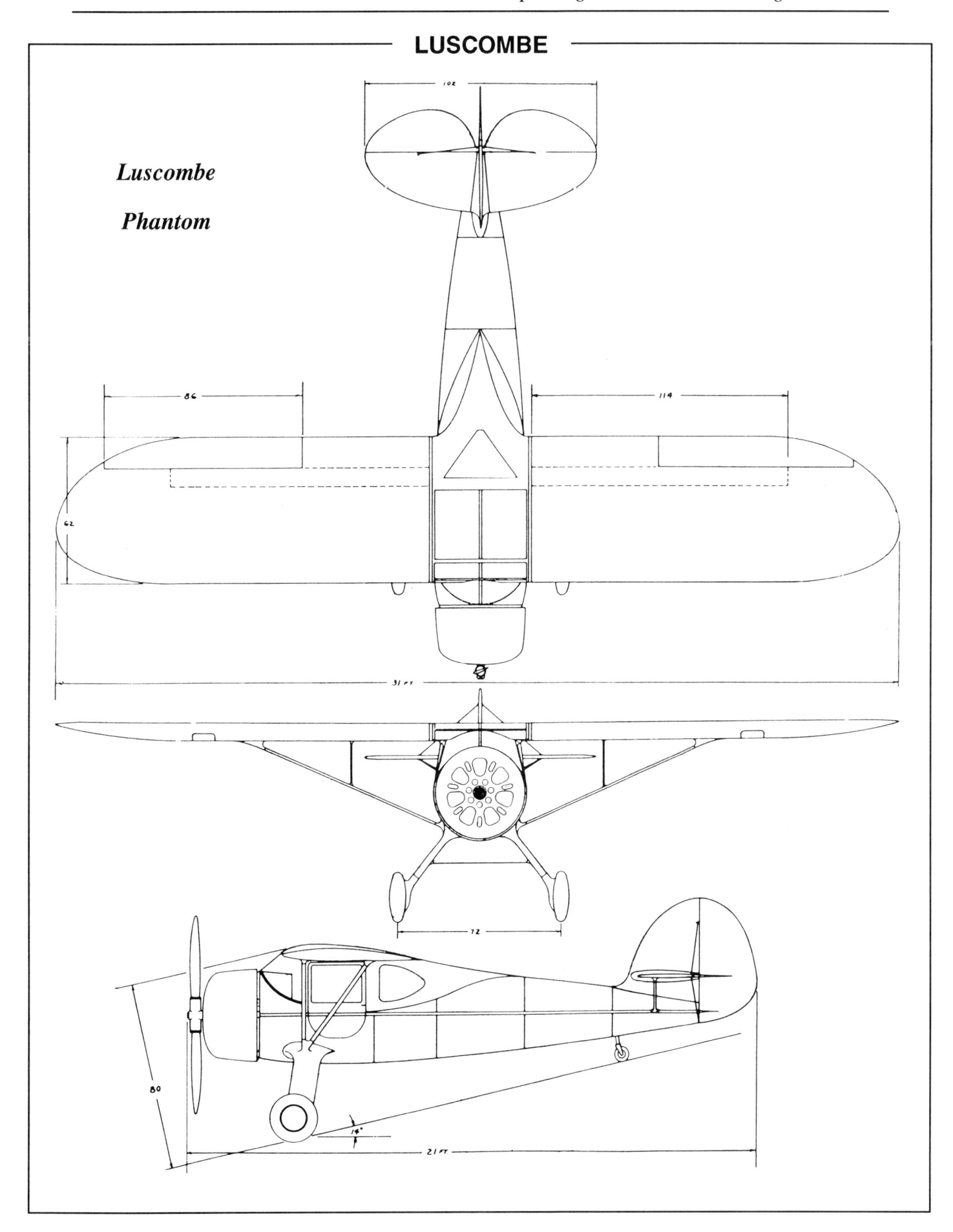

LUSCOMBE

Luscombe

Phantom

122 *Visions of Luscombe: The Early Years*

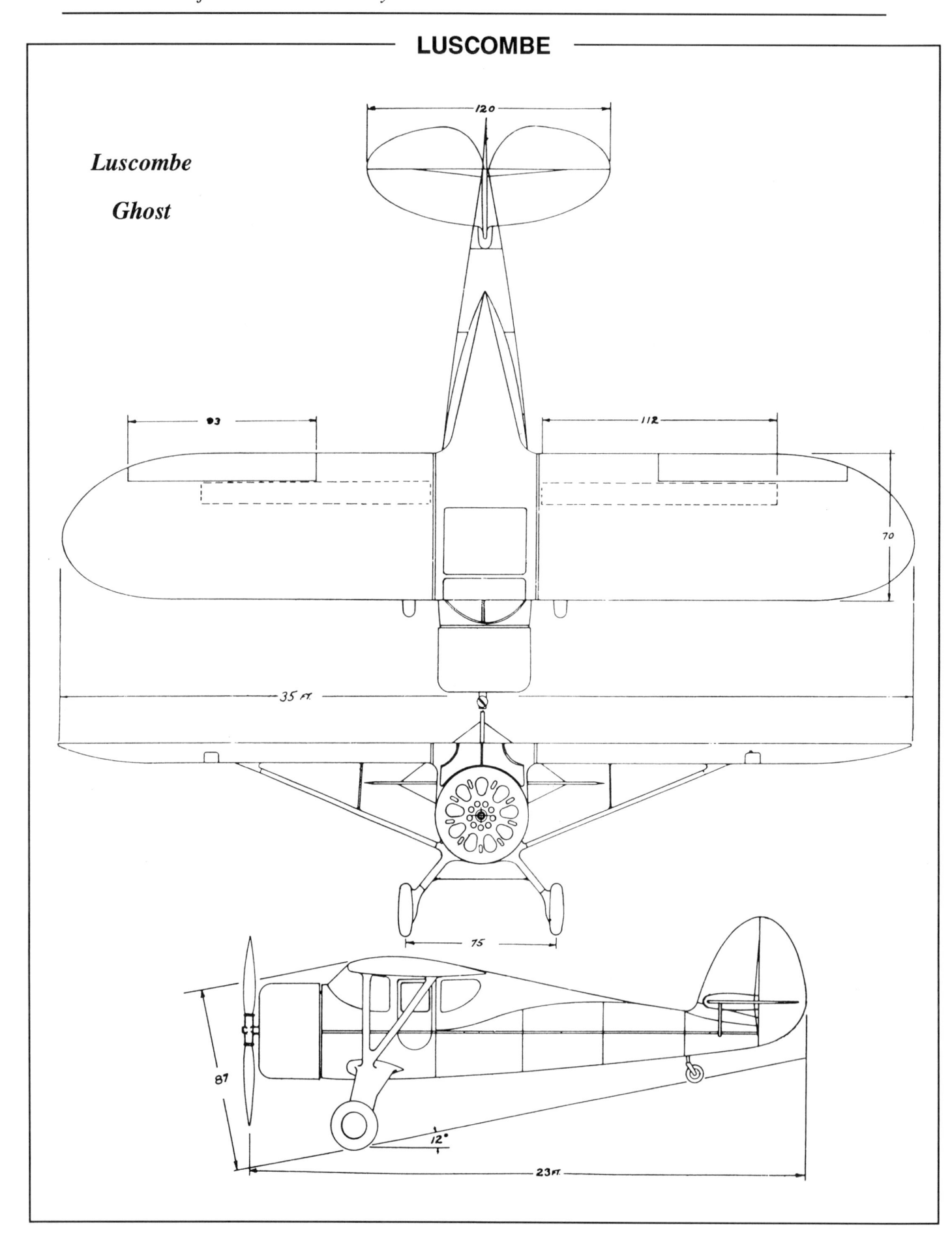

LUSCOMBE

Luscombe

Ghost

LUSCOMBE

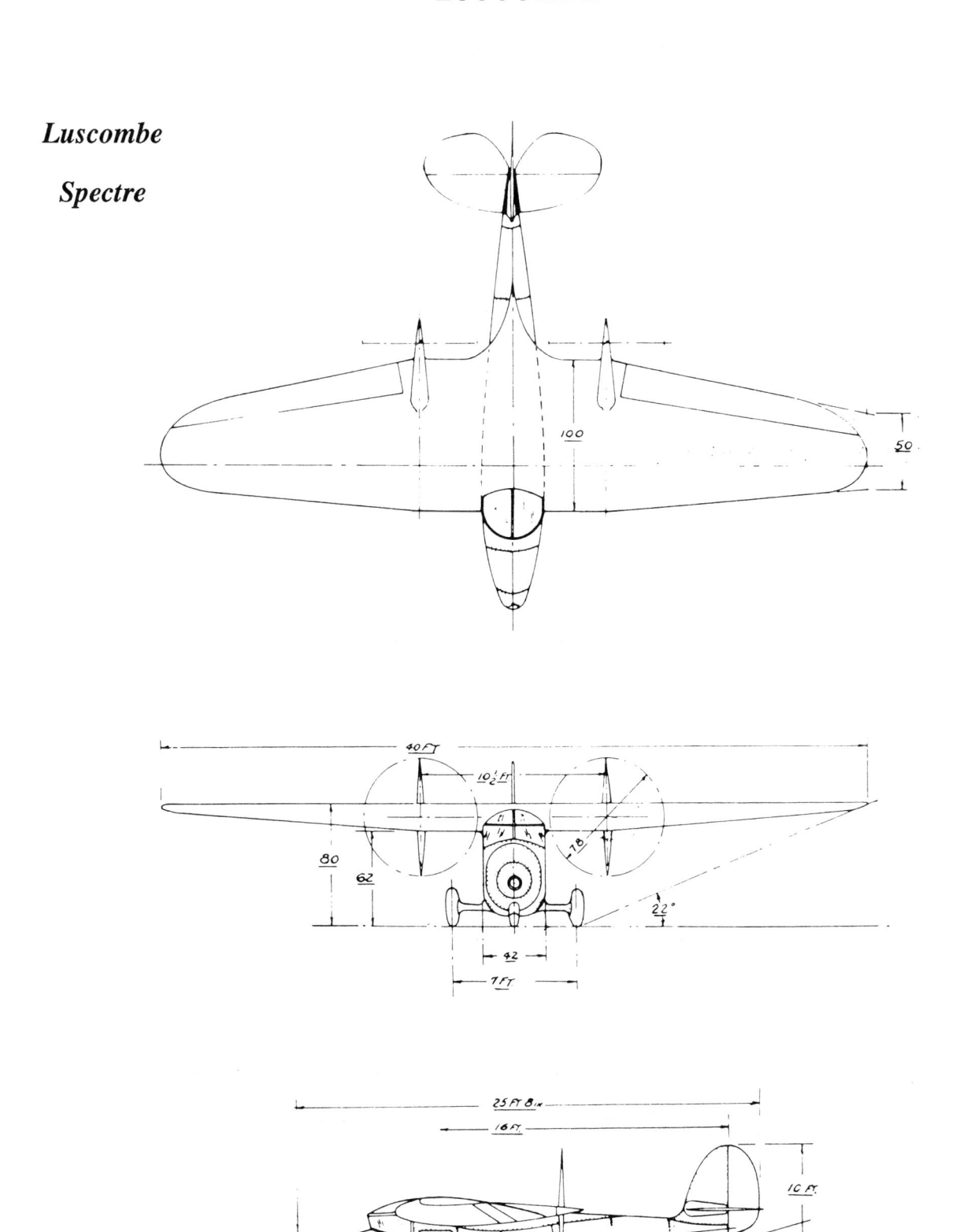

Luscombe Spectre

LUSCOMBE

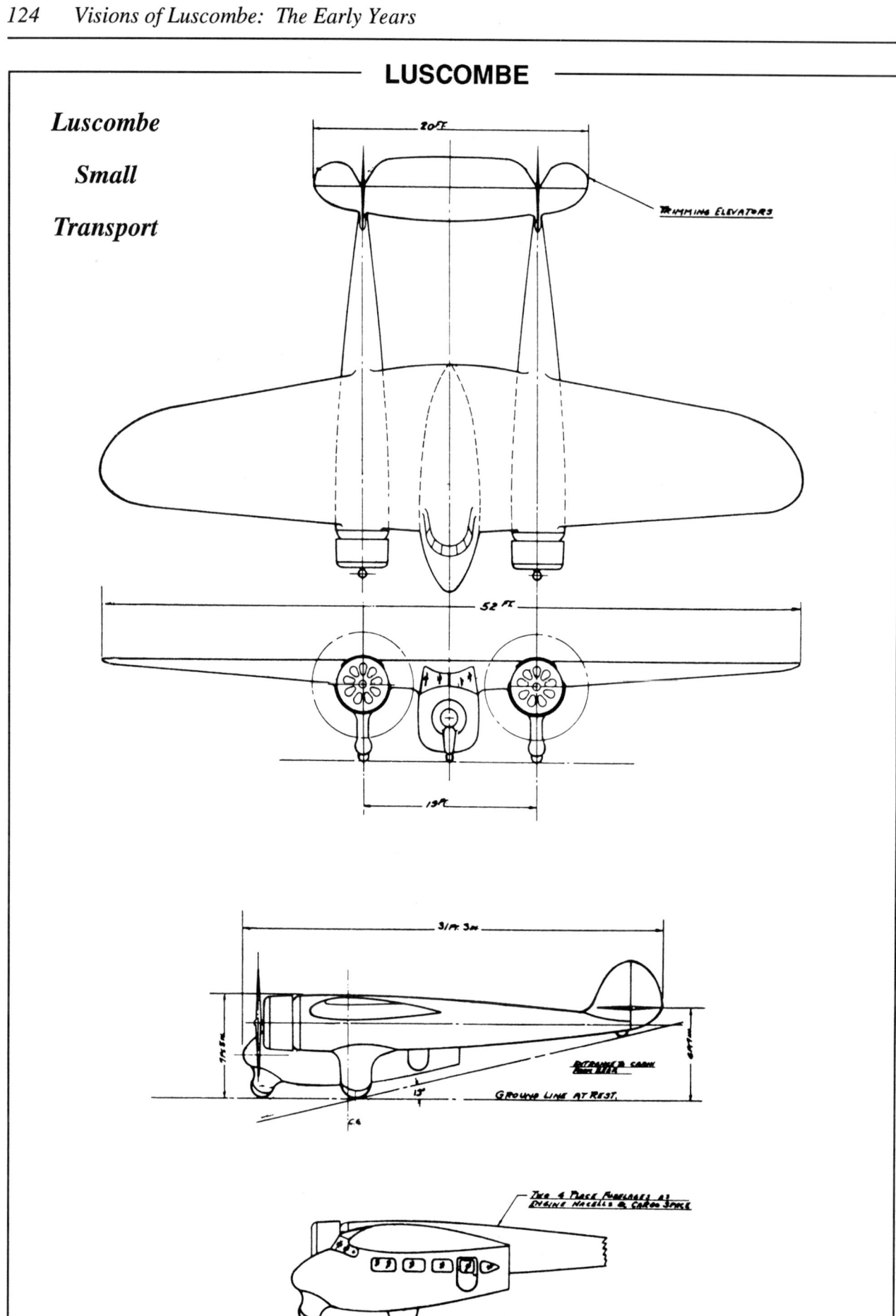

Luscombe Small Transport

Chapter Eight: New Places, Smiling Faces   125

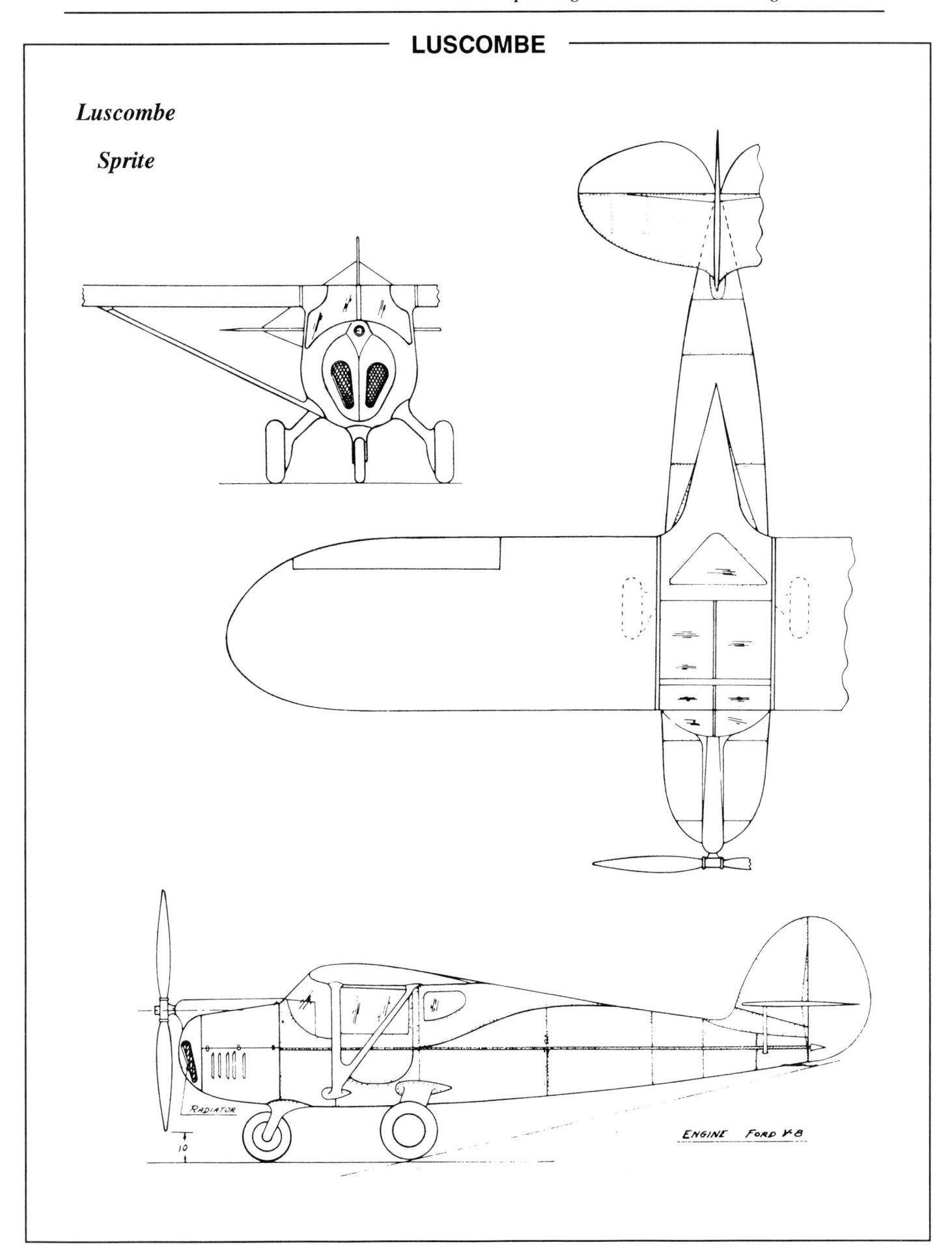

LUSCOMBE

Luscombe

Sprite

ENGINE FORD V-8

126 *Visions of Luscombe: The Early Years*

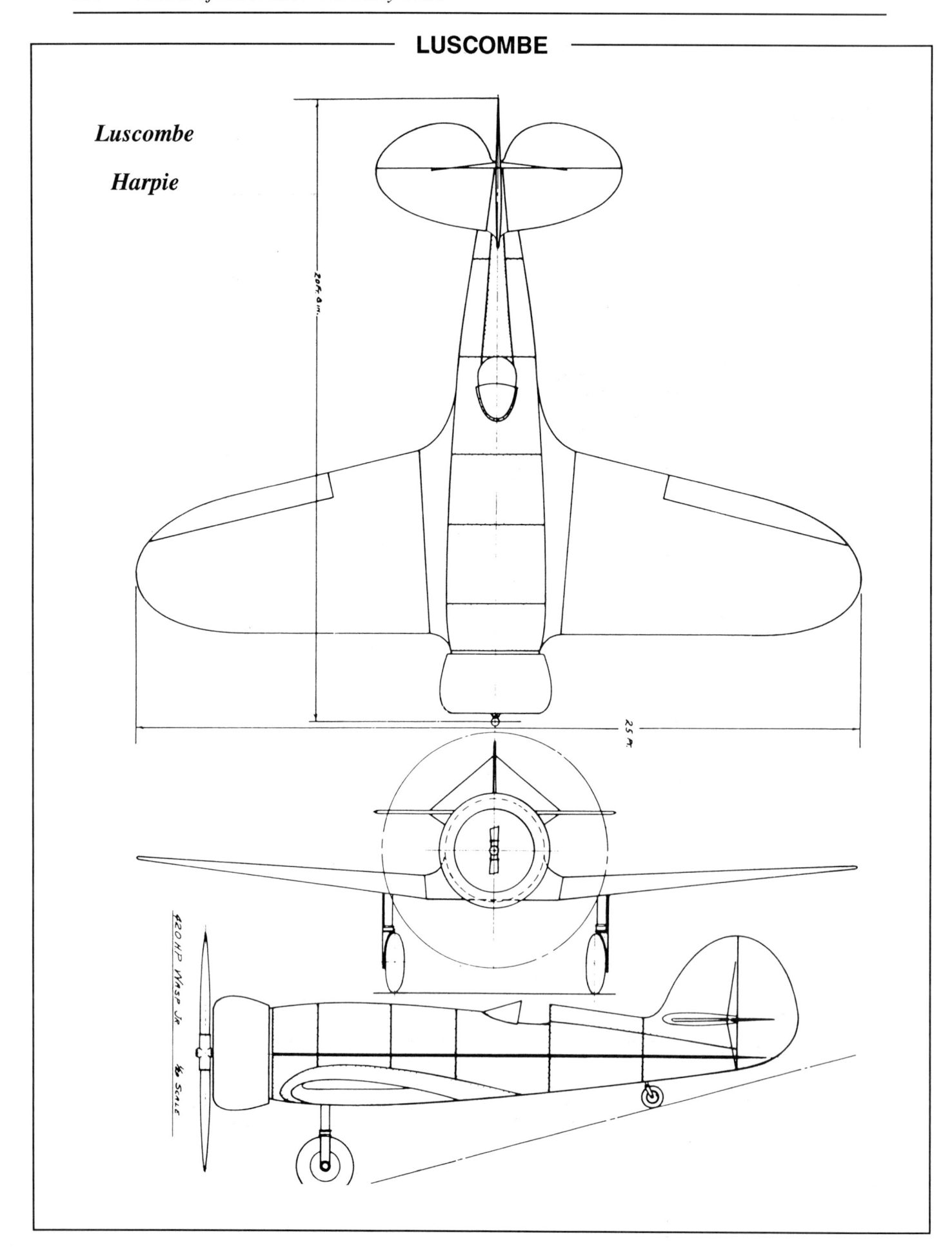

LUSCOMBE

Luscombe

Harpie

"I do not know what I appear to the world; but to myself I seem to have been only like a boy playing on the seashore, and diverting myself in now and then finding a smoother pebble or prettier shell than ordinary, whilst the great ocean of truth lay undiscovered before me."
From Brewster, Memories of Newton [1855], Vol. II, Ch. 27

Chapter Nine

Looking Up, Getting Better

The colorful STANAVO Luscombe Phantom was a popular crowd draw at air meets and aviation gatherings during its short-lived existence. HOWARD JONG

Only four Phantoms were delivered in 1935. Luscombe was discouraged when he reflected upon this depressing fact. He had hoped to have been able to build and deliver many more. At least, his intent had been to build and deliver twenty-five Phantoms. Furthermore, the few flying Phantoms needed repairs constantly.

Bryan Sheedy had nosed over his airplane in Watermill, Long Island, New York, the previous summer (1935) and incurred major damage. He had it repaired at the factory and during October 1935, had a pair of Edo Aircraft Corporation 44-2425 metal floats installed on the airplane at Edo's, College Point, Long Island, New York, factory. Thus this Luscombe Phantom became the *only* ever so equipped with floats. The Luscombe Airplane Development Corporation fabricated the fittings to attach the aft float struts to the fuselage.

This airplane was reregistered with the Department of Commerce as a "Phantom 1S" shortly after its conversion to floats. Sheedy retained the original paint scheme briefly, then opted for something more eye-catching. Within weeks after his Phantom had emerged from the shop with floats, he had his ship repainted an overall bright red with a black trim, except for the floats, float struts and spreader bars. This flashy Phantom became a well-known sight along the East Coast waterways between New York and Palm Beach, Florida, and was quite a hit with his Sportsman Pilots Association buddies.

Not unexpectedly, a disgruntled Sheedy complained to Don the floats degraded the Phantom's performance. Don could only offer to replace the floats with the original landing gear. Sheedy decided to wait until April 1936 before undertaking the change. Despite Sheedy's complaints, these repairs and

(Left) Phantom 276Y sits on the Edo Aircraft Corporation ramp shortly after its conversion to floats. The aircraft retained its original color scheme until it was repainted an overall, bright red with black trim.

(Below) The same Phantom painted an overall bright red.

modifications generated much-needed income to pay LADC workers. Every dollar helped keep Don's vision alive to see another day.

Meanwhile, Don continued to make attempts to lure Ivan Driggs back to the company. He related his feelings about the Fleetwings proposals in a letter to Driggs by saying, *"They seem to yearn for the parts that have been our biggest headaches."* Once more, Driggs chose not to respond to Don's letters. Not withstanding Driggs' lack of response or the many financial problems at hand, Luscombe held his chin high and remained consistently optimistic. He "knew" things would get better. Why else would he continue to pursue this difficult, often fraught-with-frustration endeavor into 1936?

Fortunately, the "apprentice program" was well under way and each student's tuition money offered the company a small measure of financial breathing room. Don used his previously developed and innovative formulas to cover overhead.

The cost of the first "apprentice program" course was set at $500 per student and included coveralls, tools and text books. In turn, each student was paid a $15 per week salary. Additionally, if the student had previous aviation maintenance experience or demonstrated a keen ability to learn and work, Don added $10 in Luscombe Airplane Development Corporation stock.

These initial courses ran twenty-six weeks, which meant each student was paid $390 overall. Thus, Luscombe had $110 to use as he needed. As a bonus, he got twenty-six weeks of "free" labor from each student. Fifteen dollars a week was meager wages in the mid-1930s, but a single fellow could live on this amount if necessary. This pay was comparable to what "relief workers" made digging ditches for the U.S. Government's Works Progress Administration. Nearby living quarters were available at a nine dollar weekly average and often included any charges for board.

There were fifteen students in this first class. About half the students in this group were college graduates and came from families, a few quite affluent, who could afford to pay the course's tuition. The balance scrimped and saved their precious money to attend the course.

The first class started in early January 1936, but there was no formal classroom instruction until Cy Terry completed his Winter Term teachings at Cornell University later in the month prior to taking a leave of absence to teach at LADC. In the meantime, the students were given actual on-the-job training and work.

Terry arrived in early February and quickly organized his classes and classroom. One or two hours of classroom instruction were scheduled before lunch. Studies included airplane design, stress analysis, production planning, stock control, sales, and cost accounting. Practical on-the-job training and shop experience consumed the balance of the day.

Students were assigned to various departments and rotated somewhat, but not on a regular schedule. Individual capability and department requirements determined who would be assigned where. Those with aeronautical engineering backgrounds went to engineering; others were assigned to detail parts (equipped with one old lathe, possibly two drill presses), sheet metal, welding, fuselage, wing or control surface departments. Later, a few students were assigned to final assembly.

Ross Funk's detail parts department. Funk instructed apprentice students in various metal working skills while parts were made, eventually to be used in Phantom production. LYLE FARVER

Two books were used by the students. The first, *Technical Aerodynamics*, was written by Cornell University professor, K.D. Wood. The second, *An Airplane Design,* was written by Professor Wood, also. At the time, Niles and Newell's *Airplane Structures* was considered by many instructors and engineers to be the "bible" regarding structures, material strengths and so forth, and was referenced on many occasions.

The combination of students and employed workers on the production floor was a curious one. Perhaps no where else did an aircraft company use student labor to build airplanes except, possibly, Parks, Aeronca, Spartan, Ryan, etc., which had established flight and mechanics schools. Though the students did not make any critical parts, such as cowlings or fuselage skins, they made and assembled, nevertheless, many small Phantom detail parts.

Terry had few major problems to confront. One major annoyance, however, was the incessant noise from Nick Nordyke's power-hammer. It was deafening and disrupted the classroom instruction. The classroom was a small room located above the stockroom inside the main hangar. Nordyke's power-hammer was downstairs,

Factory employee Kenneth E. Cericola is dwarfed by the cowl of a visiting Waco Cabin. KENNETH E. CERICOLA

not far from the classroom. Terry appealed to Luscombe to build facilities expressly for the school.

Don recognized the current hangar and side office facilities offered little room for expansion and made plans to remedy the situation. He contracted to have a trio of new buildings erected adjacent the West Trenton hangar. One of these buildings would house the classroom and school shop.

The other two buildings would house the dope/paint shop and the sheet metal shop, respectively. The second floor of the sheet metal shop building would be occupied by the engineering department.

Word of Luscombe's training program spread quickly and a second class started a few weeks after the first. Now, almost thirty young men were in some form of apprentice training and instruction. Ken Cericola was among this group of students.[43] The "Apprentice Program" continued the balance of the year, accepting students as new classes were organized.

Despite the income generated from student tuition, Don Luscombe continued to seek money from friends and backers. But, many of his New York City friends, including Pete Brooks, Bryan Sheedy and George Thorne, began to lose interest in the company and Don's glowing talk of mass production and all-metal airplanes. Perhaps the glamour and expectation of success were no longer there or perhaps politics were involved, the final result was the same — Don was left hanging and this fact distressed him greatly. If not for the immediate influx of deposit money from Eddie Davis and Ig Sargent for their Luscombe Phantoms, and the income from student training, Don's airplane endeavors might have collapsed quickly.

Don remained resourceful, however, and he continued to meet new people willing to offer financial support. George B. Cluett, II, and Daniel Simonds were but two of several financially endowed gentlemen who answered Luscombe's call for help.

Cluett, a somewhat short individual in his mid-thirties, was keen to aviation and aircraft manufacturing. Ig Sargent, Eddie Davis and Don Luscombe were aware of this fact and combined their salesman talents and aviation contacts to interest Cluett in the company. Cluett, an heir to the Cluett-Peabody family fortune (Arrow collar and shirt business known for the patented "Sanfordizing" process), was most anxious to assist Luscombe in his continuing endeavors. For his efforts, Cluett became a director in the company.

However, before Don Luscombe or his company received any money, Cluett attached a major string. He insisted Don hire Roger H. Johnson to handle the company's financial affairs. Cluett wanted to make sure his investment was in good hands and handled properly as there was then no one with solid accounting and financial background in the Luscombe organization.

By way of introduction, Johnson graduated from the Pierce School of Accounting in Philadelphia, Pennsylvania, in 1926, which was followed by two years of post graduate work. Johnson was employed during the daytime as an Industrial Accountant by Middishade, Inc., of Philadelphia, manufacturers of men's clothing, and instructed the night classes at the Pierce School for two years.

In late 1934, he became Comptroller of Hall, Hartwell and Co., Inc., manufacturers of men's shirts, in Troy, New York. During this employment, Johnson became associated with George Cluett. He returned to Philadelphia during the fall of 1935, and became a semi-senior certified public accountant. In March 1936, Johnson left this position and became associated with the Luscombe Airplane Development Corporation as office manager and accountant, eventually assuming the secretary and treasurer positions. Johnson was most anxious to see Luscombe succeed. Soon, these two gentlemen developed a close rapport. Roger Johnson had an easy-going personality which meshed well with Don Luscombe's friendly and persuasive style of conducting business.

The second investor, Daniel Simonds owned and presided over Simonds Saw Company in Massachusetts. Much like Cluett, Simonds enjoyed flying and was keen to aviation. During this time frame, at least three Phantom airplanes were in various stages of construction. These included Ig Sargent's and Eddie Davis' airplanes.

At the start of 1936, only the bottom half of Sargent's airplane was in the jig. The top half was added within a month, completed and removed from the jig. As soon as Sargent's airplane left the jig, Eddie Davis' airplane was readied. Sargent's fuselage was completed by late March and was painted an overall Diana cream shortly afterwards.

In the meantime, a third Phantom was under construction for STANAVO, the Standard Oil Development Company of New Jersey. When completed, this aircraft was destined to sport the fanciest paint scheme of any Phantom built.

To meet the increasing workload, Luscombe hired several new employees. Joining the employee roster were Lou Coghill, Ralph Coston, Henri D'Estout and Jules De Crescenzo. Louis Coghill, a very qualified mechanic and a rated pilot, joined the Luscombe team in early 1936. His experience was badly needed. Coghill was placed in the wing department and worked under Fritz King, who was department foreman.

Eventually, King relinquished his position to Coghill so he could devote full time to final assembly department duties, which included repairing damaged Phantoms, flight training and running the gas and vending machine concessions. The latter were mostly after-work, personal endeavors which Fritz undertook to make money on the side and were not part of his job.

Ralph Coston of Clifton, Texas, was a student assigned to the detail parts department under Ross Funk. After hours, he worked with Fritz King flight instructing and pumping fuel. These two aviators soon formed a side-business on the field called the K & C Flying Service, of which the LADC received a percentage of its profits.

Henri D'Estout, formerly an Army Air Corps mechanic, was hired and was placed in charge of the paint and fabric department. His skill and ability contributed immensely to the inherent beauty of the West Trenton-produced Phantoms. D'Estout's painting abilities rivaled, if not surpassed, those of any other painter at any competing airplane manufacturer.

Jules De Crescenzo brought with him a vast aviation background. Having worked in the Philadelphia area for almost fourteen years as an aircraft mechanic and instructor prior to his employment with Luscombe, Don hired De Crescenzo as the factory's sub-assembly inspector.

Several Yale University graduates joined the Luscombe sales staff during this energetic period. Hiram Mallinson of New York City, heir to the Mallinson

Chapter Nine: Looking Up, Getting Better 131

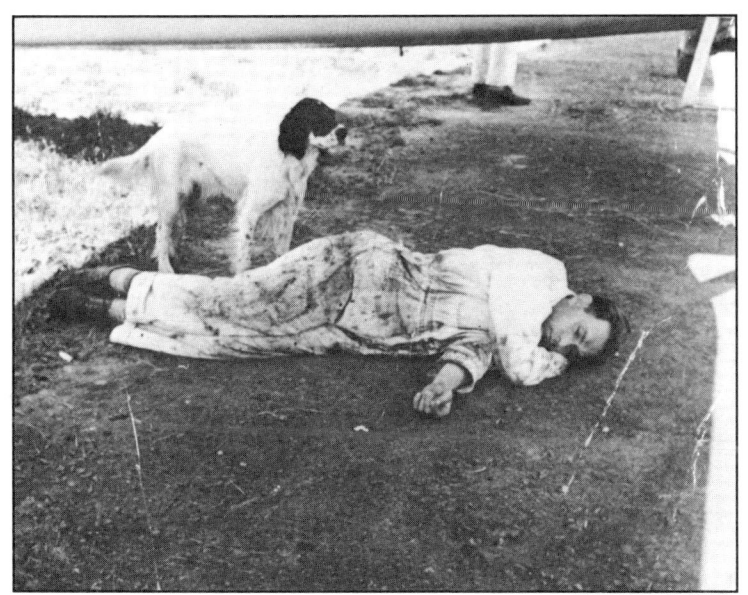

Fritz King takes a quick, mid-afternoon snooze. One of Don Luscombe's dogs stands nearby to ensure King is not disturbed. CHARLES E. BURGESS

Ralph Coston IGNATIUS SARGENT

silk fortune, invested heavily in Luscombe's endeavor and was later rewarded with a Director position within the company. In time, this congenial relationship would sour as Mallinson had the unnerving ability of wrecking Phantoms.

Another Yale graduate, John Polhemus, joined the company and enrolled in the apprentice program. Likewise, Yale graduates Thaddeus Longstreth, Richard Fabian and investors Don O'Conner and Lew Lawton were entered on the employee rosters, most working in the sales department.

Carl Aa, a young and generous Canadian, became associated with the company about this time. Aa was hired for his ability to splice cable — a skill very much in demand within Luscombe's developing company. To earn extra money on the side, Aa arose early to milk the cows on dairy farms not far from the factory.

Aa's unusual last name was not his given name. Instead, it was a name he adopted. Aa was concerned the company could fold at any time and wanted to be sure he would be first in line to receive any paychecks before the money ran out.

Aa owned an Aeronca C-2 which he rented to students and employees for two dollars per hour. He organized a small flying club called the Flying Stooges Flying Club. Members would buy and sell "shares" in this limited partnership flying club. As one member left, he would sell his share to a prospective new member.

Incidentally, Carl Aa was not the first student to have his airplane available to employees and students. Ig Sargent and Eddie Davis owned a Monocoupe 90 they rented for $5 per hour. Ironically, this airplane was the same airplane Wes Smith had flown *through* the Mercer County Airport's open and, fortunately, empty hangar a couple years earlier.

Other airplane rental arrangements were made by other employees. Instructor Cy Terry and "apprentice program" student Bill Shepard leased a Kinner-powered Bird biplane from an Fixed-Base Operation in Ithaca, New York, during May 1936. The aircraft was rented to LADC employees and students who had pilot's licenses. After two weeks, however, the FBO needed the Bird returned and exchanged it for a 40 hp Taylor E-2 Cub.

After witnessing some of the flying hijinx at the Mercer County Airport, one would think the Flying Stooges Flying Club was named appropriately. These experiences were often the brunt of much laughter around the factory.

One day, Ig Sargent got into a delicate situation after returning to Mercer County Airport. Shortly after landing, the Aeronca's engine quit because the idle speed was set too low. Sargent, deciding not to inconvenience any employees, jumped out to hand-prop the engine. However, he had opened the throttle too much and the engine roared to life. As the airplane began to move, the hapless pilot jumped out of harm's way. By now, the Aeronca was moving too fast to reach the cockpit, so all he could do was grasp one of the wing-tips or wing struts to prevent the errant airplane from departing sans pilot.

Workers and students at the LADC factory, eating lunch at the time, ventured into the field to assist but were laughing so hard by the time they reached the Aeronca and pilot they were of little help.

All were moved almost to tears to see the hapless pilot holding onto his whirling Aeronca while it traced a bouncing, circular path, a large ring.

After a few minutes, Ralph Coston was able to approach the aircraft, get "inside" the ring, and turn off the magneto switches, much to the relief of an embarrassed pilot.

As word and praise of Luscombe's new school spread, other eager and aviation-hungry individuals joined the LADC organization. From an initial cadre of less than a dozen men, the company was able to boast thirty or more full-time employees on its employee roster.

Interestingly, with so many "well-heeled" individuals running about the grounds either visiting, enrolled in the school or working for Don, the Mercer County Airport became known by some as "the Luscombe Country Club."

With the apprentice program in full-swing and several Phantoms in various stages of construction, the engineering department had time to expand upon new ideas. Under Chief Engineer Lyle Farver's direction, this department attempted to improve the Phantom's wily handling characteristics, simplify some construction aspects and advance the Model 2, a four-place Phantom design concept.

Several significant engineering changes were incorporated in the post-Kansas City Phantoms. The most notable change involved relocating the tailwheel to the fuselage bulkhead station immediately forward of the vertical fin's leading edge. There, it was attached to the bulkhead and supported by a shock absorber system fully enclosed in the fuselage. The supporting bulkhead, originally a stamping, was changed to a casting. Later, after a tailwheel ripped out the lower lug, this lug was reinforced with a "U" bolt to take the tension loads.

However, this design change did not improve the aircraft's ground handling characteristics. In fact, the Phantom's groundloop potential was increased because the aircraft's turn radius was decreased. The airplane still demanded it be flown by an experienced pilot. In an effort to lessen the treacherous groundloop tendency, a tailwheel locking mechanism was in the works, but was not ready to be tested for several months. Eventually, the Department of Commerce, Bureau of Air Commerce, approved the tail wheel redesign for future production in late 1936.

Another, yet more subtle design change involved the pilot's and passenger's seat rivet pattern around the door frame area. The Kansas City-built Phantom fuselages had a curved seat bottom and exhibited three curved rows of rivets where the edge of the gracefully curved seat was attached to the skin. Starting with serial number 106 (NC1286), the seat was flat and the rivet pattern attaching the sides of this seat to the skin was a straight line from the bottom center of the door frame back to the next aft bulkhead. Additionally, a new door hinge was designed and incorporated. This new hinge was larger and operated more smoothly.

A significant production improvement involved the method in which the Phantom's bulkheads were fabricated. Previously, these bulkheads were beat-out by hand. Chuck Burgess recognized this problem and developed a novel and very functional solution. Using his previous steel mill experience, Burgess fabricated a set of rollers on a machine lathe. Then, he built a framework to hold the rolls and anchored it to the building's concrete floor. Power to turn these rollers came from an old truck that was jacked-up and anchored to the floor.

Ig Sargent's Phantom (s/n 106) under construction. Note the many improvements to the landing gear and door hinge. LYLE FARVER

Chapter Nine: Looking Up, Getting Better   133

One wheel was locked and the other was removed.

The drive to the rollers was taken from the truck's axle. By adjusting the pressure on the rollers, Burgess was able to make perfectly circular bulkheads with the angle slightly open or closed as necessary to adjust for the fuselage's streamline taper.

Don rewarded Chuck for his insightful invention by giving him 1000 shares of stock in the company. Often, while Don showed his company to a prospective client, he would have Burgess fire-up the rolling machine to demonstrate the "mass-production" processes being used in the company.

Even as these changes on the Phantom were designed, approved and put into effect, work continued on the Model 2 design. On paper, this four-place project featured a longer fuselage, a larger wingspan and a slightly revised tail group over its two-place cousin, the Luscombe Phantom 1. Likewise, the engineers envisioned this aircraft would be powered by a Jacobs 285 hp radial engine or, surprisingly, a 420 hp Pratt and Whitney power plant.

Drawings circulated in late 1935 and throughout 1936 referred to this design as the Luscombe "Ghost." Nevertheless, the engineering effort was more towards a four-place project and not a five-place airplane as paraded in various company brochures.

Bill Benckert and Charlie Barnett, two students assigned to engineering, assisted Lyle Farver with this project. Other engineering department employees at that time included Eddie Tarencz, Bob Humphreys, F. Dunford and P.V. Cheng.

At one point, Farver explored the feasibility of a

Chuck Burgess' innovative Phantom bulkhead rolling mill. Power was taken from the rear axle of a Ford pick-up truck and transferred to adjustable rollers used to make the bulkhead ring.   CHARLES E. BURGESS

(Upper Right) Luscombe Model 2, four-place wood mock-up, circa summer 1936. From left to right — factory salesman Ken Kuchawa, Bill Shepard, Bill Benckert, Lyle Farver and Lou Coghill.

WILLIAM B. SHEPARD

(Lower Right) Wood model of the Luscombe "Ghost," a proposed four-place follow-on to the Luscombe Phantom. Factory engineer Bill Shepard built the cowl whereas other employees built the fuselage. The wings were built by New York University students.

LYLE FARVER

retractable landing gear version of the "Ghost." He soon discovered the extra weight penalty was unacceptable and quickly killed this idea. The Luscombe "Ghost" development never progressed beyond a rudimentary, wood-frame mock-up of the cabin area and a series of wind tunnel model tests at New York University in New York City during the summer of 1936.

Originally, the plan was to test only the design's airfoil shape in the wind tunnel, but further study dictated a one-tenth scale model of the four-place design be constructed. While the university wind tunnel staff built the wing, Luscombe employees built the fuselage.

After the model was assembled and hung inverted in the wind tunnel chamber, tests commenced to determine the viability of the project. The design, though feasible, exhibited less than expected performance results and the concept was eventually abandoned.

Interestingly, the impetus for this testing was not as much to actually test a new design as it was an innovative way for Luscombe to "cultivate" a new friend and potential source of money. In this case, Luscombe attempted to woo the support of New York University's Dr. Alexander Klemin and the university as a whole. Overall, Don's efforts were unsuccessful.

With the greater part of this project behind them, the engineering staff directed their efforts towards a lighter, lower horsepower, potentially lower priced airplane. The Phantom's $6000 price tag continued to discourage buyers and Luscombe wanted a new design that would appeal to a cost-conscious, sportsman pilot.

Farver and his small staff studied ways to pare down the Phantom's robust and compound curve structure so it could fly satisfactorily on a lower horsepower engine. They soon discovered the Phantom's robust structure could not be compromised. Ivan Driggs' design remained intact. Farver then decided the best approach would be to design a new fuselage structure altogether. These efforts occupied his at-

The Luscombe "Ghost" model hangs inverted in the New York University's wind tunnel. LYLE FARVER

tention the balance of the year.

In the meantime, Phantom NC272Y was disassembled and its fuselage and wings stored in the main hangar's overhead rafters. Thus, a fuselage and a set of wings were readily available for any engineering design and related flight testing.

During late May and early June 1936, another group of "apprentice program" students arrived to begin classes. Luscombe could now count almost fifty students engaged in some form of training or apprentice work on the floor. William E. "Bill" Force and Paul McCormick were among this new group of students. Like many young men of the day, each were infatuated with flying and desired a career in aviation.

Paul McCormick stayed on the school and factory grounds until November 1936, and built many of the Phantom stabilizers and elevators. Bill Force, on the other hand, remained to work for Don for many productive years.

By way of background, William Force was born in Glen Ridge, New Jersey, in 1915 and attended the local schools there until the family moved to Fryeburg, Maine, when he was a young boy. He continued his education in Fryeburg, and graduated from the Fryeburg Academy in 1932.

An advertisement in a newspaper caught his eye and he pleaded with his folks to help him attend Luscombe's new training program. Excited, he wrote Mr. Benjamin Kauffman in New York City, then Luscombe's agent to solicit students, for more information.

Force's parents were most concerned the training could involve flying of some type and begged their son not to fly. Bill allayed their fears and promised he would not. In the end, his parents relented and allowed him to attend the new apprentice program. Bill Force, on the property for barely a few weeks, noted sweeping changes were taking place around him.

Commencing in late spring or early summer of 1936, ground was broken for the first two of the three buildings to be erected. As they were completed, the Paint Shop, Sheet Metal, and Engineering departments moved into their new facilities. A third building, dedicated to the apprentice program, was erected shortly thereafter.

Located behind and to the rear left of the main hangar, the first building housed the paint shop. This structure was 40 ft. by 20 ft. and was constructed of sheet metal. It was equipped with air pressure guns for spraying and a ventilation system with vapor proof switches for safety to provide even temperatures throughout the year.

Next to it was the Sheet Metal and Engineering Building, a two story, 40 ft. by 20 ft. frame building which housed the sheet metal shop on the first floor and the engineering department on the second floor. Nick Nordyke's bumping hammer was moved from the main hangar and was repositioned on the new building's ground floor. Noise was still a problem.

The third building was devoted to the school. This frame building measured 40 ft. by 20 ft. and had three rooms inside. The ground floor room housed the school shop. Upstairs, the space was divided into two rooms with a small office for the instructor in between. The room nearest the hangar was the classroom and the back room was used for engineering drafting instruction.

By late May and early June, Ig Sargent's Phantom (s/n 106) began to look like an airplane. The fuselage was complete and on its gear. The tail feathers were attached, but not rigged. Only the wings needed to be finished and attached. Similarly, the instruments had yet to be installed.

Soon, three Phantom fuselages were completed

The first two of three supplemental buildings built to handle the Luscombe Airplane Development Corporation's growing student and airplane business. The building on the left was the paint shop. The Sheet Metal and Engineering Building is the adjacent two story building. Note the primed Phantom fuselage behind the tree. Circa summer 1936. LYLE FARVER

Phantom s/n 106 fuselage and wings under construction in the foreground. To the far left is Phantom s/n 109. The ship in the middle under construction is Phantom s/n 107. LYLE FARVER

136 Visions of Luscombe: The Early Years

Phantom construction at the West Trenton factory. Phantom s/n 107 is under construction in the foreground. HOWARD JONG

and out of the jig, Eddie Davis' Phantom (s/n 107), the Standard Oil Development Company of New Jersey's (STANAVO) Phantom (s/n 109), and an unpurchased Phantom (s/n 108). Available manpower was used to complete the first three mentioned airplanes before further effort was expended on any subsequent production. When production resumed, a new fuselage was produced every two to three weeks.

In mid-June, Ig Sargent's Phantom was assembled and made ready for its maiden flight. The six-foot-two-inch Sargent, wearing a pair of white coveralls with red lettered "LUSCOMBE AIRPLANES" embroidered on the back, held his Phantom's wing panels while Fritz King, Henri D'Estout and employee Lionel Quellette bolted the wing to the fuselage. Don Luscombe and a few other employees stood nearby and observed the ambitious activity.

On June 20, 1936, Ignatius Sargent climbed aboard, started the engine and proceeded to test fly his own Phantom airplane. This flight was the first time he had ever flown a Phantom. The experience was exhilarating!

Though a generally smooth test flight overall, it was not without incident. A hard landing broke one of the landing gear wires. Quickly repaired, Sargent was back in the air within a few days, building hours and confidence in his new airplane.

Ig Sargent, left, lifts the left wing of his Phantom (NC1286, s/n 106) during final assembly. HOWARD JONG

Chapter Nine: Looking Up, Getting Better   137

(Top) A good inside view of the Luscombe hangar. Ig Sargent's NC1286 is under construction in the foreground. Circa June 1936.

(Lower Right) Ig Sargent and Ralph Coston make a brake adjustment on NC1286.

(Lower Left) The cockpit of NC1286.

Ig Sargent's Luscombe Phantom, NC1286, is rolled-out.   IGNATIUS SARGENT

The scalloped red trim paint scheme on Ig Sargent's Phantom shown to a good advantage.   IGNATIUS SARGENT

In the rush to build more airplanes, more employees had to be hired. Among those hired was Francis "Frank" Bonneau Johnson. He joined the Luscombe Airplane Development Corporation in an "apprentice worker" capacity, but did not attend the school as a student.

Frank Johnson, son of an Episcopal minister, was born in Roanoke, Virginia, in 1911, yet he claimed Franklin, North Carolina, as his home in later years. A bright and intuitive youngster, he learned to use a slide rule before he was fifteen. An older brother (Frank was the fourth of six brothers) was an engineering student at the University of North Carolina in Chapel Hill and brought his slide rule home often. Johnson followed his older brother's footsteps and attended the University of North Carolina between 1930 and 1933, where he majored in mechanical engineering with an aeronautical option.

Johnson left school and got a surveyor job in South Carolina with the United States Forest Service. During the spring of 1936, he visited Don Luscombe and was advised that apprenticeship positions were open. Some weeks later, Frank received an anxious telegram from Don Luscombe stating, *"When can you*

Chapter Nine: Looking Up, Getting Better   139

report? We need your help." Frank Johnson joined the company in early July.

Johnson's first assignment was in the sheet metal shop. There, he worked with Nick Nordyke fabricating various Phantom parts. During Nick's absence, Johnson would fabricate some of the Phantom's intricate, compound curvature skins on the bumping-hammer. Yet, the final products were approved by Nordyke or Chuck Burgess. When Johnson arrived, he secured quarters in the old farm house turned "dormitory" near the factory. Within a week, however, this arrangement changed.

Nick Nordyke and Frank Johnson — HOWARD JONG

Roger Johnson, the company's treasurer and no relation to the aforementioned Frank Johnson, set about to find better quarters for apprentice program students and company employees. He embarked upon a brief search to find a suitable building large enough to accommodate twenty or more students.

Using money provided by George Cluett, II, and George Gallitan, an affluent LADC school student, Johnson purchased outright or secured a long-term lease for a structure known at one time as the Mountain View Inn. This large, late eighteenth century Prussian farmhouse and its accompanying estate were not far from the West Trenton facilities and offered students a tremendous improvement in living conditions over any previous quarters.

Ig Sargent beams proudly before his Luscombe Phantom. — IGNATIUS SARGENT

This three story building had at least eight bedrooms, one large living room and a spacious dining room. Likewise, the kitchen was well-equipped and offered much storage space for canned and boxed items. The new facility was called the "Jolly Roger," no doubt a nickname derived from the friendly Roger Johnson whom managed the facilities. This endearing nickname was applied originally to the old, original dormitory and was used infrequently. When the

The "Jolly Roger" as it appeared in 1936. This Luscombe student and employee boarding house had a checkered history. — HOWARD JONG

new dormitory was bought, the name followed.

Students and employees alike lived in the "Jolly Roger." On weekends, Roger Johnson would organize social activities at the house. The weekends were festive times for the residents of the Jolly Roger, with many students playing a variety of musical instruments while others danced to the beat of the music.

Beginning in late 1936, a Mrs. Elsie Thatcher was hired to run the house for Roger Johnson and served as a sort of "housemother." Her teenage daughter, Becky, did some modeling in New York City.

Rumors abounded then as today regarding the true, historical background of the "Jolly Roger." One whimsical account states it was used as a brothel during General George Washington's tenure in the area. Another tattle states the buildings and land once belonged to a wealthy family that became broke and destitute, eventually deeding the premises to the state to meet financial obligations. Regardless of this inn's true nature, the history of the "Jolly Roger" adds much to the Luscombe lore.

numbers painted on the wings, this Phantom's out-of-sequence delivery allowed the Standard Oil Development Company and its contracted paint shop personnel more time to complete the intricate, bright red eagle on a base white paint scheme. A similar, very distinctive paint scheme had been applied previously on at least three STANAVO-owned airplanes, a Lockheed Vega and two Monocoupe 90As. The STANAVO airplanes were well-recognized wherever they flew.

The name *STANAVO* was synonymous with quality aviation fuels and lubricants. Capt. Edwin E. Aldrin, Standard Oil Development Company of New Jersey Aviation Manager (and astronaut Edwin "Buzz" Aldrin's father), took great pride in his fleet of gala painted airplanes. The Phantom would carry the STANAVO name proudly.

This Phantom's delivery and subsequent sale gave Luscombe much needed cash to further production of other airplanes. In early July, Don Luscombe appealed to the Department of Commerce, Bureau of Air Commerce, to approve a smaller license number for the STANAVO Phantom. The Department had assigned a five digit number originally, but this number proved virtually impossible for D'Estout to paint on the wing surfaces and still comply with the Department's regulations. In his letter, Luscombe suggested NC105, NC106 and included the customer's request, 7734. The Department approved 7734. The imputation behind this number's selection was a curious one. "7734," when

WILLIAM B. SHEPARD

(Above) The Standard Oil Development Company of New Jersey (STANAVO) Luscombe Phantom, s/n 109, was delivered to its new owners in an overall base white, except for the painted registration numbers.

(Right) Taken from virtually the same angle as the previous photograph, the STANAVO Luscombe Phantom displays its unique red eagle paint scheme.

JOHN LENGENFELDER

Meanwhile, back at the plant, at least two more Phantoms were prepared for their respective first flights. The STANAVO Phantom was ready to test its wings. Eddie Davis' airplane, NC1007 (s/n 107), was not far behind it.

Ironically, the STANAVO Phantom was destined to be completed, test flown and delivered before Davis' airplane. Finished and delivered in an overall egg shell white except for the large, black registration

written with a slightly opened "4," spells "hell" when viewed from an inverted angle. Perhaps STANAVO was making a bold, if not defiant statement to its competitors.

The Standard Oil Development Company of New Jersey applied for a Commercial Airplane License in late June 1936. The application was approved and the aircraft inspected as airworthy by Department of Commerce, Aeronautics Branch in-

Chapter Nine: Looking Up, Getting Better   141

STANAVO Luscombe Phantom, NC7734.   JOHN LENGENFELDER

spector George Gay on July 27, 1936.

George Gay, a little guy with an Errol Flynn-type moustache, was one of the very few early inspectors who understood completely the Phantom's intricate construction and its touchy ground handling nature. Gay approved and actually flew many of the Phantom airplanes produced by Luscombe in Kansas City and West Trenton. Gay's signature of approval is found on many of the company's early Applications for Commercial Airplane License forms (Department of Commerce, Aeronautics Branch, Form AB-9).

On August 14, 1936, Ig Sargent took Phantom NC7734 (s/n 109) aloft for its first test flight. Three days later, he was in the air again checking-out the STANAVO pilots in their new company airplane.

Barely eight days later, Eddie Davis test flew his Phantom (NC1007). Eager to compare his best friend's Phantom's flight characteristics to his own, Sargent made a test flight in Davis' airplane the following day.

Noteworthy, both Ig Sargent's and Eddie Davis' Phantom airplanes sported identical paint schemes, with one exception — the trim color. Both aircraft had a gloss Diana cream base coat, but Sargent's airplane displayed a bright Stearman red stripe trim with scalloped pattern on the wing and horizontal stabilizer, whereas Davis' airplane used a dark blue trim with the scallop pattern.

There had been somewhat of a quiet rush to get Sargent's and Davis' ships completed. Both gentlemen planned to fly their respective airplanes to Cali-

Fritz King, Ben Melcher and Lou Coghill load sandbags on the tail of Eddie Davis' Phantom, s/n 107.   LYLE FARVER

142   Visions of Luscombe: The Early Years

(Left and below) Except for some paint and gear fairings, Eddie Davis' Luscombe Phantom (NC1007) nears completion.

JAMES B. ZAZAS COLLECTION

JAMES B. ZAZAS COLLECTION

(Left) Eddie Davis' Luscombe Phantom being masked prior to painting the "NC1007" registration.

IGNATIUS SARGENT

Chapter Nine: Looking Up, Getting Better 143

Ig and Sissie Sargent take a break during an outing in their Luscombe Phantom.

fornia and attend the National Air Races at Los Angeles. In the end, the Davis ship was completed barely four days before he and Sargent left on their six week, company-sponsored Phantom sales and promotion adventure.[44]

As their respective airplanes were completed, Sargent and Davis realized they would soon be out of a "job." Don Luscombe appreciated this possibility and proposed they remain as the company's test pilots and sales managers. Both Sargent and Davis accepted gladly.

While Sargent and Davis prepared to leave on their trip, Cy Terry bid a fond adieu to his students and the company. His leave of absence from Cornell University was over and it was time for him to return. Don asked Terry's former college student and, of late, apprentice program student, Bill Shepard, to take over the class until a full-time instructor could be hired. Shepard agreed.

While he was an "apprentice program" student, Shepard worked with Ross Funk in the detail parts department. There, he learned how to rivet, run the lathe and function in other shop duties. Funk was impressed by his new charge and was quite happy to have Shepard working for him. However, Funk became quite upset when he learned Shepard was going to teach at the school. It meant he was going to

A youthful Howard Jong stands beside Eddie Davis' Phantom.

lose his best worker.

To ease ruffled feathers, Shepard wore two hats. He continued to work for Funk, but took two hours each day to prepare and teach the academics portion of the class. Shepard remained in this capacity until November when Luscombe hired a full-time instructor to take over the classes. Meanwhile, Chuck Burgess filled-in temporarily as the shop instructor during the shop portion of the class.

In early September 1936, Howard "Johnny" Jong joined the Luscombe Airplane Development Corporation. Like so many of the young men working at the company, Jong lived, ate and breathed aviation. By way of background, Jong was born and raised and attended schools in Los Angeles, California. A brilliant and gifted student, Jong graduated from the Curtiss-Wright Technical Institute, Grand Central Air Terminal, Glendale, California, in 1935 with an aeronautical certificate. Shortly after graduation, he went to work briefly for Hawley Bowlus of the Bowlus Sailplane and Trailer Company in San Fernando, California, between 1935 and 1936.

One day in mid-1936, Jong saw his first Luscombe Phantom parked on the Grand Central Air Terminal line. It was Frank Spreckles' cream with maroon trim airplane, NC277Y. Jong was enamored with this finely crafted airplane. He made up his mind to go to work for Luscombe.

Thus, in early September 1936, Jong began as an apprentice worker. His first assignment was in the detail parts department under Ross Funk's watchful eye, then in the metal shop working for Nick Nordyke and Frank Johnson.

Johnson taught Jong the art of aluminum welding. Many of his first jobs involved welding the Phantom's fuel tanks and fabricating other Phantom parts, including the speed cuffs on the aircraft's wing struts. Jong's welding ability soon caught the attention of everybody in the shop.

Jong proved to be an adept welder with his work rivaling the best in the shop. Very few shop personnel could match his ability for a constant ripple. At one point, a class of students from the Casey Jones

School of Aeronautics, Roosevelt Field, New York, made a special visit to the Luscombe factory to observe and learn Jong's welding techniques.

Jong did not like repetitive work. He sought new challenges to keep his hands and mind active. As such, Jong demonstrated his innate mechanical and engineering talents in many areas. During his spare time, Jong worked with Fritz King and Ralph Coston maintaining the airplanes. At the same time, Jong was able to log some dual flight instruction.

When Jong went to work for Luscombe, he was only nineteen years old! During this time, a new apprentice program class started which brought another twenty-five or more people into the company. Tuition was raised to $800, and if the money was paid in advance, the weekly take-home pay was increased to $20 per week. Additionally, the course was extended to nine months.

To help a few of the more unfortunate souls, the Pennsylvania Department of Welfare underwrote the schooling of a number of handicapped or disabled individuals who attended Luscombe's "Apprentice Program." The Department theorized Luscombe's training would be a good chance for these folks to get a good job during a time when the Depression still held a tight grip on the scarce job market.

One of the students starting in this class was Marty Eisenmann. He saw an ad in a newspaper and decided this program was what he needed to complete work towards his mechanic's license.[45] On his first day on the job, Eisenmann was assigned to work in the detail parts department. On his second day, he was reassigned to the sheet metal department and worked under Nordyke and Johnson. Nordyke was away on an extended and much-needed vacation to his native Holland, so Johnson did most of the instructing. Much of Eisenmann's work was making Phantom fairings and engine cowlings.

Eisenmann made most, if not all, of the nose cowls for the Phantom after serial number 107. However, Frank Johnson was tasked to make the de Bustamente cowling, always under the watchful eye of its future owner. The early nose cowls were made from .032 soft aluminum and were prone to dings and dents. Eisenmann suggested to Nordyke the next nose cowl order should be made of .040 half-hard aluminum, thus, eliminating most dents. Nordyke agreed and the balance of the Phantom nose cowls were made with .040 half-hard aluminum.

During his employment at Luscombe, Jong stayed at the "Jolly Roger." Often, when a few Jolly Roger residents went home for the weekends, Jong and others would meet in Johnson's spacious room on the second floor and discuss airplane design. They talked about a design they hoped to enter in a future Cleveland air race with Ralph Coston as pilot. But, with no financing immediately available, this idea was quickly dropped.

A second joint endeavor involved designing a two place airplane similar to the Cub, Aeronca or Taylorcraft class. Eventually, their efforts would revolutionize the light airplane industry and inspire other airplane corporations to adopt metal construction techniques.

The Luscombe Model 8 design originated from this humble Jolly Roger boarding house table. After work hours drafting sessions in Frank Johnson's room set the basis for what became one of the most beloved, two place, all-metal airplanes. HOWARD JONG

Johnson and his eager young buddies enjoyed these sessions to sharpen their engineering skills. Howard Jong, in particular, relished in these informal discussions. During the course of these weekend hobby efforts, Frank Johnson and his "students" laid the fundamental groundwork for the Luscombe "50," or as it became better known, the Luscombe Model 8.

THE BERRYLOID FLEET — NUMBER TEN OF A SERIES

Red-winged BLACKBIRD

The *Monocoupe* and

Berryloid

AIRCRAFT FINISHES

Mono Aircraft Corporation's first ship was finished 100 per cent with Berryloid as are the planes now coming off the production line. The Red-winged Blackbird inspired the combination on the above Monocoupe —International orange, Boeing yellow and black.

AERO DIGEST, January 1930

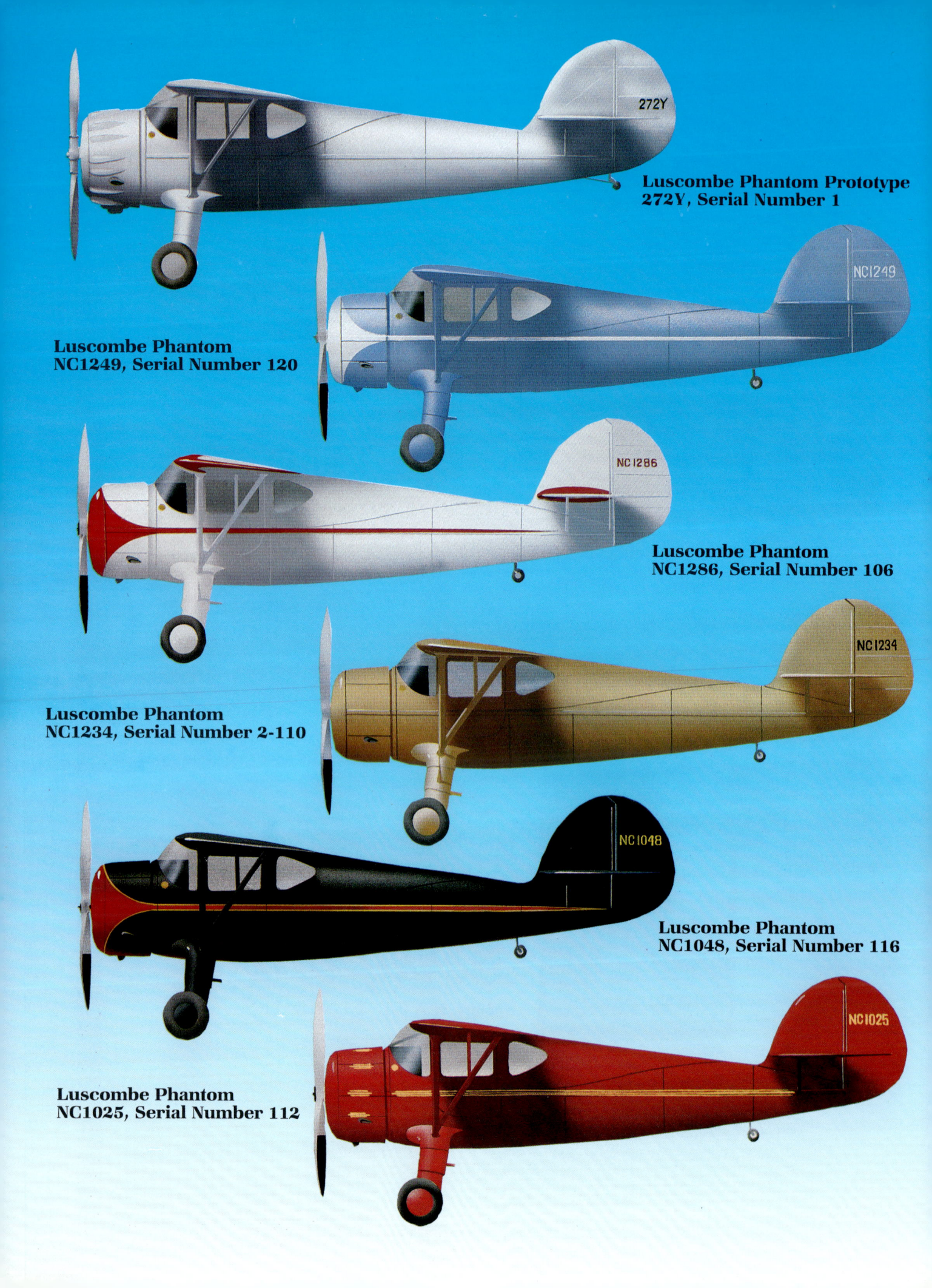

Luscombe Phantom Prototype
272Y, Serial Number 1

Luscombe Phantom
NC1249, Serial Number 120

Luscombe Phantom
NC1286, Serial Number 106

Luscombe Phantom
NC1234, Serial Number 2-110

Luscombe Phantom
NC1048, Serial Number 116

Luscombe Phantom
NC1025, Serial Number 112

"The country needs and, unless I mistake its temper,
the country demands bold, persistent experimentation.
It is common sense to take a method and try it.
If it fails, admit it frankly and try another.
But above all, try something."

Franklin Delano Roosevelt (1882 - 1945)
Address at Oglethorpe University,
Atlanta, Georgia, May 22, 1932

Chapter Ten

"Well... We Tried Everything Else"

The 1017 airplane was a quick, lash-up job. The airplane used the fuselage from NC272Y and production Phantom wings and tail group. Flight testing revealed the airplane was much too heavy for the laboring Warner "Scarab Junior," 90 hp engine.

LYLE FARVER

The last quarter of 1936 proved the busiest, if not the most productive, period of time in the company's brief history to date. Six Phantom airplanes were built and delivered to mostly satisfied customers. Likewise, a new prototype airplane took to the air for the first time, a 90 horsepower design using a Phantom fuselage and wing structure. Finally, almost a hundred men had passed through the apprentice program, and most were now working for the company full time. But this excitement was tempered by sadness. A Phantom was involved in a fatal accident and another was involved in a potentially fatal mishap.

September 1936 was a busy month at the Luscombe Airplane Development Corporation. The production floor hummed with activity. Two Phantoms were completed, at least three fuselages waited to be mated to their matched sets of wings and another five airplanes were in various stages of construction.

The first Phantom finished in September was George A. Humphreys' ship, NC1008 (s/n 108). Though the airplane was completed during September, official Department of Commerce documents disagree whether the correct month of manufacture was September or October.[46]

Ig Sargent, just back from his successful six week Western United States sales tour, flight tested NC1008 on October 15, 1936. He checked-out Humphreys' on October 25. Humphreys took delivery of NC1008 later in the month. For unknown reason(s), the official Bill of Sale is dated January 11, 1937.

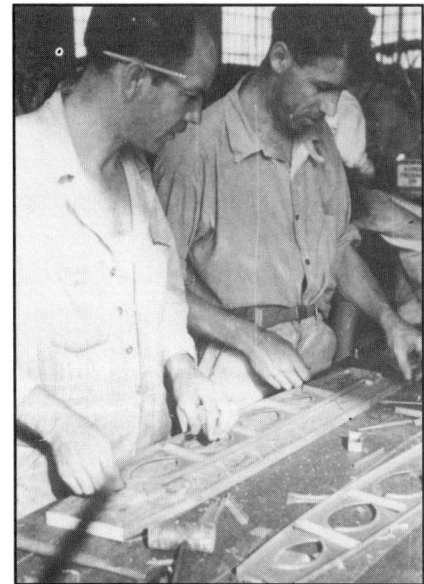

146   *Visions of Luscombe: The Early Years*

(Above right) Two employees attach the wingtip bow to a Phantom wing.

(Top left) Factory employees Eddie and Mose Grigg buildup a Phantom wing rib.

(Far left) Shown here, the completed left wing of a Luscombe Phantom is ready for cover.

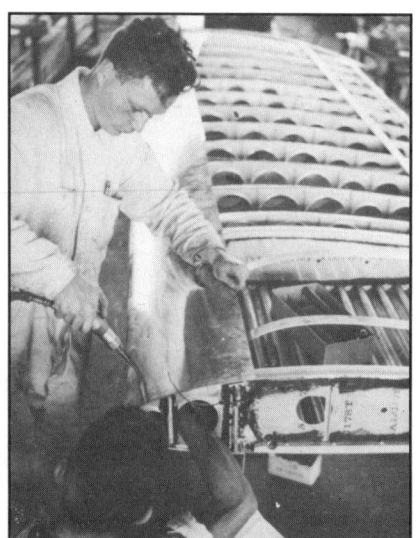

(Left) The metal leading edge is attached to a Phantom wing.

(Bottom left) A Phantom wing under construction.

(Below) A Phantom wing being covered.

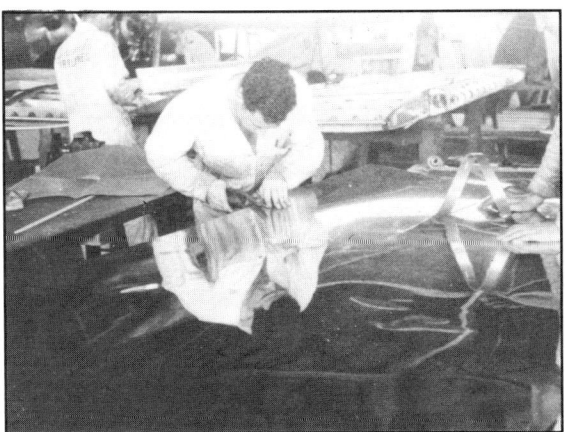

Chapter Ten: "Well... We Tried Everything Else" 147

(Above) Care had to be taken when cutting sheet aluminum so that very little was wasted.

(Top right) Phantom tail assembly required a careful eye and close jig tolerances to ensure proper fit and alignment.

(Middle right) The engineering department. Circa 1937.

(Bottom left) Rudder and brake pedal installation of a West Trenton-built Luscombe Phantom.

(Bottom middle) Employee Bob Humphries looks over some engineering drawings. Note the "Ghost" drawing on the wall.

(Bottom right) Phantom fin construction.

HOWARD JONG

CHARLES E. BURGESS

HOWARD JONG

LYLE FARVER    HOWARD JONG    HOWARD JONG

148 Visions of Luscombe: The Early Years

(Left) Phantom construction at its peak saw almost a new fuselage completed every three weeks.

(Below) Final assembly of Phantom NC1008 was completed in early October 1936.

HOWARD JONG

The second Phantom completed in September was NC1234 (s/n 2-110) and was built for Hiram "Hi" Mallinson, a prominent LADC backer. (Mallinson became a LADC Board member on January 20, 1937.) Ig Sargent took this airplane, painted an overall copper-bronze paint scheme (complementing Mallinson's favorite brand of beer "Ballantine"), aloft for its maiden flight on October 8, 1936. Once again, there exists some paperwork confusion as to the correct date of manufacture. [47]

The ink was hardly dry on the Bill of Sale when Mallinson gently nosed-over his Phantom on his first landing. He landed rather long and hot, zig-zagged a bit, then slowly went over on his back.

CHARLES E. BURGESS

Embarrassed, he told associates he cranked-in the parking brake instead of trim. In reality, Mallinson was unfamiliar with the aircraft's very sensitive braking characteristics. As was often the case, any substantial braking above a moderate taxi speed could result in an embarrassing nose-over for the hapless Phantom pilot and airplane.

LADC employees and students ventured onto the grass runway, righted the ship and pushed it back to the factory for repairs. In this instance, the damage was very minor and Mallinson was soon back in the air. This airplane was the first of several Mallinson damaged or destroyed during his tenure with Luscombe. Miracu-

The aerodynamically clean lines of the Luscombe Phantom fuselage are shown to a good advantage.   HOWARD JONG

Chapter Ten: "Well... We Tried Everything Else" 149

(Above) Painted an overall bronze color, Hiram Mallinson's Luscombe Phantom, NC1234, basks in a warm New Jersey sun.

(Left and Below) Ooops! Phantom NC1234 after a gentle, noseover accident.

lously, he would walk away from each accident with barely a scratch.

Mallinson's second Phantom flight was not without its "incident," also. Shortly after he landed, one of the apprentice program students approached Mallinson and queried how he groundlooped his airplane. Mallinson was stunned! His landing was perfect. He ran back to his ship to check for damage. Employees and students walked over to the metallic, bronze-colored ship to inspect the wingtips.

Scratching his red hair, Mallinson was totally bewildered by what he saw. There,

Spun-in from 800 feet, the gala painted STANAVO Phantom, NC7734, and its pilot met a fiery demise on October 6, 1936, near Stroudsburg, Pennsylvania. LYLE FARVER

for all to see on the right wing was a clump of grass, indicative of a minor groundloop. The gig was up when Mallinson observed the smirks and smiles on several employees' faces. Somebody had placed the grass on the wing-tip. They all had a good laugh for the moment.

But Mallinson's earlier mishap was only a small ripple in the company's affairs of the previous two weeks. The gala-painted, red and white STANAVO Phantom had crashed and burned on October 6, 1936, near Stroudsburg, Pennsylvania, killing the pilot, Frederick "Red" McPhaul. Ben Melcher and Lou Coghill flew to the accident scene at Stroudsburg's Pipher Airport in Coghill's Waco PCF to seek some early answers. This was the first fatal accident in an LADC-built airplane and both gentlemen had a lot of questions.

Factory workers were stunned by this accident, also. Gone was one of the most colorfully painted of the Phantoms. Even more disquieting was the strongly suspected reason for this accident, pilot error. McPhaul had just dropped off his sister, taken off and started his climb when, at 800 feet, the left wing dropped. The hapless plane and pilot entered a low altitude spin.

McPhaul was known by several pilots to enjoy low altitude aerobatics. One of his favorite maneuvers included a low-altitude spin, often recovering at the last possible second. Most likely, when McPhaul recovered from his spin this time, he did not have enough altitude to pull-out from the dive and crashed within a hundred yards of his sister. [48]

After the Department of Commerce had completed their initial investigations, the burned wreckage was returned to West Trenton for further study. Workers and engineers who examined the wreckage were amazed to find some major portions had survived the high impact forces.

Fortunately, the Phantom's stout construction would save a life six weeks later.

Two more Phantoms were completed in October. The first airplane, NC1010 (s/n 111), was destined for Charles A. "Bunnie" Hinsch. Hinsch was a banker from Cincinnati, a company investor and had been a close friend of Don Luscombe from earlier Monocoupe days. Sadly, Hinsch's Phantom would see more time in the shop for repairs than in the air due to Hinsch's many nose-over accidents. Fortunately, he never hurt himself or any passenger in these embarrassing mishaps.

The second airplane was bought by famed Cuban sportsman pilot Gustavo S. de Bustamente, yet registered in his wife's name, Helen R. de Bustamente, an American citizen. They were members of the Sportsman Pilots Association and met Don Luscombe through the same organization.

The burned remains of the STANAVO Phantom revealed much about the Phantom's stout construction and crashworthiness to Department of Commerce inspectors and Luscombe factory engineers. CHARLES E. BURGESS

Chapter Ten: "Well... We Tried Everything Else"   151

The de Bustamentes' Phantom was registered NC1025 with serial number 112. It was was test flown by Ig Sargent on October 16, 1936. Hinch's airplane, in turn, took to the skies on November 7, 1936.

The bright red and Diana cream trimmed de Bustamente airplane was loaded with options, virtually cancelling a major portion of the airplane's useful load capabilities. An engine compartment fire-extinguisher system was installed in the airplane and built-in parachutes in the seats were added. The cabin and seat cushions were upholstered with genuine pigskin. As an additional safety measure, a cabin door quick-release system was installed. Finally, all available options were crammed into the instrument panel, space permitting.

Mr. de Bustamente was a demanding and precise individual. No detail escaped his attention. He hovered over workers like a mother hen while various parts were made for his airplane. Prior to accepting delivery, de Bustamente demanded the aircraft be recoverable from four-turn left and right spins. Furthermore, he wanted verified tests flown to determine the aircraft's service ceiling. Ig Sargent complied dutifully and flew all tests to de Bustamente's satisfaction.

(Right) The bright red with Diana cream trim de Bustamente Luscombe Phantom was made under Mr. de Bustamente's exacting standards. No detail escaped his discerning eye.

(Below) Mr. and Mrs. Gustavo de Bustamente stand beside their Luscombe Phantom.

HOWARD JONG

CHARLES E. BURGESS

The de Bustamentes elected to keep their Phantom based at the Mercer County Airport to avoid any potential Cuban certification problems. Additionally, the airplane was licensed as a U.S. airplane and had an "NC" number because it was registered to Mrs. de Bustamente who was an American citizen.

Though several more fuselages were built, only two Phantom airplanes were completed and delivered during the balance of the year. The first, NC1028 (s/n 113), was assembled during late November. Ig Sargent test flew this metallic blue and silver trimmed airplane on December 11, 1936, prior to its sale to Henry C. Olmsted, Hiram Mallinson's brother-in-law, on December 12, 1936.

The last Phantom manufactured during 1936 went to H.J. Crummer of Orlando, Florida. This airplane, NC1043 (s/n 114), was flight tested by Eddie Davis on December 21, 1936, and by Ig Sargent the

Luscombe Phantom NC1043 (s/n 114) was the last Phantom produced in 1936. Nine Phantoms, including six built in the last quarter were built and delivered to satisfied customers, more than in any year during the company's turbulent history. AVIATION HERITAGE LIBRARY

following day. The Bill of Sale was signed on December 22, 1936.

Eddie Davis set out on a cold December 22 day to deliver the aircraft to Crummer. His journey to Florida took three days, often circumnavigating bad weather to get this latest Phantom to the customer. Davis returned via a commercial, Eastern Air Lines flight.

With this sale, the Luscombe Airplane Development Corporation could boast more Phantom airplanes were sold in one year than in any year previously, nine airplanes altogether. History would disclose more Phantom airplanes were sold during 1936 than in any year in the company's turbulent history.

In retrospect, the year was marred only by the tragic STANAVO accident and Hiram Mallinson's unusual accident in his ship, NC1234, on November 20, 1936. The latter occurred as the young, red-haired Mallinson headed towards New Hampshire in his metallic bronze Phantom to visit friends and family. Just before he boarded his airplane, he told a surprised Frank Johnson, *"I just talked to my insurance agent and told him to turn on the insurance for this trip."*

A unique line-up of six Luscombe Phantoms. Left to right — NC1008, NC1028, NC1025, NC275Y, NC1286 and NC1007. CHARLES E. BURGESS

Chapter Ten: "Well... We Tried Everything Else" 153

(Left) Incredibly, pilot Hiram Mallinson walked away from this accident with barely a scratch! The Phantom's stout construction saved a life.

(Below) Though subjected to horriffic loads and stresses during its high-speed dive and ensuing crash, owner/pilot Hiram Mallinson's Phantom NC1234 wing structure remained relatively intact.

HOWARD JONG

HOWARD JONG

Enroute to his destination, Mallinson decided to see how high he could climb. Unfortunately, he experienced hypoxia — aviation's insidious altitude sickness caused by a lack of oxygen. Disoriented, Mallinson apparently stalled, spun, recovered and finally dove his aircraft so fast the leading edge nose ribs buckled in several places on both wings. Miraculously, he had control enough to land his crippled Phantom in an apple orchard.

The ensuing crash was horrific, but Mallinson walked away unscathed. After the Department of Commerce had completed their initial investigations, the wreckage was returned to the factory. Once more, LADC engineers and employees were amazed to find the Phantom's structure withstood the many forces applied to it. All were more astonished that Mallinson survived, let alone unhurt.

Engineers later estimated Mallinson exceeded 320 mph airspeed during his plunge, well in excess of the aircraft's designed maximum diving speed of 294 mph. Previously, the most anybody recorded, or *dared* to report they recorded, was 300 mph.

Shortly before this accident, Luscombe concluded negotiations to build a large storage hangar behind the paint shop, sheet metal building and school building. J. Noel Macy of Croton Point, New York, funded the project and planned to lease it to the corporation. Ground was broken during late October or early November 1936.

This 121 ft., 5 in. by 40 ft. storage hangar was located 120 feet behind the rear of the paint shop. It featured sliding glass and steel doors and a roof constructed of steel truss members braced with tie rods and covered in corrugated and galvanized roofing. The side walls were made from corrugated and galvanized siding sheets.

Though Macy owned the building and secured all rights to remove it from the premises should he so desire (via a lease with Mercer County), he later sold the building in early 1937 to George B. Cluett, II. In turn, Cluett leased this double hangar to the Luscombe Airplane Development Corporation for a dollar per year. Fritz King sub-leased this hangar from Luscombe, using and maintaining this hangar for his fixed base operation. He stored LADC airplanes in it, as well.

Meanwhile, as stated in a preceding chapter, the engineering staff had been tasked to develop a lower horsepower airplane that would appeal to the cost-conscious sportsman pilot as per Don's wishes. Farver took these basic requirements to heart and sought a way to satisfy his boss' mandate. In the end, two separate, 90 hp designs emerged.

The staff's initial design effort was a quick "lash-up" and drew hardly a round of notice, much less applause, from most factory workers, students or even the aviation media that occasionally frequented the plant. This "lash-up" airplane made its first appearance in late October or early November 1936. It was an ungainly aircraft that used a Phantom's fuse-

154 Visions of Luscombe: The Early Years

Factory employees assemble a Monocoupe 90A in front of the completed storage hangars erected behind the rear of the Luscombe Airplane Development Corporation paint shop.   CHARLES E. BURGESS

lage, tail group and wings, but the similarities stopped there. The landing gear, designed to fit the Phantom's landing gear fittings, was a truss-type, reminiscent of a Ryan "Brougham" or a Fairchild 24 landing gear arrangement.

In an effort to keep related engineering and fabrication costs low, the Phantom prototype fuselage, NC272Y, was removed from the rafters and was employed in this project. Since the original tail section had been removed previously as a repair for Bryan Sheedy's damaged Phantom, a production tail section was spliced to the fuselage at the sixth bulkhead station, just forward of the original fin and stabilizer location.

A wide, spindly landing gear was used to save cost and weight and was supposed to improve the aircraft's ground handling characteristics. Finally, the prototype (NC272Y) Phantom's wings were used with the flaps and flap mechanism removed. The resulting space was covered by a fixed sheet of aluminum alloy.

All that remained was adding a motor. A Warner "Scarab Junior" 90 hp engine was obtained and mounted on the nose. To compensate for the lighter engine's weight, a new motor-mount was constructed that moved the motor forward a foot or more to keep the airplane's center of gravity at the correct location.

The LADC applied for an Unlicensed Aircraft Identification Mark assignment on November 4, 1936. The date of manufacture was shown on the Department of Commerce Form 9 as November 4, 1936, and the serial number was denoted as 100. This documentation reflected this new airplane was called, simply, the "Luscombe."

The government issued "1017" as the airplane's identification number. Thus, to many employees, this

Ig Sargent's Phantom sits on the Mercer County Airport ramp. Note the sign above the hangar doors has been repainted to reflect the new tenant's desires.   JAMES B. ZAZAS COLLECTION

Chapter Ten: "Well... We Tried Everything Else"   155

(Left) A good view of the Luscombe Airplane Corporation buildings in November 1936. Note the additional hangars being constructed behind the existing factory buildings.

HOWARD JONG

(Right) An aerial view of Mercer County Airport. Circa October 1936. Note the outline of the new hangar foundation just to the left of the factory buildings. The winding road on the right leads to the "Jolly Roger." Interstate 95 cuts a wide path along the road today.

HOWARD JONG

airplane became known as the "1017 airplane" or "1017 Project." However, to other employees — including Sargent — this airplane was logged as the "Sprite I."

The first time Don Luscombe saw the airplane and the slender wing struts it had, he hit the ceiling. *"The struts are too small!"* he yelled at his engineering staff. *"They look more like a Heath!"* Lyle Farver was away at the time, so Bill Benckert answered the charges and explained the struts were adequate to handle all air loads and stresses.

Luscombe became more persuasive. *"I don't care what the book says, they are not strong enough and no customers are going to buy something like that. They have to LOOK strong."* Benckert relented and put larger and stronger struts on the airplane. Don was correct in demanding stronger struts for another reason — they would have been damaged by ground handling, pushing, etc.

The aircraft's first flight occurred on November 3, 1936, with Ig Sargent at the controls. Sargent returned from this brief, twenty-five minute flight with less than sterling praise for the new ship. It was underpowered for the weight and needed to be rerigged. After all, the aircraft was essentially a Phantom mated to a ninety horsepower engine.

During this flight and most subsequent test flights, Ben Melcher rode as a "bonafide crew member" (as required by Department of Commerce regulations pertaining to test aircraft) and took notes relating to the aircraft's performance. However, much like his Phantom work, Melcher never flew this aircraft solo.

Fritz King made his one and only flight in the 1017 airplane two weeks later in an effort to determine what changes could be made to improve the aircraft's mediocre performance. Even Lou Coghill made a few test flights to determine what could be done. At one point, the airplane was flown uncowled! Eddie Davis' first of two flights occurred December 3, 1936. After a brief fifteen minute flight, he returned with concerns and comments that echoed those of Sargent.

These test flights underscored the aircraft's inadequate performance, almost to the point of being dangerous, with two people aboard. A few more test flights were conducted before the project was abandoned altogether. Analysis revealed the design was too heavy for the laboring 90 hp power plant.

Furthermore, the landing gear was not without its share of problems. It deflected badly on taxiing and

156 *Visions of Luscombe: The Early Years*

LYLE FARVER

(Above) Construction the "lash-up" airplane, a production Phantom tail is spliced to NC272Y's fuselage. Circa September 1936.

landing, almost in a "walking" motion. Serious concerns were raised about its ability to withstand any hard landings.

Despite its many shortcomings, the development and subsequent flight testing of the "Luscombe" was not without its humorous moments.

Various combinations of wing struts were used in an effort to improve the airplane's flying characteristics. In absolute frustration, Lou Coghill and Bill Force put a set of Phantom struts on the aircraft. *"Well,"* Coghill sighed, *"we've tried everything else."*

The net result was an airplane that looked like a child's model airplane with an exaggerated dihedral. Incredibly, the 1017 airplane was flown a couple times in this configuration and proved very stable, though grossly underpowered.

The "boss" was not amused. After one test flight, Don stepped from the balcony sales office (his office was on the ground floor) and cried, *"What the hell did you boys do to my airplane?"*

Coghill responded, *"Well, we tried everything else and we though it might make a difference."*

Don didn't go along with the idea. One afternoon, after much testing had been completed, he flew the airplane himself to see what the problem was. Don returned frustrated and disgruntled.

Meanwhile, a second 90 hp airplane was taking shape on the main hangar floor and it promised vastly improved results. Farver had worked day and night to finalize a new design that would give Luscombe what he wanted in a lighter airplane. He endeavored to eliminate the labor and complications involved in making the compound curvature skins.

Eventually, he hit upon the idea of using flat sheet Alclad wrapped around the top and bottom of oval bulkheads, all tapering towards the tail. Called "bunting sections," there was no compounding in it.

Between these curved sections was a gap on the sides of 5 to 7 inches to be covered by a flat sheet.

The initial layouts of this second, more innovative 90 hp design effort looked very promising. Benckert, Tarencz, Humphreys and others in the engineering department expanded upon Farver's ideas and worked to solve the various geometry and stress problems. These problems were solved shortly with Terencz completing most of the stress engineering.

Nick Nordyke was a frequent visitor to the engineering department. He often wondered aloud how much work he would

(Left) Pilots who flew the experimental 1017 airplane expressed concerns the airplane's landing gear deflected badly and would not withstand any hard landing.

HOWARD JONG

HOWARD JONG

Clarence Chamberlin's Curtiss Condor transport biplane was a frequent visitor to the Mercer County Airport. Here, the experimental 1017 airplane can be seen under the Condor's lower left wing. Circa November 1936.

have if this new design was built. Likewise, he offered many constructive ideas how to pare labor and reduce weight without sacrificing strength. Nordyke questioned Farver constantly if this new design would have butt joints or lap joints. A butt joint arrangement required two rivet rows whereas the lap joint required only one.

Moreover, butt joints were costly to install because each adjoining pair of skins had to be hand filed and fitted to match. In addition, several trial fittings were required to get a good fit all around the bulkhead. Obviously, this process was slow, expensive and unsuitable for Luscombe's overall cost-effective, mass-production plans.

The lap joint, Nordyke debated, could use thinner fuselage skins and, thus, save weight. Yet both Farver and Nordyke acknowledged a lap joint presented problems for the paint shop. The paint would be rubbed off along the lap after repetitive cleaning and polishing. In the end, the lap joint was selected and used.

By this time, Don had developed a keen interest in the second 90 hp design. Farver went to great lengths to describe in detail the new airplane design to his boss. He explained why certain sections were constructed the way they were and how his team was able to solve the various stress problems.

Farver explained why the horizontal stabilizer needed to be positioned mid-way up the vertical stabilizer. His work, supported by various N.A.C.A. studies and Ivan Driggs' previous efforts, condemned a tail assembly design with the horizontal tail down low and the vertical and horizontal leading edges in line — fore and aft — because it could produce unacceptable spin characteristics.

Don listened carefully to Farver's convincing arguments, but shook his head; this arrangement was not what he wanted. Don stated the horizontal stabilizer *"didn't look right"* placed mid-way up the vertical stabilizer, much like the Phantom's tail arrangement. He wanted the stabilizer and elevator positioned lower, at or near the junction where the vertical stabilizer joins the fuselage. [49]

Farver and Luscombe argued vigorously over this point. In the end, Don won his argument. Still,

Lyle Farver at work in his ground floor office at West Trenton. LYLE FARVER

Eddie Tarencz stands in front of a Vought Corsair. KENNETH B. CERICOLA

Farver did not want to be responsible for any flat spin related accidents resulting from this tail arrangement.

Luscombe once bragged to investors while Farver was present he *"...designed the Monocoupe D-145 and the Luscombe Phantom with the toe of his boot in the sand."* This comment irritated Farver to no end for it demonstrated to Farver, at least, Don's lack of respect for the talents his engineering team possessed.

Likewise, he was becoming weary of Don's constant meddling in the engineering department's work. Furthermore, the paychecks were arriving less regularly. For the first time during his employ with Luscombe, Farver entertained plans to leave the Luscombe organization.

Despite these differences, Don liked what he saw in the new 90 hp design and quickly authorized a prototype be built. Metal was soon cut for the new fuselage. Tucked away in a corner of the main hangar, shop personnel and a few students slowly shaped the first fuselage of the new design. Other employees were busy building

(Left) Fuselage assembly foreman Chuck Burgess works on a Phantom. Note the fuselage jig in the foreground holding the first, proof-of-concept "Ninety."

LYLE FARVER

(Right) Howard Jong inspects the proof-of-concept "Ninety" fuselage under construction. The oval shaped bulkheads are shown to a good advantage. Some employees referred to this airplane as the "Sprite." Circa November 1936.

LYLE FARVER

new Phantoms, repairing broken Phantoms and flight testing same. The LADC floor hummed with activity.

The repairing of broken Phantom airplanes kept a much-needed cash flow coming into the factory. A few ships required almost complete rebuilding. As was often the case, a complete or nearly complete fuselage, or major components of same, replaced the parts of the broken bird. To keep the factory records in order, Phantom production serial or constructor's numbers were deleted from fresh fuselages. Hence, gaps were created in the serial number chronology. One example was the total rebuild of George Thorne's Phantom, NC278Y. Thorne wrecked his ship several months earlier in a forced landing near Sugar Creek, Ohio, in the Allegheny Mountains. In turn, he had it trucked to the company for repairs.

The cost of repairs was extensive and Thorne elected to part company with his Phantom. Shortly after its first post-rebuild test flight by Ig Sargent on December 7, 1936, a disgusted Thorne sold this airplane to the Luscombe Airplane Development Corporation.

Meanwhile, several significant changes took place within the apprentice program. Bill Shepard, who had been filling the school instructor role temporarily, happily relinquished his duties to Penn Muhlowney. Muhlowney hailed from Raleigh, North Carolina, where he was an engineering instructor at North Carolina State College. Luscombe hired him to run the school.

In turn, Shepard went back to work full time in the Detail Parts Department. Also, he joined a class conducted by Henri D'Estout to earn his mechanic's license, one of several employees asked by Don Luscombe to earn this license.

During the latter part of 1936, while Phantom production was increasing, the Department of Commerce inspector assigned to monitor the LADC pro-

Chapter Ten: "Well... We Tried Everything Else" 159

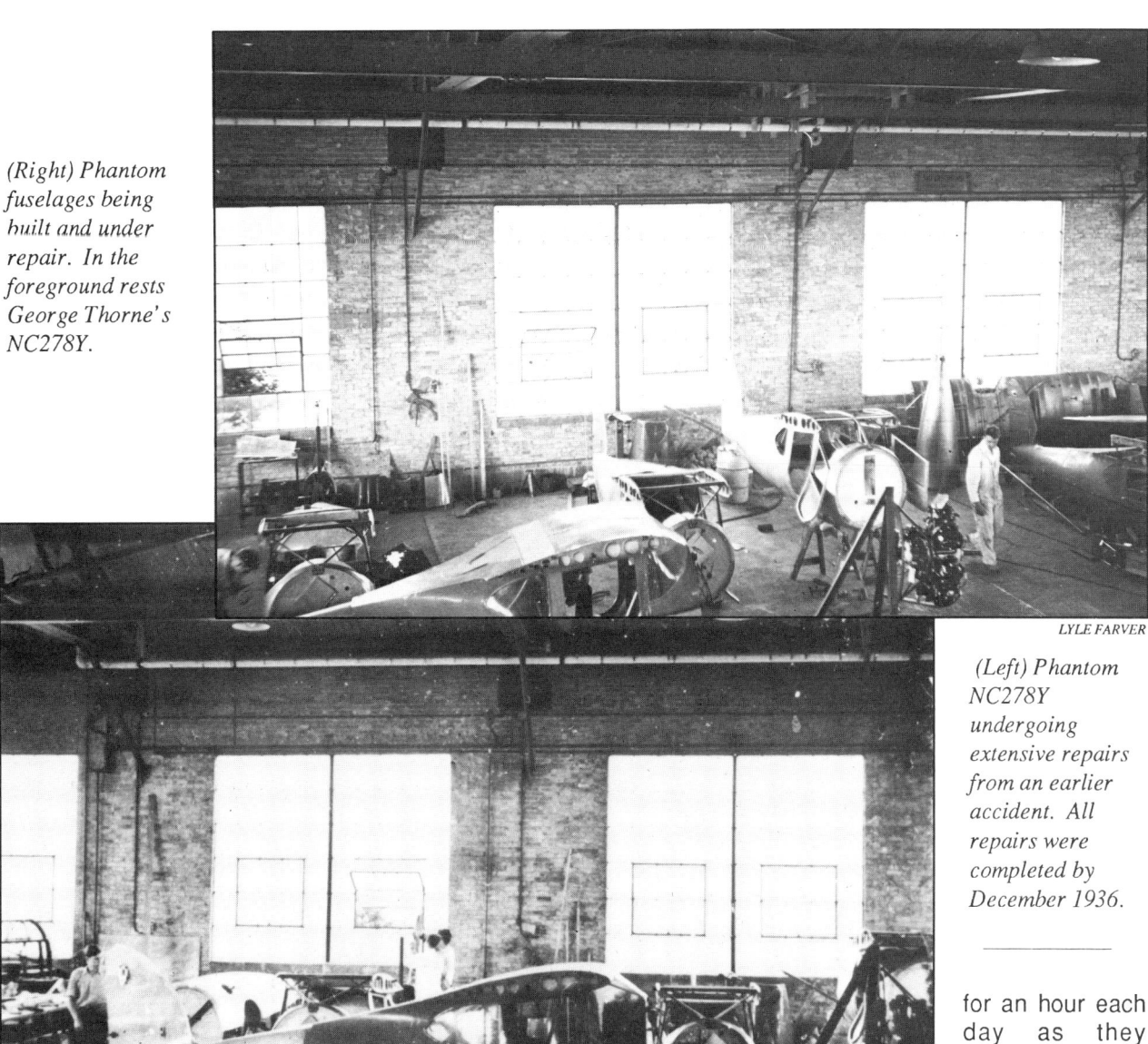

(Right) Phantom fuselages being built and under repair. In the foreground rests George Thorne's NC278Y.

LYLE FARVER

(Left) Phantom NC278Y undergoing extensive repairs from an earlier accident. All repairs were completed by December 1936.

LYLE FARVER

duction observed there were not enough government certificated aircraft mechanics in the shop to assure the quality of the work at hand. He suggested to Don those individuals who had the prerequisite one year's training get a license.

At the time, only Fritz King (then the final assembly foreman), Lou Coghill (wing department foreman), Henri D'Estout (paint shop foreman), and Fred Brunton (an engineering student) had the required licenses. Luscombe approached D'Estout, a former Army Air Corps mechanic, to teach the class for one or two hours per day. He agreed.

A dozen people, including Bill Shepard and Chuck Burgess, attended the two week course (only for an hour each day as they worked in their respective departments the rest of the time) and passed the written test afterwards. The inspector waived the practical test as he had seen everybody working in the factory at one time or another. Presto! The factory now had a dozen new licensed mechanics.

Shortly before the year ended, Penn Muhlowney left the school for a position at Glenn L. Martin Aircraft in Baltimore, Maryland. Muhlowney had given as his reason to leave to return home to teach at North Carolina State College. In turn, Don asked Frank Johnson to take over the whole school operation. Frank had been the shop instructor for a few weeks. Johnson accepted gladly.

Don was aware Johnson had been doing some design work for Lyle Farver and had been working with a few of the boys at the "Jolly Roger" on some design drawings, but nothing specific. He decided to tap Johnson's drafting ability. Luscombe pulled Johnson aside and shared his vision for a new and innovative airplane design.

"Frank, we have to have a good school project. Penn has been building a quarter-sized Phantom as a school project. I even bought a bunch of one-sixteenth inch rivets. But there is no useful product there. We've got all this cheap labor around here and no way to use them. They really don't have the skill to make something like the Phantom without a lot of direction. And we can't make enough Phantoms because they are too damn expensive. And this '90,' I am having second thoughts about it. I have been over in engineering working on it with Lyle Farver. It is not enough of an airplane to be a good cross-country airplane and it is too damn expensive to fly with that five-cylinder Warner for flying around the field. We need something like a Taylor Cub or something like an Aeronca. It's got to look like an airplane! What can you come up with? I want you to look at that instead of what Penn had as the school project," Luscombe said.

Frank Johnson scrapped the quarter-scale Phantom idea immediately. He knew his young charges would learn much more by building and problem solving a full-scale airplane design. Borrowing heavily from the preliminary engineering hobby work he, Jong, and others had undertaken at the "Jolly Roger," Johnson instructed his students to consider a two-place, side-by-side design about the same size as a Taylor Cub or Aeronca. For the power plant, Johnson suggested to his students they use a four cylinder, Continental Motors horizontally opposed A-40 or the new, then experimental A-50.

This design would be the "new" school project.

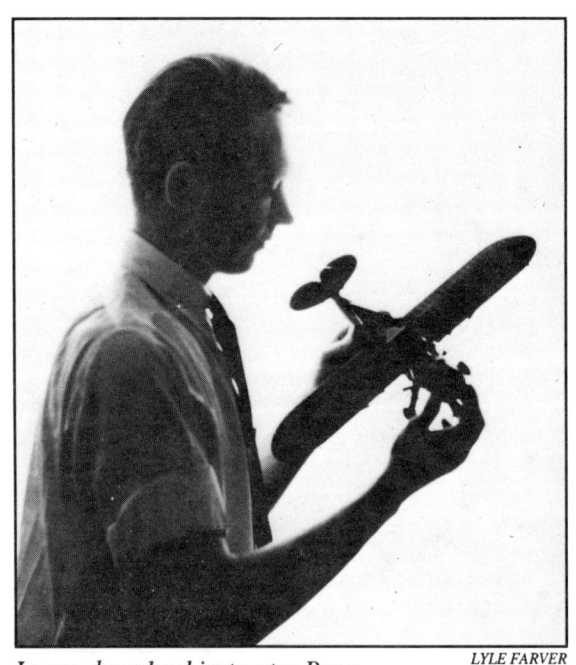

Luscombe school instructor Penn Muhlowney holds a model of a Luscombe Phantom. LYLE FARVER

*"Just as wood bridges gave way to steel,
just as wood railway coaches gave way to steel,
just as wood automobiles gave way to steel,
SO TOO must airplanes be made of metal if lives are to be saved
and automatic machine operations are to be introduced into production
and satisfactory price levels reached."*

Luscombe Airplane Corporation advertising brochure

Chapter Eleven

Making The Grade —
The Quest For An All-Metal Airplane

The "Ninety" sits in the hangar being fitted with the Bill Shepard-designed production wings.
The square block area to the right-center housed the Department of Commerce weather reporting and teletype office.

Don Luscombe was quite happy to show his honored guest and close friend, Charles A. "Bunnie" Hinsch, the company and the surrounding buildings. It was New Year's, Hinsch was visiting and Luscombe was in a festive mood.

Taking his guest in arm, Don showed "Bunnie" Hinsch how his money was being put to work. So much had been built and accomplished in only two short years. Likewise, he explained in great detail the apprentice program and the successful income it was generating for the company.

Luscombe restated his firm belief that an all-metal airplane, made from die-cut and interchangeable parts, was the means to mass production and the choice of airplane builders of the future. Additionally, he believed firmly this production method would lower overall costs by producing more airplanes.

To prove his point, Don could point proudly to at least five Phantom fuselages and five sets of wings in various stages of final assembly. Two airframes were nearly complete. The balance of the airframes were to be mated to their matched, serial numbered wings at a later date upon receipt of a firm order.

Don Luscombe and Charles A. "Bunnie" Hinsch. ELEANORE LUSCOMBE SHURTZ COLLECTION
A banker, Hinsch was one of Don's keenest financial backers.

Hinsch, on his behalf, was most pleased by what he observed. His financial input to Don's concern was being put to good use. Airplanes were being built and new orders were being booked during an era when few could afford a new car, much less a new home. A new design was on the floor almost ready to test its wings and new designs were taking shape on the engineering department's drafting tables. And the level of employed talent was increasing, with many of the new employees coming from the ranks of the school graduates.

Although Don was quite happy the way his company was growing, he confided his many concerns to his banker friend from Cincinnati, Ohio. Don was worried about his company's future and discussed the prognosis of the company. Money, or the lack of it, was always his constant concern and he wondered aloud if the difficult financial problems at hand would improve to the point when they would no longer be a source of so much anxiety.

The money situation was tight, indeed. Phantom airplane sales were generating very little income. Only the novel "Apprentice Program" was providing the company with a much-needed constant cash flow. At least thirty students were currently enrolled.

Hinsch had an idea. He asked Don to join him for a few days in Cincinnati to talk to his banker friends. Perhaps they could help Don ease his financial crisis and his worries. Thus, during the second week of January 1937, Luscombe traveled to Cincinnati with his friend, Hinsch. While there, Don was asked by a reporter from the respected *Cincinnati Inquirer* newspaper to share his views on some of the "development trends" in aviation. As printed in the January 17, 1937, issue, Don responded:

"Metal is the conclusion of the airplane manufacturers today. The Army, Navy and transport companies have accepted metal and the civil market will follow in the footsteps of these leaders."

When asked to share his views about mass-production and its future potential, Luscombe replied, *"Overhead in today's system is what eats the manufacturer 'out of house and home.' When we can get around to the mass production system, we will upset the vicious circle of the last ten years. Each year aircraft arrive on the market at a price higher than the year previous. Fewer planes are sold and the price necessarily becomes higher. Reverse that process, more planes will be sold each year and the price will decline with each successive year."*

Luscombe concluded his interview by discussing the difficulties he was experiencing finding capable individuals to build his metal airplanes. *"Throughout the entire industry, this condition is extremely acute. Manufacturers have gone so far as to obtain injunctions to restrain a competing company from enticing its men away,"* he said.

Overall, Don's visit to Cincinnati was brief and proved generally unsuccessful. Company business in West Trenton required his attention. At a stockholders' meeting on January 20, 1937, the affairs of the company were reviewed and discussed. A "resolution of confidence" voted upon was unanimous. It was obvious to all, the company's overall outlook was improving and the chances were excellent for continuing in that direction.

However, the financial set-up of the current Luscombe Airplane Development Corporation was

Chapter Eleven: Making The Grade — The Quest For An All-Metal Airplane 163

Half-completed Phantom fuselages beg to be bought by customers. These airframes tied-up important funds and factory space. Circa December 1936. JAMES B. ZAZAS COLLECTION

determined to be inadequate for any appreciable manufacturing program. As such, the officers were instructed to negotiate with investment brokers and bankers in an effort to secure additional working capital. To this end, Hiram Mallinson was elected to the Board of Directors.

After several weeks of negotiations, it was determined such financing was too costly and would dilute the stockholders' holdings. Consequently, the officers and other active participants in the corporation assumed the task of securing additional capital on a non-commission basis.

Concurrently, a new, partially completed

The proof-of-concept "Ninety," called the "Sprite" by some employees, is shown under construction. Note the straps employed to 'pull down' the fuselage skins around the bulkheads which were handmade by Nick Nordyke. LYLE FARVER

164   *Visions of Luscombe: The Early Years*

The completed fuselage of the "proof-of-concept" airplane. This "Ninety" was built to test Lyle Farver's fuselage design, a design which did prove to be very successful.

LYLE FARVER

The Warner "Scarab Junior" from the 1017 airplane waits to be mated to the new "Ninety."

LYLE FARVER

Chapter Eleven: Making The Grade — The Quest For An All-Metal Airplane 165

(Left) The handmade fuselage bulkheads of the new "Ninety" are shown to a good advantage. Note the absence of the fuselage splice strip in this particular airplane.

(Below) The internal structure of the "Ninety's" vertical and horizontal stabilizers were bolted to the airplane prior to being covered by sheet aluminum.

CHARLES E. BURGESS

LYLE FARVER

design occupied a small corner in the main hangar. Months of earlier engineering and assembly work quickly became a prototype reality. This experimental airplane was unlike anything that had graced the LADC factory floor previously.

The fuselage was a monocoque duraluminum structure, the skin tapering gently aft in straight sections to the tail cone. The fuselage shape was maintained by oval-shaped, dural bulkheads with .032 duraluminum skins riveted to them. Unique to this design, these bulkheads were handmade by Nick Nordyke and were flat on the sides unlike later bulkhead stampings that exhibited a slightly rounded side.

Uniquely, this first fuselage did not employ the seven inch splice strip as Farver had envisioned. Instead, during assembly, 17ST duraluminum sheet was pulled over and down the bulkheads by wide straps and lap-jointed, along the lower rivet line, to the skins that wrapped around the bottom of the bulkheads. A small angle section ran the length of this rivet line to add strength and rigidity.

The cabin superstructure consisted of a pair of bulkheads attached to chrome molybdenum steel tubing. The cabin's bottom half consisted of handmade bulkheads while the top half had a cleverly attached steel tubing arrangement.

The compound curvature skins around the cabin were handmade with Nick Nordyke adding to his incomparable ability. Wide, rounded-on-the-bottom doors allowed easy access. A large, "D" shaped window was positioned on each side of the fuselage just aft of the cockpit.

Riveting the skins to the "Ninety's" horizontal stabilizer.   LYLE FARVER

Ben Melcher, right, checks the workmanship on a Luscombe Phantom.   LYLE FARVER

The wide tread landing gear was robust. Unlike the unpredictable Phantom gear which could scarcely withstand any side-loading forces, this gear was designed to absorb tremendous punishment and come back for more.

The main gear struts passed through holes in the side of the fuselage where each strut attached to a short, oil-draulic shock strut (oleo) surrounded by a stout spring. The pivot points for the landing gear legs were positioned just inside the fuselage's skin on an aluminum forging which, in turn, formed a common support for the wing strut. The oleos were located close together on either side of the fuselage centerline.

These oil-draulic shocks were positioned between the dual bulkhead, bridgework-type structure of the lower cabin. Thus, each gear leg had its own, individual shock absorber/spring assembly. When one leg was deflected, it would spring quickly to its original position without adversely affecting the other gear leg or the aircraft's overall handling.

A simple tail skid was provided. Later flight testing revealed this arrangement behaved like an old Victrola record player needle on a phonograph record. The tail skid's scrapping sounds were amplified through the aircraft's conical, comparatively open interior structure.

The first set of wings installed on this latest design endeavor were the reworked Phantom wings from the 1017 airplane. These wings had the flaps and flap operating mechanism removed and the areas covered with pieces of aluminum sheet.

The vertical fin and horizontal stabilizer consisted of a spar and rib internal structure, all covered in alclad sheet. These surfaces were interchangeable with only minor modification, a process designed to save labor and pare overall costs.

Grade "A" fabric and dope covered the control surfaces. To add rigidity, the vertical fin was braced by streamline tubing struts attached to each side of the horizontal stabilizer.

Chapter Eleven: Making The Grade — The Quest For An All-Metal Airplane   167

CHARLES E. BURGESS

(Above) The new "Ninety" undergoes a series of structural checks. Note the old 1017 airplane is the third airplane from the left.

(Right) The "Ninety" rests on its gear. Circa January 1937.

LYLE FARVER

The Warner "Scarab Junior" 90 hp engine, removed from the 1017 job, was enclosed in a smooth, N.A.C.A. cowl. Given this power plant, this new design became known as the "Ninety."

The new "Ninety's" landing gear was very robust, quite a contrast to the wobbly gear of the 1017 airplane that preceded it. Each gear leg in this "Ninety" used two, independent oil-draulic shocks, one for each gear leg. CHARLES E. BURGESS

Many employees referred to this new airplane as the "Luscombe 90" or "Ninety." Others called the airplane the "Sprite," most likely in reference to the sales brochure drawings made earlier. Yet, according to a Department of Commerce Application for Identification Mark, dated March 24, 1937, the aircraft is referred to as the "Luscombe Model 4."[50] As recorded in a Department of Commerce, Aeronautics Branch, Form AB-9, this airplane's identification mark assignment was 1253. The recorded serial number was 400.[51] Only a few details remained to be completed before this "Ninety" was ready for its maiden flight.

Everybody in the metal working shop, including Nick Nordyke, Howard Jong, Marty Eisenmann, Cameron Story and others, could proudly claim they contributed to this new airplane. Others outside this department, including Ben Melcher, Bill Force, Chuck Burgess, Ross Funk, Lou Coghill, Fritz King, Ralph Coston and welding department foreman Bill Keegan, added their hands and hearts to the project.

All but completely disassembled, the 1017/272Y fuselage was eventually returned to the main hangar's overhead rafters for storage. The flimsy landing gear used on the 1017 airplane was placed in storage, also. Farver was excited to see his design take shape during the last few months of 1936 and early 1937. So were Ig Sargent and Eddie Davis, as both were anxious to test fly the new design.

But the overall picture at hand was not as bright as it appeared, however. There was much friction in the air. Differences between Don Luscombe and the engineering department were reaching an impasse, the resolution of which had a profound influence on the corporation's future course.

Farver became increasingly disillusioned by what he perceived to be Luscombe's engineering shortsightedness on the new 90 hp design. Though Farver agreed marketing potential had its place in any airplane design, he felt Luscombe was trading sound engineering principles for eye appeal and marketing potential.

Much like his mentor, Ivan Driggs, Farver cared deeply that his designs possess inherent stability and strength. And like Driggs, Farver decried the phenomenon that an airplane's design should be based on the whims of a consummate marketeer.

In reality, Don Luscombe wanted an airplane of unquestioned structural integrity with excellent performance and handling characteristics. More important, he wanted an airplane that would sell. As a result, his views often differed with the views of those around him.

Moreover, Farver had his share of money problems with Don Luscombe. Much like Driggs' earlier experience, Don was tardy on several occasions with Farver's paychecks. Lyle Farver's differences with Don peaked during January and he resigned as chief engineer on January 30, 1937. In short order, virtually all of the engineering staff followed Lyle Farver's departure.

Within weeks after his departure, Farver went to work at Martin Aircraft in Baltimore, Maryland. There he joined his close friend and former colleague, Ivan Driggs.

Others within the engineering department echoed Farver's concerns. Benckert, Humphreys, Dunford, and Terencz left for positions at Martin Aircraft in Baltimore, Maryland; Sikorsky Aircraft in Stratford, Connecticut, Brewster Aircraft in Johnsonville, Pennsylvania, or Pitcairn Autogiro in nearby Willow Grove, Pennsylvania. Cheng, not being an American citizen, returned to his native China.

This mass exodus of engineering talent left Luscombe in a lurch. He needed qualified design and stress engineers to complete or refine current and

Chapter Eleven: Making The Grade — The Quest For An All-Metal Airplane 169

future designs under development. Don turned to his old friend and former associate Fred Knack. Knack was working at Bellanca Aircraft in New Castle, Delaware, as the company's assistant chief engineer when Luscombe paid him a visit. During their meeting, Don described the new, ninety horsepower design taking shape and the potential for further designs. Knack was intrigued by Luscombe's offer.[52]

Don continued. He told Knack of his plans to create a new company, one that would absorb the current Luscombe Airplane Development Corporation and replace it with a new identity and purpose.

Then, Don sweetened the pot. Besides offering Knack the company's chief engineer position, Luscombe offered the company's vice president job, also. Knack was hooked and he gave Bellanca his notice to leave in early March.

Meanwhile, airplanes were still being built and sold. Phantom, NC1235 (s/n 115), was finished for the Warner Aircraft Company, of Detroit, Michigan. An early February 1937 delivery was anticipated.

Luscombe Phantom, NC1048, under construction inside the main hangar. HOWARD JONG

A second Phantom, NC1048 (s/n 116), was meticulously handcrafted for the Luscombe Airplane Development Corporation itself. There was an air of urgency to get this airplane completed by the end of January as it was scheduled to be the corporation's "star" at the non-flying National Aviation Show being held January 28 to February 6 in New York City's Grand Central Palace.

Henri D'Estout and his paint staff worked overtime to paint, polish and buff this new company demonstrator Phantom to a high luster. Finished in an overall gloss black (ten coats!) with a red and gold trim, the airplane was striking! Not to take any chances or risk damage, Don directed company personnel to disassemble the airplane and truck it to the New York City show. It would be at least two months before Ig Sargent would test fly this new Phantom.[53]

The Phantom proved to be, indeed, the "star" of the show. An ad in the February 1937 *Aero Digest* claimed the aircraft to be *"the outstanding MODERN airplane for the American Sportsman."*

The star of the New York "National Aviation Show" was this polished black with red and gold trimmed Luscombe Phantom, NC1048. ELEANORE LUSCOMBE SHURTZ COLLECTION

170   Visions of Luscombe: The Early Years

Occupying space number four on the main display floor, the Phantom was one of 33 airplanes and 100 manufacturers of engines, accessories and aeronautical products displayed. The event was sponsored by Aviation Post #743 of the American Legion. Three floors of the Palace were used to house exhibits. Virtually every major airframe and engine manufacturer had a display.

Ironically, for all the effort the company expended on this show, no new airplane orders came forth. But the effort was not in vain. Ig Sargent summed up the event best by whimsically stating, *"Nothing came out of the New York Show other than a good drunk!"*

On February 9, 1937, Ig Sargent took the striking gloss black and red trim Warner Aircraft Corporation Phantom aloft for the first time. He returned fifteen minutes later pleased with its performance. He conducted three more test flights the following day, even taking

HOWARD JONG

(Above and right) Henry Olmstead's gleaming blue and silver trimmed Luscombe Phantom, NC1028.

HOWARD JONG

Henry Olmstead's Phantom, NC1028, and Ig Sargent's Phantom, NC1286, are shown together in this factory photograph. Note the rivet detail around the door area on Olmstead's Phantom.

JAMES B. ZAZAS COLLECTION

Chapter Eleven: Making The Grade — The Quest For An All-Metal Airplane 171

Don Luscombe aloft on one test flight.

Eddie Davis, on his behalf, undertook some test flights in the Warner airplane on February 10. His airwork included stalls and seven turn spins. On February 11, Sargent took-off for Detroit, Michigan, to deliver this new Phantom to the Warner Aircraft Corporation.[54]

On February 18, word arrived at the factory another Phantom had been damaged extensively. In this case, the broken bird was NC1028, Henry Olmstead's gleaming blue and silver trimmed Phantom.

As the details of this mishap became known, it became apparent Hiram Mallinson was flying the ship when he experienced a forced landing or a severe groundloop near Stelton, New Jersey. The landing gear had been sheared off, the fuselage was severely bent to the fourth bulkhead, both wings had severe rib and fabric damage, and the engine mount was bent.

Henry Olmstead's wrecked NC1028. HOWARD JONG

When Department of Commerce inspectors completed their investigations, LADC workers loaded the damaged Phantom aboard a trailer and returned to the factory for repairs. These repairs were never undertaken, however, and the airplane was salvaged for parts.

Fred Knack arrived in early March. Knack sat down with Don Luscombe and carefully reviewed all of the programs in progress and planned. The new, 90 hp job captured the bulk of their immediate attention.

Knack quickly organized his engineering department. He brought with him Jim Rising, a knowledgeable and capable stress expert from the Bellanca Aircraft Company. Rising hailed from Norfolk, Virginia, and was a true "Southern Gentleman." He held a masters' degree in aeronautical engineering from New York University. Rising was a brilliant engineer and, together with Fred Knack, offered Don's fledgling company an almost enviable light airplane engineering team. Rising was given the chief designer position.

Desiring to tap the qualified labor and engineering resources within the company, Knack approached Ben Melcher for suggestions who, within the present company, was qualified to work in the engineering department. Melcher mentioned Frank Johnson and Bill Shepard, to name a couple. Knack agreed they were all excellent choices. Frank Johnson, on his behalf, already had a drawing board and manuals in the engineering room where he worked on his new lightplane designs at night and on weekends.

Meanwhile, the classroom behind the main hangar building became a beehive of activity as Apprentice Program students worked on Frank Johnson's off-beat school project. A wood mock-up was slowly coming together and its unveiling was still several months in the future.

In early April, Melcher told Bill Shepard and Howard Jong that Fred Knack needed some extra engineering help. Both reported to Knack the next morning. In time, Melcher would ask other employees to move into this department.

Shepard's first assignment was to lay out a wing for the first production "Ninety." His instructions from Knack were simple, *"Use as many Phantom wing parts as you can, but lighten it up. Space the ribs a little further apart, put on trailing edge flaps, etc."*

This assignment became a most challenging task for Shepard. He had no previous aeronautical engineering experience except for the little he gained in a course in introductory airplane design at Cornell University.

Other factory departments found themselves immersed with an increasing workload. The sales department, for one, remained quite busy. Hiram Mallinson initiated work towards obtaining foreign interest in the company's airplanes and designs. Richard Fabian, another sales office member, sought Phantom buyer interest on a national level. Though he probably sold more airplanes than anybody else in the office, Ig Sargent maintained his busy Phantom test flying, ferry and delivery schedule.

Eddie Davis, on his behalf, spent most of March in Florida with several Sportsman Pilot Association buddies. His Phantom was a hit with his friends and churned much interest in Don Luscombe's West Trenton-based factory.

During this period, a third Phantom, NC1249 (s/n 120), came together. This aircraft was a replacement for Henry Olmstead's wrecked NC1028. The Warner power plant and Curtiss metal propeller from Olmstead's wrecked Phantom were salvaged, overhauled and placed on this new airplane. Sargent would not test fly this Phantom until May 25, 1937.[55]

On March 10, company personnel assembled on a cold, windswept Mercer County Airport ramp to witness the new, 90 hp experimental aircraft make its first flight. The day was partly cloudy and blustery when Ig Sargent fastened his seat belt in the new bird. With minimal fanfare, Sargent took the 1253 airplane aloft, sans landing gear fairings, and tested her wings. Before the day was out, Sargent made three successful test flights in the new experimental job. Don Luscombe joined Sargent on one of these initial test flights. Ben Melcher joined Sargent on a later flight during the day.

Unlike the almost dangerous sluggish performance exhibited by the "1017" airplane, this new "90" job was quite fun to fly. Everybody who flew with Sargent that day was generally pleased with the new airplane. Each realized there was much production and sales potential in this new design.

Shortly after their flight together, Don shared a personal, if not somewhat disparaging observation with Sargent. He complained that most aeronautical engineers did not test fly their airplanes. Luscombe said, *"There is only one decent chief engineer in the business."*

A somewhat surprised Sargent asked, *"Who is that?"*

Don responded, *"That is Ted Wells of Beech Aircraft. Because the S.O.B. had to bail-out of one of his own airplanes!"*

Al "Fritz" King made his first test flight in the new airplane on March 11. King, generally one not to smile, returned all smiles after his brief thirty minute flight.[56] Eddie Davis, who eventually made the largest number of test flights in the new experimental airplane, did not make his first flight in 1253 until April 3, 1937.

Ig Sargent's early test flights were not without their share of engine problems. The 90 hp Warner cut-out repeatedly, often forcing Sargent to make a hasty return to the airport. Within a few days, the trouble was corrected and an appreciative Sargent was soon undertaking a variety of other flight tests.

The experimental "Ninety" was flown by several employees over the next several months. Don Lus-

Ig Sargent pilots the first flight of the "Ninety" on a blustery day, March 10, 1937.

HOWARD JONG

combe, Lou Coghill, Ralph Coston and, later, Bill Shepard took turns flying 1253.

Early flight tests revealed the new airplane had a top speed of 135 mph, a cruising speed of 118 mph and a docile 40 mph landing speed. Initial company literature stated this new monoplane would be priced to sell at $3975 Flyaway Factory if it went into production.

Desplte the fun nature of the aircraft, serious testing needed to be done. Many of Sargent's test flights in 1253 involved checking stability and determining airflow paths around the wing root and wing lift strut attach points. One quick flight was made to nearby Pitcairn Airfield to obtain some preliminary speed tests.

The method in which these speed tests were conducted irked Lou Coghill. With everybody flying the new airplane with its uncalibrated instruments, there was no reliable and standardized test data coming from the field. Widely different top speeds and other unreliable performance data filtered to Coghill. He wanted solid performance data obtained from timed runs over a measured course, not just speeds read from the airspeed indicator.

Coghill was the wing department foreman and had no responsibility for flight test data and had no real need for it. But Coghill believed in an informal tradition prevalent at the factory at the time: *"If you see something that needs doing, go ahead and do it and pretty soon it will become your job."* Thus, Lou Coghill made it his job to obtain some data to evaluate the various changes that were being made from time to time.

Coghill sought and obtained Luscombe's and Knack's permission to make some speed runs over a measured course to calibrate the airspeed indicator with Bill Shepard running the stopwatch and recording the data. Likewise, this calibration would be used to assess the effect on speed of any changes made to the airplane.

During mid-March, Lou Coghill made several flights in the new airplane with Bill Shepard. A stretch of Pennsylvania Railroad track near Princeton, New Jersey, became very familiar. Both gentlemen made repeated, full throttle speed runs between the mile posts during their investigations. They rarely flew above 100 feet during these tests!

Except for the initial engine problems, the new airplane proved to be quite a sprightly and reliable performer. However, the airplane demonstrated a darker side barely a month later.

On April 16, Eddie Davis took 1253 aloft for some spin tests. Commencing the spins at 10,000 feet, Davis discovered the airplane had a tendency to flatten out in a left hand spin. Deciding to pursue the problem further, Davis undertook another spin test the following day.

Starting at 10,000 feet once again, Davis kicked the airplane into a left spin. Five turns later, the airplane flattened out completely. Davis tried everything he could to effect recovery, but to no avail. Employees on the ground were horrified to see the new airplane plummet towards the ground. Many clenched their fists in tension, others prayed silently Davis would bail out.

With barely a thousand feet remaining, Davis was able to recover the errant aircraft and land safely. When questioned by others how he managed to recover the aircraft, the shaken pilot could not offer a plausible explanation.

Lou Coghill expressed his concerns regarding the flat spin problem and decided to undertake his own flight tests. When he spun the "Ninety," it went flat, but Coghill recovered quickly. The company's engineers went to work immediately to seek a solution to the "Ninety's" flat spinning tendencies.

During mid-April, the corporation undertook a major metamorphosis. On April 12, 1937, the Luscombe Airplane Corporation was organized under the laws of the State of New Jersey, the only State in which it was qualified to do business, and succeeded to do the business of the Luscombe Airplane Development Corporation.

This new corporation's goals and functions were simple:
 1. Manufacturing and Sales.
 2. Technical Education.
 3. License arrangement with importing nations.

A meeting of the stockholders on April 23, 1937, approved the liquidation of the Luscombe Airplane Development Corporation.

The officers of the new Luscombe Airplane Corporation included the following individuals:

Don A. Luscombe	President and Chairman of the Board
Frederick J. Knack	Vice President
Roger H. Johnson	Secretary and Treasurer
George B. Cluett, II	Director
Hiram R. Mallinson	Director
Ignatius Sargent	Director
Richard B. Fabian	Director

There were varied reasons for this reorganization. One reason, as described in a later Stock Prospectus dated October 6, 1937, stated:

"The development work was so far completed that it was deemed unnecessary longer to retain the word 'Development' in the corporate title; because the Corporation needed additional capital, and to simplify the capital structure."

A second reason concerned some serious and pending cost matters. In a letter to the company's stockholders dated May 17, 1937, Don Luscombe stated the creation of a larger corporation and its

174   Visions of Luscombe: The Early Years

(Left) Phantom NC1249 was intended originally to be a replacement for Henry Olmstead's wrecked NC1028, but title was transferred to the Luscombe Airplane Development Corporation.

(Below) Herb Kraft climbs aboard NC1265. An American Airlines pilot, he had this airplane painted to match his airline's silver with red trim colors.

JAMES B. ZAZAS COLLECTION

HOWARD JONG

subsequent registration with the Securities and Exchange Commission would have cost the company almost $10,000 when all legal accountants, appraisers' fees, attorney fees, etc., were factored. Likewise, there would have been at least a 90 day filing process delay if any new funds raised or generated exceeded $100,000.

Therefore, he informed the stockholders that the corporation's officers decided to limit the corporation liability to $100,000 in raising new funds which would reduce the complex and often ambiguous SEC requirements to a simple filing solution. Thus, a long delay was avoided and overall costs were pared to less than $4,000.

With respect to the stock held by the Development Corporation, Luscombe and his officers devised a simple plan. The LADC exchanged all of its assets, subject to liabilities, to the new corporation in return for 100,000 shares of capital stock of the new company. In turn, the old corporation would be liquidated and dissolved and the shares distributed pursuant to stockholder approval and the laws in force at that time.

Two Phantom airplanes were completed and test flown during April and May 1937. The first Phantom was NC1265 (s/n 122). Ig Sargent tested this airplane's wings on May 13, 1937 — barely minutes after its inspection and approval by Department of Commerce Inspector George Gay.

Originally painted a dark blue, this airplane was stripped to bare metal by several factory employees and had only its control surfaces repainted to reflect the new owner's wishes. This airplane remained at the factory until it was sold to American Airlines pilot Herb Kraft on August 9, 1937.

The second Phantom completed and test flown was Henry Olmstead's replacement airplane, NC1249 (s/n 120); however, title had been transferred to the Luscombe Airplane Corporation earlier as per an agreement with Olmstead, the insurance company that covered Olmstead's original loss, and the defunct Luscombe Airplane Development Corporation. Ig Sargent took this Phantom aloft for the first time on May 25, 1937.

Between April through June, at least five more Phantom fuselages were produced, but there were no buyers for complete aircraft. Don soon realized the airplane had reached the limit of its useful sales appeal and decided to suspend most Phantom production. Enough fuselages and parts then existed in stock to complete several new airplanes, if so ordered, or repair any which might be damaged.

Don's opinion of the Phantom began to change about this time. He began to view the Phantom as an experimental airplane, to demonstrate to company investors and prospective owners the many superior advantages of an all-metal airplane. To this end, the Phantom succeeded. New dies and tools were created to build the Phantom using innovative production methods. Furthermore, the Phantom's robust construction and design requirements laid the engineering and manufacturing groundwork for future all-metal private airplane designs.

Concurrently, Don Luscombe viewed the new "Ninety" with mixed feelings. He did not want to build a new airplane that drained the company's scarce resources as the Phantom had. Yet, the "Ninety" held the potential to fulfill his dreams for an airplane which would be produced and sold in volume despite any preliminary performance or production shortcomings. Don decided to persevere with this design.

Extensive flight testing of the new Luscombe "90" continued. Sargent made at least eleven test flights during April and May while Davis made at least a dozen. The "Ninety's" flat spinning tendency continued to plague the test program. Davis encountered

Chapter Eleven: Making The Grade — The Quest For An All-Metal Airplane

Lou Coghill's Waco PCF was often used for flight training and recreational activities. HOWARD JONG

several flat spin situations while flying with various ballast weights, but he was able to recover each time. Knack, Rising and others associated with this project were at a loss as to how to resolve this recurring problem.

A suggestion was made to limit the elevator travel, thus, theoretically, preventing a stalled condition from ever happening. This idea was vetoed as being impractical for a tail-dragger type airplane. Another suggestion involved adding weights at key places to enhance the aircraft's spin recovery characteristics. This idea was nixed due to an unacceptable loss of performance due to the additional weight. Another unsuccessful solution involved further streamlining of the main gear fairings.

While the engineers struggled to correct the "Ninety's" pesky spin problems, the lack of steady orders gave students and employees ample free time to pursue various recreational activities on the Luscombe Airplane Corporation property. Extended lunch hours became the norm rather than the exception. Often, a spirited softball game would be played on the grounds. Other students and employees took to the tennis and trap shooting facilities available on the premises.

Don and Brownee Luscombe, being avid trap shooter enthusiasts, had two trap shooting pits installed between the main hangar and his home. On weekends, students or employees could make a few extra dollars pulling the traps. The call, "Pull," became an often heard word from the Luscombe back yard.

Another favorite pastime was watching the Switlik Parachute Company test its products. This Trenton, New Jersey, based company used the Mercer County Airport to develop new parachutes and parachute containers. Unknowing visitors were startled on many occasions to see a flailing human form fall to the ground, sometimes without parachute, only to learn later the object was a wood and cloth dummy.

Some employees took flying lessons in Fritz's Fleet while others were treated to a local area ride in a visitor's airplane. Well-known barnstormer Clarence Chamberlain was a frequent visitor in his large Curtiss B-20 Condor biplane and enjoyed selling rides to Luscombe's employees and students as well as to the general public.

On rare occasions, when the weather was poor for test flying and hopping passengers was nil, em-

Looking more like a cowboy of the old West, Don Luscombe visits Jeff's hamburger stand for a quick meal. LYLE FARVER

ployees and students alike were treated to an unusual display of airmanship. In one case, the principals in this display included Fritz King and his Kinner powered Fleet, Jerry Fielder and his J-5 powered Travel Air and, finally, a Gregg Gregorson and his OX-5 powered Challenger.

Quite often, these individuals frequented a small hamburger stand barely a stone's throw from the paved tarmac in front of the main hangar. Known as Jeff's Hamburger Stand, or "The Greasy Spoon" in local parlance, this "four counter" establishment was popular with transient pilots, company employees and school students alike.

A friendly discussion over a cup of coffee would turn into a lively argument as to the merit of each aircraft mentioned previously. Quite often, the argument would end in a friendly "showdown" with the winner being awarded several cans of beer. The contest rules were simple, who could takeoff in the shortest distance.

One at a time, the pilots would board their respective aircraft and taxi over to a fence separating the tarmac from Bear Tavern Road. Because the aircraft used in this contest lacked brakes, Howard Jong and Ralph Coston held the wingtips while the pilot revved his engine to full power. After a simple head nod, he was released and on his way.

Almost universally, Fritz King and his Fleet were declared the winners, but by scant inches on many occasions. If the winds were brisk from the west, all airplanes were airborne before the edge of the ramp on the other side, a distance of some 150 feet!

These recreational activities and flying contests were not the only "diversion" from work for employees. On several occasions, Pete Brooks would fly to West Trenton to visit his buddy, Don Luscombe. Pete was not content to simply land and taxi his souped-up Monocoupe to the ramp. He had to announce his arrival with a low, high-speed pass over the hangar, the Monocoupe's Warner engine screaming. As the hangar and shops emptied, Pete would be performing a graceful series of acrobatics. Ben Melcher, on his behalf, was furious and would tear at his hair, what little he had. Work was NOT getting done with everybody outside watching Pete Brooks' aerial display.

But one event burned a vivid memory in the minds of many employees — the fiery demise of the great airship *Hindenburg* on an overcast, May 6, 1937, evening. Lakehurst, New Jersey, was barely an hour's drive from the factory and several employees made the trip to see the twisted, charred remains of a once proud airship. For others, the emotional, "live" commentary of WLS of Chicago radio reporter, Herbert Morrison, was enough to cast a gloomy pall for the day without a curious visit.

Amid the many moments of fun and diversion from the serious work at hand, there was a noteworthy accomplishment. Frank Johnson and students Ed Yulke, Dick Cavin, Bert Rowe, Mike Melfa and several others finished a preliminary mock-up of their school project. Complete with windshield and stub-wings, the mock-up was positioned on a large piece of wood supported by two flimsy wood saw horses. Other aircraft components and layouts were close at hand to show the design's various wing, fuselage and tail lines. The cabin featured a close, side-by-side seating arrangement. The instrument panel was a piece of plywood with templates showing where the instruments were to be positioned. Simulated control sticks were installed.

Using Carl Aa's Aeronca C-2, a Monocoupe and other airplanes based on the field as examples, Frank Johnson measured these airplanes' cabins to give him a rough idea for his mock-up's interior size, then he added a bit more. The result was a thirty-six inch wide cabin at the seat and thirty-eight inches at the shoulders.

The fuselage was envisioned to be a monocoque structure with flat-wrapped aluminum skins shaped around squared ellipse bulkheads. There were to be no stringers or stiffeners. Johnson had several drawings and layouts nearby to show any inquisitive visitor how this arrangement would work.[57]

Impressed with the Aeronca's high aspect ratio wing, Johnson decided the school project would feature a high aspect ratio wing utilizing a NACA 4412 airfoil. The wings would span thirty-five feet and have a fifty inch chord with tapered tips.

To further save costs, Johnson made sure there was minimal fuselage skin curvature where the wing's trailing edge met the cabin. Thus, labor costs were reduced since no fillets were necessary in this area.

Though the mock-up had only high mounted stubs for wings, the plans called for a fabric covered, two spar, Vee-strut braced wing with a few parts coming from the Phantom wing design. Lighter spar extrusions were needed to accommodate the mock-up's smaller wing chord and thickness.

In an effort to save extrusion costs and use readily available parts, the forward spar of the school design used a Phantom's extruded I-beam rear spar. Additionally, the mock-up's rear spar was a highly modified Phantom rear spar.

To reduce its height, this rear spar was fabricated by removing a one and three-eighths inch wide slice from the center section web. Then, .025 aluminum strips were riveted on each side to splice the web together. Though the effort reduced potential extrusion costs, the modified spar exhibited a greater weight than an extruded spar, if one had been made. For production, an extrusion of the required size could

Chapter Eleven: Making The Grade — The Quest For An All-Metal Airplane

be purchased.

The wingtips, if built, were to be rounded. Likewise, the ailerons, starting at their mid-section would feature a gentle, upward bend as they faired towards the wingtip. Interestingly, the outboard wing and wingtips were designed to be easily repaired in the event of an accident. In his initial layouts, Johnson provided a "C" channel extension to the extruded I-beam spar at the point where the tapered tip slanted. The ailerons outboard ends were rounded to approximate the tip taper. (Though this idea was not employed in the mock-up, it became very successful in a later Luscombe Airplane Corporation design, the Luscombe Model 8 series.)

The wing ribs developed in the school shop were of aluminum alloy tube construction. They were light, strong and easy to build. Basically, they were a Warren truss of 1/4 inch 4S aluminum tubing flattened on the inside of the bends made by using a special set of tools, resembling pliers, made by the students.

Johnson had his students build a few examples and subject them to various stress tests on a specially prepared test stand behind the school shop. Eventually, this type of rib structure was used in the prototype Luscombe "50" design. The planned power plant was to be a Continental A-40 or the new A-50, the latter not available for several months to come.

Johnson and his students were proud of their project. In jest, some students called their effort the "Luscombe Elf" or the "Luscombe Pond Hopper." Others were content to call it the "mock-up."

Sometime during late April or early May 1937, Don Luscombe was asked to view the school's ambitious endeavor. He stood before the mock-up momentarily before hopping into it. He felt a little bit insecure as the cabin gently swayed atop the work bench.

"Hmm, a little bit tight," he commented. Turning to Frank Johnson, he added, *"Frank, it doesn't matter if you are buying a two thousand dollar airplane or a six thousand dollar airplane, your ass is just as big!"*

Johnson replied, *"I am trying to keep it light and simple, you know."*

Luscombe nodded approvingly. *"That's right. But see what you can do."*

The plans were redrawn slightly. The changes reflected a full 40 inch wide cabin instead of the 38 inch wide cabin used in the mock-up.

Later in the evening, Frank and Don walked together across the asphalt tarmac in front of the main hangar. Don was adrift in his thoughts, but he shared a few of his feelings with Frank. He sat down on the horizontal stabilizer of a nearby Phantom.

Using a trick he often enjoyed sharing with friends and associates, Don ground out a cigarette on the aircraft's metal fuselage. *"Frank, I don't know if we can build that metal job. I was thinking of something somewhere between an Aeronca and a Monocoupe, fabric covered, of course."*

Frank looked squarely at Don. He could sense his boss was somehow disillusioned with the prospect of building the design completely from metal. Perhaps, the mock-up's small size or the idea of a *small*, all-metal airplane ran against Don's marketing beliefs to cater to "well-heeled" clientele. Johnson tried a little persuasive salesmanship.

Frank Johnson's original wood mock-up served as basis for a school project. This project evolved into the popular Luscombe Model 8 series.

FRANK JOHNSON

"We can't build a stick and rag job as cheap as Taylor and Aeronca can," Johnson began. *"They can't build a metal airplane as cheap as we can. You want an airplane that looks like an airplane. We can build a metal airplane as cheap as we can build a stick and rag airplane. You have spent all these years and all this effort preaching metal. This is the way you can prove the point."*

Don nodded approvingly. *"Frank, you are right. I'll give you six hundred dollars appropriation to get started."*

Frank Johnson had barely started refining the former school project when word came from the main office that the project was going to engineering. Fred Knack and Jim Rising would complete the design and see it through prototype development.

Johnson may have been upset not to complete the design, but he never showed it. He was content knowing his efforts, and those of his students, had made a "passing grade" with Don Luscombe.

the more MODERN METAL *Phantom*

is now offered at prices comparable with stick and wire and fabric airplanes. It has new standards for strength, durability and affords lower maintenance costs.

It is designed and built to the higher standards best appreciated by the market which is airplane wise.

Our production capacity will now permit additional dealer contracts for the new Phantom and other metal airplanes shortly to be announced.

As an airplane owner you will want the fire resistance and strength of metal construction—as a dealer your future is best associated with a product leading the field in advanced construction.

For information address inquiries to:

LUSCOMBE AIRPLANE CORPORATION
WEST TRENTON, N. J.

The Luscombe (Metal) Phantom

Acclaimed at the Air Show as the outstanding MODERN airplane for American Sportsmen.

Information on request

LUSCOMBE AIRPLANE DEVELOPMENT CORPORATION

West Trenton, New Jersey

"The man of virtue makes the difficulty to be overcome his first business, and success only a subsequent consideration."
Confucius (551 - 479 B.C.)

Chapter Twelve

Prelude To Success

The new Luscombe "Fifty" prototype, registered 1304, is prepared for its first flight. Note the small "4" in the registration number on the upper right wing. HOWARD JONG

Fred Knack and Jim Rising deliberated Frank Johnson's resourceful mock-up and plans. Both gentlemen marveled at the many ingenious ideas Johnson, Jong and others employed to create the apprentice program's proposed airplane. The aircraft's proposed construction simplicity and overall strength were noteworthy.

Essentially, the initial airplane design depicted was a lower horsepower version of the "Sprite." Factory school brochures touted this design as the Luscombe "Elf," a Continental A-40 powered, two place airplane. The same fuselage construction was there, as was the strut-braced tail. As Knack and Rising examined the many drawings and notes, they realized this two-place design had tremendous production potential.

Don realized this fact, too. He had given his engineering department a tidy sum of money to study, refine and expand upon the school project idea. Now it was time for them to develop something "workable." Luscombe needed a good, solid, cost-effective design to lift him from his production woes and keep him competitive.

Don was frustrated. He had a reasonably well-equipped shop (though he lacked large production machinery), lots of experienced and inexpensive labor, and an airplane that was *"too damn expensive to build."* The Phantom cost too much. Yet, he was not about to rule the airplane a failure.

To add insult to injury, many of the same metal airplane concepts he preached were being put into actual practice by at least two potentially competitive concerns — Ryan Aircraft in San Diego, California, and the recently formed Stearman-Hammond Aircraft Company in San Francisco, California. The former produced the Ryan S-T, a single-engine, all-metal monocoque fuselage design with fabric-covered, metal-structure wing and tail surfaces, whereas the latter company began to produce a twin-boom, pusher-engine, all-metal airplane.

Don turned his attention to the Model 4 program. Priced to be almost $4000, this design was expensive

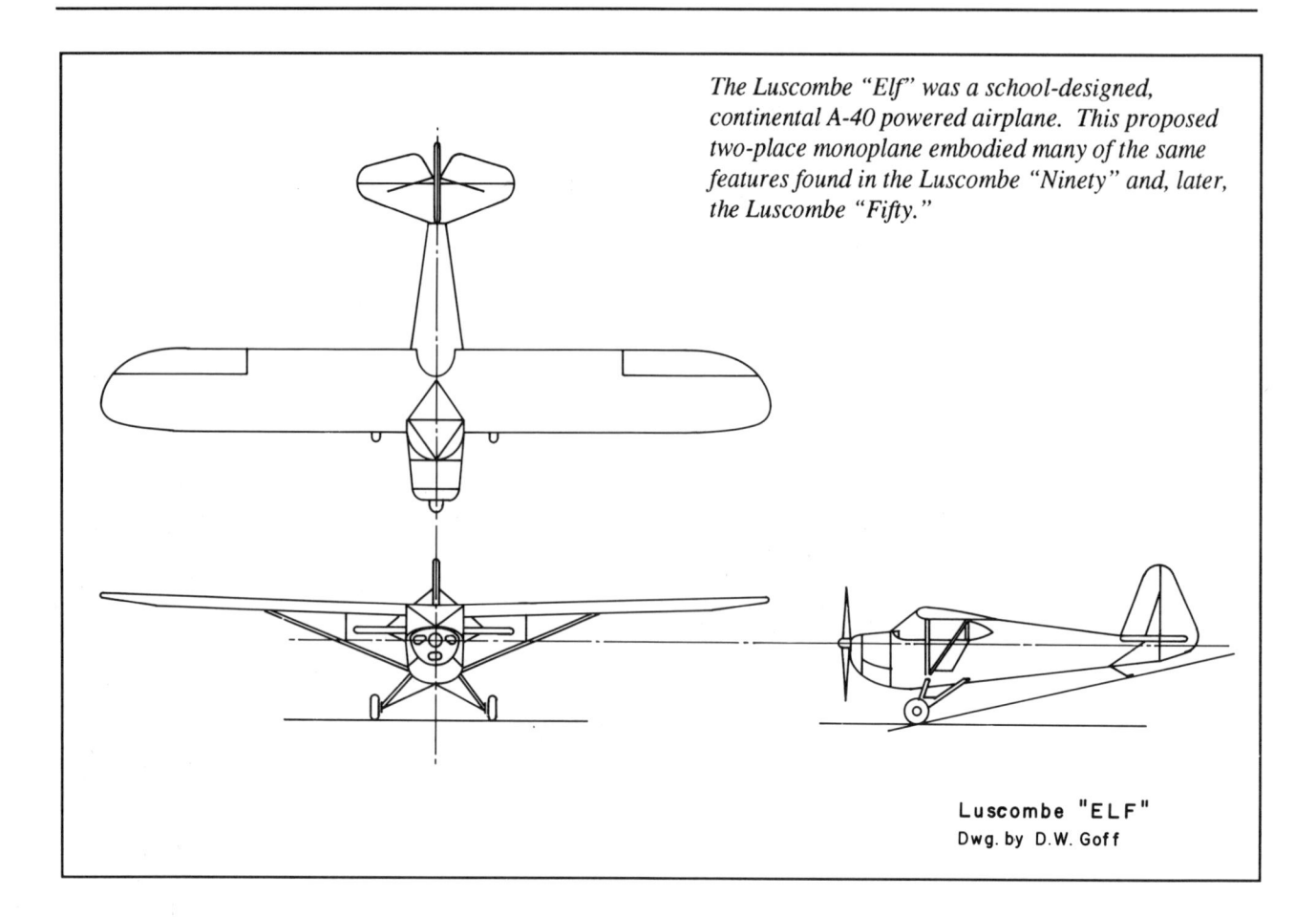

The Luscombe "Elf" was a school-designed, continental A-40 powered airplane. This proposed two-place monoplane embodied many of the same features found in the Luscombe "Ninety" and, later, the Luscombe "Fifty."

Luscombe "ELF"
Dwg. by D.W. Goff

when compared to competitors' airplanes of comparable size and performance. However, it could be the aircraft that would keep him in business. Hence, the "Ninety" held great promise.

Furthermore, Luscombe faced a sobering reality — he had invested too much of his stockholders' money to abandon this Warner "Scarab Junior" powered design. Any hesitation on his part to develop the airplane would signal to stockholders his passionate "all-metal airplane" dialogues were only a scheming promoter's dream, not those of a man with a credible vision. In light of his predicament, Don chose the only viable option left to him — he called for an acceleration in the Model 4's development.

At the same time, Don took a closer look at the new design on the drawing boards and the horizontally-opposed engine it proposed to use. At first, Don took exception to Johnson's original power plant ideas. He believed a flat-opposed engine was unreliable and, therefore, unsuitable.

His hesitancy was rooted in the flat-opposed engine's poor reliability, especially when he looked at the Continental A-40's record. Early examples exhibited blown head gaskets, broken crankshafts and magneto failure, all adding to a very short useful life. However, Don's opinions changed quickly.

He was very encouraged by Continental Aircraft Engine's consistent efforts to improve the reliability of this simple, four-stroke. A second magneto was added in late 1936, as was a second spark plug to each cylinder. Blown head gaskets became a problem of the past. The crankshaft failure problem was solved by adding a thrust bearing to the front of the crankshaft. The final result was a very capable and reliable performer. [58]

To remedy these many past problems, Continental Motors Corporation, Aircraft Engines Division management all but abandoned the original A-40 design and developed, virtually from scratch, the Model A-50 engine. Luscombe's conversations with Continental Motors Corporation representatives convinced him this new power plant would be ideal for any new design. Yet, as of May 1937, the A-50 was still an experimental engine. [59]

During these conversations, Luscombe learned his major competitors planned to use or substantially increase their use of Continental power plants. Piper, Taylor, Taylorcraft, Aeronca, Porterfield and others had affordable, light airplane designs ready to accept the advantages of a flat-opposed engine's improved reliability and performance. Luscombe had none. [60]

Don acted swiftly. He gave a firm "go-ahead" for

Chapter Twelve: Prelude To Success 181

development-to-prototype of the new, fifty horsepower airplane design. Don wanted a prototype ready by year's end. To meet the competition, he needed a $1500 class airplane. The fifty horsepower design was his answer.

In an effort to keep development costs low, Don instructed his engineering staff to use as many parts in common with the Model 4 as possible, a point they had assumed already. To this end, he insisted the department make use of the oval shaped bulkheads as used in the "Ninety."

Luscombe's frugal approach was not an unwillingness on his behalf to spend more money for a new fuselage bulkhead design or parts. Quite simply, he did not have the money to spend and it made good sense to save design and tooling costs where possible.

With two experimental airplane designs in concurrent development, Don recognized there had to be a means to differentiate between these two programs. The answer was simple. The Model 4 was known to many as the Luscombe "90" or "Ninety." Why not call the new, A-50 powered design the Luscombe "50," or "Fifty" for short? Interestingly, engineering department drawings of the period referred to the new design as the "Model 8."

Meanwhile, "Ninety" test flights were virtually an everyday occurrence. Wedged between their various sales and Phantom demonstration flights, Eddie Davis and Ig Sargent took turns testing the experimental Luscombe "90." Fritz King and Lou Coghill assisted by making several flights, as well.

A set of wings with full span, narrow-chord ailerons was built for the "Ninety" as an attempt to reduce stick loads, but was never used. WILLIAM B. SHEPARD

During May 1937, Bill Shepard completed the Model 4 "production" wing design. His drawings were checked by Fred Knack and stress analyzed by Jim Rising before they were approved by Knack and sent to the shop. In turn, the new wings were produced quickly and installed on the experimental airplane.

The first set of production wings for the Luscombe "90" were almost completed before Fred Knack had approved the drawings. Lou Coghill, wing department foreman, and Bill Shepard often shared rides to work. During their morning drive to work and evening return home, Bill would describe his work at length to Lou. From these conversations, together with visits to the Engineering Department and studies of the preliminary blueprints, a very intuitive Coghill was able to build the wing's basic structure before the final drawings were approved.

A good view of the "Ninety" showing its wire-braced tail and production "Ninety" wings. LUSCOMBE SCHOOL OF AERONAUTICS BROCHURE, JAMES B. ZAZAS COLLECTION

182 Visions of Luscombe: The Early Years

Always a practical joker, Peter Brooks added his own humorous comments to one of Don Luscombe's Phantom brochures.

ELEANORE LUSCOMBE SHURTZ COLLECTION

Chapter Twelve: Prelude To Success 183

Consisting of left and right panels, similar to those used on the Phantom, these aluminum alloy structured, fabric-covered wings featured metal-framed, fabric-covered ailerons outboard and trailing edge flaps from the ailerons inboard to the wing root. The I-beam extruded spars were made from the same extruded sections used for the Phantoms. Phantom ribs were used, also. A 15.5 gallon fuel tank was installed in the root end of each wing. [61]

Another important feature found on these production wings was the detachable wingtip spars. Much like the detachable wingtip spar extensions employed on Johnson's wing design, these spar tips reduced the chance of damaging the extruded portions of the main wing spars and offered easy repair with minimal labor. Though Shepard's "detachable wing-tip" design evolved concurrently with Johnson's "detachable wing-tip" plans, it was no doubt Fred Knack who nudged Shepard towards this innovative idea.

On June 5, 1937, Ig Sargent made the first test flight with the new wings. Upon Sargent's return, Eddie Davis flew the airplane and put the "Ninety" through its paces during a brief fifteen minute flight. Both gentlemen were quite pleased by the aircraft's improved handling. Sargent made two more test flights (June 7 and June 9) in the airplane before concluding "Ninety" flight tests for the month.

Incidentally, neither Sargent nor Davis would fly the "Ninety" again until early or mid-July as other duties required their attention. Sargent flew to Chicago, Illinois, to give a series of demonstration flights in his Phantom. Davis, in turn, stayed in the local area checking out pilots in the Phantom before heading to Massachusetts for a much-needed vacation.

Meanwhile, Don Luscombe pursued a variety of ways to generate more cash flow for his company. To encourage Phantom sales and possibly dispense remaining Phantom fuselages and parts stock on hand, Don placed advertisements in *Aero Digest*, *Aviation* and other prestigious aviation periodicals during the 1937 summer months. Some ads were aimed to appeal to a prospective purchaser whereas other ads touted the availability of Phantom dealer franchises.

One full-page advertisement, carried in the June 1937 issue of *Aero Digest*, listed 46 attributes of the Phantom and asked the reader to *"check and total the score in comparison with any other plane."* Upon looking at this slick piece of marketing, any reader would have a difficult time disputing the intrinsic "value" of the Luscombe Phantom, despite the advertised $5675 price.

But a few of Don Luscombe's friends had their own ideas about the Phantom. Always a practical joker, Pete Brooks took a copy of a similar brochure and added his particular comments. After looking at Brooks' handiwork, Don laughed and said the changes would make a better advertising copy than the one placed in the *Aero Digest* magazine.

Ironically, tucked neatly within the classified section of the same issue was an advertisement from the Warner Aircraft Corporation. Their Phantom, with less than seventy-five hours total time, was for sale.

Though the Warner ad was one of the first non-Luscombe Aircraft Corporation advertisements to appear in a major aviation publication offering to sell a Phantom airplane, it was not to be the last. Soon, Don Luscombe would read more ads in more publications as more used Phantoms became available on the open market.

Undaunted by this competitive, if not sobering, marketing fact, the Luscombe Airplane Corporation Board of Directors approved the formation of a dealer

A tranquil view of the Mercer County Airport grounds. Circa February 1937.   HOWARD JONG

franchise system. Previously, all Phantoms had been sold by the company directly to the customer. This new program was announced in the July 1937 issue of *Aero Digest*.

Don and his small sales staff went to work immediately. Within thirty days of this announcement, major territories of the United States had been assigned to dealers. Additionally, by the end of the year, the quotas of airplanes to be sold by these dealers totaled almost 345 airplanes, a most optimistic figure!

Amidst this swirling flurry of Luscombe Airplane Corporation activity, Agnew Larsen, Pitcairn Autogiro Company's chief engineer, paid Don Luscombe a cordial visit. Pitcairn Autogiro, an established airplane and autogiro manufacturer in nearby Willow Grove, Pennsylvania, was developing a series of roadable autogiro aircraft.

The company wanted to build an all-metal roadable, jump-takeoff autogiro, but lacked the necessary metalworking experience and labor to construct the design. Hence, Harold Pitcairn, president of the company that bore his name, at Larsen's suggestion, agreed that his chief engineer should seek Don's help and Nick Nordyke's expertise.

Within a short time, a contract was produced for the Luscombe Airplane Corporation to develop and produce a duraluminum metal autogiro fuselage, as per Pitcairn's specifications, on a straight time and material basis. Labor charges were set at $1.50 per hour. The Luscombe Airplane Corporation would be reimbursed for the cost of materials. Furthermore, Pitcairn agreed to pay Luscombe semi-monthly upon receipt of all invoices for labor spent upon and material used making the fuselage.

Don Luscombe was elated! He had another source of positive cash-flow. Additionally, he anticipated he would get more contracts for all-metal fuselage work should Pitcairn commence work on their production models.

Fred Knack, on the other hand, recognized a potential problem from the Pitcairn contract — it would drain needed manpower from his small, six to eight person engineering staff. Knack gently reminded Don that all efforts were directed towards the "Ninety" and the new "Fifty," and he had barely enough help to meet *these* requirements.

Don agreed, but told Knack the company needed the Pitcairn work to survive. Knack, very much aware of the company's difficult financial position, resolved this problem quickly. He assigned one engineer to undertake the autogiro's fuselage design, Bill Shepard.[62]

Initially, Shepard was tasked to design the autogiro's entire fuselage, but this requirement changed quickly. When Larsen discovered Shepard was the only engineer assigned to the project, he decided to divide the work between Shepard and Pitcairn's engineering department. Pitcairn engineers would be responsible for the design of the forward fuselage and rotor pylon, while Shepard would be responsible for the fuselage aft of the cabin doors, including the tail surfaces.

This contract provided Luscombe's company with much needed working capital and cash flow. Meanwhile, Luscombe pursued the potentially lucrative foreign market.

Starting in May 1937 and continuing through the summer, Luscombe surveyed the export market and found considerable foreign interest to build factories for the manufacture or assembly of the moderately-priced Luscombe Airplane Corporation designs. Besides taking into account any cash considerations, Luscombe would furnish engineers, designers, instructors and any equipment necessary for these projects. Negotiations were conducted with interested individuals from Canada, England, France, Greece and the Republic of Argentine (Argentina).

Talks with a prominent Canadian company looked especially promising. They proposed establishing a Luscombe Associate Company as a subsidiary. A detailed review of Luscombe's airplane(s), the plant and manufacturing processes was favorable. Likewise, Hiram Mallinson traveled throughout Europe for the LAC and elicited substantial interest in France and England. His diligent efforts proved very successful.

Mallinson met Jacques Negrier, son of the president of the Aero de France (French Aero Club). The two discussed at length the requirements of a low cost training airplane as specified in the "Aviation Populaire" program of the French Air Ministry. The new Luscombe "50" met these requirements quite handily.

Encouraged, Negrier talked to his father at length about the Luscombe "50." Negrier's father was a senior executive in the Caudron Corporation and was quite involved in the parent company, the Renault Automobile Company. At the time, Caudron built wood and fabric airplanes, mostly low-wing multi-seat designs. The idea of building, under license, an all-metal airplane appealed to the senior Negrier. Very quickly, an oral agreement was made between the Luscombe Airplane Corporation and Caudron to sell airplanes to the Aero de France. The airplane of choice was the yet-to-be-produced "Fifty."

This agreement stipulated Caudron would furnish the necessary capital to assemble the "Fifty" in France under a French License at such time as the Luscombe Airplane Corporation obtained the necessary Service Technique license required for fabrication of airplanes in France. Both parties agreed in principle the LAC would receive one-third of the shares in the proposed new French corporation's capital stock plus $20,000 cash. Furthermore, Luscombe would provide blueprints, engineering data, free access to all tools and processes, and exclusive sales rights in France and her Colonies.

The agreement was strengthened further by another voiced agreement with Monsieur Luc, the French Minister of Education. He assured Caudron the Ministry of Education would subsidize the annual training of forty men at the French corporation's aeronautical school.

Mallinson's efforts in England also netted potentially handsome returns. Once again, a prominent manufacturer agreed orally to advance one-half the capital needed to establish a Luscombe licensee company. The only consideration was obtaining a Certificate of Airworthiness from the British Air Ministry on the Luscombe "Ninety" modified for a Gypsy Major engine installation.

Luscombe was ecstatic! His personal celebrations, however, were short-lived. With the prospects of such production potential becoming available, Don faced a problem he hadn't encountered since his Monocoupe days — lots of potential orders, but not enough floor space to build the airplanes to fulfill these orders.

Don needed an extension to his building and his Mercer County Airport lease. The former problem was a simple matter of contracting a firm to design and build a building to specification. The latter required some careful negotiations with the Mercer County Board of Freeholders.

On July 27, 1937, Luscombe submitted a letter to this Board in which he stated his desire to obtain a ten year lease for an additional fifteen acres of land at the Mercer County Airport with an option to renew this lease for an additional fifteen years at an increased rental rate. Don stated he needed the land to build an additional factory building adjoining the main hangar and office space for a proposed expansion. In closing his letter, Luscombe hinted he would move his company to another airport if his terms were not met.

Soon, Don was before the Board contending he needed an expeditious approval so he could include the terms of the new lease in a prospectus for the Securities and Exchange Commission. These arguments upset the Board and delayed approval.

Board members debated Luscombe's proposals vigorously for several weeks. Many members wanted to see manufacturing continue at the airport, but did not want to see the airport grounds damaged. Others feared such an expansion would severely impact flying operations at the airport.

Luscombe tried to quell these fears by saying, *"I think I am more interested in that than anyone in this town. When I fly airplanes out of there, I risk my life and I don't want anything that will be an obstruction."*

While the Mercer County Board of Freeholders haggled with the lease issues, Luscombe signed a contract with the Austin Company of Cleveland, Ohio, to build a one-story factory addition plus a one-story addition to the office. The new factory was planned to extend some 120 feet east from the existing main hangar. Total cost of the new expansion was estimated to be $36,000.[63]

Faced with the prospect of losing much-needed county revenue and fearful the airport would fall into disuse, the Board, on August 17, 1937, passed a resolution approving Luscombe's expansion plans. This lease became effective October 1, 1937. Though all buildings were on the leased property, the Luscombe Airplane Corporation had the right to remove the Paint Shop, the Sheet Metal and Engineering Building, and the School Building. The lease could be cancelled upon the sale of the airport at public auction. In such an occurrence, the LAC would be reimbursed to the full extent of any depreciated value of the buildings.

Barely three days before the Board's approval, Don Luscombe concluded a Memorandum of Agreement with Peter Vanech of Athens, Greece, to form a limited company under the laws of Greece and a convenient State in the United States of America. This corporation was to be called the Hellenic Luscombe Aeronautic Corporation. Other suitable names were approved, also.

This partnership's purpose was to organize a company to manufacture, assemble, and sell Luscombe airplanes in Greece. Additionally, a training and apprentice program similar to the Luscombe Apprentice Program would be established.

Beyond the terms of the agreement as included in an August 23, 1937, Registration Statement filed with the Securities and Exchange Commission, very little further information is known regarding the aforementioned plan. Likewise, very little information is known about Mr. Vanech, his background or his airplane building experience.

Meanwhile, the Luscombe Airplane Corporation managed to sell two Phantoms. The first Phantom sold went to Herbert Kraft of Burbank, California, an American Airlines captain. He bought his airplane on August 9, 1937. Kraft had his Phantom painted similar to his company's colors — bare metal fuselage with red control surfaces. This glistening airplane had been test flown by Sargent three months earlier.

The second Phantom sold during August was NC1278 (s/n 117). Fritz King tested this Phantom's wings on August 13, 1937, in the blue skies above the Mercer County Airport. This airplane was purchased by the Falcon Aircraft Corporation of Los Angeles the following day.[64] No more Phantoms were produced for the balance of the year. Yet, many changes took

Luscombe Phantom NC1278 (s/n 117) under construction.

place in the school and on the floor.

Seeking better design engineering opportunities, Frank Johnson left the company in mid-August to pursue a job with a design team building a new, two-place airplane in Camden, New Jersey. In turn, Luscombe asked Lou Coghill and Jim Rising to fill the school instructor void until a suitable replacement could be hired. [65]

In the meantime, the apprentice program underwent a major metamorphosis. Originally conceived as a means to train men exclusively for the Luscombe Airplane Corporation, the apprentice program was changed into a separate and self-sustaining concern, but kept the same education philosophy. Don made it clear to his Board of Directors and investors these changes were necessary for the company's long-term growth and survival. He cited several reasons.

First, the apprentice program was very popular and had gained a positive reputation within the aircraft industry. Don did not want to disturb this favorable attention. Though many graduates remained with the Luscombe organization, other graduates secured lucrative positions with other prestigious airplane manufacturers.

Second, Luscombe and his Board of Directors had to adopt a program that would mesh well with any foreign educational programs. A bonafide school would satisfy this need. Future United States Government approval was considered, also.

Third, the current lack of work at the factory forced Don to hire fewer men from the apprentice program ranks. Too many men were completing the curriculum to be absorbed readily into the Luscombe Airplane Corporation. The school's reorganization would make it easier for Don to hire what graduates he needed when he needed them.

Fourth, the use of student labor to build airplanes had to end. Before the school's reorganization, Department of Commerce inspectors tended to cast a blind eye towards any students building parts for any Luscombe airplane, e.g. the Phantom. Now, student labor on production line aircraft was no longer condoned.

Finally, as usual, Don's company was strapped for money. He needed the school to be a self-sustaining, yet credible source of income. By reorganizing the apprentice program into a subsidiary of the parent Luscombe Airplane Corporation, Don would reap the benefits of school-generated income and dispel any lingering suspicions that the student's tuition money might be used improperly.

The LAC Board of Directors met in late August to consider Luscombe's "apprentice program" reformation. Don assured Board members this new school would still specialize in metal airplane engineering, instruction and construction. With minimal fanfare, the Board approved Don's ideas.

Don wasted no time announcing his new school to the public. A full-page ad, placed in the September 1937 issue of *Aero Digest*, heralded the new Luscombe School of Aeronautics, a division of the Luscombe Airplane Corporation.

During this same period, Luscombe filed a stock offering prospectus with the Securities and Exchange Commission. This offering consisted of 195,000 shares at 50 cents-par-common stock of which 145,000 shares were offered through Knight and Company, the underwriters, at $2.50 per share. In turn, the underwriters were optioned 35,000 shares and another 15,000 shares were optioned to key men and officers of the Luscombe Airplane Corporation. Proceeds were to pay for new buildings, machinery, equipment and development and working capital.

Despite his many and innovative attempts to raise capital, the critical money situation continued to plague Luscombe. The nation was still gripped by the crippling Depression and more financially tight times were forecast. The company's only major income sources during this difficult period were the bi-monthly Pitcairn Autogiro Company payments, student tuitions and a percentage of Fritz King's gas sales on the

Chapter Twelve: Prelude To Success 187

field. Occasionally, a Phantom or two would return for repairs or modifications. [66]

Likewise, Don's backers were most discouraged when they looked at any future return on their invested funds. Many investors tried to reason with Don and explain why many aspects of the company's financial picture were suspect.

Don was not good with intricate accounting principles and often turned a deaf ear to his investors' pleas for sound fiscal policy and sense. Frustrated and discouraged, many investors shunned Don's repeated pleas for more capital. Several investors elected not to pour any more money into the Luscombe Airplane Corporation "money pit."

To this end, Richard Fabian resigned his position as an LAC Director at a special Board of Directors' meeting held on October 21, 1937. Daniel Simonds was elected to fill this vacancy. A normal businessman would be very discouraged by these events, but Don was not an "ordinary" businessman — he worked best during these hardships. He enjoyed the challenge to rally people around his goals during difficult times.

Always concerned for the welfare of his employees, Don often took long walks on the factory floor to see how his people were doing, what they needed and if they would work a little longer without a paycheck. Don knew who could stand to have a paycheck delayed and who could not, so he was selective in withholding them. Don may have lost a few employees during this difficult time, but most stayed to satisfy his all-metal airplane dreams because they enjoyed working there and aircraft jobs elsewhere were very difficult to find.

Meanwhile, "Ninety" test flying all but ceased for the balance of the year. Except for a few test flights by Don Luscombe, Ig Sargent, Eddie Davis and Lou Coghill, including a brief flurry of proficiency flights by Bill Shepard, aircraft 1253's logbook had few entries after September. [67]

Though the company entered a "quiet," non-flying phase for the balance of the year, it was far from being dormant. Three major projects occupied the engineering department and the production floor. The first of these projects was an improved Luscombe "90." Plans were finalized and jigs were fabricated to build this prototype "production" model, a job many estimated would not be completed until early 1938.

Anticipating the "Ninety" would go into production, Don had ordered almost twenty-five sets of drop-hammered fuselage bulkheads from the Teicher Manufacturing Company. A goal was set to obtain the Approved Type Certificate by the middle of 1938.

The second project was the smaller Luscombe "Fifty," a task that kept the engineering, fuselage and control surfaces departments quite busy to meet Don's end-of-the-year prototype goal. Throughout October and November, the final plans were released by the engineering department to the shop for manufacture.

The third project was the Pitcairn contract job. This one project could be considered the most important financially for Don. There were no orders for Phantom airplanes, none were being produced and neither the "Ninety" nor the "Fifty" were ready for production.

The Pitcairn PA-36 wood mock-up form arrives at the Luscombe Airplane Corporation hangar. This form was used to ensure proper fit of all metal parts prior to actual assembly. HOWARD JONG

The PA-36, as it became known, was unlike any engineering or construction challenge ever built by a small airplane manufacturing concern. Using their very limited financial resources, engineering talent, and available manpower prudently, the Luscombe Airplane Corporation and the Pitcairn Autogiro organization created a very aesthetically appealing and functional jump-takeoff roadable autogiro.

The PA-36 borrowed heavily from the PA-35, an earlier steel tube and fabric covered Pitcairn autogiro design. The PA-36 evolved, however, into an all-metal, two place, side-by-side cabin aircraft powered by a Warner "Super Scarab," 165 hp engine. The engine, located behind the cabin, drove a four-blade propeller via a shaft through the cabin and, through an ingenious clutch arrangement, drove a large, steerable tailwheel in the rear. Engine cooling was provided by a fan. A fuselage pylon supported the rotor system. For initial pre-takeoff spin-up, this rotor was connected to the engine via a fuselage mounted transmission and clutch.

All fuselage, pylon and steerable landing gear stub components were made of sheet duraluminum riveted to intricately formed duraluminum bulkheads. Interestingly, the sheet metal seat structure and the lower cabin skin, with all joints sealed, formed the fuel and engine oil tanks.

Besides being flyable, the PA-36 was to be "roadable." That is, the autogiro could be driven on a road, much like an automobile via a clutch arrangement to the rear wheel. In actual practice, however, this complicated arrangement was not used.

As envisioned originally, a pilot would "drive" the PA-36 to the airport, switch engine power from the tailwheel to the rotor via a clutch, bring the rotor up to proper speed, whereupon the pilot would increase rotor blade pitch and literally cause the autogiro to "jump to altitude" — about thirty feet or so off the ground.

The Pitcairn PA-36, fuselage number 1, under construction at the Luscombe factory. Luscombe needed this project to stay in business. Chuck Burgess stands to the right of this all-metal fuselage. CHARLES E. BURGESS

Then, very quickly, the pilot would shift power from the rotor blades to the front-mounted propeller, which was rotating at half speed during rotor spin-up. Upon this shift, the propeller would turn at full-speed while the main rotor blades autorotated. Now, the pilot would fly the PA-36 much like any other autogiro.

The motivating theory was workable, but proved very complicated when put into actual practice. Luscombe's engineers and workers were burdened with many headaches and frustrations while they built the Pitcairn PA-36's aft fuselage section.

As soon as Shepard completed his PA-36 design work and the drawings were approved by Agnew Larsen, Luscombe added a second shift to expedite completion of the autogiro fuselage. Chuck Burgess was assigned the first shift, generally a daytime period. Bill Shepard, on the other hand, had the night shift.

Nick Nordyke was tasked to work when he was needed which, quite often, was during both shifts. Soon, however, he reverted to a more "normal" workday schedule to fabricate necessary parts. A wood mock-up was first built to help solve any unforeseen space, engineering or fabrication problems. Nick Nordyke used this mock-up extensively to visualize how certain items should be formed and fitted.

Starting in late October, the first metal was cut for the PA-36. It was at this development stage Chuck Burgess and Bill Shepard began to sweat blood on some perplexing manufacturing problems. The PA-36, due to its complex nature, required adherence to very small tolerances on the location of the rotor hub.

As the weather got colder, the angle iron jigs wreaked havoc between the day and night shift personnel, particularly between Burgess and Shepard.

After the heat was turned on in the morning, the jig members supporting the fuselage/rotor pylon would start to expand. By noon, an adjustment of an eighth of an inch or more would be required. Burgess would make a checkpoint mark for Shepard to show where the jig should be set. When Shepard came to work in the evening, the heat was turned down and, in turn, the jig shrank. Burgess' mark was now off an eighth of an inch or more on the small side.

Shepard would make his jig adjustments and make a new mark for Burgess. When the heat was turned on in the morning, the frustrating process started once more. After some serious discussions with Pitcairn engineers, a Department of Commerce inspector and Jules De Crescenszo, the factory sub-assembly supervisor and a company "key man," everybody agreed the eighth inch error was acceptable.

Another major PA-36 headache was the fuselage fuel tank which formed as part of the fuselage structure. It had to be sealed with neoprene tape, then

Chapter Twelve: Prelude To Success 189

(Left and Below) The completed Pitcairn PA-36. Luscombe engineers and employees designed and fabricated the autogiro's gleaming aluminum fuselage and tail aft of the door post. This activity produced a positive cash flow that kept Don Luscombe's struggling company in business. Flight tests of this finely crafted aircraft commenced in 1939 at the Pitcairn factory in Willow Grove, Pennsylvania. Sadly, this PA-36 and a partially completed twin were scrapped at the start of World War II.

riveted to the rest of the fuselage with at least one tank wall being the fuselage skin itself. In turn, the tank had to be vibration tested to ensure there were no leaks and to reduce the chance of leaks developing in service. The completed tank was sent to Pitcairn for testing.

Filled with water, the tank's first vibration test shook the tank apart completely and sprayed its contents over the hapless observers. Quick inspection showed the seals failed and allowed the structure to become completely unbalanced in the test stand.

Undaunted, Luscombe personnel went to work on the problem, but Larsen didn't have the time or money to invest in improving this tank. He contracted with Fleetwings in nearby Bristol, Pennsylvania, to build another tank. In the end, their vibration test was less "vigorous" than the first test. The second tank withstood the pounding and was pronounced acceptable for installation in the fuselage.

Nick Nordyke was somewhat "double-teamed" during this period. He had to form the compound curve duralumin parts for the PA-36 and the new Luscombe "Fifty" taking shape beside it. Occasionally, Nick would become quite frustrated forming a particularly difficult part and his ensuing anger would get the best of him.

Once, Nick was having a tough time forming and fitting a piece of PA-36 fairing between the top of the fuselage and leading edge of the center fin pylon. After several unsuccessful attempts, he slung the piece across the shop in disgust, cursed the piece and walked out the door telling all present he had enough and quit! Nick then proceeded to the nearest tavern to quell his nerves with a drink.

Upon hearing what Nick had done, Don hastened to the tavern to see Nick, share a drink and try to hire him back. While they chatted, Don offered Nordyke "one for the road" before saying good-bye to a valuable employee. Nick could see through Don's good-natured ploy, apologized to Don for making a fool of himself and returned with him to the factory.

Nick's small staff became quite frustrated on several occasions, also. Several of the sheet metal mechanics, including Bert Rowe, Les Lynch and Cameron Story, had to hand-form the autogiro's duralumin bulkheads over maple wood forms.

In order to form the metal to the required shape, the bulkheads had to be annealed before being sent to another factory to be heat-treated. They soon learned too much heat melted the bulkhead, whereas too little heat made the bulkhead very brittle and difficult to form.

Bill Force, control surface department foreman, was another company "key man" who endured the PA-36's subtle horrors. He and his small staff had to build the PA-36's complicated, triple vertical tail surfaces in addition to the steel tube and fabric control surfaces for the prototype Luscombe "50" airplane. Though he often pulled at his hair, Force maintained his cool. He did not want to upset Luscombe or

(Left) Joe Kotula's pencil rendition of the production Luscombe "Ninety."

(Below) Joe Kotula's pencil rendition of the proposed Luscombe "Fifty." Note the "bug-eye" cowling. This drawing sparked Don Luscombe's interest to seek a similar cowl in the prototype "Fifty."

LAC FACTORY BROCHURE, JAMES B. ZAZAS COLLECTION

LAC FACTORY BROCHURE, JAMES B. ZAZAS COLLECTION

Pitcairn's Larsen who often visited the factory. However, other LAC employees were not so gracious with their respect towards the complex PA-36. Speaking in hushed tones, many called this autogiro, "Larsen's Goon."

Though the PA-36 design was finalized, the Luscombe "50" final design was not. Input came from many sources advising how to improve this new airplane, even as metal was cut. Using simplicity as their goal, ideas were tossed back and forth as to how to pare labor costs, yet retain a structurally sound airplane without sacrificing performance.

For example, Jim Rising suggested a simplified landing gear. He proposed using independent landing gear legs, both attached to a single Luscombe "Ninety" oil-draulic shock cylinder mounted in the center of the fuselage under the cabin floor, instead of the dual oleo system employed on the "Ninety." The lower gross weight of the proposed airplane allowed for such a change.

Furthermore, Rising argued, a semi-cantilever constructed, single oleo system would keep the airplane on a generally even keel while taxiing, therefore minimizing or eliminating any adverse or uncomfortable rocking motions as demonstrated in the prototype "Ninety."

Knack studied Rising's simple landing gear idea, liked what he saw and approved it. The absence of an external oleo strut shock cord gave the gear a slender, streamlined appearance.

Howard Jong, who was assigned to the engineering department shortly after the school mock-up was unveiled, proposed an engineering change at the wing's root end. Aware the major intent of this new "Fifty" was to build it as cost-effectively as possible, Jong suggested his notched trailing edge idea, an idea conceived during some early "Jolly Roger" drafting sessions. Instead of fairing the wing root to the

The prototype Luscombe "Fifty" fuselage being assembled. This same jig was used to build the proof-of-concept Luscombe "Ninety."

JAMES B. ZAZAS COLLECTION

Chapter Twelve: Prelude To Success   191

fuselage as depicted on early engineering drawings, why not cutout the trailing edge wing-root at the rear spar, taper it to the first rib and cover all with a light fairing? Jong showed his pencil sketches to Knack. Once more, Knack studied the idea closely and agreed to the change.

This wing-root modification has been attributed erroneously to many individuals including Fred Knack, Jim Rising and Ben Mclcher. The idea evolved in late 1936 while Frank Johnson and Howard Jong sought ways to pare labor costs on their joint designs.

Further investigations revealed this modification would improve rearward visibility. As a direct consequence and as a cost saving move, the small "D" window originally planned to be installed aft of the door posts was eliminated.

Another and very consequential idea came from an unlikely source — a commercial artist. Desiring to get some initial drawings of the Luscombe "90" and the proposed Luscombe "50" on the market in a slick sales brochure, Don Luscombe hired renowned aviation artist Jo Kotula to make some sketches of the two airplanes. Using photographs, engineering drawings, miscellaneous data and the then flying "Ninety" prototype, Kotula made his sketches. In August 1937, he submitted his snappy drawings to Luscombe.

Don was most pleased with Kotula's work, but became quite startled. The "Ninety" looked all right, but the "Fifty's" exposed engine cylinder heads were covered by a pair of bugeye fairings attached to the cowlings. Don liked the idea.

Without hesitation, Don asked Nick Nordyke if he could fabricate such cylinder covers integral with the cowl for the "Fifty." Nordyke said he could after Knack's engineers determined the correct size for proper cooling. The final result was a pressure-type cooling cowl that looked very similar to the Jo Kotula drawings.[68]

Surprisingly, one of the biggest arguments centered around the Luscombe "50's" control system. Don wanted a stick, the engineers argued a wheel or yoke system would be cheaper and easier

(Right) This type of oil-draulic spring/shock assembly was used in the Luscombe "Ninety" and "Fifty" designs.

(Below) Howard Jong's original pencil sketches showing his ideas for a "notched" trailing edge at the fuselage.

LYLE FARVER

(Below) Another Howard Jong pencil sketch depicting his idea for a "notched" trailing edge at the fuselage. This idea was used in the "Fifty" and significantly reduced the airplane's overall production costs.

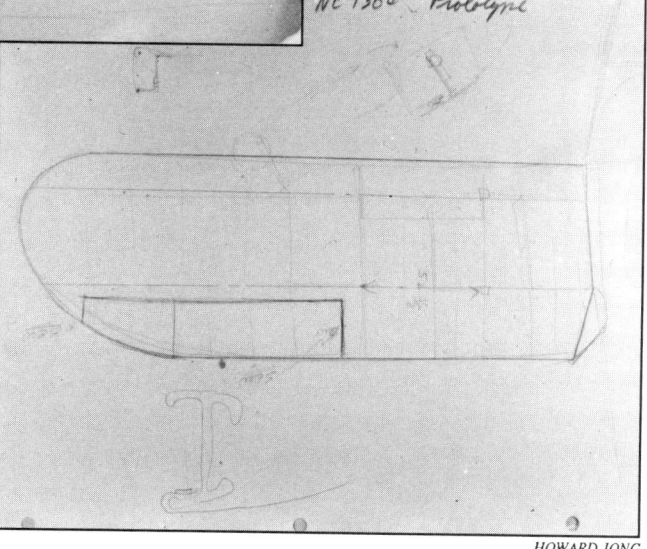

HOWARD JONG

HOWARD JONG

Supporting several tons of sand, the prototype Luscombe "50" fuselage undergoes a series of required government tests. — JOHN UNDERWOOD

to build. In the interest of simplicity and cost, the control wheel idea was adopted, though only for this prototype design. Subsequent production models of the "Fifty" featured a control stick arrangement.

At the time, a control stick arrangement presented some very difficult engineering challenges. Allowed more time, these challenges were solved and incorporated in the production aircraft.

Designed by Howard Jong, the control yoke arrangement was unlike most control wheel systems of the period in that the yoke itself did not move upwards as it was moved backwards. Instead, this prototype's yoke moved straight forward and aft. This design used a bicycle chain to move the ailerons. Linked to the yoke via a sprocket, this chain ran along the aft side of the firewall to just below the cabin floorboards where it was connected, in turn, to the aileron cables.

The new "Fifty" came together while the engineers brainstormed the finer points of the Luscombe "50" design and construction. All but lost in this activity was another Phantom sale. H.T. Cole of Atlanta, Georgia, bought the all-black company demonstrator, NC1048 (s/n 114), on December 4, 1937. Within days, this well recognized Phantom was on its way to the Peachtree State.

Don knew the unveiling and subsequent first flight of the prototype "Fifty" was near. Thus, he applied to the Department of Commerce, Bureau of Air Commerce on December 9, 1937, for a permanent identification mark assignment. The reply confirmed an earlier, experimental identification mark assignment — 1304. In turn, this black painted number was applied to the aircraft's silver-doped fabric wings and rudder.

In mid-December 1937, this labor of many Luscombe employees was unveiled. A dainty, two place, side-by-side machine stood before their eyes. Sprouting gracefully long, round-tipped wings, the all-metal fuselage glistened in the clear, cold air. An early model, upward exhaust Continental A-50-1 engine (loaned to the company for experimental flight test purposes) was mounted on the nose. A brass-tipped, Sensenich wood propeller complemented the airplane.[69]

Many employees and students contributed to this project and all were proud to be involved in building this Luscombe "50" prototype. Don Luscombe was most happy, too! The airplane fulfilled Don's simple request to use as many parts as possible common to the "Ninety." The metal horizontal and vertical stabilizers were the same, as were the fabric covered control surfaces. Likewise, the fuselage was the same as the "Ninety" from the fourth bulkhead aft.

Keen observers noticed other unusual features about this prototype "Fifty." The second bulkhead exhibited a little hump or bump at the point where the airplane's wing struts joined the fuselage. This bump, an integral part of the actual bulkhead form, was intended to smooth the turbulent airflow and decrease the drag at this juncture. However, this feature was costly to make, proved ineffective in actual practice, and was removed in future Model 8 production.

Another unusual feature was the firewall mounted fifteen gallon fuel tank. Subsequent models would exhibit a stronger and safer fuselage fuel tank design located aft of the passenger's seat. Finally, a small amount of room was provided behind the passenger seats to serve as a baggage compartment. The capacity was 40 pounds.

Contrary to a popular belief, Luscombe did not order his engineering department to make the Luscombe "Fifty's" firewall round should the Continental A-50 prove unsuitable, thus, requiring a return to a "round" engine. The almost-round shape of the firewall developed was a logical means to bring together the fuselage geometry and cabin lines into a functional and structurally sound cabin firewall.

Furthermore, Don observed early in the airplane's development that a flat engine was ideal for a small, side-by-side seating airplane because it matched the width required for two passengers. Additionally, Don defended the horizontally-opposed engine by saying,

Chapter Twelve: Prelude To Success

"If you're going to have a side-by-side airplane anyway, the flat engine doesn't make the airplane any wider and you can see over the nose better."

Even if Luscombe decided to return to a "round" engine, virtually none were, or would be, available during the production life of the Model 8. Warner Aircraft phased-out Warner "Scarab Junior" production in late 1937, whereas the 80 hp Le Blond (Ken-Royce) engine was not available in any meaningful quantity until late 1938. By then, Luscombe's airplane competitors were running away with successful, flat-opposed engine powered designs.

By mid-December, the new airplane was assembled and, in turn, underwent a series of taxi tests in preparation for its first flight. Company employees Tom Foley, Jr., and Jules De Crescenzo taxied the airplane on several occasions over the hard, frozen ground. They quickly discovered the airplane was extremely light in the tail and required ballast.

Inexplicably, this weight and balance calculation was missed by the engineering department. To correct the potentially dangerous center-of-gravity problems, an 18 pound sandbag was installed in the tail to hold it down during these taxi tests.

Behind these festive scenes, a small debate arose as to who would make the first test flight in the prototype "Fifty." Everybody assumed it would be Ig Sargent. After all, he had made most, if not all the first test flights in the West Trenton-produced Phantoms, the 1017 airplane and the experimental, proof-of-concept "Ninety."

Tom Foley, Jr., a somewhat opinionated individual with a stock of gray hair that made him look years older than his twenty-five-year-old age would suggest, approached Don Luscombe and asked him if he could make the first flight.[70]

Foley worked for Chuck Burgess in the fuselage department as supervisor of the group that built the 1304 fuselage, some of the work accomplished by unpaid volunteers after regular hours. Also, Foley managed the employees' Flying Stooges Flying Club and lived at the "Jolly Roger." He was well-liked by the students and fellow employees.

With the first flight imminent, Foley appealed directly to Don. Why not let a licensed pilot from the shop make the first flight? Don listened to Foley's arguments, pondered them for a few moments, then agreed to let him fly the 1304 airplane. On December 17, 1937, when the first "Fifty" took to the skies over Mercer County Airport, Tom Foley was at the controls.[71]

Don Luscombe's vision for an affordable, mass-produced airplane for the private owner was now a proud reality. More important, Don had a flat-opposed engine powered airplane that could meet, if not better, the competition. Success was within his grasp.

Tom Foley preflights the new Luscombe "50" prior to making the first test flight, December 17, 1937. HOWARD JONG

Announcing

LUSCOMBE
SCHOOL OF AERONAUTICS

THE LUSCOMBE PLAN of apprenticeship training, originally designed to train men exclusively for THE LUSCOMBE AIRPLANE CORPORATION, has now been extended and broadened by popular demand into a separate and self-sustaining institution. The success of LUSCOMBE trained men throughout the aviation industry has been responsible for the organization of THE LUSCOMBE SCHOOL OF AERONAUTICS to continue and augment the original LUSCOMBE plan.

YOU can now receive the training that has been proven by experience to be so successful in training others for technical positions in aviation.

We offer YOU a nine months technical training, embracing a thorough background in theory and the practical application so vital to well-rounded experience. Close association with the developments in the LUSCOMBE factory where new processes, designs and production methods are being tried and proved enhances each student's knowledge and adds to his training a useful interest in the vital problems of an actual manufacturing unit.

The training you receive now will affect your future progress in aviation. Send us the attached coupon immediately and we will show you why LUSCOMBE trained men are in demand.

DON'T just wish for a place in aviation—let us show you how to get it!

THE LUSCOMBE SCHOOL OF AERONAUTICS
Specialized training in metal airplane engineering and construction
WEST TRENTON   NEW JERSEY

LUSCOMBE SCHOOL OF AERONAUTICS
West Trenton, New Jersey

Please send me, without obligation, full particulars concerning your nine months technical training course in all-metal airplane engineering and construction.

NAME_____

STREET_____

CITY_____ STATE_____

EDUCATION_____ AGE_____

"Envy is a pain of mind that successful men cause their neighbors."
Onasander (fl. A.D. 49)
The General, Ch. 42, Par. 25

Chapter Thirteen

No Wood! No Nails! No Glue!

The prototype Luscombe "Fifty" with the original fabric tail. A.R. KRIEGER

The Luscombe "50" was a sheer delight to fly! The airplane was light on the controls and very responsive to a pilot's input. Tom Foley was most enthusiastic upon his return to "terra firma" after his brief flight.

Ig Sargent and Eddie Davis, on their behalf, chomped at the bit to make their initial flights in 1304. Meanwhile, the weather had soured and a few rigging problems needed to be corrected before they could fly the prototype Model 8. Their three day wait must have seemed like an eternity to these youthful, eager aviators.

Their opportunity arrived on December 20, 1937. Sargent and Davis each made a brief twenty to thirty minute flight. Fritz King made his first flight in the 1304 airplane the following day. Virtually overnight, the little "Fifty" became the darling of the Luscombe Airplane Corporation. The employees and students were proud of their handiwork.

Word of the new Luscombe "50" spread quickly. Curious spectators flocked to see the new airplane being put through its paces. The aviation periodicals were anxious to get the scoop on Luscombe's new venture. The local newsprint media heralded

An early photograph of the Luscombe "Fifty." Note the stylized IGNATIUS SARGENT
"Luscombe 50" name on fin. This writing was used for publicity purposes and was removed shortly after dedicated flight testing commenced.

Luscombe's new airplane as the "Flying 'Tin Lizze.'"

Interestingly, many factory employees were not on hand to watch the "Fifty's" momentous first flight or the very early subsequent test flights. Don, in an effort to save money and spread a little Christmas cheer, gave all employees and students two weeks off. Thus, many were on holiday when Foley, Sargent, Davis and King made their first flights.

Notwithstanding the lack of factory personnel on hand, flight testing of the new "Fifty" continued at a brisk pace during the last two weeks of December 1937. Sargent flew the new airplane six more times before the end of the year. Davis flew the Luscombe "50" only two more times before heading to his New England home to spend the holidays with family and friends.

During this adventurous period, Ben Melcher rode with Sargent several times to record flight test data. His observations included rigging, engine temperature readings, airspeed calibrations and so forth. Much like his earlier Phantom and Luscombe "90" work, Melcher did not fly the airplane solo on any test. He rode with another pilot and served as a bonafide crew member.

Early testing revealed some potentially serious Continental A-50 carburetor icing problems. During one early test, Sargent was flying the airplane when the engine began to lose power. He applied full power, but engine rpm decreased steadily. Sargent was barely able to return to the field before the engine quit entirely.

After discussing the problem with Luscombe, Melcher, Shepard, and a few other employees present, Sargent decided to undertake another test flight the next day. Sargent asked Bill Shepard to join him.

Sargent was airborne for almost half-an-hour when the A-50 engine began to lose power once more. Sargent turned tail and headed for the Mercer County Airport. Once more, he was just able to make the field before he lost all power.

Not wasting time, Sargent, Shepard, Melcher and Luscombe uncowled the engine. The outside of the carburetor throat was coated with frost. The onlookers were dumbfounded to see so much frost. *"It looks like a mint julep!"* Luscombe exclaimed. Everybody present had a cheerful laugh.

The carburetor icing problem was soon solved after numerous inquiries to Continental Motors. Because this early flat-opposed engine had no provisions for carburetor heat, the first solution attempted involved a series of baffles for the air intake to straighten the airflow onto the carburetor intake. Initially, Continental thought the problem was a mixture problem. After the "mint julep" flight, they designed a carburetor heat scoop and included one with each new engine.

Other tests revealed the Continental engine was prone to heating problems. The firewall bulkhead insulation was changed as a quick stab to correct the problem. Yet, despite the cold ambient temperature, the engine still got too hot. Efforts continued to remedy the overheating difficulty. Serious attention to baffling solved the problems.

During one interesting test on December 30, Sargent took his Phantom aloft and observed the first "Fifty" spin tests. Most likely, Lou Coghill or Tom Foley flew the "Fifty" during these tests. Unlike the Luscombe "90" chancy spin characteristics, no problems were reported during any "Fifty" spin entry and recovery investigations.

Noteworthy, Don Luscombe never flew the "Fifty" prototype airplane solo during any of these early or subsequent flight tests. He elected to remain on the ground, observe and let the assigned employees do the necessary and possibly dangerous work.[72]

Don's time was not wasted, however. He snapped a few pictures of his new creation and prepared his marketing plans. Additionally, he sent information about the new Luscombe "50" to various aviation periodicals in an attempt to spread news of the airplane to the general public. A small, two paragraph story appeared in the January 1938 issue of *Aero Digest* announcing the news.

No doubt the competition chewed their fingernails as Luscombe's creation took to the skies. Priced at $1895, the new Luscombe "50" was definitely a thorn in their marketing plans. Fortunately for them, Luscombe was many months from obtaining an Approved Type Certificate for the design.

Early flight tests confirmed most of the engineering department's paper performance figures. Top speed was 103 mph, cruising speed was 94 mph, landing speed was 37 mph. The rate-of-climb was 750 fpm and the service ceiling was 13,000 feet. Since no tests had been conducted yet outside the local area, cruising speed range was still listed as 400 miles in early company literature.

Other impressive figures were listed in the literature. Gross weight was 1,130 lbs, useful load was 500 lbs with a maximum payload of 223 lbs with a full fuel tank. These weights were supported on the ground with a sturdy, 73 inch tread, semi-cantilever landing gear. The airplane's overall dimensions enhanced its consumer appeal. Length was 20 feet, 7 inches, the wingspan was 35 feet and the height was 5 feet, 6 inches.

In another shrewdly prepared flyer, Luscombe promoted his airplane as "America's Most Advanced Light Plane Powered with Continental A-50 Engine." He concluded his descriptions with what soon became the design's most well-known and endearing phrase, *"No Wood! No Nails! No Glue!"*

As flight testing continued well into 1938, Don held high hopes for this new airplane and his company. He knew the year ahead would be a "make or

Chapter Thirteen: No Wood! No Nails! No Glue! 197

break" proposition. Either the new "Fifty" and "Ninety" would see him clear of his difficult financial problems, or he would admit defeat in his all-metal personal airplane dreams and be forced to close his factory's doors.

The Luscombe Airplane Corporation's 1937 end-of-year Analysis of Inventories revealed readily why Don was concerned — too much capital was tied-up in unused and possibly unsalable parts and material. The company owned one complete, unneeded Phantom (NC1249, s/n 120). Eleven Phantom fuselages and ten sets of Phantom wings were stored in the main hangar's rafters. On the floor below, eleven partially completed Luscombe "90" fuselages were neatly stacked on end. There items and the parts necessary to complete these airplanes added a tremendous financial burden which appeared in the company's accounting records.

Though there were many behind-closed-doors concerns voiced regarding the company's financial future at the close of 1937, one could never tell there was anything less than totally optimistic thoughts on the faces of almost thirty-five young men that arrived at the plant during late December. They came from all parts of the country to attend a new Luscombe School of Aeronautics class scheduled to start January 1, 1938.

Production Luscombe "Ninety" fuselages are stacked in a corner. Identical fuselage sections were used in production "Ninety" and "Fifty" airplanes.

JAMES B. ZAZAS COLLECTION

Most students came predominantly from the northeastern United States. Some arrived by car, others by train and a couple flew their own planes to school. Glen Kauffman, Tom Murphy, Linwood Lawrence, and Rolfe Gregory were included in this group of eager students. While most students secured room and board in the nearby "Jolly Roger," others found lodging in homes around the West Trenton, New Jersey, area.[73]

Tuition was set at $55 per month or $660 per year for this class. For their hard-earned money, the students were issued the same equipment as previous classes

JAMES B. ZAZAS COLLECTION

(Above) Jim Rising instructs a Luscombe School of Aeronautics class.

(Right) Drawing and blueprint reading was an important part of the Luscombe School of Aeronautics' school program.

JAMES B. ZAZAS COLLECTION

— two pairs of white coveralls with "Luscombe Airplanes" embroidered on the back, one tool box with a hammer, pliers, diagonal cutters, tin snips, 6" scale, dividers, center punch, combination square and a six foot tape. Their textbook was *Airplane and Engine Maintenance* by Daniel J. Brimm and H. Edward Boggess, both airplane mechanic instructors at the New York City School of Aviation Trades.

The course's duration was twelve months. The first three months were spent in the school, as were months five, seven, nine and eleven. The other months were spent honing their learned skills in the factory. Outside of some cable splicing, detail parts production or riveting certain assemblies, such as riveting reinforcement plate(s) to a bulkhead, these students built few, if any, production airplane parts. For their efforts, these students were paid 35 cents per hour, eventually raised to 40 cents per hour.

Jim Rising, Dick Rude and Jim Hammer were the instructors. Rising instructed the academic portion of the class, Rude taught the shop portion and Hammer taught the drafting.

Rude was a good shop man, yet he exhibited a very testy personality. This unfavorable trait was overlooked as he shared his vast metal working experience and abilities with his young charges.

A typical school day started at 8:00 a.m. with two hours of aeronautical engineering taught by Rising. Other studies taught by Rising included aerodynamics, structures, stress analysis, Department of Commerce regulations, mathematics, engines, propellers, accounting and so much more.

Then, from ten until noon, Hammer taught aeronautical drawing. Following lunch, which was from noon until 1:00 p.m., Dick Rude taught the "shop" portion of the class. Studies involved metal working, welding, brazing, fitting tubing for welded structures, layout and making of small parts, until quitting time at 5:00 p.m.

As this program grew and developed, the class sizes dictated they be divided into two sections, an "A" section and a "B" section. While one section was in the classroom, the other would be learning and practicing various "shop" skills.

For several students, particularly those who lived at the "Jolly Roger," the day started well before dawn. For example, Tom Murphy, the first to wake-up in the morning, would go downstairs into the building's large kitchen, open the draft to a coal-fired stove, load the coal and light the fire. He would then wake up another student who, in turn, would help get things ready for the cooks. Murphy would take the housemother's Dodge automobile and pick up the two cooks. Upon their return, Murphy would help his assistant set the table for the thirty or so hungry LAC students and employees who resided in the dorm. After work, Murphy and his assistant would set the table for supper. When the meal bell rang, the place would explode with the guys acting like they hadn't eaten in a month.

While this new group of students started to learn the ropes of metal airplane construction, the metal parts department fabricated a new beaded surface rudder for the Luscombe "50." The idea for this metal rudder originated during a conversation between Don Luscombe and Ben Melcher. A Stearman-Hammond, an all-metal, low wing, twin boom, pusher-type two place airplane, had visited the field earlier and Melcher was intrigued by the airplane's corrugated control surfaces.

He called to Don and asked, *"Say, Luscombe, you want to see a good way to make a control surface?"* Don was intrigued by Melcher's idea and told him to pursue it. In turn, Ben Melcher asked Fred Knack for his engineering opinions and Nick Nordyke for his fabrication opinions. All agreed the metal control surface had merit.[74]

A Stearman-Hammond visits the field. Note the corrugated rudder design employed on this airplane. A similar idea was adopted for the Luscombe "Fifty." HOWARD JONG

Knack made his engineering drawings and forwarded them to Nordyke. Quickly, Nordyke made a grooved maple wood block and formed the beads in 17ST aluminum alloy skin by forcing it in the grove by hammering on a wedge-shaped maple block. Nordyke made two matched sections with rudder contour, placed them back to back, with the beads facing outward, and riveted them together along the trailing edge. While the leading edges of these formed panels were spread apart, a 17ST dural channel-shaped spar was inserted between them with the legs facing outward. The corrugated sheets were then riveted to the spar legs. Hinge fittings and a control horn were added.

The result was a rudder that weighed less than a steel tube and fabric design, was stronger and used less parts to make. As a bonus, the beaded surface provided adequate drainage. After undergoing a series of static load tests, this new all-metal rudder replaced the original steel tube and fabric rudder. Braving a blustery cold winter day, Ig Sargent made a brief, twenty minute test flight with this new rudder on January 20, 1938. No problems were encountered.[75]

The Luscombe "50" was one step closer to being truly an all-metal airplane.

Within a short time, the "Fifty's" elevator control surfaces were made of similarly constructed, corrugated Alclad sheet. Upon completion of the required Department of Commerce static load tests, these new all-metal control surfaces were incorporated into the production airplane's final design. The ailerons followed a similar development path a couple months later.[76]

These new control surfaces were not the only project keeping the production floor busy. A new model Luscombe "Ninety" fuselage was on its landing gear and sported the Bill Shepard-designed production wings. Balanced, metal-framed ailerons were an integral part of this wing design, as were the manually operated trailing edge wing flaps.

This "new" Luscombe "90," or Model 4 as written in the official Department of Commerce (Bureau of Air Commerce) paperwork, was built on the production fuselage jig, employed production construction techniques and utilized production parts. However, the company had no intention to sell this particular airplane to any buyer. Instead, it remained a company-owned, prototype airplane to be used only for obtaining the Approved Type Certificate.

The Model 4's final dimensions and performance were established with this pre-production airplane. The length was 20' 11", the height was 6' 6", and the wingspan was 32' 1". The NACA 2412 airfoil exhibited a 62" wing chord. The performance figures were computed to give a top speed of 136 mph, 120 mph cruise speed, 47 mph landing speed with no flap, 40 mph with flaps; and a 580 mile cruising range. The service ceiling was shown as 15,000 ft. The weights were listed as 1725 lbs gross, 1103 lbs empty, 622 lbs useful load, 258 lbs payload with both 15 gallon wing tanks full, and a 60 lbs baggage capacity.

A Sensenich wood prop, normal engine and flight instruments, navigation lights, carburetor air heater, fire extinguisher and first-aid kit were standard equipment. Goodyear 18x8-3 "Airwheels" with brakes, a Hamilton-Standard metal propeller, radio gear, electric starter and battery were optional. Of course, performance would be degraded slightly if these options were added.

Don planned to offer his newest airplane for $3995 from the factory. Early company literature referred to this airplane as the "Luscombe 'Ninety' De Luxe." A casual observer could easily miss the many subtle differences inherent in this "new" pre-production Luscombe "90" and the proof-of-concept, experimental "Ninety" that preceded it.

One obvious contrast was the point where the airplane's streamlined Vee-strut and landing gear leg attached to the fuselage. Much like the flying Luscombe "50" prototype, a drag-reducing bump was seen at the second bulkhead, but was slightly larger.

The prototype Luscombe "Fifty" with a new, all-metal rudder. This airplane design was one step closer towards achieving Don Luscombe's all-metal airplane production goals. JAMES B. ZAZAS COLLECTION

Another readily noticeable change was seen on the airplane's tail. Unlike its predecessor, this latest Luscombe "90" did not have a strut-braced tail or external bracing wires.

In addition, the fuselage, landing gear and cockpit areas revealed some subtle engineering changes. Whereas the previous Luscombe "90's" fuselage possessed hand-made, flat-sided (in a fore and aft direction) bulkheads and did not use the Farver-designed splice strip, this new airplane had stamped, slightly rounded, 17ST duraluminum bulkheads surrounded by two aluminum sheet conical sections joined by a seven inch splice strip on each side of the fuselage. Likewise, the landing gear

200   *Visions of Luscombe: The Early Years*

HOWARD JONG

(Above) The first production Luscombe "Ninety" fuselage being assembled in jig.

(Right) Riveting fuselage skins to the first production Luscombe "Ninety."

(Below) The first production Luscombe "Ninety" fuselage nears completion. Note the small bump on the fuselage. This fairing was intended to smooth the airflow around the wing strut/fuselage junction.

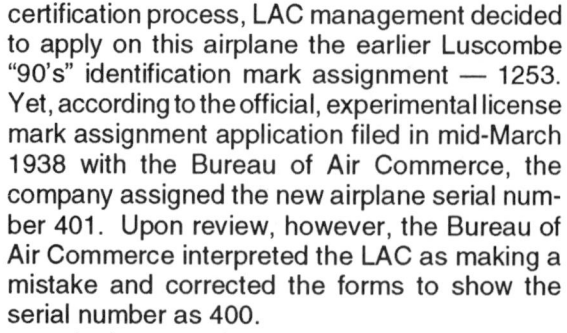

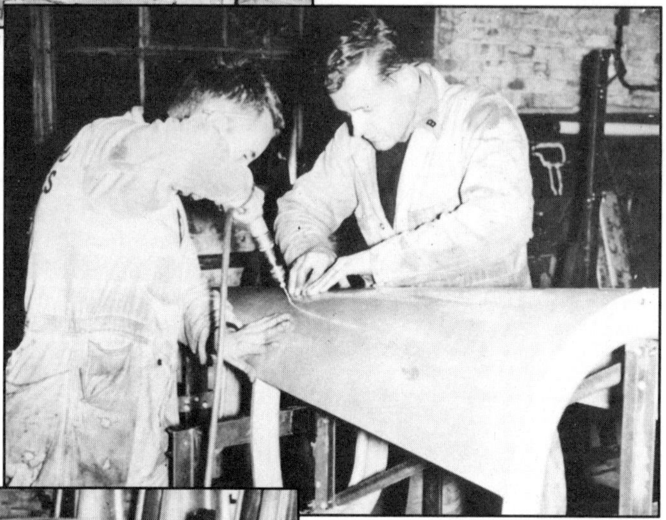

HOWARD JONG

HOWARD JONG

fairings were smaller.

Finally, the cockpit windshield on the "new" Luscombe "Ninety" exhibited a more rounded corner near the door post bulkhead. Furthermore, this improved model's doors tapered almost to a point at the door post station unlike the somewhat square, rounded bottom doors as used on the earlier "Ninety."

To save paperwork and time during the lengthy certification process, LAC management decided to apply on this airplane the earlier Luscombe "90's" identification mark assignment — 1253. Yet, according to the official, experimental license mark assignment application filed in mid-March 1938 with the Bureau of Air Commerce, the company assigned the new airplane serial number 401. Upon review, however, the Bureau of Air Commerce interpreted the LAC as making a mistake and corrected the forms to show the serial number as 400.

At the same time, the Bureau approved an experimental license for this airplane. Hence, plain 1253 became NX1253. Thus, two completely different Luscombe Airplane Corporation airplanes possessed the *same* Department of Commerce issued identification mark assignment and the *same* serial number, though *not* at the same time.[77]

Perhaps the only items in common with this "new" pre-production prototype and its "proof-of-concept" predecessor were the 90 hp Warner "Scarab Junior" engine and the Hamilton-Standard metal propeller. These items were removed from the earlier experimental proof-of-concept Luscombe "90" and installed on this later model.

Meanwhile, the "old" 1253 fuselage was pushed aside, eventually into a dark corner of the main hangar. Within a few weeks, this fuselage was dismantled completely by Luscombe School of Aeronautics students.

Ig Sargent made the first flight in the "new" Luscombe "90" airplane on January 22, 1938, with Fred Knack serving as observer. Their brief flight ended with the tailwheel breaking upon landing. Quickly repaired, the plane was back in the air four days later undergoing more tests.

Don reviewed the Luscombe "90" and Luscombe "50" programs. He renewed his goal to have an Approved Type Certificate on both airplanes by mid-year. Confident in the Luscombe "90's" future, he set his sights towards an initial production run of twenty-five airplanes.

Don knew he had to sell his company's designs to stay in business. With the Phantom out of production, except for an occasional special order, he would have to demonstrate the "Fifty" and "Ninety" quite regularly and successfully. Salesman/test pilots Sargent and Davis realized they would be quite busy during the next few months.

In a most fortuitous sequence of events, a delegation from the Aero Club of France arrived in early February at a time when both the pre-production version Model 4 and the prototype Model 8 were airworthy. The team, headed by Jacques Negrier, Jr., wasted no time evaluating both designs, though their visit's intended purpose was to evaluate primarily the Luscombe "50."

On February 5, Eddie Davis took Mr. Negrier aloft in a Luscombe Phantom (NC1049), the Luscombe "Ninety" and the Luscombe "Fifty." Mr. Negrier was impressed!

Don hoped the junior Negrier's report to the senior Negrier would be favorable. Company director Hiram Mallinson's earlier European efforts laid the groundwork for this moment and Don trusted these demonstrations would seal the oral agreements made previously.

Before the junior Negrier returned to France, he informed Don he wanted a Luscombe "50" sent overseas as soon as one was available. Don told him he would receive the second production built Model 8. This most important deal with Caudron to build the Luscombe "50" overseas was all but consummated.

Within days, a delegation from Canada visited the West Trenton facilities. They were most eager to follow-up on their earlier discussions with Hiram Mallinson and pursue a potential joint production and marketing venture with Luscombe. Once more, Don promised these visitors they would receive an early production Model 8.

While Don Luscombe, Ig Sargent and Eddie Davis employed their best salesman tactics, Fred Knack, Jim Rising, Howard Jong, Howard Green, Fred Brunton, Chuck Holloway and other engineering department members directed their attention towards a production wing, fuselage and nose cowling design for the Luscombe "50." Much like the many differences that existed between the proof-of-concept Luscombe "90" and its subsequent production version, there were many differences between the prototype 1304 airplane and the Model 8 production version that followed.

The aluminum tube rib wing structure utilized on the prototype Luscombe "50" was deemed unsuitable for production as being too costly to make. Additionally, portions of this wing's structure were not strong enough to meet the stringent Department of Commerce requirements for a certificated airplane. This inherent weakness was demonstrated aptly by Don Luscombe's old friend, Pete Brooks, with almost fatal results.

When word reached him the new "Fifty" was flying, Brooks flew to Mercer County Airport in his "Clipped-wing" Monocoupe 110. Upon landing, he immediately inspected the new prototype and hurriedly asked Don if he could make a flight in the aircraft. Don obliged, but warned him the wings were not stressed for any hard aerobatics. Fred Knack echoed these concerns.

Brooks threw caution to the wind and nearly lost his life because of his reckless actions. He took off, climbed to altitude and executed a graceful series of loops, rolls and snap rolls

Jacques Negrier, Jr., (shown here) worked with LAC director Hiram Mallinson to negotiate a deal to produce the Luscombe "Fifty" in France.

The first production Luscombe "Ninety," 1253, s/n 400. This airplane adopted the same number and serial number of its predecessor, due partly to simplify factory and government paperwork.

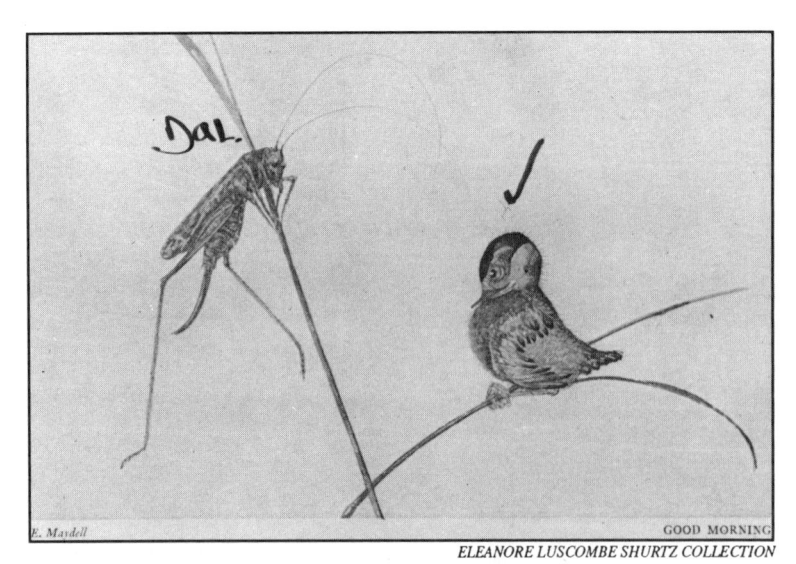

The close friendship between Don Luscombe and Pete Brooks is described aptly by this postcard sent by Brooks to Don.

over the astonished Luscombe employees assembled below. Brooks soon returned to the field, flushed with excitement from his exhilarating flight.

Upon landing, several employees came over to congratulate Brooks on his superb aerial display, but were aghast when they inspected the "Fifty's" wing. They found a major section of the right wing's trailing edge was bent noticeably upward. The left wing fared little better. The trailing edge ribs had pulled away from the rear spar and, quite literally, only the wing's fabric held the trailing edges in place.

Don Luscombe was furious. He chided his friend for breaking the new airplane. In reality, Don was more upset his friend could have become a grim statistic from this premeditated lapse of good judgement. Moreover, any accident would have produced very bad publicity for the new Model 8, at a time when favorable publicity was needed most.

Lou Coghill and Fritz King inspected the damage. They told Don the repairs would be simple and accomplished quickly. There would be no appreciable delay flight testing the "Fifty."

Capitalizing on Brooks' flight, other production wing changes were proposed and adopted. Externally, the most noticeable alteration involved changing the shape of the wingtip bow. Fred Knack utilized a wingtip concept he had developed during his tenure at Bellanca and applied it to the Luscombe "50." The prototype wingtip with the rounded wingtip bow would be replaced using a squared-end, 17ST duralumin stamping.

Another visible external feature involved gently tapering each wing panel's leading edge aft from the third rib outward. This change enhanced the wing's aesthetic appearance while facilitating the "detachable wingtip" design idea as used in the Luscombe "90" production wing.

Internally, the aluminum tube rib structure, as used on the Luscombe "50" prototype, was abandoned. As per a suggestion by Ben Melcher to Fred Knack, Vierendiehl truss construction ribs, comprised of extruded dural capstrip T-sections and 17ST dural vertical channels, took their place. These capstrips were pre-drilled to allow rapid assembly. The ribs were riveted to Aluminum Company of America extruded aluminum alloy I-beam spars.

Furthermore, the 17ST duraluminum alloy stamped nose ribs were riveted to the main spar. A single drag truss was used and employed dural tubing drag struts and inexpensive steel tie rods fitted with spoke and nipple end fittings, an idea of Ben Melcher, also.

Sporting an experimental registration on it wings, the first production Luscombe "Ninety" takes to the sky. Note the outlined "X."

The wing's outboard section retained the channel section spliced to the end of each main spar. Designed to give way quickly in the event of any wing damage accident, this idea would save future Model 8 owners the grief and expense of having to rebuild an entire wing panel.

Finally, a single wing truss of welded steel tubing was bolted to both spars just outboard of the wing lift struts to add torsional rigidity. This truss idea was later found to be unnecessary and was not used after the first thirty-two airplanes had been produced. Employee Rolfe Gregory welded these structures.

Interestingly, the nipples were stock motorcycle spoke nipples. Likewise, the tie rods were made especially from the same wire as motorcycle spokes, but were threaded on both ends. Special fittings were used at the ends to connect them to the rest of the structure. They were very strong and less expensive than MacWhyte tie rods used previously.

Much like the prototype Luscombe "50," the production wing's leading edge nose and upper surfaces inboard of the strut connection were aluminum covered. Also, outboard of the connection, the upper, lower and nose sections were aluminum covered. In turn, the entire wing was covered in "Flightex" with sufficient holes for inspection.

While the production wing underwent several crucial alterations, significant changes were introduced in the production fuselage. For example, the bump at the second bulkhead where the landing gear and wing Vee-strut joined the fuselage was removed as being difficult to fabricate, costly and unnecessary. Additionally, a bulkhead was eliminated from the tail cone which pared labor and simplified production without sacrificing strength.

Other notable changes were adopted. Early 1304 flight tests revealed forward center of gravity problems when the firewall fuel tank was full and two persons occupied the cabin area. As such, Jim Rising suggested relocating the fuel tank behind the passenger compartment. Hence, the space between the third and fourth bulkheads was lengthened slightly to accommodate a fourteen gallon, fuselage mounted fuel tank behind the cabin area.

At first, Don Luscombe expressed some crash survival and post-crash fire concerns regarding this arrangement. He was worried the tank could break loose in an accident, come forward and seriously injure the occupants. Furthermore, if the tank ruptured, the ensuing fire would most certainly be fatal. Future sales would be hurt immeasurably if the public perceived the fuel tank as unsafe.

Fred Knack assured Don such an arrangement was very safe and very sturdy and only a non-survivable accident would give cause for the tank to "break loose." In production, the oval-shaped tank was mounted via cables and wood cradles to the top center, triangular-shaped reinforced fuselage skin just behind the third bulkhead. Despite a few faint-hearted comments from the competition to the contrary, required Bureau of Air Commerce tests and actual service experience practice demonstrated this tank location to be extremely safe, sturdy and solved the pesky center of gravity problems. [78]

The production Luscombe "Fifty's" wing was a vast improvement over the aluminum tube-rib structure as used in the prototype "Fifty." The type of wing structure shown in this photograph was used in Model 8 serial numbers 801 to 832.

JAMES B. ZAZAS COLLECTION

More cockpit room was another tangible benefit derived by this new fuel tank installation. Removing the firewall fuel tank allowed the instrument panel to be moved forward, which, in turn, allowed more cockpit room. Folks like Ig Sargent, whose large stature created problems in small cockpits, were most grateful for the extra space.

The fuselage bulkheads were eventually respaced to lower production costs. Early Model 8 airplanes, s/n 801 through s/n 835, possessed eight bulkheads. Commencing with s/n 836, the number five and number six bulkheads were eliminated and replaced with one bulkhead. As a result, fewer skins and bulkheads had to be fabricated and handled.

As an extra safety feature, adopted from Phantom and Luscombe "90" experience, the 4130 welded steel tubing engine mount was bolted to an Edward G. Budd Mfg. Co. (Philadelphia, Pennsylvania) stainless steel stamped firewall at three points. The upper, most-stressed section of the mount was designed to transmit its load directly to a Vee made of 4130 steel tubes which, in turn, was bolted to the fuselage at the wing root spar connection. In the event of a noseover, the airplane's occupants were protected by this steel Vee structure.

To comply with stringent Department of Commerce certification requirements, the fuselage, wings and landing gear were subjected to a series of torturous loading, dynamic and drop tests. Some tests were made with 115 percent design failing load with no distortion. At least the following static tests were included in the certification process:
1. High angle of attack.
2. Three point landing.
3. Maximum horizontal and vertical tail surface loads.
4. Drag component of landing gear loads in three point and level landing.
5. Control system loads.
6. Fuel tank loads.

Finally, the hand-made, pressure cooling cowling covers were abandoned. A new nose bowl was fabricated from half-hard aluminum, drop-hammered stamping. Thus, this piece, like many other parts being changed from a hand-made product to an easily produced stamping, reduced labor costs in the production process and enhanced the airplane's "mass production" potential.

As the first production Luscombe "50" came together, the question was broached regarding the type of interior materials that should be employed. A whimsical answer came while production manager Ben Melcher and Don Luscombe discussed this very subject.

Melcher, being a very practical and no frills sort of individual, took his job very seriously. As such, he was often the butt of some of Don's jokes. Melcher was looking into the cabin of the nearly completed first production Model 8 when he called to Don. *"What kind of upholstery job do you want in this airplane, Luscombe?"*

Don pondered the question for a moment and replied, *"I want a tufted bassinet."* Melcher was startled, but he resigned himself to comply with his boss' wishes.

Later in the day, Melcher shared Don's comments with control surface department foreman, Bill Force. In his characteristically slow, Missouri drawl, Melcher asked Force, *"What did the 'old man' mean by 'tufted bassinet?'"* Bill Force could barely hold back his laughter.

However, another practical joke was not as successful and somewhat backfired on its perpetrators. The joke this time involved the Pitcairn PA-36 autogiro. The PA-36 project was still an important part of the overall Luscombe production work and earnings during the first six months of 1938. Outside of the very few cash infusions from generous financial backers (George Cluett, II, mostly) or school tuition, Don could count on income from this autogiro building contract to provide badly needed funds every two weeks. As such, Don strived to maintain a good image for Pitcairn's chief engineer, Agnew Larsen, and his engineers who often visited the Luscombe Airplane Corporation plant to check on the autogiro's progress.

Don recognized many of his employees were disgruntled working on "Larsen's Goon." Often, the only way they could vent some of their pent-up frustrations was through snide comments or harmless practical jokes.

One day, Henri D'Estout took a workman's rubber glove, filled it with water and attached to the PA-36's fuselage just forward of the tailwheel. To all who saw the arrangement, the autogiro appeared to have sprouted a cow's udder.

Unfortunately, Agnew Larsen dropped by the plant as the employees were laughing at D'Estout's joke. Larsen may have been upset by this prank, but he never showed it. In fact, he may have shared the humor. Don Luscombe, on his behalf, was somewhat embarrassed about the whole episode. In turn, D'Estout was abashed for embarrassing Don.

Despite the infrequent practical jokes, there was still the serious work to be done in the factory and school. Students were enrolling in the Luscombe School of Aeronautics for successively larger classes. Bill Robinson and Mike Melfa were among the thirty or so students that started in the March 1st class. Once again, the vast majority of students came from northeastern or eastern United States.[79]

Surprisingly, a Phantom order materialized during the early spring months. William C. Haines of Philadelphia, Pennsylvania, wanted a Phantom and placed his order through Ig Sargent, a friend of Haines.

A fuselage was pulled down from the main hangar's overhead storage rafters. A pair of wings followed. Under Dick Rude's watchful eye, this Phantom came together as a Luscombe School of Aeronautics senior class project. Fearful the government inspector would object to this student labor, Don assigned a few employees to make this airplane and had the students "assist" them.

On April 2, 1938, the company applied for an identification mark assignment for Haines' Phantom. The Department of Commerce issued NC20620, but quickly rescinded it when Luscombe informed the Department the number was too big to paint on the Phantom's wings. The Department issued NC1323 as the new identification mark assignment.

On April 16, 1938, Ig Sargent took Phantom NC1323 (s/n 121) aloft for the first time. His check flight routine was much like his many earlier Phantom test flights — smooth, simple and short. On April 20, Eddie Davis checked out Mr. Haines in his Phantom.

Meanwhile, the flight test schedule remained brisk. It was not uncommon to see Sargent take 1304 out for a test flight while Davis returned in 1253.

The company's marketing plans and the media's attention began to pay handsome dividends. Advertisements and written stories about Luscombe's new airplanes began to appear regularly in various publications, including *Air Trails* and *Aero Digest*. Curious pilots and airplane owners wrote letters to Luscombe seeking more information. Professional and amateur photographers dropped by the airport with increasing frequency to catch a glimpse of Luscombe's new designs.

The competition fretted. Luscombe was getting closer to an Approved Type Certificate on both airplanes. Of greater concern to them, both airplanes — predominantly the Luscombe "50" — were gaining a strong and devoted following. Taylor, Piper, Aeronca, Rearwin, and other light airplane manufacturers began to stand up and take notice of Don's all-metal designs. They wondered, would their mostly steel tube and fabric designs fall by the wayside as Don's "all-metal" creations took to the skies? No doubt the competitions' management was most concerned.

They had to be disturbed. Luscombe was gaining a stronger market share of interest every day — and his Model 4 and Model 8 airplanes hadn't yet entered into production!

Don was overjoyed to receive such public reception of his airplanes, but was humbled when he realized he did not have enough production floor space to meet any appreciable demand. True, he had a signed contract with the Austin Company to build an extension to the main hangar, but the lack of money held Don back from starting construction.

To raise construction capital and pay some developmental costs at the same time, the Luscombe Airplane Corporation presented another stock offering. On May 9, 1938, a brief article in the financial section of *The New York Times* revealed the terms of the offering: *"A group of dealers headed by Eugene J. Hynes & Co. will offer today 155,160 shares of 50 cent-par-value common stock of the Luscombe Airplane Corporation at $1.25 per share. The offering was subject to the prior subscription by the officers, directors and present stockholders of the company to the extent of not more than 59,997 shares.*

With the exception of $15,000 to be used to retire current obligations, the proceeds from the sale will be used by the company for new capital purposes, including the increase of inventories, purchase of additional machinery, tools and equipment, and for the expansion of manufacturing facilities, according to the prospectus."

Luscombe Phantom, NC1323 (s/n 121). This Phantom, painted an overall gloss black with red trim, was delivered to William C. Haines of Philadelphia, Pennsylvania. JAMES B. ZAZAS COLLECTION

Don hoped this stock issue would give him the capital he needed to fulfill his immediate goals. However, very few people took advantage of the available stock. Don bit his lip and pressed onward. Somewhere, somehow, he would get the money he needed.

Meanwhile, the first Model 8 built from production tooling came together. At the same time, at least three Model 4 airplanes were in various stages of final completion, even though this design had not yet been granted an Approved Type Certificate. The production floor became a very busy place.

The main offices became quite hectic, also. A flurry of paperwork virtually inundated the office staff. Company Treasurer Roger Johnson found himself signing form after form. Ben Melcher, a Notary Public, signed the same documents.

On or about May 3, the company applied to the Department of Commerce, Bureau of Air Commerce, for an experimental identification mark assignment for the first production Model 8 soon to make its debut. The Department's reply was 1327.

Concurrently, the company applied to the Department of Commerce for an unlicensed identification mark for at least one, soon-to-be-completed, Model 4 airplane. The Department issued 1325.

On June 2, 1938, Don applied to the Department of Commerce for a Commercial License for the currently experimental licensed Model 4, NX1253. On the same day, Fred Knack signed a Temporary Certification Agreement with the Department of Commerce, Bureau of Air Commerce to carry a temporary "NC" registration for aircraft NX1253. Quickly, the "NX" was changed to an "NC" on the airplane.

Other Model 4 unlicensed identification numbers would be changed to "NC" numbers upon completion of required Department of Commerce inspections prior to the formal issuance of the Approved Type Certificate.

Three days later, the labors of many individuals rolled through the main hangar's open doors. The first production Model 8 greeted the warm New Jersey sunshine. The airplane was assigned NX1327 and possessed serial number 801. The airplane was taxi-tested and its rigging checked before Don Luscombe and Fred Knack gave their OK for a test flight.

On June 7, Ig Sargent tested this proud new airplane's wings for the first time. His thirty-five minute flight was wildly successful. Eddie Davis followed later in the day and made a shorter, fifteen minute flight. Other employees soon had the opportunity to fly NX1327, also. Ben Melcher joined Sargent on a test flight the following day and on other test flights during the balance of the week.

Don Luscombe waited more than a week before he flew NX1327 solo. Most likely, Don Luscombe flew with Ig Sargent or Eddie Davis during a couple of these early test flights before he flew NX1327 solo.

On June 8, the company applied for another unlicensed identification mark for another Model 4. The Department of Commerce, Bureau of Air Commerce's reply was 1344.

On June 10, Ig Sargent took the company's "first" production Model 4, aircraft 1325 (s/n 402), aloft for its initial test flight. Once more, Eddie Davis followed, making his first test flight in 1325 later in the day.

Shortly after Davis landed, Sargent and Luscombe boarded 1325 and flew to Roosevelt Field, New York, to get the airplane licensed. The airplane was inspected and approved for a commercial license. Plain 1325 became NC1325.

On June 11, NC1325 was sold to A. Lincoln McNeal of Chester, Pennsylvania. He owned this airplane barely two weeks before he was involved in a serious, non-fatal accident with it. News of this accident filtered quickly through the plant. Except for a few corporate officers and key men,

HOWARD JONG

(Above) A rare shot of the second production Model 4, NC1325 (s/n 402) and the first production Model 8, 1327 (s/n 801), pose together on the Mercer County Airport ramp.

(Right) Nick Nordyke poses with Luscombe "Ninety" NC1325.

HOWARD JONG

(Left) Standing beside fourth production built Model 4, Ig Sargent talks with Franklin T. Kurt (back to camera) at the Aviation Country Club in Hicksville, L.I., New York. This aircraft was lost in 1943 in a fatal accident.

(Below) Early Model 4 cockpit.

most employees were too busy to be concerned about the mishap.

On June 13 and June 14, the company applied for unlicensed identification mark assignments for two more Model 4 airplanes. The Department of Commerce issued 1337 and 1344 for Model 4 serial numbers 403 and 404 respectively.

On June 22, Bill Shepard had his opportunity to test fly Luscombe "50" NX1327. He was most enthusiastic about the airplane's sprightly handling and performance. On June 24, Sargent test hopped Luscombe "90" 1344 (s/n 404). No discrepancies were noted.

Later in the day, he flew to Roosevelt Field to get the airplane licensed. Within minutes after the airplane was certificated, Sargent flew to nearby Hicksville, New York, to demonstrate the airplane to writer Franklin T. Kurt for a *Sportsman Pilot* magazine review. Kurt wrote an excellent and popular column called "The Sportsman Test Pilot."

Upon his return, Sargent hopped into Eddie Davis' Phantom with Ralph Coston and flew to Chester, Pennsylvania, to view McNeal's broken airplane and undertake some preliminary investigative analysis. Davis and Melcher flew to the crash site the following day in Phantom NC1249. Shortly after the Department of Commerce had completed their investigations, NC1325 was released to Mr. McNeal who, in turn, promptly trucked the airplane to the company for repairs.[80]

The unyielding efforts of so many involved with the Model 4 design, development and construction culminated in an Approved Type Certificate dated June 25, 1938. The company was issued ATC #687. Thus, the Luscombe Airplane Corporation's Model 4 was certificated and approved for production.

However, the airplane proved to be not as popular as many employees had hoped. Very few Model 4 orders were on the books and even less were anticipated. The sprightly Model 8 garnered all the attention and accolades.

Don realized this fact. He ordered most Model 4 parts and stock removed from the main hangar and stored in the large hangar nearby. This move gained the company badly needed production floor space for the increasingly popular Model 8.

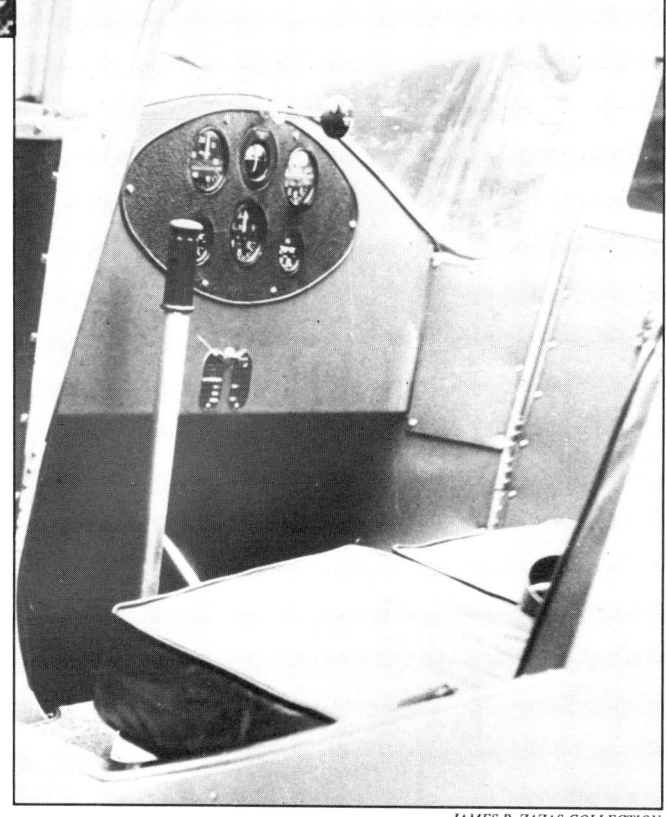

Another bulky item left the floor, too. The PA-36 fuselage was completed during June and was promptly picked-up by Pitcairn employees. They came by the factory, loaded the autogiro on a truck and returned to Willow Grove. Luscombe was all too happy to see the difficult project leave and free the extra floor space.

Despite the mayhem the month of June presented, Don and his employees were able to catch their breath briefly on Sunday, June 26. A major airshow and fly-in was hosted that day on the Mercer County Airport grounds. Pilots from miles around brought their fine airplanes to display and fly in various aerial parades.

208 *Visions of Luscombe: The Early Years*

Airshows were always popular and well attended event at the Mercer County Airport. Here, a wide variety of Waco, Aeronca, Taylor, Fairchild and other manufacturers' designs grace the grass around Bear Tavern Road. Don used shows such as this June 1938 event to promote his company's designs.

HOWARD JONG

Many who came to see the show were more interested in seeing the Luscombe "90" and the "No Wood! No Nails! No Glue!" Luscombe "50." Don did not miss this opportunity to promote his airplanes and company.

One visitor who came to watch the festivities was Henry K. Boller of Baltimore, Maryland. Boller arrived from Hagerstown, Maryland, flying a red, Ranger-powered Fairchild 24 owned by his girlfriend, a Vera Montgomery. He spoke very broken English and demonstrated a "haughty" attitude towards many around him.

Boller owned a small, struggling engine manufacturing company in Hagerstown called the Boller Motor Company. The main thrust of this company was to develop and perfect several commercial diesel engines Boller claimed he had designed. Like Don, Boller was having difficulty financing his company.

Boller expressed a keen interest in Don's airplane designs and hinted he might be interested in purchasing an example. However, with little further discussion, Boller took off for his return flight to Hagerstown.

Don was not sorry to see him go.

Don Luscombe's pretty nieces, Lucille Luscombe (Kapitan) and Betty Luscombe (Numerof) await their turn for a flight in NC1327, the first production Luscombe Model 8 airplane.

BETTY LUSCOMBE NUMEROF

*"Now this is not the end. It is not even the beginning of the end.
But it is, perhaps, the end of the beginning."*
Sir Winston Churchill (1874 - 1965)
Speech on Dunkirk, House of Commons
[June 4, 1940]

Chapter Fourteen

Rainbow's End

October 24, 1938, Alfred "Fritz" King takes Luscombe "Fifty" NC20663 (s/n 826) into the air for the first time. The Luscombe Model 8's high aspect ratio wing is shown to a good advantage in this photograph. JAMES B. ZAZAS COLLECTION

The air around the factory and school crackled with impatient anticipation and almost rowdy excitement. The Luscombe "50's" bright future provided this twitter.

If the hectic activities of June 1938 served as any indication, the late summer and early autumn months of July, August, September and October were predicted to be very busy months at the Luscombe Airplane Corporation.

Don Luscombe was excited, too. He was anxious to obtain the "Fifty's" Approved Type Certificate as quickly as possible. Fortunately, the bulk of the required engineering and structural tests was behind him and only the Bureau of Air Commerce flight tests remained to be completed.

Anticipating the Bureau of Air Commerce would issue the Approved Type Certificate shortly, Don ordered at least five Luscombe "50" airplanes to be built. Additionally, he petitioned the Bureau of Air Commerce to issue a small block of sequential license numbers. Thus, the wait for an airplane's license mark assignment was shortened considerably, even though the company was still required to file the appropriate paperwork for each airplane individually. The initial batch of numbers issued were 2589 through 2593, inclusive.[81]

The company's mailbox filled rapidly. Dealer and private owner inquiries had been arriving steadily since the prototype Model 8 was unveiled six months earlier. What started as a trickle of information requests soon developed into a small avalanche. Furthermore, the few published early photographs and stories of the "Fifty" and "Ninety" contributed to this climbing volume of interest as did equally important word-of-mouth.

While Luscombe "50" inquiries accounted for the vast majority of these requests, a few private owners and dealers desired "Ninety" information. Sadly, most Model 4 requests originated from dealers saddled with contracts to buy a Model 4 demonstrator. These contracts had been made with the company months earlier and did not reflect actual purchases by customers.

Luscombe "Ninety" (Model 4), NC1344, s/n 404. Note the drag reducing bump at the wing strut/main landing gear junction point. Originally intended to streamline airflow over this area, this design idea was abandoned on later built airplane designs, e.g. the Model 8, which employed a similar fuselage structure. JAMES B. ZAZAS COLLECTION

Most requests were handled through the sales department. Ig Sargent, Eddie Davis and a few other personnel soon acknowledged the almost "country club" atmosphere, once prevalent at the LAC sales department, was about to end. Each realized free time would be at a premium while they maintained a hectic flight test schedule in addition to their demonstration rides and check-out flights for company backers and prospective customers.

Don reprinted a small, three-fold brochure to meet this rush for information. Much like an earlier version that depicted the 1304 Luscombe "50" airplane and various exterior and interior black and white pictures, this brochure showed the NC1327 airplane. Of course, the airplane's major selling points were highlighted — all-metal construction, sprightly performance and a very attractive $1895 Flyaway Trenton price.[82]

Though the Model 8 garnered the bulk of the Luscombe Airplane Corporation's mid-summer attention, two production Model 4 airplanes had been built and delivered to customers by the end of June.

On June 29, Sargent made a pre-delivery flight of Model 4, NC1344. Within minutes after his return, ownership was transferred to LAC dealer Air America, Inc., of Leominster, Massachusetts, as per an earlier sales agreement. Noteworthy was the fact that LAC director, Daniel Simonds, was president of Air America, Inc.

Additionally, work was started on at least two more Model 4 airplanes during June and July. However, astute employees noticed there was no particular rush to build more Model 4 fuselages and wings. A few began to wonder if this design would be all but abandoned as the company's energies were directed towards the smaller, more promising Model 8. In time, their "gut" feelings proved wholly accurate. It was a "top level" decision to quickly fill the five "Ninety" orders and discontinue this model because there were lots of "Fifty" orders. All the shop space was needed to build these airplanes.

Meanwhile, extensive Luscombe "50" flight testing continued well into July. Engine cooling, airspeed calibration, rigging, and spin tests, plus so much more needed to be performed and completed. No longer needed in the ATC certification program, the 1304 airframe was disassembled and stored in a corner of the main hangar. What became of the airplane after it was stored is not known by this author.

During the first and last weeks of July 1938, Ig Sargent and Eddie Davis performed the vast majority of flight tests in NX1327. Likewise, Fritz King and Lou Coghill each made one or more test flights in the airplane.

The "boss" decided to also undertake his own

series of challenging flight tests with his new Luscombe "50." With scant notice given to the Bureau of Air Commerce, Don Luscombe embarked on a an early to mid-June, two week cross-country sales and demonstration tour in NX1327. His stops included: Cincinnati, Ohio; Lexington and Louisville, Kentucky; Detroit, Michigan; Cleveland, Ohio; Erie, Pennsylvania; and Buffalo, Rochester and Syracuse, New York. Don logged almost twenty-five hours flying time during this ambitious tour.

Don did not make the trip alone. Brownee joined him on this tour. The couple looked like a pair of movie stars before they left. Don wore a white summer suit, a white Panama hat, and black and white shoes. Brownee wore clothes that complemented Don's attire.

Don had barely returned to West Trenton when Ig Sargent and NX1327 were in the skies over West Trenton for more ATC test and demonstration flights. Additionally, now as a matter of routine, a few flights were staged photo opportunities for magazines and newspapers.

On July 26, Ig Sargent completed the last test flight in NX1327 required to satisfy the requirements for an Approved Type Certificate. Three days later, company treasurer Roger Johnson completed and filed the official paperwork for the Approved Type Certificate. Dutifully, Ben Melcher notarized the forms.

On the same day, Fred Knack signed a Temporary Certification Agreement with the Bureau of Air Commerce. Thus, the company was allowed to apply an "NC" registration on completed Model 8 airplanes, pending appropriate inspections and documentation, in lieu of an "NX" registration or no registration at all. As such, NX1327 became NC1327.

The practical effect of this Temporary Certificate Agreement was it permitted the paint shop to put the "NC" numbers on the wings and rudder before assembly instead of having to do it after weighing and after

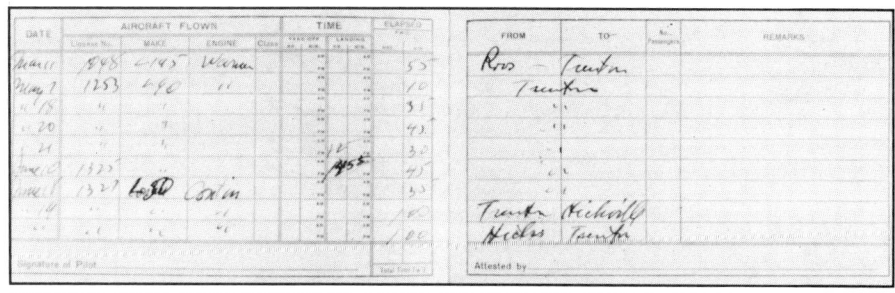

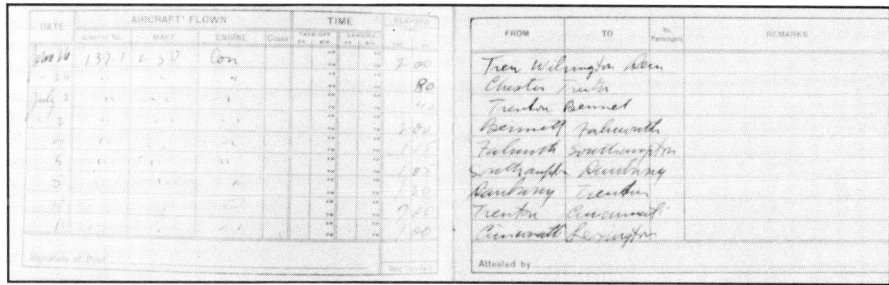

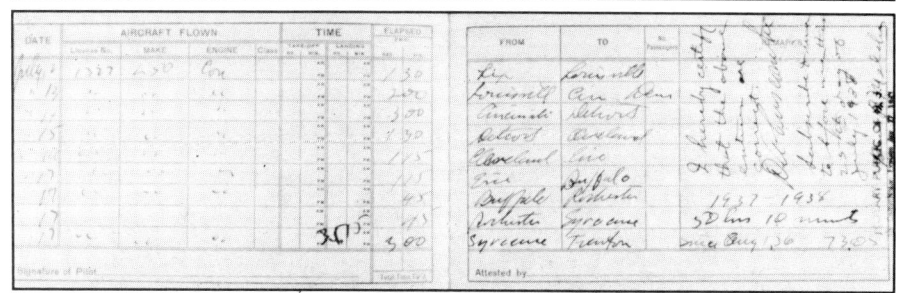

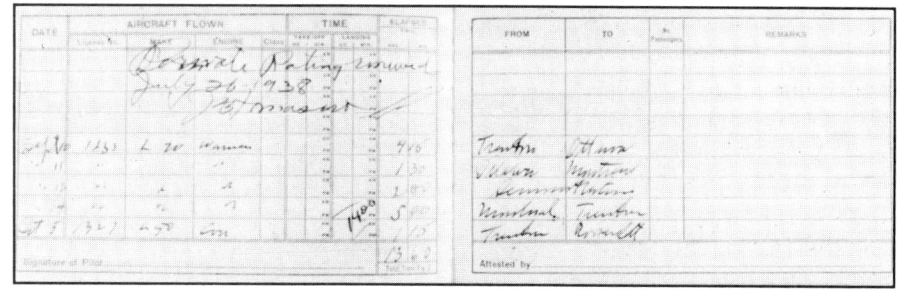

In mid-June 1938, Don and Brownee Luscombe took the first production "Fifty" on a promotional tour. The pages, from Don's pilot logbook, record this event. Note the renewal of Don's private pilot rating. ELEANORE LUSCOMBE SHURTZ COLLECTION

an inspector had licensed the completed airplane.

Prior to this accord, Don maintained legality and ordered (or was required to order) all completed Model 8 airplanes held on the West Trenton property, except those flown to Roosevelt Field, New York, for Bureau of Air Commerce licensing, before they were sold. The company had come this far in benefiting from the cooperation of the government's certification bureaucracy and Don did not want any potentially disruptive violation problems interfering with Model 8 production, sales, or delivery.

The swift speed with which the Luscombe Airplane Corporation completed the test for and, later, received the Model 8 ATC was due in large part to on-

The first production Luscombe Model 8 in flight shortly after receiving its "NC" registration. JAMES B. ZAZAS COLLECTION

site Department of Commerce Inspector John B. Fornasero. He ensured no unusual snags or surprises developed during the overall certification process.

Fornasero worked closely with the LAC staff and shepherded the Luscombe "50" through its many structural loading, weight and balance and subsequent ATC flight tests. Always a pleasant individual, Fornasero offered help when help was needed. Otherwise, he stood silently nearby and observed.

While Don and his key employees waited for the ATC to be issued formally, a small amount of Luscombe Model 4 flight testing and airplane construction continued. Ig Sargent took NC1337 (s/n 403) aloft for the first time on July 30, 1938, for an uneventful twenty minute test flight. Five days later, he took NC1335, serial number unassigned, into the air. Both airplanes were deemed ready for sale after his brief test flights.[83]

On August 4, the second production Luscombe "50" graced the asphalt ramp at the Mercer County Airport. Possessing serial number 802 and sporting a flashy red-trim over a gleaming natural metal surface, this airplane was destined to be sent to France as part of the previous sales agreement between Luscombe and Caudron.

United States Department of Commerce regulations forbade French identification letters being placed on the airplane prior to certification. Thus, the numbers 2589 were taped to the fin and used temporarily. On August 5, Ig Sargent tested this airplane's wings during a forty-five minute flight. Eddie Davis, anxious to fly the future Aero de France airplane, undertook his own fifteen minute test flight shortly after Sargent's flight.

Content everything was in order, Ig Sargent re-boarded this airplane and flew to Roosevelt Field to have it weighed and licensed according to U.S. standards, one of the conditions of the contract between Luscombe and Caudron. At the time, the resident airplane inspector was not on the field, so Sargent made arrangements with the Bureau of Air Commerce to have the airplane inspected at the Roosevelt Field Bureau of Air Commerce field office.

Luscombe "Ninety," NC1337 (s/n 403). RON PRICE

At the request of Fred Knack, Bill Shepard joined Sargent on this journey to compute the required weight and balance information. As they boarded the airplane, Sargent turned to Shepard and commented, *"I'll fly up and you can fly it back."* Shepard was eager to fly this newest "Fifty."

Shortly after their arrival, Bill Shepard set about

his duties. To obtain some proper weight and balance figures, he had to drain the "Fifty's" fuel into some five gallon cans. When all calculations were competed, the fuel was returned to the "Fifty's" fuel tank.

The return trip home proved more exciting than either Shepard or Sargent had expected. Just as the "Fifty's" wheels broke ground at Roosevelt Field, the A-50 engine coughed once or twice, then died — in full view and earshot of the Air Commerce inspectors that had just licensed the airplane!

Instinctively, Sargent grabbed the controls and landed the Luscombe "50." A quick, yet thorough, inspection revealed the fuel was contaminated by water. Further investigation revealed the source of the problem was the five gallon cans used to drain the fuel.

The problem was corrected and a somewhat embarrassed Sargent and Shepard headed home. Very shortly after their return to West Trenton, the airplane was disassembled and crated for shipment to France. Within two weeks, this Model 8 was loaded aboard the *Isle de France* and headed for France.

Production Model 8 flight testing commenced at a fast and furious rate as more airplanes were completed. On August 8, Sargent took NC2590 (s/n 803) aloft for the first time. Three days later, he followed with a similar test flight in NC2592 (s/n 805). Luscombe "50" NC2591 (s/n 804) would not be ready to be test flown for at least four days after NC2592's flight test.

Only a week or so earlier, Jerry Coigny of Grant's Pass, Oregon, arrived at the factory to pick-up a new Luscombe "50" he had ordered. Coigny had been working for the Douglas Aircraft Company repairing DC-3s at United Air Lines' Cheyenne, Wyoming, repair base when a he spotted an advertisement in *Western Flying* depicting the prototype Luscombe "50."

Coigny was hooked and had to have one. He traded in his 40 hp Taylorcraft to get the necessary down payment and quickly placed an order for a new Luscombe "50" which, incidentally, was to be the third production Model 8.

Though Douglas offered a bright future, Coigny had other employment plans and soon resigned his position. He envisioned having his own Luscombe dealership and a flight school while doing a little barnstorming on the side. Thus, he associated himself with Falcon Aircraft Corporation of Los Angeles, then the Luscombe Airplane Company distributor for the Western states.

Carlton Darneal, one of the partners of Falcon Aircraft (Tom Warner was the other partner), came to Cheyenne in Warner's Waco cabin biplane to pick up Coigny. Jerry joined a trio of other pilots who were flying with Warner to pick up a Phantom, a Luscombe "90" and two Luscombe "50" airplanes. A day later, the group was on their way to West Trenton.

Shortly after they arrived, Coigny was informed his Luscombe "50," NC2590, was ready. But the second Luscombe "50" being prepared for delivery to Falcon Aircraft, NC2591, would not be ready for at least one, possibly two weeks.

Coigny and his party were somewhat distressed. They had planned to return to California as a group since a couple of the pilots had very limited, long cross-country experience. Coigny, however, was in no particular hurry to return West. Thus, he relinquished his airplane to Tom Warner and, in turn, accepted NC2591 to be his airplane.

Now, all but stranded in West Trenton, Coigny told Don Luscombe he could not wait long — he was low on money. In an effort to keep his customer happy and take advantage of Coigny's vast sheet metal experience, Don offered Coigny the opportunity to help build his airplane and earn some money, a prospect accepted readily. Soon, Coigny was driving rivets into his own airplane. Furthermore, Don offered Coigny the chance to assist Sargent and Davis with the flight testing load. Coigny declined.

Before Don put Coigny on the payroll, however, Tom Warner arrived at Trenton from the Bahamas where he had been honeymooning. Warner took the pilots from California, including Coigny, to Atlantic City Beach for a brief vacation. While there, a policewoman tried to arrest Tom Warner for wearing Bermuda Shorts on the Boardwalk which, at the time, was "illegal." Coigny almost ran afoul of the law when walked into the surf with trunks but no uppers, which he found out later was "illegal," also.

Barely a day after the group returned to West Trenton, Jerry Coigny met Lucy Rago, who had just returned from Atlantic City as well on a family vacation. He was anxious to meet this very lovely and petite lady with dark brown hair and eyes that sparkled.

Lucy Rago was a Trenton, New Jersey, native and had been employed with the company for a couple years as Don's secretary. Besides her secretarial duties, Lucy and her family assisted the company by sewing the wing cover envelopes for the Model 4 and early Model 8 airplanes, often on their living room floor. On many occasions, Brownee Luscombe would visit the Rago family and join the sewing party.

Jerry was drawn initially to Lucy by a photograph he had seen posted on a wall showing Lucy sitting inside the prototype Luscombe "50" holding its control wheel. Walking over to Jeff's Hamburger Stand, Coigny's opening line to Lucy was, *"Will you be my first passenger in the '50'?"*

With a twinkle in her eye, Lucy said, *"Yes."*

Lucy Rago poses with two of Don Luscombe's dogs. She was hired in 1935 to be Don's secretary. — JERRY & LUCY COIGNY

Thereupon, Jerry invited her to see the movie "Alexander's Ragtime Band" at a Trenton theater. When the couple arrived in the foyer, half of the factory employees were there waiting for seats. The "cat was out of the bag" and a romance was started, despite the best efforts of other employees to set up blind dates for Jerry with other girls from the West Trenton area.

During his stay in West Trenton, Jerry Coigny roomed with Rolfe Gregory at the "Jolly Roger." Always a warm and friendly individual, Jerry became goods friends with everybody around him.

On August 11, 1938, Don Luscombe received the news he had long waited to hear. The Department of Commerce granted the Model 8 design Approved Type Certificate number 694. The Luscombe Airplane Corporation was now free to commence Luscombe Model 8 production.

Don was ecstatic! Perhaps more than any other accomplishment, Don savored this crowning achievement. His singular vision and virtually unyielding passion to develop an affordable, production airplane made from uniform and interchangeable metal parts was now fulfilled.

If other light airplane manufacturers showed any competitive anxiety before this day, they were definitely concerned now. Don's new Model 8 was a competitive "winner." Don knew it! And a begrudging competition knew it!

All-metal durability and safety, coupled with performance and price that could compare favorably with any airplane in its class, the Model 8 became the design to match. For one proud moment in time, Donald A. Luscombe could boast he found his pot of gold at the end of a glorious rainbow.

All but lost in the rush to obtain the Approved Type Certificate was the surprising order for a Luscombe Phantom. This unexpected order originated from a most unusual source, the Brazilian Navy. Amidst the "Fifty" and "Ninety" hustle and bustle, a very colorful Luscombe Phantom took shape on the main hangar floor.

Acting through their agent, J. Sumner Ireland, officials within the Brazilian Navy were intrigued by Don Luscombe's robust machine and desired to have one. Though the stated reason to obtain such an airframe may have been maritime patrol or training, this Phantom was destined most likely to be the private airplane of some ranking Brazilian Navy officer or official.

The photograph that started a lifelong romance! Here Lucy Rago holds the control wheel in the prototype Luscombe "Fifty" (s/n 800), the only Model 8 to be so equipped. — JERRY & LUCY COIGNY VIA JOHN SWICK

Don cared little about the owner's intended purpose — he was delighted to sell another Luscombe Phantom 1 airplane. The corporation had at

Chapter Fourteen: Rainbow's End 215

least six more Phantom fuselages in storage, including one complete airplane which was used infrequently as a company demonstrator. This sale was very much needed to reduce the corporation's Phantom inventory and convert the tied-up cost of labor and material into income.

Like all remaining Phantom fuselages and wings, this airplane's fuselage and wings were constructed somewhat earlier, most likely in late March or early April 1937. When no buyers came forward at the time, this unused fuselage and wing set were stored in the main hangar's overhead rafters.

Before the airframe was assembled, the company's consummate painter, Henri D'Estout, applied an overall navy blue base paint scheme. The fabric rudder was painted with vertical yellow, blue and green stripes. Roundels depicting the Brazilian nationality were applied to the wing's polished upper and lower surfaces. Additionally, a white anchor was painted underneath each wing, no doubt to function as a readily recognizable aid for Brazilian ground and sea observers.

combe School of Aeronautics students assisted more experienced factory personnel to assemble the airplane.

When all was ready, Ig Sargent took this newest Phantom, s/n 118, aloft for a quick test flight on August 16. He made several more flights in the MARINHA Phantom before the day's sun settled below a lazy, New Jersey horizon. Then, Sargent hurried home to pack for his upcoming trip to France to demonstrate

JAMES B. ZAZAS COLLECTION

(Above) Ig Sargent prepares to test fly the Brazilian Luscombe Phantom, D1L-204.

(Left) Delivery fast approaching, a LAC employee makes a few wheel adjustments on the Brazilian Luscombe Phantom, D1L-204.

JAMES B. ZAZAS COLLECTION

Finally, the airplane's individual identification numbers were added. A large, white "2-D-1" was painted on each side of the fuselage. Likewise, "D1L-204" was painted on the side of the fuselage just forward of the horizontal stabilizer, yet in a much smaller size. A black lettered "DIL" was painted on the fin over a black lettered "MARINHA."[84]

At least two weeks' labor was required to paint, assemble and prepare this Phantom for its flight test and subsequent delivery. Once more, senior Lus-

the serial number 802, Model 8 airplane. During Sargent's absence, Eddie Davis made his own test flight in the Brazilian Phantom two days later.

Only the day before (August 15), a hard working Sargent flight tested Jerry Coigny's Model 8. When Sargent departed for France, Eddie Davis assumed the majority of the flight test load.

Within minutes after Sargent's test flight, Jerry Coigny made his own test flight with Lucy aboard and fulfilled an earlier promise he made to her that she

Congratulations LUSCOMBE "50"

On obtaining your A·T·C· on your new Model "50"...powered with the brilliant new **Continental A·50 Engine**

50 H. P.
at 1900 R. P. M.
WGT.—150 LBS.

Continental Motors Corporation
Aircraft Engine Division

AERO DIGEST, SEPTEMBER 1938

would be his first passenger. Both returned to earth ecstatic!

But Coigny was worried. He confided to Rolfe Gregory he might not be able to cover his first month's airplane loan payment, then about one hundred dollars. Gregory was more optimistic. He looked at his new friend and said, *"Jerry, let's go barnstorming!"*

Rolfe Gregory convinced his colleague there were dozens of small towns between New Jersey and South Carolina, with adequate landing fields, where they could hop passengers for $2 a head.

On August 19, Coigny and Gregory took off for Baltimore's Logan Field, their first stop. They filled the gas tank and headed for Hoover Field in Washington, D.C., but not before calling the control tower to ask permission to land. Even in those days, airplanes were not welcome without a radio at the airport near the nation's capital. (Incidentally, the airport then sat very near the same spot the Pentagon occupies today.)

Jerry had never been to the East Coast before and wanted dearly to make a side trip to the Smithsonian Institution. But his hopes were dashed when the tower operator said a firm *"No!"* to the request to land — that is, until Jerry mentioned he was flying a new Luscombe "50." The operator's attitude changed abruptly and said he expected an "open slot" shortly.

When Coigny and Gregory arrived at Hoover Field, they saw a man frantically wave them toward his direction. He was on the opposite side of the field from where a sign said "Visiting Pilots." The man was standing near the base of the control tower and next to the passenger terminal.

The propeller had barely stopped turning and the doors cracked open when Coigny and Gregory were besieged by an avalanche of questions. *"How fast does it cruise?" "What is the top speed?" "How long does it take to get one?"* The traveling duo had never seen any new airplane get so much attention.

The tower operator told Coigny and Gregory he would watch over their new airplane while the two went sight-seeing. He even took their baggage up to the tower for safe keeping! Hours later, Coigny and Gregory returned and were soon on their way south. They made a special trip to visit Rolfe's parents in Petersburg, Virginia.

On August 22, a tired but very happy Jerry Coigny and Rolfe Gregory returned to West Trenton. Don Luscombe was quite pleased, also, as the trip had given the Model 8 a lot of positive, albeit free, publicity.

Meanwhile, Ig Sargent and his wife, Sissie, were heading east towards France in the luxurious spacious comfort of the ocean liner *S.S. Normandie*. The Sargents had every intention to combine business and pleasure on this trip. Their host, Jacques Negrier, had grand plans in store for them in Paris and the surrounding French countryside.

The Sargents arrived in France and had three weeks to sight-see and visit. When the Luscombe "50" arrived, a well-rested Ig was hustled to the Caudron Aerodrome near Versailles to supervise the Model 8 assembly and rigging in preparation for its test flights. A few problems developed, such as the use of Metric versus English-calibrated tools, but the overall assembly went smoothly.

However, Ig Sargent's initial test flight went less than smooth. Confident all was in order after a thorough preflight inspection, Sargent hopped into the gleaming monoplane, fastened his lap belt and motioned to one of the nearby French mechanics to pull the propeller to start the engine. In an instant, the engine roared to life — *at full power* — and a very startled Sargent found himself on his way for a sooner-than-anticipated takeoff. The poor mechanic who started the engine was barely able to clear the propeller's swirling arc before Sargent and the Luscombe "50" lurched over the chocks and bounded forward.

Ig Sargent was dumfounded! Instinctively, he knew something was amiss, but what? Perhaps there was excess fuel in the carburetor. He pushed forward on the throttle hoping to clear the engine. Strangely, the engine went to idle. Not wanting to kill the engine, Sargent retarded the throttle — and the engine roared to full power once more. Quickly reaching flying speed, Sargent elected to make a takeoff, which he did effortlessly.

Once airborne, Sargent quickly took stock of his predicament, but failed to understand totally the reasons for the throttle problem. However, he reasoned correctly the throttle was installed backwards somehow. Only after he landed did he discover the reasons why.

The throttle arm was installed "backwards" as per the French light plane aviation requirements in force at the time. In other words, American-built airplanes used an aft throttle position for an idle power setting and a forward position for a power setting. The French, on the other hand, operated their throttle settings in reverse.

Sargent soon learned the French mechanics who had reworked the throttle-to-carburetor linkage did so according to their particular requirements, but neglected to tell the famous Luscombe Airplane Corporation test pilot of the change. They "assumed" he knew of this change.

As a result, Sargent learned quickly one of the first rules followed by any seasoned test pilot, "Be prepared for the unexpected!" When Ig Sargent returned to the field, one Caudron mechanic was ready to break his neck and his French Aero Club friends were laughing so hard they almost broke theirs.

Despite the throttle "problem," the airplane was re-rigged slightly and was test flown a few more times. Satisfied with its handling, Sargent dutifully turned the airplane over to the Caudron chief test pilot for his flight in the polished aluminum and red-trimmed "Fifty."

Dressed in a white cotton coverall flight suit, complete with a white silk scarf, the French pilot who was rather obese — he weighed almost 300 pounds — had a difficult time belting into the Luscombe 8's small cabin. His ensuing takeoff roll was a bit uncomfortably long, but once airborne, the laboring Luscombe "50" carried him into the air with little effort. Upon his return, the French test pilot wore a smile rarely seen by those individuals who knew the Caudron pilot.[85]

The rigging and test flights were soon completed. Once more, the Sargents could relax for a few days and joined the junior Negrier on a grand tour of Paris and the surrounding countryside. Notre Dame, the Louvre, the Seine River and so much more were "must see" items on their long list of places to visit.

Uniquely, the Sargents trod over much of the same territory Don Luscombe had done some twenty-one years earlier. And, once more, war clouds on a distant horizon threatened to destroy the peace and beauty of the pastoral French countryside.

While Ig and Sissie Sargent enjoyed their scenic tour and gracious host's hospitality, their closest friend back home, Eddie Davis, had no time to rest. He was busy with test flights, demonstration rides and sales pitches.

Meanwhile, Flying Associates, Limited, a small Canadian charter firm based in Winnipeg, Alberta, Canada, purchased what was to become the first Model 8 delivered to a Canadian customer. Don agreed to provide a Luscombe "50" as soon as one was available. The fifth production Model 8 (s/n 806) was selected and was registered as CF-BKW. Incidentally, this charter firm became the first Luscombe airplane dealership in Canada.

Davis, on his behalf, spent most of the third week of August preparing this Model 8 for its Canadian customers. His first flight in CF-BKW was on August 19 and followed with another flight on August 20. On August 21, he departed the Mercer County Airport with Ronold Giguere, the buyer. Over the next two days, the duo flew to a small airport near the United States-Canadian border. After clearing Customs, the new owner flew his new prize to its Canadian home. The airplane was registered in Canada on August 25, 1938.

A pair of Canadian buyers take delivery of the first Luscombe "Fifty" to go to Canada. Left to right — unknown, Don Luscombe, Eddie Davis, Ronold Giguere and Ig Sargent.   IGNATIUS SARGENT

An exhausted Davis had barely returned to West Trenton when he was tasked to undertake two more test flights in Coigny's airplane, one on August 25 and the other a day later. Once more, Jerry Coigny joined Eddie Davis on one of these test flights.

Coigny remained on the factory grounds until the start of the 1938 National Air Races at Cleveland. Thereupon, he bid his new friends a fond farewell. Coigny promised his sweetheart, Lucy Rago, he would keep in touch and return soon.

Howard Jong joined Jerry Coigny on the trip westward. Jong was homesick and longed to return to his Los Angeles home. Coigny invited Jong to join him, but hinted he would be making several stops along the way to see family and friends, including an extended stop at the National Air Races. Jong cared little — he was going home. He gave little, if no advance notice, he was leaving, a point that surprised many of his friends.[86]

Coigny, Jong and the Luscombe "50" were welcomed like royalty at Cleveland. Mr. Evington, who was working with the Sensenich Propeller Company of Lancaster, Pennsylvania, to develop the "Everal One Blade Propeller," asked Coigny to install the new prop on his Luscombe "50." Coigny agreed and flew his Luscombe "50" in the daily "Parade of Progress." All expenses were paid by Mr. Evington.

The Everal propeller shook the Model 8 badly as it was designed for a 40 hp motor. Coigny cared little — he was doing a brisk business checking out pilots before and after the show.

As a humorous sidelight, Jerry Coigny was addressed as "Mr. Doug Corrigan" while entering the elevator at the Carter Hotel in Cleveland. Coigny and Corrigan arrived at the Cleveland airport at the same time, stayed at the same hotel and wore the same type of leather jacket and Army "pinks." From that moment on, the fun began, especially when the real Douglas Corrigan left in his Curtiss Robin the next day.

In the company of crack stunt pilot Mike Murphy, Coigny pulled several pranks, one of them posing as "Wrong Way" Corrigan. Thus, he and Howard Jong

Jerry Coigny's Luscombe "50" at the 1938 National Air Races at Cleveland. The Everal propeller and Continental A-50 combination performed satisfactorily, but shook badly in flight as the prop was designed for A-40 use.   JOHN LENGENFELDER

were able to sit in a swank, $75 seat at the first pylon in the company of some notable folks, including Helen Jones, who was daughter of Jess Jones, Sensenich Propeller Company's test pilot. The usher was afraid to throw out Coigny thinking he was Corrigan.

Meanwhile, confirmed orders for the Model 8 arrived daily. The ensuing rush to build airplanes threatened to overwhelm the existing facilities. In a situation reminiscent of earlier Monocoupe days, Don Luscombe could foresee he was going to have major problems meeting the demand. The main hangar was too small to build the Model 8 in any appreciable quantity. He needed the new addition now!

Don was stymied. He knew he had to start construction of the factory addition very shortly or risk being unable to deliver a quality product on time, a point the competition was acutely aware. Once more, the lack of capital prevented him from commencing work on the much-needed factory building.

A large amount of stock was outstanding. If sold, then Don's worries would be alleviated temporarily. Yet, very few people were interested in investing in a small, private airplane company during the late 1930s. Those individuals involved in Don's concern either owned stock in the corporation, had already invested money in the corporation or had thrown up their hands in disgust over the company's affairs and walked away.

Additionally, Don was forced to consider another disquieting aspect of his beleaguered company. Model 8 production was limited by the amount of time required to build each airplane. Though many Model 8 parts were drop-hammered or used punch pressed stampings, each airplane was still a labor-intensive, handmade product.

Despite the many improvements Don and his staff made to pare labor and improve productivity, the mass production goals were nowhere near those Don envisioned. As a result, tempers often frayed as frustrations and the production bottleneck worsened.

Don needed an interim solution before the new addition was built. He tasked production manager and plant superintendent Ben Melcher and fuselage department foreman Chuck Burgess to develop the means to increase production. While Melcher tackled the overall problem, Burgess chewed on the fuselage production problem a very short while before he found some solutions.

Burgess made some drill templates for the aft fuselage skins and matching ones for the aft fuselage frames. This made it possible to pre-drill these parts and then assemble skins to frames temporarily with fasteners to form fuselage cones before placing them in the fuselage jig for riveting and final assembly.

This process ensured the accuracy of the location of each rivet and made possible the concept of interchangeable parts for repairs as well as to reduce considerably the time required for assembly.

In mid-September, he unveiled this process and a new fuselage jig that virtually halved the time to build a complete fuselage. Now, a fuselage could be built in four hours instead of the previously required eight hours.

Burgess was anxious to prove the jig's worth. He challenged control surfaces department foreman Bill Force to an informal contest. Burgess wagered he could build a fuselage and pop it out of the jig in less time than Force's department could build a complete set of tail surfaces.

An incredulous Force glanced at his friend and retorted, *"Aw, Chuck, you're crazy!"* Then, within earshot of many workers in the plant, he added, *"I'll kiss your ass in Macy's (Department Store) window if you beat me."*

The challenge was accepted!

The time of day to start the contest was selected and a worker was chosen to blow a whistle to announce the start and stop of the competition. When each team signalled they were ready, the whistle was blown. The contest was underway!

Ben Melcher couldn't understand what all the commotion was outside his office. Don Luscombe was surprised, too. Both were startled to learn of the "contest" in progress, but did nothing to stop it. Both agreed it was a great morale

Control surfaces department foreman, Bill Force (right) assists a fellow employee rivet a Luscombe "Fifty" horizontal stabilizer leading edge. JAMES B. ZAZAS COLLECTION

boost for the employees.

The seconds turned into minutes and then into hours. Rivet guns clattered as Alclad fuselage skins joined stamped duraluminum bulkheads. Metal brakes bent carefully cut aluminum sheet for the tail surfaces which, in turn, was riveted to press brake formed spars. Both teams worked feverishly while their fellow workers cheered them.

Then, slightly less than four hours into the contest, the whistle blew.

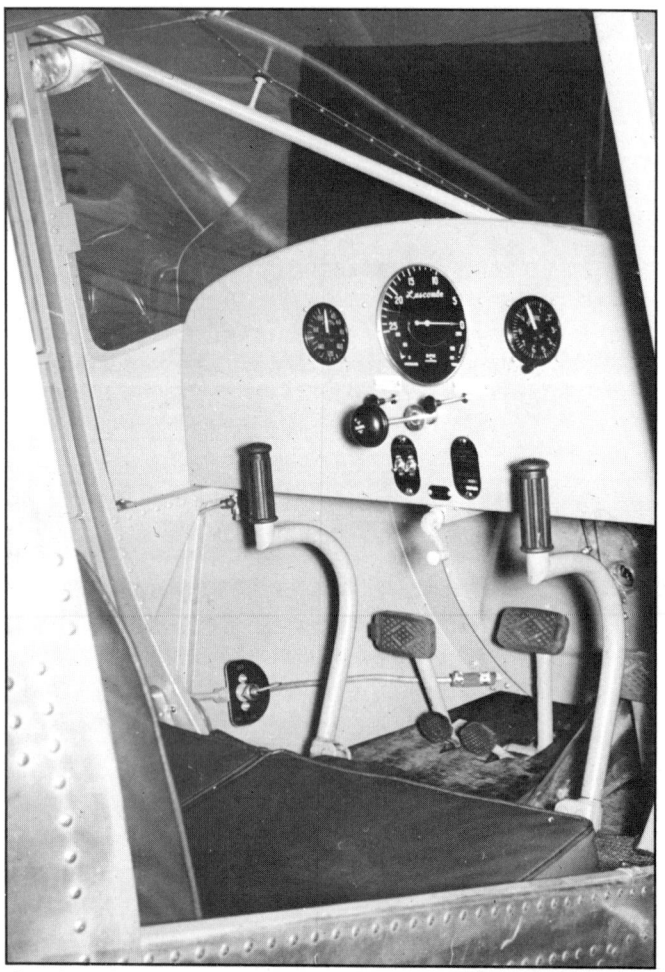

Good cockpit view of an early production Luscombe "Fifty," NC2336 (s/n 812). JAMES B. ZAZAS COLLECTION

A triumphant Chuck Burgess stood beside a shiny new Model 8 fuselage perched beside its angle iron jig. Then, looking squarely at his vanquished foe, who himself was within minutes of completing the tail surfaces, Burgess walked over to Force, turned around, bent over and pointed to his derriere.

The thick brick walls of the Luscombe Airplane Corporation's main hangar reverberated with the hoots, howls and laughter of several dozen employees. A very red-faced Bill Force acknowledged the cheering assemblage and conceded defeat. Ben Melcher soon ordered everyone back to work. After the congratulatory handshakes and pats on the back, the plant's work environment returned to a more serious mood.

Don was excited when he reviewed the June, July and August production and delivery figures. At least five Model 8s, four Model 4s and one Luscombe Phantom were built and delivered. September's forecast promised at least ten Model 8s to be built and delivered. October's estimate was an outstanding fifteen, possibly more, Model 8 airplanes.

In only four short months, Don's growing company produced more airplanes than it did during the whole of the previous year.

Further production forecasts were more optimistic and promised sizable profits. Model 8 production alone would generate sufficient revenues to meet obligations. In turn, Don realized he would have to depend less on the income generated by the school to stay in business. However, he entertained no plans to abandon his primary source of qualified mechanics and employees.

Visitors and customers came to the plant with increasing frequency. All clamored for a peek of the Model 8. The Luscombe Airplane Corporation was fast becoming aviation's new "Mecca" and Don Luscombe its new "Guru."

Henry Boller was one of these visitors. However, Boller astonished Don when he said he wanted to purchase a Luscombe Phantom instead of a shiny new, Luscombe "50." Don was uneasy with Boller's coarse, if not occasionally obnoxious attitude, but he was happy to sell him an airplane.

Unlike the other remaining Luscombe Phantom airplanes stored in the main hangar's rafters, the airplane sold to Boller was completed prior to the order. NC1249 had been stored intact for a "quick sale" with only an occasional flight to insure all was in order. Interestingly, the Warner 145 "Super Scarab" power plant and Curtiss metal propeller, each overhauled a year earlier, were salvaged from Henry Olmstead's wrecked Phantom, NC1028.[87]

September presented Luscombe employees a very busy, if not a very exciting month. As expected, Ig Sargent and Eddie Davis were engaged in test flying the new Model 8 airplanes. The duo test flew at least nine, possibly more, airplanes that month.

Don Luscombe, realizing the demand for his new design was literally "taking off," tried to convince Continental Motors Corporation to extend credit on its engines which, until then, had been shipped upon receipt of payment or a Cash-On-Delivery basis. Continental, on their behalf, balked when they studied Don's less-than-sterling credit record.

This engine supply problem, of course, was due

primarily to the lack of adequate working capital. The LAC did not have a good enough credit rating to persuade Continental to ship engines as ordered and then bill Luscombe when shipped. Therefore, payment had to accompany the order for each engine (about $600 at the time) or have the engine shipped Cash-on-Delivery. As the production rate increased, larger inventory of engines was needed if final assembly was not to be delayed waiting for engines.

The production bottleneck caused by this limitation infuriated company treasurer Roger Johnson. He was faced with the proverbial "chicken and egg" situation. How could he deliver an airplane to a customer and receive payment if the airplane was not complete? The company could not make money operating in this manner.

Johnson knew the only way to make a profit from the Model 8 was to boost production or raise prices. The second option may have alleviated the company's dire financial picture, but this possible option was never implemented. Instead, Johnson bit his lip and soldiered onward. Soon, the new addition would be completed, thereby ensuring increased production and profits.

Eventually, a compromise was hammered out between Luscombe and Continental Motors whereby Continental would ship its engines to a bonded warehouse in the Trenton area. When Don received an order, he or a factory representative could go to the warehouse and draw an engine only after it had been paid. Thus, any shipping delay from Continental's Detroit, Michigan, plant was minimized. In time, as the Luscombe Airplane Corporation's credit record improved, Continental Motors reevaluated its terms with Don and his company.

Other events during September tried the employees' patience. A New York studio descended

Lights! Camera! Action! Movie magic descends upon Luscombe's humble company. JAMES B. ZAZAS COLLECTION

upon the company during the third week of September. Their purpose was to make a short, five minute clip showing the construction techniques employed building the then radical Luscombe 8 "metal" airplane.

In the "good old days," many feature movies were preceded by a short cartoon or newsreel. Hence, a documentary film made at Luscombe became one of these short pre-feature movie clips. Warner Brothers was the major studio that made the clip. Once they agreed, the studio expended a tidy sum of money transporting men and equipment in trucks from their New York City offices.

For two days, the movie folks quite literally took over the company. The movie crew almost outnumbered the factory workers. Large, black electrical cables lay about the hangar floor and were strung through the overhead rafters. A bewildered Don Luscombe surveyed the scene and must have thought his beautiful company was being invaded by creatures from space.

Several employees became the actors and those who weren't in the movie were the spectators. Several airframes were rubbed with a special wax to cut-down on glare from the bright lights. There was a feeble attempt to work, but any serious effort was soon abandoned as the director called, *"Lights! Camera! Action!"*

The filming was interrupted occasionally by the weather outside — it was atrocious! Rain and wind pounded the main hangar. The hangar doors were closed to cut down on the wind and the wet that tried to stream inside. It mattered little to the movie crew portions of their 440-volt cables were laying in pools of water. A few employees thought otherwise and sought safety on the main hangar's wood balcony.

Space inside the main hangar became a premium when the main doors were closed. Completed airplanes, normally parked outside during the day, were shoved next to almost-completed airplanes. There was virtually no room left to do any serious work. Only the movie guys had the room to work, and even they were complaining about the cramped quarters.

By the end of the second day, most of the filming was completed. However, the inclement weather outside prevented them from completing the final scene in which Brownee Luscombe was to hop into a shiny new Luscombe "50," give a wave and take off. The director said he would return within a few days to complete the clip when the weather was better.

In the end, the movie was completed and enjoyed a limited distribution. The final clip showed the various construction operations needed to build a Luscombe "50" airplane. Various parts were neatly arranged before the camera while a fast-speaking narrator lead the viewer through a step-by-step assembly of the airplane. It ended with the very attractive Brownee Luscombe making her flight.[88]

And why was the weather outside the hangar so dreadful during the initial filming? Unbeknown to the crew and workers, an unforecast hurricane of incredible force passed off the East Coast within a hundred miles of the plant. During September 21, 22, and 23, the states of New Jersey, New York, and the balance of the northeast states were pummeled by this great hurricane of 1938. Beachfront homes and property sustained an almost incomprehensible amount of damage.

Fortunately, neither the factory nor any of the new airplanes sustained any damage and the company returned to a more normal state of affairs. Test flying and customer deliveries resumed on an almost daily basis.

On October 3, Boller's airplane was made ready. Don asked Ig Sargent to check-out Mr. Boller on the many unique intricacies involved in flying a Phantom. During their brief, ten minute flight, Boller learned the Luscombe Phantom was not at all like his more docile Fairchild 24. The airplane required a gentle hand while landing, a point Boller refused to readily accept.

Boller soon departed with his new airplane. However, within a few days, word reached the company Boller had groundlooped his Phantom and sustained some minor damage. Sargent ferried the airplane to the factory to effect repairs. Boller remained nearby while his airplane was in the shop.

Barely a week later, Boller had another groundloop. Once more, his Phantom was returned to the factory for repairs. And once more, Boller visited the factory on a regular basis while his Phantom was fixed.

Henry F. Boller and Ignatius Sargent. KENNETH E. CERICOLA

During these repairs, perhaps as early as his initial order, Boller discussed with Don at length the problems he was having raising capital to support his own company, the Boller Motor Company in nearby Hagerstown, Maryland. He stated the company's purpose was to develop diesel engines for commercial, maritime and aviation use. Boller emphasized several of the engines were his own design, a point Luscombe found hard to accept.

Then, chewing on the stem of a pipe he carried with him, Boller asked Don bluntly if he, Don, could refer him to any financial backers willing to support his venture.

Don was flabbergasted by Boller's forward nature! He replied he was having too many problems with his *own* company and financial backers to worry about any *other* concerns. He related why a new addition needed to be built to handle the growing influx of Model 8 orders, but the lack of sufficient capital prevented him from proceeding. No doubt Don revealed a huge block of stock was still outstanding and hinted its purchase, or any sizable cash infusion, would help the present situation tremendously.

Then Boller turned the tables. He told Don he knew of someone who might be able to help, but declined to offer any names. Perhaps, Boller believed he had in his pocket a solution agreeable to both gentlemen's current financial woes. Though he was rebuffed previously by many wealthy investors, Boller hoped he would succeed in his own ventures when he mentioned the Luscombe Airplane Corporation's immediate needs.

Don became increasingly suspicious of his customer's chatty and boastful nature. Not long after Boller departed in his Phantom, Don made a few inquiries to learn more about Boller's cloudy background. Don began to think of Boller as a sly fox in the hen house, poised to seize any opportunity offered or not.

By way of background, very little is known about Heinrich Frederick Boller. Immigration records state he was born in Bergen, Germany, on October 23, 1909, and immigrated to the United States, arriving on May 26, 1930, at the Port of New York on the *S.S. Dresden*. He worked as a mechanic in various cities from 1930 to 1937. In 1932, he returned briefly to Germany to convince his parents and brother to return with him to the United States, but they elected to remain in Germany. Boller, however, returned to the United States.

In light of the very tense and developing international situation in Europe during the mid to late 1930s, Boller was held in suspicion by several government agencies, including the Federal Bureau of Investigation and the Naval Investigative Service. The latter service was alerted to Boller due to his constant diesel engine inquiries with the Navy Department. Later, when questioned about his political affiliations, Boller maintained steadfastly he was anti-Nazi. To this end, he filed his declaration to become a U.S. citizen on February 7, 1939 at the District Court in Baltimore, Maryland.[89]

In the course of his many attempts to raise capital for his diesel engine ideas, Boller met Vera Montgomery, a petite woman with black hair and dark eyes. Montgomery was a customer's woman for the brokerage firm Winslow, Douglas and McEvoy in New York City. Reportedly, the two became romantically involved.[90]

Boller hoped Montgomery, through her many contacts, would be able to locate someone who would be interested in his diesel engine ideas. Montgomery turned to several clients, yet all turned her down.

Then she approached a young, twenty-eight-year-old German-born gentleman friend living in Montreal, Canada. He owned an investment business that dealt primarily in the stock of commercial aviation companies. His name was Leopold Hugo Paul Klotz.

Klotz was quite wealthy and was very knowledgeable of banking and financial matters. Yet, like so many characters being drawn into the affairs of the Luscombe Airplane Corporation at that time, Klotz's background holds much mystery.

According to wartime Vested Claims Committee records, Klotz was born in Berlin, Germany, on September 12, 1910. He attended various schools in Berlin and finished his primary schooling in 1928. He got a job working in an investment firm and, between 1928 and 1931, attended the University of Berlin where he studied law and economics.

In 1931, the conditions in Germany became so acute that the family moved to Switzerland, as they had done briefly once before shortly after the end of World War I. In 1932, Klotz went to Paris for six months where he attended the Sorbonne, taking a course in economics and banking. Later in the year, he traveled to England and resided in London where he was employed by some investment brokers.

While he lived in England, he applied for citizenship, but was denied. During the summer of 1938, he traveled to Canada to find ways to invest the family fortune. In the process, he applied for Canadian citizenship, but was denied once more.[91] The nature of his business required several trips to New York City. During one of these trips, he met Vera Montgomery.[92]

Initially, when Mrs. Montgomery presented Boller's diesel engine ideas, Klotz was interested and offered some financial backing. Reportedly, he went as far as approaching influential contacts within the United States Navy Department on Boller's behalf. However, he quickly shunted Boller's ambitions aside when Mrs. Montgomery mentioned a brighter prospect — a small, floundering light airplane company in nearby West Trenton, New Jersey. The company had perfected and was producing an all-metal airplane.

Klotz's interest was piqued. He demanded more information.

Both Boller and Montgomery provided what little information they knew about the Luscombe Airplane Corporation, but endeavored to provide more. The more information they provided, the more Klotz became interested in the company.

Within days of learning about the factory, Leopold H.P. Klotz requested a meeting with Don Luscombe to discuss ways to assist Don's capital-starved corporation.

THE Luscombe..50

Two wide doors and deep cushions that hold their shape afford comfort for two large adults.

The cowling encloses the engine and exhaust manifolds affording aerodynamic and windshield cleanliness.

Generous cargo space behind the seat gives complete protection to fine luggage.

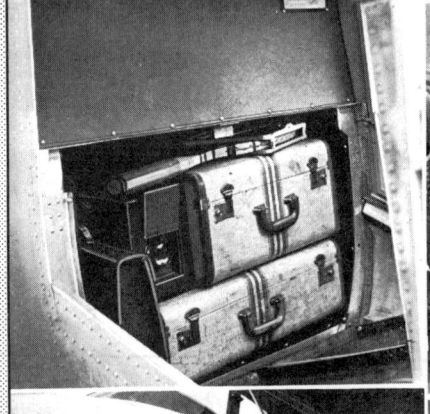

By lifting the hinged hood your engine is as accessible as the motor in your car.

In keeping with careful streaming the semi-cantilever undercarriage keeps its oildraulic struts inside the airplane.

Unobstructed visibility on the ground and in the air is a welcome refinement.

A full cantilever tail for efficiency and beauty is a distinctive feature of this design.

A quick acting window for ventilation is mechanically trouble free.

*"Whither is fled the visionary gleam?
Where is it now, the glory and the dream?"*

Intimations of Immortality from
Reflections of Early Childhood [1807]
William Wordsworth (1770 - 1850)

Chapter Fifteen

Forces Greater Than He

Leopold H.P. Klotz traveled to West Trenton for the first time on or about November 2, 1938. His meeting with Don Luscombe and company treasurer Roger Johnson was cordial.

Luscombe and Johnson were intrigued by Klotz's plans to make a sizeable investment in the Luscombe Airplane Corporation. Each wondered to what extent Klotz was willing to put up to come aboard. Numbers were bantered about, but no specific figures were given. Soon, they had an answer.

Though Don was very open to Klotz's offers of money, he viewed him more as a "banker-type" individual than an optimistic investor truly concerned with the company's future prosperity. Hence, he was somewhat wary of Leopold's true intentions. In spite of his reservations, Don was blinded by Klotz's generous offers and failed to realize the magnitude and end result of the forthcoming transactions Klotz, on his behalf, masked any future plans for the Luscombe Airplane Corporation behind the dire financial conditions that existed within the company.

On November 3, 1938, company treasurer Roger Johnson sent a letter to Board member George B. Cluett, II, detailing Klotz's visit to the factory and his subsequent offer to provide funding. In this letter, Johnson referred to Klotz sarcastically and said, *"Our little German boy who visited us yesterday sent in asking us to please give him a few days or so before we accept any other bids."*

Other offers on the table at the time included a $25,000 proposal from a wealthy New York investor.

JAMES B. ZAZAS COLLECTION
Leopold H.P. Klotz was only 29-years-old when he made his play to take over the Luscombe factory.

Though "Bunnie" Hinsch verified the merits of this potential investor, this deal proved to be smoke in the wind.

Within days of receiving Johnson's letter, Klotz revealed his initial investment intentions to Don, but not his long-term plans relative to acquiring the company. Klotz would invest at least $10,000 in Don's foundering company in the form of a loan payable by January 2, 1940, and bearing an interest rate of 5 percent per year.

On November 9, 1938, Don Luscombe and Roger Johnson inked a letter to Klotz confirming an agreement whereby Klotz was to advance $10,000 as a loan. Furthermore, each agreed if Klotz decided to buy stock in the company, then this loan would be cancelled by issuing 10,000 shares of common stock.

This loan was the foothold Klotz needed to gain access into the company's corporate affairs. It didn't take a banker's sixth sense to tell Klotz of the company's difficult financial condition and that its Board of Directors would be receptive to virtually any offer of more funds.

Barely a week later, Klotz made another move. He astounded Luscombe with an almost unbelievable offer. Klotz offered to purchase 85,000 shares of common stock for $85,000. Don could not accept so much money without his Board of Directors' approval. A special meeting of the Board was scheduled at the Hotel Lexington, New York City, New York, for November 18, 1938, to consider Klotz's most generous proposal.

Don Luscombe, Roger Johnson and Board members Ig Sargent, George Cluett, II, and Hiram Mallinson attended this meeting. Leopold H.P. Klotz attended as a guest. Don, presiding as the Board Chairman, presented Klotz's offer in one hand and a tentative letter of agreement in the other.

A budget was presented detailing the figures used to consummate the deal. Likewise, these figures were used to serve as a guide for the company's projected growth through June 30, 1939. A discussion followed concerning the need for additional floor space and the need for adequate funds to build this proposed expansion.

George Cluett, II, offered to build the additional floor space, financing the project from his own pocket. In turn, he offered to take stock or keep the buildings in his name and charge the Luscombe Airplane Corporation rent. Klotz objected and said the budget amounts were sufficient to cover the expansion.

However, after further discussion, it was determined the budget amount was not sufficient. Klotz offered to take care of the building program if he was allowed to increase his stock holding to 105,000 shares. Thereupon, Mr. Cluett withdrew his offer to help financially with the proposed expansion project. A vote was taken by the Board approving Klotz's offer of increased stock purchase plus the building program financing.

Additionally, Klotz received an option to purchase another 35,000 shares of stock between the date of the meeting and December 31, 1941. These shares would be bought at $1.25 net to the Corporation.

These additional shares were the shares optioned previously to the Corporation's underwriter, Eugene J. Hynes and Company, for the sale of 90,000 shares of stock, which they failed to exercise. A cancellation agreement was signed by Eugene J. Hynes and Co. as outlined in the stock prospectus of May 6, 1938. (The corporation's outstanding unissued stock as of December 31, 1938, was 280,998 shares.)

At the conclusion of these negotiations, the Board informed Klotz the Securities and Exchange Commission would be notified of these transactions. Klotz had no objections.

Shortly after this meeting, Don Luscombe and Roger Johnson sent a letter to Leopold Klotz inviting him to join the Board of Directors at any time desired. Or, if this invitation was impractical, a competent nominee of his choice would be acceptable.

Klotz opted for the latter, but refrained from mentioning any names. Yet, his mind was already set. It would be Henry Boller. Incidentally, Boller was now a frequent visitor to the plant and often reported his observations to Klotz.

Don had high hopes his future relationship with this new, enthusiastic and very wealthy investor would be fruitful and profitable for all concerned. Don closed a letter to Klotz dated November 21, 1938, by stating, *"We sincerely believe that the relationship into which you intimated your intention to enter will prove to be a pleasant and profitable undertaking and we wish to welcome you as an important member of our group which has tried so diligently to produce a finer product for the flying public."*

Little did Don realize this relationship would sour and fragment within a few short months, even weeks. Events within the Luscombe Airplane Corporation management

CHARLES E. BURGESS

(Above) The new factory addition comes together. Circa December 1938.

(Right) Another view of the soon-to-be-completed new factory addition.

CHARLES E. BURGESS

structure would test and eventually upset Luscombe's patience and his relationship with Klotz.

Though his intentions may have been otherwise at the beginning of his dealings with Don Luscombe, Klotz's later relationship with Don and other factory employees took on a more acrimonious tone. In time, Klotz cared little if his relationship with Don Luscombe was productive or friendly.

No doubt Klotz was well aware of the potential ramifications of his investment actions and the tense difficulties these actions might present. As the opportunities arose, Klotz loaned more money and, in turn, converted these loans into stock, all the while solidifying his control over Don's financially fragile company.

During November and December, Klotz advanced $90,000 to the Luscombe Airplane Corporation. On December 31, 1938, the corporation issued 90,000 shares of stock to effectively cancel this loan.

An aerial view of the Luscombe factory grounds as it existed in December 1938. WILLIAM ROBINSON

With a generous supply of money in hand, Don was able to start construction on the proposed factory expansion. Once more, the Austin Company of Toledo, Ohio, was contracted to build the new addition. In late November, ground was broken to erect this new structure.

The influx of money benefited the engineering department, also. This department was undertaking two major projects to improve the Model 8. The first project involved increasing the aircraft's gross weight to 1200 lbs. The second endeavor involved adding a more powerful engine.

Throughout the autumn months, Fred Knack and his engineering team sought ways to improve the Model 8's performance and utility. Originally certificated at 1130 lbs, Knack realized the airplane's gross weight could be increased. Though preliminary stress and structure analysis studies were started in September, the final paperwork was not completed and submitted to the Department of Commerce for certification until November.

To accommodate this gross weight increase, the wing's internal structure was modified slightly. Basically, the reinforcement on the main spar at the spar/strut attachment was lengthened.

On December 7, 1938, Ig Sargent took Model 8, NX20685 (s/n 839), through a series of takeoff tests leading towards government approval of the 1200 lbs gross weight certification. On December 8, Sargent flew a series of spin tests, at gross weight, in the same aircraft. No problems were encountered.

On December 12, Sargent flew the aircraft several more times for Department of Commerce approval tests. Department of Commerce inspector Joe Fornasero flew with Sargent during these tests. Shortly afterwards, the Luscombe Model 8 was approved for the increase to 1200 lbs gross weight.

The second improvement involved the installation of a more powerful power plant, a Continental A-65 motor. Continental Motors had been seeking ways to improve its very popular and very reliable A-50 power plant. The logical outgrowth of this development was the Continental A-65, an engine that provided sixty-five horsepower at 2350 rpm.

Aware the Luscombe Airplane Corporation could now meet their immediate financial obligations, the Continental Motors Corporation relaxed their previous credit restrictions. Furthermore, they made available a new, uprated to sixty-five horsepower engine for testing and eventual use. Don accepted one of these new engines in early December 1938.

In turn, the engineering department calculated the various stress, performance and weight and balance changes this new power plant would produce. Coupled with Continental Motors Corporation's figures, all computations pointed towards some remarkable performance gains.

To test this new airframe/engine combination, the first production Model 8, NC1327, the company demonstrator, was removed from service. Its Continental A-50-1 engine was removed and replaced with a Continental A-65-1 power plant. In turn, NC1327 was re-registered NX1327 to satisfy government regulations.

Ig Sargent braved a cold, West Trenton winter day and test flew this new combination for the first time on December 31, 1938. He returned from his one-and-a-half hour flight extremely pleased with the new increased performance.

On New Year's Day, 1939, Ig Sargent and Eddie Davis took turns flying NX1327. Both were quite surprised by the sprightly aircraft's new flight figures — 116 mph top speed, 102 mph cruise speed and an outstanding 1000 fpm initial rate of climb. True, the cold weather enhanced the performance, but Sargent and Davis both agreed the extra fifteen horses turned Luscombe's all-metal aircraft into a very responsive tiger. At least six more weeks of A-65 powered Model 8 test flying was undertaken, mostly by Sargent and Davis, before the improved airplane was approved for production.

But Sargent's and Davis' flight testing schedule was not limited to the two aforementioned airplanes. Each maintained an exhaustive pre-delivery test flight schedule of new production, Continental Motors A-50 powered Luscombe Model 8 airplanes. Sargent test flew at least six Model 8s in October, twelve in November and fifteen in December. Davis, on his behalf, test flew only one Model 8 in October, one in November and three in December.

One of the more unusual test flights occurred on December 27, 1938. Fritz King test flew NC22002 (s/n 852) the first U.S. registered Model 8 modified with a snow ski landing gear. Except for replacing the wheels with skis, the only difference between the standard gear and the ski gear was a tubular strut in place of the streamline wire. In-

CHARLES E. BURGESS

(Above) Luscombe "Fifty" construction inside the main hangar.

(Right) At least six Luscombe "Fifty" and "Sixty-Five" airplanes crowd the Luscombe Airplane Corporation hangar floor. Shortly after this photograph was taken, the new addition was opened easing production bottlenecks.

CHARLES E. BURGESS

terestingly, most, if not all, of the early Model 8s exported to Canada had this strut modification, yet the ski arrangement was not tested prior to their initial delivery.

Don was most pleased when he reviewed the October through December production figures. Almost fifty-five Model 8 airplanes were built during this period. Furthermore, Don was pleased by the progress made on the factory addition. The steel truss structure would be ready for occupancy within two or three months. Then, Don thought, mass production of his all-metal airplanes would begin in earnest shortly thereafter.

But December 1938 and January 1939 did not pass without their share of severe management and financial problems. Hiram Mallinson resigned abruptly as an LAC board member on December 13, 1938. In turn, he sold all of his stock in the corporation. Concurrently, company investor and former Phantom owner Henry Olmsted sold his LAC stock holdings, also.

Luscombe informed Klotz of these transactions, as he was obliged to do per an earlier agreement. Basically, this agreement stipulated neither Don nor any board member would sell any stock without informing Klotz. In turn, Klotz agreed not to issue any buying orders behind Don's back.

Yet, despite these covenants, Klotz's desires to gain total control of the LAC were strong. Soon, more stock, often obtained through dubious means, found its way into his control. Meanwhile, the price of the stock began a slow but steady upward climb, indicative that buying orders were being placed. Don noticed this fact and became furious.

In a scathing telegram to Boller dated January 4, 1939, Luscombe inquired, *"36,000 shares held in what appears as dummy names at Guaranty Trust Company in addition to shares held by other brokers. Stop. Please wire immediately what knowledge you have in matter."*

Boller responded quickly to Luscombe's inquiries, vigorously denying any knowledge of these actions. Later in the same day, Don penned a biting letter to Boller restating his feelings regarding the Guaranty Trust stock situation, *"I must state I cannot imagine who would give this bank buying orders for this amount or more. The Cluett-Melady stock is accounted for. Leopold has continually assured me that he has not issued buying orders and so long as he must rely on the whole-hearted support and trust of this organization, I cannot bring myself to suspect that he would in any way jeopardize the confidence we all have in him by such a breach of faith."*

Then Don dropped his own bombshell. Aware of the fact Klotz had acquired shares sufficient to give him control of the corporation, Don believed he would soon be ousted as president of the corporation. Don concluded his letter by stating: *"In view of our anxiety regarding these manipulations, I can only recommend that this corporation contract for the services of its President for the next several years without delay."*

Before the month was over, Don's worries proved accurate. Klotz recanted his denials and stated he was obliged to protect his interests. Thus, he admitted he had issued the buying orders. Furthermore, Klotz believed the LAC management was attempting, according to a January 30, 1939, letter from Don Luscombe to George Cluett, II, to, *"put things over behind his back."*

Leopold Klotz believed his comments were justified. LAC stock was appearing on the market from unknown sources. Fearful another party might attempt to buy the stock and gain or retain control of the company, Klotz had no choice but to buy these shares to protect his interests.

Little did he realize Don had been selling portions of his stock. The stock, once fifty cents a share, was now selling for almost three times that amount. Don, fully aware of Klotz's true intentions, made sure this wealthy investor was going to pay the price.

The surreptitious ploy to sell some of Don's holdings actually began sometime during late December, very shortly after the December Board of Directors meeting. Don called company employee Keith Funk to his office for consultations. Funk had been handling Don's stock transactions for several years and was intimately familiar with his boss' holdings.

Don looked at Funk and vented a few of his observations regarding the Klotz situation, but resolved to work closely with this investor. But the opportunity to make some money was great, Thus, Don asked Funk to broker or sell some of his, Don's, holdings.

At first, the amounts discussed were quite small and almost insignificant. A month later, however, this situation changed dramatically. Shortly after Don learned Klotz had, in fact, issued large buying orders, Don resolved to hit Klotz where it hurt the most — his pocketbook. Don exclaimed, *"If the #!?# wants the stock so bad, then we are going to make him pay for it!"*

Don and Keith Funk devised a plan whereby Don would sell or transfer portions of his stock to Funk. In turn, Funk would put the stock on the market in such a manner that it could not be traced back to Don.

As this stock came on the market, Klotz had no choice to but to buy it to protect his investment. Slowly but surely, the price went up as more buying orders were issued. Klotz spent more money and Don became a little more wealthy.

It took Klotz another month or more before he learned of Don's activities. When he did, a verbal confrontation ensued in Don's office the likes of which the Luscombe Airplane Corporation had never before heard.

Concurrently, another major stock-related concern weighed heavily on Don's already overburdened mind. This concern was the inability of the Luscombe Airplane Corporation to license airplanes in its name or obtain United States Army Air Corps contracts because of the corporation's dominant ownership by a foreign national. In this case, it was Mr. L.H.P. Klotz.

Don was keenly interested in bidding on a contract to furnish airplanes for a new Army Training Program. But affairs within the company, as well as current government regulations, hindered this lucrative goal.

At the time, Section 521 (b) of the Civil Aeronautics Act of 1938 provided: *"An aircraft shall be eligible for registration if, but only if — (1) It is owned by a citizen of the United States and is not registered under the laws of any foreign country."*

Furthermore, Section 401 (13) of the same Act defines *"Citizens of the United States"* as, among other things: *"a corporation or association created or organized under the laws of the United States or of any State, Territory, or possession of the United States, of which the president and two-thirds or more of the board of directors and other managing officers thereof are such individuals and in which at least 75 percentum of the voting interest is owned or controlled by persons who are citizens of the United States or one of its possessions."*

Incidentally this Act created the Civil Aeronautics Authority (CAA). Shortly thereafter, the Civilian Pilot Training Program (CPTP) came into being, a plan formulated by the new CAA and approved by then President Franklin D. Roosevelt who explained to an excited press, this plan, *"would boost the private flying industry by annually teaching 2,000 college students how to fly."*

Both Don Luscombe and Roger Johnson were frustrated by these obstructions and endeavored to find an acceptable solution. Each voiced his concerns regarding this delicate matter in a series of personal letters to Klotz.

In one letter to Klotz dated January 19, 1939, a concerned Luscombe stated: *"We are submitting our bid to the army on the small ships they will select for the Civilian Training program. It is, of course, necessary to make affidavit relative to stock owned by others than U.S. citizens. Since so many shares are now held by nominees, I am embarrassed with the question."*

On January 24, 1939, Don sent Klotz a telegram stating: *"We cannot accept Army bid unless three quarters stock held by United States citizens and Board must be 100 percent American. Can you arrange?"*

On January 28, Roger Johnson wrote to Klotz and suggested: *"The complication is that we can license ships for customers but we cannot license them in our own name unless we comply with this section of the Act. My suggestion is that we, in order to satisfy everyone concerned, get lined up within the next six months to list our stock somewhere and then we cannot in any way be effected in both Army and civil business."*

On January 30, 1939, Don wrote to George B. Cluett, II, and stated: *"More serious than the army business is C.A.A. itself, which demand two-thirds American ownership. At the present moment we dare not license an airplane in the Corporation's name. Although Leopold will put his stock in the name of American citizens, again I must be asked to put my tongue in my cheek when signing my name under oath as to the ownership of that stock."*

On February 3, 1939, Johnson wrote to George Cluett, II, and stated Klotz: *"called me yesterday and said that he was working as fast as possible on a way to have his stock listed in other person's names so that we would be able to accept government contracts and license ships in our own name."* [93]

When the dust finally settled regarding the aforementioned issues, Klotz was somewhat successful in getting a substantial portion of his stock listed in other individuals' or companies' names. Most, if not all the names listed were American citizens or corporations controlled by American citizens. Thus, the company had the opportunity to make a "legal" bid on the Army contracts.

Moreover, the question of registration with the Civil Aeronautics Authority was resolved completely six months later with the formation of the North American Investment Company. Klotz transferred enough shares of Luscombe Airplane Corporation stock to this new corporation, or holding company of sorts, to bring ownership of the Luscombe Airplane Corporation technically within the C.A.A. regulations.[94]

Don Luscombe was left emotionally and physically exhausted by these events. Yet, there was to be no rest. His problems with Henry Boller, festering for several months, soon developed into a most difficult impasse. Sadly, the resolutions of these problems would cost Don his company and his airplane manufacturing visions.

Don could scarcely contain his anger towards Boller at times. Moreover, Don was incensed Klotz entrusted so much authority in an individual man Don considered, at best, inept.

The differences between Luscombe and Boller began to fester almost from the moment Boller set foot on the LAC property several months earlier. His haughty attitude endeared himself to few people, particularly Luscombe.

Now, serving as Klotz's confidant, Henry Boller took a more active role in the company's day-to-day affairs. At first, Don bit his tongue regarding Boller's interference so as not to upset Klotz or any amicable working relationship each sought to achieve. Within a short time, however, Don began to make his feelings known as conditions deteriorated. Boller's affairs within the company's overall history offers much insight into the difficult conditions that soon prevailed.

Shortly after Klotz made his initial cash infusions, Boller began to make frequent visits to the factory to discuss marketing plans and sales. Hired initially by Klotz as a sales manager within the Luscombe organization, Boller thought he had this right. However, the coarse methods he employed to keep track of production and marketing goals and report all to Klotz, only served to infuriate the Luscombe Airplane Corporation management.

Company treasurer Roger Johnson made a note to Don Luscombe on December 15, 1938 and complained of Boller's developing tactics: *"It seems Leopold is going to hold us to every remark we make, so maybe we had better get together on statistics so that we can enjoy a smooth business life and not have Boller dropping in here every few days to ask for explanations."*

Boller then made another surprising demand. In mid-December 1938, shortly after Mallinson's resignation, he insisted he should be elected to the Board of Directors by virtue of the 9,600 shares of LAC stock in his possession, evidently obtained from Mallinson's and Olmsted's previous holdings. Klotz suggested management call a Board meeting before the first of the year to put Boller in as Klotz's nominee. Thus, Klotz would be represented if the Securities and Exchange Commission balked or did not approve Klotz's massive stock purchases.

A Board meeting convened shortly before Christmas and Boller was duly elected to the Luscombe Airplane Corporation Board of Directors. He filled the vacancy left by Mallinson. But Boller's interference in corporate matters did not stop with sales or as a Board member, however. It extended to areas in which Boller had absolutely no experience — air racing.

In one particular case, Boller countermanded Don Luscombe's decision not to participate in a Miami, Florida, light airplane air race. The results wreaked havoc with Don's Model 8 marketing plans. Lacking proper preparation, Luscombe airplanes were overwhelmed by the competition, most notably Aeronca airplanes.[95]

Don could no longer contain his displeasure with Boller. He lodged a formal complaint with Leopold Klotz. In a letter to Klotz dated January 9, 1939, Don drew upon his previous air derby and racing promotion experience and stated emphatically: *"Henry Boller, in his own overzealousness to accomplish certain ends, countermanded my judgment and submitted the entrance fees out of his own pocket. This permitted all the Luscombes in Miami to enter the race, and with their standard engines competing against the more powerful ones found themselves being led to the slaughter. This puts Aeronca in a position to make their proclamation to the world and all the aviation journals that they have won the race, which included Luscombes, and therefore enjoy the reputation for being the fastest American light plane. It simply means that it makes our sales effort throughout the nation about five times as hard as they would have been otherwise, and definitely puts us in a position where we cannot refute their statement to the export market.*

I am obliged to go on record at this point to advise you that, I cannot assume any responsibility for the success of this enterprise if our judgment and policies are to be interfered with by willing but inexperienced enthusiasts."

Klotz chose not to respond formally to Luscombe's letter. His mind was preoccupied with the stock ownership and C.A.A. problems. Yet, during a series of meetings held between Don Luscombe and Leopold Klotz in Montreal, Canada (Klotz's home at the time), during the third week of January, the problems with Boller were aired and discussed at great length.

During these meetings, Luscombe learned Klotz had no intention of replacing Boller. In fact, Klotz resorted to arm twisting and insisted Don and the company accept Boller into the organization, virtually at all costs. Don returned to West Trenton dejected and felt *"my week's salary must be charged off as a loss so far as any productive contributions to the business."*

Don summed-up his sour feelings regarding the whole Klotz-Boller matter in an incredibly candid and insightful letter to George B. Cluett, II, dated January 30, 1939. (Another portion of this letter is cited in an earlier paragraph in this chapter.) In this lengthy and most frank letter, Luscombe stated: *"Pressure is being exerted to make us accept Boller into the organization. This will result in the departure of existing members of our personnel, who I am sure will neither accept this exertion of force graciously nor mutely. Embarrassing investigations will follow and I will not relish inquiries to determine my qualifications as a perjurer. Although acquitted I am sure our competitors would be ungenerous enough to dub us the little German company at West Trenton. Henry Boller meeting the trade would hardly dispel the suspicion.*

Leopold has been influenced in his opinion of Boller by Miss Montgomery. I have been obliged to tell him that I cannot accept responsibility of the company if Boller is forced upon us. Boller's record is bad, and I am in a position where I cannot go into personal phases of his history, but must confine my remarks to his lack of qualifications. As a Sales Manager I question his ability to write an English letter, since he can only speak broken English. This should be enough, but the bond of the Vaterland [sic] has dulled Leopold's perception of this connection, and I suspect he has committed himself about Boller to Miss Montgomery, whose judgment he esteems. Any attempt to discredit motives in this quarter could result in a Hannibal victory and I could hardly be forgiven for having presented the type of embarrassment so detrimental to male pride.

Despite Leopold's early life, which may have provoked a highly suspicious nature regarding all strangers, I still regard him as a cultured and fine young man. He has a banker's point of view and will I believe take advantage in money matters. Our difficulty in establishing confidence has been impaired by the Boller-Montgomery combine. Boller has fish to fry, and Miss Montgomery, I suspect, has provoked mistrust down here that Leopold will feel the need of Boller as a major-domo [sic]. Once in this position Boller and Miss Montgomery dare aspire new worlds to conquer. This is the Boller admission. It's all legitimate enough except that we are caught in the middle of the ambition which has maneuvered us into a corner where we can't do business legally and stick to the whole truth.

Leopold's attempt to strengthen his position has only weakened it. He must also learn that he is better off letting us, who know pretty well what we are doing, alone rather than sending us someone who doesn't know, to disturb and tear the heart out of the organization."

Don aimed to clarify many of the differences that existed between himself, Klotz and Boller at a special Board of Directors meeting held at the Hotel Waldorf-Astoria in New York City on February 23, 1939. Yet, quite the opposite occurred. Despite Don Luscombe's many and constant objections, Boller was employed by the Board of Directors as production manager.

The Board accepted Klotz's recommendations of Boller in lieu of the usual references and recommendations. The Board, obliged to fulfill their fiduciary responsibilities, had little choice when confronted with the company's principal stockholder.

At this same meeting, Boller resigned his Board position to accept the production manager position. This action allowed Ernst Oberhumer, Klotz's closest financial and corporate legal advisor, to be elected to the Board to fill the vacancy left by Boller.[96]

Don Luscombe's proposed contract was discussed at length. A minimum salary of $7,800 per year, to be paid yearly from January 1, 1939 to December 31, 1942 was approved. Additionally, Don Luscombe would participate in a profit sharing program, generally 5 percent of the annual net profits.

As an extra perk, Don was permitted to enjoy free occupancy and use of the Caretaker's House, the two car garage, the tennis court and skeet grounds for at least five years after termination of his contract, regardless of the reason for such termination. Oberhumer consented to review the contract as written to clarify any ambiguities and insert any amendments as outlined.

Boller's inept skills as production manager became apparent almost immediately. Half-completed airplanes, waiting for certain parts to be built or ordered, became the norm rather than the exception. Communications between the shop foremen and Boller all but broke down completely. Worse, Boller preferred to spend more time in New York City on "business" than taking care of his responsibilities within the factory.

Former production manager Ben Melcher, now stripped of his position, was assigned to select and oversee installation of new production machinery in the factory's new addition. This building was all but finished by late February, and lacked only the essential tools and machinery necessary to start full-scale, assembly line production of Luscombe airplanes.

Even though Melcher had responsibility in this area, Boller often dictated what pieces of equipment would be bought and where they should be placed. Boller had Klotz's ear. Melcher did not. Even while Don and his management team were emotionally ravaged by the many preceding events, much productive factory and sales work was accomplished.

In early January, Otis Massey, owner of Massey and Ransom Flying Service — a Luscombe distributor in Denver, Colorado, — placed an order for a Luscombe Model 4. This airplane, NC22026 (s/n 405), was quickly assembled from the Model 4 parts on hand.

On January 19, 1939, the Bill of Sale was signed transferring ownership to Massey. However, inclement weather prevented any test flights until a week later. On January 26, Alfred "Fritz" King took this newest Model 4 aloft for a quick, pre-delivery test flight. All was in order, so he turned the airplane over to Massey. On the following day, Massey and his airplane headed west for Denver. This Luscombe Model 4 was the last of its type to be built and sold by the Luscombe Airplane Corporation.

Almost eighteen Model 8 airplanes were produced during January 1939, with eleven more Model 8s produced during February. The flight testing schedule remained quite heavy for Ig Sargent and Eddie Davis. Fritz King and Lou Coghill helped as needed.

Ironically, many of these planes could not be delivered due to bad weather. For a brief period during late January and early February, the company became a "second home" to several ferry pilots and owners waiting to fly their new, all-metal Luscombe 8 airplanes home.

Furthermore, as conditions allowed, several Luscombe Model 8 airplanes were ferried to nearby Pitcairn Field to be stored in the spacious Pitcairn Aircraft hangar. Many of these airplanes were purely stock and remained in their bare metal state without so much as a painted stripe.

Throughout the early 1939 months and weather permitting, flight testing of the Continental A-65 powered Luscombe Model 8 continued at a brisk pace. Approval to use this new power plant was expected by early March.

In an effort to obtain more accurate performance figures and solve unforeseen engineering problems, a newer production Model 8, NX22055 (s/n 881), was pulled from the line and replaced NX1327. Interestingly, its A-65 power plant came from NX1327. This newer Luscombe Model 8 became the primary aircraft to be used in the ATC certification tests.

For its part, NX1327, refitted with an A-50 engine, was returned to its company demonstrator role and was often used for other ATC related tests including wheels, brakes, engine cooling, etc.

Noteworthy, the 65 hp airplane became known as the Luscombe "Sixty-five" within the Luscombe Airplane Corporation organization. Marketing plans were undertaken to tell the aviation world of this new airplane as soon as certification was imminent. The marketing strategy planned to advertise the Luscombe "65" as the sporty cousin to the Luscombe "50."

Meanwhile, the Army entertained bids for its new Civilian Pilot Training Program (CPTP) airplane. Don Luscombe was invited to enter the Model 8 into this competition.

On February 27, both Sargent and Davis departed West Trenton, New Jersey, and headed for Wright Field near Dayton, Ohio. Sargent flew NC22056, a stock 50 hp Luscombe 8. Davis, opting to fly a different route to Dayton, flew NX22055, the 65 horsepowered Luscombe 65.

Sargent made his demonstration flights on February 28. Davis followed with a couple of brief flights two days later. The evaluating Army Air Corps personnel were impressed by the performance each Luscombe Model 8 aircraft possessed. They informed Sargent and Davis a decision would be made shortly and added little else.

Meanwhile, events in West Trenton were less optimistic. Luscombe Airplane Corporation management and workers became increasingly disillusioned

Ig Sargent flew this stock Luscombe "Fifty" to Wright Field, Dayton, Ohio, to participate in an Army evaluation for the Civilian Pilot Training Program.

U.S. ARMY AIR FORCES PHOTO NUMBER 18-WP-63345

with Boller. Quiet conversations often spilled over into open debate regarding the man's abilities.

Don was aware of this developing strife and he made repeated efforts to inform Klotz of the problem. Klotz, in turn, told Don to make do with what he had. Don was exasperated! He decided to force the Boller issue to a head. Don reasoned a collective strategy might capture Klotz's attention and result in some positive action.

On the first Sunday in March 1939, Don called his shop supervisors and other key employees to a meeting at the nearby Bear Tavern Inn. At this meeting, Don explained the problems he encountered trying to dismiss Boller and suggested a group effort might be more successful.

In an action that may have been a "first" for a corporation president, Don Luscombe asked these employees to "strike" or "walkout" as a statement of protest regarding Boller. Don hoped this threat would force Klotz to remove Boller because production would grind to a halt. Don acknowledged there was great risk in that everybody could lose their positions, but he cautioned the options were worse.

On March 13, 1939, the several employees of the Luscombe Airplane Corporation, designating themselves as "Keymen," addressed a petition (written by Don Luscombe) to the Chairman of the Board of Directors requesting the dismissal or resignation of Henry Boller on the following grounds:
1. Demoralization of factory organization.
2. Evident lack of experience with manufacturing.
3. Lack of the quality of leadership and judgment in handling personnel.

The "Keymen" who signed this petition included Nick Nordyke, William E. Force, Duwen Johnson, Robert Kittler, Charles Burgess, Jules E. DeCrescenzo, Louis W. Coghill, Keith G. Funk, Rhys P. Jones, Ralph Coston and William B. Shepard.

Upon receipt of this petition, Don fired Boller. In turn, Don went upstairs to the Production Control office and told everyone present, quite excitedly, *"I just fired Boller."* Then, turning to Bill Shepard, he added, *"Bill, you're production manager."*

Bill Shepard had been writing shop production orders with Rolfe Gregory during this period. In fact, during Boller's brief, two week period as production manager, Boller approached Shepard and flatly stated, *"Oh, you're somebody else I have to get along with."*

Don called Klotz who was furious when he received the news! Faced with the prospects "his" airplane company would all but shutdown if the walkout took place, Klotz suspended Boller temporarily until a complete and thorough review of the facts had been made. Leopold H.P. Klotz intended to face Don Luscombe head-on. Klotz arrived on the property the next day and asked Don for the opportunity to interview the workmen who presented the petition. This request was granted.

Klotz gave the men two days to withdraw their petition. They did not and it was presented once more the following morning. Klotz stayed on the property two days interviewing the signators individually and collectively, with and without Boller present. The tone during these conversations was often quite threatening with respect to any future employment in the company.

At a meeting of the factory's foremen, Klotz sent a strong signal, *"Right now, Don controls the Board of Directors, but there is not always the same Board of Directors."* No doubt Klotz's comment was in reference to a forthcoming shareholders' meeting scheduled for March. Still, the Boller matter was not resolved. A special Board of Directors' meeting was called by Klotz.

Concurrently, he asked Ernst Oberhumer to study the matter carefully. Similarly, he asked Oberhumer to report on the legality of any extended services contracts Don Luscombe had or might make with the Board of Directors.

On March 29, 1939, Don Luscombe, Roger Johnson and Board members George B. Cluett, II, Ernst Oberhumer, Ignatius Sargent and Daniel Simonds met at the Hotel Lexington in New York City to discuss the current situation. Oberhumer informed the Board that Leopold Klotz was present within the hotel and was available to appear when it was agreeable and convenient to the Board.

From the outset, a very eloquent Oberhumer made it clear he represented the best interests of Klotz and other principle shareholders. As such, he said he would cast any vote based strictly on facts, as any good attorney would, not emotional bias. Don, on his behalf as the chief officer of the company, made it clear he felt *"obliged to decline any suggestion that we have any more representatives of the Klotz interests."* The meeting lasted better than an hour-and-a-half. These discussions often became quite heated, yet tempers remained checked.

As a possible solution to the Boller crisis, Oberhumer suggested an outside engineering firm be contracted to investigate Boller's competency. This idea was vetoed by other Board members and the bulk of the discussions remained centered on Boller's competency and his working relationship with the men on the production floor.

Before the meeting ended, the Board voted to settle the Boller matter via mail ballots postmarked no latter than April 5, 1939. Similarly, the Board voted that no one would be hired to replace Boller until the votes were counted. Furthermore, it was voted upon that Boller's "vacation" would be continued indefinitely.

Shortly before the meeting ended, the following discussion took place, as recorded in the Stenographer's Minutes:

"MR. LUSCOMBE [sic]: We have had a tentative proposal from Mr. Klotz relative to the purchase of certain shares of stock which seem to stand in the way of your exercising your opinion as to how this business should be conducted.

MR. OBERHUMER: Right. There are various ideas in the air. What we want to decide here is the broad future of the company. Have you any idea what you want to do, whether you want to give up your shares or not to give up your shares, whether you want to retire from the management or you want to be in the management? It is an incompatible combination.

MR. LUSCOMBE [sic]: If it continues to be incompatible, as I rather suspect it will be, if we are to have certain figures in the company, I can see there is nothing else for me to do but retire."

Even as Don made his comments, he made it clear to all present he had "an obligation towards the people who have sponsored this thing from the beginning and I have the same concern for their holdings." This point was acknowledged by all present. Though Don's days at his company were obviously numbered, he made it clear he was not to sink without a good fight. Don made one last appeal to his Board to sway their vote.

Attaching a copy of the aforementioned petition, the following letter from Don Luscombe to the LAC Board of Directors, dated March 31, 1939, aptly describes the state of the company's affairs as of that date as well as Don's sensitive feelings regarding the whole affair:

"Attached herewith is a copy of the petition which has been signed by the foremen; a copy of a letter to Mr. Klotz; and a copy of a letter to Mr. Oberhumer, who requested information relative to a situation involving Mr. Boller.

A threatened walkout in protest to Mr. Boller has necessitated a suspension of Mr. Boller's services until the Board has had occasion to review the case from various angles. In view of the fact that your president has gone on record in protesting Mr. Boller's qualifications and being possessed of strong convictions not favorable to Mr. Boller, and since Mr. Boller has been sponsored by a principal stockholder, who has been equally persistent in championing Mr. Boller's virtues, deference to this stockholder is again suggested by appealing to the Board rather than to the president for proper action.

The minutes of February 23rd, 1939 read as follows:

It was made plain that Mr. Boller would be an employee and could be discharged by the president, subject to action of the Board of Directors. This position was in no way guaranteed.

A telephone call from Mr. Oberhumer on Sunday, March 19th, intimated that the president had not been empowered to act alone.

Mr. Klotz asked for the right to interview the workmen who had presented the petition. This right was granted. The men were then given a day to withdraw their petition, with the result that this petition was again presented on the following morning. Mr. Klotz was on the property for two days where he discussed the situation with the men individually and collectively both with and without Mr. Boller. During the course of these discussions he belittled the efforts and competency of the existing management and implied that unless the men would cooperate with Mr. Boller no more money would be put into the business, which would rapidly go broke and leave the men without jobs anyway.

Mr. Klotz has stated that the Board of Directors have no right to contract with Mr. Luscombe for extended services, quoting Mr. Oberhumer's findings on extended contracts. Mr. Klotz further states his lack of satisfaction with Mr. Luscombe's business judgment and stated his intention to withhold an effective contract.

Mr. Klotz and Mr. Boller have continued to intimate their intention to change the Board of Directors that officers more to their liking might be appointed.

Mr. Klotz has interfered in the purchase of equipment, in the purchase of materials, personnel, and sales. He has attempted to intimidate the management with threats and has assumed coercive tactics as above stated.

He has made the statement that he held enough proxies at the first stockholders' meeting to have carried the election.

The act relative to citizenship reads in part — 'of which the president and two-thirds or more of the Board of Directors and other managing officers thereof are such individuals and in which at least seventy-five percentum of the voting interest is owned or controlled by persons who are citizens of the U.S. or one of its possessions.'

Legally the stock in Mr. Klotz's name is within proper limits. His recent assumption of details of management, however, seems to be indicative of his

LUCKY BUYERS IN 1939 WILL GET A "LUSCOMBE 50"

ADVANTAGES!

FASTER
LONGER RANGE
BETTER VISIBILITY
MORE LUGGAGE
LONGER LIFE
LESS MAINTENANCE
FIRE RESISTANT
BIG PLANE PERFORMANCE
STUDENTS FLOCK TO IT
EASY PAYMENT TERMS IF DESIRED

PERFORMANCE

TOP SPEED	109 MPH
CRUISING	96 MPH
LANDING	37 MPH
SERVICE CEILING	14000 ft.
CLIMB 1st MIN.	750 ft.
RANGE	400 mi.

SPECIFICATIONS

SPAN	35 ft.
LENGTH	20 ft.
HEIGHT	5 ft. 10 in.
TREAD	6 ft. 4 in.
WING AREA	140 sq. ft.
WING LOADING	8.07 lbs.
POWER LOADING	22.6 lbs.
EMPTY WEIGHT	650 lbs.
USEFUL LOAD	550 lbs.
GROSS WEIGHT	1200 lbs.
BAGGAGE	55 lbs.
GAS CAPACITY	15 gal.

The only all-metal lightplane in production. New factory facilities permit early deliveries on orders placed immediately. A few dealer franchises yet available

LUSCOMBE AIRPLANE CORP., West Trenton, N. J.

AERO DIGEST, FEBRUARY 1939, P. 80

---

control. An ever growing doubt as to how this control might withstand Federal investigation becomes troublesome to your officers who are expected to temporize with the fact and make affidavit that the ratios of ownership are legal and proper."

Klotz was incensed, no doubt, by Don Luscombe's statements. Yet, Klotz waited to hear from Oberhumer before he acted. Two days later, Oberhumer's report arrived.

Basically, this report summarized the management friction, the personnel issues and the legal questions. Oberhumer addressed each area and offered his suggestions to remedy the problems at hand.

With respect to management, Oberhumer suggested a new management team must be instituted, irrespective of whose claims were right or wrong. He observed, *"This conception had been accepted,"* but he did not elaborate who accepted this conception.

Furthermore, Oberhumer advised caution when dealing with the workers. If the old management left in anger, production would be crippled. These men would not suffer appreciably from such actions as there was a heavy demand for men with such metalworking experience. Oberhumer suggested a cooperative and smooth transition from the old management to new management to avoid any unnecessary production or financial losses.

Touching upon the Boller situation, Oberhumer suggested keeping Boller away for at least three months, possibly longer, until the old management helped the new management get established. Oberhumer conceded Boller could become a valuable man based upon his flying experience, but suggested he should return to a position *"where he can learn the engineering end of aviation."*

Finally, Oberhumer stated the legal issues were raised *"only from personal issues and represent actions of the Luscombe group in building up a legal case in furtherance of their claims."* Oberhumer believed these issues would *"disappear automatically with the solution of the personal issues."*

When the votes were counted, it became to all who were present at the March 29 meeting that Don's days as president of the corporation he founded and held so dear were over. The differences between Luscombe and the principal shareholders had reached an impasse.

The only acceptable solution was Don Luscombe's resignation.

Thus, Donald A. Luscombe's airplane manufacturing dreams, goals and visions would soon disappear with a stroke of a pen.[97]

"The basic fact of life today is the tremendous pace of change in human life."
Jawaharlal Nehru (1889 - 1964)
Credo. Reprinted in *New York Times*
[September 7, 1958]

Chapter Sixteen

Post Luscombe, Luscombe

Don Luscombe took a long, deliberate, reflective walk around the factory grounds. Lost in thought, Don replayed the hectic events of the previous months in his bedraggled mind and tried to make sense of what went wrong. He felt a slight tinge of betrayal and tried to figure who or what forces conspired against him.

Besides Oberhumer, somebody on the Board cast their support towards Klotz. Don knew it wasn't Cluett or Sargent. Was it Roger Johnson, or Daniel Simonds, perhaps?

Though Don was disheartened, he gazed towards the future with an unwavering optimism. True, he had worked so hard and so diligently in a futile attempt to attain his dreams, but other productive endeavors lay before him. Don knew life presented many challenges. He knew life presented many rewards, also.

Don was concerned his company was being taken from him by individuals whom, Don thought, were amateurs and knew nothing about airplane manufacturing. As such, he was genuinely distressed for the well-being of his men, the many workers who shared his vision over the previous difficult years and had, literally, sweat blood to see these visions become reality.

Don did not know what would become of these gentlemen as Leopold H.P. Klotz developed the company to meet his own airplane production goals. Don knew the "family" atmosphere that had grown and prospered around the Luscombe Airplane Corporation would all but disappear under Klotz's sometimes arrogant and impulsive leadership style.

Only Klotz's legal advisor, Ernst Oberhumer, showed any methodical or logical foresight in his management style, though he never worked at the company. Instead, Oberhumer remained behind the scenes and exercised his position through the LAC Board of Directors.

If Don could have foreseen in early April 1939 that Klotz would actually improve upon many of Don's original all-metal airplane mass production ideas, such as an overhead conveyor system (an idea conceived originally by Ben Melcher and the first of its

Don Luscombe   ELEANORE LUSCOMBE SHURTZ COLLECTION

What Don Luscombe might have seen if he had remained with the company he founded. Here, Luscombe Model 8 fuselages advance along an overhead conveyor assembly system, perhaps the first of its kind installed in a light airplane manufacturing operation. JAMES B. ZAZAS COLLECTION

type to be used in light airplane manufacturing), he may have been impressed somewhat with the efficiency and future production goals the youthful investor from Montreal had in store for the company.

But Klotz wasn't talking about his future plans, except to his closest advisors and investors. Don was left to face a most uncertain future.

For now, at least, Don was still president of his company and still had work to do, even if it was in a "figurehead" role. Airplanes had to be built and delivered to customers and dealers. Advertising was still important in the company's sales plans. Don tended to his duties as best he could under the circumstances.

Ernst Oberhumer and Leopold H.P. Klotz, meanwhile, worked to draft an "agreement" detailing the conditions of Don's resignation. It would be at least mid-April before this document was ready for the signatures of all principal parties.

Many Luscombe Airplane Corporation workers were aware of the difficult and often testy situation between Don Luscombe and Leopold Klotz. Though rumors ran rampant, most knew enough "facts" to realize Klotz was "taking over" the operation. Many workers and students harbored strong feelings regarding the current situation, but most chose to remain quiet and keep their opinions to themselves. They were still employed and wanted to continue working.

Despite the mayhem of February and March, at least nineteen new Model 8 airplanes rolled off the assembly line, eleven in February and eight in March. Likewise, at least ten airplanes rolled through the company's doors during April.

March's sluggish sale record was attributable, in part, to the introduction of the Luscombe "65." This airplane was identical to the "Fifty" except for the more powerful engine mounted firmly on the nose. The production line needed only a few days to adjust, but

JOHN LENGENFELDER

(Left) The graceful lines of the Luscombe "65" are highlighted in this photograph. This particular Model 8 was photographed in Tulsa, Oklahoma. Circa April 1939.

(Right) Luscombe "Sixty-Five" NC22093 (s/n 922) was the first Model 8 to be equipped with Edo Aircraft Corporation floats. First flown by Alfred "Fritz" King on May 20, 1939, this version was priced to sell for $3179.

JAMES B. ZAZAS COLLECTION

these few days robbed the company of a couple new airplanes.

Additionally, there may have been a temporary slump in customers taking orders due to a bad midwinter's weather. At least four Luscombe "50" airplanes were ferried to Pitcairn Field in January and February for a month's storage in a hangar until dealers or customers came to pickup their airplanes.

Ig Sargent and Eddie Davis continued to test fly and demonstrate these new airplanes. Many tests involved such things as new mufflers, Shinn wheels and tires, and improved motor mounts. NC1327 was used to undertake the majority of these tests. To be legal, the "C" in the NC1327 had to be X'd out with tape for any flight with parts or equipment not approved previously for use on the airplane.

On February 25, Ig Sargent flew an exhaustive series of tests for the "Sixty-five" Approved Type Certificate. His efforts proved successful and the Luscombe "65" was approved for production within days.

Dimensionally, the Luscombe "65" was the same as the Luscombe "50." But the extra fifteen horses on the nose offered a startling leap in performance. The airplane's cruise speed was now 104 mph, unlike the "Fifty's" 96 mph. Additionally, maximum speed was listed as 115 mph, as compared to the "Fifty's" 109 mph.

Luscombe "65" production began in March. The price was set at $1975 Flyaway Factory. Advertisements heralding the Luscombe "65" were carried in many magazines including *Aero Digest*, *Western Flying* and *Sportsman Pilot*. Five months later a Luscombe "65" floatplane joined the Luscombe airplane family and was priced to sell for $3170.[98]

Though Luscombe "50" production continued, the days were numbered for this no frills, A-50 powered airplane. The more powerful A-65 was a proven and reliable power plant, and very popular with many buyers. Pilots clamored for a shiny new, all-metal Luscombe airplane powered by the Continental A-65. Their call, *"I'll take an all-metal Luscombe"* echoed many of the advertisements that appeared during the period.

Innovative advertising continued to draw hundreds of inquires for the Luscombe "50" and "65." One Luscombe airplane was displayed in the heart of New York City. Carl Evers, the New York area Luscombe distributor, rented a modest showroom on New York City's Park Avenue beginning in August 1939. A Luscombe "65" — sans right wing — was placed on permanent display in what was the country's first airplane showroom. The idea was Evers' and business proved to be excellent with half of the airplanes eventually sold being Luscombe floatplanes.

In time, other Luscombe airplane showrooms were set-up in Indianapolis, Indiana; Perth Amboy, New Jersey; Philadelphia, Pennsylvania; Grand Rapids, Michigan; Chicago, Illinois; and the Exhibition Hall at the 1939 World's Fair in New York City. Other cities were added eventually.

The Luscombe "65's" spirited performance soon caught the eyes and ears of racing enthusiasts, most notably, famed aviatrix Jacqueline Cochran. She was determined to set a new speed record in one of the lightplane classes.

With the full backing of the Luscombe Airplane Corporation, a stock Luscombe "65," NC22070 (s/n 896), was selected for this record attempt. On April 8, 1939, Ig Sargent piloted NC22070 to an anxiously waiting Miss Cochran at Floyd Bennett Field, New York. Jackie Cochran flew a 100 km speed course at 105.6 mph establishing a new lightplane record. This record would stand for many months to come.[99]

During this ambitious period, new equipment was installed in the modern, 9200 square foot factory addition. Shears, air drills, rivet hammers, die making equipment, heat treating equipment and other items were added. This latest equipment would boost production many fold. The new building was scheduled to be ready for production use by mid-summer 1939.

Once more, Chuck Burgess was instrumental in solving some thorny production and labor reduction problems. Several months earlier (September or October 1938), Burgess made some drill templates for the aft fuselage skins with matching templates for the aft fuselage frames. Thus, it was now possible to pre-drill these parts and then assemble the skins to the fuselage frames with sheet metal screws or fasteners to form the fuselage cones before placing them in the fuselage jig for final riveting.

This process ensured the accuracy of the location of each rivet. Furthermore, the concept of interchangeable parts for production and repairs became reality. Just as important, the labor to produce each part was reduced considerably.

An often printed photograph shows several aft fuselage cones standing on end at the Luscombe Airplane Corporation factory. These cones are a result of Chuck Burgess' foresight and hard work.

When the press brake was installed in the new addition during the spring of 1939, Burgess had it set up with gang punches and dies to punch all the rivet holes in one edge of a skin in one stroke. After punching one edge of all the skins called for in the shop order, the dies were rearranged to punch the other edge until the fore and aft edges of the fuselage skins had been punched.

Quite obviously, this process was faster and

more accurate than locating and drilling the holes in each skin individually. However, the matching holes in the fuselage frame flanges still had to be drilled one at a time, using the appropriate drill template for the frame. This permitted assembling the skins and bulkheads with sheet metal screws.

When production operations commenced in the new addition in early August 1939, the Luscombe Airplane Corporation production capability increased from barely two or three new airplanes a week to a new airplane daily. Within a year, this number swelled to two, sometimes three airplanes a day.

Don took a sanguine approach to the events unfolding around him. One balmy April night, shortly before he resigned, Don invited Bill Shepard to his home. Stretched out on the floor, his head and shoulders propped on the living room sofa, Don commented, *"It's getting soggy, Bill."*

Don resigned himself to the fact "his" company was lost. Now it was time to admit the facts at hand, sign the agreement and move forward. On April 13, 1939, Ernst Oberhumer presented Don a ten page document detailing the terms of Don's resignation from the Luscombe Airplane Corporation. Reviewing this document, Don realized it was fair, yet most specific in its terms.

The terms of the agreement between Donald A. Luscombe and Ernst Oberhumer, who was serving as proxy to Leopold Klotz, included the following salient points. Luscombe agreed:

1. To resign as president and director of the Luscombe Airplane Corporation.

2. To procure the resignation of George B. Cluett, II, as a Director of said corporation.

3. To sell 12,500 shares of his (Don's) stock holding in Luscombe Airplane Corporation to Oberhumer, his nominee or assigns, at a price of $2.25 per share, free of commissions.

4. To procure the sale by Mrs. Luscombe of 3,500 shares of said corporation to Oberhumer, his nominee or assigns, at the same price and terms.

5. To give an option, good until August 30, 1939, to Oberhumer, his nominees or assigns, to purchase all or any part of 2,731 shares of Luscombe's stock holdings in Luscombe Airplane Corporation at the price of $2.50 per share, free of commissions, and a further option, good until January 10, 1940, to purchase all or any part of 2,730 shares of Luscombe's stock holdings in Luscombe Airplane Corporation at $2.50 per share, free of commissions.

6. To vacate the Caretaker House dwelling located on the grounds leased by the Luscombe Airplane Corporation not later than April 30, 1939.

7. To release and relinquish any contractual agreements or other rights which he may have against Luscombe Airplane Corporation or its Board of Directors, whether such rights be in writing or not.

8. To, within a period of one year from the date the agreement was signed, not directly or indirectly, design, produce, sell or offer for sale any airplane of 65 horsepower or less which carries two people, nor any airplane that can be offered for sale for less than $2,100 without accessories, nor any airplane that embraces the essential features of design found in the Luscombe Model 4, which sells for $4,000, or the Luscombe Phantom, which sells for $6,000.

9. To, within a period of three months from the date hereof not, directly or indirectly, employ or become associated with any person who was an officer or employee of the Luscombe Airplane Corporation.

10. To turn over to a representative of Oberhumer forthwith all available information (including original drawings and engineering data) necessary for the production of the current models of airplanes of the Luscombe Airplane Corporation, and would expressly specify and explain those points on which no written records are available.

11. That during the period of one year from the date hereof he would hold himself available to the Board of Directors of said corporation, its president and general manager, for consultation and advice, at such times and places as may be mutually convenient.

12. That during the period of one year from the date hereof he would not make any statements or do any act that will be detrimental to the interest of the Luscombe Airplane Corporation or violate any terms of this agreement.

Ernst Oberhumer, on the other hand, agreed to several conditions, also. The following are the more salient terms agreed by Oberhumer:

1. Would purchase and pay for the 16,000 shares of Luscombe Airplane Corporation stock (12,500 shares held in Don's name; 3,500 held in Mrs. Luscombe's name.)

2. Would cast his vote as a Director of the Luscombe Airplane Corporation and to use his best efforts to persuade the other Directors to vote for payment to Luscombe of the sum of $7,800 as a part of the consideration for the entry into this agreement, which sum shall be payable in twelve monthly installments of $650, commencing with the month of April 1939.

3. Would, upon the vacation of the premises by Luscombe, cast his vote as a Director of the Luscombe Airplane Corporation for the payment by said corporation to Luscombe of the sum of $2,000 as compensation for the improvements made by Luscombe to said dwelling.

4. Would forthwith pay said amount to Luscombe in the event the Luscombe Airplane Corporation does not agree to the provisions listed above.

Finally, it was mutually understood and agreed upon that the only announcement of the severance of Luscombe's relations with the Luscombe Airplane Corporation would be in the form of a written statement satisfactory to both parties. In turn, this announcement would be posted on the bulletin board of the Luscombe Airplane Corporation.

Other paragraphs within the agreement detailed the means by which Luscombe was to relinquish his shares, his wife's shares, and those of George B. Cluett, II, to Oberhumer, his assigns or nominees.

Don Luscombe resigned officially on April 15, 1939. George B. Cluett, II, resigned the same day.

The announcement describing Don's departure was simple and direct as illustrated below:

NOTICE

Having sold my interests in the Luscombe Airplane Corporation, I have resigned as President and Chairman of the Board of that Corporation and have severed all my connections therewith. This step has been taken by me in order to pursue other activities and to

(Top) Don Luscombe's Gwynedd Valley, Pennsylvania, estate.

(Above) Don Luscombe's study in his Gwynedd Valley home.

(Left) The living room area in Don Luscombe's Gwynedd Valley home.

(Left) An aerial view of the Gwynedd Valley estate in 1939.

(Below) Don and his dogs.

ELEANORE LUSCOMBE SHURTZ COLLECTION

take care of my personal affairs.

I am happy to announce that other interests have taken over the control and operation of the Corporation's business and affairs. I wish them and the Corporation the best of success and good fortune and especially request the staff show the new management the same loyalty and cooperation which has united me with them for the past years.

Dated: April 1939
DON A. LUSCOMBE

Thus, with a simple notice on the employees' bulletin board, Don Luscombe bid a fond farewell to many of his friends, associates, workers and students. Though several would join Don in his new endeavors, others were content to remain with the new leadership.

When all transactions were completed, Don Luscombe had a check in his hand for almost $36,000 — a lot of money in 1939! In turn, the Luscombe Airplane Corporation came under the total control and domination of Leopold H.P. Klotz.

Flush with a sizeable amount of money, one of Don and Brownee Luscombe's first purchases included a new Luscombe "65," NC22085 (s/n 907). This airplane featured a Phantom style instrument panel arrangement, maroon striping, carpet, maroon upholstery, dual ignition, tailwheel, brakes and 18 inch tires. Both Don and Brownee, now a licensed pilot herself, would find many hours of flying enjoyment in this craft.

ELEANORE LUSCOMBE SHURTZ COLLECTION

Ig Sargent made the test flights in this airplane on April 17 and 19. Incidentally, he would make only one more Luscombe "65" test flight (April 20, 1939) before he severed his employment ties with the Luscombe Airplane Corporation.

In late April, the Luscombes vacated the Caretaker House and moved to nearby Gwynedd Valley, Pennsylvania, a Philadelphia suburb, where they rented (and later purchased) a stately home on ten acres on Meetinghouse Road. Eventually, Don increased his estate to almost ninety acres by purchasing parcels of land on either side of the original property and one in front, across Meetinghouse Road.

This spacious home was three stories high and had four bedrooms, a large living room, a well lit library, an ample kitchen and a separate building housing a garage/workshop, an office and an open upper floor, later converted to guest quarters. Don built a darkroom in one of the outbuildings.

The grounds featured a tennis court, a stable and several large, open fields. There was ample room for the horses to graze and Brownee to take-off and land her Luscombe "65." Don built a well-equipped dog kennel for his Pointers and English Setters, all twenty-three of them!

Normally, Brownee Luscombe kept the "65" at Wings Field, but after World War II started and private flying was prohibited along the Atlantic Coast, she ferried it to the estate for long-term storage in a barn on the estate.

This picturesque estate was barely twenty-five miles west-southwest of the West Trenton factory. Thus, Don was able to remain close to the factory and fulfill any contractual obligations.

More important, however, Don was still near his many aviation friends and potential sources of money. He was not about to abandon his aviation related dreams.

Don's bird hunting interests remained keen, also. In late 1939, he and Brownee began spending the winter months in lodges in South Carolina hunting quail. Eventually, the couple bought 150 acres and leased another 5000 acres near Bamberg, South Carolina. The purchase proved invaluable in Don's future business promotions.

Several of Don's friends followed his example and built their homes along the road Sherman used on his march into Bamberg. The locals dubbed Don's and his neighbors' homes "Damned Yankee Row."

Don's position remained vacant until mid-June when an L.A.C. Board of Directors' meeting elected respected businessman John H. Torrens of Trenton, New Jersey, to fill the vacancy.

Fred Knack, the corporation's vice-president and chief engineer, resigned his position on May 24, 1939. Shortly thereafter, he went to work for Pitcairn. Not long afterwards, he established an engineering consulting firm operating from a second living room at his Willow Grove, Pennsylvania, home. He called his business the F.J. Knack Engineering Company.

Jim Rising was given the chief engineer position after Fred Knack's departure. Under his capable direction, the popular Luscombe Model 8 series was improved continuously. During his tenure, the Luscombe "50" became known as the Luscombe 8 whereas the Luscombe "65" became known as the Luscombe 8A.[100]

New models included the Luscombe 8B (a Lycoming O-145 powered airplane), the Luscombe 8C (a plush, Continental A-75 powered airplane) and the Luscombe 8D (also, a Continental A-75 powered airplane designed to cater to a new U.S. Government Civilian Pilot Training Program that developed shortly after Don's departure). Other refinements and creative advertising kept the Luscombe Model 8 at the forefront of light airplane sales until wartime aluminum allotments suspended further Model 8 production.

Leopold H.P. Klotz, on the other hand, refused to become an executive or director in his own company for many months. Though elected as vice president at an August 25, 1939, LAC Board of Directors meeting, Klotz declined and the position remained vacant until December 12, 1939, when the Board asked Mr. Klotz to reconsider his decision. Klotz took office on that date.

An always effervescent Brownee Luscombe poses in front of the Luscombe "65" she and Don bought shortly after Don's resignation. ELEANORE LUSCOMBE SHURTZ COLLECTION

Henry Boller returned to the factory, but in a lesser role. Acting through his Board of Directors, Klotz discharged Boller in August 1939, because of personal financial difficulties.

While Don negotiated his departure, Ig Sargent and Eddie Davis could see their future prospects at the Luscombe Airplane Corporation were dim, also. They had sided with Don on every issue. No doubt Klotz was anxious to see these two Board members retire quickly, quietly and move on.

Seeking a future career, both Ig Sargent and Eddie Davis interviewed and were accepted into the

New Jersey Air National Guard. However, each would not report to the Guard until late April or early May of 1939. Both desired to see Don through his final days at his company and help him any way they could during the transition. Sargent and Davis resigned officially from the Luscombe Airplane Corporation on May 24, 1939.[101]

Ig Sargent and Eddie Davis remained close friends with Don for many years. Often, one or both of these gentlemen invested in Don's post-West Trenton ventures. Each never lost a dime with Don and frequently received a sizeable return on their money.

Nick Nordyke realized his days were numbered, also. With Don's assistance, Nick placed a few feelers with Agnew Larsen at Pitcairn Autogiro and was promptly accepted. Much like Sargent and Davis, Nick wished to remain with Don until he left West Trenton.

Ben Melcher decided to leave with Don, also. He knew Don had "plans" after his departure and wished to help his good friend. Ben was an excellent production manager and was most willing to help Don in any future endeavor.

With no work available in the immediate future, however, Melcher sought employment, with Don's assistance, at Pitcairn Autogiro and was accepted. He started work in early May.

Keith Funk and Bill Force chose to stay with Don and each went to work for Pitcairn in early May. Like other former Luscombe Airplane Corporation employees, they soon joined Don Luscombe in many of his post-Luscombe Airplane Corporation endeavors. Within a couple years, Howard Greene would leave the Luscombe Airplane Corporation and join Don.

Interestingly, these and other former employees were never formally employed by Pitcairn. Instead, these former associates, or employees, gained employment at Pitcairn because Don had initiated an agreement with Agnew Larsen, Pitcairn's plant manager and chief engineer, to "loan" them until such time as Don needed them for his own development projects. Additionally, Don arranged to obtain the use of shop space if and when he needed it.

Larsen, on his behalf, was quite happy to have these men with metal aircraft design and construction experience. They were sorely needed to complete work on a second Pitcairn PA-36. Knack and Melcher assisted in the engineering work, Nordyke and Force fabricated the metal pieces, and Keith Funk was placed in charge of purchasing.

Chuck Burgess thought long and hard about what he would do. He was close to Don, but he had a good career at the Luscombe Airplane Corporation with ample room for advancement. Though Klotz often exhibited a testy personality towards Burgess, Burgess was able to work quite well with this young German. In time, Chuck would be promoted to production manager and, later, vice-president of the Luscombe Airplane Corporation.

Roger Johnson, like Chuck Burgess, sensed his career opportunities were better served if he remained with the corporation. Thus, Johnson remained the corporation's treasurer until he left in 1943 or 1944.

Fritz King was another worker who decided to stay, but in a different capacity. King had resigned his position with the company sometime earlier and devoted his attention to his on-site K & C Flying Service business, which was doing quite well. But once Sargent and Davis had left, King was hired to undertake most of the Model 8 test flying. These test flying duties began in late April. King left the Luscombe organization in early 1942 and became a pilot for Delta Air Lines.

Ralph Coston, the other half of the K & C Flying Service, stayed with his buddy Fritz King until the outbreak of hostilities in World War II. Coston, who now had his instructor's license, went to California and settled near San Diego where he became a Civilian Pilot Training Program instructor. Tragically, he was killed in late 1941 when a student flew a Ryan ST trainer into some power lines.

Bill Shepard elected to stay, but only until the end of July. Like King, Shepard would undertake a Model 8 test pilot role, mostly during May and early June. Not long afterwards, he decided to return to school at Purdue University in Lafayette, Indiana, and pursue his Master's Degree in aeronautical engineering.

After receiving the degree and working for slightly less than a year at Vought-Sikorsky, Shepard rejoined Don and most of the gang in Louisville, Kentucky, during Don's Reynolds Metals Company employment stint.

Lou Coghill left the Luscombe Airplane Corporation shortly after Don's departure for a position at Martin Aircraft in Baltimore, Maryland. Coghill was made foreman of the wing department that made bombers for export. Within a couple years, he left this position and rejoined Don at Reynolds Metals. After Reynolds, Coghill went to work for Continental Airlines in Denver, Colorado, where, eventually, he became foreman of the airline's maintenance night shift.

Jules De Crescenzo chose to leave the company and pursue a more rewarding role in aviation. From 1940 to 1942, De Crescenzo served as the director of training and chief instructor for the U.S. Army Air Forces in Philadelphia. Thereafter, De Crescenzo spent 32 years as an air safety inspector and airframe and power plant mechanic examiner for the Civil Aeronautics Authority, later, known as the Federal Aviation Administration.

Rolfe Gregory remained with the company and occupied various positions from welding lift struts to working in production planning. In 1942, he was appointed the company's assistant chief engineer and project engineer on the wartime contracts with nearby Eastern Aircraft. In January 1944, Gregory was appointed chief engineer, a position he held until he resigned from the company in September 1945. Shortly thereafter, he accepted a position with Fairchild Aircraft as a staff engineer, a position he held for the next 18 years.

One very bright story did have a happy ending during this arduous period. Jerry Coigny and Lucy Rago were married. Ever since Jerry had returned to the West Coast in his Luscombe "50" in late August 1938, he corresponded daily with Lucy, though a lot of his news dealt with barnstorming and racing experiences in his Luscombe airplane.

Similarly, Jerry's official correspondence to Don often included a touching, *"Tell Lucy Hello."* Occasionally, Don included a couple of Jerry's letters in company advertising literature. In turn, a customer would inquire, *"Who's Lucy?"*

On December 25, 1938, Keith Funk paid a visit to the Rago home. He had in his hand a "special gift" from Jerry, an engagement ring. As far as Lucy was concerned, this gift made Keith Funk *"the greatest Santa Claus in the world."*

In time, Jerry sold his well-worn Luscombe "50." In early July 1939, he sent a deposit for a new Luscombe "65." This airplane became known as the "Honeymoon Special."

Jerry returned to West Trenton on July 1. He brought many gifts for the Rago family. However, a minor problem developed — the family said a firm *"NO!"* to their wedding plans. Jerry was Protestant and Lucy was Catholic. The couple decided to elope.

Using Rolfe Gregory's car as not to draw any undue suspicion, the girls in the office helped Lucy smuggle personal items from home into the factory. Jerry, meanwhile, prepared their "Honeymoon Special" for their journey and life together.

On July 12, the Luscombe "65," decorated with signs and crepe paper, was loaded with Lucy's belongings. Company president J.H. Torrens made a farewell speech and presented the couple a new Lear Radio. After many tearful goodbyes, the lovely couple flew to nearby Doylestown, Pennsylvania, where they were married in a brief civil ceremony.

Afterwards, they flew to Wings Field in Ambler, Pennsylvania, where Don and Brownee Luscombe waited to take the newlyweds to the Luscombe's new home in nearby Gwynedd Valley, Pennsylvania. The honeymooners spent the first night there before continuing towards Grant's Pass, Oregon, where Jerry had his home and had established his flying school and fixed base operation.

As mentioned previously, many of Don's former associates worked for Pitcairn Autogiro. While there, these individuals and veteran Pitcairn employees completed construction of the first PA-36 autogiro and built a second Pitcairn PA-36 autogiro fuselage. Interestingly, this second autogiro was never completed beyond a basic skeletal frame. Flight testing of the Luscombe Airplane Corporation-built PA-36 continued for a year or two more before Harold Pitcairn abandoned the PA-36 program altogether.[102]

Though Don was stymied somewhat by his "contract" with Oberhumer, his airplane dreams remained clear. He wished to enter the market with a high performance, four-place airplane. Don contacted Fred Knack in August 1939, and asked him to

The Honeymoon couple, Jerry and Lucy Coigny stand beside a specially prepared Luscombe 8A called "The Honeymoon Special."

design a new, experimental four-place, high-wing airplane.

Shortly thereafter, Don called together many of his former associates. Ben Melcher, Nick Nordyke, Keith Funk, Bill Force and a few others converged on Don's estate to share Don's new airplane and manufacturing visions.

Concurrently, war clouds were gathering on a distant, European horizon. A fanatic dictator named Adolf Hitler was gaining a sizable portion of the world press' daily attention. These facts mattered little to Don at the moment, however. He cared only for the new, four place personal airplane design coming together in a workshop on his Gwynedd Valley estate that would best anything the competition would have to offer, including the Luscombe Airplane Corporation. Being a four-place, it did not violate his agreement with Klotz.

Beginning in August or September 1939, drawings were started for the new airplane. Fred Knack, who was working at the Pitcairn Autogiro Company at the time, hired A. Edgar Mitchell, a young, bright and intuitive engineer to make the majority of the engineering drawings.

Still employed in the Standards and Aircraft Design Section at the Naval Aircraft Factory in Philadelphia, Mitchell worked from Knack's Willow Grove home on evenings and weekends. Shortly thereafter, however, Fred Knack divorced himself entirely from the Pitcairn Autogiro Company employ while Ed Mitchell relinquished his Civil Service commission with the Naval Aircraft Factory Design Section. These actions enabled both individuals to devote full time efforts to design Don's new airplane.

Knack would determine what Don needed in the new airplane and then discussed the design details with Mitchell who, in turn, proceeded with detailed drawings. Ed Mitchell made 85 percent of the drawings for the Luscombe "Four-Place," as Don Luscombe and some associates called the airplane, or Luscombe "Gull-Wing" as it was known by others. The latter name was applied due to the gentle, gull-wing shape planform of the wings. Contrary to popular myth, this development was never dubbed the "Colt" while owned by Don Luscombe.

The Luscombe "Gull-Wing" featured a monospar design where each rib section was used twice in each of both left and right wing panels. Where a rib was placed in the area between the root and the thickest (greatest chord) of the gull planform, the same rib configuration was utilized outboard between the thickest part of the gull-wing and the wing-tip. Of course, the spacing between ribs was greater in the outboard section as compared to the inboard section.

Over the next year, a roomy four place airplane evolved in Don's well-equipped and efficient shop. Metal frame wings, intended to be fabric-covered, were built but never covered. Eventually, they were mated to the robust aluminum fuselage at one point. A Continental 185 hp engine, sans rods, pistons and other internal parts, was borrowed and mounted on the airframe, but was never run.

Though the airplane was virtually completed, work on the "Four Place" was suspended when aluminum became extremely difficult, if not impossible, to obtain during mid-1940. Don's lack of government priority prevented the purchase of needed material, i.e. aluminum, instruments and engine parts; hence, the project was terminated in November 1940.

Interestingly, Leopold H.P. Klotz was made aware of this project in a letter from Oberhumer to Klotz describing the potential merits of this airplane. No further action was undertaken.

At this point and time, through the mutual consent and understanding of Don Luscombe, Fred Knack accepted a position as chief engineer with the Cluett Aircraft Company located in Falmouth, Massachusetts. He took Ed Mitchell along as his assistant. Incidentally, George B. Cluett, II, a former LAC major stockholder and former LAC director, owned this enterprise![103]

The Luscombe "Four Place" or "Gull-Wing" under construction at Don's Gwynedd Valley home. This airplane was sold to another concern and later called the Weatherly-Campbell "Colt." JAMES B. ZAZAS COLLECTION

Chapter Sixteen: Post Luscombe, Luscombe   247

(Left) The Luscombe-built, television guided bomb after a successful air drop test at Muroc Dry Lake Bed. Circa September 1941.

(Below) Don Luscombe, Fred Knack and Ben Melcher assemble the Luscombe "Four-place" ("Gull-wing") at Don's Gwynedd Valley home.

BEN MELCHER

ELEANORE LUSCOMBE SHURTZ COLLECTION

(Right) A good view of the Luscombe "Four-place." As originally designed, these wings were to be covered in Grade A Flightex.

ELEANORE LUSCOMBE SHURTZ COLLECTION

(Left) The Luscombe "Four-place" in front of Don's well equipped shop. Tight wartime controls and scarcity of aluminum forced suspension of further work on this design at this stage in development.

ELEANORE LUSCOMBE SHURTZ COLLECTION

The Luscombe "Four-Place" or Weatherly-Campbell "Colt," as it was known in 1945, prepares for a test flight in Dallas, Texas, in 1945.

The Luscombe "Four-place" as it appeared in 1985 in Texas. Don Luscombe sold this airplane to Ray Weatherly and Bill Campbell in 1942 who, in turn, invested $100,000 in its redesign with plans to enter full production. Joe Johnson of Alvarado, Texas, acquired the "four place" in 1972 and spent considerable time restoring this lovely airplane. Damaged severely by a tornado in May 1988, the author now owns this proud plane and is undertaking a careful rebuild.

The Luscombe "Four-place" instrument panel and throw-over control wheel as redesigned by Weatherly-Campbell. Originally, the cockpit sported a pair of control sticks.

Shortly thereafter, Don and his group were tasked to develop, build and test an experimental television guided bomb under sub-contract to the Radio Corporation of America. This work was done under the auspices of the National Defense Research Committee, a Department of War scientific committee headed by Dr. Hugh Dryden of the Bureau of Standards and, later, the National Advisory Committee for Aeronautics (NACA).

Work started on this project in late 1940, and ended with several successful (and unsuccessful) drop tests from a Douglas B-23 bomber at Muroc Dry

(Right) A Luscombe Engineering-built P-40 snow ski installation at Wings Field, Pennsylvania, in December 1942. Luscombe's company built a couple hundred of these skis. Most were shipped to the Soviet Union in World War II.

Lake Bed in California during the fall of 1941.

During this same period, several of Don's "employees" developed wood and metal snow skis for Curtiss P-36 and P-40 fighter airplanes. The P-36 skis were fixed or non-retractable whereas the P-40 skis were retractable.

Concurrently, Don became the Aircraft Parts Division head of Reynolds Metals Company's Louisville, Kentucky, plant. Melcher, Shepard, Force and Howard Greene joined Don at this factory.

By early 1942, Don resigned his position at Reynolds Metals and started a new business in North Wales, Pennsylvania, called the Luscombe Engineering Company, Inc. Always keen to cost effective, mass production of aviation parts and components, Don's small but efficient company obtained several lucrative War Department contracts and sub-contracts.

The company improved the P-40 ski assemblies and built 270 sets. After a series of tests at Ladd Field in Alaska, it was deemed these skis were unsuitable for Army Air Force operations. Eventually, most of these skis were exported to the Soviet Union.

At the same time, the company built retractable snow ski assemblies for North American P-51 and Bell P-63 fighters. Actual field tests were undertaken in Manchester, New Hampshire (P-51), and St. Jouite, Quebec, Canada (P-63), in late 1944 and met with mixed success.

During the mid to later war years, the company built Sikorsky R-4 helicopter welded fuselage assemblies and R-5 helicopter welded fuselage sub-assemblies, industrial routers, cold storage boxes for blood plasma, insulated cases for holding frozen meals on

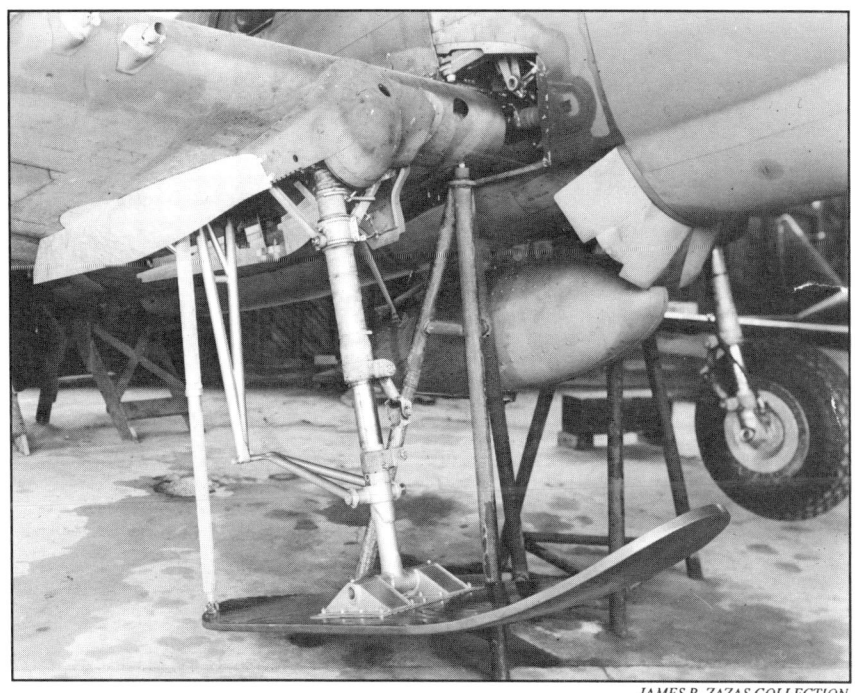

JAMES B. ZAZAS COLLECTION

(Above) Luscombe designed and built retractable snow skis installed on a P-51 aircraft. Later flight and taxi tests proved such installations on fighter aircraft as impractical.

WILLIAM B. SHEPARD

Martin flying boats, P-47 wingtip assemblies, welded aluminum pontoon boats for bridging rivers in Europe and other high quality, all-metal components.

Additionally, from September 1942 to mid-1943, many personnel of the Luscombe Engineering Company's "job shop" engineering team were farmed-out to Waco Aircraft of Troy, Ohio, to assist in the design of a military cargo airplane, the Waco C-62. When Waco's contract was cancelled, this team was

250 *Visions of Luscombe: The Early Years*

ELEANORE LUSCOMBE SHURTZ COLLECTION

(Above) One of Don's post-war activities included manufacturing a line of children's slides and swingsets.

(Right) Another post-war endeavor involved the manufacture of an insulated cooler, or "Coldtainer."

transferred to Sikorsky to assist with design of the Sikorsky R-5 helicopter.

Post-World War II activities saw Don and his company build children's playground equipment, including slides and swings. These brightly painted, high quality items were displayed in many of the better known children's toy stores of the period, including F.A.O. Schwarz Toys, Inc.

When this endeavor did not prosper, Don developed and promoted a post-retirement job opportunities program called "Second Careers." One of Don's printed brochures described this new venture as *"an unusual educational experience for men age 60, and over who aspire to be lucid at 90."* "Second Careers" was designed to utilize *"guided luncheon study-discussion groups in search of better ideas to augment income after 65."*

Don once said, *"Luncheon meeting moderators are paid $50 for chairing and managing each session. Venerable, long, white beards create no objection in this capacity."* Sadly, divorce, bouts with alcoholism, bankruptcies and re-marriage were in Don's future, also.

Don's mind remained clear in his many endeavors. He knew not what drove him, but being so driven, he usually received credit for his many accomplishments. Donald A. Luscombe faced life's challenges with a positive anticipation and complete dedication. No problem was insurmountable.

Once, when he was asked to pinpoint his strongest points, Don said he could *"offer a seasoned toughness without inhibiting the visionary attributes."* Consequently, the visions of Luscombe remained intact, and an aviation legend continued.

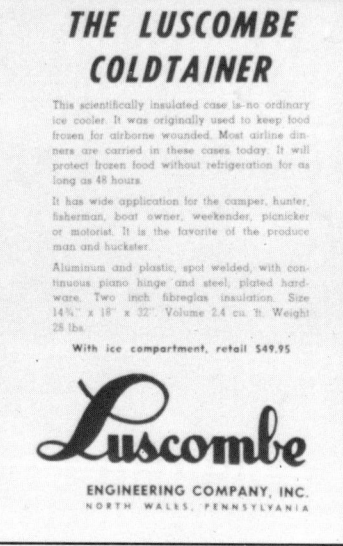

THE LUSCOMBE COLDTAINER

This scientifically insulated case is no ordinary ice cooler. It was originally used to keep food frozen for airborne wounded. Most airline dinners are carried in these cases today. It will protect frozen food without refrigeration for as long as 48 hours.

It has wide application for the camper, hunter, fisherman, boat owner, weekender, picnicker or motorist. It is the favorite of the produce man and huckster.

Aluminum and plastic, spot welded, with continuous piano hinge and steel, plated hardware. Two inch fibreglas insulation. Size 14¾" x 18" x 22". Volume 2.4 cu. ft. Weight 28 lbs.

With ice compartment, retail $49.95

Luscombe
ENGINEERING COMPANY, INC.
NORTH WALES, PENNSYLVANIA

JAMES B. ZAZAS COLLECTION

ELEANORE LUSCOMBE SHURTZ COLLECTION

Second Careers

—AN UNUSUAL EDUCATIONAL EXPERIENCE FOR MEN AGE 60, AND OVER WHO ASPIRE TO BE LUCID AT 90

Guided luncheon-study-discussion groups in search of better ideas to augment income after 65

MAIN OFFICE: SKIPPACK & BUTLER PIKES
MI 6-7994

AMBLER, PENNSYLVANIA

Paying Jobs for Oldsters

Luncheon meeting moderators are paid $50 for chairing and managing each session. Venerable, long, white beards create no objection in this capacity.

Men who prepare themselves for this responsibility will be recruited largely from Second Career students. This is a second career, emotionally rewarding within the Second Career movement.

This capitalizes and sublimates the individual's retirement anxiety and satisfies the need for being wanted and useful in a dignified endeavor. When five meetings a week become too heavy a schedule, the participant may choose the extent of his energies to be employed.

D. A. LUSCOMBE
Chairman

Then and now... The Mercer County Airport

(Left) The Mercer County Airport, West Trenton, New Jersey, as it appeared in 1934.

(Right) The same view taken in October 1991. The Mountain View Country Club Golf Course, developed in the mid-1950s, occupies a major portion of the former airport grounds today. Note: Interstate 95 follows the former northeast/southwest runway.

Footnotes

CHAPTER 1

[1] Luscombe did not like to use his formal, given name when addressing or signing letters, documents or certificates. Instead, he preferred to sign his name simply "Don A Luscombe." Interestingly, Don often hinted to friends he did not have a middle name and chose the "A" because it *"was the first letter of the alphabet and it sounded good."*

[2] While pursuing his family roots, Don Luscombe discovered the family name, Luscombe, was an anglicized adaption of the French surname "Les Combes."

[3] According to Betty Luscombe Numerof, one of Don's living nieces, *"As a child, Don was instructed always to retain the final 'e' in the spelling, since some branches of the family had already dropped it, thus making 'Luscomb.'*

"... in addition, Uncle Don was contacted originally by the British authorities who were trying to resolve the inheritance problem, because he had tried to offer a home to British children who were being evacuated during World War II."

[4] Most likely, this citation refers to the Allied offensive operations conducted east and northeast of Paris during July, August, and September, 1918. All major combatants suffered tremendous casualties during these bitterly-fought campaigns.

[5] Eleanore True was born on October 7, 1899, and grew up near Iowa City. Sadly, Eleanore's parents divorced in the early 1900s, virtually an unheard event at the time. Her mother remarried a local lawyer. Though never adopted by her step-father, Eleanore took his last name, True.

CHAPTER 2

[6] The Jenny which Don purchased was built by the St. Louis Street Car Company. The OX-5 engine was built by the Wyllis-Morrow Company and the wood propeller was labeled by the Liquid Carbonic Corporation.

[7] Don's younger brother, Bob, became an officer of Central States Aero Company by accident. Don approached Bob for a hundred dollars to be applied to the company. When Bob handed Don the money, Don stated, *"You are now a co-owner of an airplane company."*

[8] In later years, 1936 and 1939, Folkerts designed and built racing airplanes for the National Air Races. He sent his designs to well-known engineer Fred Knack for stress analysis. Folkerts' intuition for selecting the correct sizes of tubing for structural members, without calculating the actual design loads, was uncanny. Often, Knack had few, if any, corrections to suggest. Several more noteworthy designs include the 1936 Folkerts SK-1, a 185 hp Menasco racer flown by Harold Neumann in several events, including the Greve and Thompson Trophy races. Always improving on a winning combination, Folkerts built the Folkerts SK-3 in 1937, with the pilot winning the Greve and Thompson Trophy races. The Folkerts SK-4 followed in 1938, but experienced serious wing flutter problems and did not race. SK-4 pilots included Del Bush and Roger Don Rae.

Folkerts went to work for Waco Aircraft in 1940 designing gliders and trainers where he contributed his vast experience to the War effort. He left Waco in 1948 and retired to his farm near Iowa Falls, Iowa, with his wife. Folkerts died in 1965 at the age of 67.

[9] The Detroit "Air-Cat" was an Eddie Rickenbacker sponsored and former Wright Field Chief Engineer Glenn D. Angle design.

CHAPTER 3

[10] What became of this airplane may be found in a letter dated February 27, 1928. Don Luscombe advised the Department of Commerce this airplane had been dismantled and condemned at the Central States Aero factory. Furthermore, Don wrote: *"Our first airplane, and although everything seemed to be in perfect condition, the fuselage contained several members with 22 gauge tubing (with which) we are not entirely satisfied with the welding. We are using the wing for further experimental work on a new type aileron."*

[11] The name "Flying Flivver" was used by the press in 1926 and applied originally to a Henry Ford-built airplane design powered by a 36 hp, 3-cylinder Anzani engine. This unique design boasted an incredible 100 mph cruise speed. Charles A. Lindbergh flew a "Flying Flivver" and reportedly deemed it to be one of the *"worst airplanes"* he ever flew.

[12] Ryan, in turn, took a Monocoupe dealership in San Diego, California. However, he did not carry the honor of having the first Monocoupe dealership. This honor went to George A. Weis.

[13] The Cirrus engine was created as a result of Geoffery deHavilland's request to the British ADC (Aircraft Disposal Corporation, a British government company created to dispose of World War I surplus aircraft, engines and parts) to build a smaller, lighter engine using the cylinders from a basic Royal Aircraft Factory RAF 4D, an in-line, 240 hp engine. The net result was a durable and light engine, one that made the light airplane movement in Great Britain possible.

[14] Interestingly, over 270 companies in the United States were making automobiles in 1927. However, in 1928, only two companies that built automobiles were still controlled by their founders; Willard L. Velie of the Velie Motors Corporation and Henry Ford of the Ford Motor Company of Detroit.

CHAPTER 4

[15] Phoebe Fairgrave Omlie, born in Des Moines, Iowa, on November 21, 1902, was the first female to receive a Transport Pilot License and the first woman to receive an airplane and mechanic's license.

Omlie started her meteoric aviation career after watching a Ruth Law air show. She started making parachute jumps and wing walks in 1920, eventually organizing and promoting her own "flying circus" from 1920 through 1928. Husband Vernon Omlie taught her how to fly in a Curtiss "Jenny" during 1926 and 1927. The duo barnstormed before they founded Mid-South Airways of Memphis, Tennessee.

Though Phoebe Omlie's transport license (number 199) is dated June 30, 1927, she actually passed the exam for this license some three months earlier. During the same year, Omlie earned an early mechanics license, number 422. Her post-Monocoupe work included campaigning for Franklin Delano Roosevelt's 1932 presidential campaign, eventually earning several government posts involving aviation and air safety. Her two most important were Special Assistant for Air Intelligence on the National Advisory Committee for Aeronautics and, later, Senior Private Flying Specialist, Civil Aeronautics Authority, Department of Commerce.

Shortly after Vernon Omlie died in a 1936 commercial airline accident, Phoebe Omlie returned to the Memphis area to direct the Civilian Pilot Training Program (C.P.T.P). Within a year, Omlie established in Nashville, Tennessee, the first Women's Aviation Instructor Aviation Training Program.

Phoebe Fairgrave Omlie died on July 16, 1975, in Indianapolis, Indiana, and was buried beside her husband, Vernon, in a Memphis, Tennessee, cemetery.

[16] During the 1920s and early 1930s, various aircraft engine manufacturers asked the United States Navy to test and "approve" their engine's airworthiness. With such a blessing in hand, these manufacturers could allay a questioning public's fear about reliability by stating their engine met and passed strenuous U.S. Navy testing, even though no formal U.S. Government requirement existed to do so at the time. This military/commercial relationship gave kudos to the U.S. Navy while "enhancing" the reputation of the aircraft engine manufacturer.

Eventually, however, the government did require aircraft engines to be certified for manufacture in a program much like the legislated airplane ATC program. To this end, the Velie M-5 was awarded Approved Type Certificate number four.

CHAPTER 5
[17] Upon completing his work at Studebaker, Lederer went to Aero Insurance Underwriters as their chief engineer. In 1940, he joined the Civil Aeronautics Board as its first director of safety.

In 1947, Lederer was appointed managing director of the two year old Flight Safety Foundation (FSF), a position he held for the next twenty years! He left the FSF in 1967, to head the Apollo safety program after the disastrous Cape Kennedy (Canaveral) fire. In 1970, he was appointed director of safety for all of the National Aeronautics and Space Administration. He retired from this position in 1972, to serve as a lecturer and consultant to the Institute of Nuclear Power where he applied his aviation safety experience to the nuclear power industry.

As of this writing, Lederer travels extensively expounding his many aviation safety philosophies. Interestingly, Lederer was never a rated pilot, his eyesight did not allow him to pass the stringent tests of the time, but he has done more to enhance aviation safety than any other aviation-minded individual.

[18] Lambert's airplane had a metal propeller which had been bent and straightened a number of times. It was believed this constant bending made the blade brittle. Furthermore, Lambert often operated his airplane's engine at a high power setting and this activity may have caused the blade to fail. When the aircraft nosed down, the Lambert H-106 engine may have slipped off the seat beside Lambert and jammed the controls, thus, making any recovery impossible.

CHAPTER 6
[19] C.B. "Scotty" Burmood continued in the employ of Mono-Aircraft, Inc. until late 1932, at which time he ferried five Monocoupe "Mailplanes" to Columbia via Cuba. He stayed in South America as an airline operator.

Tiresome of his work, he returned to the United States in 1934, and went to work for the Monocoupe Corporation of St. Louis. Shortly thereafter, he went to work for Walter Beech of Wichita, Kansas, selling airplanes. In 1936, Burmood went to China and sold two Beech D-17R airplanes to Generalisimo Chiang Kai-Shek's Headquarters squadron.

In early 1937, Burmood accepted a job to fly Chinese government officials in the D-17Rs, DC-2s and Boeing 247s. Contrary to popular belief, Burmood never served as Generalisimo Chiang Kai-Shek or Madam Chiang's personal pilot, though he liked to tell stories to this effect.

Burmood often flirted with death from Bogata, Colombia, to Chungking, China. His heroic exploits ranged from retrieving a downed Monocoupe, virtually single-handed, in a snake-infested South American river to evading Japanese bombs while ferrying Chinese officials to and from the front lines in wartime China. Reportedly, his reward for "services rendered" was $12,000.

Once reported dead by the press, Burmood surfaced alive and healthy. Shortly thereafter, was employed as a ferry pilot working for the U.S. Ferry Command, but was fired shortly thereafter. In early 1943, Burmood took a job with B.F. Goodrich in Akron, Ohio, as flight operations manager. Afterwards, he worked for Shell/Merida in Columbia, then returned to the United States to crop dust. He tried gold mining, also.

[20] Vern Roberts stayed in the Moline area at least until 1934. He left with his wife, Henrietta, and son, Ken, and moved to New Mexico to do some gold mining. After struggling for four years, the family returned to Moline where a fully recovered Roberts became the manager of the Moline Airport after Rusty Campbell died, and established the Moline Air Service, an FBO that eventually trained World War II pilots. Also, Roberts established the Moline Engine Service. Vern was forced to retire from both enterprises in 1949 due to health problems. A heart attack claimed Vern Roberts' life in 1964.

[21] "Group 2 Approval" certificates were usually awarded to individuals or small organizations making airframe changes or modifications without needing a full-blown Approved Type Certificate.

Originally intended to be a simpler way to gain the government's stamp of approval, "Group 2 Approval" was awarded to a design that was to be built in limited numbers. Quite often, "Group 2 Approvals" were given to aircraft with ATCs, but possessing design changes such as rearranged seating, increased fuel capacity or different engine configurations.

[22] Reportedly, Don Luscombe "fired" Knack for marrying his secretary, Grace. At the time, the company was alive with much conjecture as to the real reasons for his departure from

Monocoupe Corporation, but suffice it to say his departure was quite sudden and unexpected.

[23] Driggs had other technical memorandums published, but was cognizant the layman could be confused by the many and often difficult mathematical descriptions presented. To help these individuals understand the basis of aeronautical engineering and theory, Driggs wrote several articles with the layman in mind. Notable examples include "Why an Airplane Flies" and "Choosing Your Own Wing Curve." These articles appeared in the 1930 edition of *Flying Manual*, a publication of *Modern Mechanics and Inventions* magazine.

[24] Though Driggs organized the company, he did not own it. Driggs Aircraft Company was owned by several Lansing, Michigan, area bankers. The corporation's officers held prestigious positions in other companies, also. H.F. Harper, the president, was president of Motor Wheel Corporation. H.B. Lundberg, the vice-president, held an executive position at Michigan Screw Corporation. E.C. Shields, Driggs Aircraft Co. treasurer, was a prominent banker.

Sadly and quite unexpectedly, the company folded in 1931, when one of the backers decided to close the company rather than reimburse Driggs for the cost of a boxcar loaded with newly delivered engines.

[25] The Driggs Dart Model 1 was a single seat monoplane developed to satisfy an Army Air Corps request. Powered by a 30 hp, 2 cylinder Wright-Moorehouse motor, this closed-in cabin airplane was a refined example of the Driggs-Johnson DJ-1, a high-wing monoplane that captured the interest of many at the 1924 Dayton Air Races.

The Driggs Coupe followed and was a two place, enclosed cabin monoplane. It was powered by the Detroit Aircraft Co. "Air-Cat" engine, the first airplane to use this engine.

The Driggs Dart Model 2 was next. It was a tandem seating biplane powered by a 35 hp, 3 cylinder Anzani radial engine. Steel tubing, an unusual feature inherent in this design, was used in lieu of wires for bracing and absorbing various stresses.

The Driggs Model 2 was awarded Approved Type Certificate #15 in October, 1927, but was later rescinded when the aircraft exhibited unsatisfactory spin characteristics — it would NOT spin. Despite repeated tests to spin the airplane, it proved "spin-proof." Even Department of Commerce conceded this fact and deemed the Driggs design unsuitable for flight training schools.

The final aircraft to pass through the Driggs Aircraft Company doors was the Driggs Skylark (ATC #303). The Skylark was designed to be a primary trainer or an affordable sportsman pilot aircraft. Powered by an in-line, 4 cylinder 75 hp Michigan Aero Engine "Rover," the Skylark possessed a top speed of 100 mph, cruised at 80 mph and landed at 40 mph. The price of the Skylark was $3485 Flyaway, Lansing.

[26] When finally certificated on March 23, 1934, this airplane, known as the Monocoupe D-145, became one of the more respected, though not generally loved, airplanes in the immensely popular Monocoupe airplane design series. The Approved Type Certificate for the Model D-145 (ATC #529) was awarded on March 23, 1934.

Don Luscombe once called the D-145, *"my last and worst Monocoupe."*

[27] By way of background, Ora May "Brownee" Luscombe was born in 1906, in San Diego, California. The daughter of an upper-middle class road contractor, Charles Chapman Taylor, Brownee and her sister grew-up in an area called Mission Hills, which overlooked what is Lindbergh Field today.

When she was a freshman in high school, Brownee was thoroughly smitten with flying. Her parents, however, were totally opposed to her dreams.

Thinking she could do as she pleased if she were married, Brownee ran off with the most popular boy in her school, Lawrence Dilworth Wellington. Both families were close and the fact Lawrence was a fine and upright sort of person, Brownee's parents had few objections to the marriage. Of course, it didn't work out the way she planned. The newlyweds lived in their respective homes. Then, after Lawrence left school, he joined an orchestra and went to Australia.

Brownee completed her three remaining years of high school and spent one year at the State Normal School learning to become a teacher. Another year at the San Diego Business College followed. However, Brownee's desires to fly remained strong.

By now and in almost desperation, her poor parents decided to send her to her uncle in Kansas City. Brownee soon found a secretarial job at the Kansas City Airport and her uncle allowed her to do as she pleased. Though she met another man who loved flying as much as she did, a flight instructor on the field, Don Luscombe had her heart.

In time, Brownee became Don Luscombe's most avid listener. . . and the rest is history.

CHAPTER 7

[28] In 1911, Longren designed the first successful airplane to be built in the state of Kansas. He went on to design and build a series of popular airplanes, eventually associating himself with Alexander Industries of Denver, Colorado. This company later produced the well-known Alexander Eaglerock airplanes.

[29] Kansas City, in 1933, was a rough town, controlled politically by some unsavory, unscrupulous bootlegging individuals. Thomas Pendergast, owner of a ready-mix concrete plant, all but "controlled" the local politicians. Rival concrete firms often had tires slashed, sugar put in the gas tanks, etc. A local haberdashery owner and former associate of Mr. Pendergast became President of the United States. His name was Harry Truman. This author was unable to uncover any evidence if Don's airplane concerns were ever "influenced" or at any time "threatened" by local organized crime.

[30] During the early days at Kansas City, Ben Melcher and Ivan Driggs roomed together in a small furnished apartment. Don Luscombe and Brownee lived at the President Hotel near the Country Club Plaza, which, incidentally was one of the first shopping center malls in the United States.

[31] Over the balance of his engineering career, Farver worked with Driggs on many different occasions (January 1929 to May 1930, August 1930 to September 1930, November 1933 to February 1935, February 1937 to September 1939 and October 1939 to early 1952, at which time Ivan Driggs

left McDonnell Aircraft to assume a position as the U.S. Navy's Chief Scientist at the service's Johnstown, Pennsylvania, Naval Air Development Center.

Farver's post-Luscombe employment included the Glenn L. Martin Company of Baltimore, Maryland, (February 1937 to September 1939), McDonnell Aircraft Corp. of St. Louis, Missouri (September 1939 to February 1962) and, finally, Aerotronics of Florissant, Missouri, as Chief Engineer (February 1962 to August 1964). Upon his retirement, Lyle Farver was responsible for designing various main-frame computer systems and space capsule control thrusters.

Lyle and Carol Farver retired to a quiet life in Englewood, Florida. Tragically, Lyle Farver lost his life on July 4, 1989, in an automobile accident.

[32] Fritz King made the small fairing windows by dipping Plexiglas in hot water and molding it around a wood form. King worked in final assembly, also. He mounted all engines to the airplanes and made the early annealed-copper, wrapped-in-rubber gas lines until Neoprene gas lines became available.

[33] It has often been recorded erroneously that Ben Melcher, Barton Stevenson or even Pete Brooks, undertook these early flights. According to personal and telephone interviews conducted by this author with former Kansas City LAC employees, none of these gentlemen undertook the prototype Phantom's first flight. Furthermore, interviews conducted by this author with Ben Melcher revealed he never flew the aircraft on any solo flight, even though he was a rated pilot.

[34] A study of Aline Brook's logbook reveals she either flew the Phantom or flew with Don Luscombe as a passenger in Phantom NC272Y on August 31, 1934. The routing was North Beach, New York, to Cleveland, Ohio, via Bellefonte, Pennsylvania. Bellefonte, located in the Pennsylvania Allegheny Mountains, was a stop for the early mail pilots.

Furthermore, the logbook states they flew back to North Beach on September 3, 1934, via Albany, New York, in "lousey" (sic) weather.

[35] Upon his return to Kansas City, Luscombe recounted his mishap to his engineering staff. They were quite surprised by his comments the tail simply "sheared off" in the accident and the repairs consisted of "pushing the tail back into place" and re-riveting.

Driggs, Farver and Melcher were more surprised the rivet holes had not been elongated by the shearing force, as they had expected. The only explanation they could offer was the rivets had been heat treated improperly or soft rivets had been used. All agreed Don was very lucky the damage was minimal.

[36] Unwittingly, Don Luscombe almost "made a deal with the devil." Though very generous in their discussions with Luscombe, these Wall Street investors cleverly neglected to tell him the deal, if consummated, would require Luscombe relinquish 51 percent control of his firm to them. Fortunately, Don Luscombe never signed on the proverbial dotted line.

[37] There has been much conjecture regarding the Phantom serial numbering system. One idea suggests Luscombe used the higher numbers as a savvy marketing ploy to imply more airplanes were produced than actually were. Another theory suggests a single digit numbering system implied to a potential customer he was buying a new, possibly unproven design. No doubt Luscombe adopted the former system as the latter method left too much to question in a buyer's mind.

Additionally, the use of the model number as the first digit of a three digit serial number identified the model of the new airplane. However, this idea had to be abandoned when the Model 8 series proved to be very successful.

CHAPTER 8
[38] George Thorne, Jr., was connected with the first Byrd Antarctic Expedition. At the time of his Phantom order, he was involved with some Canadian mining operations.

[39] Driggs' resignation triggered a "battle of letters." Luscombe wrote Driggs often trying to sway him to return to the company. Driggs would have none of it and insisted he be paid for the services he rendered to the company.

Initially, Luscombe stated his obligations were to those individuals still under his employ and offered to help Driggs when he was able. In one letter, Luscombe sent Driggs several promotional booklets and stated, ". . . *any trick you turn would immediately offset your account.*"

However, over the course of a year, the letters from Luscombe became increasingly heated, argumentative and disrespectful of Driggs' impeccable integrity, personal dignity and respected engineering talents. Eventually, Luscombe blamed Driggs for the corporation's inability to remain solvent and stated flatly Driggs' demands for payment of wages due served only to exacerbate a difficult situation.

Eventually, the matter was resolved legally and Driggs was paid a total of $300, excluding legal fees, of the $380 due him. This issue was concluded in late November 1936.

[40] Luscombe would order a Phantom's instruments, Warner engine and Hamilton-Standard (later, Curtiss) propeller upon receipt of a confirmed order.

Additionally, as best as can be determined via interviews by this author with former employees, at no time did the company assemble any Phantom aircraft only to later disassemble it for future sale. Tight finances and lack of manpower prevented this needless endeavor.

[41] The Phantom's engine overheating problem was a recurring problem and a constant complaint from owners. Though the company made repeated efforts to correct this problem, it was never resolved fully.

[42] Luscombe Phantom NC272Y's registration was cancelled on June 27, 1935, at the written request of Don Luscombe. Therefore, it is most likely the airplane was in this dismantled state as per Luscombe's request rather than being prepared to fly again. (History would later show this airplane or various components of this airplane did, indeed, fly under several guises).

CHAPTER 9
[43] Kenneth E. Cericola's personal background is typical of many Luscombe "apprentice program" graduates. All were bright, intuitive individuals with a strong, if not overriding desire, to fly and work on airplanes.

Cericola was born August 10, 1914, in Philadelphia, Pennsylvania.

He attended schools there, taking Latin and scientific courses during his high school years. He built and flew model airplanes as a hobby. Cericola had his heart set on attending New York University and majoring in aeronautical engineering, but the Depression forced him to rethink his life's goals.

From June 1930, through January 1933, Cericola took any part-time job he could find. In January 1933, he got a job working at the Philadelphia Art Club doing everything from serving as bellhop to filling basic cashier and accountant functions. In late 1935, he read an advertisement in a newspaper about the Luscombe Airplane Development Corporation's training program. Always interested in flying and aviation, Cericola signed-up for the course immediately.

While at Luscombe, Cericola bucked the rivets on the Phantom's fuselage aluminum longitudinal splice strip which joined the upper and lower skins together. Later, he assembled many of the Luscombe "50" corrugated aluminum ailerons for Carl Aa, another apprentice program graduate. Cericola left Luscombe briefly in late 1937 for a short stint working on Coast Guard flying boats at Hall-Aluminum. He returned to Luscombe and stayed until October 1939, at which time he went to work at the U.S. Naval Aircraft Factory (NAF) at the Philadelphia Naval Base, Philadelphia, Pennsylvania. There he made parts and ribs for N3N biplanes and OS2U Kingfishers, installed radomes on Grumman Avengers, did modification work on Martin PBMs and made bomb racks for various model Grumman fighters.

He left the NAF in April 1952, and went to work for Piasecki Helicopter (later, Vertol then Boeing-Vertol) where he held a variety of engineering and production planning positions. He retired on February 1, 1980, as a production engineer.

[44] Joining Davis and Sargent on this journey were Ralph Coston and Frances "Sissie" Sargent. Coston flew with Davis most of the time while Sissie flew with her husband.

Their visit to the National Air Races at Los Angeles was rewarding. Frank Spreckles won the Ruth Chatterton Sportsman Trophy Race in his Phantom. Additionally, the appearance of three Luscombe Phantoms at one major event provoked quite a bit of interest in the airplane.

Likewise, while enroute, their respective Phantom airplanes garnered a tremendous amount of attention from curious pilots, spectators and reporters. Perhaps one reason for this interest was Franklin T. Kurt's "The Sportsman Test Pilot" review of the Phantom in the August 15, 1936, issue of *The Sportsman Pilot*.

On the flight out, a landing gear tie rod fitting weld broke on Sargent's Phantom while landing in Winslow, Arizona. The only person capable of doing a creditable repair was the local blacksmith.

Realizing the landing gear was heat treated and any weld on its surface carefully made, the blacksmith took great care with the broken tie rod and made a secure fix. It held until the Sargents and NC1286 were safely back in West Trenton five weeks later, at which time the weld broke. In the meantime, the weld had withstood the rigors of multiple demonstration flights throughout the Los Angeles and San Francisco areas!

Davis and Coston left the Sargents' company in California and headed back east via Arizona, New Mexico and Texas. Wherever the duo stopped, onlookers and aviation enthusiasts were astonished by the Phantom's pleasing lines and sprightly performance.

At one stop near Palestine, Texas, Davis allowed a local cropduster, a C.W. Blackwell, the opportunity to fly the Phantom. Davis was treated to the most dazzling aerobatic display he had ever seen. When Mr. Blackwell returned, he summed-up his Phantom flight with a simple, *"Nice airplane."*

[45] Marty Eisenmann grew up in northeastern Ohio under the New York-to-Cleveland Mailroute. Marty was enthralled seeing the DH-4 mailplanes fly overhead. Yet, it wasn't until Lindbergh made his historic flight in 1927 that set Marty's generation's desire to fly "on fire."

Though he took flying lessons while attending high school, he found out he did not qualify for a Class I medical certificate. Thus, he opted to attend the Dallas Aviation School, Dallas, Texas, for six months to earn credits towards his mechanics license. He returned home to work in the family business. Not long afterwards, he read the Luscombe advertisement.

CHAPTER 10

[46] The unique registration versus serial numbering system alludes to an interesting fact. Though it has been rumored Luscombe hoped to match serial numbers to registration numbers through the balance of Phantom production, there is no documented effort on his behalf to do so.

Most likely, as the bookkeeping of serial numbers versus "NC" registration numbers was handled by the sales department personnel, e.g. Ig Sargent and Eddie Davis, et al., there was a conscious effort to match NC1007 (s/n 107) and NC1008 (s/n 108) as a potential sales effort.

Out-of-sequence deliveries took place occasionally, especially if a customer had an urgent reason for an expedited delivery. Thus, it is possible this circumstance created a situation whereby an airplane was pulled off the floor out of sequence, sent to the paint shop and delivered to the customer with a serial number different than originally assigned. No doubt it was easier to change the initial paperwork than repaint the airplane.

[47] When this aircraft was registered initially, the original Form 9, Application for Identification Mark, was dated October 11, 1936, and showed this airplane's serial number as 2-109. However, a voided Application for Commercial License dated October 9, 1936, shows this aircraft's serial number to be 110. When the original Unlicensed Aircraft Identification Mark was issued on October 11, 1936, it showed 2-109 as the serial number. However, the "109" portion was crossed out and "110" was inserted. The company informed the Department of Commerce, via written correspondence, to make the appropriate changes whereupon it was approved. Perhaps this serial number snafu related to the situation or condition as explained in the previous footnote.

[48] Reportedly, McPhaul did this low-level stunt quite often. During an interview with this author, Bill Force related an incident involving McPhaul.

One day, after an afternoon of

flying over the Jersey Meadowlands area, he came into the Teterboro, New Jersey, airport white as a sheet. His mechanic asked him, *"What's the matter, Red?"*

The shaken 24-year-old McPhaul replied, *"I dragged my wheels in the hay when I came out of a spin!"*

[49] Farver asked Frank Johnson to work overtime a few nights to layout the fuselage top and tail installations. These ideas were incorporated on the new Luscombe "90" and, later, on the Luscombe "50."

CHAPTER 11

[50] This nicknaming of new designs created quite a research problem for this author, and the problem has not been resolved totally. The following descriptions attests to this research predicament.

Entries in Ig Sargent's logbook refer to the 1017 airplane as the "Sprite." Similar entries in Eddie Davis' logbook denote the same airplane as the "Luscombe 90" whereas later entries refer to this aircraft as the "Sprite."

Sargent's logbook entries refer to this "first" 1253 airframe as the "Sprite." Later entries refer to 1253 as the "Sprite II."

Furthermore, interviews with Howard Jong and Lyle Farver refer to the "1253" airplane as the "Sprite." Yet, a stock prospectus dated August 17, 1937, shows a photograph of the airplane and is captioned "Luscombe 90."

[51] At the time, it was legal to fly an unlicensed aircraft in New Jersey. Paperwork and delay were eliminated because the original design and subsequent changes did not have to be approved by the United States Department of Commerce until an application for an Approved Type Certificate was made.

[52] Prior to returning to work for Luscombe and after he had left Monocoupe in early 1933, Knack worked as a checker at General Aviation Corporation, Dunkirk, Maryland, 1933; chief stress analyst of the Bellanca Aircraft Corporation, New Castle, Delaware, 1934-1935; structural design engineer at Douglas Aircraft Company, Santa Monica, California, 1935-1936; and, project engineer at Bellanca Aircraft Corporation, New Castle, Delaware, 1936-1937.

[53] Sargent's first test flight in this airplane was on March 30, 1937. The airplane remained with the company as a demonstrator until sold to H.T. Cole, Atlanta, Georgia, on December 4, 1937.

[54] Several months later, Don Luscombe received a surprising letter from L.A. Faunce, vice-president of the Warner Aircraft Corporation. Faunce forwarded, under separate cover, a tobacco pipe he found while inspecting the Phantom's brake installation. In his letter, he said the *"pipe was found under the rear floor compartment where the aileron and elevator controls are located. We are returning this thinking possibly you might like to return this pipe to the owner who carelessly left it in such a place."*

A red-faced Lou Coghill was grateful when Don returned his pipe.

[55] The new Olmstead airplane was listed as a contingent liability in a May 31, 1937, Stock Prospectus. Evidently, Olmstead assigned a $2900 claim to the LADC for damages to his airplane. He assigned this claim as an advance payment for rebuilding his airplane. The corporation was to hold title to the airplane until it was sold in the normal course of business. Mr. Olmstead agreed to accept, at the time of sale, his equity in the airplane which amounted to the amount paid by the insurance company.

[56] Fritz King was known to be gruff at times, but never abusive. His sometimes coarse attitude is best described by a humorous incident.

One of the younger men at the factory, a Bob Behal, bought an old Velie Monocoupe. Behal had very little flying experience and asked King to give him some instruction. One day, about the noon hour and directly over the Luscombe factory, Behal and King were returning to the Mercer County Airport in the Monocoupe when the engine revved-up fast and quit. Gliding to the runway was no problem; however, the prop was observed to be stopped in the vertical position, not an ideal position for any forced landing. LADC employees on the ground were dumbfounded when over the edge of the field they saw the prop move, almost magically, to the horizontal position. When some employees ran over to the crippled airplane after it landed, they discovered the crankshaft had broken just inside the crankcase.

A shaken Behal replied, *"King just cussed it until it finally moved!"*

[57] To give the reader some scale of Frank Johnson's squared ellipse fuselage design, the Cessna 120/140 fuselage design of today closely approximates his original idea for the Luscombe school project.

CHAPTER 12

[58] According to Herschel Smith in his admirable book, *A History of Aircraft Piston Engines,* the Continental A-40 engine *"did more to keep private flying alive during the Depression than any other engine."*

[59] In an effort to determine a direction for future aircraft engine development, Continental Aircraft Engine Company (a division of the parent Continental Motors Corporation) polled various aircraft manufacturers to see what they desired in an airplane power plant. Luscombe was one of these manufacturers included in the survey conducted by then Continental Motors president, William R. Angell, Jr. The review disclosed all wanted something like the A-40, but with more power, better reliability and a cheaper price.

Likewise, Carl Bachle, one of the Continental Motors senior engineers involved with the original A-40 development, recommended management dump the A-40 and pursue a power plant with more power and better reliability. From his impassioned pleas, plus the aircraft manufacturer's survey, staff changes were made within the Continental Motors organization for the development of the 50 hp Model A-50 power plant which evolved to be a very worthy successor to the A-40. In turn, superior engines developed from the A-50 included the A-65, A-75 and C-85 power plants.

The overwhelming success and acceptance of the A-50 and its successors cannot be underscored enough. In his superb work, *Continental! Its Motors And Its People,* author William Wagner cites the prophetic words of Dr. Chester L. Peek of Oklahoma City University, *"Development of the horizontally opposed, air-cooled aircraft engine was perhaps the single most important factor in the growth of our modern private aircraft industry."*

[60] Designs adapted to the Continental A-50 included the Piper Cub and the Aeronca K.

[61] Prior to being fitted with the new wings, a set of full-span, narrow chord ailerons were load tested, but never flown, on the "Ninety" in an attempt to reduce stick loads.

Bill Shepard related to this author some tests undertaken during the summer of 1937 regarding these full-span ailerons: *"During operation tests of the early ailerons when one aileron was loaded with the required weight of sandbags and the stick moved full over to raise that aileron, cable stretch and pulley bracket deflection were large enough that the aileron did not move the required amount.*

One suggested solution was to use narrow chord, full span ailerons which might reduce the required torque and still provide sufficient roll control."

These ailerons were not satisfactory, either. The actual solution was to make the pulley brackets and mounting structure more rigid. Also, the bellcrank arms were lengthened to reduce the tension loads on the cables.

[62] As best as can be determined, the engineering department personnel at the time consisted of Fred Knack, Jim Rising, Bill Shepard, Howard Jong, Chuck Holloway, Ed Tarencz, Ray Klisher and Ed Yulke. Howard Greene and Charlie Duthie, both apprentice program students, joined the engineering team in August 1937.

[63] Shortly before the lease terms and extension were approved, LAC treasurer Roger Johnson told Mercer County Counsel Phillip S. Vine construction of the new building would not start for two years. In turn, this information was relayed to the Board, which subsequently approved the lease.

[64] A Thomas W. Warner, Jr., owned the Falcon Aircraft Corporation. A popular rumor states Mr. Warner was related to the famous Warner Brothers of Hollywood, California, fame. In reality, Mr. Warner was related to Warner family of the Stewart-Warner Company in Detroit, Michigan.

Warner's West Coast company was the first of many concerns to sign a Dealer's Franchise Agreement with the Luscombe Airplane Corporation. One of the terms of this agreement required Falcon Aircraft Corp. to purchase a Phantom within four days of signing the agreement, which they did.

[65] Frank Johnson continued to enjoy a productive airplane design career. Shortly after his work in Camden, New Jersey, Johnson went to work for Rearwin Aircraft in Kansas City, Missouri, as structures engineer. He then joined Porterfield Aircraft Company, Kansas City, Missouri, as the company's chief engineer where he produced the "Collegiate" series. He held this position until his employment with the Stinson Airplane Company shortly before the start of World War II.

During the war years, he was the design group engineer responsible for the flaps, ailerons, controls and empennage of the Consolidated (later Convair) B-24, B-32 and B-36. He developed the first large aircraft applications of full span flaps, spring-tab boost controls and waffle-grid skin panels. As Chief Engineer of Convair's Stinson Division, Johnson design responsibilities included the L-5 "Sentinel," Model 108 "Voyager" and the short takeoff and landing L-13.

After Convair, Frank joined Lockheed Aircraft Company where he worked on the Little Dipper project. Tragically, Frank was critically injured in this prototype's crash when the test pilot attempted a takeoff with too little flying speed and subsequently stalled. Though Frank never fully recovered from his injuries, he nevertheless continued to pursue a successful and rewarding career with Lockheed.

Later positions within Lockheed included design group engineer on the P2V aircraft, assistant project engineer responsible for the B-29 rebuild program, the C-130 fuselage, landing gear and hydraulic systems. Additionally, he was the project engineer, Special Projects Division, which developed the C-130 ski-wheel landing system and the aerial delivery systems.

In the mid-1960s, Johnson was in charge of the Propulsion Systems Design on the Lockheed super-sonic transport. During this period, he was the manager of the Missile Design Division on the Polaris-Poseidon missile program.

Johnson retired from Lockheed in the late 1970s as the senior research and development engineer for Advanced Concepts, Rotary Wing New Design Division. Not one to retire from aviation, Johnson devoted many hours to a nearby Experimental Aircraft Association chapter. Similarly, his drawing board at home held many, future airplane ideas.

This great engineer died March 10, 1991, at his Norcross, Georgia, home.

[66] One Autumn day was particularly successful for King. A United Airlines Boeing 247, unable to land at Newark Terminal due to weather, diverted to Mercer County Airport. The airliner's captain instructed King to fill the tanks while he prepared to take-off for another try at Newark.

Running out of fuel from his own tanks, King had to call for a fuel truck from Trenton. The airliner's fuel needs had emptied the K & C Flying Service fuel tanks. King pumped more fuel into this one airplane than he had pumped in all other airplanes during the entire month.

[67] Bill Shepard forfeited his summer vacation to complete the "Ninety" production wing design and PA-36 aft fuselage and tail surfaces design. In a deal negotiated with Don Luscombe, Bill was given ten hours flying time in the "Ninety," instead. Bill put the total time to good use and renewed his Limited Commercial License. In 1937, 10 hours flying time were required to be logged every 6 months to renew this grade of license.

[68] This type of cowling represents one of the earliest known examples of light airplane pressure cowling engineering. This idea evolved into the production cowlings found on later Luscombe Model 8 aircraft.

Kotula returned to the factory later in the year to make some sketches of the PA-36.

[69] The Luscombe "50" was one of the first, if not the first, production light airplanes to use a Continental A-50 power plant.

[70] Though Tom Foley had a known heart problem, he never stopped enjoying life to its fullest.

Once, during a party at the "Jolly Roger," Foley was asked to make the "punch" for a party as he was known for his ability to make a super party punch. He added gin, vodka, whiskey and other ingredients, always taste testing his concoction until he deemed it was "ready." By this time, however, poor Tom became too drunk to enjoy the party and passed-out. Several friends carried him to his room.

Tragically, Tom Foley died within a year or two of his Luscombe "50" test flight from a heart attack while attending a hockey game in Boston. The news stunned Luscombe students and employees.

[71] No doubt this statement will bring the ire of many Luscombe "purists" who insist Ig Sargent made the first flight. Yet, as determined through numerous interviews with Luscombe factory alumni, newspaper accounts and logbook studies, this author believes steadfastly Foley made the *prototype* "Fifty" flight and Sargent made the first *production* "Fifty" flight some six months later.

CHAPTER 13

[72] A study of Ig Sargent's logbook suggests Don Luscombe flew with Sargent during one of his early test flights in that the passenger column is marked. However, there is no notation of any 1304 flight time in Don Luscombe's log book.

[73] Glen Kauffman, a Gap, Pennsylvania, native, arrived in late 1937 flying his American Eaglet. At least one other student, a George DuVall, owned an OX-5 powered Waco 10. Incidentally, this Waco 10 was rebuilt by the class as one of their school projects.

[74] Another theory regarding the metal rudder states the idea originated between Ig Sargent and Don Luscombe while an Aeronca C-2 visited the field. This airplane possessed corrugated aluminum aileron control surfaces.

A third theory states Bert Rowe and several LAC students went to the crash site of a Stearman-Hammond, retrieved a piece of the rudder and returned same to West Trenton for further study.

[75] All control surfaces on the Luscombe "50" were made of "Alclad." Alclad, the trade name for the Aluminum Company of America (ALCOA), was 17ST Dural which had a thin coat of aluminum. This thin coating provided corrosion resistance and a shiny surface at a very small sacrifice of strength. Dural possessed an unattractive gray color.

For example, the ultimate tensile strength of 17ST dural was 60,000 pounds per square inch whereas 17ST Alclad was 54,000 pounds per square inch for a given piece of material.

[76] The static load test demanded by the Department of Commerce was very rigorous. As stated in a later Luscombe Airplane Corporation *Operators Hand Book*:

The surfaces were static tested to the following unit loads without suffering permanent distortion:

Stabilizer	84.0 psf
Fin	29.5 psf
Elevator	43.1 psf
Rudder	26.5 psf
Aileron	26.2 psf

[77] This historical "blip" has, no doubt, confused some Luscombe enthusiasts who believe only *ONE* Luscombe "90" airplane, possessing the 1253 identification mark and 400 serial number, was ever built. In reality, *TWO* completely different airplanes—though somewhat similar in appearance — shared these same numbers.

[78] As best can be determined, no fatalities have been attributed directly to any failure of this fuel tank design. Perhaps, these early "false" reports were veiled attempts by some unscrupulous competitors to bring some "bad publicity" to bear upon the Luscombe Airplane Corporation.

[79] In light of the increasing student workload, it is amazing Jim Rising ever had time to instruct or fulfill his engineering duties.

[80] According to a Department of Commerce, Bureau of Air Commerce Repair and Alteration Form, NC1325 was virtually rebuilt. Except for the engine, cockpit instruments and both wings, a new fuselage was used as were new wing struts and vertical fin components. The airplane was returned to service in mid-September 1938.

CHAPTER 14

[81] These block license numbers were apportioned by the Bureau of Air Commerce to an airplane manufacturer in sequence. When all the assigned numbers were used, a new block of numbers were issued.

[82] Interestingly, two virtually identical brochures were prepared, one slightly preceding the other, each with one noticeable difference. The first brochure showed the 1304 airplane in the centermost photograph, whereas the second brochure showed the 1327 airplane.

[83] Luscombe Model 4, NC1335, posed an enigma during this author's research for this book. Though this airplane is listed in Ig Sargent's logbook, no official Federal Aviation Administration records attest to the existence of this particular airframe.

[84] The Brazilian D1L-204 flash number is decoded as follows:

D = general purpose aircraft
1 = first model built by Luscombe
L = Luscombe.

Official Brazilian aircraft registry records paint an interesting history for this particular Phantom. Originally certified as D1L-204 for the Marinha de Brasil (Brazilian Navy), this airplane became PP-TPT in 1942 when it was donated to the Aeroclube do Brazil by the Forca Aerea Brasileira, or FAB (Brazilian Air Force). The FAB was created in January 1941 by the amalgamation of the Army and Navy aviation services.

Interestingly, PP-TPT was registered officially on June 19, 1943, and its serial number, or constructor number, was listed as 121, not 118 as evidenced by FAA records. This Phantom's registration was cancelled from the official records on October 27, 1948 for unknown reasons.

[85] Other than the fact the airplane was registered F-W-0116 by French officials, very little is known what became of this Luscombe Model 8 after Ig Sargent's work with Caudron. One popular theory states the airplane was converted to a radar-controlled drone shortly before the outbreak of World War II, but no evidence known by this author at this time supports this theory.

[86] In the rush to leave with Coigny, Howard Jong told virtually no one at the factory he was leaving. It came as quite a shock to many when they learned Jong had returned to California. Enroute to California, Coigny made an extended stay in St. Louis. Jong decided to continue to California via a bus.

Jong continued to enjoy a successful career in a variety of aeronautical engineering endeavors. He joined Douglas Aircraft, Northern Division, shortly after he arrived home. Much to his delight, he was assigned to the landing gear group. There, he spent the next 23 years designing landing gear assemblies for everything from World War II fighters to early passenger transports to modern day commercial airliners.

In the early 1960s, Jong was transferred to Douglas' biomedical group responsible for cockpit design. Jong designed several control knobs and switches that were readily identifiable by feel only.

When Douglas Aircraft merged with McDonnell Aircraft of St. Louis, Missouri, and consolidated all engineering activities in Long Beach, California, Jong was moved to the Commercial Aircraft Interior Design Group. There, he designed improved lavatories, public address systems, oxygen mask systems, food service systems, etc.

Jong retired from the McDonnell-Douglas Corporation in 1976, and has remained very active in various sport and law enforcement aviation activities. One successful project involved the first ultralight ever employed for use by a police department (Monterey Park, California) for patrol purposes. This ultralight hangs in the Smithsonian Institution today.

[87] Boller's airplane was assembled a year earlier and flight tested by Sargent on May 25, 1937. The Luscombe Airplane Corporation had retained ownership of this Phantom. The airplane, when sold, was used to satisfy any financial encumbrances that existed between the corporation, Henry Olmstead, and his aviation insurance company.

[88] The short subject film was made in cooperation with *Mechanix Illustrated Magazine*. The clip, filmed on a perishable nitrate-base film stock, was called "Take to the Air" and ran about five minutes.

The completed clip today resides in the Library of Congress film archives, but is rapidly deteriorating due to its nitrate film composition. Requests by this author to view the film were denied due to its fragile nature.

Various rights to this film are retained by the Turner Entertainment Company of Los Angeles, California, who bought the Warner Brothers' film library during the mid-1980s.

[89] U.S. Government investigations conducted during World War II concluded Boller, as a teenager, may have participated in alleged acts of sabotage against occupying French, World War I forces. When questioned about these activities by U.S. officials, Boller reportedly stated any acts of sabotage were done under instruction from superiors and were done well before he came to the United States. Boller stated he and his friends resented the post-World War I French Occupation of the Rhineland.

[90] If Boller's background is clouded, then Vera Montgomery's background, though better documented, is just as obtuse.

According to wartime Vested Claims Committee documents, Mrs. Montgomery was born Vera Pavlow in Sofia, Bulgaria, on April 1, 1908. She lived in Bulgaria until 1922, at which time she moved to Switzerland and remained there until 1929. She married in August 1929, but was divorced four years later. She came to the United States in September 1929, resided in New York City, and became a naturalized citizen on January 5, 1931.

While she lived in New York City, Mrs. Montgomery was employed with several brokerage houses. She became very successful in the role of a "customer's woman." Through her work at Beverly Bogert & Company (later renamed Winslow, Douglas and McEvoy), she met Henry Boller for the first time in 1932, but not again until 1938.

In late 1936, she purchased a weekly newspaper called the *Yorkville Advance*, later changed to the *New York Advance*.

[91] A study of various United States Department of Justice, Vested Claims Committee documents relate Klotz had acquired Liechtenstein citizenship by degree of the Prince of Liechtenstein. Klotz's Liechtenstein passport was dated December 29, 1937. Interestingly, his parents held Liechtenstein citizenships, also dated December 29, 1937.

Contrary to any popular notion, the Klotz family was not Jewish and did not flee Germany for their lives. The family feared the German government, then coming into power, would seize all family money. Thus, they fled Germany to retain control of their money.

[92] Klotz's personal and family fortune evolved from the activities of his grandfather, Leopold Koppel, the father of Klotz's mother. Koppel was the founder of Osram Lamp Company, GmBH. in Berlin, Germany. Furthermore, he owned another company in Zurich, Switzerland, and held major interests in several companies throughout Germany and Europe. These companies virtually dominated the electric lamp business in Europe.

Shortly after the end of World War I, Koppel began to liquidate his vast holdings. He continued to do so until his death in 1933. In 1928, the International General Electric Company purchased a major portion of the Osram Lamp Company.

The subsequent liquidation of the Koppel estate amounted to almost $2,500,000 (1933 dollars). These holdings decreased substantially due to various levies imposed by the German government during the period. Likewise, the family was obligated to pay a large "flight tax," reportedly 25 percent of their net worth, when they left Germany in 1931. The family fortune, then worth roughly six million dollars, was divided into three equal shares. L.H.P. Klotz's immediate family share was approximately two million dollars.

In 1936, believing Holland was a safe haven from German seizure of the family money, Klotz decided to keep the family funds there. He formed the company, Stribbe & De Vries N.V. as a means to protect and invest the family fortune. At the start of World War II, upon hearing the Germans had entered Holland, Klotz wisely withdrew all funds and transferred them to the Chase National Bank in New York City. In turn, he assigned control of approximately half the funds to his father, Paul Klotz, and retained slightly more than one million dollars for his own use.

CHAPTER 15

[93] Henry Boller became an American citizen on February 7, 1939. Thus, the Luscombe Airplane Corporation Board of Directors consisted of 100 percent American citizens.

[94] The North American Investment Company was formed in December 1939 as a means to solve the Civil

Aviation Administration 75 percent stock ownership problems. Virtually all of Klotz's and Oberhumer's Luscombe Airplane Corporation stock was transferred to this corporation. In turn, Oberhumer, a naturalized American citizen, purchased all of this new corporation's capital stock.

[95] A series of lightplane races were held in Miami, Florida, on January 8 and 9, 1939. The first race was called the Firestone Elimination Race and was held on January 8. The second race, held the following day, was called the Firestone Trophy Race. Luscombe "50," Aeronca K, Aeronca Chief and Taylorcraft airplanes participated in this two day event. An A.B. Muzzy placed first in the first event flying a Luscombe "50" with an average speed of 94.72 mph. His prize was $75. Ig Sargent took fifth place flying a Luscombe "50" (NC22007) at an average speed of 89.48 mph.

On the following day, the Luscombe aircraft were overwhelmed by Aeronca K airplanes in the Firestone Trophy Race, a thirty mile race consisting of six laps around a five mile course. A.B. Muzzy placed third flying a stock Luscombe "50" with an average speed of 93.61 mph.

[96] According to U.S. Government records, Ernst Oberhumer was born in Germany on June 24, 1892. He entered the United States during August 1923, and became a naturalized citizen in 1929.

Oberhumer was a 1917 graduate of the University of Vienna and held a Bachelor of Law and a Doctor of Mechanics degrees. Shortly after graduation, Oberhumer was employed by various banks in Europe before he came to the United States.

Shortly after he arrived in the United States, Oberhumer joined the J. Henry Schroeder Banking Corporation of New York. Thereafter, he became a registered representative with various New York stock firms. His record and ability were highly regarded and respected.

Oberhumer was introduced to Leopold H.P. Klotz by Vera Montgomery. Klotz was quick to recognize Oberhumer's careful and analytical approach to financial, legal and management matters. Within a short time, Oberhumer became Klotz's closest financial and legal advisor and confidant.

[97] Though possibly never before revealed publicly, Don came close to losing his company in another stock takeover attempt before Klotz's takeover. Several Yale University graduates made a concerted effort to obtain enough stock to oust Don Luscombe. This group believed the company would be better served without Don at the helm.

One conspirator commented (referring to Pan Am founder and Yale graduate Juan Tripp), *"If he can do it, we can run this outfit."* According to another anonymous conspirator who corresponded with this author, *"We lost, but not by much."*

CHAPTER 16

[98] The Luscombe 65 Seaplane, or floatplane, was equipped with Edo 1340 floats and received its ATC in August 1939.

[99] Cochran's record was broken on January 30, 1940, when Philadelphia, Pennsylvania, Luscombe distributor Edward J. Waltz flew a highly-modified Luscombe "65," NC25180, to a blistering 118.7 mph over the same 100 km course Cochran flew. As of this writing, this record still stands.

To improve performance, Waltz removed the washout in his wings and tail. Similarly, he added specially made wheel pants and installed a Freedman-Burnham adjustable propeller for speed.

[100] James Rising resigned his chief engineer position in 1941 and accepted a direct commission in the Army Air Forces as a Captain. He was stationed in Florida.

When the war ended, he took a position with Pan American Grace Airlines as chief engineer. Several years later, he went to work with for Chase Aircraft in West Trenton, New Jersey.

Shortly thereafter, Rising left Chase and went to New York City. In 1964, while staying in one of New York City's many hotels, Rising heard a woman scream for help down a desolate hallway. Always a southern gentleman, Rising went to her aid. The woman's assailant wielded a knife and, there in a dimly lit hallway, James G. Rising lost his life.

[101] Both Ig Sargent and Eddie Davis rose to the rank of Colonel in the United States Army Air Force. Both received their baptism by fire in World War II with Sargent flying fifty-eight B-17 combat missions in the Far East. Both later commanded military installations during this conflict, each being highly decorated for exemplary service. Sargent and Davis left the active-duty service shortly after the War ended.

Afterwards, Sargent joined some friends, including Davis and ran Wings Field in Philadelphia. They started a new corporation called the Philadelphia Aviation Corporation, which later became Wings Field, Inc. They had the distributorships for Beechcraft airplanes and Republic Seebees.

Sargent and Davis remained in the U.S. Air Force Reserves and were both called to active duty during the Korean War. Sargent was assigned to War Plans in the Pentagon, checking-out in various jet aircraft during his tenure. Sargent's more exciting jet flights included a 30 minute flight as co-pilot in a North American B-45 at Edwards Air Force Base,

After retiring from the service, Sargent went into private industry, selling electronic equipment to the government. Additionally, he and his wife, Sissie, founded a very successful Washington, D.C., based travel agency.

As of this writing, Ig Sargent and his wife travel extensively in their Cessna 310 airplane.

Eddie Davis retired from the service and elected to enjoy a comfortable retirement on the South Carolina coast.

Ig Sargent and Eddie Davis remain the closest of friends today.

[102] After trying unsuccessfully to obtain a military contract for further PA-36 production, Harold Pitcairn ceased further flight testing of the PA-36. In turn, he ordered both airframes destroyed and the aluminum components donated to a wartime (World War II) scrap drive.

[103] Ed Mitchell, a 1936 Aero Engineer graduate and a licensed pilot, became the chief engineer of Cluett Aircraft Company following Fred Knack's departure some time later.

Subsequently, Mitchell accepted a position at the Luscombe Airplane Corporation during February 1944, and eventually became the company's acting chief engineer during a rapidly growing segment of post-West Trenton history.

Appendix A

You Certainly Look Funny In That Outfit

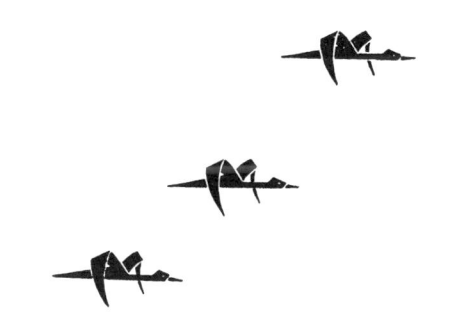

Mono-Aircraft Corporation
Moline, Illinois, U. S. A.

You Certainly Look Funny In That Outfit!

HI HO! Take for yourself a look. The swashbuckling Jenny expert appears—swaggers right up without blushing. What's the idea of the boots mister?—Oh yes, to keep the wind from blowing up your pant leg. But the breeches?—going horseback riding? They bind you around the knee. Yes, of course, we should have known, you like them that way—being tight helps reduce knee vibration, when you are asked to fly a modern airplane that doesn't look like a Jenny.

That leather jacket too, that's natty—hard to tell whether you look more like a dilapidated army officer or a taxi driver.

We'll bet you are one of these daring bird men—picturesque fellows who can tell the youngsters and natives just about all there is to be known about aviation and airplanes. Sure, you've had four thousand hours, sure!—not counting the dusk to dawn flying when you hand out advice about every airplane made, whether you have ever flown anything but your Jenny or its close modification.

Better get next to yourself big boy. Times are changing without waiting for you. If you're thinking like you did a year ago about most anything, you're slipping.

Perhaps you have been the backbone of commercial aviation during the chili and hot dog period but, if you don't get over the cheap heroics and burlesque you will be regarded a great menace rather than a contributing factor to aeronautical progress.

You have been so engrossed in your personal grandeur you have felt the public would pine away with a yearning to duplicate your picturesqueness and arrogance. You have attracted a few irresponsible boys and occasionally you are called upon by a person of mature judgment who gets sold on aviation in spite of you.

You haven't found a single, logical, economic reason why anyone should own an airplane. To be able to wear goggles and helmet and astonish ones friends may appeal to youngsters with barely enough money to buy the goggles, but it isn't reason enough for the class of people with money enough to buy an airplane if they choose.

The trouble with most of the helmet and goggle boys is that you are thinking too much in terms of a $3 passenger ride than a $300 commission.

Remember always that the only logical excuse for an airplane is to render fast, economical transportation. Too many have been trying to sell the thrill of merely getting up in the air, staggering around, and the right to look picturesque. It doesn't go over well enough to make any of you any real money in the short season you can operate your open face, drafty, whistle-wire, tandem, bumpy crates.

Take it point for point—a plane that is comfortable in all weather without getting dressed up to look funny. It's companionable—you can smoke and talk, no weather too rough, one man moves it in and out the hangar, a power plant that requires no more attention than you give your car, one that you can rebuild after the second year for $75—with a landing speed of less than 37 miles an hour—guaranteed top speed of 120 miles an hour and a fuel cost of less than 1½ cents a mile—an initial cost far below anything on the market, and regardless of some of the queerest yarns, some of the Jenny experts who have never flown such an airplane tell it is so easy to fly that it's almost a shame to tak money for showing a prospect how to operate it.

264 Visions of Luscombe: The Early Years

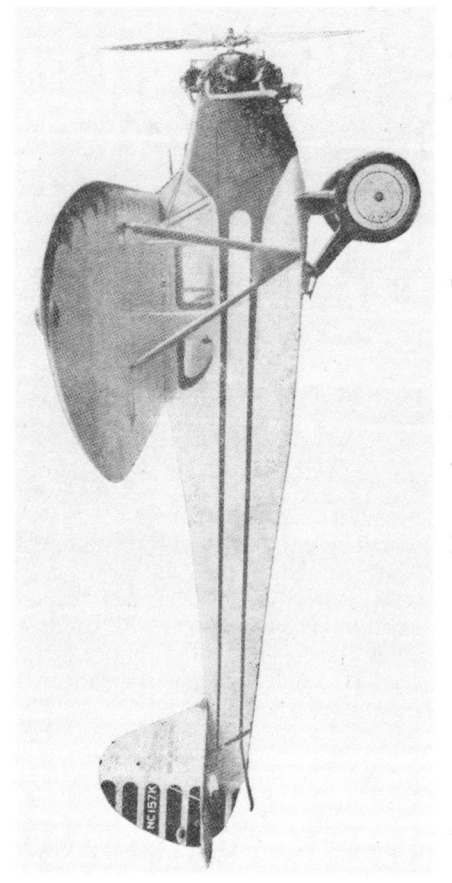

The Monocoupe "90" powered by Lambert R266, 90 H.P. Engine, giving the plane a high speed of 120 M.P.H. Price flyaway, Moline, $3375.00.

This $75.00 Lambert R266 engine repair kit includes all of the wearing parts and enables one to completely overhaul his engine with a minimum expense.

The Monocoupe 90
Registered Trade Mark

In the Monocoupe "90" you will find the fulfillment of your fondest dream of the qualities an airplane should possess—Speed, comfort, economy of operation, stability, complete equipment (including brakes and steel propeller), visibility and dependability, all are embodied in this new model at a price that represents airplane value never known before.

A glance at the accompanying illustration of this plane reveals at once its clean lines and sturdy construction. Note the tapered wing, braced wing struts, streamlined tail group, wide door and trim nose cowling

Within the cabin you find dual controls with one set quickly detachable if not desired, a wide comfortable seat built to accommodate parachute seat packs, and an instrument panel complete to the last detail. Brakes are actuated from the left side only and throttle and carburetor mixture controls are located in center of instrument panel, easily accessible to either occupant. Pulling the back of seat forward reveals a large luggage compartment. Under the edge of seat is the Bungee control for adjustment of elevator. A cabin heater can be found in the fire wall, opening into the cabin by the occupants feet where it will be most effective during cold

[7]

weather. At the side of the pilot is a large window that opens out and is held in that position if desired by a special lock. Overhead is a large window in the wing which permits perfect vision. In flight the tail is well up and the pilot can look straight ahead over the engine.

Two fifteen gallon gasoline tanks are located one on each side of fuselage in the wing and are equipped with direct reading gauges. The floor of cabin is covered with carpet and interior finish is in attractive colors. A step beneath the door permits easy access to cabin.

The fuselage is constructed of welded steel and chrome molybdenum steel tubing, covered with finest grade Flightex fabric.

The wing is made of specially selected spruce spars and ribs. MacWhyte tie rods are used for internal drag bracing. Sheet aluminum is fitted over the nose ribs forming a very sturdy and even leading edge. The entire wing is covered with Flightex.

A choice of five color combinations can be had for external finish.

SPECIFICATIONS

Span, 32 ft. 0 in.
Chord, 5 ft. 0 in.
Overall length, 20 ft. 5 in.
Overall height, 6 ft. 11 in.
Wing area, 132.2 sq. ft.
Wing section, Clark "Y"
Landing gear tread, 63 in.
Inside width of cabin, 35 in.
Height, floor to roof, 3 ft. 8 in.
High speed, 120 M.P.H.
Landing speed, 37 M.P.H.
Cruising speed, 105 M.P.H.
Cruising range, 525 miles
Climb, 1200 ft. per. min.
Ceiling, 20,000 ft.

Equipment: Navy specification consolidated instruments including altimeter, tachometer, oil gauge, temperature gauge, air speed meter, wheel brakes, Hamilton steel propeller, heater and gasoline gauges. Engine set in rubber.

[9]

The Lambert R266

This engine has been developed as a result of the experience gained from the Velie M5 that has proven so dependable for its hundreds of owners. Due to its slightly larger bore, increased engine speed and refinement the Lambert R266 develops 90 h. p., while its predecessor, the Velie M5, although of nearly equal size, develops only 65 h. p. Furthermore by using lighter alloys in the crank case and by improvement in design the 90 h. p. motor actually weighs less than the 65 h. p. engine.

The most outstanding feature of the R266 is the fact that, due to its construction it is possible to furnish a repair kit (illustrated on page 8) consisting of five cylinder barrels, five pistons with rings fitted, ten rocker arm bushings, ten valve guides, ten spark plugs and a complete set of gaskets—ALL FOR $75.00. Nowere else can such value be found! This kit enables one to fly the plane all year and at the end of this time replace all worn engine parts for only $75.00. Replacing of parts has been made so simple that any average mechanic can easily make the necessary changes. No more worries about the high cost of engine overhauls.

Gasoline consumption at 2150 R.P.M. (cruising speed) is about six gallons per hour. Oil consumption is proportionately small.

Untold hours of testing under actual flight conditions have proven definitely that this engine will stand abuse that heretofore no one would think of imposing upon an aircraft power plant. The Lambert R266 now holds the altitude record for light planes.

SPECIFICATIONS

Type, 5 cyl., air cooled, radial
Bore, 4.25 in.
Stroke, 3.75 in.
Displacement, 266 cu. in.
85 h.p. at 2250 R. P. M.
90 h.p. at 2375 R.P.M.
Weight less equipment, 214 lbs.
Length overall, 30⅜ in.
Diameter overall, 33 in.
Ignition, Two Scintilla magnetos
Carburetor, Stromberg NA-R3
Spark Plugs, 2 per cyl., Champions

SETTING TONGUES A-WAGGING

MONO-AIRCRAFT CORPORATION
MOLINE   ILLINOIS

Setting Tongues A-Wagging

WHEN women wore mutton sleeves and the gay bucks about town went in for the thrilling and daring sport of bicycling, the smart thing in bikes was a two seater—tandem arrangement. This vehicle exposed to the elements was a bit drafty, like other two seaters of the day so ably described by our friend "Chic" Sales.

The race was virile in those days and the drafts didn't matter. Modern plumbing hadn't progressed far and knitting mills worked overtime to supply the demand for female underwear of the full length variety.

Some of these bikers were more daring than the great run of their brothers and were first to venture into aircraft. They left the imprint of their times and for years we have had to accept the drafty, unsociable tandem bike arrangement in our airplanes.

At any rate this was all we had when most of us learned to fly. When the War came along we learned, more or less, how to push around a Jenny. We astonished our friends who in their hero worship for our daring rather set up a standing of aeronautical expert for us. We swaggered about

[3]

with this reputation to maintain for so long we came to accept the rating.

Of course, our experience has been entirely around this one design or its slight modification but, since all the other experts like ourselves came out of the same school, our position of authority was not challenged.

It was difficult to accept some of the new ideas which came along about the time the general public became interested. It was rather a shock to our standing to have new ideas in aircraft upon which we could only advance conjectures.

Youngsters were coming home from school talking a jargon of aeronautical formula which left us gaping. The Department of Commerce came out with a list of comparatively simple questions to answer and we were embarrassed. Fortunately the inspectors displayed certain deference to our background and our position as expert again became bonafide with a license to prove it.

Then and there, however, we formed a new alliance to our alma mater and became most cynical toward new things we didn't understand and that threatened to impede the traditions dating back to the bicycle days.

Possibly the mutton sleeves, the rigid corset stays, the heavy underwear weren't much inducement to side by side sociability in those days.

[4]

Flying was largely a matter, too, of astonishing ones friends and customers. Getting up in the air was the thing. Controls weren't especially responsive and we didn't think in terms of fast, economical transportation. We got used to slow controls, it didn't matter as long as our planes had plenty of resistence to insure slow, sloppy landings.

When the new planes that were clean in line and carried the same weight at faster speed yet with half the horsepower came out, responsive controls and higher speeds again rather upset the old order of things. The modern idea was playing havoc with Army traditions and what good would our Army be without traditions.

Those of us, however, who cling to our preference for the planes of yesterday are losing ground. Sooner or later the man who flies will not choose to be called a pilot or chauffeur and much of the picturesqueness of flying will be lost.

The trappings on the race track—the boots, breeches, helmets and goggles will go the way of gauntlet gloves, dusters, flowing veils, mutton sleeves and the telephone booths out in the back yard.

Mono Aircraft was first to plan its future on this belief and each day forcefully bears out the soundness of the conviction.

[5]

To Dominate

its field in 1930 — beyond a question of doubt

MONO-AIRCRAFT *Offers*

. . . a new two place, cabin monoplane with a top speed in excess of 120 miles an hour (—*yet with a fuel cost less than* 1½ *cents per mile*).

. . . new smartness in appearance, greater comfort, improved vision and incomparable stability.

. . . a new approved 90 h. p. engine, second to none in the world for dependability, accessibility, simplicity and economical maintenance. (*We will supply a kit of five cylinder barrels, pistons with rings fitted, valve guides, rocker arm bushings, gaskets and spark plugs for $75.00 list.*)

. . . complete accessories contributing to added safety such as brakes, steel propeller, parachute pack seats, air speed indicator and the best instruments money will buy.

. . . a price, as usual, below anything else in the field

Nineteen Thirty Will Be a Mono Aircraft Year

Full information is yours for the asking.

The New 1930 Model

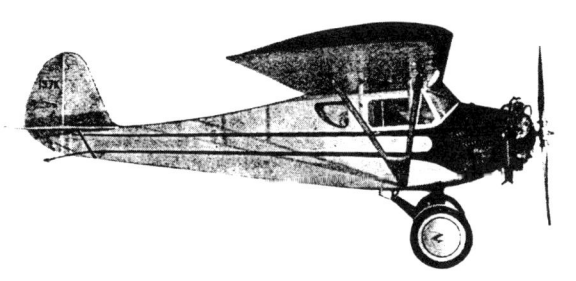

clean lines and absence of external bracing. Every exposed fitting on the plane is streamlined in production and no pains have been spared to make this job the utmost in efficiency and yet not sacrifice the comfort of the passengers.

A very novel and yet extremely practical device, operated by the pilot by a small crank, exerts pressure on the elevator control wires in such a way as to offset any nose or tail heaviness of the plane. Its effect is exactly the same as an adjustable stabilizer but is much lighter and offers no additional drag.

A specially built lock on the left window provides for opening it and holding it open in such a way that the pilot has perfect vision straight ahead. This will prove to be a great help to landing in bad weather.

Color combinations will be varied and to a certain extent optional with the purchaser.

Close investigation will prove our claim that the plane represents America's most outstanding airplane value.

The performance of this plane will be a startling revelation to all of you who have flown. Its speed, rate of climb, ease of maneuverability and the sense of security from the ninety horse motor—all will tend to establish new standards of comparison.

Within the cabin you will find comfort in its wide seat, excellent visibility and a complete set of Navy specification instruments including air speed indicator. A luggage compartment of ample size is provided at rear of seat. The seats are of a type suitable for wearing parachute pack if desired. The throttle control is located in the center of instrument panel thus making it accessible for either occupant in case dual controls are used.

As can be seen from the photograph, the external appearance is exceptionally trim. The whole plane represents the utmost in streamline design. Especial attention is called to the empennage. Notice the

The Lambert Model R-266

The Lambert R266 engine has been developed as a result of vast experimental work and after a great deal of experience from manufacturing the Velie M5 engine, an engine that has gained an enviable reputation for dependable service.

In spite of its increase of horsepower the Lambert R266 is twenty pounds lighter than the Velie M5. This is accomplished by cleanness of design and use of lighter magnesium alloys.

The short stroke enables high speed and yet the piston travel is comparatively slow. The crank case is made of two piece magnesium alloy split on a plane through the cylinder centers. Cylinder heads and pistons are of heat treated heat resisting aluminum alloy. Cylinder barrels are of a high strength nickel iron, and due to having a loose fit in the head the barrels can be replaced with little expense. The crank shaft is of two pieces, constructed of heat treated chrome nickel steel, single throw and is carried on three ball bearings. Lubrication is of the pressure dry sump type.

Its construction is such that for $75.00 sufficient parts (listed elsewhere herein) can be purchased to make the motor practically brand new and the labor required can easily be done by any competent mechanic without the use of special tools and machines.

SPECIFICATIONS LAMBERT R266 ENGINE

Type	5 cyl., air cooled, radial
Bore	4.25 in.
Stroke	3.75 in.
Displacement	266 cu. in.
85 h. p. at 2250 R. P. M.	
90 h. p. at 2375 R. P. M.	
Weight less equipment	214 lbs.
Length overall	30⅝ in.
Diameter overall	33 in.
Ignition	Two Scintilla magnetos
Carburetor	Stromberg NA-R3
Spark Plugs, two per cyl.	Champions

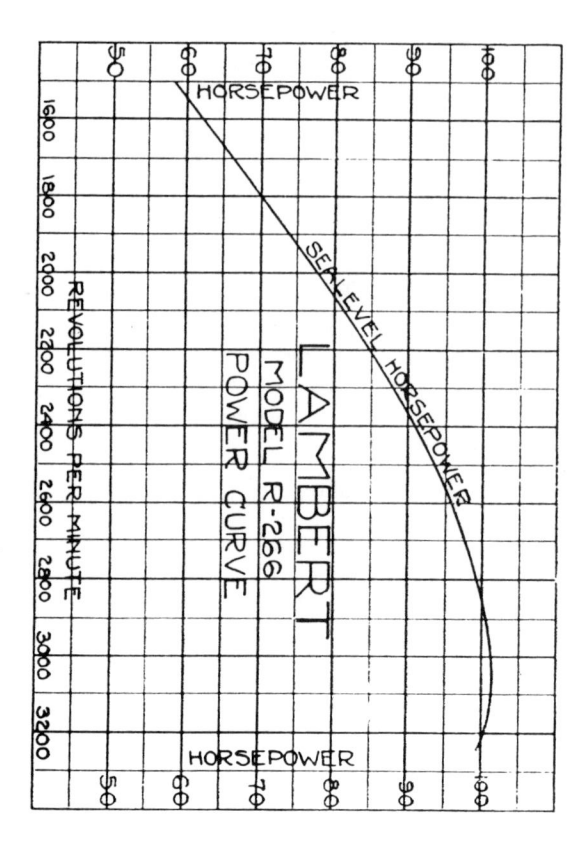

Appendix B

Monocoupe Specifications

CENTRAL STATES MONOCOUPE 2-place ATC 22
(Anzani powered version)

Specifications: Wingspan 30' with 60" chord
Length 19' 9"
Height 6' 3"
Wing area 143 sq. ft. ("Clark Y" airfoil)
Empty weight 700 lbs.
Gross weight 1175 lbs.
Useful load 475 lbs.
Payload 185 lbs.
Fuel capacity 20 gals.
Oil capacity 2 gals.
Performance: Maximum speed 102 MPH
Cruising speed 87 MPH
Landing speed 35 MPH
Service ceiling 8000 ft.
Rate of climb 700 ft./min.
Cruising range 400 miles
Engine: Anzani 60 hp
Price: $2375 FAF

CENTRAL STATES MONOCOUPE 2-place ATC 22 (1-28)
(Detroit Air-Cat powered version)

Specifications: Wingspan 30' with 60" chord
Length 19' 9"
Height 6' 3"
Wing area 143 sq. ft. ("Clark Y" airfoil)
Empty weight 749 lbs.
Gross weight 1224 lbs.
Useful load 475 lbs.
Payload 185 lbs.
Fuel capacity 20 gals.
Oil capacity 2 gals.
Performance: Maximum speed 95 MPH
Cruising speed 80 MPH
Landing speed 38 MPH
Service Ceiling 8000 ft.
Rate of climb 600 ft./min.
Cruising range 400 miles
Engine: Detroit Air-Cat 60 hp
Price: $2285 FAF

JIM HARVEY

MONOCOUPE MODEL 70   2-place   ATC 70   (9-28)

Specifications: Wingspan 32' with 60" chord
Length 19' 9"
Height 6' 3"
Wing area 143 sq. ft. (Clark "Y" airfoil)
Empty weight 795 lbs.
Gross weight 1350 lbs.
Useful load 555 lbs.
Payload 215 lbs.
Fuel capacity 25 gals.
Oil capacity 2 gals.
Performance: Maximum speed 98 MPH
Cruising speed 85 MPH
Landing speed 37 MPH
Service ceiling 10,500 ft.
Rate of climb 550 ft./min.
Cruising range 500 miles
Engine: Velie M-5 (55-65 hp)
Price: $2500 FAF
$2835 FAF
(October 1929)

JOHN UNDERWOOD

BILL MEEHAN/JIM HARVEY

MONOCOUPE MODEL 113   2-place   ATC 113   (2-29)

Specifications: Wingspan 32' with 60" chord
Length 19' 9"
Height 6' 3"
Wing area 143 sq. ft.
(Clark "Y" airfoil)
Empty weight 848 lbs.
Gross weight 1350 lbs.
Useful load 502 lbs.
Payload 172 lbs.
Fuel capacity 25 gals.
Oil capacity 2 gals.
Performance: Maximum speed 98 MPH
Cruising speed 85 MPH
Landing speed 37 MPH
Service ceiling 11,000 ft.
Rate of climb 580 ft./min.
Cruising range 500 miles
Engine: Velie M-5 (55-65 hp)
Price: $2675 FAF (1929 introductory price)
$2835 FAF (August 1929)

JAMES B. ZAZAS COLLECTION

FRAN FITZWILLIAM

Appendix B: Monocoupe Specifications

MONOCOACH 201 4-place ATC 201 (8-16-29)

Specifications: Wingspan 39' with 75" chord
Length 26' 8"
Height 7' 8"
Wing area 230 sq. ft.
(USA-35B airfoil)
Empty weight 1919 lbs.
Gross weight 3092 lbs.
Useful load 1173 lbs.
Payload 578 lbs.
Fuel capacity 63 gals.
Oil capacity 6 gals.
Performance: Maximum speed 128 MPH
Cruising speed 110 MPH
Landing speed 48 MPH
Service ceiling 18,000 ft.
Rate of climb 900 ft./min.
Cruising range 550 miles
Engine: Wright J5 "Whirlwind" 220 hp
Price: $6500 FAF (1928 introduction with Velie ML-9 engine)
$7950 FAF (October 1929)

FRAN FITZWILLIAM

MONOPREP MODEL 218 2-place ATC 218 (8-30-29)

Specifications: Wingspan 32' with 60" chord
Length 21' 0"
Height 6' 3"
Wing area 143 sq. ft.
("Clark Y" airfoil)
Empty weight 783 lbs.
Gross weight 1288 lbs.
Useful load 505 lbs.
Payload 250 lbs.
Fuel capacity 15 gals.
Oil capacity 1.5 gals.
Performance: Maximum speed 92 MPH
Cruising speed 80 MPH
Landing speed 37 MPH
Service ceiling 9000 ft.
Rate of climb 680 ft./min.
Cruising range 290 miles (4 gal/hr)
Engine: Velie M-5 (55-65 hp)
Price: $2675 FAF (1929 introduction)
$2835 FAF (1929)
$2575 FAF (1930 price reductions)

FRAN FITZWILLIAM

JAMES B. ZAZAS COLLECTION

272 Visions of Luscombe: The Early Years

MONOSPORT MODEL 1 **2-place** **ATC 249 (10-4-29)**

Specifications: Wingspan 32' 3" with 60" chord
Length 21' 5"
Height 7' 1"
Wing area 133.2 sq. ft.
("Clark Y" airfoil)
Empty weight 1056 lbs.
Gross weight 1650 lbs.
Useful load 594 lbs.
Payload 205 lbs.
Fuel capacity 32 gals.
Oil capacity 4 gals.
Performance: Maximum speed 129 MPH
Cruising speed 110 MPH
Landing speed 42 mph
Service ceiling 18,000 ft.
Rate of climb 1000 ft./min.
Cruising range 520 miles (6.5 gal/hr)
Engine: Warner 110 "Scarab" 110 hp
Price: $6350 FAF (1929)
$4500 FAF (1930 price reductions)

FRAN FITZWILLIAM

MONO-AIRCRAFT FACTORY BROCHURE, JAMES B. ZAZAS COLLECTION

MONOSPORT MODEL 2 **2-place** **ATC 250 (10-4-29)**

Specifications: Wingspan 32' 3" with 60" chord
Length 21' 5"
Height 7' 1"
Wing area 133.2 sq. ft.
("Clark Y" airfoil)
Empty weight 1053 lbs.
Gross weight 1650 lbs.
Useful load 597 lbs.
Payload 208 lbs.
Fuel capacity 32 gals.
Oil capacity 4 gals.
Performance: Maximum speed 129 MPH
Cruising speed 110 MPH
Landing speed 42 MPH
Service ceiling 17,500 ft.
Rate of climb 990 ft./min.
Cruising range 550 mile (6 gal/hr)
Engine: Kinner K5 100 hp
Price: $5750 FAF (1929)
$4250 FAF (1930 price reductions)

JAMES B. ZAZAS COLLECTION

Appendix B: Monocoupe Specifications 273

MONOCOACH 275 4-place ATC 275 (11-13-29)

Specifications: Wingspan 39' with 75" chord
Length 26' 9"
Height 8' 7"
Wing area 230 sq. ft. (USA-35B airfoil)
Empty weight 1883 lbs.
Gross weight 3100 lbs.
Useful load 1217 lbs.
Payload 626 lbs.
Fuel capacity 63 gals.
Oil capacity 6 gals.
Performance: Maximum speed 133 MPH
Cruising speed 112 MPH
Landing speed 48 MPH
Service ceiling 18,000 ft
Rate of climb 1200 ft./min.
Cruising range 550 miles (12.5 gal/hr)
Engine: Wright J6 225 hp
Price: $8250 FAF

AERO DIGEST

MONOCOUPE MODEL 90 2-place ATC 306 (4-2-30)

Specifications: Wingspan 32'
Length 20' 10"
Height 6' 11"
Wing area 132 sq. ft.
("Clark Y" airfoil)
Empty weight 859 lbs.
Gross weight 1490 lbs.
Useful load 631 lbs.
Payload 266 lbs.
Fuel capacity 30 gals.
Oil capacity 2.5 gals.
Performance: Maximum speed 116 MPH
Cruising speed 100 MPH
Landing speed 40 MPH
Service ceiling 15,000 ft.
Rate of climb 850 ft./min.
Cruising range 500 miles
(5.5 gal/hr)
Engine: Lambert 90 hp
Price: $3375 FAF (1930)
$2885 FAF (1933 price reductions)

JIM HARVEY

274 Visions of Luscombe: The Early Years

MONOCOUPE MODEL 110   2-place   ATC 327   (6-16-30)

Specifications: Wingspan 32' with 60" chord
Length 20' 4"
Height 6' 11"
Wing area 132 sq. ft.
 ("Clark Y" airfoil)
Empty weight 991 lbs.
Gross weight 1611 lbs.
Useful load 620 lbs.
Payload 247 lbs.
Fuel capacity 30 gals.
Oil capacity 3.5 gals.
Performance: Maximum speed 133 MPH
 (142 MPH*)
Cruising speed 112 MPH
 (120 MPH*)
Landing speed 45 MPH
Service ceiling 16,000 ft.
Rate of climb 1050 ft./min.
Cruising range 450 mile (7 gal/hr)
Engine: Warner 110 "Scarab" 110 hp
Price: $4500 FAF (1930)
$4750 FAF (1931)
Notes: Items denoted by an asterisk (*) reflect a Model 110 equipped with wheel pants and a Townend speed-ring engine cowling.

JOHN UNDERWOOD

JOHN UNDERWOOD

MONOCOUPE MODEL 90-J   2-place   ATC 355   (8-20-30)

Specifications: Wingspan 32' with 60" chord
Length 20' 10"
Height 6' 11"
Wing area 132.3 sq. ft.
 ("Clark Y" airfoil)
Empty weight 902 lbs.
Gross weight 1511 lbs.
Useful load 609 lbs.
Payload 244 lbs.
Fuel capacity 30 gals.
Oil capacity 2.5 gals.
Performance: Maximum speed 118 MPH
Cruising speed 102 MPH
Landing speed 40 MPH
Service ceiling 15,000 ft.
Rate of climb 850 ft./min.
Cruising range 500 mile
 (5.5 gal/hr)
Engine: Warner 90 "Scarab Junior" 90 hp
Price: $3950 FAF (1930)

U.S. CIVIL AIRCRAFT BOOK, VOLUME 4

Appendix B: Monocoupe Specifications

MONOCOUPE MODEL 125 2-place ATC 359 (8-23-30)

Specifications: Wingspan 32' with 60" chord
Length 20' 8"
Height 6' 10"
Wing area 132.3 sq. ft.
 ("Clark Y" airfoil)
Empty weight 1007 lbs.
Gross weight 1590 lbs.
Useful load 583 lbs.
Payload 203 lbs.
 (1 passenger @ 170 lbs.
 and 33 lbs baggage)
Fuel capacity 30 gals.
Oil capacity 4.5 gals.
Performance: Maximum speed 133 MPH
 (144 MPH*)
Cruising speed 113 MPH
 (124 MPH*)
Landing speed 45 MPH
Service ceiling 18,000 ft.
Rate of climb 1100 ft./min.
Cruising range 460 miles (7.5 gal/hr)
Engine: Kinner B5 125 hp
Price: $4500 FAF (1930)
 $4750 FAF (1930, later price increase)
Notes: Items denoted by an asterisk (*) reflect a Model 125 equipped with wheel pants and a Townend speed-ring engine.

JOHN UNDERWOOD

MONOCOUPE MODEL 70-V 2-place ATC 492 (9-1-32)

Specifications: Wingspan 32' with 60" chord
Length 20' 10"
Height 6' 10"
Wing area 132.3 sq. ft.
 ("Clark Y" airfoil)
Empty weight (unknown)
Gross weight (unknown)
Useful load (unknown)
Payload (unknown)
Fuel capacity 30 gals.
Oil capacity 4.5 gals.
Performance: Maximum speed (unknown)
Cruising speed (unknown)
Landing speed (unknown)
Service ceiling (unknown)
Rate of climb (unknown)
Cruising range (unknown)
Engine: Velie M-5 65 hp
Price: $2395 FAF (1932)
Note: Factual data was unavailable regarding this particular model airplane.

U.S. CIVIL AIRCRAFT BOOK, VOLUME 5

Approved Type Airplanes Now in Production (Continued from April Issue of Aero Digest)

Specifications: (Models 90, 110, 125, respectively) Span, 32 feet. Length overall, 20 feet 10 inches; 20 feet 4 inches; 20 feet 8 inches. Height overall, 6 feet 11 inches. Wing area (including ailerons), 132.3 square feet. Lambert R-266 at 90 horsepower; Warner Scarab 110 horsepower; Kinner B-5 of 125 horsepower. Wing loadings, 11.3;

MONO
MONOCOUPE 90, 110, 125
Mono Aircraft Corporation
Moline, Illinois

12.25; 12 pounds per square foot. Power loadings, 16.6; 14.7; 12.7 pounds per horsepower. Weights empty, 859; 991; 1,007 pounds. Useful loads, 631; 620; 583 pounds. Gross weights, 1,490; 1,611; 1,590 pounds.

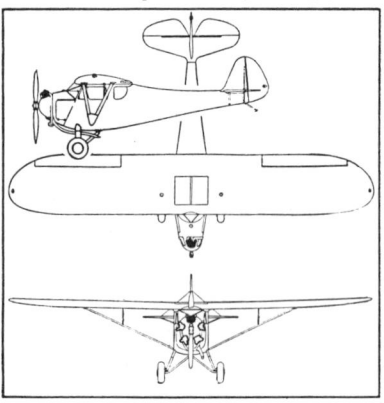

Performance: High speeds, 116; 133 (or 142 with ring); 133 (or 142 with ring) miles per hour. Cruising speeds, 100; 112; 112 miles per hour. Landing speeds, 40; 45; 45 miles per hour. Rates of climb, 900; 1,200; 1,200 feet per minute. Service ceilings, 15,000; 18,000; 18,000 feet. Radii, 540; 460; 420 miles. Gasoline capacities, 30 gallons, all three models.

The fuselage of all three models is of welded steel tubing, engine mount being integral with fuselage. Covering is Flightex. Ailerons are unbalanced. Framework of the tail surfaces is of welded steel tubing, braced. Wings are one-piece, conventional two-spar construction. Two persons are accommodated. Landing gear is of the divided type. Equipment includes Hartzell wood or Hamilton-Standard propeller, Aircraft Products brakes, Pioneer instruments, Monoil oildraulic shock struts, Goodrich tires, Townend ring, wheel pants. Model 90 approved for Edo float installation.

Two persons are accommodated. Models 110 carries 33 pounds of baggage; model 125, 29 pounds; and model 90, 52 pounds.

Specifications: Span, 39 feet. Length overall, 26 feet 8 inches. Height overall, 7 feet 8 inches. Wing area (including ailerons), 222 square feet. Wright J-6 of 225 horsepower. Power loading, 14 pounds per horsepower. Wing loading, 14 pounds per square foot. Weight empty, 1,883 pounds. Useful load, 1,217 pounds. Gross weight, 3,100

MONO
MONOCOACH 275
Mono Aircraft Corporation
Moline, Illinois

pounds.

Performance: High speed, 133 miles per hour. Cruising speed, 112 miles per hour. Landing speed, 55 miles per hour. Rate of climb, 1,200 feet per minute. Service ceiling, 18,000 feet. Radius, 350 miles. Gasoline capacity, 63 gallons.

The framework of the fuselage is constructed of welded steel tubing (1025 steel except in highly stressed members which are 4130). The engine mount is integral with the fuselage. Covering is Flightex. The ailerons are Frise type, wood construction with aluminum leading edge. The framework of the tail surfaces is of welded steel tubing, braced. Stabilizer is adjustable in the air, fin on the ground. The wings are two-piece, conventional two-spar construction. Spars are spruce, ribs picture frame with basswood webs and spruce capstrips. The leading edge is covered with aluminum. The landing gear is the divided type, heat treated 4130 steel tubing.

Propeller is Hamilton-Standard; instruments, Pioneer; shock absorbers, Aircraft Products oildraulic struts; brakes, Bendix. Wheels are 30 inches by 5 inches. Four persons without parachutes and 114 pounds of baggage or 34 pounds of baggage and parachutes are accommodated. Dual controls are provided.

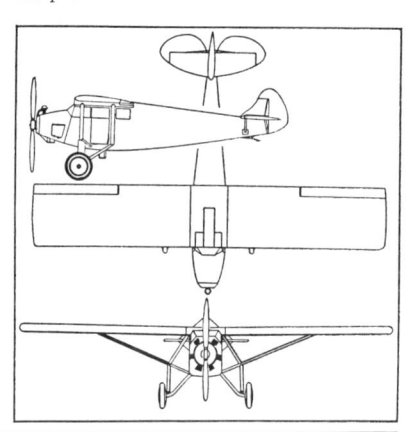

Specifications: Span, 32 feet 3 inches. Length overall, 21 feet. Height overall, 6 feet 3 inches. Wing area (including ailerons), 143 square feet. Velie M-5 of 55 horsepower. Wing loading, 9 pounds per square foot. Power loading, 23.4 pounds per horsepower. Weight empty, 783 pounds. Useful load, 505 pounds. Gross weight,

MONO
MONOPREP 218
Mono Aircraft Corporation
Moline, Illinois

1,288 pounds.

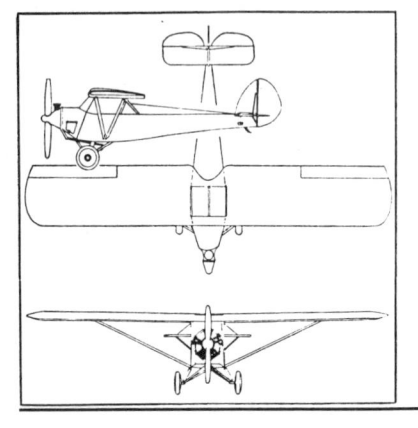

Performance: High speed, 90 miles per hour. Cruising speed, 78 miles per hour. Landing speed, 40 miles per hour. Rate of climb, 600 feet per minute. Services ceiling, 9,000 feet. Radius, 240 miles. Gasoline capacity, 14.6 gallons.

The framework of the fuselage is constructed of welded steel tubing (1025 steel). The engine mount is integral with the fuselage. The covering of the fuselage is Flightex. The ailerons are plywood, unbalanced, inset slightly from the tip. The framework of the tail surfaces is of welded steel tubing, braced. The wing is one piece, conventional two-spar construction. Spars are spruce, ribs picture frame with basswood webs and spruce capstrips. The landing gear is of the divided type, heat treated 4130 steel tubing. Monoil oildraulic shock struts are provided.

The propeller is Hamilton-Standard. Instruments are Consolidated. Tires are 26 inches by 4 inches. Aircraft Products brakes are provided as optional equipment. Shock absorbers are Monoil oildraulic.

The Monoprep accommodates two persons, including crew. Twenty-five pounds of baggage and parachutes are accommodated, or 65 pounds of baggage less parachutes. Seating arrangement is side by side. Controls are dual.

AERO DIGEST, MAY 1931

Appendix C
Individual Luscombe Phantom Model 1 Histories

LUSCOMBE PHANTOM, NC272Y, Serial Number 1

STATUS—Aircraft Deregistered
REASON—Owner's Request
AIRCRAFT SERIAL NUMBER—1
DATE of MANUFACTURE—May 1934, manufactured at the former Butler Blackhawk Plant, Kansas City Municipal Airport, Kansas City, Missouri.
POWER PLANT—Warner 145 "Super Scarab", serial number (?).
PROPELLER—Hamilton-Standard with 7056F hub and 19B 1/2-16 blades, serial numbers (?).
Department of Commerce Form AB-9 application filed June 11, 1934 for Identification Mark. Inspector's recommendation was 272Y. This number was already displayed on the aircraft.
Fuel capacity—33 gallons, Empty weight—1320 lbs, gross weight—1950 lbs, useful load— lbs, payload—236 lbs, cargo—66 lbs.

JAMES B. ZAZAS COLLECTION

Approved Type Certificate No. 552 awarded July 28, 1934.
Operation Inspection Report, Form AB-80, filed on July 29, 1934 by Inspector George Gay.
Unlicensed identification mark of 272Y cancelled September 4, 1934. New mark was NC272Y.
Repairs to aircraft's structure made in Boston, Massachusetts during September 1934. Repairs included replacement of rivets on top part of fuselage next to last bay. Dents bumped out of fuselage in same section. Straightened top of rudder and fin. Repaired small cuts on top of wing. All repairs undertaken at the direction of Mr. Luscombe according to Form AB-80 filed 9/25/34.
Letter from Department of Commerce to Don A. Luscombe reminding him license for NC272Y, Luscombe Phantom 1, will expire August 1, 1935. In reply, DAL sent letter to Department of Commerce, dated June 24, 1935, "subject airplane which was for experimental and test purposes has been completely dismantled and cancellation is requested".
Cancellation was granted on June 27, 1935.

LUSCOMBE PHANTOM, NC275Y, Serial Number 101

STATUS—Aircraft currently registered
REASON—
AIRCRAFT SERIAL NUMBER—101
DATE of MANUFACTURE—December 13, 1934, manufactured at the former Butler Blackhawk Plant, Kansas City Municipal Airport, Kansas City, Missouri.
POWER PLANT—Warner 145 "Super Scarab", serial number SS 106 E.
PROPELLER—Hamilton-Standard, serial number 23314. Changed to Curtiss-Reed, model number 55511, serial number ?.
First test flight December 18, 1934. Pilot- Barton Stevenson.
Application for Commercial License submitted on December 19, 1934.
Sold to Carl B. Haun, Blackwell, Oklahoma, on December 19, 1934.

JAMES B. ZAZAS COLLECTION

Aircraft inspected and approved by Inspector James N. Peyton on December 19, 1934. Inspection undertaken in Blackwell, Oklahoma.
Sold to Luscombe Airplane Company, Kansas City, Missouri, on December 24, 1934.
Sold to Mr. Reginald L. and Aline R. Brooks, New York, New York, on January 12, 1936.
Sold to Aline Rhonie Brooks, New York, New York, on June 1, 1937.
 (Aline resumed her maiden name after divorce from R.L. Brooks.)
Registered to Aline H. Rhonie on April 22, 1941.
Sold to Herbert L. White, Van Nuys, California, on October 23, 1941.
Sold to Roy Taylor, Fort Worth, Texas, on August 4, 1942.
Sold to Johney Cockburn, Artesia, New Mexico, on April 19, 1943. Stated purpose of sale to War Production Board was "Pipeline Patrol".
Sold to Roy R. Taylor, Fort Worth, Texas, on December 22, 1943.
Sold to Carl Richard Kraff, Fort Worth, Texas, on February 5, 1944.
Sold to Mrs. Phil Brown (A.K.A. Antoinette Agnes Leprohon), Bakersfield, California, on May 5, 1945.
Sold to Thomas W. Foxworthy, Los Angeles, California, on August 1, 1947.
Sold to Lawrence Zanutto, Los Angeles, California, on June 26, 1952.
Sold to David J. Considine, Oakdale, California, July 23, 1953.
Sold to Lt. Fred Serenson, USN, NAS Moffett Field, California, on March 27, 1963.
Sold to B. Peter Bowers, Cupertino, California, on January 4, 1967 and remains the current owner as of December 15, 1991.

LUSCOMBE PHANTOM, NC276Y, Serial Number 102

STATUS—Aircraft Airworthiness Certificate Expired
REASON—Aircraft destroyed in fatal accident, April 13, 1941, Holyoke, Colorado.
AIRCRAFT SERIAL NUMBER—102
DATE of MANUFACTURE—January 5, 1935, manufactured at the former Butler Blackhawk Plant, Kansas City Municipal Airport, Kansas City, Missouri.
POWER PLANT—Warner 145 "Super Scarab", serial number SS 15 E.
PROPELLER—Hamilton-Standard, serial number 21696, blade design 19B 1/2-16.
Fuel Capacity—33 gals, empty weight—1311 lbs, gross weight—1950 lbs, maximum payload with full fuel—236 pounds, cargo—66 lbs.
Aircraft Application for Identification Mark applied January 5, 1935.
Sold to Bryan D. Sheedy, Roosevelt Field, Garden City, New York on January 5, 1935. (Of special interest, the paperwork was signed in Kansas City, Missouri.)
Application for Commercial License submitted on January 6, 1935.
Airplane inspected and approved by Inspector Oscar L. Wallace on January 6, 1935. Inspection undertaken at Roosevelt Field, New York.

ELEANORE LUSCOMBE SHURTZ COLLECTION

Aircraft involved in nose-over accident, July 31, 1935, Watermill, L.I., New York. Pilot was Bryan Sheedy.
Extent of damage included crumpled rear and tail bulkhead, motor mount bent, left forward strut fitting broken, propeller bent, left wing tank cracked and engine cowling dented.
Aircraft was returned to the Luscombe Airplane Development Corporation for repairs which included new fuselage section from station 6 and back was replaced, new stabilizer rear spar support, fin entirely rebuilt, rudder rebuilt, left elevator rebuilt, two ribs straightened on left wing, five ribs straightened on right wing, new engine cowl and new strut ends for lift wing struts.
Prester Propeller Service of Jackson Heights, New York repaired the propeller.
Auxiliary fin and pontoons installed by Edo Corporation during October 1935. Edo model 44-2425 floats were used.
Aircraft reregistered and referred to as Luscombe Phantom 1S in all Department of Commerce paperwork and correspondence.
Aircraft returned to landplane condition as per Official Inspection Report, Form 80, dated April 24, 1936.
Aircraft involved in ground-loop accident, May 3, 1936, Ridgeland, South Carolina. Pilot was Byran D. Sheedy. Extent of damage was crushed right wing tip, both legs of undercarriage damaged beyond repair, main bulkhead pushed in by right leg of undercarriage, left wheel broken off and dented in fuselage behind baggage compartment, engine cowling mashed and propeller bent.
Aircraft returned to the Luscombe Airplane Development Company for repairs. Repairs included a new right wing, repair of the left wing leading edge, revised gas tank in left wing (engineering improvement?), new landing gear, new engine

mount, number 1 bulkhead repaired, number 2 bulkhead replaced, lower skins number 1 and 2 replaced, leading edge of fin repaired, new engine installed (Warner 145 "Super Scarab", serial number SS 292 E) and new propeller installed (Curtiss model 55511, serial number M 5172).

Sold to Ford Collins, Seversky Aircraft Corp., Farmingdale, L.I., New York on May 27, 1937 (Another listed address was the Racquet Club, St. Louis, Missouri).

Sold to St. Louis Flying Service, Robertson, Missouri, on March 7, 1939.

Sold to St. Louis Air Lines, Robertson, Missouri, on March 10, 1939.

A lien was placed against this aircraft by Aero Discount Corporation of Robertson, Missouri, on March 29, 1939.

Aircraft involved in cross-wind landing ground loop on March 22, 1939 at Lambert-St. Louis Municipal Airport, Robertson, Missouri. Pilot was Willis G. Wood. Extent of damage was landing gear torn off, propeller bent, nose cowl bent and right wing-tip damaged.

Aircraft repaired by Parks Air College, Inc., East St. Louis, Illinois. Repairs made in accordance with CAR Part 18. Repairs completed by June 7, 1939.

Sold to Arthur William Beal, Ovid, Colorado, on July 26, 1939.

Aircraft involved in landing accident, October 13, 1939, Glendale, California. Pilot was Arthur W. Beal.

Accident synopsis—aircraft had landed and during roll after landing, the propeller blast from a Central Airways of Mexico DC-2 aircraft caused the Phantom to ground loop. Extent of damage was damaged rear spar on right wing, damaged right wing tip bow, rivets sheared on rear compression members and damage to fabric covering at tip.

Aircraft repaired by Timm Aircraft Corporation, Grand Central Airport, Glendale, California. All repairs made in accordance with CAR Part 18. Repairs completed October 16, 1939.

Aircraft involved in groundloop accident on May 19, 1940 at James H. Douglass Airport, Ovid, Colorado. Pilot was Arthur W. Beal, passenger-Kenton Beal (son). Extent of damage was fuselage body twisted and caved-in at rear bulkhead, vertical fin damaged, propeller damaged, leading edges of both wings damaged and trailing edges of both wings damaged.

Repairs completed by John W. Dearing of Brule, Nebraska. All repairs made in accordance with CAR Part 18. Propeller repaired by Curtiss Propeller Division, Clifton, New Jersey. All repairs completed by August 19, 1940.

Aircraft destroyed in fatal accident, April 13, 1941, Holyoke, Colorado. Pilot was Arthur W. Beal, passenger-Kenton Beal (son).

Accident synopsis—the aircraft was observed pulling out of a power dive. After pulling out of the dive, fabric was observed leaving the right wing. It was reported two rolls followed and then a steep turn started. The aircraft entered a right spin and crashed resulting in fatal injuries to both occupants.

A Civil Aeronautics Board report, dated October 4, 1941, lists the probable cause as failure of the wing fabric during a dive and subsequent pull-out. Contributing factors were damaged rib stitching (from mouse activity in wing) and unsatisfactory condition of the fabric along the aileron hinge.

LUSCOMBE PHANTOM, NC277Y, Serial Number 103

STATUS—Aircraft Deregistered
REASON—Aircraft damaged in accident near Faison, North Carolina on December 25, 1944.
AIRCRAFT SERIAL NUMBER—103
DATE of MANUFACTURE—January 1935, manufactured at the former Butler Blackhawk Plant, Kansas City Municipal Airport, Kansas City, Missouri.
POWER PLANT—Warner 145 "Super Scarab", serial number SS 121 E.
PROPELLER—Hamilton-Standard, hub design 7056F, serial number 23315, blade design 19B1/2-16, serial numbers 50719 and 50720.
First test flight date unknown.
Sold to Donald D. Cooke, Tenafly, New Jersey, on January 22, 1935 in Kansas City, Missouri.
Application for Commercial License submitted January 22, 1935.
Aircraft inspected and approved January 22, 1935 by Inspector James W. Peyton.
Sold to Frank Spreckels, Coronado, California, on July 6, 1935.
Aircraft altered on December 17, 1936. Alterations included installation of new landing gear, new motor cowling made, new leather installed on tailwheel and entire aircraft repainted.

ELEANORE LUSCOMBE SHURTZ COLLECTION

Aircraft repaired after groundloop accident. Repairs included overhaul of engine, propeller repair, new motor mount installed and repair of left wing tip leading edge. Repairs completed February 18, 1937.

Aircraft involved in accident at Burns, Oregon on February 26, 1937. Details of accident are not recorded in current FAA records.

Confusion exists as to correct owner of aircraft at time of accident. The accident report stated that a Mr. Edward N. Brown of Burns, Oregon, was the proper owner whereas the Department of Commerce records listed Mr. Frank Spreckles as the current owner. Information of sale was obtained from accident which occurred at Burns, Oregon.

Aircraft was involved in another accident on April 17, 1937 at Silver Lake, Oregon. The name of the pilot flying is unknown. The following damaged was reported: Vertical fin wrinkled, top rudder crushed, rear of fuselage near tail badly wrinkled throwing vertical fin out of line, fuselage dented at fitting of oleo strut near braces, propeller bent and motor mount out of line."

Eventually, the sale was voided as the Civil Aeronautics Authority determined the purchaser failed to submit necessary documents for transfer of title. The license was cancelled on June 26, 1937.

Sold to Archie A. Baldocchi, San Francisco, California, on June 29, 1938.

Sold to Racquel Baldocchi, San Francisco, California, on February 10, 1939.

Aircraft repaired from accident of April 17, 1937 by Aircraft Industries Corp., Glendale, California. Repairs completed August 28, 1939. Repairs included replacing all of fuselage from station #5 to rudder attachment; rudder, stabilizers and elevators recovered and refinished; all paint removed from fuselage, inspected and refinished; new left and right fuel tanks installed; right and left wings repaired; both wings recovered and finished.

Sold to R.J. Wilson and W.D. Hull, Santa Maria, California, on July 1, 1940.

Sold to Halmond K. Stanfield, San Antonio, Texas, on October 2, 1940.

Aircraft's flaps shortened 58 1/2 inches as per a Form 337 filed June 6, 1941. The purpose of this alteration was to improve aileron control during landing.

Sold to Dwen R. Younger, San Antonio, Texas, on September 24, 1941.

Sold to Aircraft Sales Company, Fort Worth, Texas, on February 7, 1942.

Sold to Oscar O. Cooke, Omaha, Nebraska, on May 24, 1942.

Sold to Hunter Flying Service (D.F. Hunter), Spencer, Iowa, on August 3, 1942.

Sold to O.E. Kuhlman, Kansas City, Missouri, on March 18, 1944.

Aircraft damaged in accident on May 20, 1944 at the Kansas City Municipal Airport, Kansas City, Missouri. The pilot was a Daniel Rose. According to the accident report, "Pilot Rose was making an approach to landing when approximately two feet from the ground, the airplane ballooned. Power was applied, but too late to effect recovery. Aircraft struck the ground in a stalled position, shearing off bolts that hold streamline wire fitting to left landing gear leg, resulting in fracturing the upper left jack strut fitting."

Damage repaired by Daniel Rose. All repairs completed May 27, 1944.

Sold to Ernest A. Taylor, Jr., Faison, North Carolina, on June 14, 1944.

Aircraft damaged severely in accident on December 25, 1944. The pilot was the owner. According to the Inspector's Report of Non-Carrier Accident, the "landing gear, both wings, control surfaces, engine and fuselage sustained major damage. In addition to damage in the forward sections, the fuselage is snapped almost completely off just forward of the tail surfaces. Engine was torn completely out of the aircraft."

Report from Civil Aeronautics Board stalled the aircraft while making an emergency landing following engine stoppage. A contributing factor was the pilot's failure to keep the engine warm during a prolonged descent.

The aircraft was reportedly scrapped.

LUSCOMBE PHANTOM, NC278Y, Serial Number 104

STATUS—Aircraft Deregistered
REASON—Owner failed to reply to correspondence regarding status
AIRCRAFT SERIAL NUMBER—104
DATE of MANUFACTURE—May 14, 1935, fuselage manufactured at the former Butler Blackhawk Plant, Kansas City Municipal Airport, Kansas City, Missouri; balance of aircraft manufactured and assembled at the Mercer County Airport, West Trenton, New Jersey.
POWER PLANT—Warner 145 "Super Scarab", serial number SS 234 E.
PROPELLER—Hamilton-Standard Metal, hub design 7056F, serial number 22548, blade design 19B 1/2-16, serial numbers 48920 and 48921.

Sold to George A. Thorne, Jr., New York, New York on May 14, 1935.

Application for Commercial License submitted July 8, 1935.

Aircraft inspected and approved by Inspector George Gay on July 8, 1935. Inspection completed at Roosevelt Field, New York.

Aircraft damaged substantially in accident at Sugar Creek, Ohio on April 26, 1936. Pilot was George Thorne, Jr. The causes of this accident are unknown.

Aircraft was returned to the factory for repairs.

ELEANORE LUSCOMBE SHURTZ COLLECTION

Repairs included overhaul of propeller and engine by respective manufacturers. The number two bulkhead was replaced as were the number one and number two lower skins. The number six bulkhead was replaced as were all fuselage and vertical fins aft of station number six. (Note: The entire tail group was replaced using the tail group from the dismantled NC272Y airplane.) New landing gear and tail wheel assembly installed as per approved drawings for serial number 106 and up. Revised gas tank bays as per approved drawings applying to ships #106 and up. Installed complete new rudder system as per approved drawings applying to ships #110 and up. Wings, elevator and rudder recovered. New engine installed, Warner 145 "Super Scarab", serial number SS 154 E. New Hamilton-Standard propeller installed, blade serial number 48926 and 48927. Repairs completed December 12, 1936.

Sold to Luscombe Airplane Development Company, West Trenton, New Jersey on January 20, 1937.
Sold to Alvah Crocker, III, Fitchburg, Massachusetts on June 24, 1937. Sold to Inter City Aviation, Inc., Boston, Massachusetts on June 6, 1941.
Sold to Edward Sturgis, Jr., Brookline, Massachusetts on August 29, 1941. Sold to Forrest M. Bird, Long Beach, California on April 9, 1945.
Sold to Hallice H. Beckett, Pendleton, Oregon on June 1, 1945.
Sold to Robert P. and John L. Heasley, Heasley Flying Service, Rosemead, California on July 2, 1945.
Aircraft registration cancelled July 8, 1948 because owner failed to reply to correspondence.

LUSCOMBE PHANTOM, HB-EXE, Serial Number 105

STATUS—Aircraft Deregistered
REASON—Accident in Africa, April 8, 1937
AIRCRAFT SERIAL NUMBER—105
DATE of MANUFACTURE—July 11, 1935 according to Application For Certificate for Export (E-1519). Fuselage fabricated at the former Butler Blackhawk Plant, Kansas City Municipal Airport, Kansas City, Missouri; balance of aircraft manufactured and assembled at the Mercer County Airport, West Trenton, New Jersey.
POWER PLANT—Warner 145 "Super Scarab", serial number SS 167 E
PROPELLER—Hamilton-Standard with 7056H hub, 19B1/2-16 blades, serial number 54417 and 54418.
Sold to Dr. K. Tschudi, Bergamo, Italy, July 15, 1935.
Registered in Switzerland on August 6, 1935.
Aircraft damaged or destroyed in accident in Africa, April 8, 1937.
No other information is known.

ELEANORE LUSCOMBE SHURTZ COLLECTION

LUSCOMBE PHANTOM, NC1286, Serial Number 106

STATUS—Aircraft Currently Registered
REASON—
AIRCRAFT SERIAL NUMBER—106
DATE of MANUFACTURE—June 25, 1936
POWER PLANT—Warner 145 "Super Scarab", serial number SS 169 E.
PROPELLER—Curtiss-Reed, Model 55511, serial number 5374.
First test flight June 20, 1936. Pilot was Ignatius Sargent.
Sold to Ignatius Sargent, New York, New York on June 25, 1936.
Application for Commercial License submitted on June 25, 1936.
Aircraft inspected and approved by Inspector George Gay on June 25, 1936.
Sold to Wings Field, Inc., Ambler, Pennsylvania on September 6, 1939.
Sold to Theodore F. Steiner, Upper Darby, Pennsylvania on September 21, 1939.
Sold to John C. Collingswood, Staten Island,

IGNATIUS SARGENT COLLECTION

New York on November 27, 1940.
New factory right wing and strut replaced July 31, 1941. Old flap mechanism and fuel tank transferred from old wing.
Sold to May Brother (Thayer May, Doing Business As), Garden City, Louisiana on May 26, 1942.
Sold to John C. Collingswood, Staten Island, New York on May 29, 1942.
Sold to Jack Stinson, Long Island, New York on July 10, 1942.
Sold to Charles Haas and Mount Robb, Elmhurst, New York on September 12, 1951.
Sold to Varner Williams, Patchoque, New York on February 21, 1953.
Sold to Leon Joseph Heffron, Smithtown, New York on November 2, 1953.
Fuselage replaced by factory fuselage; modified tailwheel installed as per Eveland Aircraft Service drawings; rudder and both wings recovered in linen; all windshield, side doors and skylight windows replaced; aircraft assembled with all new hardware. Work completed August 7, 1956.
Sold to Eugene D. Ruder, Weaton, Illinois, on March 11, 1964.
Left wingtip damage repaired, October 21, 1964.
Doors, tail fairings and other small parts lost in hangar fire in Rockford, Illinois, in July 1989.

LUSCOMBE PHANTOM, NC1007, Serial Number 107

STATUS—Aircraft Airworthiness Expired
REASON—Aircraft damaged in accident, Bettis Airport, Dravosburg, Pennsylvania on June 15, 1939.
AIRCRAFT SERIAL NUMBER—107
DATE of MANUFACTURE—August 28, 1936
POWER PLANT—Warner 145 "Super Scarab", serial number SS 288 E.
PROPELLER—Curtiss-Reed, model 55511, serial number M 5386.
Fuel capacity—33 gallons, empty weight—1322 lbs, gross weight— 1950 lbs, maximum payload with full fuel load—234 lbs, cargo— 110 lbs.
First flight test August 26, 1936. Pilot was Ignatius Sargent.
Application for Commercial License submitted on August 27, 1936.
Aircraft inspected and approved by Inspector George Gay on August 27, 1936.
Sold to Edgar S. Davis, New York, New York, August 28, 1936.
Engine changed at 292 hours. New Warner 145 "Super Scarab", serial number SS-286 E, installed.
Sold to Stanley Washburn, Jr., New York, New York, on February 18, 1939.
Total time to date was 470 hours.

JAMES B. ZAZAS COLLECTION

Aircraft involved in accident at Richmond, Virginia, Richard E. Byrd Field, on April 10, 1939.
Accident synopsis—pilot landed on NE-SW runway during gusty wind conditions. Right wing touched resulting in a ground loop damaging the engine mount, propeller, both wing tips, tail wheel fork, landing gear and fuselage.
Sold to Joe George Marrs, Sandston, Virginia, on April 12, 1939.
The aircraft was sent to the factory for repairs. Repairs included new motor mount, left landing gear fitting, upper left jack strut fitting, landing gear tie rod, tail wheel assembly, left wing panel, right wing tip bow, engine cowl, landing gear fairings and propeller. Repairs completed May 26, 1939.
Aircraft involved in another accident on June 15, 1939, Bettis Airport, Dravosburg, Pennsylvania.
Accident synopsis—pilot overshot field and rolled down 75 foot bank and rolled over on its back. The aircraft was completely washed out.
Aircraft Airworthiness Certificate expired September 15, 1939.

LUSCOMBE PHANTOM, NC1008, Serial Number 108

STATUS—Deregistered
REASON—Unknown
AIRCRAFT SERIAL NUMBER—108
DATE of MANUFACTURE—September 15, 1936 (some paperwork states October 1936).
POWER PLANT—Warner 145 "Super Scarab", serial number SS 295 E.
PROPELLER—Curtiss-Reed, model 55511, serial number M 5385. Fuel Capacity—33 gallons, empty weight—1348 lbs, gross weight—1950 lbs, maximum payload with full fuel—208 lbs, cargo—78 lbs.
Application for Commercial License submitted on October 9, 1936.
Aircraft inspected by Inspector George Gay on October 9, 1936.

Appendix C: *Individual Luscombe Phantom Model 1 Histories* 283

First flight test October 15, 1936. Pilot was Ignatius Sargent.
Sold to George A. Humphreys, Southampton, New York, on January 11, 1937.
Sold to John M. Warner, Greenwich, Connecticut, November 5, 1938.
Repair and Alteration Form 337 submitted on March 9, 1940 to install a 21 gallon aux fuel tank behind seat. Modification approved.
Sold to Obed Chester Hall, Grand Rapids, Michigan on October 10, 1942.
Sold to David H. Wilson, Louisville, Kentucky on August 27, 1943.
Aircraft reported scrapped October 7, 1947.
Sold to John M. Butler, Pearland, Texas on March 25, 1953.
Aircraft deregistered September 14, 1971.

CHARLES E. BURGESS

LUSCOMBE PHANTOM, NC7734, Serial Number 109

STATUS—Aircraft cancelled on Office records October 6, 1936.
REASON—Aircraft accident, October 6, 1936
AIRCRAFT SERIAL NUMBER—109
DATE of MANUFACTURE — June 1936
POWER PLANT—Warner 145 "Super Scarab", serial number SS 299 E.
PROPELLER—Curtiss Reed, model 55511, serial number M 5387.
NC7734 number chosen by Standard Oil Development Company of New Jersey. Letter of July 8, 1936 from DAL to Robert Reining, Department of Commerce, requesting this number. Department of Commerce approved request on July 24, 1936.
Application for Commercial Airplane License made by Standard Oil Development Company of New Jersey on June 24, 1936.
Aircraft inspected and approved by Inspector George Gay on July 27, 1936.
First test flight August 14, 1936. Pilot was Ignatius Sargent.
Bill of Sale from Luscombe Airplane Development Corporation to Standard Oil Development Company of New Jersey dated August 14, 1936.

HOWARD JONG COLLECTION

Confusion exists as to aircraft true date of manufacture. Application for Commercial License/Identification Mark shows date of June 1936. A notarized Bill of Sale from Luscombe Airplane Development Company shows date of August 15, 1936. CAA changes date to reflect Bill of Sale; however, most likely June 1936 as per date on Application for Commercial Airplane License.
Aircraft destroyed in accident in Stroudsburg, Pennsylvania on October 6, 1936. The pilot, Frederick "Red" McPhaul, was killed.

LUSCOMBE PHANTOM, NC1234, Serial Number 2-110

STATUS—Aircraft Airworthiness Certificate Expired
REASON—Aircraft washed-out in accident, November 20, 1936.
AIRCRAFT SERIAL NUMBER—2-110 (2-109 on original Form 9 dated September 11, 1936).
DATE of MANUFACTURE—September 1936 (October 1936 on Form 9 dated
October 9, 1936).
POWER PLANT—Warner 145 "Super Scarab", serial number SS 300 E (changed to SS 310 E on Form 9 dated October 9, 1936).
PROPELLER—Curtiss-Reed, model 55511, serial number M 5389
(changed to M 5391 on Form 9 dated October 9, 1936).

Application for Airplane Identification Mark filed September 10, 1936.
First test flight October 8, 1936. Pilot was Ignatius Sargent.
Application for Commercial License submitted October 9, 1936.
Aircraft inspected and approved by Inspector George Gay on October 9, 1936.
Sold to Hiram R. Mallinson, Mercer Airport, Trenton, New Jersey on October 21, 1936.
Aircraft washed-out in accident on November 20, 1936. Location is unknown. Pilot was Hiram R. Mallinson.

LUSCOMBE PHANTOM, NC1010, Serial Number 111

STATUS—Aircraft Registration Cancelled
REASON—Aircraft Destroyed in San Diego Air Museum Fire on February 21, 1978.
SERIAL NUMBER—111
DATE of MANUFACTURE—October 1936
POWER PLANT—Warner 145 "Super Scarab", serial number SS 316 E.
PROPELLER—Curtiss-Reed, model 55511, serial number M 5385.
Application for Airplane Identification Mark filed October 2, 1936.
Application for Commercial License filed November 7, 1936.
Aircraft inspected and approved by George Gay November 7, 1936.
First test flight November 7, 1936. Pilot was Ignatius Sargent.
Sold to Charles A. Hinsch, Cincinnati, Ohio on November 19, 1936.
Aircraft damaged in groundloop accident, Waycross, Georgia, on March 2, 1937. Pilot was Charles A. Hinsch.
The aircraft was taken to Jacksonville, Florida to effect repairs. New parts were shipped from factory. A wing was loaned by the factory and the damaged wing was returned to the factory. Aircraft was then flown to Cincinnati and held in storage until original wing was repaired and ready for installation. Aircraft was then flown to Trenton, New Jersey where repaired wing was installed at the factory. Final inspection was made by George Gay at Roosevelt Field on April 27, 1937.
Aircraft's landing gear removed and shipped to factory for repair on August 26, 1937. New bow strip in left wing installed at same time. Repairs made by Queen City Flying Service, Cincinnati, Ohio. (Portion of company owned by Hinsch.)
Aircraft damaged in groundloop accident, February 23, 1939, near Miami, Florida. Temporary repairs made to left wingtip bow until aircraft could be ferried to Cincinnati to complete repairs. Temporary repairs completed March 7, 1939.
Aircraft damaged in taxiing accident, Atlanta Municipal Airport, Atlanta, Georgia on March 13, 1939. Pilot was Charles Hinsch. Wind got under tail and the aircraft went up on its nose damaging the propeller and engine cowling.
Sold to Warner Industries, Inc., Cincinnati, Ohio, on April 8, 1943.
Front fuselage and rear landing gear bulkheads repaired. Major sections of cabin area skin replaced. Repairs not made as a result of groundloop accident.
Sold to M.D. Ator and Harold Bothwell, Western Springs, Illinois, on January 24, 1945.
Sold to E.A. Spence, Sturgis, Michigan, on July 19, 1945.
Sold to U.S. Airlines, Inc., St. Petersburg, Florida, on January 1, 1946.
Sold to Roy C. Davis, St. Petersburg, Florida on November 20, 1946.
Sold to Charles A. Dayton, Jr., St. Petersburg, Florida, on February 7, 1947.
Sold to Carolina Aviation, Municipal Airport, Greenville, South Carolina on October 1, 1948.
Sold to Stanley O. Kelley, Asheville, North Carolina, on January 16, 1950.
Sold to Frank Williamson at some point (?).
Sold to Broward Aviation, Inc., Ft. Lauderdale, Florida, on March 22, 1952 in a Broward County Sheriff's Sale.
Sold to Marion F. Parkinson, Pascagoula, Mississippi, on August 26, 1952.
Sold to Charles W. Pyeatt, Troy, New York, on November 7, 1955.
Sold to C.V. Hazelton, Williamsville, New York, on January 23, 1956.
Sold to William Wessel, Cincinnati, Ohio, on February 7, 1959.
Sold to William A. Roberts, Cincinnati, Ohio, on June 8, 1959.
Sold to M.A. Norman, Sebring, Florida, on October 12, 1959.
Sold to Charles Farmer, Denver, Colorado, on April 23, 1960.
Sold to Shelly L. Abramson, Louisville, Kentucky, on June 17, 1968.
Sold to Jim Dewey, Santa Paula, California, on (date unknown).
Aircraft destroyed in San Diego Air Museum fire, February 21, 1978. All aircraft records were lost in the fire.

ELEANORE LUSCOMBE SHURTZ COLLECTION

Appendix C: Individual Luscombe Phantom Model 1 Histories 285

LUSCOMBE PHANTOM, NC1025, Serial Number 112

STATUS—Aircraft Currently Registered
REASON—
SERIAL NUMBER—112
DATE of MANUFACTURE—October 1936
POWER PLANT—Warner 145 "Super Scarab", serial number SS 312 E.
PROPELLER—Curtiss Aeroplane Motor Co., model 55511, serial number M 5390.
Application for Commercial License filed October 16, 1936.
Aircraft inspected and approved by George Gay on October 16, 1936.
First test fight October 16, 1936. Pilot was Ignatius Sargent.
Sold to Helen R. de Bustamente, Havana, Cuba, on October 16, 1936.
Sold to Fairhaven Flying Co., Inc., New York, New York, on June 29, 1937.
Sold to Grace K. Liebman, New York, New York, on January 23, 1939.
Sold to Crocker Snow, Boston, Massachusetts, on April 5, 1940.
Aircraft damaged in groundloop accident on April 23, 1943. Pilot was Crocker Snow.
Repairs included minor repairs to outboard ribs of right wing, recover outer 5 feet of right wing, repairs to outboard three ribs of left wing, minor repairs to rudder and recover same, repair nose cowling. Repairs completed May 3, 1940.
Croker Snow applied to Department of Commerce to use aircraft for Coastal Patrol and Anti-Submarine Patrol on June 2, 1943. The request was approved.
Sold to Claire W. Grove, Cleveland, Ohio, on October 25, 1943.
Sold to Carl E. Schultz, Detroit, Michigan, on March 21, 1944.
Sold to Meinrad Wirtz, Detroit, Michigan, on January 9, 1946.
Aircraft involved in extensive rebuild/restoration project during Summer 1946. Repairs included replacement of leading edge, nose ribs, tip bow and tip cover of right wing; reinforcement of six ribs at tip of wing; spliced rudder spar and replacing counterbalance; replaced skins below seat and replaced bulkhead below seat with factory part; repaired motor mount; Warner engine overhauled; wings, elevators and rudder recovered; Curtiss-Reed propeller removed and replaced with wood propeller; new wheels and brakes; new weight and balance computed. Repairs completed for inspection August 3, 1946. All repairs undertaken by owner.

ELEANORE LUSCOMBE SHURTZ COLLECTION

Sold to Robert E. Bristle, Port Huron, Michigan, on November 15, 1949.
Sold to Clarence B. Green, Sidnaw, Michigan, on June 14, 1950.
Sold to Koichi Kiyomura, Los Angeles, California, on March 7, 1951.
Motor mount, aileron skins and fabric covering of wings and tail surfaces replaced. All repairs undertaken by owner and completed November 11, 1954.
Sold to Auto Rebuilders, Los Angeles, California, on February 11, 1956. (Koichi Kiyomura was owner/president of company.)
Sold to Harvy L. Aberle, Rivera, California, on July 15, 1958.
Sold to L.E. Dunavant, Gardena, California, on August 13, 1961.
Sold to Joseph R. Johnson, Bedford, Texas, March 5, 1971.
Aircraft completely restored by Johnson. Restoration completed February 22, 1972.
Sold to George T. Ramin, Houston, Texas, on June 27, 1973.
Aircraft placed in EAA Air Museum, Franklin, Wisconsin, on loan July 1977.
Aircraft currently on display, EAA Air Museum, Oshkosh, Wisconsin.

LUSCOMBE PHANTOM, NC1028, Serial Number 113

STATUS—Cancelled on Office Records, May 16, 1937
REASON—Aircraft not inspected for relicensing
AIRCRAFT SERIAL NUMBER—113
DATE of MANUFACTURE—November 1936
POWER PLANT—Warner 145 "Super Scarab", serial number SS 331 E.

PROPELLER—Curtiss Reed, model 55511, serial number M5392.
Fuel Capacity-33 gallons, Empty weight-1323 lbs, gross weight-1950 lbs, maximum pay load with full fuel-233 lbs, cargo-63 lbs.
First test flight December 11, 1936. Pilot was Ignatius Sargent.
Aircraft Application for Identification Mark applied for November 20, 1936.
Sold to Henry C. Olmsted, New York City, New York on December 12, 1936.
Application for Commercial License submitted December 12, 1936.
Aircraft inspected and approved by Inspector George Gay on December 12, 1936.
Severely damaged in accident, February 18, 1937, Stelton, New Jersey. Pilot was Hiram R. Mallinson.
Damage report of March 13, 1937 reported damage was: landing gear sheared off, both wings-fabric torn, ribs and spars bent, fuselage dented back to fourth bulkhead, cowling bent, motor shaft out of line (sent to factory for overhaul). Aircraft not inspected for relicensing as of May 16, 1937.

HOWARD JONG

LUSCOMBE PHANTOM, NC1043, Serial Number 114

STATUS—Aircraft Currently Registered
REASON—
AIRCRAFT SERIAL NUMBER—114
DATE of MANUFACTURE—December 1936
POWER PLANT—Warner 145 "Super Scarab", serial number SS 328 E.
PROPELLER—Curtiss-Wright, model 55511, serial number 5030.
Application for Identification Mark filed December 12, 1936.
Application for Commercial License submitted on December 21, 1936.
Aircraft inspected and approved by George Gay on December 21, 1936.
First test flight December 21, 1936. Pilot was Edgar S. Davis.
Sold to H.J. Crummer, Orlando, Florida, on December 23, 1936.
Sold to Stinson Aircraft Corp., Wayne, Michigan, on January 8, 1938.
Sold to Kosmos Portland Cement Company, Kosmosdale, Jefferson County, Kentucky, on May 20, 1938.
Aircraft damaged in groundloop accident on March 24, 1939.
Repairs undertaken by Louisville Flying Service, Bowman Field, Kentucky.
Repairs included replacing the bottom fuselage skin between bulkheads #4 and #5, reconditioning the propeller (sent to Curtiss Wright Propeller Co.), replacing engine cowl with new cowl, recovering the left wing, replacing entire rudder assembly with new unit supplied by manufacturer. Repairs completed June 8, 1939.
Sold to Chester Shimp, Huron, South Dakota, on January 20, 1945.
Sold to Garrett A. Adam, Huntingburg, Indiana, on October 2, 1945.
Sold to Joe Gillette, Cincinnati, Ohio, on August 20, 1949.
Sold to Nicholas H. Melvin, Cincinnati, Ohio, on September 27, 1950.
Sold to Paul R. Heiders, Cleveland, Ohio, June 20, 1951.
Sold to E.C. Broxon, Cincinnati, Ohio, September 13, 1951.
Sold to Jack Mitchell, Xenia, Ohio, June 24, 1954.
Sold to John Hazy, Reynoldsburg, Ohio, on January 21, 1955.
Sold to Edward Eckert, Cleveland, Ohio, on September 15, 1956.
Sold to Frank H. Fennen, Houston, Texas, on February 1, 1958.
Sold to W.S. Compton, Jr., Houston, Texas, on February 11, 1959.

AVIATION HERITAGE LIBRARY

Sold to Richard E. Larsen, Houston, Texas, on January 12, 1959. (Author has been unable to determine proper sequence in the above two transaction dates based upon Bills of Sale...)
Sold to John J. Carrig, Houston, Texas, on June 21, 1960.
Sold to George T. Ramin, Houston, Texas, on March ?, 1971.
Sold to Kenwood G. Cassens, Allendale, New Jersey, on July 1, 1973.

LUSCOMBE PHANTOM, NC1235, Serial Number 115

STATUS—Sold (?), Aircraft wrecked
REASON—Purchaser Failed to Comply with Civil Aviation Regulations. However, subject aircraft was wrecked in an accident, August 1949 and subsequently sold.
AIRCRAFT SERIAL NUMBER—115
DATE of MANUFACTURE—January 1937
POWER PLANT—Warner 145 "Super Scarab", serial number SS 358 E
PROPELLER—Curtiss-Wright, model 55511, serial number M 5389
Application for Identification Mark filed January 27, 1937.
Aircraft assigned "1235" February 9, 1937.
Application for Commercial License submitted February 9, 1937.
Aircraft inspected and approved by Inspector George Gay on February 9, 1937.
First test flight February 9, 1937. Pilot was Ignatius Sargent.
Sold to Warner Aircraft Corp., Detroit, Michigan, on February 10, 1937.
Aircraft groundlooped El Paso, Texas. Repairs to both wingtips made there and subsequently inspected at Ryan School of Aeronautics, San Diego, California.
Sold to W.L. Graves, Payson, Arizona on November 15, 1938.
Sold to William V. Skall, Los Angeles, California on September 2, 1939.
Aircraft tailwheel assembly modified and made steerable.
Sold to John Swope, Phoenix, Arizona on August 10, 1941.
Aircraft lower left motor mount discovered bent. Lower left hand motor mount repaired.
Sold to A.W. Hawks, Canyon, Texas on March 20, 1942.
Sold to Seth Burton Ford, Jr., Dallas, Texas on May 20, 1943.
Transaction approved by War Production Board, pursuant to order L-262, on June 8, 1943.
Aircraft's torque arm, dual control torque tube to elevator push rod replaced by fabricated parts. Work done by Ray Weatherly of Dallas, Texas. Repairs completed October 2, 1943.
Aircraft's rudder pedal brackets reconstructed and reinforced after one failed while recoving from spin demonstration. Repairs completed October 12, 1943.
Aircraft's leading edge skin reinforced at all nose ribs and main ribs. Repairs done by Ray Weatherly. Repairs completed March 3, 1943.
Aircraft's wings recovered with Grade A fabric. Entire aircraft cleaned, primed and painted. Work completed March 21, 1944.
Aircraft's engine overhauled by Sparan School of Aeronautics. Work completed on August 22, 1944.
Sold to E.W. Caperton, Tyler, Texas on August 31, 1946.
Sold to J.D. Roop, Tucumcari, New Mexico on January 15, 1947.
Sold to Western Flying Service, (Raymond G. Spaulding, owner), Clovis, New Mexico on August 25, 1947.
Aircraft involved in groundloop accident. Two pieces of vertical skin replaced; both wings recovered with Grade A; left and right front lift struts repaired; all windshield and window glass replaced. Work completed April 1, 1948.
Sold to Robert J. Thompson, Manitowac, Wisconsin on June 15, 1949.
Aircraft totally wrecked in accident during August 1949.
Sold to Alfred Muchen Metal, Co., Manitowac, Wisconsin on August ?, 1949.
Aircraft registration cancelled. Owner failed to comply with Civil Air Regulations.

LUSCOMBE PHANTOM, NC1048, Serial Number 116

STATUS—Aircraft Deregistered
REASON—No reply to audit questionnaire
AIRCRAFT SERIAL NUMBER—116
DATE of MANUFACTURE—January 1937
POWER PLANT—Warner 145 "Super Scarab", serial number SS 300 E.
Propeller—Curtiss-Wright, model 55511, serial number M 5389.
Application for Identification Mark filed January 13, 1937.
Identification Mark "1048" issued January 15, 1937.
New tailwheel assembly installed during February 1937.
First test flight March 30, 1937. Pilot was Ignatius Sargent.
Application for Commercial License filed April 1, 1937.
Aircraft inspected and approved for license by Inspector George Gay on April 1, 1937.

JAMES B. ZAZAS COLLECTION

Aircraft's ownership retained by Luscombe Airplane Development Company, West Trenton, New Jersey. Aircraft was painted an overall gloss black with gold trim.
Sold to H.T. Cole, Atlanta, Georgia, on December 4, 1937.
Aircraft involved in groundloop accident on February 21, 1938. The location of the accident and the extent of damage are unknown. All repairs were completed May 26, 1938.
Aircraft damaged in groundloop accident on August 6, 1938. Repairs included installing new fin and tail assembly furnished by the factory, installing new right lift strut assembly furnished by factory, straightening kink in leading edge of left wing and repairing top of rudder post. Repairs completed October 15, 1938 by Eastern Air Schools, Inc., Atlanta, Georgia.
Sold to John J. Farris, Cynwyd, Pennsylvania, on October 23, 1940. Sold to Ferris Thomas, Knoxville, Tennessee, on May 27, 1941.
Sold to Eugene Patterson, Jr., Chattanooga, Tennessee, on October 1, 1941.
Sold to Hilyer A. DuBois, Hempstead, New York, on May 23, 1942.
Aircraft damaged in forced landing on May 27, 1942, location unknown. Repairs included replacing lower half of fuselage skin from firewall back to the second bulkhead, replacing lower half of fuselage skin between bulkheads two and three, replacing bulkhead #4, replacing lower half of skin between bulkhead four and five, replacing damaged portion of firewall, installing new motor mount, new left hand strut installed and all control cables in fuselage replaced. The wings were completely inspected, all internal bracing checked, all rivets tightened where necessary, all ribs and spars coated with Zinc Chromate and wings recovered, doped and painted. Repairs undertaken at Roosevelt Field, Inc., Mineola, New York and completed October 1, 1943.
Further repairs included complete overhaul of Warner engine. This overhaul was completed March 2, 1944. The aircraft was reassembled and rerigged on September 8, 1944. Final inspection was completed on September 12, 1944 and was approved for return to service.
Sold to Paul J. Rennard, Oil City, Pennsylvania, on December 4, 1944.
Sold to Don S. Penn, Sturgis, Michigan, on March 31, 1945.
Sold to Arthur A. Werkhaven, Sturgis, Michigan, on August 11, 1945.
Sold to Albert F. Kloer, Fort Wayne, Indiana, on March 14, 1946.
Sold to Charles F. Rettig and Dan L. Merkey, Fort Wayne, Indiana, on March 19, 1947.
Audit questionnaire sent to owners during February 1956. There was no reply; thus, the aircraft's registration was cancelled.

LUSCOMBE PHANTOM, NC1278, Serial Number 117

STATUS—Airworthiness Certificate Expired
REASON—Aircraft accident
AIRCRAFT SERIAL NUMBER—117
DATE of MANUFACTURE—August 1937
POWER PLANT—Warner 145 "Super Scarab", serial number SS 373 E.
PROPELLER—Curtiss-Wright, Model 55511, serial number M 5724.
Application for Commercial License filed August 13, 1937.
Aircraft inspected and approved by Boudwin on August 13, 1937.

First test flight August 13, 1937. Pilot was Alfred "Fritz" King.
Sold to Falcon Aircraft Corporation, Los Angeles Municipal Airport, Los Angeles, California on August 14, 1937. T.W. Warner, Jr. listed as company president.
Tailwheel lock removed January 28, 1938.
Sold to David Grey, Santa Barbara, California on or about September 12, 1938.
Sold to Catherine de Bernard Leigh, Beverly Hills, California on February 3, 1939.
Aircraft severely damaged in ground loop accident at New Castle, Delaware on November 21, 1939. Pilot was Catherine de Benard Leigh.
Extent of damage consisted of wrecked landing gear, bent tail wheel fork, buckled fuselage aft of cabin door, motor mount broken, left wing tip badly damaged and minor right wing tip damage.
As stated in the Inspectors Report of Non-Carrier Accident, the pilot was "practising simulated forced landings while accompanied by certificated instructor. When leveling off for landing sudden gust ballooned aircraft about ten feet into air and fell off on right wing. Pilot failed to open throttle in time to recover control and due to fact that throttle was located at extreme left side of plane the check pilot was unable to reach same in time to recover control. Plane cartwheeled from right wing to left wing and came to stop heading down wind." There were no injuries in this mishap.
Aircraft was sent to Luscombe factory for repairs, but owner decided not to repair aircraft.

LUSCOMBE PHANTOM, PP-TPT, Serial Number 118

STATUS—Aircraft Deregistered
REASON—Unknown
AIRCRAFT SERIAL NUMBER—118 (Official Brazilian registration records list serial number as 121).
DATE of MANUFACTURE—August 1938 (Awaiting verification)
Fuselage was completed in March or April 1937.
POWER PLANT—Warner 145 "Super Scarab", serial number (?)
PROPELLER—Curtiss Wright, model 55511, serial number (?)
First test flight August 16, 1938. Pilot was Ignatius Sargent.
Aircraft delivered to Brazilian Navy in August 1938.

IGNATIUS SARGENT

Aircraft painted an overall dark blue with following exterior markings: Fin, DIL placed over MARINHA; Fuselage sides, 2-D-1 in large print; Rear fuselage just forward of stabilizer, D1L-204
Aircraft transferred to Aeroclube do Brazil on June 11, 1942 and registered PP-TPT.
Aircraft registration cancelled October 27, 1948.

LUSCOMBE PHANTOM, NC30449, Serial Number 119

STATUS—Aircraft Deregistered
REASON—Purchaser failed to comply with FARs.
AIRCRAFT SERIAL NUMBER—119
DATE of MANUFACTURE—March 1937
POWER PLANT—None
PROPELLER—None
Sold to Carl Evers, New York, New York, on February 3, 1941 in an "as is" condition. Aircraft was disassembled and included no motor or propeller. The record does not state if wings, tail surfaces and landing gear were included in the sale.
Sold to Jeanette Eastman Jacobs, Miami, Florida, on June 12, 1944.
Sold to Joseph Haag, Williamsport, Pennsylvania, on June 16, 1944.
Sold to Howell C. Jones, Jr., Augusta, Georgia, on May 20, 1953.
This sale was later invalidated for reasons unknown.
Sold to L.J. Heffron, Smithtown, Long Island, New York, on January 12, 1954.
In response to an Aircraft Registration Eligibility and Activity Report, Mr. Heffron stated "the aircraft was purchased by me in 1955. It was minus engine and landing gear. After (2 yrs) (1957) being unable to obtain a landing gear, I sold remaining parts of aircraft to various buyers throughout the country. When it was in my possession it never flew."

LUSCOMBE PHANTOM, NC1249, Serial Number 120

STATUS—Aircraft Currently Registered
REASON—
AIRCRAFT SERIAL NUMBER—120
DATE of MANUFACTURE—March 1937
POWER PLANT—Warner 145 "Super Scarab", serial number SS 331 E.
PROPELLER—Curtiss-Wright, Model 55511, Serial Number M5392.
Application for Identification Mark filed March 26, 1937.
Aircraft assigned "1249" April 3, 1937.
Application for Commercial License submitted May 24, 1937.
Aircraft inspected and approved by Inspector George Gay on May 24, 1937.
First test flight May 25, 1937. Pilot was Ignatius Sargent.
Aircraft title transferred from Luscombe Airplane Development Company to Luscombe Airplane Corporation during April 1937.
Listed in Stock Prospectus of October 6, 1937 as "completely rebuilt". Does this entry denote a previous damage history?
Sold to Boller Motors Company, Curtiss-Wright Airport, Baltimore, Maryland on October 4, 1938. Henry K. Boller listed as president.
Aircraft damaged in groundloop accident at Hagerstown, Maryland on October 14, 1938. Pilot was Henry K. Boller. Left wingtip damaged slightly.
Sold to Fairchild Aircraft Corporation, Hagerstown, Maryland on November 22, 1938.
Aircraft damaged in groundloop accident at Hagerstown, Maryland on November 25, 1938. Pilot was Henry Boller. Fin and last section of fuselage damaged, top of rudder and front section of fuselage damaged, propeller bent.
Repairs undertaken at Luscombe Airplane Corporation, West Trenton, New Jersey. Repairs included new fuselage from factory including fin, rudder and motor mount. The wings, landing gear, stabilizer, elevators, engine, controls and instruments were removed from the original fuselage, inspected and installed in the new fuselage. Repairs were completed on January 19, 1939 and all paperwork was signed by Alfred G. King.
Sold to Curtiss M. Henderson, Washington, D.C., on November 17, 1939.
Sold to Noah Fry, Elsa, Texas, on January 25, 1943.
Aircraft damaged in groundloop accident on February 6, 1943. Only left wingtip was damaged slightly.
Repairs completed by Fullwood Flying Activities, McAllen, Texas on February 24, 1943.
Sold to J.D. Reed, Houston, Texas, on September 20, 1943.
Aircraft damaged in groundloop on September 21, 1943. Leading edge and three nose ribs damaged, vertical skin wrinkled.
Repairs completed November 19, 1943.
Sold to Clyde J. Bristow, Kokomo, Indiana, on February 19, 1944.
Sold to George T. Purves, Jr., Indianapolis, Indiana, on July 25, 1945.
Aircraft damaged extensively in groundloop accident, date circa September 1946.
Repairs completed October 22, 1946.
Aircraft damaged extensively in groundloop accident, date circa September 1947.
Repairs completed by Roscoe Turner Aero Corp., Indianapolis, Indiana, October 18, 1947.
Sold to Loren E. Devers, Indianapolis, Indiana, on July 14, 1953.
Sold to Charles E. Dee, Indianapolis, Indiana, on November 8, 1958.
Sold to Eugene D. Ruder, Maple Park, Illinois, on March 21, 1970.

LUSCOMBE PHANTOM, NC1323, Serial Number 121

STATUS—Sold (?)
REASON—Purchaser Failed to Comply with Federal Regulations
AIRCRAFT SERIAL NUMBER—121
DATE of MANUFACTURE—March 1938
POWER PLANT—Warner 145 "Super Scarab", serial number SS 12 E.
PROPELLER—Hamilton-Standard, hub design 7056E, serial number (?), blade design 19B1/2-16, serial numbers 46448 and 46449.
Application for Commercial License or Identification Mark originally had NC20620 as assigned ID. However, in a Department of Commerce letter of April 9, 1938 (interoffice correspondence, it said the five letter issued to Luscombe on April 6, 1938

HOWARD JONG

was too large and 1323 was issued to them on April 8, 1938).
Propeller changed to Curtiss-Wright, Model 55511, serial number M5725 on April 16, 1938.
Application for Commercial License submitted April 16, 1938.
Aircraft inspected and approved by Inspector J.B. Fornescero on April 16, 1937.
First test flight April 16, 1938. Pilot was Ignatius Sargent.
Sold to William C. Haines, Philadelphia, Pennsylvania on April 16, 1938.
Aircraft's engine replaced May 17, 1940. New Warner 145 "Super Scarab", serial number SS 427 E, installed.
Sold to M. Caller Traver, Trenton, New Jersey on April 3, 1941.
Letter from CAA was sent to Mr. Traver requesting information on status of aircraft registration. Mr Traver replied the aircraft had been sold to "Wing's Field" in 1942. A subsequent letter was sent to Wing's Field, Ambler, Pennsylvania, on July 21, 1954 requesting registration information. A reply from Wing's Field on August 27, 1954 stated Wings, Inc. never possessed the aircraft.

LUSCOMBE PHANTOM, NC1265, Serial Number 122

STATUS—Aircraft Deregistered
REASON—Owner failed to comply with CAA/FAA registration regulations
AIRCRAFT SERIAL NUMBER—122
DATE of MANUFACTURE—May 1937
POWER PLANT—Warner 145 "Super Scarab", serial number SS 419 E
PROPELLER—Curtiss-Wright, model 55511, serial number M 5709.
Application for Commercial License submitted on May 13, 1937.
Aircraft inspected and approved by Inspector George Gay on May 13, 1937.
First test flight May 13, 1937. Pilot was Ignatius Sargent.
Sold to Herbert G. Kraft, Burbank, California, on August 9, 1937.
Sold to Thomas A. Drummond, Randsburg, California, on March 23, 1940.
Aircraft damaged in groundloop accident on December 5, 1940. The location is unknown.
Repairs included installation of a new windshield and roof pyralin, installation of new factory left hand flying struts, installation of a new motor mount, installation of new fairings and brace wires on landing gear, and replacement of leading edges on both wings and recover of both wings.
Repairs completed on June 21, 1941 by Pacific Airmotive, Burbank, California.
Sold to John H. Nagel, Long Beach, California, on September 26, 1944.
Sold to Robert Marks, Los Angeles, California, on December 23, 1944.
Aircraft damaged in groundloop accident on December 23, 1944. The location is unknown.
Repairs included repair and replacement of various rudder and fin parts. Airframe and motor mounts repairs complete March 8, 1946.
Sold to Authur J. Murphy, Culver City, California, on May 23, 1947.
Sold to Clyde R. Swanson, Hawthorne, California, on July 20, 1955.
Aircraft's wings and control surfaces recovered with Grade "A" fabric, the propeller was overhauled and all control cables replaced. New tires were installed. These repairs completed March 26, 1956.
Sold to John R. Strang and Bette J. Strang, Lomita, California, on April 4, 1956.
Sold to James N. Brink, Yuma, Arizona, on September 27, 1956.
Sold to Charles M. McClure, M.D., Lindsay, California, on July 17, 1957.
Sold to James G. Saftig, San Diego, California, on October 18, 1958.
Owner failed to sign and submit an Aircraft Registration Eligibility, Identification and Activity Report to the Federal Aviation Administration, Aircraft Registry Branch, as required by FAR 47.44 (a).
Aircraft was deregistered by the FAA on September 29, 1971.

HOWARD JONG

LUSCOMBE PHANTOM, NC25234, Serial Number 126

STATUS—Aircraft Deregistered
REASON—Groundloop accident, Municipal Airport, Atlanta, Georgia, August 8, 1940.
AIRCRAFT SERIAL NUMBER—121
DATE of MANUFACTURE—March 1938

POWER PLANT—Warner 145 "Super Scarab", serial number SS 373 E.
PROPELLER—Hamilton-Standard, hub design 7056F, serial number (?),
  blade design 19B 1/2-16, serial numbers (?).
Sold to Frank A. Orme, Washington, D.C. on August 3, 1940.
Application for Commercial License submitted on August 3, 1940.
Aircraft inspected and approved by Inspector V.L. Gardner on August 3, 1940.
Aircraft damaged in a groundloop accident at the Atlanta Municipal Airport, Atlanta Georgia on August 8, 1940. The pilot
  was Frank Orme.
The Inspector's Report stated the damage was limited to the motor mount bent, fin and rudder damaged, both wingtips
  damaged and fuselage twisted.
Sold to Thomas D. Schall, Jr., Hyattesville, Maryland on August 24, 1940.
No further known effort was made to repair the aircraft.

LUSCOMBE PHANTOM, NC28799, Serial Number 131

STATUS—Aircraft Currently Registered
REASON—
DATE of MANUFACTURE—June 1941
POWER PLANT—Warner 145 "Super Scarab", serial number SS 261 E.
PROPELLER—Curtiss Reed, model 55511, serial number 175314.
Department of Commerce, Administration of Civil Aeronautics Application for Registration for All Types of Aircraft applied
  for March 26, 1941. Roger Johnson, company sec/treas, signator.
"N" number used was NC28799.
Aircraft Registration Certificate issued May 23,
  1941 to Luscombe Airplane Corporation;
  however, incorrect "N" number was used
  on form.
New Aircraft Registration Certificate issued
  July 2, 1941 to Luscombe Airplane
  Corporation.
Sold to Ailor Sales Corporation, Bloomsburg
  Airport, Bloomsburg, Pennsylvania. The
  aircraft was described as a "PHANTOM
  145, Model Phantom 1" with a June 1941
  date of manufacture.
Sold to Aircraft Service Consolidated,

ELEANORE LUSCOMBE SHURTZ COLLECTION

  Bloomsburg Airport, Bloomsburg, Pennsylvania on February 27, 1943.
Sold to Charles Benjamin, Springfield Gardens, L.I., New York on February 23, 1944.
Aircraft was damaged substantially on July 9, 1944 after flipping over after a hard brake application. The former ring which
  carried the tail wheel and the aft end carrying the fin, rudder, stabilizers and elevators were completely wrecked.
  Additionally, there was substantial damage to the wings, cowling and related structures.
The aircraft was sent to the Aircraft Development Company, Washington, D.C., for repairs. Repairs were effected with the
  battery box being relocated between the pilot's seat and the baggage compartment. Also, the outboard half of the flap
  assembly was disconnected and sealed as an effort to improve aileron control during landing. The aft sections of the
  fuselage were replaced with parts available on hand via parts salvage. During assembly, it was discovered the rivet
  holes were not jig-drilled at the factory and the replacement piece rivet holes did not coincide with the rivet holes of
  the original airframe. Wing construction required a complete disassembly with replacement ribs available through the
  Luscombe factory.
The aircraft was deemed airworthy on January 25, 1947.
Sold to John R. Mathieu, Arlington, Virginia on August 18, 1945.
Sold half-interest to Victor C. Bunting, Alexandria, Virginia on April 11, 1947.
Sold to Alfred E. Straughan, Silver Springs, Maryland on October 6, 1948.
Sold to Lyman Rice, Laconia, New Hampshire on February 3, 1951.
Sold to Air Repair, Inc., Municipal Airport, Bridgeport, Connecticut on July 20, 1951.
Sold to M. Schine and M. Kaufman, Fairfield, Connecticut on August 4, 1951.
Sold to Baron G. Clift, Cincinnati, Ohio on July 26, 1952.
Sold to Theodore Hayduk, Brooklyn, New York on September 18, 1952.
Sold to Robert E. Lipper, Daleville, Alabama on March 17, 1965.
Sold to Kenneth D. Wright, Palmetto, Georgia on September 12, 1977.
Aircraft re-registration to "NC272Y" sought on December 14, 1978 via letter to Federal Aviation Administration, Aircraft
  Registration Branch.
Aircraft Assignment of Special Registration Numbers "NC272Y" approved December 16, 1978.
Sold to Robin P. Collard, Weslaco, Texas on October 8, 1981.
Sold to P. Douglas Combs and Linda G. Gamble, Incline Village, Nevada on April 11, 1988.

Appendix D

Individual Luscombe "90" Histories

LUSCOMBE EXPERIMENTAL 1017, Serial Number 100

STATUS—Aircraft Airworthiness Expired
REASON—Aircraft dismantled permanently
AIRCRAFT SERIAL NUMBER—100
DATE of MANUFACTURE—November 4, 1936.
POWER PLANT—Warner 90 "Scarab Junior", serial number V 27
PROPELLER—Hamilton-Standard, serial number 26832
First test flight November 3, 1937. Pilot was Ignatius Sargent.
Department of Commerce Form AB-9,
   Application For Commercial, Restricted or Experimental Aircraft License or Unlicensed Identification Mark for All Types of Aircraft, made on November 4, 1936 by the Luscombe Airplane Development Corporation.
Aircraft had two, 16.5 gal. wing fuel tanks, one 2.5 gal oil tank
Aircraft title transferred to Luscombe Airplane Corporation on February 11, 1938.
Aircraft was referred to as a Phantom in a letter to the Chief, Registration Section, Department of Commerce dated December 23, 1936.
According to letter sent by Roger Johnson, LAC Treasurer, dated March 1, 1938, ship 1017 was completely dismantled.
   The aircraft's Unlicensed Aircraft Identification Mark Assignment card was included in this letter.
This letter was acknowledged by the Department of Commerce, Bureau of Air Commerce on March 7, 1938.

HOWARD JONG

LUSCOMBE MODEL 4, NC1253, Serial Number 400

STATUS—Aircraft Airworthiness Expired
REASON—
AIRCRAFT SERIAL NUMBER—400
DATE of MANUFACTURE—March 1937
POWER PLANT—Warner 90 "Scarab Junior", serial number V 27
PROPELLER—Hamilton-Standard, hub model 7005-C, serial number 26832, blade design 25V2-0.
Application for Aircraft Registration filed on February 5, 1937.
Recorded by Department of Commerce on March 24, 1937.
Unlicensed Aircraft Identification Mark Assignment was 1253.
First test flight "proof-of-concept" Luscombe "90" March 10, 1937. Pilot-Ignatius Sargent.
First test flight of "production prototype" Luscombe "90" January 22, 1938.

HOWARD JONG

Reassignment Application was filed on February 5, 1938 for the purpose of testing new model in order to obtain ATC.
Title of aircraft transferred from Luscombe Airplane Development Corporation to the Luscombe Airplane Corporation on February 11, 1938.
Department of Commerce Form 9 was filed on March 15, 1938 and was approved on March 21, 1938. (NX1253 approved

this date).

This form further showed the aircraft would possess two, 15 gallon fuel tanks and one 2 gallon oil tank.

Aircraft had logged 6.75 hours flight time up to this point.

Wheels were Goodyear Air 18 x 8-3, 4 ply tires, tailwheel was a Universal 6.00 x 2.

Department of Commerce Form 9 filed on June 2, 1938 for Commercial license. Approved for Approved Type Certificate on that date.

Empty weight-997 lbs, Gross weight-1598 lbs. Max payload is 230 lbs with 31 gallons fuel. Max cargo was 60 lbs.

Airworthiness Certificate expired on June 15, 1939.

HOWARD JONG

LUSCOMBE MODEL 4, NC1325, Serial Number 402

STATUS—Aircraft Airworthiness Expired
REASON—Aircraft wrecked in accident, June 25, 1945
AIRCRAFT SERIAL NUMBER—402
DATE of MANUFACTURE—June 1938
POWER PLANT—Warner 90 "Scarab Junior", serial number V-77E
PROPELLER—Hamilton-Standard adjustable metal, model 7005-D, serial number (?), hub design 25V2-0, blade serial numbers 70081 and 70082.

First test flight June 10, 1938. Pilot was Ignatius Sargent.

Department of Commerce Form 9 filed on May 3, 1938 for uncertified identification mark 1325.

Department of Commerce Form 9 filed on June 10, 1938 for certification of NC1253.

Empty weight was 1063 lbs, gross weight was 1650 lbs, maximum payload was 216 lbs with 31 gallons of fuel, cargo was 46 lbs.

Sold to A. Lincoln McNeal, Chester, Pennsylvania on June 11, 1938.

Aircraft damaged substantially in landing accident, Chester, Pennsylvania, on June 24, 1938.

Repairs were made by Luscombe Airplane Corporation, supervised by William B. Shepard. Repair and Alteration Form 466, dated September 2, 1938, details these repairs.

Repairs included following:
-Both wingtips repaired
-Left wingtip recovered
-Nine nose ribs and entire right wing leading edge replace and entire wing recovered
-Right lift struts replaced
-Fin replace with new fin
-Rudder tailing edge straightened
-New fuselage provided with exception of superstructure
-New engine cowl
-Propeller repaired by Pester Propeller Service

Tailskid shoe replaced by a 3" tailwheel bolted to the end of a tailspring on August 12, 1940. Alteration was accomplished by Charles E. Burgess, A&E 15516.

Aircraft destroyed in accident Monday, June 25, 1945, 2:35 pm.

Accident synopsis: Approximately 12 miles east of Baltimore, engine cutout. Pilot made a forced landing, but aircraft went over on its back. Pilot was Arnold L. McNeal. No further known effort was made to repair or salvage aircraft.

HOWARD JONG

LUSCOMBE MODEL 4, NC1337, Serial Number 403

STATUS—Aircraft Currently Registered
REASON—
AIRCRAFT SERIAL NUMBER—403
DATE of MANUFACTURE—June 24, 1938.
POWER PLANT—Warner 90 "Scarab Junior", serial number V 83 E
PROPELLER—Hamilton-Standard adjustable metal, model 7005-D, serial number 31311; blade model 25V2-O, serial numbers 73462 and 73485.
First test flight July 30, 1938. Pilot was Ignatius Sargent.
Department of Commerce Form 9 filed June 14, 1938 for Identification Mark 1337.
Temporary Certification Agreement signed July 30, 1939.
Department of Commerce Form 9 filed August 2, 1938 for Commercial License NC1337.
Aircraft Inspection Report list empty weight of 1023 lbs, gross weight of 1650 lbs, useful load of 256 lbs with 31 gallons fuel, 75 lbs cargo with passenger, 90 lbs cargo without passenger.
Sold to Falcon Aircraft Corporation, Inglewood, California, on August 6, 1938.
Sold to Herbert L. White, Los Angeles, California, on January 24, 1939.
Sold to Edward K. Hertford, Los Angeles, California, on September 27, 1941.

JOHN UNDERWOOD

Sold to Charles H. Babb, Los Angeles, California, on May 23, 1942.
Sold to Weber College, Ogden, Utah, on May 23, 1942.
Sold to J.W. Bonham, Glendale, California, on October 15, 1946.
Sold to Richard W. Smith and Lack L. Penix, Los Angeles, California, on July 8, 1947.
Sold to Alfred A. Longons, Torrence, California, on June 11, 1950.
Sold to James H. Elkin and Wm. R. Elkin, San Francisco, California, on May 25, 1957.
Sold to Orange Airport, Stockton, California, on August 6, 1959.
Sold to Elmer F. Guy, San Francisco, California, on September 27, 1959.
Sold to Walter A. Feldmann, Burlingame, California, on December 7, 1967.
Sold to Ron and Donna Price, Menlo Park, California, on May 10, 1978.

LUSCOMBE MODEL 4, NC1344, Serial Number 404

STATUS—Aircraft Airworthiness Expired
REASON—Aircraft destroyed in accident, August 1, 1943
AIRCRAFT SERIAL NUMBER—404
DATE of MANUFACTURE—June 13, 1938
POWER PLANT—Warner 90 "Scarab Junior", serial number V 82 E
PROPELLER—Hamilton-Standard hub design 7005-D, blades serial numbers 73838 and 73839.
First test flight June 13, 1938. Pilot was Ignatius Sargent.
Department of Commerce Form 9 filed June 13, 1938 for Identification Mark 1344.
Department of Commerce Form 9 filed June 24, 1938 for Commercial License NC1344.
Aircraft Inspection Report lists empty weight of 1040 lbs, gross weight of 1650 lbs, useful load of 239 lbs with 31 gallons fuel, 69 lbs cargo.
Sold to Air America, Inc., Leominster, Massachusetts on June 29, 1938.
NOTE: Daniel Simonds was president of Air America, Inc. He was, also, a director of the Luscombe Airplane Corporation.
Sold to Samuel Slone, Fitchburg, Massachusetts on October 19, 1939.
Sold to Claud Adelbert Herrick, Rochester, New York, on November 13, 1939.
Sold to Arthur C. Lohman, Rochester, New York, on January 12, 1940.
Sold to William H. Masters, Rochester, New York, on June 1, 1940. Tail skid shoe replaced by full swivel tail wheel on

June 12, 1940.
Involved in accident, July 7, 1940, Carmel, New York.
Accident synopsis-W.H. Masters was giving a ride to a Miss Lea Hammond when subject aircraft was damaged while trying to land in a small field. Pilot made downwind landing with tail coming up and nosing over. Repairs to propeller, firewall, leading edge of both wings, fin and rudder were completed August 5, 1940.
Sold to Eugene L. Ward and Albin J. Marn, Cleveland, Ohio, on June 29, 1942.

JAMES B. ZAZAS COLLECTION

Aircraft destroyed in accident on August 1, 1943 during a local pleasure flight near the Lake County Airport, Willoughby, Ohio. The pilot and passenger were fatally injured.
Accident synopsis—According to the Civil Aeronautics Board report, the pilot displayed poor judgement in attempting a low altitude, wingover maneuver. The aircraft impacted the ground at a 45 degree angle, power on, and disintegrated as it slid forward. Both occupants were Naval Aviation cadets on leave, having completed basic flight training with the Navy.

LUSCOMBE MODEL 4, NC22026, Serial Number 405

STATUS—Aircraft Registration Expired
REASON—
AIRCRAFT SERIAL NUMBER—
DATE of MANUFACTURE—January 1939
POWER PLANT—Warner 90 "Scarab Junior", serial number V 86 E
PROPELLER—Hamilton-Standard model 7005-D, serial number 29167, blades serial numbers 70083 and 70084.
First test flight January 26, 1939. Pilot was Alfred "Fritz" King.
Department of Commerce Form 9 filed January 5, 1939 for Identification Mark 22026.
Department of Commerce Form 9 filed January 26, 1939 for Commercial License NC22026.
Sold to Massey and Ransom Flying Service, Inc., Denver, Colorado, on January 19, 1939.
Aircraft damaged in ground loop on July 15, 1939 at Municipal Airport, Denver, Colorado. Repairs to right wing tip, bottom of rudder, stabilizer tip, elevator tip and tail wheel fitting repaired August 1939.
Sold to James H. Peden, Long Beach, California, on February 23, 1940.
Aircraft was altered substantially with the addition of radio equipment to fulfill Civil Air Patrol coastal patrol role. Lear radio receiver and transmitter, Lear Antenna reel, Lear Rotatable Loop, Lear Wind Driven Generator, Pioneer sensitive altimeter and Elgin 8 day clock added.
Sold to Associated Engineers, Inc., Houston, Texas, on December 9, 1943. A lien of $2000 was owed to Edwin W. Ritchey, Meacham Field, Ft. Worth, Texas.
Sold to Milton T. Ramsey, Abiline, Texas, on March 11, 1944.
Sold to Bryce Bostic, Post, Texas, on April 2, 1946.
NOTE: Author's research into fate of this aircraft and Mr. Bostic failed to produce further information.

Appendix E

Dealer Franchise Agreements

August 1937 - January 1938

DATE	NAME OF COMPANY	TERRITORIES ASSIGNED
August 8, 1937	Falcon Aircraft Company, Los Angeles, California	California, Washington, Oregon
August 12, 1937	Fitchburg-Leominster Airways, Inc. Fitchburg, Massachusetts	Maine, Vermont, New Hampshire Connecticut (except Faifield, New Haven, Middlesex and New London counties)
August 23, 1937	Queen City Flying Service, Cincinnati, Ohio	Ohio (southern half)
August 23, 1937	Sundorph Aeronautical Group, Cleveland, Ohio	Ohio (northern half)
August 23, 1937	Illinois Aircraft Sales Co., Glenview, Illinois	Illinois, Lake and Porter counties of Indiana and tier of counties in southern Wisconsin
August 23, 1937	Muncie Aviation Co., Muncie, Indiana	Indiana except Porter and Lake counties
August 24, 1937	Robert I. McKee Salisbury, North Carolina	North Carolina
August 25, 1937	Karl Voelter, Inc Miami, Florida	Florida (southern half including Orlando and Tampa)
August 25, 1937	George B. Cluett, II Troy, New York	New York State (excluding Manhattan and Long Island)
September 24, 1937	Salzman-Leonard, Inc. Detroit, Michigan	Michigan (except the Upper Peninsula)
September 28, 1937	St. Louis Flying Service, St. Louis, Missouri	Missouri and Kansas Inc. City and environs
September 28, 1937	Louisville Flying Service, Louisville, Kentucky	Kentucky
September 29, 1937	Marines, Des Marais Aircraft and Distributors, Inc Phoenix, Arizona	Arizona, New Mexico, Utah
October 2, 1937	Campbell Aircraft Company, Dallas, Texas	Texas
November 16, 1937	Sioux Skyways, Inc. Sioux Falls, South Dakota	North Dakota, South Dakota, Nebraska and western tier Iowa counties
December 15, 1937	C.M. Booker Marion, Kansas	Oklahoma
December 18, 1937	Iowa Airplane Company Des Moines, Iowa	Iowa (except western tier counties)
January 7, 1938	Otis T. Massey and Harry T. Gaines Denver, Colorado	Colorado

298 *Visions of Luscombe: The Early Years*

—and now the new Luscombe "90" takes its place in America's finest line of METAL AIRPLANES

JUST as Luscombe designs of ten years ago offered the basic pattern for most small private airplanes presented for sale today, the new METAL Luscombe airplanes point the way to more modern standards of styling, strength and performance.

Farsighted dealers will ask for details concerning the Luscombe Metal Line which will start with two-place models in the $1500 price field.

LUSCOMBE AIRPLANE CORPORATION
WEST TRENTON NEW JERSEY

AERO DIGEST — AUGUST 1937.

One of Don Luscombe's favorite cartoons. This cartoon originally appeared in the April 16, 1936 issue of THE SATURDAY EVENING POST.

ELEANORE LUSCOMBE SHURTZ COLLECTION

Appendix F

Luscombe Phantom, Luscombe "90", Luscombe "50" and Luscombe "65" Specifications

LUSCOMBE PHANTOM   2-Place   ATC 552   (8-18-34)

Specifications:
Wingspan 31' with 62" chord
Length 20' 10"
Height 6' 9"
Wing area 143.25 sq. ft. (NACA 2412 airfoil)
Empty weight 1320 lbs.
Gross weight 1950 lbs.
Useful load 630 lbs.
Payload 236 lbs.
Baggage 66 lbs.
Fuel 33 gals.
Oil 3.5 gals.

Performance:
Maximum speed 168 MPH
Cruising speed 142 MPH
Landing speed with flaps 45 MPH
Service ceiling 19,000 ft.
Climb 1400 ft./min.
Cruising range 560 miles

Engine: Warner 145 "Super Scarab", 145-hp at 2050 RPM
Price: $6,000 (1934) $6,500 (1935) $6,800 (1936)

JAMES B. ZAZAS COLLECTION

LUSCOMBE "90"   2-place   ATC 687   (6-25-38)

Specifications:
Wingspan 32' 1" with
Length 20' 11"
Height 6' 6"
Wing area 140 sq. ft. (NACA 2412 airfoil)
Empty weight 960 lbs.
Gross weight 1275 lbs.
Useful load 765 lbs.
Payload 258 lbs.
Baggage 125 lbs.
Fuel 30 gals.
Oil 2 gals.

Performance:
Maximum speed 136 MPH
Cruising speed 120 MPH
Landing speed with flaps 40 MPH
Service Ceiling 15,000 ft.
Rate of climb 850 ft./min.
Cruising range 600 miles

Engine: Warner 90 "Scarab Junior", 90-hp at 2025 RPM
Price: $4,000 FAF (1938)

JAMES B. ZAZAS COLLECTION

LUSCOMBE "50" 2-place ATC 694 (8-11-38)

Specifications:
- Wingspan 35'
- Length 20'
- Height 5' 10"
- Wing Area 140 sq. ft. (NACA 4412 airfoil)
- Empty weight 630 lbs.
- Gross weight 1130 lbs.
- Useful load 500 lbs.
- Payload 214 lbs.
- Baggage 44 lbs.
- Fuel 14 gals.
- Oil 1 gal.

Performance:
- Maximum speed 109 MPH
- Cruising speed 96 MPH
- Landing speed 37 MPH
- Service ceiling 13,500 ft./min.
- Rate of climb 750 ft./min.
- Cruising range 400 miles

Engine: Continental A-50, 50-hp at 1900 RPM
Price: $1,895 FAF (1938)

JAMES B. ZAZAS COLLECTION

LUSCOMBE "65" 2-place ATC 694 (8-11-38)

Specifications:
- Wingspan 35'
- Length 20'
- Height 5' 10"
- Wing Area 140 sq. ft. (NACA 4412 airfoil)
- Empty weight 665 lbs.
- Gross 1200 lbs.
- Useful load 535 lbs.
- Payload 225 lbs.
- Baggage 55 lbs.
- Fuel 14 gals.
- Oil 1 gal.

Performance:
- Maximum speed 115 MPH
- Cruising speed 104 MPH
- Landing speed 37 MPH
- Service Ceiling 15,000 ft.
- Rate of climb 900 ft./min.
- Cruising range 350 miles (4.5 gal/hr)

Engine: Continental A-65, 65-hp at 2350 RPM
Price: $1,975 FAF (1939)

JOHN LENGENFELDER

Appendix G

Phantom, Luscombe "90," Luscombe "50" and Luscombe "65" First Flight Analysis

May 14, 1934 through August 22, 1939

The following information was gleaned from a study of the pilot's logbooks of Donald A. Luscombe, Ignatius Sargent, Edgar S. Davis, William B. Shepard and Alfred G. "Fritz" King.

SERIAL NUMBER	"N" NUMBER	ENGINE	DATE	PILOT/COMMENTS
1	NC272Y	W-145	05-14-34	Don Joseph
101	NC275Y	W-145	12-17-34	Bart Stevenson
102	NC276Y	W-145	01-??-35	?
103	NC277Y	W-145	01-??-35	?
104	NC278Y	W-145	??-??-35	?
105	HB-EXE	W-145	07-15-35	? (Ben Melcher rode as bonifide crew member.)
106	NC1286	W-145	06-20-36	Ignatius Sargent
107	NC1007	W-145	08-26-36	Edgar S. Davis
108	NC1008	W-145	10-15-36	Ignatius Sargent
109	NC7734	W-145	08-14-36	Ignatius Sargent
2-110	NC1234	W-145	10-08-36	Ignatius Sargent
111	NC1010	W-145	11-07-36	Ignatius Sargent
112	NC1025	W-145	10-16-36	Ignatius Sargent
113	NC1028	W-145	12-11-36	Ignatius Sargent
114	NC1043	W-145	12-21-36	Edgar S. Davis
115	NC1235	W-145	02-09-37	Ignatius Sargent
116	NC1048	W-145	03-30-37	Ignatius Sargent
117	NC1278	W-145	08-13-37	Alfred "Fritz" King
118	D1L-204	W-145	08-16-38	Ignatius Sargent
119	-	-	-	Airframe fuselage only
120	NC1249	W-145	05-25-37	Ignatius Sargent
121	NC1323	W-145	04-16-38	Ignatius Sargent
122	NC1265	W-145	05-13-37	Ignatius Sargent
100	1017	W-90	11-03-37	Ignatius Sargent
400	1253	W-90	03-10-37	Ignatius Sargent (Proof-of-Concept Design)
400	NX1253	W-90	01-22-38	Ignatius Sargent (Protoype Luscombe "90")
401	-	-	-	Unassigned Ser. No.
402	NC1325	W-90	06-10-38	Ignatius Sargent
403	NC1337	W-90	07-30-38	Ignatius Sargent
404	NC1344	W-90	06-24-38	Ignatius Sargent
?	NC1335	W-90	08-03-38	Ignatius Sargent
405	NC22026	W-90	01-26-39	Alfred "Fritz" King
800	1304	A-50	12-17-37	Tom Foley (Model 8 Prototype)
801	NC1327	A-50	06-07-38	Ignatius Sargent (First Production Model 8)
802	NC2589	A-50	08-05-38	Ignatius Sargent
803	NC2590	A-50	08-08-38	Ignatius Sargent
804	NC2591	A-50	08-15-38	Ignatius Sargent
805	NC2592	A-50	08-12-38	Ignatius Sargent
806	CF-BKW	A-50	08-19-38	Edgar S. Davis
807	NC2355	A-50		

808	NC2390	A-50	08-30-38	Alfred "Fritz" King
809	NC2391	A-50	09-04-38	Alfred "Fritz" King
810	NC2193	A-50		
811	NC2289	A-50	09-27-38	Ignatius Sargent
812	NC2336	A-50	09-15-38	Alfred "Fritz" King
813	NC2379	A-50	09-17-38	Edgar S. Davis
814	NC2381	A-50	09-22-38	Ignatius Sargent
815	NC2386	A-50	09-29-38	Ignatius Sargent
816	NC2417	A-50	09-24-38	Ignatius Sargent
817	NC20654	A-50	09-27-38	Ignatius Sargent
818	NC20655	A-50	10-04-38	Ignatius Sargent
819	NC20656	A-50	10-04-38	Edgar S. Davis
820	NC20657	A-50	10-07-38	Ignatius Sargent
821	NC20658	A-50	10-10-38	Ignatius Sargent
822	NC20659	A-50	10-15-38	Ignatius Sargent
823	CF-BLW	A-50	10-13-38	Ignatius Sargent
824	NC20661	A-50	10-18-38	Ignatius Sargent
825	NC20662	A-50	11-02-38	Ignatius Sargent
826	NC20663	A-50	10-24-38	Alfred "Fritz" King
827	NC20664	A-50	11-09-38	Ignatius Sargent
828	NC20665	A-50	11-04-38	Ignatius Sargent
829	HB-DUT	A-50	11-08-38	Ignatius Sargent
830	NC20667	A-50	11-12-38	Ignatius Sargent
831	NC20668	A-50	11-16-38	Ignatius Sargent
832	NC20669	A-50	11-22-38	Edgar S. Davis
833	NC20679	A-50	11-18-38	Ignatius Sargent
834	NC20690	A-50	11-23-38	Ignatius Sargent
835	NC20681	A-50	11-29-38	Ignatius Sargent
836	NC20682	A-50	11-30-38	Ignatius Sargent
837	NC20683	A-50	11-30-38	Ignatius Sargent
838	NC20684	A-50	12-03-38	Ignatius Sargent
839	NX20685	A-50	12-07-38	Ignatius Sargent (A/C used for 1200 lb. gross weight ATC tests)
840	NC20686	A-50	12-07-38	Ignatius Sargent
841	NC20687	A-50	12-08-38	Ignatius Sargent
842	NC20688	A-50	12-08-38	Ignatius Sargent
843	NC20689	A-50	12-12-38	Edgar S. Davis
844	NC20690	A-50		
845	NC20691	A-50	12-14-38	Ignatius Sargent
846	NC20692	A-50	12-19-38	Ignatius Sargent
847	NC20693	A-50	12-20-38	Edgar S. Davis
848	NC20694	A-50	12-20-38	Ignatius Sargent
849	NC20695	A-50	12-21-38	Ignatius Sargent
850	NC20696	A-50	12-22-38	Ignatius Sargent
851	NC22001	A-50	12-22-38	Ignatius Sargent
852	NC22002	A-50	12-27-38	Alfred "Fritz" King (First Model 8 modified for snow skies)
853	NC22003	A-50	12-27-38	Edgar S. Davis
854	NC22004	A-50	12-29-38	Ignatius Sargent
855	NC22005	A-50	12-30-38	Ignatius Sargent
856	NC22006	A-50	12-30-38	Ignatius Sargent
857	NC22007	A-50	12-31-38	Ignatius Sargent
858	NC22008	A-50		
859	NC22009	A-50	01-07-39	Edgar S. Davis
860	NC22010	A-50	01-16-39	Edgar S. Davis
861	NC22011	A-50		
862	NC22012	A-50	01-17-39	Edgar S. Davis
863	NC22013	A-50	01-19-39	Edgar S. Davis
864	NC22014	A-50	01-26-39	Alfred "Fritz" King
865	NC22015	A-50	01-28-39	Ignatius Sargent
866	NC22016	A-50	01-27-39	Alfred "Fritz" King
867	NC22017	A-50		
868	NC22018	A-50	01-31-39	Edgar S. Davis
869	NC22019	A-50	02-05-39	Ignatius Sargent
870	NC22020	A-50	02-07-39	Edgar S. Davis
871	NC22021	A-50		
872	NC22022	A-50	02-07-39	Ignatius Sargent
873	NC22023	A-50		
874	NC22024	A-50	02-17-39	Ignatius Sargent
875	NC22025	A-50	02-16-39	Edgar S. Davis
876	NC22050	A-50	02-21-39	Ignatius Sargent

877	NC22051	A-50	02-25-39	Edgar S. Davis (Service ceiling tests, 13,800 ft.)
878	NC22052	A-50		
879	NC22053	A-50		
880	NC22054	A-50	02-23-39	Ignatius Sargent
881	NX22055	A-65	02-19-39	Ignatius Sargent (Aircraft used for Cont. A-65 engine ATC tests. Also, flown by E.S.D. in Army competition, Wright Field, Ohio, March 1939)
882	NC22056	A-50	02-25-39	Ignatius Sargent
883	NC22057	A-50		
884	NC22058	A-50		
885	NC22059	A-50		
886	NC22060	A-50	03-07-39	Ignatius Sargent
887	NC22061	A-50	03-09-39	Ignatius Sargent
888	NC22062	A-50	03-15-39	Ignatius Sargent
889	NC22063	A-50	03-15-39	Ignatius Sargent
890	NC22064	A-50	03-09-39	Ignatius Sargent
891	NC22065	A-65	03-15-39	Ignatius Sargent (First Production Luscombe "65")
892	NC22066	A-50	04-03-39	Edgar S. Davis
893	XB-AKL (?)	A-50	04-05-39	Edgar S. Davis
894	NC22068	A-65	03-22-39	Ignatius Sargent
895	NC22069	A-65	03-23-39	Ignatius Sargent
896	NC22070	A-65	03-28-39	Ignatius Sargent (Used 04-08-39 for Jackie Cochran's Lightplane Speed Record Attempt)
897	NC22071	A-65	03-31-39	Edgar S. Davis
898	NC22072	A-65		
899	NC22073	A-65	03-31-39	Ignatius Sargent
900	NC22074	A-65	04-05-39	Edgar S. Davis
901	NC22079	A-65	04-05-39	Edgar S. Davis
902	NC22080	A-65	04-11-39	Ignatius Sargent
903	NC22081	A-65	04-07-39	Ignatius Sargent
904	NC22082	A-65	04-10-39	Ignatius Sargent
905	NC22083	A-65	04-10-39	Ignatius Sargent
906	NC22084	A-65	04-13-39	Ignatius Sargent
907	NC22085	A-65	04-17-39	Ignatius Sargent (Bought by Don Luscombe)
908	NC22086	A-65	05-07-39	William B. Shepard
909	NC22087	A-65	04-20-39	Ignatius Sargent
910	NC22088	A-65	04-27-39	Alfred "Fritz" King
911	NC22089	A-65		
912	NC22090	A-65	04-25-39	Alfred "Fritz" King
913	NC22091	A-65	04-27-39	Alfred "Fritz" King
914	NC22092	A-65		
915		A-65		
916		A-65		
917		A-65		
918	NC22096	A-65		
919	NC22097	A-65		
920	NC22098	A-65	05-11-39	William B. Shepard
921	NC22099	A-65	05-11-39	Wilaim B. Shepard
922	NX22093	A-65	05-20-39	Alfred "Fritz" King (First Luscombe 8A Seaplane)
923				
924	NC23000	A-65	07-14-39	Alfred "Fritz" King
925				
926	NC23003	A-65	05-23-39	William B. Shepard
927	NC23004	A-65	05-25-39	William B. Shepard
928	NC23005	A-65	05-25-39	William B. Shepard
929	NC23002	A-65	05-26-39	William B. Shepard
930	NC23007	A-65	05-27-39	William B. Shepard
931	NC23008	A-65	05-31-39	William B. Shepard
932	NC23009	A-65	06-01-39	William B. Shepard
933	NC23010	A-65	06-02-39	William B. Shepard
934	NC23011	A-65	06-01-39	William B. Shepard
935	NC23012	A-65	06-02-39	William B. Shepard
936	NC23013	A-65	06-05-39	William B. Shepard
937	NC23014	A-65	06-08-39	William B. Shepard
938	NC23015	A-65	06-08-39	William B. Shepard
939	NC23016	A-65	07-07-39	Alfred "Fritz" King
940	NC23017	A-65	06-12-39	William B. Shepard
941	NC23018	A-65		
942	NC23019	A-65		
943	NC23020	A-65	06-13-39	William B. Shepard

944	NC23021	A-65	06-12-39	William B. Shepard
945	NC23022	A-65	06-14-39	William B. Shepard
946				
947	NC23024	A-65	06-16-39	William B. Shepard
948	NC23025	A-65	06-16-39	William B. Shepard
949	NC23006	A-65	06-21-39	Alfred "Fritz" King
950	NC23027	A-65	06-17-39	William B. Shepard
951	NC23028	A-65	06-20-39	William B. Shepard
952	NC23029	A-65	06-21-39	Alfred "Fritz" King
953	NC23030	A-65	06-21-39	Alfred "Fritz" King
954	NC23031	A-65	06-22-39	Alfred "Fritz" King
955	NC23032	A-65	06-22-39	Alfred "Fritz" King
956	NC23033	A-65	06-23-39	Alfred "Fritz" King
957	NC23034	A-65	06-26-39	Alfred "Fritz" King
958	NC23035	A-65	06-26-39	Alfred "Fritz" King
959	NC23036	A-65	06-27-39	Alfred "Fritz" King
960	NC23037	A-65	06-27-39	Alfred "Fritz" King
961	NC23038	A-65	06-28-39	Alfred "Fritz" King
962	NC23039	A-65	06-29-39	Alfred "Fritz" King
963	NC23040	A-65		
964	NC23041	A-65	06-29-39	Alfred "Fritz" King
965	CF-BAC	A-65	06-30-39	Alfred "Fritz" King
966	NC23043	A-65	07-01-39	Alfred "Fritz" King
967	NC23044	A-65	07-01-39	Alfred "Fritz" King
968	NC23045	A-65	07-01-39	Alfred "Fritz" King
969	NC23046	A-65	07-06-39	Alfred "Fritz" King
970	NC23047	A-65		
971	NC23048	A-65	07-08-39	Alfred "Fritz" King
972	NC23049	A-65	07-08-39	Alfred "Fritz" King
973	NC23050	A-65	07-10-39	Alfred "Fritz" King
974	NC23051	A-65	07-11-39	Alfred "Fritz" King
975	NC23052	A-65	07-12-39	Alfred "Fritz" King
976	NC23053	A-65	07-13-39	Alfred "Fritz" King
977	NC23054	A-65	07-14-39	Alfred "Fritz" King
978	NC23023	A-65	07-13-39	Alfred "Fritz" King
979	NC23055	A-65	07-14-39	Alfred "Fritz" King
980	NC23056	A-65	07-21-39	Alfred "Fritz" King
981	NC23057	A-65	07-17-39	Alfred "Fritz" King
982	NC23062	A-65	07-26-39	Alfred "Fritz" King (Model 8A Seaplane)
983	NC23059	A-65		
984	NC23060	A-65	07-31-39	Alfred "Fritz" King (Model 8A Seaplane)
985	NC23061	A-65	07-23-39	Alfred "Fritz" King
986	NC23058	A-65	07-18-39	Alfred "Fritz" King
987	NC23063	A-65	07-23-39	Alfred "Fritz" King
988	NC23064	A-65	07-25-39	Alfred "Fritz" King
989	NC23065	A-65	07-27-39	Alfred "Fritz" King
990	NC23066	A-65	07-25-39	Alfred "Fritz" King
991	NC23067	A-65	07-27-39	Alfred "Fritz" King
992	NC23068	A-65	07-27-39	Alfred "Fritz" King
993	NC23069	A-65	07-28-39	Alfred "Fritz" King
994	NC23070	A-65	07-28-39	Alfred "Fritz" King
995	NC23071	A-65	07-31-39	Alfred "Fritz" King
996	NC23072	A-65	07-31-39	Alfred "Fritz" King
997	NC23073	A-65	08-01-39	Alfred "Fritz" King
998	NC23074	A-65	08-03-39	Alfred "Fritz" King
999	NC23075	A-65	08-04-39	Alfred "Fritz" King
1000	NC23076	A-65	08-09-39	Alfred "Fritz" King
1001	NC23077	A-65	08-09-39	Alfred "Fritz" King
1002	NC23078	A-65	08-07-39	Alfred "Fritz" King
1003	NC23079	A-50	08-08-39	Alfred "Fritz" King
1004	NC23042	A-65	08-10-39	Alfred "Fritz" King
1005	NC23081	A-65		
1006	NC23082	A-65		
1007	NC23083	A-65		
1008	NC23084	A-65		
1009	NC23085	A-65	08-21-39	Alfred "Fritz" King
1010	NC23086	A-65	08-21-39	Alfred "Fritz" King
1011	NC23087	A-65	08-21-39	Alfred "Fritz" King
1012	NC23088	A-65	08-22-39	Alfred "Fritz" King

Bibliography

BOOKS

Aeronautical Chamber of Commerce of America, Inc.; The Aircraft Year Book. Volumes 11 through 22, New York, New York: The Aeronautical Chamber of Commerce, Inc., 1929-1940.

Airports and Established Landing Sites in the United States, 1934 Edition. Hackensack, New Jersey: The Airport Directory Company, 1934.

Angle, Glenn D., ed.; Aerosphere. New York, New York: Aircraft Publications, 1939.

Beck, Emily M., ed.; Bartlett's Familiar Quotations. Toronto, Canada: Little, Brown and Company, 1980.

Bowers, Peter M.; Yesterday's Wings. Washington, D.C.: Aircraft Owners and Pilots Association, 1974.

Bridgeman, Leonard, ed.; Jane's All the World's Aircraft. New York, New York: The Macmillian Company, 1941.

deVries, Col. John A.; Alexander Eaglerock, A History of the Alexander Aircraft Company. Colorado Springs, Colorado: Century One Press, 1985.

Holden, Henry M. with Captain Lori Griffith; Ladybirds, The Untold Story of Women Pilots in America. Freedom, New Jersey: Black Hawk Publishing Company, 1991.

Juptner, Joseph P.; U.S. Civil Aircraft. Volumes 1 through 9; Fallbrook, California: Aero Publishers, Inc., 1962-1980.

Luscombe, Don A.; Simplified Flying. Moline, Illinois: Mono Aircraft, Inc., 1928.

Norcross, Carl and Quinn, James D., Jr; The Aviation Mechanic. New York, New York: McGraw-Hill Book Company, Inc., 1941.

Pellegreno, Ann Holtgren; Iowa Takes to the Air, Volume Two 1919-1941. Story City, Iowa: Aerodrome Press, 1986.

Phillips, Edward H; Cessna, A Master's Expression. Eagan, Minnesota: Flying Books, 1985.

Preston, Eric; The Aviator's Timeless Choice. Sonoma, California: Prewar Publications, 1986.

Salitri, Frank R.; The Luscombe; No Wood, No Nails, No Glue!. Hollywood, California: Agony House Publishers, 1982.

Schend, S.C. and Weaver, Truman C.; The Golden Age of Air Racing, Pre-1940. Oshkosh, Wisconsin: EAA Aviation Foundation, Inc., 1991.

Smith, Frank Kingston; Legacy of Wings The Story of Harold F. Pitcairn. New York, New York: Jason Aronson, Inc., 1981.

Smith, Herschel; A History of Aircraft Piston Engines. New York, New York: McGraw Hill, Inc., 1981; reprint ed., Manhattan, Kansas: Sunflower University Press, 1986.

Swick, John C.; The Luscombe Story; Every Cloud Has a Silvalre Lining. Terre Haute, Indiana: SunShine House, Inc., 1984.

The Editors of Time-Life Books; Shadow of the Dictators: Time Frame AD 1925-1950 (Time Frame Series). Alexandria, Virginia: Time-Life Books, Inc., 1989.

The Writers' Program of the Work Projects Administration; Who's Who in Aviation, A Directory of Living Men and Women Who Have Contributed to the Growth of Aviation in the United States, 1942-1943. New York, New York: Ziff-Davis Publishing Company, 1942.

Thomas, Stanley G.; The Luscombes. Blue Ridge Summit, Pennsylvania: TAB/Aero Books, 1991.

Towson, George A.; Autogiro, The Story of "the Windmill Plane". Fallbrook, California: Aero Publishers, Inc., 1985.

Underwood, John; Of Monocoupes and Men. Glendale, California: Heritage Press, 1973.

U.S. Department of Justice, Public Affairs Office; Vested Claims Committee Records, # D28-1466, 1941-1945.

Wagner, William; Continental! Its Motors and Its People. Fallbrook, California: Aero Publishers, Inc., 1983.

SELECTED MAGAZINES and PERIODICALS

Air Trails, April 1938.

Aviation and Aero Digest magazines, 1924 through 1941.

American Airman magazine, July and August 1961.

Armchair Aviator, December 1972.

Max-Fax, newsletters of the D.C. Maxchuters, 1974 through 1980.

Flight, September 19, 1935.

Rock Island Argus, January 12, 1965.

Shell Aviation News, November 1934.

Sport Aviation, February 1973.

Sport Aviation, February 1975.

The Ambler Gazette, September 29, 1983.

The Davenport Democrat, August 1927 through May 1931.

The Moline Daily Dispatch, December 1926 through May 1931.

The New York Times, 1933 to 1940.

The Trenton Sunday Times-Advertiser, June 9, 1935.

The Trenton Times, June 15, 1936.

Antique Airplane Association newsletters and publications, Robert Taylor, ed. 1956 to present.

Continental Luscombe Association newsletters, Loren

and Adele Bump, ed. 1975 to present.
Luscombe Association newsletters, Jay Armstrong, ed., 1975; Robert Shelton, ed. 1975 through 1980; John and Alice Bergeson, ed., 1980 to present.
Monocoupe Flyer and other newsletters of the Monocoupe Club, Jim Harvey, ed., 1964 through 1976; Bud and Connie Dake, ed., 1977 through 1983; Bob Coolbaugh, ed., 1990 to present.
Contemporary newspapers, aviation journals and anthologies.
Various National Air and Space Museum biographical files.

DRIGGS FAMILY HISTORY

1. Baker, Dorothy Driggs; notes, letters, photographs, family history.

FOLKERTS FAMILY HISTORY

1. Folkerts, Dale; notes, letters, photographs, family history.
2. Folkerts, Calvin; notes, letters, photographs, family history.

LUSCOMBE FAMILY HISTORY

1. Shurtz, Eleanore Luscombe; notes, letters, photographs and family history.
2. Luscombe, James T.; notes, letters, photographs and family history.
3. Luscombe, James H.; notes, letters, photographs and family history.
4. Luscombe, Ora May; notes, letters photographs and family history.
5. Kapitan, Lucille Luscombe; notes, letters, photographs and family history.
6. Numerof, Betty Luscombe; notes, letters, photographs and family history.

INTERVIEWS and CORRESPONDENCE
(Company Alumni and Family Members of Alumni)

1. Akers, Bruce; correspondence, 1987.
2. Brutus, Lee and Geraldine; interviews and correspondence from 1988 to 1990.
3. Burgess, Charles and Winona; interviews and correspondence from 1984 to 1990.
4. Cavin, Dick; correspondence, 1985 and 1990.
5. Cericola, Kenneth; interviews and correspondence from 1984 to 1991.
6. Coghill, Kathy; correspondence from 1986 to 1991.
7. Coghill, Louis; correspondence, 1984.
8. Coigny, Jerry and Lucy; interviews and correspondence from 1985 to 1992.
9. Davis, Edgar; interviews and correspondence from 1989 to 1991.
10. De Crescenzo, Jules; correspondence, 1985 to 1990.
11. Eggleston, J. Elliot; correspondence from 1988 to 1989.
12. Eisenmann, Marty and Bee; interviews and correspondence from 1985 to 1992.
13. Farver, Lyle and Carol; interviews and correspondence from 1987 to 1989.
14. Feldmann, Stephen; correspondence from 1987 to 1991.
15. Force, William and Dottie; interviews and correspondence from 1985 to 1988.
16. Funk, Keith; interviews and correspondence from 1985 to 1991.
17. Funk, Robert; interviews and correspondence from 1985 to 1989.
18. Funk, Ross; interviews and correspondence from 1985 to 1988.
19. Greene, Howard; interviews and correspondence from 1988 to 1992.
20. Gregory, Rolfe; correspondence from 1985 to 1991.
21. Hoernig, Otto; interviews and correspondence from 1985 to 1991.
22. Johnson, Frank and Leah; interviews and correspondence from 1986 to 1991.
23. Jong, Howard and Ella; interviews and correspondence from 1985 to 1991.
24. Kauffman, Glenn and Pauline; interviews and correspondence from 1985 to 1990.
25. Klotz, Leopold H.P.; interview 1989.
26. King, Alfred "Fritz" and Marion; interviews and correspondence from 1985 to 1991.
27. Lawrence, Linwood and Emilee, interviews and correspondence from 1985 to 1992.
28. Lederer, Jerome; interviews and correspondence from 1986 to 1991.
29. McCormick, G. Paul; interviews and correspondence from 1988 to 1991.
30. Melcher, Ben; interviews and correspondence from 1985 to 1992.
31. Melfa, Mike; correspondence from 1985 to 1988.
32. Mitchell, A. Edgar and Lorry; interviews and correspondence from 1983 to 1992.
33. Mueller, Merle and Wanda, interviews and correspondence from 1986 to 1992.
34. Murphy, Thomas and Evelyn; interviews and correspondence from 1985 to 1991.
35. Norris, Eugene and Jan, interviews and correspondence from 1986 to 1992.
36. Roberts, Ken; correspondence, 1991.
37. Robinson, William and Ginny; correspondence from 1984 to 1987.

38. Rowe, Bert; correspondence from 1985 to 1988.
39. Sargent, Ignatius and Sissie; interviews and correspondence from 1987 to 1992.
40. Shepard, William and Jane; interviews and correspondence from 1985 to 1991.
41. Winazak, Walter; correspondence from 1985 to 1991.

U.S. GOVERNMENT DEPARTMENTS and AGENCIES

1. Air Force Museum, Research Department, Wright-Patterson AFB, Ohio.
2. HQ USAF Historical Research Center, Reference Division (HD), Maxwell AFB, Alabama.
3. National Aeronautics and Space Administration, Hugh L. Dryden Flight Research Facility, Edwards AFB, California.
4. National Archives and Records Administration, Civil Reference Division, Washington, D.C.
5. National Archives and Records Administration, Military Field Branch, Washington, D.C.
6. National Air and Space Museum, Smithsonian Institution, Washington, D.C.
7. National Air and Space Museum, Smithsonian Institution, Archival Support Center, Suitland, Maryland.
8. United States Department of Justice, FOI/PA Office, Civil Division, Washington, D.C.
9. United States Department of Transportation, Federal Aviation Administration, Mike Monroney Aeronautical Center, Oklahoma City, Oklahoma.
10. United States Securities and Exchange Commission, Public Reference Branch; Washington, D.C.

FOREIGN AIRCRAFT REGISTRATION INFORMATION

1. Brazil Registration Branch, FAA Representative, US Consulate, Rio de Janeiro, Brazil.
2. Costa Rica Registration Branch, Dirreccion General de Aviatcion Civil, Ministerio de Obras Publicas y Transportes, San Jose, Costa Rica.
3. Panama Registration Branch, Direccion de Aeronautica Civil, Repulica de Panama.
4. Switzerland Registration Branch, Office Federal de L'Aviation Civile, Berne, Switzerland.

SECRETARIES of STATE

1. Iowa Secretary of State, Corporate Division, Des Moines, Iowa.
2. Missouri Secretary of State, Division of Corporate Records, Jefferson City, Missouri.
3. New Jersey Department of State, Division of Commercial Recordings, Trenton, New Jersey.
4. Commonwealth of Pennsylvania, Department of State, Bureau of Corporations, Harrisburg, Pennsylvania.
5. Office of the Secretary of State, Statutory Filings Division-Corporations, Austin, Texas.

COURTHOUSES

1. Rock Island County Courthouse, Rock Island, Illinois.
2. Scott County Courthouse, Davenport, Iowa.

PITCAIRN AIRCRAFT HISTORY

1. Gunther, Carl, correspondence, 1988 to 1991.
2. Pitcairn, Stephen, correspondence, 1988 to 1991.

PRIVATE COLLECTIONS, PUBLIC AND UNIVERSITY LIBRARIES

1. Antique Airplane Association Airpower Museum, Ottumwa, Iowa.
2. Augustina College Library, Rock Island, Illinois.
3. Aviation Heritage Library, Terre Haute, Indiana.
4. Duke University Library, Durham, North Carolina.
5. Boyd Library, Sandhills Community College, Southern Pines, North Carolina.
6. Davenport Public Library, Davenport, Iowa.
7. Elmer Holmes Bobst Library, New York University, New York, New York.
8. Experimental Aircraft Association Library/Archives, Oshkosh, Wisconsin.
9. Indianapolis Public Library, Indianapolis, Indiana.
10. John Underwood Collection, Glendale, California.
11. Lane Leonard Collection, Covina, California.
12. Los Angles Public Library, Los Angeles, California.
13. Moline Public Library, Moline, Illinois.
14. New York Public Library, New York City, New York.
15. Roy O. West Library, DePauw University, Greencastle, Indiana.
16. The University of Texas at Dallas History of Aviation Collection, Dallas, Texas.
17. The University of Southern California at Los Angeles Library, Los Angeles, California.
18. United States Library of Congress, Washington, D.C.

MISCELLANEOUS REFERENCES

1. Registrars Office, University of Iowa, Iowa City, Iowa.
2. Thomson Consumer Electronics, Public Affairs Office, Indianapolis, Indiana.
3. Turner Entertainment Company, Los Angeles, California.
4. Wichita Aeronautical Historical Association, Wichita, Kansas.

(Above and Below) Donald A. Luscombe's vision started in October 1926 with one airplane... and evolved into an incredible mass production reality.

Addendum

Four Pomona California-based pilots pose before their specially marked Monocoupe 70 airplanes. FRAN FITZWILLIAM

West Coast Monocoupe distributor, John Hinchey (standing), poses with the four California pilots. FRAN FITZWILLIAM

310   Visions of Luscombe: The Early Years

The first production Monocoach 201, C-8916, (s/n 5001), is shown here sporting a Wright J-5 "Whirlwind" engine.

FRAN FITZWILLIAM

The prototype Monoprep, serial number 6000, was powered by a Velie M-5 engine and featured a Goettingen airfoil. This airfoil was soon abandoned and replaced by "Clark Y" airfoil. Note the unusual landing gear arrangement used in this prototype.

FRAN FITZWILLIAM

Addendum 311

FRAN FITZWILLIAM

(Above and right) A pair of Monocoupe 113 airplanes, each sporting the Velie M-5 engine, are shown in these photographs.

FRAN FITZWILLIAM

The Monocoach Model 275 was powered by the 225 hp Wright J-6 engine.

FRAN FITZWILLIAM

(Right) Kinner Airplane and Motor Corporation chief pilot, Les Bowman, poses before his Kinner K-5 powered Monosport Model 2 at Glendale, California.

FRAN FITZWILLIAM

(Left) Johnny Livingston's clip wing Monocoupe 110 Special racer.

AVIATION HERITAGE LIBRARY

FRAN FITZWILLIAM

(Above and Below) The sleek racing lines of the Cirrus-powered Mono Special are shown to a good advantage in these photographs.

AVIATION HERITAGE LIBRARY

(Above) Spunky Florence Klingensmith added much to the Monocoupe's racing lore. Sadly, this lovely lady lost her life on September 3, 1933, flying a modified Gee Bee Model Y during the Frank Phillips Trophy Race at the Chicago International Air Races.

AVIATION HERITAGE LIBRARY

Addendum 313

(Left and below) Phoebe Omlie was a perennial favorite with racing fans. Omlie and her Monocoupe 113 Special airplane won and placed in many prestigious races, earning a wide variety of trophies.

JAMES B. ZAZAS COLLECTION

(Below) Phoebe Omlie stands proudly beside her famous Monocoupe 113 Special, "Miss Moline", NR8917. Note the National Exchange Club Emblem.

JAMES B. ZAZAS COLLECTION

MIKE SCHENK

314   Visions of Luscombe: The Early Years

NC22082, (s/n 904), was a stock Luscombe "65" and was test flown by Ig Sargent on April 10, 1939.

AVIATION HERITAGE LIBRARY

AVIATION HERITAGE LIBRARY

AVIATION HERITAGE LIBRARY

AVIATION HERITAGE LIBRARY

(Left) Luscombe 8, NC20663. This airplane, serial number 826, was test flown by Albert "Fritz" King on October 24, 1938.

JOHN UNDERWOOD

Index

Aa, Carl, 131, 176, 256
Abby de Chartes, 6, 7
Aeroclube do Brazil, 259, 289
Aero de France (French Aero Club), 184, 201, 217
Air Commerce Act of 1926, 21, 25
Aircraft;
  Aeronca C2, 131, 132, 160, 176, 259
  Aeronca Chief, 261
  Aeronca K, 257, 261
  Alexander Bullet, 44
  Alexander Eaglerock, 254
  American Eagle, 95
  Beech D-17R, 253
  Bell P-63, 249
  Bird, 131
  Boeing B-17, 261
  Boeing 247, 253, 258
  Cessna 120/140, 257
  Cessna 310, 261
  Challenger, 176
  Command-Aire C3C, 64
  Consolidated B-24, 258
  Consolidated (Convair) B-32, 258
  Consolidated (Convair) B-36, 258
  Curtiss B-20 Condor, 156, 175
  Curtiss JN-4 Jenny, 9, 10, 16, 17, 252
  Curtiss Kingbird, 84
  Curtiss P-36, 249
  Curtiss P-40, 249
  Curtiss Robin, 218
  de Havilland Moth, 80
  Demonty-Poncelet, 11
  Douglas B-23, 248
  Douglas DC-2, 253
  Driggs Coupe, 83, 254
  Driggs Dart Model 1, 83, 254
  Driggs Dart Model 2, 83
  Driggs DJ-1, 82, 254
  Driggs Skylark, 254
  Fairchild, 24, 154, 208, 222
  Fleet, 109, 110, 114, 115, 175, 176
  Folkerts Parasol, 26
  Folkerts #1, 13, 15
  Folkerts #2, 13-15
  Folkerts #3, 14, 15, 16
  Folkerts #4, 16
  Folkerts #5, 16
  Folkerts SK-1, 66, 252
  Folkerts SK-3, 252
  Folkerts SK-4, 252
  Folkerts Special, 66
  Gee Bee Model Y, 312
  Grumman Avenger, 256
  Heath Parasol, 90
  Laird Swallow, 9, 10
  Lockheed C-130, 258
  Lockheed Little Dipper, 258
  Lockheed P2V, 258
  Loose Special, 77
  Martin PBM, 256
  Naval Aircraft Factory N3N, 256
  North American B-45, 261
  North American P-51, 249
  Piper Cub, 180, 257
  Pitcairn PA-35, 187
  Pitcairn PA-36, 187, 188-190, 204, 207, 244, 245, 258, 261
  Republic Seebee, 261
  Ryan Brougham, 154
  Ryan S-T, 179, 244
  Sikorsky R-4, 249
  Sikorsky R-5, 249, 250
  Stearman-Hammond, 198, 259
  Stinson L-5, 258
  Stinson 108, 258
  Stinson SM8A, 44
  Taylorcraft, 213, 261
  Taylor E-2 Cub, 131, 146, 160
  "Tommy" Morse, 9
  Travel Air, 34, 80
  Travel Air 4000, 41
  Voisin, 6, 11
  Waco 10, 259
  Waco PCF, 150, 175
  Weatherly-Campbell Colt, 246, 248
  Wright Cabin Cruiser, 82
  Wright OW Aerial Coupe, 82
Aircraft engines;
  Anzani, 11, 24, 34, 252, 269
  Armstrong-Siddeley Genet, 24
  Cirrus, 24, 34, 66, 312
  Continental A-40, 160, 177, 179, 180, 213, 257
  Continental A-50, 160, 177, 180, 192, 196, 213, 218, 227, 228, 233, 257, 258
  Continental A-65, 227, 228, 233, 257, 303
  Continental A-75, 243, 257
  Continental C-85, 257
  Detroit Air-Cat, 18, 20, 22, 24-27, 31, 32, 34, 37, 83, 252, 254, 269
  Gypsy Major, 185
  Henderson, 16, 26, 82
  Jacobs, 133
  Ken-Royce, 193
  Kinner B5, 63, 79,275
  Kinner K5, 46, 48, 50, 79, 272
  Lambert H-106, 61,62, 76, 253
  Lambert R-266, 49, 50, 60, 61, 79, 81, 273
  Lawrence, 15, 16
  Le Blond, 90, 193
  Liberty, 19
  Lycoming O-145, 243
  Menasco, 252
  Michigan Aero Engine Rover, 254
  OX-5, 9, 10, 16, 89, 252, 259
  Pratt and Whitney, 133
  Royal Aircraft Factory 4D, 252
  Siemans, 31, 33, 37
  Spake Cycle Car, 14
  Velie M-5, 32, 34-37, 42, 44, 49, 79, 253, 270, 271, 310, 311
  Velie ML-9, 40, 41
  Warner 90 Scarab Junior, 63, 69, 100, 145, 154, 156, 164, 168, 171, 172, 180, 193, 200, 274, 293-296
  Warner 110 Scarab, 41, 45, 46, 63, 69, 79, 272, 274
  Warner 125 Scarab, 77, 78, 100
  Warner 145 Super Scarab, 63, 81, 84, 97, 119, 220, 277-293
  Warner 165 Super Scarab, 188
  Warner 185 Super Scarab, 63
  Wright J-5 Whirlwind, 41, 43, 271, 310
  Wright J-6, 44, 273, 311
  Wright-Moorehouse, 254
Aircraft shows;
  All-American Aircraft Show, 34, 62
  Detroit Air Show, 115
  International Aircraft Show, 60
  National Aviation Show, 169
Air Mail Service, 22
Air Meets, Tours and Races;
  All Ohio Derby (1929), 48
  California Class A Race (1928), 38
  Challenge de Tourisme International (1930), 65
  Chicago National Air Races, 312
  Cincinnati Trophy Race (1932), 81
  Civilians Closed Course Race (1930), 67
  Dayton Air Races (1924), 254
  Firestone Elimination Race (1939), 261
  Firestone Trophy Race (1939), 261
  Ford Reliability Tour (1938), 39
  Frank Phillips Trophy Race (1933), 312
  Gordon-Bennett Races (1920), 82
  Greve, 252
  Indiana Air Tour (1930), 66
  Iowa State Air Tour (1930), 65
  Light Plane Speed and Efficiency Race (1928), 38
  Miami Air Races (1931), 75, 77
  Miami Air Races (1932), 80
  Miami Beach to Cleveland Air Derby (1929), 48
  National Air Derby (1929), 46, 48
  National Air Races (1928, Los Angeles), 38, 44
  National Air Races (1929, Cleveland), 44, 46, 48, 65
  National Air Races (1930, Chicago), 66, 67
  National Air Races (1931, Cleveland), 77, 80
  National Air Races (1932, Cleveland), 77, 81
  National Air Races (1934, Cleveland), 100, 102, 103
  National Air Races (1936, Los Angeles), 143, 256
  National Air Races (1938, Cleveland), 218
  National Air Tour (1928), 38
  Nebraska State Air Tour (1930), 66
  New York-Spokane Air Derby (1927), 25
  Omaha Races (1931), 77
  Omaha Races (1932), 81
  Philadelphia to Cleveland Air Derby (1929), 44
  Rockford Air Meet (1930), 65
  Ruth Chatterton Sportsman Trophy Race (1936), 256
  Thompson Trophy, 252
  Woman's Closed Course Race (1931), 67
  Woman's Transcontinental Handicap Air Derby (1931), 78
Airports;
  Boston Airport, 103
  Caudron Aerodrome, 217
  Detroit City Airport, 115
  Floyd Bennet Field, 239
  Hoover Field, 216
  Kansas City Municipal Airport, 88, 95, 254, 277-281
  LaGuardia Airport Marine/Air Terminal, 90, 103
  Lambert Field, 76, 81
  Logan Field, 216
  Lunken Airport, 90
  McCook Field, 82, 83
  Mercer County Airport, 104, 107, 108, 112, 114-116, 131, 132, 151, 154-156, 174, 175, 183-185, 193, 196, 207, 208, 212, 217, 257
  Moline Airport (Franing Field/Weaver Farm), 19, 20, 32, 35, 37, 42, 49, 59, 63, 64, 77
  Newark Terminal, 114
  North Beach Airport, 103, 116
  Pipher Airport, 150
  Pitcairn Field, 173, 233, 239
  Roosevelt Field, 23, 144, 206, 207, 211-213

Shockley Field, 62
Wallace Field, 9, 11, 12, 18, 19, 21, 26
Wings Field, 242, 245, 249, 261
Wright Field, 59, 303
Aldrin, Edwin E., Jr. "Buzz", 140
Aldrin, Edwin E., Sr, 140
Angell, William R., Jr., 257
Angle, Glenn D., 83, 252
Atkinson, Jack, 38, 39
Augustine, Floyd, 48, 67
Aviation Country Club, 207
Aviation Heritage Library, 6, 10, 18, 25, 106, 114, 152, 312

Baker, Dorothy Driggs, 83, 91
Bachle, Carl, 257
Ball, Phil De Cameron, 75, 76, 84, 87
Barnett, Charlie, 133
Bear Tavern Inn, 234
Beech, Walter, 253
Behal, Bob, 257
Benckert, Bill, 133, 155, 156, 168
Bevelo, Anthony, 89, 90
Blackwell, C.W., 256
Block, Robert L., 12
Boller, Henry K., 208, 220, 222, 223, 225, 229, 230-236, 243, 260, 290
Bowlus, Hawley, 143
Bowman, Leslie, 48, 67, 75, 312
Bowman, Marti, 67
Brooks, Aline, 90, 105, 106, 108, 255, 278
Brooks, Reginald "Peter", 79, 90, 105, 106, 108, 113, 114, 130, 176, 182, 183, 201, 202, 255, 278
Brunton, Fred, 201
Bunch, Clare, 91
Bureau of Air Commerce, 21-23, 28, 44, 79, 132, 192, 199, 200 203, 206, 209, 211, 212, 259
Burgess, Charles "Chuck", 89, 94, 99, 100, 109, 113, 115, 117, 131-133, 137, 139, 147, 148, 150-152, 154, 158, 159, 165, 167, 168, 187, 193, 219, 220, 226, 228, 234, 239, 244, 294
Burmood, Cornelius Barnett "Scotty", 32, 34, 46-49, 61, 62, 253
Bush, Del, 252
Butterworth, Ben, 28

Caldwell, Cy, 67
Campbell, Bill, 248
Campbell, Earl K. "Rusty", 19, 20, 22, 28, 31, 34, 37, 59, 253
Carbury, Lord John E., 65
Carnahan, Art, 81
Carpenter, James B., 37
Casey Jones School of Aeronautics, 116, 144
Cavin, Dick, 176
Cericola, Kenneth E., 83, 91, 129, 255
Cessna, Clyde, 13
Chaing Kei-Shek, 253
Chamberlin, Clarence, 156, 175
Cheng, P.V., 134, 168
Civil Aeronautics Act of 1938, 230
Civil Aeronautics Authority, 230, 231, 244, 260
Civilian Pilot Training Program, 230, 233, 243, 244, 253
Cluett, George B., II, 130, 139, 153, 173, 204, 225, 226, 229-231, 234, 237, 240, 241, 246
Cochran, Jacqueline, 239, 261, 303
Coghill, Louis W., 130, 133, 141, 150, 155, 156, 159, 168, 173, 175, 181, 186, 187, 196, 202, 233, 234, 244, 257
Coigny, Jerry, 213, 214, 216, 218, 219, 244, 245, 259
Coigny, Lucy Rago, 213, 214, 218, 244, 245
Colby, Tom, 23, 90
Cole, H.T., 192, 257, 288
Cole, Robert A., 68, 69, 75
Cooke, Donald D. 90, 108, 279
Corporations (miscellaneous);
  Aero Insurance Underwriters,.253
  Aeronautical Corporation of America (Aeronca), 180, 205, 231
  Aerotech, Inc., 22, 33, 34, 59
  Air America, Inc., 210, 295
  Alexander Aircraft Company, 44
  Allied Aviation Industries, Inc., 48, 49, 67, 69, 75
  Aluminum Company of America (ALCOA), 95, 259
  American Airlines, 174, 185
  American Cirrus Company, 66
  Armstrong-Siddeley, 24
  Augustine & Co., 48
  Austin Company, 185, 205, 227
  Aviation Accessories Corporation, 49
  Bellanca Aircraft Corporation, 169, 171, 202, 257
  Berry Brothers Paints, Inc, 23, 90
  Bettendorf Railroad Car Company, 12, 21
  B.F. Goodrich Company, 253
  Boller Motor Company, 208, 222, 290
  Bowlus Sailplane and Trailer Company, 143
  Brewster Aircraft, 168
  Burgess-Dunne Company, 82
  Butler Blackhawk Airplane Company, 88, 99, 277-281
  Campbell-De Schepper Airplane Company, 19, 35, 64,
  Caudron Corporation, 184, 185, 201, 212, 217, 259
  Central States Aero Company, 12, 13, 20-26, 28, 31, 252
  Cessna Aircraft Company, 80, 89
  Chance-Vought Aircraft Corporation, 113
  Chase Aircraft, 261
  Cluett Aircraft Company, 246, 261
  Cluett-Peabody, 130
  Consolidated (Convair), 258
  Continental Airlines, 244
  Continental Motors Corporation, 180, 196, 220, 221, 228, 257
  Curtiss-Wright Aircraft Company, 59, 67, 84
  Curtiss-Wright Flying Service, 59, 64, 80
  D.A. Luscombe Airplane Company, 88
  Delta Air Lines, 244
  Detroit Aircraft Engine Corporation, 17, 26
  Douglas Aircraft Company, 213, 257, 259, 260
  Driggs Aircraft Corporation, 83, 89, 254
  Eastern Aircraft, 244
  Eastern Air Lines, 84, 152
  Edo Aircraft Corporation, 39, 127, 238, 261, 278
  Edward G. Budd Manufacturing Company, 204
  Embry-Riddle Company, 45
  Eugene J. Hynes & Co., 205, 226
  Fairchild Aircraft Corporation, 244, 290
  Fairchild Aviation Corporation, 113
  Falcon Aircraft Corporation, 185, 213, 258, 288
  F.A.O. Schwartz Toys, Inc 250
  F.J. Knack Engineering Company, 243
  Fleetwings Aircraft, 117, 128, 189
  Flying Associates, Limited, 217
  Fokker Aircraft, 67
  Fokker and Universal Aviation, 48
  Ford Motor Company, 23, 100, 252
  General Aviation Corporation, 82, 257
  General Motors Corporation, 67
  Gillis Construction Company, 34
  Glenn L. Martin Company, 113, 159, 168, 254
  Goodyear, 199
  Hall-Aluminum, 256
  Hall, Hartwell & Company, 130
  Heath Airplane and Supply Company, 13
  Hellenic Luscombe Aeronautic Corporation, 185
  Hurricane Aircraft Engine Company, 48
  International General Electric Company, 260
  John Deere & Company, 12, 27, 28
  Johnson Airplane and Supply Company, 82
  K & C Flying Service, 130, 244, 258
  Kinner Airplane and Motor Corporation, 46, 50, 312
  Knight and Company, 186
  Lambert Aircraft Engine Corporation, 48-50, 62, 64, 67-69, 75
  Lambert Engine and Machine Corporation, 76
  Lambert-Graves Auto Agency, 49
  LeBlond Aircraft Engine Corporation, 32, 90
  Libby Welding Company, 95, 101
  Lockheed Aircraft Company, 258
  Love, Bryan and Company, 48
  Luscombe Airplane Company, 88, 91, 100-102, 104, 105, 110, 278
  Luscombe Airplane Corporation (LAC), 173-175, 177, 183, 184-187, 195, 197, 198, 200, 203, 205, 207, 209, 210, 212, 214, 217, 220, 221, 223, 225-231, 234, 235, 237-246, 258-261, 290, 292, 293
  Luscombe Airplane Development Corporation (LADC), 112, 113, 116, 118, 127, 128, 130-132, 135, 139, 143, 145, 148,152-155, 1158, 159, 165, 168, 171, 173, 174, 257, 278, 281, 283, 288, 290, 293
  Luscombe Associate Company, 184
  Luscombe Company of St. Louis, 68
  Luscombe Engineering Company, 249
  Massey and Ransom Flying Service, 232, 296
  McDonnell Aircraft Corporation, 254, 260
  McDonnell-Douglas Aircraft Company, 76, 260
  Michigan Screw Corporation, 254
  Middishade Company, 130
  Mid-South Airways, 252
  Miller-Palmer Company, 12
  Moline Air Service, 253
  Moline Engine Service, 253
  Monarch Airplane Company, 32
  Mono-Aircraft, Inc., 28, 32, 33, 35-39, 45, 46, 48 50, 59, 62, 64-68, 75, 76, 253
  Mono-Aircraft Sales & Service, Inc., 42, 44, 45
  Monocoupe Corporation, 76, 77, 79, 83, 87, 89, 98, 253
  Monoplane Aircraft Company, 37
  Motor Wheel Corporation, 82, 254
  National Air Transport Company, 35, 64
  Naval Aircraft Factory, 256
  North American Investment Company, 230, 260
  Osram Lamp Company, G.mB.H., 260
  Pan American Airways, Inc., 261
  Pan American Grace Airlines, 261
  Philadelphia Air Transport Company, 45
  Philadelphia Aviation Corporation, 261
  Piasecki Helicopter, 256

Pioneer Instrument Company, 68
Pitcairn Autogiro Company, 168, 184, 186-189, 207, 243-246
Porterfield Aircraft Corporation, 180, 258
Radio Corporation of America, 248
Rearwin Aircraft Company, 205, 258
Renault Automobile Company, 184
Reynolds Metals Company, 244, 249
Reynolds Tobacco Company, 47
Royal Aircraft Factory, 252
Ryan Aircraft Company, 76, 179
St. Louis Street Car Company, 252
Sensenich Propeller Company, 218, 219
Shell Oil Company, 253
Sikorsky Aircraft Corporation, 113, 168
Singer Sewing Machine Company, 90
Simonds Saw, 130
Skyways, Inc., 39
Standard Oil Development Company, 130, 140, 283
Stearman-Hammond Aircraft Company, 179
Stevenson-Weeks Air Service, 99
Stewart-Warner Company, 258
Stribbe & De Vries N.V., 260
Stinson Aircraft Corporation, 258, 286
Stromberg Carburetor, 32
Studebaker Corporation, 59, 253
Switlik Parachute Company, 175
Taylor Airplane Company, 180, 205
Taylorcraft Aviation Corporation, 252
Teacher Manufacturing Company, 110, 187
Texas Aircraft Corporation, 34
Thropp Flying Service, 104
Travel Air Ways, 37
Turner Entertainment Company, 260
United Airlines, 213
Universal Aviation, Inc, 48
Velie Mono Sales, 37
Velie Motors Corporation, 26-28, 32, 33, 41, 49
Vought-Sikorsky Aircraft Corporation, 244
Waco Aircraft Company, 249, 252
Wallace Brothers Aero Company, 59
Warner Aircraft Corporation, 69, 77, 170, 171, 183, 258, 287
Warner Brothers Studios, 221, 258, 260
Wyllis-Morrow Company, 252
Zimmerman Foundry, 9
Cornell University, 117, 118, 128, 129, 143, 172
Corrigan, Douglas, 218, 219
Coston, Ralph, 130, 131, 132, 137, 144, 168, 173, 176, 207, 234, 244, 256
Cram, Ralph, 19
Crummer, H.J., 152, 286
Curtiss-Wright Technical Institute, 143

Dallas Aviation School, 256
Daniel Guggenheim School of Aeronautics, 22, 103, 116
Darnell, Carlton, 213
Davenport Aero Club, 19
Davis, Edgar S., 115, 116, 130, 131, 140, 141-143, 152, 155, 168, 171-173, 175, 181, 183, 187, 195, 196, 201, 205-207, 210, 212, 215, 217, 218, 228, 233, 239, 243, 256, 257, 261, 282, 286, 301-303
de Bustamente, Helen, 151, 285
de Bustamente, Gustavo S., 144, 151
De Crescenszo, Jules, 130, 131, 188, 193, 234, 244
D'Estout, Henri, 130, 136, 140, 158, 159, 169, 204, 215
Department of Commerce, 21, 22, 26, 32, 64, 79, 95, 97, 99, 100, 108, 112, 132, 140, 145, 150, 153-155, 168, 171, 174, 186, 188, 192, 199-201, 206, 207, 212, 214, 227, 256, 259, 277-296
Driggs, Ivan H., 82-84, 91, 98, 100, 108, 109, 112, 113, 116, 128, 168, 253, 254, 255
Dryden, Hugh, 248
Dunford, F., 134
Duthie, Charlie, 258
DuVall, George, 259

Eisenmann, Marty, 144, 168, 256
Elks Club, 43, 44
Evers, Carl, 239

Fabian, Richard, 131, 172, 173, 187
Fargo Aeronautics Club, Inc., 25
Farver, Carol, 109, 255
Farver, Lyle L., 89-91, 98, 100, 101, 109, 111-113, 129, 132-135, 137, 141, 145-147, 149, 150, 155-160, 163-167, 175, 191, 199, 254, 255-257
Faunce, L.A., 257
Fielder, Jerry, 176
FitzHenry, Louis, 68, 75
Fitzwilliam, Frances, 24, 27, 33, 34, 39, 42-45, 65, 270-272, 309-312
Flying Stooges Flying Club, 131, 193
Foley, Tom, 193, 195, 196, 258, 259, 301
Folkerts, Atho, 13
Folkerts, Clayton, 12-18, 21, 25, 42, 59, 60, 66, 76, 252
Folkerts, Edward, 13-15
Folkerts, Johanna Voss, 13
Folkerts, Harold, 9, 13-16, 26
Folkerts, Henry, 14
Folkerts, Minno, 14
Forca Aerea Brasilia (Brazilian Air Force), 259
Force, William E. "Bill", 134, 135, 156, 168, 189, 203, 219, 220, 234, 244, 246, 249, 256
Ford, Henry, 34, 252
Fornasero, John B., 212, 227
Forster, Burton E., 12
Frey, Harm, 13
Funk, Keith G., 95, 113, 117, 229, 230, 234, 244-246
Funk, Naomi, 90, 109,
Funk Ross, 89, 95, 109, 112, 113, 117, 129, 143, 168

Gallitan, George, 139
Gay, George, 100, 112, 141, 174, 277, 280-288, 290, 291
Giguere, Ronold, 217, 218
Gillis, Jack, 104
Graf Zeppilin, 44
Grand Central Air Terminal, 143
Greasy Spoon, 176
Greene, Howard, 201, 244, 249, 258
Gregorson, Greg, 176
Gregory, Rolfe, 197, 203, 214, 216, 234, 244, 245
Grigg, Eddie, 146
Grigg, Moss, 146
Group 2 Approval, 42, 46, 81, 253

Hadley, Clara, 7
Hagenmueller, Ernest, 21
Hammer, Jim, 198
Hard, George Wales, 90
Harding, William Barclay, 90
Hartle, George, 2
Hartle, Sarah Dansdill, 2
Hatch, Byron, 48
Harris, Douglas, 23
Harvey, Jim, 17, 21, 23, 40-43, 59, 63, 76, 78, 82, 269, 270, 273
Haun, Carl B. 90, 105, 108, 277
Haines, William C., 204, 205, 290
Haizlip, Mary "Mae", 78
Harper, H. F., 254
Heath, Ed, 13
Hinchey, John B. "Jack", 37, 45, 47, 62, 309
Hindenburg, 176
Hinsch, Charles A. "Bunnie", 90, 150, 151, 161, 162, 225, 284
Hitler, Adolf, 246
Holman, Charles "Speed", 65
Holloway, Chuck, 201, 258
Hoover, Herbert, 66
Howard, Ben O., 91
Humphreys, Bob, 133, 147, 156
Humphreys, George A., 145, 283

Ireland, J. Sumner, 214
Isle de France, 213

Johnson, Duwen, 234
Johnson, Francis B. "Frank". 138, 139, 143, 144, 159, 160, 171, 176, 177, 179, 183, 256, 257
Johnson, Joe, 248
Johnson, Roger H., 130, 139, 140, 173, 205, 211, 221, 225, 226, 230, 231, 237, 244, 258, 293
Jones, Helen, 219
Jones, Jess, 219
Jones, Rhys P., 234
Jong, Howard, 99, 127, 136, 139, 143, 144, 146-148, 151, 153, 155, 158, 161, 168-172, 174-176, 179, 183, 186, 189-193, 200, 201, 206, 208, 218, 253, 255-260, 293, 294
Jolly Roger, 139, 140, 144, 155, 159, 190, 193, 197, 198, 214, 258
Joseph, Don, 98

Kapitan, Lucille Luscombe, 208
Kauffman, Benjamin, 134
Kauffman, Glenn, 197, 259
Keegan, Bill, 112, 168
Kenyon, Theodore, 39
Khan, Roger Wolf, 90
King, Albert "Fritz", 95, 108, 109, 110, 113-115, 130, 131, 136, 141, 144, 153, 155, 159, 172, 175, 176, 195, 196, 202, 229, 233, 244, 254, 257, 258, 289, 301-304, 314
Kittler, Robert, 234
Klemin, Alexander, 103, 116, 117, 134
Klingensmith, Florence, 42, 46, 47, 78, 81, 312
Klisher, Ray, 258
Klotz, Leopold Hugo Paul, 223, 225-227, 229-231, 234 -237, 240, 241, 243, 244, 246, 260, 261
Klotz, Paul, 260
Knack, Frederick J., 22, 42, 59, 78, 81, 82, 169, 171, 173, 175, 177, 179, 181, 183, 184, 190, 191, 200-203, 206, 211, 212, 227, 243, 245, 246, 252, 253, 257, 258,
Kohn, Leo J., 128
Koppel, Leopold, 260
Korn, Tom J., 12
Kotula, Jo, 190, 191, 258

Kraft, Herb, 174, 185, 291
Krieger, A. R., 195
Kuchawa, Ken, 133
Kurt, Franklin T., 207, 256

LaJotte, Charles, 38
Lambert, Albert B., 49
Lambert, J.D. Wooster, 49
Lambert, Samual B., 49, 61, 253
Larsen, Agnew, 184, 188, 204, 244
Law, Ruth, 252
Lawrence, Linwood, 197
Lear, William "Bill", 84
LeBlond, R.K., 90
Lederer, Jerome, F. "Jerry", 22, 33, 42, 59, 104, 253
Lengenfelder, John, 140, 141, 218, 238
Libby, Hugh, 101
Lindbergh, Charles A., 24, 36-38, 49, 252, 256
Livingston, "Bite", 66
Livingston, John, 31, 37, 63, 64, 66-68, 75, 77, 78, 80-82, 312
Lochner, Walter O., 104
Longren, A.K., 88-90, 254
Longren Process, 88, 89
Longstreth, Thaddeus, 131
Loose, Chester, 21, 66, 76
Love, John A., 48
Lundberg, H. B., 254
Luscombe airplanes by design name;
  Coupe, 100
  Elf, 177, 179
  "Fifty" or "50", 177, 181, 184, 187, 189-193, 195, 196, 197-199, 201-203, 208-214, 216-220, 222, 238, 239, 243, 245, 257-259, 261, 300
  Four-Place (Gull-Wing), 246, 247, 248
  Ghost, 112, 122, 133, 134, 147,
  Harpie, 112, 126
  Luscombe, 155
  Model 2, 132, 133
  Model 4, 168, 179-181, 199, 205-207, 210, 212, 220, 233, 234
  Model 8, 144, 177, 181, 201, 205-207, 210-216, 219, 220, 221, 227-229, 231, 233, 238, 243, 244, 258, 259, 301, 302
  Model 8A, 243, 303, 304
  Model 8B, 243
  Model 8C, 243
  Model 8D, 243
  "Ninety" or "90", 158, 160, 161, 163-168, 171-175, 180, 181, 183, 184, 185, 187, 190-192, 196, 197, 199-203, 208, 210, 213, 214, 257, 258, 293-296, 299, 301
  Phantom, 92-94, 96-103, 105, 106, 108, 110, 112-118, 121, 127, 130-141, 145-159, 162, 163, 166-171, 174, 176, 177, 179, 183, 185-187, 196, 197, 200, 204, 213-216, 220, 222, 255, 256, 260, 277-292
  Phantom 1S, 127
  Pond Hopper, 177
  "Sixty-five" or "65", 228, 233, 238, 239, 242, 243, 245, 300, 314
  Small Transport, 112, 124
  Spectre, 112, 123
  Sprite, 112, 125, 155, 163, 168, 179, 257
  Sprite II, 257
  Television guided bomb, 247, 248
Luscombe airplanes by nickname;
  "Honeymoon Special", 245
Luscombe airplanes by number;
  Aircraft 1017, 145, 155, 156, 164, 167, 168, 172,

  Aircraft 1253, 168, 172, 173, 187, 200, 201, 205, 257, 259
  Phantom 272Y, 99, 100, 115, 168, 301
  Phantom NC272Y, 103, 107, 116, 134, 145, 154, 156, 255, 277, 301
  Phantom NC275Y, 105, 106, 109, 152, 277, 301
  Phantom NC276Y, 108, 109, 110, 128, 278, 301
  Phantom NC277Y, 108, 114, 143, 279, 301
  Phantom NC278Y, 111, 112, 158, 159, 280, 301
  Phantom HB-EXE, 113, 114, 281, 301
  Phantom NC1286, 132, 136-138, 152, 170, 256, 281, 301
  Phantom NC1007, 140, 141, 142, 152, 256, 282, 301
  Phantom NC1008, 145, 148, 152, 256, 282, 301
  Phantom NC7734 (STANAVO), 127, 130, 136, 140, 141, 150, 152, 283, 301
  Phantom NC1234, 148, 283, 301
  Phantom NC1010, 150, 284, 301
  Phantom NC1025, 151, 152, 285, 301
  Phantom NC1028, 151, 152, 170-172, 174, 220, 286, 301
  Phantom NC1043, 152, 286, 301
  Phantom NC1235, 169, 287, 301
  Phantom NC1048, 169, 288, 301
  Phantom NC1278, 185, 186, 288, 301
  Phantom D1L-204 (PP-TPT), 215, 259, 289, 301
  Phantom NC30449, 289, 301
  Phantom NC1249, 172, 174, 197, 201, 207, 220, 290, 301
  Phantom NC1323, 204, 290, 301
  Phantom NC1265, 174, 291, 301
  Phantom NC25234, 291, 301
  Phantom NC28799, 292, 301
  Model 4 NX1253, 206, 293, 301
  Model 4 NC1253, 206, 293, 301
  Model 4 NC1325, 206, 207, 259, 294, 301
  Model 4 NC1344, 206, 207, 210, 295, 301
  Model 4 NC1337, 207, 212, 295, 301
  Model 4 NC1335, 212, 259, 301
  Model 4 NC22026, 232, 296, 301
  Model 8 1304, 192, 193, 195, 201, 203, 205, 210, 259, 301
  Model 8 NC1327, 210, 211, 228, 239, 259, 301
  Model 8 NX1327, 206, 207, 210, 211, 228, 233
  Model 8 2589, 212, 301
  Model 8 2590, 213, 301
  Model 8 2591, 212, 301
  Model 8 2592, 212, 301
  Model 8 CF-BKW, 217, 301
  Model 8 NC2336, 220, 302
  Model 8 NC20663, 209, 314
  Model 8 NX20685, 227, 302
  Model 8 NC22002, 229, 302
  Model 8 NC22007, 261, 302
  Model 8A NX22055, 233, 303
  Model 8 NC22056, 233, 303
  Model 8A NC22070, 239, 303
  Model 8A NX22082, 314
  Model 8A NC22085, 242, 303
  Model 8A NC22093, 238, 303
  Model 8A NC25180, 261
  Model 8 F-W-0116, 259
Luscombe Apprentice Program, 128, 129, 134, 143, 144, 162
Luscombe Country Club, 132, 210
Luscombe family members and relatives;
  Luscombe, Betty (see Betty Luscombe Numerof)
  Luscombe, Donald A. see book

  Luscombe, Eleanore True (see Eleanore Luscombe Shurtz)
  Luscombe, James Liddle, 1-3
  Luscombe, James Torring (grandfather), 1, 2
  Luscombe, James Torring (brother), 2
  Luscombe, James True, 24, 25, 85, 114
  Luscombe, Lucille (see Lucille Luscombe Kapitan)
  Luscombe, Mary Liddle, 2
  Luscombe, Minnie Ellen Hartle, 1
  Luscombe, Ora May "Brownee" (Wellington), 85, 90, 91, 104, 108, 111, 112, 114, 118, 175, 211, 213, 222, 240-243, 245, 254
  Luscombe, Patricia Irene, 8
  Luscombe, Robert Hartle, 1-4, 7, 11, 17, 21, 252
Luscombe School of Aeronautics, 186, 197, 200, 204, 215
Lynch, Les, 189

Macy, J. Noel, 153
Marinha de Brasil (Brazilian Navy), 259
Mallinson, Hiram, 131, 148-150, 152, 156, 163, 171-173, 184, 185, 201, 226, 229, 231, 284, 286
Massey, Otis, 232, 233
McAlpin, Malcolm, 90
McCormick, G. Paul, 134
McNeal, A. Lincoln, 206
McPhaul, Frederick "Red", 150, 256
Meehan, Bill, 270
Melcher, Ben B., 83, 89, 91, 98, 100, 110, 114, 141, 150, 155, 166, 168, 171, 176, 196, 202, 204-207, 211, 219, 232, 238, 244, 246, 247, 249, 254, 255, 301
Melfa, Mike, 176, 204
Michigan Agricultural College, 89
Michigan State College, 82
Miller, Millton, 12, 16, 17, 20
Mitchell, A. Edgar, 246, 261
Monocoupe airplanes by design name;
  Model 22 (ATC #22), 28, 37, 269
  Model 70 (ATC #70), 37, 38, 270, 309
  Model 113 (ATC #113), 41, 42, 44, 45, 48, 60, 68, 78, 270, 311
  Model 113 Special, 48, 67, 313
  Model 90 (ATC #306), 59, 60, 61, 63, 79, 81, 90, 273
  Model 90-J (ATC #355), 63, 274
  Model 110 (ATC #327), 60, 62, 63, 67, 75, 77-80, 81, 84, 115, 116, 201, 274
  Model 110 Special, 63
  Model 125 (ATC #359), 60, 63, 64, 79, 81, 275
  Model 70-V (ATC #492), 79, 80
  Model 501, 61
  Model "D", 78, 82, 83, 84,
  Model D-145 (ATC #529), 89, 91, 157, 254
  Monocoach Model 201 (ATC #201), 43, 44, 271
  Monocoach Model 275 (ATC #275), 43, 44, 273, 311
  Mono Midget, 76
  Monoprep Model 218 (ATC #218), 44, 45, 271, 310
  Mono Special, 66, 312
  Monosport Model 1 (ATC #249), 45, 46, 272
  Monosport Model 2 (ATC #250), 45, 46, 48, 272, 312
Monocoupe airplanes by nickname;
  "Little Sweetheart", 38, 45, 48, 66

Livingston "Special", 81
"Miss Chiggers", 39
"Miss Fargo", 25
"Miss Moline", 46, 48, 313
Monocoupe airplanes by registration number;
   Model 22 1025, 23
   Model 22 1026, 23
   Model 22 1027, 23
   Model 22 1427, 25, 38
   Model 70 4138, 32
   Model 70 5877, 39
   Model 70 5878, 39
   Model 70 7323, 38
   Model 70 7838, 42
   Model 110 NC501W, 63, 82
   Model 110 NC503W (G-ABAR), 65
   Model 110 NC12345, 80, 176
   Model 110 Special NR8917, 48, 313
   Monocoach 201 X-8900, 41
   Monocoach 201 C-8916, 310
   Monocoach 201 NC8969, 44
   Monosport 1 NC105K, 46
   Monosport 2 NC113K, 48
Monocoupe prototype, 17, 18, 20, 21
Monocoupe "Rockets", 47
Monocoupe "Three Rockets", 66
Montgomery, Vera, 223, 232, 260, 261
Moritz, Rudy A., 12
Morrison, Hebert, 176
Muhlowney, Penn, 158, 159, 160
Murphy, Tom, 197, 198
Muzzy, A.B., 261

National Advisory Committee for Aeronautics (NACA), 83, 157, 248, 253
National Air and Space Museum, 188, 189
National Aeronautics and Space Administration (NASA), 253
National Defense Research Committee (NDRC), 248
Nelson, Lincoln, 82
Nemechek, Edward, 89, 91, 110, 113
Negrier, Jacques, 184, 201, 217
Newmann, Harold, 66, 77, 91, 252
Numerof, Betty Luscombe, 1-4, 7, 11, 24, 208, 252
Newstead, Dave, 8
New York City School of Aviation Trades, 198
New York University, 22, 133, 134
Nordyke, Bertha, 109
Nordyke, Nick, 95, 96, 101, 104, 111, 117, 129, 135, 139, 143, 144, 157, 163, 165, 168, 188, 189, 234, 243, 244, 246
North Carolina State College, 158

Oberhumer, Ernst, 232, 234-238, 240, 241, 245, 246, 260, 261
O'Conner, Don, 131
O'Donnell, Gladys, 67
Olmstead, Henry C., 152, 170, 171, 172, 174, 220, 229, 231, 257, 260, 286
Omlie, Phoebe, 35, 37-39, 41-43, 46, 47, 65, 67, 75, 77, 252, 253, 313
Omlie, Vernon, 252
Ortman, Earl, 91
Outman, Vernon, 96, 110

Park College, 83
Peacock, Charlie, 109
Peek, Chester L., 257
Pennsylvania Department of Welfare, 144
Pierce School of Accounting, 130
Pitcairn, Harold, 245, 261

Polhemus, John, 131
Price, Ron, 212
Propellers;
   Curtiss, 172, 220, 255, 281-292
   Everall, 218
   Hamilton-Standard, 60, 98, 199, 255, 277, 281, 290, 291, 293 -296
   Hartzell, 18
   Sensenich, 193, 199
Purdue University, 244

Quellette, Lionel, 136
Quinby, Roy T. "Stub", 34, 46-48, 65-67, 75

Rankin, John G. "Tex", 37
Rae, Roger Don, 252
Reynolds, R.J., 46
Rickenbacker, Eddie, 26, 83. 91, 252
Rising, James; 171, 175, 177, 179, 181, 186, 190, 197, 198, 201, 243, 258, 259, 261
Roberts, Herietta, 253
Roberts, Ken, 253
Roberts, Vernon L., 25, 32, 38, 40, 48, 59, 60, 64, 65-67, 75, 78, 253
Robinson William, 204, 227
Rogers, Will, 35
Roosevelt, Franklin Delano, 230, 253
Rowe, Bert, 176, 189, 259
Rude, Dick, 198, 204
Russell, Basil, 48
Russell, Joe, 48
Ryan, T. Claude, 24, 252

Sargent, Frances "Sissie", 115, 143, 216, 217, 257, 262
Sargent, Ignatius "Ig", 115, 116, 130-132, 135-138, 141-143, 145, 148, 151, 152, 154, 155, 158, 168, 169, 170-173, 175, 181, 187, 193, 195, 196, 199-201, 204-207, 210-213, 215-218, 222, 227, 228, 233, 234, 239, 243, 256-258, 261, 293-295, 301-303, 313
Schmind, Edgar, 44
Second Careers, 250, 251
Securities and Exchange Commission, 174, 185, 186, 226, 231
Shaw, C.W., 37
Sheedy, Bryan, 108, 114, 127, 130, 154, 278
Schenk, Mike, 31, 33, 35, 313
Shepard, William B., 118, 131, 133, 140, 143, 158, 159, 171, 173, 181, 183, 184, 187, 188, 196, 199, 212, 213, 234, 240, 244, 249, 257, 258, 294, 303, 304
Shields, E.C., 254
Shriker, Ray, 9, 10
Shurtz, Eleanore Luscombe, 3-8, 11, 18, 24, 25, 32, 36, 75, 78, 80, 84, 85, 87, 88, 92-94, 96, 98, 99, 104, 106, 162, 169, 182, 202, 211, 237, 241-243, 250, 252
Simonds, Daniel, 130, 210, 234, 237, 295
Simplified Flying, 38, 85
Smith, Herchel, 257
Smith, Wesley, 67, 131
Smith, Clifford T., 22, 42
Smithsonian Institution, 260
Snow, Croker, 39, 285
Sorbonne, 223
Sportsman Pilot Association, 127, 150
Spreckles, Frank, 114, 143, 256, 279
SS Dresden, 223
SS Normandie, 216
Stange, George A., 28, 44,

Stevenson, Barton, 65-67, 78, 99, 105, 255, 277
Stoeble, "Pops", 89-91, 95, 110,
Story, Cameron, 168, 189
Stout, Bill, 34
Sunday, Billy, 21
Sweeny Automobile School, 101
Swick, John, 93, 214

Tarencz, Eddie, 134, 156, 157, 258
Terry, Cy W., 117, 128, 129, 131, 143,
Thatcher, Becky, 140
Thatcher, Elsie, 140
Thorne, George A., Jr., 90, 112, 114, 130, 158, 159, 255, 280
Torrens, John H., 243, 245
Tripp, Juan, 261
Truman, Harry, 254
Tschudi, A.K., 113, 281
Turner, Roscoe, 91

Underwood, John, 10, 11, 20, 41, 45, 47, 48, 66, 95, 106, 128, 192, 270, 274, 275, 287, 295
University of Belin, 223
University of Chicago, 82
University of Cincinnati, 90
University of Iowa, 4-7
University of North Carolina, 138
University of Vienna, 261

Vanech, Peter, 185
Velie, Anne Floweree, 28
Velie, Emma Deere, 28
Velie, S. H., 28
Velie Villa, 27, 62
Velie, Willard L., Sr., 26-28, 31, 32, 38, 41, 252
Velie, Willard L., Jr., 26-28, 31, 41, 48, 49
Vested Claims Committee, 223, 260
Vine, Phillip S., 104, 258

Wagner, William, 257
Wallace, Frank, 9, 11, 12, 17, 19, 32
Wallace, Frederick, 59
Waltz, Edward J., 261
Warner, Thomas W., 213, 258
Washburn, Beverly "Bud", 21
Weatherly, Ray, 248
Weigel, A.R., 41
Wellington, Lawrence Dillworth, 254
Wells, Ted, 172
Weis, George A., 23
Whelan, Bud, 22, 42
Wilson, Woodrow, 5
Wittman, Steve, 80, 91
Wood, K.D., 117, 118
Works Progress Administration, 128
Wright, Eva, 82
Wright, Jack, 81, 82
Wright, Orville, 82

Yale University, 130, 131, 261
Young, Clarence, 90
Yulke, Ed, 176, 258

Zeuch, Frederic E., 12
Zeuch, Warren T., 12
Zimmermann, Fred, 37